RICHARD III

RICHARD III

LOYALTY BINDS ME

MATTHEW LEWIS

AMBERLEY

First published 2018

Amberley Publishing
The Hill, Stroud
Gloucestershire, GL5 4EP

www.amberley-books.com

British Library Cataloguing in Publication Data.
A catalogue record for this book is available from the British Library.

ISBN 978 1 4456 7154 3 (hardback)
ISBN 978 1 4456 7155 0 (ebook)

Typesetting and Origination by Amberley Publishing.
Printed in the UK.

Contents

SCOTLAND

TOWNS & CASTLES

edinburgh

berwick
-upon-
tweed

middleham
castle

england

king's lynn

ludlow

fotheringhay

wales

london

corfe castle

calais

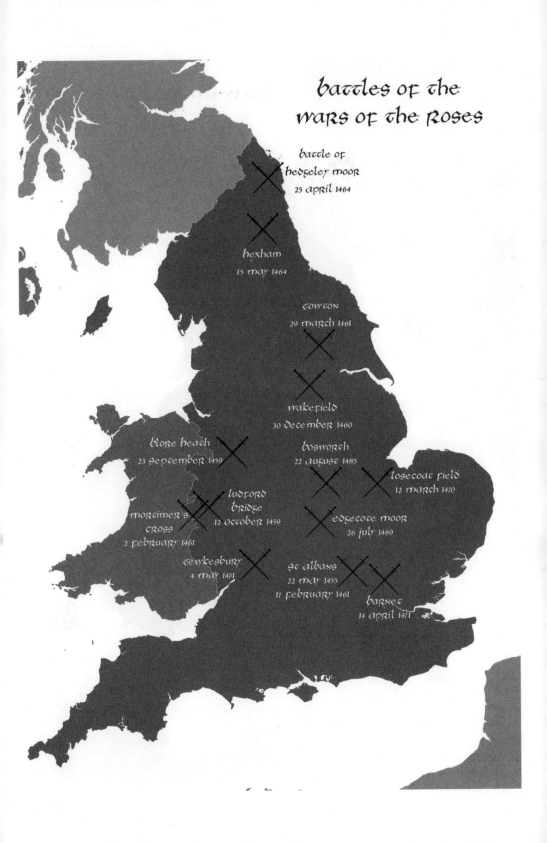

battles of the
wars of the Roses

battle of
hedgeley moor
25 april 1464

hexham
15 may 1464

towton
29 march 1461

wakefield
30 december 1460

blore heath
23 september 1459

bosworth
22 august 1485

losecoat field
12 march 1470

mortimer's
cross
2 february 1461

ludford
bridge
12 october 1459

edgecote moor
26 july 1469

tewkesbury
4 may 1471

st albans
22 may 1455
17 february 1461

barnet
14 april 1471

exile in burgundy

1461 & 1470

texel
alkmaar
leyden
the hague
utrecht
veere
wielingen
bruges
antwerp
king's lynn

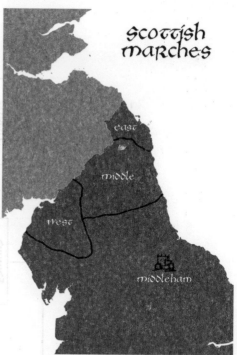

scottish marches

east
middle
west
middleham

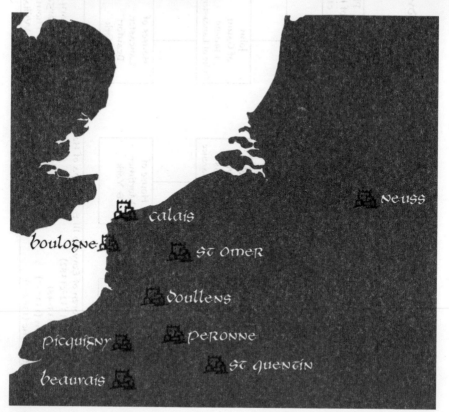

Neuss
calais
boulogne
st omer
doullens
picquigny
peronne
st quentin
beauvais

The French Campaign

Descendants of Edward III

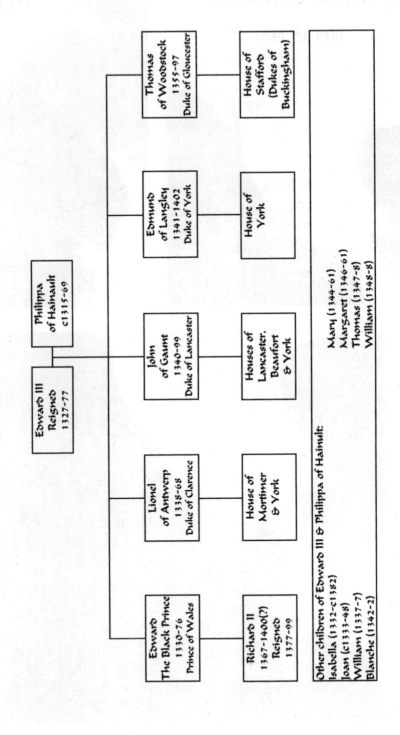

Edward III Reigned 1327–77 — **Philippa of Hainault** c1315–69

Edward The Black Prince 1330–76 Prince of Wales
- **Richard II** 1367–1400(?) Reigned 1377–99

Lionel of Antwerp 1338–68 Duke of Clarence
- **House of Mortimer & York**

John of Gaunt 1340–99 Duke of Lancaster
- **Houses of Lancaster, Beaufort & York**

Edmund of Langley 1341–1402 Duke of York
- **House of York**

Thomas of Woodstock 1355–97 Duke of Gloucester
- **House of Stafford (Dukes of Buckingham)**

Other children of Edward III & Philippa of Hainault:
Isabella (1332–c1382)
Joan (c1333–48)
William (1337–7)
Blanche (1342–2)

Mary (1344–61)
Margaret (1346–61)
Thomas (1347–8)
William (1348–8)

Descendants of Edmund of Langley

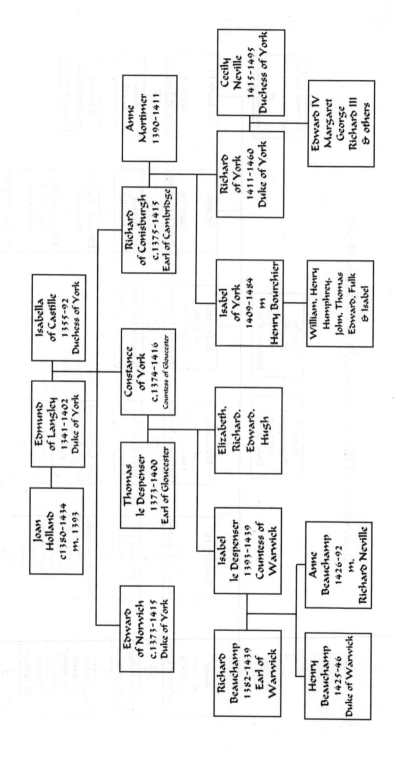

Descendants of Richard, Duke of York & Cecily Neville

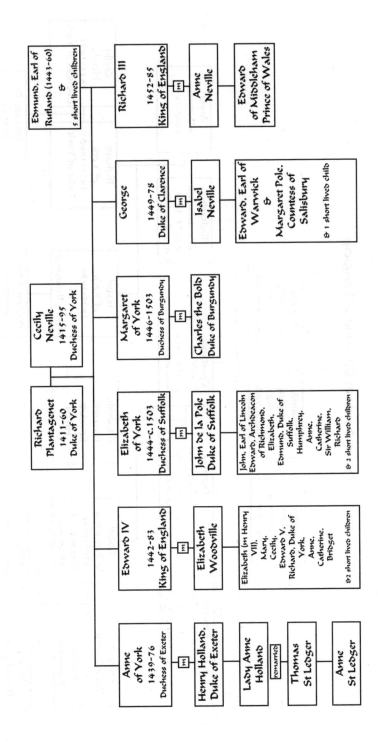

Descendants of Lionel of Antwerp

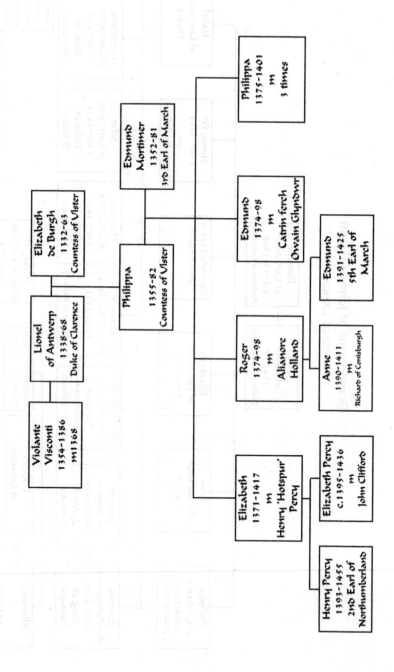

Descendants of John of Gaunt
House of Lancaster

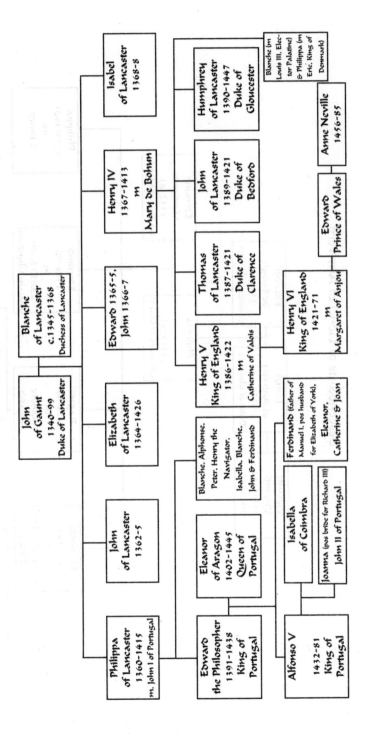

John of Gaunt 1340–99 Duke of Lancaster

Blanche of Lancaster c.1345–1368 Duchess of Lancaster

Philippa of Lancaster 1360–1415 m. John 1 of Portugal

John of Lancaster 1362–5

Elizabeth of Lancaster 1364–1426

Edward 1365–5, **John** 1366–7

Henry IV 1367–1413 m Mary de Bohun

Isabel of Lancaster 1368–8

Edward the Philosopher 1391–1438 King of Portugal

Eleanor of Aragon 1402–1445 Queen of Portugal

Blanche, Alphonse, Peter, Henry the Navigator, Isabella, Blanche, John & Ferdinand

Henry V King of England 1386–1422 m Catherine of Valois

Thomas of Lancaster 1387–1421 Duke of Clarence

John of Lancaster 1389–1421 Duke of Bedford

Humphrey of Lancaster 1390–1447 Duke of Gloucester

Alfonso V 1432–81 King of Portugal

Isabella of Coimbra

Joanna (pos bride for Richard III)

Ferdinand (father of Manuel 1, pos husband for Elizabeth of York), Eleanor, Catherine & Joan

Henry VI King of England 1421–71 m Margaret of Anjou

Blanche (m Louis III, Elec- tor Palatine) & Philippa (m Eric, King of Denmark)

Edward Prince of Wales

Anne Neville 1456–85

Descendants of John of Gaunt
House of Beaufort

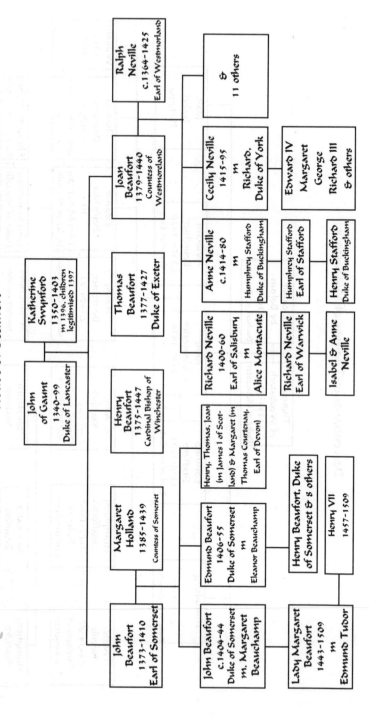

John of Gaunt
1340–99
Duke of Lancaster

Katherine Swynford
1350–1403
m 1396, children legitimised 1397

Ralph Neville
c.1364–1425
Earl of Westmorland

Margaret Holland
1385–1439
Countess of Somerset

Henry Beaufort
1375–1447
Cardinal Bishop of Winchester

Thomas Beaufort
1377–1427
Duke of Exeter

Joan Beaufort
1379–1440
Countess of Westmorland

& 11 others

John Beaufort
1373–1410
Earl of Somerset

Edmund Beaufort
1406–55
Duke of Somerset
m
Eleanor Beauchamp

Henry, Thomas, Joan (m James I of Scotland) & Margaret (m Thomas Courtenay, Earl of Devon)

Richard Neville
1400–60
Earl of Salisbury
m
Alice Montacute

Anne Neville
c.1414–80
m
Humphrey Stafford
Duke of Buckingham

Cecily Neville
1415–95
m
Richard,
Duke of York

John Beaufort
c.1404–44
Duke of Somerset
m. Margaret Beauchamp

Henry Beaufort, Duke of Somerset & 8 others

Richard Neville
Earl of Warwick

Humphrey Stafford
Earl of Stafford

Edward IV
Margaret
George
Richard III
& others

Lady Margaret Beaufort
1443–1509
m
Edmund Tudor

Henry VII
1457–1509

Isabel & Anne Neville

Henry Stafford
Duke of Buckingham

Descendants of Thomas of Woodstock

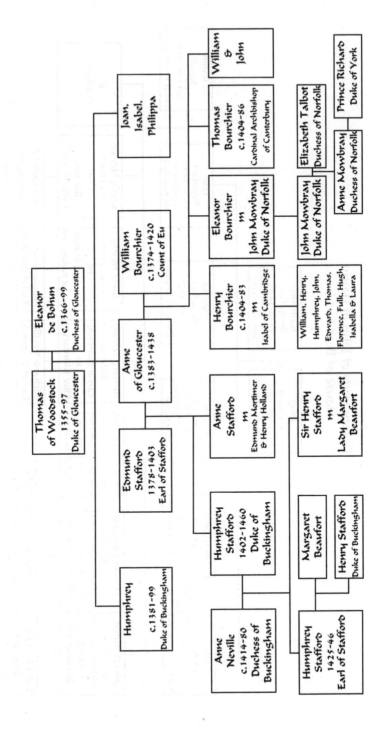

Thomas of Woodstock 1355–97 Duke of Gloucester *m* **Eleanor de Bohun** c.1366–99 Duchess of Gloucester

Humphrey c.1381–99 Duke of Buckingham

Anne of Gloucester c.1383–1438

Joan, Isabel, Philippa

Edmund Stafford 1378–1403 Earl of Stafford

William Bourchier c.1374–1420 Count of Eu

Humphrey Stafford 1402–1460 Duke of Buckingham

Anne Stafford *m* Edmund Mortimer & Henry Holland

Henry Bourchier c.1404–83 *m* Isabel of Cambridge

Eleanor Bourchier *m* John Mowbray Duke of Norfolk

Thomas Bourchier c.1404–86 Cardinal Archbishop of Canterbury

William & John

Anne Neville c.1414–80 Duchess of Buckingham

Sir Henry Stafford *m* Lady Margaret Beaufort

William, Henry, Humphrey, John, Edward, Thomas, Florence, Falk, Hugh, Isabella & Laura

John Mowbray Duke of Norfolk *m* **Elizabeth Talbot** Duchess of Norfolk

Humphrey Stafford 1425–46 Earl of Stafford

Margaret Beaufort

Henry Stafford Duke of Buckingham

Anne Mowbray Duchess of Norfolk *m* **Prince Richard** Duke of York

Introduction

King Richard III has perhaps been the cause of more spilt ink in the five centuries since he became the last Plantagenet King of England and the last holder of that title to die in battle than any other domestic figure. The growth of social media has propelled debate on his life and its myriad facets further to the forefront. Increasingly bitter and entrenched views have found new homes and new champions on both sides of the debate. Somewhere, lost in the melee, is a man who lived his life, the final years of it in controversy and tragedy. As the mists of time have shrouded the shrinking, distant past, that man – the real, tangible, feeling person – has become lost, a vapour that can be moulded to take any form to match the expectations, preconceptions and prejudices of anyone.

The discovery of Richard III's mortal remains in September 2012 beneath a Leicester car park have ignited a further spark of interest. His skeleton made available to us a wealth of new information. The remains confirmed that Richard had scoliosis that caused a curvature of the spine, a revelation that caused shock amongst Ricardians who had long believed the evidence of doctored portraits meant that a raised shoulder was a later invention intended to darken Richard by the medieval association of a physical condition with the corruption of a soul. For those who espouse a more sinister interpretation of Richard, it was viewed as proof that everything history has said of him must be true. If anything, the severe scoliosis revealed by the examination of his skeleton, which showed that it caused his spine to curve, adds another layer of interest to the man. His breathing and movement would have been heavily restricted, and his back would have caused him almost constant pain, yet his reputation on the battlefield remained fearsome until the very moment of his death and is the one aspect of his character even his fiercest detractors have never denied.

There are two Richard III caricatures in wide circulation. The Black Legend, as Desmond Seward's biography named him, and the White Knight called up by his defenders to give battle to this dark evil. As the two ethereal riders joust for supremacy, they tilt against each other endlessly, sometimes the Dark Legend scoring a hit, sometimes the White Knight striking his opponent's shield. The argument becomes far too monochrome to reflect any reality we might recognise, or that might engage a more casual spectator. The biggest problem with this polarised approach is that it completely ignores human nature and all the shades of colour encapsulated within it. Just as television and film moved on from black and white, so the study of history in general, and Richard III in particular, should adopt a technicolour approach. The Black Legend and the White Knight must hang up their spurs for a while. A Hollywood notion of the incorruptible hero and the irredeemable villain must be washed away.

England in the fifteenth century was a riven land of deep political manoeuvring. The interests of great noble houses, made rich and filled with hope by the promise of Henry V's successes in France but left to stagnate and bloat under the distant, distracted watch of his son Henry VI, ground into each other like icebergs in the polar seas. Those who had looked across the Channel for wealth, fame and honour found themselves frustratedly looking at their domestic neighbours in the hope of gain instead. Across an increasingly divided land, each cast furtive, suspicious glances at the other and saw in return the same mistrust cast over himself. Children born into such uncertain times can hardly have been unaffected by them. It is striking that the two most directly and drastically affected might have been the future kings, Richard III and Henry VII. Their stories are not as dissimilar as history might suggest: not least an insecure childhood leaving them buffeted by events beyond their control. For both men, their experiences culminated in them taking the throne of England to the shock and amazement of their contemporaries. Fate made them adversaries. History has made them enemies. To hold a favourable view of Richard III should not require the painting of an equally disparaging portrait of Henry VII. If Richard was a man of his times, who did what was necessary, the same courtesy of excuse must be extended to Henry VII.

The Tudors who followed Richard III have long been deemed not only his enemies on the field of battle, but also in the eternal struggle for his reputation that followed it. This is a far too simplistic view. Writers who gave permanent form to their views, opinions and remembrances in the years, decades and centuries that followed the Battle of Bosworth undoubtedly created a polemic that condemned Richard, reaching a ringing climax in Shakespeare's masterpiece that bears the king's name without even a distant resemblance to his history. The Tudors actually contributed very little to the creation of this myth, other than the fact of sitting on the throne. The notion of a concerted attack sponsored by successive Tudor monarchs cannot be evidenced. Instead, the fiction and moralising that frequently masqueraded as 'history', a word with meanings that have shifted and evolved over centuries before becoming what we might recognise it to be today, was merely a rolling stone that gathered moss.

From John Rous, who rewrote his own version of history in the immediate aftermath of Bosworth to create a new image of Richard as an ambitious monster, the mould was taking form. Polydore Vergil built upon this notion to present the advent of the Tudor dynasty as a blessing bestowed upon a nation in need of a saviour. Sir Thomas More, the first famous architect of Richard's evil reputation, is unlikely to have written what we would recognise today as history, but rather a classicist's exercise in the examination of the nature of tyranny that required little regard for literal fact and placed a far greater emphasis on moral instruction. Hall's *Chronicle*, compiled in the mid-sixteenth century, made the story racier still in order to outdo More. Shakespeare's work was merely the booming crescendo to a cacophony over a century in the building. Each retelling of the story added a layer, a dramatic flourish or a new crime to excite audiences who knew the old tale. Ultimately, Shakespeare was in the business of selling tickets.

I know what you're thinking, and you're not wrong. Matt's in the business of selling books. Quite right, I hope. This is another vehicle for the telling of Richard's story. It is only right that I disclose from the outset that I consider myself a Ricardian and that this biography is the culmination of a long interest. So why would you read *another* Richard III book? I hope that by setting aside the distracting, eternal joust of the caricature knights, a more rounded and more colourful Richard III will emerge. Whilst it is true that I begin this exploration from a position of believing Richard was wronged by the historical memory held in the collective consciousness, this book does not simply seek to redress a perceived imbalance since such a perception will necessarily be not only personal and entirely subjective, but also of narrow and limited appeal. The purpose of writing this narrative history of King Richard III is to place an authentic man in the complex context of his times. The interpretation of events in which the dry historical record can offer little insight into motive or intention will remain an unavoidable necessity, but I intend to provide a measured and balance opinion.

As ever, any mistakes are entirely mine and for any that have evaded editors, I apologise.

Your challenge, gentle reader, is to leave whatever baggage you have brought to this doorway outside and enter with a mind freed from its weight. When you depart, you may pick it up again if you wish, but my hope is that you will sift through it to see what is worth keeping before continuing on your own journey to find Richard III.

When we cease to question what we are told is the truth, then we have ceased to study history.

Matthew Lewis

A Note on Sources

A significant problem with any attempt to disentangle fact from fiction in the story of Richard III's life is the available sources. There is a substantial body of evidence in existence, but each presents its own problem, and there is one glaring hole that remains to be filled. The issues encountered cannot and should not be used to negate the importance of any source, but by understanding the sometimes cryptic and obscure reasons for writing what they wrote, the correct weight and caution can be given to their words. Primary sources, the record of those living through the events they describe or writing within living memory, remain the sharpest weapon in the armoury of any pursuit of historical truth but are no less a product of their times and the prejudices of those wielding a pen than any other source.

The fifteenth century represents something of a void in the transition of the recording of our history. In previous centuries, monkish chroniclers slavishly crafted their beautifully illuminated Latin words, meant to offer moral lessons from the events of their days and reserved for those their equal in education who could read the language of God and the law in which they wrote. Whilst the gist of what they recorded can usually be relied on, the layers of righteous indignation would need to be carefully peeled away and separated from the facts at the core of any story. Chronicles originating from holy houses would frequently equate freak weather conditions or the appearance of fantastical signs with years in which momentous events also buffeted the country. By the fifteenth century, these sources were becoming scarce, though one notable exception is of great use still.

Government paperwork was little changed over the previous 200 years. The recording of the workings and decisions of Parliament that began during the reign of Edward I (reigned 1272–1307) added to the existing Patent Rolls, Close Rolls and Fine Rolls to offer a dry presentation of government decisions. Although policy that may be particular to a monarch or a moment in time can be drawn from otherwise one-dimensional statements of grants or arrangements, these sources are generally devoid of analysis or opinion helpful in understanding the broader context of what they can relate. The explosion in State papers that came with the reign of Henry VIII, championed by Thomas Cromwell, was yet to arrive in England to provide the depth of record keeping beginning in Italy and Spain during this century.

Citizen chroniclers, writing in the vernacular rather than Latin and concerned with economic rather than spiritual and moral matters, were an emerging trend during this period. *The Paston Letters* represent a treasure trove of information for the fifteenth century, but though some of what has survived is nationally important, the bulk reflects the local and litigious preoccupations of the family. Many other such chronicles, like those of Gregory and other London writers, offer a merchant's perspective whilst frequently betraying a partisanship in the tensions that grew throughout the second half of the century into sporadic periods of open warfare. When reporting national events that took place outside the capital, they are not eye-witness accounts but the reproduction of news reaching the capital, albeit using the testimony of eye-witnesses. Embellishment and gossip can easily become woven into the fabric of such evidence.

Most of the controversy surrounding Richard III dates from the spring and summer of 1483 when tumultuous events overtook the kingdom. The movers and their actions are a matter for later in the story, but there are a handful of accounts traditionally relied on for studying these months. Each presents a problem that is insurmountable, and although they cannot be discounted entirely, each must be approached with a degree of caution and understanding about the writer's position and motives.

Perhaps the most widely vaunted contemporary source is known as *The Usurpation of Richard III*, written in December 1483 by Dominic Mancini, an Italian who was in England when Edward IV died and during the upheavals that followed, leaving sometime before the end of the summer. Mancini's account was rediscovered less than a hundred years ago in 1934, hidden in a library in France. The apparent value inherent in Mancini's writing stems from his position as an eye-witness to the events in London with no axe to grind on either side. That is not entirely correct, or at least does not provide the full picture. The first problem with using Mancini's account lies in the current translation in wide use, produced by C.A.J. Armstrong in 1969 and republished in a second edition in 1984. Entitled *The Usurpation of Richard III*, Mancini's original Latin title is *De Occupatione Regni Anglie per Riccardum Tercium*, which translates more accurately as *The Occupation of the Throne of England by Richard III*. There are Latin words for usurpation, but Mancini did not use them. The translation is therefore weighted from the very beginning for a dark interpretation of events.

In examining the critical events of 1483, Mancini's testimony will come to the fore, but it is essential to establish his reliability. Mancini dedicated his work to his patron Angelo Cato, Archbishop of Vienne, at whose request he set down what he had seen in England. Mancini's account begins 'You have often besought me, Angelo Cato, most reverend father in God, to put in writing by what machinations Richard the Third, who is now reigning in England, attained the high degree of kingship, a story which I have repeatedly gone over in your presence. Since you thought the original account worth recording, you considered that you would be doing a pleasing service to Frederick prince of Taranto, if you presented for him to read the story which you yourself gladly heard.'[1] Cato was a member of the French court, acting as personal physician to King Louis XI for a time. This connection is crucial given the French opinion of Richard III and the condition of internal politics in France in late 1483. For reasons that will become clear, France eyed Richard III with suspicion, and a tale of his evil ambitions fitted in well with a French narrative at the end of 1483. Mancini makes a catalogue of errors that betray his lack of understanding of English politics.

Much of his information appears to originate with Italian merchants in London, since he spoke no English. It is apparent that his sources were not friendly to Richard, and Italian merchants in London were to develop particular reasons to be hostile to Richard III. The only informant Mancini names is Dr John Argentine, a physician who served Edward V but was dismissed. Argentine made his way onto the Continent, which is most likely where this Italian speaker encountered Mancini. Dr Argentine would end up at the faux-court in exile of Henry Tudor and would eventually act as physician to Prince Arthur Tudor, so his personal animosity toward Richard III and favouring of the Tudor cause is clear to see. Mancini's testimony is perhaps handled best as that of an honest reporter of both what he saw and what he heard, since there is little reason to believe he lied. Instead, we must be cautious of where his information came from to fill the obvious and gaping void in his own knowledge of England and its politics.

The second contemporary source crucial to an understanding of this brief period of intense activity is one of the few chronicles still maintained by a religious house. *Ingulph's Chronicle of the Abbey of Crowland*, more commonly referred to as *The Crowland Chronicle* (sometimes also *The Croyland Chronicle*). Crowland Abbey was an immensely wealthy Benedictine religious house in Lincolnshire. The abbey maintained a chronicle spuriously claimed to date from the seventh century, but which contains two continuations from the thirteenth and fifteenth century that are valuable. The second continuation, which details the events of the Wars of the Roses period, was written, the anonymous writer informs us, 'at Croyland, in the year of our Lord, one thousand four hundred and eighty-six, in the space of ten days: the last of which was the last day of the month of April in the said year.'[2]

It has long been believed that the writer was Bishop John Russell, who was Richard III's Lord Chancellor for much of his reign, but doubt has recently been cast upon this. The writer provides verifiable insights that demonstrate he was a man somewhere at the heart of government under Edward IV and Richard III. He mentions having acted as an envoy for Edward IV on an embassy to Burgundy and whilst his information is invaluable, he appears to disapprove of Richard III. Despite this prejudice, as a source he remains vital and may not have been quite as anti-Richard as he might appear on the surface. He wrote during the reign of Henry VII, so although he might hope to preserve his anonymity, care would have been required. It seems unlikely that it is mere coincidence that the only copy of *Titulus Regius*, passed by Parliament during Richard's reign and not only revoked unread by Henry VII but also ordered to be destroyed, was found hidden at Crowland Abbey too. Without it, this significant piece of historical evidence would have been lost entirely. It is worth considering whether the writer, or perhaps group of collaborators, came together at Crowland to record their version of recent history before it could be erased by time and the machinery of Tudor government.

Two later sources that are all too frequently treated as contemporary, primary sources are the histories produced by Polydore Vergil and Sir Thomas More. Vergil was engaged by Henry VII to write a history of England. He began his work around 1505, completing his first compiled manuscript in 1513, though it remained unpublished until 1534. Sir Thomas More commenced his *History of King Richard III* around 1513 when he was Undersheriff of London. Before completing his work, he embarked on a career in royal service that led to it being set aside. The manuscript was edited, completed and published by More's nephew William Rastell in 1557, more than two decades after Sir Thomas's execution. Despite demonstrable flaws in their information, their distance from the subject and inherent bias, these two writers have been treated as sacrosanct for centuries. They may have still had access to informants alive in 1483, but their information would have been tainted by three decades of Tudor government that may have been the corruption feared by the writer sitting down at Crowland Abbey in 1486 to set out his version of events.

The final hurdle in trying to seek out a balance in the available material is the utter lack of any surviving account that might be considered to have originated from within Richard's own faction, or even within the north of England, where more sympathy for him might be expected. Serious efforts to unearth a more sympathetic view of Richard III began almost immediately after the Tudor dynasty ended, but these writers were presented with problems of time and distance even more significant than those which must be ascribed to the likes of Vergil, More and Edward Hall. When Edward IV returned to the throne in 1471, his exploits were recorded by an unknown member of his army in intense, if openly biased, detail. Had Richard triumphed at Bosworth, perhaps such a version of the campaign would exist to tell his side of the story. As it is, his death meant that there was no need for such a text, no audience to receive it and danger inherent in attempting it. So many of Richard's close friends and advisors fell with him that there were few left even to try to tell a more positive tale. Those who did survive were quick to distance themselves from Richard's regime in order to secure space within the new one sweeping him away. As John Rous would demonstrate, the flow was inexorably toward the negative, and none was willing to stand against the tide, entirely understandably. Nevertheless, it leaves us with a dearth of accounts from Richard's side and only adverse reports to pick through. This lack of balance is unhelpful, but unresolvable at present.

Richard III can appear a distant and one-dimensional villain from the evidence available and widely relied on, without questioning its veracity or motive. The challenge in writing a biography is to bring the man a little closer, draw him into focus and give a rounded picture of him. Taking the villain we have long sneered at with a pinch of salt, we must take care not to try so hard to balance the scales as to offer an opposite and equally flat picture of a heroic Richard without fault. Much of what follows will necessarily be this writer's interpretation of events and sources, which the reader may freely disagree with. Such is the beauty of history, and hence a book can still be written more than 500 years after the subject's death. In seeking balance, a degree of sympathy unpalatable to some, but evinced by the source material, may be expected from the pages that follow.

Prologue

Richard, 3rd Duke of York, was the most senior nobleman in Henry VI's England. His authority was second only to the king's, and his wealth was unsurpassed, even by his cash-strapped monarch, who stood in hundreds of thousands of pounds of debt.[1] He was a proud man, who had served twice as Lieutenant-General of France and as Lord Lieutenant of Ireland, who was considered by many to be the king's heir until Henry fathered a son of his own; Richard regarded himself as Henry's loyal servant. On Friday 10 March 1452, none would have known it. He was forced to ride through London's streets in front of the king and his entourage like a prisoner. His 'gallows' were to be the altar of the immense St Paul's Cathedral, where thousands could be crammed in to watch the royal duke recite an oath of fealty to his king. Although a calmer reflection might have acknowledged that he was lucky to escape an appearance at very real gallows, or at least on the executioner's block as his rank would usually have allowed; the burning rage, fuelled now by embarrassment, made the duke rue his decision to trust Henry.

York had, just a week earlier, led an army to Blackheath where he had sent the king a demand that Edmund Beaufort, Duke of Somerset, should be arrested. Somerset, who had been York's successor in France, was, York asserted, the root cause of all the kingdom's problems. He must answer for the recent losses in France and ongoing problems in England that had, just two years earlier, seen London overrun by an organised force of rebels from Kent led by the mysterious and enigmatic Jack Cade. For York, his time forced to the sidelines of politics was to be ended. The Beaufort family were close to Henry VI both in blood and affinity, representing an alternative line that might lay claim to the childless king's throne. How much this notion drove York cannot be known, but recent events would have made it only too plain for all to see.

Just before Cade's invasion of London, William de la Pole, Duke of Suffolk, had been banished from the kingdom, saved from the execution the crowds and Parliament bayed for, only to be assassinated as he crossed the Channel to begin his exile. Suffolk had been impeached by

Parliament, charged with an array of general crimes against the king and country, made more specific at Henry's insistence. The king was determined to save his favourite, his most trusted advisor, but it became increasingly impossible to ignore Parliament's demands. One of the specific charges brought against Suffolk was that he had married his own son to Lady Margaret Beaufort, the niece of the present Duke of Somerset, in an attempt to position his own family to take the throne. Parliament charged Suffolk with 'claiming and pretending her to be the next to inherit the crown of this your realm'.[2] The accusation may have been meant to alienate the Beauforts from the king through fear of their name, but it had failed. If Henry instead began to consider the option a viable one, the ploy would have backfired spectacularly. The possibility of a Beaufort succession was now a cat well and truly out of its bag.

When an MP with links to York named Thomas Young tried to bring a petition to have York recognised as Henry's official heir until the king had a son, Henry furiously brought the session to an end. Young was thrown into the Tower, an episode for which he would claim compensation in 1455 for a breach of his right to free speech in Parliament.[3] York had been marginalised with little cause and less hope of restoration, so he had taken matters into his own hands.

As he knelt before the altar at St Paul's Cathedral, delivering the oath that would procure his freedom, the duke must have felt more frustrated and isolated than ever before. He swore never again to take up arms against the king, to come whenever he was summoned and to expose any plots against Henry that he became aware of.[4] At Dartford, he had secured Henry's promise that Somerset was under arrest and York had disbanded his army at this news before going before the king. As he entered Henry's presence, any faint smile and sense of victory was immediately erased. Somerset was not the prisoner. It was York who was taken into custody and paraded to London like a prisoner. As his words rang out around St Paul's, the duke found himself in the jaws of court politics. Doubtless, he realised he had not been undone by Henry himself, but rather by the queen, Margaret of Anjou, and the man who, from this point on, would become his mortal enemy, Somerset.

York withdrew to his fortress at Ludlow on the Welsh border, stung and branded by his attempts to impose himself on English politics. The court was a fickle place filled with dangerous men and overseen by a feeble, disinterested king. Self-preservation required the duke to endure his time on the margins of political power, preserving his family's vast wealth and sprawling estates until the tide might turn in their favour again. Something else, such as a conscience, but more archaic and detached than any internal moral wrangling, must have gnawed at Richard, Duke of York, to cause him to adopt a different path. The quiet life lay in rural Shropshire, administering the Marcher lordships of his mother's

Mortimer family, or even at home within the walls of Fotheringhay Castle in Northamptonshire, the seat of the House of York bequeathed by his paternal uncle Edward, Duke of York. Richard chose to turn his back on the quiet life in pursuit of something else. Cynics might believe he sought power and glory. Sympathisers would assert a sense of noblesse oblige, the obligations of nobility, compelled him to try to help the king, even if the king didn't want his help.

What was clear by March was that the forty-year-old duke's wife Cecily, who was thirty-six, was pregnant yet again. Whether this served to remind York of his responsibility to his children, perhaps especially one yet to be born, is uncertain. This baby would be born into a family facing the chill of royal suspicion, the warmth of the king's patronage fading. The child would enter a kingdom on the brink of war with itself, as foreign glory became a burnished memory. By the time this great couple's final surviving child was born, York had learned hard lessons. Once bitten, he would be twice shy. The child would be a son. He would take his father's name, and in time he would walk a remarkably similar path. What York cannot have known is the impact this boy would have on English history and on the fate of the House of York.

1

Richard Liveth Yet

Deformed, unfinish'd, sent before my time
Into this breathing world, scarce half made up,
And that so lamely and unfashionable
That dogs bark at me as I halt by them
William Shakespeare, The Tragedie of Richard
the Third, Act 1, Scene 1

Fotheringhay Castle once loomed majestically over the slow bend in the meandering River Nene. Today only a single lump of stone, fenced off at the bottom of the mound of earth on which it once stood, remains to offer a hint of past splendours. Fodringeia is listed in William the Conqueror's Domesday Book and was rendered as Foderineye by the Tudor poet and antiquary John Leland. Foderingeye means a foddering enclosure, referring to a part of a forest that has been partitioned from the rest for the production of hay.[1] The village, once a market town huddled under the wing of the castle, boasted a market each Wednesday and an annual fair lasting three days. Richard, Duke of York, had the right to the fair confirmed and moved the date from its original commencement on the eve of St Michael, Michaelmas, to the anniversary of the death of St Thomas Becket,[2] perhaps due to a personal devotion.

The castle that stood on the eastern side of the town was built by Simon de St Liz, 2nd Earl of Northampton, in the late eleventh or early twelfth century. Under Edward III, the castle and lordship of Fotheringhay reverted to the Crown and was granted to the king's fifth son, Edmund of Langley, later 1st Duke of York. During Edmund's minority the castle fell into disrepair to the extent that upon taking possession, Edmund all but rebuilt it. The keep was layed out in the shape of a fetterlock, which, combined with a falcon, was to become a favourite device of the House of York.[3] With Edmund's death in 1402, his titles and lands passed to his oldest son Edward, whose death at Agincourt led to them falling to his nephew, Richard, 3rd Duke of York, in 1415. Richard was the only son of Edward's younger brother Richard, Earl of Cambridge, who had been executed for plotting against Henry V shortly before he left on what would become the Agincourt campaign. Young Richard was a month short of his fourth birthday when his father was executed, leaving him orphaned, but after many years of his minority, he seems happy to have adopted Fotheringhay as the continued seat of the House of York.

St Mary and All Saint's Church lies just to the west, its spire clearly visible from the site of the castle. Edward, 2nd Duke of York had established a college within the church that his nephew was tasked with completing and in which Edward had requested his body be buried. The link between the town's church and the Yorkist lords based within its castle is plain to see today as windows display brightly coloured coats of arms, and falcon and fetterlock images or white roses are to be found in almost every corner of the remaining church. The college was destroyed during the Dissolution of the Monasteries, but the parish church still proudly advertises its connection to this royal house.

It was here, within the comfortable surroundings of his family's principal residence, that a boy, named Richard for his father, was born on Monday 2 October 1452, just more than six months after his father had been tricked and forced to participate in an embarrassing spectacle at St Paul's in London. This son would be the last child the couple had to survive infancy, but he was not short of siblings. Richard, Duke of York, and his duchess Cecily Neville, were at the pinnacle of English society and had enjoyed unrivalled wealth that had, in earlier years, supported a lavish lifestyle.[4] York was a great-grandson of Edward III through his father, descending from that king in the male line through his fourth surviving son Edmund but also through his mother through Edward III's second son Lionel, Duke of Clarence. Richard was therefore also Edward III's great, great-grandson through Lionel's daughter Philippa.

Cecily Neville's ancestry was hardly less illustrious. The youngest daughter of the second marriage of Ralph Neville, Earl of Westmoreland, her northern pedigree was exceptional. The Neville family had been gradually accruing power and influence in the region for generations, culminating in Ralph's promotion to an earldom under Richard II. Despite the joining of the two great northern families a generation before Ralph, the Neville family found themselves rubbing up against their Percy neighbours in the constant quest for land and influence.[5] Neville family relations were made more complicated by Ralph's favouring of the fourteen children of his second marriage over the eight children of his first union to Margaret Stafford. Although the earldom of Westmoreland was entailed to his oldest male heir, the first son of his first marriage, Ralph ensured that the majority of his lands passed to the children of his second wife. His reason was not hard to discern. Ralph's second marriage had been to Joan Beaufort, a daughter of John of Gaunt and his long-term mistress and later wife, Katherine Swynford. The Beaufort children had been born before the couple married but had been legitimised by Richard II in Parliament and, by Papal dispensation, deemed capable of inheriting lands and titles. This legitimisation was ratified by Henry IV and, despite long belief, no legal mechanism prevented these children from inheriting the crown.[6] This connection made Cecily a great-granddaughter of Edward III herself, meaning that the couple's children could claim descent from the second, third and fourth sons of King Edward III.

The duke and duchess had been married for more than ten years before the arrival of their first child in February 1438. Named Joan, probably after her grandmother, the child did not survive long. Over the years that followed the couple had twelve further children, six of whom were thriving when Richard was born. Their oldest surviving child was Anne, already thirteen and married when her youngest brother was born. Her husband was the young Henry Holland, Duke of Exeter, who had been York's ward. A son was born in 1441 and named Henry, probably in honour of the king, but he did not survive. During their time in Normandy, Edward had been born in 1442, Edmund in 1443 and Elizabeth in 1444. None of these siblings were nearby when their youngest brother was born. Edward, aged ten and created Earl of March, and Edmund, the nine-year-old Earl of Rutland, had been installed within their own household at the Marcher fortress of Ludlow Castle, part of the inheritance Richard had acquired on the death of his maternal uncle Edmund Mortimer, 5th Earl of March. The significance of the March title to the House of York is reflected in York's decision to pass it to his oldest son. The earldom of Rutland had formed part of the Yorkist inheritance and had belonged to Edward before he became the 2nd Duke of York. Elizabeth, aged eight in 1452, was being educated within another household, as was traditional, and would be married to John de la Pole, Duke of Suffolk, in a few years' time.

The oldest York child still in the nursery at Fotheringhay when young Richard arrived was Margaret, born at the castle in 1446 and now aged six. Two more short-lived sons, William and John, followed in 1447 and 1448 respectively, before the birth of George in Dublin whilst York was Lord-Lieutenant of Ireland in 1449. Not quite three years old when Richard was born, he was the closest in age to Richard. The year before, in 1451, a boy named Thomas had died in infancy, and although the couple would have a daughter named Ursula in 1455, she would also fail to survive, leaving Richard as the youngest surviving child.

With four sons and three daughters, in 1452 the duke and duchess offered a stark contrast to King Henry VI and his wife Margaret of Anjou, who remained childless. In 1447, Henry had overseen the arrest of his last paternal uncle, Humphrey, Duke of Gloucester, amid suspicion that the fifty-six-year-old childless former Protector of the Realm was plotting to seize the throne from his nephew. Within a few days of his arrest, Gloucester was dead. The most likely cause of death was a stroke brought on by the stress of the episode, but rumour quickly sprang up that Gloucester had been poisoned. The king's uncle, the last surviving brother of Henry V, had clung steadfastly to the idea of conquest in France. He had been a vocal, and popular, opponent of the peace process the king insisted on and more than any real suspicion of his desire to be king, it was this that sealed his fate. His death on 23 February 1447 set in motion the wheels that would lead to civil war. Loyal opposition, for the first time, had no home within the House of Lancaster. Gloucester had identified York with his own cause, and it was to York that Gloucester's popular support turned. With popular acclaim came the accompanying suspicion of the king and queen. York was no childless old man.

Later mythology would begin with Richard's birth. Shakespeare's villain was, he tells his audience, 'Cheated of feature by dissembling nature, Deformed, unfinish'd, sent before my time Into this breathing world, scarce half made up'.[7] In contrast, John Rous's revised work, written after Henry VII's accession, has Richard portentously born after two years in his mother's womb, with teeth, and with hair down to his shoulders. Biology would tend to give the lie to these allegations. A difficult birth suited the later desire to paint Richard as a monster from birth, destined to bite the world with those antenatal teeth and steal a throne. Three sources suggest the infant Richard was a sickly child in some way, but each can be shown to be flawed. The Victorian historian James Gairdner, whose writing tends to suggest that he disapproved of Richard, claimed that 'it would seem that Richard himself was slender and sickly.'[8] This assertion was based entirely on a passage in *History of England During the Middle Ages*[9] by one of Gairdner's contemporaries, who 'found evidence somewhere, as he believed, that Richard had serious illness as a child'. Gairnder was forced to concede that Turner 'was not able to refer to the sources of his information'[10].

The second cause of speculation has been a poem written around 1456. *The Dialogue at the Grave of Dame Joan of Acres* contains a description of the children of York and his duchess.

> Sir aftir the tyme of longe bareynesse,
> God first sent Anne, which signifyeth grace,
> In token that at her hertis hevynesse
> He as for bareynesse wold fro hem chace.
> Harry, Edward, and Edmonde, eche in his place
> Succedid; and after tweyn doughters cam
> Elizabeth and Margarete, and aftir William.

John aftir William nexte borne was,
Which bothe be passid to Goddis grace:
George was next, and after Thomas
Borne was, which sone aftir did pace
By the path of dethe into the hevenly place.
Richard liveth yet: but the last of alle
Was Ursula, to him whom God list calle.[11]

The brief snippet 'Richard liveth yet' has been used, by Gairdner amongst others,[12] to suggest that something was surprising in his continued life. In the absence of other evidence, that seems to stretch a small mention in a rhyme a little too far. The son born before Richard and the daughter born after him had been lost and there is perhaps no more to this than the acknowledgement that the duke and duchess had lost several children. Although Richard was only about four years old and not yet free from the perils of infant mortality, nevertheless he was a living child. His unremarkable status as the youngest son might be all that can be inferred from the reference.

The final hint at a problematic birth originates from the pen of Richard's mother, Duchess Cecily. A letter in which she refers to 'encomerus labour, to me full paynfull and unesy'[13] has been linked to Richard's birth, but J.L. Laynesmith is clear that this letter, in fact, refers to a 'disease and infirmite' afflicting Cecily in early 1453. Given the passage of several months since Richard's birth, it is unlikely to be connected.[14] Of the two contemporary sources used to suggest that Richard's birth was difficult or that he was a sickly child, neither stand up to interrogation as satisfactory evidence that anything untoward affected his carriage, birth or early childhood. Gairdner's later reporting of hearsay he could not substantiate is typical of what followed Richard's death. Writers sought to find some sign or portent that he was destined to be a monster because in that knowledge lay the comfort that evil can be predicted, it can be seen coming if one is wise enough to heed the warnings. In reality, Richard was, as far as can be discerned, a normal, unremarkable child. The fourth son of a duke, he may have been destined to struggle to find his own way in the world or for a lofty position within the Church. Hindsight might tell us otherwise, but in 1452, he was fourth in line for his father's inheritance and likely to get little or nothing he didn't find for himself.

We are able to pinpoint the date of Richard's birth with a degree of certainty not always available for younger sons of the nobility. A Book of Hours owned by Richard, which would come into the possession of Lady Margaret Beaufort, contains a note, possibly in Richard's own writing, against 2 October. The Latin addition tells the reader 'on this day was born Richard III King of England at Fotheringhay AD 1452'.[15] Noting his position as king, the inscription must have been added more than thirty years after his birth. The need to mark it in something as personal as his own Book of Hours might demonstrate an awareness of his own origins as a younger son, destined to be of little consequence, and just how far he had risen despite such a beginning.

With a baby boy safely delivered, the most pressing matter on the medieval mind was now the baptism of the child. Until the moment the child had been washed of the original sin the Church taught all babies were delivered into, the soul remained in the gravest peril. If a child should die unbaptised, the passage of its soul into Heaven could not be assured. Cecily would have taken to her lying-in chamber at least a month before the baby was due and would not leave it for some weeks afterwards. She, as a new mother, must be churched before resuming her position in the temporal world to cleanse her of the taint of blood and bodily fluids involved in giving birth. For the squalling newborn child, there was no time to waste. A high infant mortality rate always made baptism a time-critical matter, and the duchess knew only too well the perils a newborn faced, having lost five children before this delivery.

The location of Richard's baptism is not recorded. It may have taken place within the castle's chapel, or at the Church of St Mary and All Saints nearby. Given the family's close ties with the church and college there, the latter is perhaps more likely. The rite of baptism had many regional variations throughout the Middle Ages, but one of the most contemporary versions is contained within the York Manual of 1509. The subject of the baptism was referred to as the catechumen. After asking the child's name, given by godparents who stood in the mother's place, the priest would breathe into the baby's face three times to drive out unclean spirits, invoking the Holy Spirit to enter into the space created. Next, the priest would make the sign of the cross on the child's forehead, then on the breast before placing his right hand on the baby's head and offering prayers.

Next, Richard would have undergone the exorcism of salt. In the sixth century, John the Deacon explained that blessed salt was used as part of the exorcism process 'so the mind which is drenched and weakened by the waves of this world is held steady.'[16] The salt could be applied to the forehead in the shape of the cross whilst the priest intoned, 'I exorcise you, creature of salt,' adding 'Richard, receive the salt of wisdom' before offering more prayers for the child. A particular set of prayers for male children would have been recited next, differing slightly to those provided for girls. The York Manual calls next for the reading of Matthew 19:13–15, in which Jesus chided those who tried to prevent people bringing children to him, telling them 'Let the little children come to me, and do not hinder them, for the kingdom of heaven belongs to such as these.' A further exorcism rite called an *effeta* was performed in which purifying oil was applied to the right ear, the nose and then the left ear.

Godparents were then called upon to confirm 'Our Father, Hail Mary, I believe,' a sentiment repeated by the priest. Unfortunately, there is no record of who acted as Richard's godparents at his baptism, but it was usual for a boy to have two godfathers and one godmother. Their role was to speak for a baby who could not confirm its own Christian belief yet. After being formally introduced into the family of the Church, the baby was blessed at the font in a manner perhaps more familiar to those attending a modern christening. A litany was spoken, and the priest had a range of available ceremonial to chose from at the font, from making the sign of the cross in the water with his finger to breathing on the water to drive out evil. Candle wax might be dropped into the font water, or chrism[17] could be added.

The York Manual next calls for the credal interrogation to be made three times. In the case of an infant, the enquiry would be made of the godparents whether the baby will believe in God. Once these questions had been answered satisfactorily, the child would be immersed in the purified water of the font three times before being anointed. The ceremony closed with readings from Mark 9:17–29, the exorcism of a deaf-mute spirit from a child, and John 1:1–14; 'In the beginning was the Word, and the Word was with God, and the Word was God.'[18] The entire baptism ceremony was an exorcism designed to remove every trace of the original sin the Church taught all babies were born into, and to replace that evil with the Holy Spirit. The symbolism of water washing the skin as the blessings it holds wash clean the soul is plain, and the use of salt and breathing are all aimed at driving out evil. The repetition of elements three times relates to the invoking of the Father, the Son and the Holy Spirit to guide and protect the infant. The role of the godparents is to vouch for the child's future faith and to offer their commitment to ensuring the baby will grow up to believe in God and accept the Church's teachings. In essence, baptism seeks to return the receiver to the same blameless, sin-free state that Adam enjoyed before his temptation. At a time of high infant mortality, the compulsion to see it done quickly is easily understood.

With this most crucial of matters completed, Richard would have taken his place within the York family nursery at Fotheringhay in the company of his sister Margaret and brother George. A wet nurse would have been employed to breastfeed the new baby since to do so reduced fertility and noblewomen had a responsibility to continue producing issue for their husbands for as long as their bodies would allow. Richard was Cecily's sixth child in six years and twelfth in fourteen years of childbearing. It would be three more years until she bore her final child, Ursula, who did not survive. Richard would have been tightly swaddled during his early months, an ancient practice believed to ensure the child's limbs grew straight and without deformity. The thirteenth-century knight and poet

Walter of Bibbesworth instructed in his Treatise that 'When the child is born he must be wrapped. Then lay him in a cradle and get a nurse.'[19]

The first seven years of Richard's life would pass by in the kind of unrecorded obscurity that might be expected for the fourth son of a duke. During that time, his parents and older siblings were being drawn deeper into a spiral of opposition to the king and his court that could have little but direct conflict at its heart. After seeming to put York in his place following Dartford, Henry had appeared reinvigorated, and 1453 began with the first good news from France in many years and, after eight years of marriage, the pregnancy of his wife Margaret of Anjou. By August, the promise was lost. A renewed offensive in France collapsed and the Battle of Castillon on 17 July 1453 was lost. Henry's premier general, John Talbot, Earl of Shrewsbury, was killed in the encounter that would become the last of the epic Hundred Years' War between England and France. The conquest that had claimed Henry's father's life was undone. The English were expelled from all of France except Calais.

At home, law and order were breaking down. The Neville and Percy families in the north took advantage of a king distant in both geography and personality to bring their grievances with each other toward open warfare. On 24 August, an armed force led by the Earl of Northumberland's second son, Lord Egremont, attacked a party returning from celebrating the wedding of Thomas Neville, fourth son of Richard Neville, Earl of Salisbury. Dubbed the Battle of Heworth Moor, the skirmish had no recorded casualties, and little real fighting as the Neville group retreated behind the thick walls of their nearby fortress at Sheriff Hutton Castle. Henry's favourite, Edmund Beaufort, Duke of Somerset, now marked as the enemy of York, was embroiled in a bitter feud of his own. He disputed an inheritance claimed on behalf of his wife but held by Richard Neville, Earl of Warwick, Salisbury's oldest son and a magnate of increasing wealth and voracious ambition. Warwick had been in possession of the lands Somerset wanted for years, but Henry ordered Warwick to make way for Somerset, heightening the sense that the duke's position at the king's side allowed him to ride roughshod over what was right. Warwick had no intention of rolling over quietly. The Neville influence had not been built by moving backwards.

Unsurprisingly, Henry selected this dispute centring on Cardiff Castle to tackle, coming to the aid of his beloved Somerset. At the royal hunting lodge of Clarendon in Wiltshire, England's problems took a new and potentially disastrous direction. Whether it was news of the loss at Castillon and death of Shrewsbury that arrived, or reports of the erupting feud in the north, is unclear; but perhaps the culmination of all this trouble proved too much for a fragile mind. Henry's grandfather, Charles VI of France, had been afflicted by repeated episodes of mental illness that had ultimately left France exposed to English invasion. Now, England's king fell away from the world, lost to the present and unable to function. Precisely what caused Henry's catatonic state is hard to pinpoint at such a distance, but his inability to lead government proved even more problematical than the incompetence he had displayed to date. Medieval government relied on the monarch for the ratification of all decisions. Without a head, the body simply could not operate.

On 13 October 1453, Queen Margaret was delivered of a son, the eagerly awaited male heir the House of Lancaster had lacked for so long. Born on the feast day of St Edward the Confessor, the boy was given the name Edward and baptised by William Waynflete, Bishop of Winchester. His godfathers were Cardinal John Kempe, Archbishop of Canterbury, and Edmund Beaufort, Duke of Somerset. His godmother was the Duchess of Buckingham, Cecily's sister Anne.[20] King Henry was unable to acknowledge his son despite several attempts to present the baby to him. The Council tried to continue government in the king's name and managed to keep Henry's incapacity secret for many months until matters were brought to a head by the death of John Kempe, Archbishop of Canterbury, in March 1454. Royal approval was an unavoidable step in appointing a replacement. Parliament orchestrated a test to try to establish Henry's mental state, but they found a shell of a man unable to feed himself, stand up or respond to any question. Something would have to be done.

In January 1454, Queen Margaret made her case to be permitted to hold regency powers on behalf of her husband and their son. She asked that she be given 'the hole reule of this land' and be permitted to make all senior appointments such as the Chancellor and Treasurer. Margaret also requested that she should have authority to appoint bishops as the king would, that a sufficient income should be provided for her, her husband and their son, and a fifth item that was not noted by John Stodeley in writing his newsletter.[21] What Margaret asked was not, to her sensibilities at least, unreasonable. In France, it was usual for a woman to take on the role of regent during the minority or incapacity of a son, husband or brother. Adèle of Champagne had acted as regent while her son Philip II had been on crusade in 1190. During the minority of Louis IX, his mother Blanche of Castile was regent and would serve in the role again when Louis was on crusade. Within living memory, Isabella of Bavaria had been regent for her mentally unstable husband Charles VI between 1417 and Henry V's assumption of that role in 1420. Following Isabella's example, the natural play for Margaret to make for her security and that of her son was to assert her right to rule during a regency period.

Margaret would never quite manage to understand that she was not in France anymore. A request that might have chimed harmoniously in Paris rang harshly in the ears and panicked minds of the misogynistic English nobility. For the lords at Henry's court, the notion of being ruled by a woman was beyond their comprehension, or at least it was not a concept they were willing to dabble with. Salic Law in France prevented the succession of a woman or the transmission of a claim through a female line, and this offered a failsafe that made the temporary exercise of royal authority by a woman acceptable. In England, no such mechanism existed. Aside from the potential risk of a longer-term usurpation of power, men with no reference point for submitting to the superiority of a woman were sent into spirals of panic at the mere thought of such a thing.

John Stodeley's newsletter next mentions the widespread rumour that Richard, Duke of York was due to arrive in the capital on 25 January.[22] The choice for those in power in London was simple. If they didn't want Margaret in charge, they needed to turn to an alternative. Somerset was one option, but he was closely aligned with the queen and had been placed under arrest on charges of treason brought by the Duke of Norfolk when York had been called to attend Parliament in November, probably to help resolve the mounting problems. The most senior royal male in the country was the obvious choice to provide a hand on the tiller, except that he was currently languishing beyond the warmth of royal favour. Even after York's recent actions at Dartford, his humiliation at St Paul's and subsequent exclusion from the court, he was a more appealing option than the queen. Stodeley reported that York was coming to London with his oldest son Edward, Earl of March, then aged just eleven. He added that an armed retinue was expected with the duke and that he was to be accompanied by his brother-in-law the Earl of Salisbury, Salisbury's son Warwick and Henry's two half-brothers Edmund and Jasper Tudor, Earls of Richmond and Pembroke respectively.

On 27 March 1454, York was appointed Protector and Defender of the Realm and Church, the arrangement formalised in Parliament on 3 April. Just before taking up the mantle, York had overseen the creation of Henry's son as Prince of Wales on 15 March, perhaps to allay any fears the queen and others might have as to his own motives and intentions. It was an intoxicating moment for a man on the fringes of national politics for years to find himself suddenly, albeit temporarily, in complete command. York's Protectorate is notable for his even-handed approach in spite of fears he might become too partisan. With the exception of Somerset, those close to Henry remained on the Council and meetings were regular. York set about redressing the disastrous royal finances and bringing under control the expenses of the royal household. Somerset languished in prison, and Margaret fumed at the affront to her regal position. They might have been the only two praying for a miraculous recovery by the king, but their wish was to be granted.

In what was heralded as a Christmas miracle, on Christmas Day 1454, Henry emerged from his catatonic state as quickly and unexpectedly as he had entered it. If his illness had created political difficulties, Henry's recover was to doom the country. Within weeks, York was removed from his role as Protector and frozen out again. Somerset was released from prison and resumed his position at Henry's right hand. York had proved that even-handed, responsible government was possible but had his efforts thrown back in his face. Before Richard was three, the tension the king could not relieve between two of his most significant subjects would spill out into open warfare. When Henry summoned a Great Council to meet in the Midlands, the power base of the Lancastrian king, York, as well as Salisbury and Warwick, who had become closely aligned with the duke, were ordered to attend. Fearing a repeat of the fate of Humphrey, Duke of Gloucester, at Bury in 1447, the lords were, perhaps justifiably, cautious, but when caution takes the form of raising an army, it manifests as aggression.

York led his force toward the king, sending letters at each stop to pledge his allegiance and raise his concerns about the state of government.[23] There was a suspicion that Somerset was intercepting these messages and preventing the king from seeing them. *An English Chronicle* noted Somerset was now the man 'be whom at that tyme the kyng was principally gided and governed', adding 'duke Edmond ever kept hym nygh the kyng, and durste nat departe fer [far] from his presence, dreding alwey the power of the seyde duk of York.'[24] As a clash became inevitable, the Yorkist force caught up with the king's while the latter was encamped within the town of St Albans. The Earl of Warwick managed to bypass the barricaded gates by breaking into some unprotected gardens at the edge of the town and, in the hail of arrows his men unleashed on the unprepared royal forces, Henry and the Duke of Buckingham were amongst those injured. As the rest of the Yorkist army breached the gates, in the ensuing panic Somerset was slain, as was the Neville family's bitter rival Henry Percy, Earl of Northumberland, and Lord Clifford. Somerset's son, another Henry, was also seriously wounded.

Despite Shakespeare's later dramatic reimagining of the battle, it was not the two-and-a-half year old Richard who killed the Duke of Somerset, however amusing the thought of a toddler swinging a mace at a grown man might be. Portions of the history of the Wars of the Roses were condensed and contracted to fit Shakespeare's desired timeline. Having Richard present at the First Battle of St Albans to kill Somerset was simply foreshadowing for the villain we would later be asked to see. In the aftermath of the fighting, York had the king, an open wound at his neck where an arrow had caught him still bleeding, treated at the Abbey after professing his loyalty once more. On their return to London, though, there could be little doubt in the minds of the watching crowds who was now the power behind Henry's throne.

On 18 November, York again took on the mantle of Protector, having been asked to do so by a pliant Parliament. Henry was absent, though there is no clear indication that he was ill again. York resurrected his efforts at improved government, but when he set about implementing an Act of Resumption to undo a good deal of Henry's free-handed gifting away of his own livelihood, the king suddenly re-emerged to dismiss York once more on 25 February 1456. His ascendancy had again been short-lived and undone by the vested interests of those who prospered under Henry's weak leadership. Back in the political wilderness, York and his family had few dealings with the court over the next two years until, in March 1458, Henry decided to make a concerted effort to bring an end to the ongoing rivalries. Henry Beaufort, now Duke of Somerset in his father's place, had joined with the new Earl of Northumberland and the son of Lord Clifford in trying to extract vengeance for St Albans and – at last – Henry thought he should intervene.

The Love Day held on 25 March 1458 celebrated the peace that Henry had extracted. The Yorkist lords were made culpable for the deaths at St Albans, and York was ordered to pay compensation to Somerset's family totalling 5,000 marks, though he was to be allowed to assign this from debts owed to him by the Crown.[25] The Earl of Warwick was required to compensate Lord Clifford for his father's loss, the Earl of Salisbury to cancel some debts owed to him by the Percy family and all three Yorkist lords were obliged to pay £45 per year to fund prayers at St Albans Abbey for those killed in the action. The only sanction against the court party saw Lord Egremont, the troublesome younger brother of the new Earl of Northumberland, bound over for 4,000 marks to keep the peace for ten years.

Henry was delighted. The Love Day parade saw him lead the reconciled parties. Behind him walked Queen Margaret, holding York's hand and followed by Salisbury clasping hands with Somerset, and Warwick with the Duke of Exeter. There must have been some sweaty, uncomfortable hand squeezing as they strolled behind the jubilant king. The crowd were delighted. The poet John Lydgate wrote the catchily titled *Upon The Reconciliation Of The Lords Of The Yorkist Faction With The King And His Adherents*, pouring hope onto the much-vaunted new peace.[26] To others, particularly with the invaluable benefit of hindsight, it was nothing more than a sham. The Tudor antiquary Richard Grafton summed up the event almost a century later by sneering, 'As by this cloked Pageant, and dissemblyng Procession, hereafter shall plainly be declared. For their bodies were joined by hande in hand, whose heartes were farre asunder: their mouthes lovingly smyled, whose courages were enflamed with malice: their wordes were swete as sugar, and their thoughtes were all envenomed: but all these dissimulyng persons, tasted the vessell of wo, as the wise man sayd: and fewe or none of this companie were unblotted, or undestroyed by this dolorous drinke of dissimulation.'[27]

Nothing was really solved. Deep cracks had been thinly papered over, but Henry lacked the force of personality to bring these running disputes to a definitive conclusion. York returned to his exclusion. A new Somerset took his place beside the king and queen. Few joined York's party, but when they included the Earl of Salisbury and his son the Earl of Warwick, they were enough to unsettle the rickety apple cart of Henry's England. Until this point, little of any permanence had been achieved or lost; the events of Richard's first years might well have passed him by as he learned to walk and talk. Thought may have been given to his future, and a post in the Church might have been considered for him or George, as younger sons. Cardinal Henry Beaufort had served his family's interests well as Bishop of Winchester, and George Neville was soon to become a powerful ally in the Church for his brother Warwick. The influence a high-ranking cleric might bring to the House of York would hold no small amount of appeal.

Unaffected by the broader machinations of the country's mightiest lords, even those of his father, Richard had been sheltered within the Yorkist nursery at Fotheringhay Castle. The comfortable seat of his family provided insulation from the storms beginning to batter the fortunes of his father, his uncle Salisbury and his cousin Warwick. It would not last long. As the wind blew harder and the waves crashed down from a greater height, the fingers of the swelling tempest began to reach into the warmth of Fotheringhay Castle. Richard's life was about to change drastically. For the first time, in 1459, the Wars of the Roses were to begin to shape one of its most controversial figures.

2

Caught in the Wheel

And for no thing but for thy chivalrie,
Thay in thy bed have slayn thee by the morwe.
Thus can fortune the wheel governe and gye
And out of joye bringe men into sorwe.
Geoffrey Chaucer, *The Canterbury Tales*, The Monk's Tale[1]

The *Rota Fortunae*, or wheel of fortune, would have been a familiar construct to those in the fifteenth century. Nowhere is it more applicable than in the tales of the improbable rises and spectacular falls of the second half of that century. A large wheel was turned, sometimes slowly and sometimes more quickly, causing some to rise and those who were once at the pinnacle to fall. Fortune was always a woman, usually blind, who turned the wheel unpredictably. The imagery was meant as a reminder to all that fortune was fickle and erratic. Those in power might lose it in an instant, and those who felt the crushing weight of fortune's wheel on their chests might suddenly rise to new peaks. It is a metaphor frequently applied to the period of the Wars of the Roses because it fits so perfectly and would have been in the minds of those living through the troubles every bit as much as it is referred to by historians.

An *English Chronicle* lamented the sorry state of England by 1459. Despite Henry's triumphant belief that he had settled the old scores, no one else was fooled.

In this same tyme, the reame of Englonde was oute of alle good governaunce, as it had be meny dayes before, for the kyng was simple and lad by covetous counseylle, and owed more then he was worthe. His dettes encreased dayly, by payment was there none; alle the possessyons and lordeshyppes that perteyned to the croune the kyng had give awey, some to lordes and some to other simple persones, so that he had almoste noughte to live onne.'[2]

The anonymous writer is unashamedly pro-York and was dismayed by the fall of the Duke of Gloucester in the previous decade, but his was becoming the populist view of Henry's incompetent government, for 'the hertes of the peple were turned away from thayme that had the land in governance, and theyre blyssyng was turnyd in to cursyng.'[3]

Queen Margaret was singled out by this chronicler as the chief cause of the mounting problems as she 'with such as were of her affynyte rewled the reame as her liked, gadering ryches innumerable.'[4] *The Brut Chronicle* noted that 'the governance of the Reame stode moste by the Quene and her Counsell,' adding 'the great princes of the land wer nat called to Counceil bot sett A-parte.'[5] Men such as James Butler, Earl of Wiltshire, who were no friends to York, were relentlessly promoted. Wiltshire became Lord Treasurer, a post from which he 'peled the pore peple'.[6] The writer also notes another rumour sent out to sow discord. Margaret 'was defamed and desclaundered'[7] by accusations that Edward, Prince of Wales, was begotten of adultery and was not the king's son. In response, Margaret sought to craft a niche in the prince's earldom of Chester that would be loyal to him personally, handing out livery badges showing a swan.[8] Ultimately, the writer believed that Margaret meant to increase her own authority by causing her husband to abdicate in favour of the prince.[9] The accusation about Prince Edward's legitimacy has lingered unproven ever since, with some asserting that his real father was Edmund Beaufort, Duke of Somerset. In 1459, just as now, no one can really have been certain, but the aspersions cast upon Henry's dynastic pretensions and Margaret's fitness to rule in the child's name were what mattered. If Margaret were planning to promote her son's affinity and perhaps even persuade Henry to abdicate, it would be so that she could control government in the prince's name; mud, as it was designed to do, stuck.

A building cold war dominated most of 1459. Margaret and the court party raised men in Chester and the Midlands. York began to gather men at Ludlow. Salisbury was drawing the vast Neville affinity to his banner. Warwick was Captain of Calais, a post that gave him access to the garrison, the only full-time army in the pay of the Crown. He was becoming ever more popular with London merchants for his exploits in keeping the seas free from pirates. This was not to be a prolonged stand-off, though. In September, Salisbury marched his men south-west towards Ludlow. Queen Margaret ordered a force, nominally loyal to her son and wearing his swan badge,[10] to intercept them. The two armies met at Blore Heath in Staffordshire on 23 September, and despite bringing twice as many men, Lord Audley's royal contingent was tricked into attacking Salisbury over a brook by a feigned retreat. As men enthusiastically poured into the stream to catch the retreating enemy, Salisbury's men turned and unleashed hails of arrows on those suddenly incapacitated by the terrain and the surprise. Lord Audley was amongst the dead whose blood caused the brook to run red. Two of Salisbury's younger sons, Thomas and John Neville, were taken prisoner along with Sir Thomas Harrington, but with reports of another royal army somewhere nearby, there was no time to try to recover them. Salisbury paid a friar to fire a cannon all night to create the illusion that the battle was still going on and to disorientate any other army in the vicinity.

When Salisbury arrived in Ludlow a few days later, it must have raised alarm to see men who had already been forced to fight for their lives trudging wearily into the town. Within a few more days, Warwick arrived with the Calais garrison to give a significant boost to the force taking shape at Ludlow. He may have been concerned to hear of the capture of two of his brothers by the queen's army, and his and his father's resolve can only have been hardened, though they needed to take care not to bring about the execution of the two men by the actions they would undertake next. This moment was a significant one for the York family too, and it represents Richard's first exposure to the revolutions of the wheel of fortune. His secluded childhood at Fotheringhay was about to be brought to an abrupt end as the events that had been causing tremors around the country finally began to impinge on this six-year-old.

At some point as summer turned to autumn, York decided that Fotheringhay was no longer a suitable place for the youngest members of his brood, nor for his wife. They were isolated, and Fotheringhay was not really meant as a fortress to withstand sieges. If matters got out of hand in the coming months, his wife and three youngest children might become a target, either for vengeance or the gaining of leverage, if they remained there. The family was moved, brought within the walls of the less comfortable but considerably more defensible Ludlow Castle. Lying on the Welsh Marches, a stone castle had been begun on the site within a decade of the Conquest. Since then, it had formed an essential link in the chain that kept the Welsh from attacking across the border into England. York had acquired the castle from his Mortimer uncle, the Earl of March. Raised high on an outcrop and held safe in the crook of the River Teme protecting it on the west and south and by the River Corve to the north, it is easy to see why early border barons selected the spot. The town to the east provided the only safe approach to the castle, but the streets and timber-framed buildings provided an adequate barrier of their own.

The outer bailey, amongst the largest in England, was encircled by high, stout walls accessed through a gatehouse from the town's market square. Buildings propped up against the outer walls serviced the castle's needs, from the blacksmith to the stables. Opposite the gatehouse stood Mortimer's Tower, added by Roger Mortimer, the 1st Earl of March, who had deposed Edward II and acted as regent for Edward III. Nestled just to the side of the tower was St Peter's Chapel, built by Roger to commemorate his escape from the Tower of London on 1 August 1323. The open grassed area of the outer bailey was perfect for mustering troops or to shelter the population of the town if they ever needed to retreat there for safety. The equally stout walls of the inner bailey were protected by a dry moat that could be filled with spikes and sharp objects in the event of an attack because the porous stone would not hold water. The original gatehouse was transformed into a keep, though the old entrance can still be seen today, bricked up. Its replacement, immediately to the right, provided access across a drawbridge to the more comfortable apartments, the great hall, kitchens, well and other essential amenities necessary to withstand a long siege. The beautiful and unusual chapel of St Mary stands in the space near the centre of the inner bailey, its Norman circular design meant to copy that of the Church of the Holy Sepulchre in Jerusalem and its presence an assurance that religious worship could continue during a time trapped within the castle.

York chose it as his base of operations during this troubled period for the same reason it had been located there nearly 400 years earlier. As men poured into the town and the castle from York's lordships along the border and in Wales, from Salisbury's northern lands and from across the Channel with Warwick at their head, it must have been a heady, exciting sight. Few can have been more impressed than the duke's youngest son, the six-year-old Richard. These weeks represent the first, and last, time all four sons of York can be confidently placed at the same location. It may well have been the first time Richard had ever met his older brothers Edward and Edmund, who had been at Ludlow for years receiving their training. The first impression they made must have left a mark on Richard.

Edmund was the sixteen-year-old Earl of Rutland, just old enough to be involved in any fighting that the coming days might bring. A deep brand must have been left on the little boy when he saw his oldest brother: Edward, Earl of March, was seventeen and stood 6 feet 4 inches tall at a time when the average height for a man was 5 feet 7 inches.[11] He was a giant who would develop a fearsome reputation on the battlefield, and no six-year-old boy could fail to be in awe of such a physical specimen. The fact that he was Richard's brother must have held out some hope that one day, he too could grow into such an imposing and impressive figure. Watching all of the preparations for war must have been a bewildering excitement after the quiet seclusion of Fotheringhay.

Richard passed his seventh birthday during all these preparations. It seems unlikely there was much in the way of a celebration, but the intoxicating feeling of being around his father, his older brothers, his uncle Salisbury and his famous cousin Warwick might have been more than sufficient substitute for any other revelry. Within a few days, York led his gathered host out of Ludlow, leaving Duchess Cecily, Margaret, George and Richard within the safety of the castle's walls. His plan seems to have been similar to that of 1452 when he had marched to Dartford. Henry VI was in London, and Queen Margaret was in the north-west championing her son's cause. York perhaps meant to catch the king away from his wife and press his complaints directly to his pliant cousin. He reached Worcester but shortly after moving on again, news arrived of a terrifying development. An army estimated to be twice the size of York's was heading directly towards them.[12] What made it worse was that Henry himself was at the head of the force, encased in his armour and flying the royal banners.

To take the field against the king himself would constitute treason and risk the loss of everything a man had. Given that kings were considered to have been appointed by God and were anointed to the role in the religious ceremony of coronation, it could be construed as a blasphemy that risked a man's immortal soul too. York's army retreated to Worcester, for taking mass at the Cathedral, and the lords pledged their allegiance to the king before the Bishop of Worcester. From there, they moved back to Ludlow, setting up their defences in the broad fields just over the Teme. *The Brut Chronicle* records that they 'had made ther felde in the strongest wise, and had proposed verily to abyden and have foughten',[13] suggesting that they were prepared for Henry to attack.

Whatever plan York had, it fell apart during the night of 12 October. *The Brut Chronicle* records that 'in the nght Andrew Trollop and al tholde soudioures of Caleys, with A gret felasship, sodenly departed out of the Dukes oost [host] and went strayt unto the Kynges feld, wher thei wer receyved joyously, for thei knew the entent of the othir lordes, and Also the maner of ther felde.'[14] Andrew Trollope was a well-respected soldier, the leader of the Calais garrison brought by Warwick. His defection should not have come entirely as a surprise. Henry Beaufort, Duke of Somerset, was the newly appointed Captain of Calais in Warwick's place.[15] Somerset's father had been Captain, and some of the men present may have served under him, retaining some lingering affection or loyalty for the Beaufort name and the Lancastrian king it supported. Trollope himself had been part of John Beaufort's 1440 campaign in France. Besides all of that, there was still the question of committing treason against the Crown and these men were in its pay. Whatever their motivation, the garrison took with them intelligence of York's defences and perhaps even his plans, if Trollope had been briefed as to what would be expected of him and his men. There was also the danger that others might see an example in Trollope's defection into the waiting arms of the king and his pardon. A terrible situation had got significantly worse.

Henry had ignored a letter the Yorkist lords had addressed to him on their return to Ludlow pleading their allegiance.[16] There was a later rumour, albeit promulgated by the Parliament that met in November 1459 to condemn the Yorkist lords, that York had 'brought in certeyn persones bifore the people, to swere that ye were decessed, doyng masse to be said and offeryng, all to make the people the lesse to drede to take the feld'.[17] Saying masses for the dead for one still alive was sinful, and the story was doubtless meant as a signal of York's desperation. The Parliament Rolls record the additional charge that York and his force had 'falsely and traiterously rered werre ayenst you, and than and there shotte their seid gonnes, and shotte aswele at youre most roiall persone, as at youre lordes and people with you than and there beyng'.[18]

Sent into a panic by Trollope's defection with the garrison, the Yorkist lords moved back into the castle in the middle of the night for a conference, ordering their men to keep the banners flying and await their return.[19] The instruction, and the promise of their return, would not only prevent the spread of panic amongst their force in the dead of night, but it would also buy them precious time for what they felt they had to do. When the lords gathered within Ludlow Castle, their choices were limited and stark. They could stand their ground and risk being attacked by the king's larger force. With Trollope's intelligence, their chances of defending Ludford Meadows were significantly reduced, and the castle itself was probably not provisioned for a long siege. The resolve of their men might falter too when King Henry appeared at the head of the opposing army.

Surrender was a possible avenue. Parliament would note that because Henry was 'a most Christian prince whose clemency is to be noted as long as the world endures'[20] he had offered pardons 'to all those accompanying the same duke and earls who would leave them'.[21] The king also 'sent word to the same duke of York and earl of Warwick that you would give them pardon and grace of their lives, livelihood and goods,'[22] if they should request it within six days. What made the offer unpalatable was the exclusion of 'a few persons proclaimed after the death of the Lord Audley,'[23] a list that included Salisbury. It would mean York turning his back on his most potent ally and Warwick abandoning his father. Besides, York was wary of trusting Henry's word. If it were a trick, he was unlikely to get away as lightly as swearing an embarrassing oath at St Paul's this time. The king was far more likely to take their heads despite his promise of clemency.

The only option that would save their lives, at least for now, and those of their men, was also the least honourable one. If they fought, they left themselves open to charges of treason and risked their lives in the uncertainty of battle. Surrender was just as much of a risk and consigned Salisbury to a certain death. They could run. They would have several hours headstart under cover of night and the confusion in the morning would take time to unravel and resolve. Wrestling against abstract notions of chivalry and less ethereal ideas of cowardice, they accepted this option as the least likely to bring about their immediate destruction. York took his second son Edmund, Earl of Rutland, into Wales and eventually reached Ireland, where his recent stint as Lord Lieutenant and his Mortimer heritage ensured him a warm, protective welcome. Salisbury and Warwick took York's oldest son Edward, Earl of March, south, reaching the coast and taking ship to Calais, which still obeyed young Warwick as its Captain despite his recent displacement.

As the sun rose on 13 October, confusion ran like wildfire through the Yorkist camp when no senior commander could be found. In the absence of orders and confronted with the king's host, those emerging from their tents to huddle under Yorkist banners in Ludford Meadow lay down their arms, relying on the king's promise of a pardon. They were excused, but the town of Ludlow attracted the king's bitter wrath for the support it had provided to its lord in his preparations to oppose Henry. His army, denied the chance to vent adrenalin on the Yorkists, was unleashed on the town instead. *Gregory's Chronicle* records that 'The mysrewle of the kyngys galentys at Ludlowe, whenn they hadde drokyn i-nowe of wyne that was in tavernys and in othyr placys, they fulle ungoodely smote owte the heddys of the pypys and hoggys hedys of wyne, that men wente wete-schode in wyne, and thenn they robbyd the towne, and bare a-waye beddynge, clothe, and othyr stuffe, and defoulyd many wymmen.'[24] The castle did not escape the marauders' attentions either. *Hearne's Fragment* relates that they 'spoiled the Town and Castle'[25] and *The Brut Chronicle* states they 'despoiled the Castel'.[26]

The shocking discovery the looters made was that the Duke of York had left his wife and three youngest children behind.[27] A later legend sprang up that Duchess Cecily took Margaret, George and the seven-year-old Richard out to the Butter Cross in the market square, where they waited to confront the oncoming royal army. There is no contemporary support for this romantic scene, perhaps meant to encapsulate the notion of 'Proud Cis', as the duchess was called. *Hearne's Fragment* clearly suggests that the duchess was in the castle when King Henry arrived there. York must have taken the hard, and seemingly cold decision that his wife and youngest children would be safe in the king's hands and that taking them with him in his haste would have been impractical. Cecily represented York's best hope of salvaging anything within England. She was on good terms with Queen Margaret, despite the queen's suspicion of York, and, as a woman, she should also have been above retribution for her husband's actions. Although politics was usually beyond the scope of behaviour seen as acceptable for medieval women, their ability to equate themselves with the Virgin Mary made peacemaking a suitable activity for them. In leaving his wife, perhaps with her approval or at her suggestion, York left himself a foot in the door within England.

Even if they were not found standing at the Butter Cross, York's children endured the looting of the castle that had only days earlier seemed like the impregnable fortress of their father and older brothers.

Combined with the noise of drunken pillaging and rape ringing out from the town beyond the castle walls, it must have been a terrifying experience for the youngsters. The thirteen-year-old Margaret might have felt some maternal, protective responsibility for her younger brothers after their years in the nursery together. George was a week short of his tenth birthday, and Richard had only just turned seven. If the build-up to York's departure had been an exciting, heady experience, mingling with armoured men preparing for war and watching their impressive older brothers sparring in the outer bailey, then their abandonment was an unfathomable and terrifying betrayal. The overnight shift of fortune and their desertion by those from whom they should have expected protection compounded their fear with the shock of betrayal.

The faith York had displayed in his wife's ability to weather the storm proved well placed, though the dangerous risk the couple had engaged in became starkly apparent soon enough. Cecily, Margaret, George and Richard were taken into custody, but it was to prove a comfortable confinement. They were placed under the care of Humphrey Stafford, Duke of Buckingham, and his wife Anne, who was Cecily's sister. *An English Chronicle* notes that 'the noble duches of York unmanly and cruelly was entreted and spoyled'[28] at Ludlow. One interpretation of this is that Cecily was physically mistreated and perhaps even raped, in line with the experiences of the rest of the town, but it seems likely that more would have been made of such a breach of a noble lady's honour. *The Brut Chronicle* simply reported that Henry 'sent the Duches of York, with hir childer, to the Lady of Bokingham, hir suster, where she was kepte long aftir.'[29] Gregory described Cecily being 'kept fulle stryte and many a great rebuke'[30] being endured, suggesting that her husband's behaviour was thrown at her, but there is no further hint of a physical attack on her at any point.

No evidence survives as to the cordiality or otherwise of the relationship between Cecily and Anne Neville. Cecily was forty-four by this time, just a year younger than Anne and both had been married to their respective husbands for around a quarter of a century, but they would have spent their early years together in their parent's nursery at Raby Castle in the sprawling beauty of County Durham's countryside. Cecily and her children may well have enjoyed their gentle confinement at Buckingham's Maxstoke Castle in Warwickshire.[31] The stunning moated, red sandstone castle was built in the middle of the previous century by William de Clinton, Earl of Huntingdon, with imposing octagonal towers at each corner of its rectangular layout. Richard may well have been made to feel comfortable and secure during his time with his Aunt Anne, even if Cecily felt the brunt of frustration at her husband's disruption of the kingdom.

Richard would spend nine months under Buckingham's care. It may have represented a return to normality after a brief and chaffing exposure to the cold winds of national politics. Being in the company of Margaret and George could have radiated the reassuring warmth of something similar to the family home at Fotheringhay, where his father and brothers had always been a distant notion. Now, however, they were very tangible, and they had abandoned Richard to a fate they may have been confident he would survive, but which he can hardly have understood. If he overheard the news seeping out from the Parliament that met at Coventry, he might have comprehended enough to know that things were getting worse for those who had left him. No barrier of age or protection within his aunt's walls could shield him from the effects of what was being done by the jubilant court party.

Acts of Attainder were enthusiastically passed through Parliament. The eagerness reflected not only the ravenous exactions of the victors from their defeated foes but also the taking into royal hands of vast amounts of property and income that might not only help to balance the royal accounts but also open the floodgates to fresh waves of patronage from the open-handed, uncomprehending Henry. An attainder was a tool available to the king as a sanction against those who had committed high treason. His subject was tried in the Court of Parliament with no right to a defence nor to appeal. Once passed, the attainted person was instantly stripped of all lands and titles and became an outlaw if they were still alive. The benefit to the Crown was both in acquiring new property and in denying it to those who might use their wealth against the monarch in future. It was not a widely used tool until the second half of the fifteenth century when civil strife made it a convenient expedient; the promise of a possible reversal of an attainder might regain loyalties that had been lost.

At Coventry, York was finally attainted. It had taken Henry eight years since the duke's first direct action at Dartford to decisively deal with him. Along with York, his two oldest sons Edward, Earl of March, and Edmund, Earl of Rutland, also stood attainted.[32] The effect on the York family was devastating. At the moment the Act was passed, they lost everything. Their fall could hardly have been more spectacular even after a decade of quarrelling with those about the king. They had begun the summer as the country's second family and ended the year as penniless, landless outlaws. York had nothing of his own, nothing to leave to his children. Edward and Edmund were deprived of what they held in their own right, but none of the brood would get anything their father had once owned either. For Cecily and her three youngest, it begged the question of how they would survive.

Alongside the York family, several other significant men were attainted. Unsurprisingly, Salisbury and his son Warwick were prominent. Two of Salisbury's other sons, Thomas and John, who had been captured at Blore Heath, appeared on the list along with John, Lord Clinton, the only other baron to appear amongst York's allies, a comment on the lack of breadth to his support amongst the nobility. Thomas Harrington hailed from an influential northern family who held estates in Yorkshire and Lancashire. The Harringtons were to become important figures later in Richard's story. John Wenlock's career would improve from his attainder in 1459, and William Oldhall was a close associate of the Duke of York. Thomas Vaughan appeared on the list and was to continue to be closely associated with York's family. William Stanley is a notable inclusion too. His brother Thomas, Lord Stanley, escaped the Commons' attempt to have him attainted, and it is possible this close call in at least appearing to take the side of the House of York scarred the brothers and directed their future activities. Amongst those who appear on the Bill of Attainder is Thomas Parr, the great-grandfather of Catherine Parr, who would be the sixth and final wife of Henry VIII.

The most striking aspect of those named is the individual to whom more blame was apportioned than any other, including York. Alice Montacute, Countess of Salisbury, headed the list of those attainted. The wife of Richard Neville, Earl of Salisbury, in whose right he held the earldom, Alice had attracted the vitriolic retribution typical of some of Henry's later dealings with those he identified as enemies. Often lax in his punishing of those who deserved it, he was occasionally prone to vicious reprisals that seem out of character and may have been an effect of the mental illness that troubled him.[33] Parliament claimed that Alice, with William Oldhall and Thomas Vaughan, had 'falsely and traiterously ymagyned and compassed the deth and fynall destruccion of you, soverayne lord'. On 4 July, it was claimed, she had 'traiterously labored, abetted, procured, stered and provoked the seid duc of York, and the seid erles of Warrewyk and Salesbury, to doo the seid tresons, rebellions, gaderynges, ridynges and reryng of werre ayenst youre moost roiall persone'.[34]

Alice's culpability in the events at Blore Heath and Ludlow is hard to fathom. It might point to weakness in the men that they allowed themselves to be ruled by one of their wives, which might make it significant for the future that Cecily was not selected to take that particular fall. An alternative, or perhaps complementary, possibility is that blaming Alice allowed the door of forgiveness to remain open to the men she had supposedly coerced into treason. Salisbury owed his title and some of his lands to his wife's Montacute father, but Warwick was in the same position if ensuring more land was snatched was the prime consideration. In the bitter aftermath of York's fall, which some had waited for years to see, it seems odd that a possible route back into favour was preserved for him. There had not at any point been even a hint of personal animosity between York and Henry. The pious and intermittently clement Henry may have desired a way to undo such a drastic action taken against the most powerful noble in his kingdom and a prince of the blood royal.

Yorkist propaganda would later dub this session the Parliament of Devils for the attack on their cause, but the notion that the king had constructed a path for York to return to favour is supported by the remarkably generous manner in which Cecily and the children who remained in her care, including Richard, were provided for. Alice Montacute's shocking fate offered a stark warning that York's decision to leave his wife behind had been a dangerous one, or that it had proven wise. When Cecily was installed at Maxstoke Castle, she was only about 10 miles north-west of Coventry and ideally placed to plead to the king on her husband's behalf. John Bocking wrote to Justice William Yelverton, John Paston and Henry Filongley on 7 December 1459 that, amongst many other things, 'the Duchesse of York come yestereven late',[35] suggesting her arrival had been on 6 December as Parliament was winding down. However, as J.L. Laynesmith suggests, it seems far more likely that Cecily was engaged in more protracted negotiations with the king over the fate of her husband.[36]

Gregory's Chronicle notes that Cecily came to the Coventry Parliament and 'submyttyd hyr unto hys grace.' She petitioned the king to show her husband mercy and to allow him to 'come to hys answere and to be ressayvyd unto hys grace.'[37] Henry and York do not appear to have indulged in personal animosity, and later events would demonstrate that Henry had great faith in his cousin and probably affection for him as a kinsman. The odd way in which Henry seemed to separate his fear of the threat York represented from his personal relationship with the man himself may have been a manifestation of Henry's mental illness or a symptom of the whispering campaign York had been subjected to by the queen and her party. Whatever the cause, Cecily clearly felt able to speak directly to Henry about salvaging her husband's position. It worked, too, though probably to a lesser degree than was at first apparent.

Gregory reported that 'the kynge fulle humbely grauntyde hyr grace, and to alle hyrs that wolde come with hyr, and to alle othyr that wolde com yn with yn viii dayes.'[38] Many men, 'knyghtys and squyers', were able to take advantage of the king's grace period of eight days to obtain forgiveness, which they owed to Cecily. It is unlikely that eight days was ever going to be enough time to get a message to York in Ireland or the other members of her family in Calais and for them to return. Indeed, it is doubtful they would have placed enough faith in Henry's offer, after all that had gone before, to venture to Coventry. Nevertheless, the offer of a pardon combined with the overarching blame attached to Alice Montacute, Salisbury's wife, suggests that Cecily may have engineered a backdoor for her husband, a way out of the mess he was in now. She and her children were at Maxstoke, close to Coventry, so she might have used her relationship with the king and queen and her ability to operate as a peacemaker to continue to fight her husband's corner. If Alice shouldered most of the blame, the men ensnared in the imagined trap she had operated could be excused and eventually rehabilitated.

The duchess managed to ensure that she, and the children who remained with her, were provided for too. Her success in this endeavour is, if anything, even more remarkable. King Henry set aside an annual income of 1,000 marks 'for the relief of her and her infants, who have not offended against the king'.[39] The income was to be drawn from York's forfeited possessions in Northamptonshire, Essex, Hertfordshire, Suffolk, Shropshire and Herefordshire and represented a more than generous settlement. It would amply support Cecily, Margaret, George and Richard, even if York were unable to find his way back to favour, serving as more than a comfortable baronial income. The estates of the young Prince of Wales had been valued the previous year at less than £900[40] and Cecily's 1,000 marks equated to £666,[41] so it is clear that she was not being punished because of her husband's fall from grace.

The year 1459 saw Richard's first contact with the cold realities of politics in an England beset by weak government and liable to the fickle winds of fortune. Lifted from the cosy nursery that had protected him since birth, Richard was suddenly propelled into the front line of preparations for war. Such exposure can only have been a dizzying source of excitement for a six-year-old boy. He was surrounded by a family who had, through no fault of his, been distant for most of his life. What kind of impression did his huge oldest brother Edward leave on such an impressionable little boy? Richard could not help but have hoped to match Edward in stature one day; and as he passed his seventh birthday with both his parents and almost all his siblings for the first time ever, he might have felt another step closer to meeting that goal.

A ubiquitous depiction of blind Fortune turning her wheel, propelling some to greatness whilst crushing others at the same time, might have held a new significance for Richard by the end of 1459. Any exuberance, any feeling of being part of a larger family and of being protected by them was torn away. His father and the two older brothers he had been admiring as they practised with sword and mace in the outer bailey of Ludlow Castle had run away and left him. Their reasons might be fathomable to one able to appreciate the whole complicated web closing in around them, but to a seven-year-old boy, it must have felt like a terrifying betrayal. Who could be trusted, if not those old enough to defend him? His mother, his sister Margaret and his brother George had stayed at his side, but what impression would these weighty experiences leave on a child? Could Richard perceive some sense that he might have a duty to protect those left with him, however impossible the physical realisation of that mission might have been? Did he learn what it meant to be abandoned? Did he nurture a nagging recognition, the sort that is hard to shake off once it settles into a young mind, that he couldn't really trust anyone but himself?

Cecily had deftly sheltered her children from the worst of the fallout. At their aunt's house, however Cecily might have been chided for her husband's actions, the children were probably spared that abuse. Their mother had secured a comfortable future for them too. Perhaps Richard could reflect that things could have been a lot worse, but that gnawing sense of the loss of something could prove hard to let go of. The type of mark left by his experiences in 1459 on Richard cannot be confidently identified, but neither can he have been altogether unblemished by them.

Any peace he found was to prove short-lived as blind Fortune set about her unpredictable work once again.

3

Fear and Sorrow

It cannot be long before we hear some great news, though it cannot be good, unless some satisfactory agreement is arranged between them; otherwise great shedding of blood cannot be avoided, and whoever conquers, the Crown of England loses, which is a very great pity. May the Most High intervene and save this kingdom and everyone who dwells here, although, amid such disturbances great fear and sorrow cannot be absent from the spirit of anyone who happens to be here! If such fear and sorrow were allayed we could put up with the absence of events.

Letter from C. Gigli to Michele Arnolfini,
14 February 1461[1]

Over the two years that followed his experiences at Ludlow in 1459, Richard was to undergo a transformation that may have seemed miraculous to an observer of his fortunes as that year came to an end. Often, a transformation requires the endurance of pain and change. The more dramatic the alteration, the greater the discomfort to be tolerated to achieve it. None of this would offer comfort to a seven-year-old boy unable to divine where his trials and tribulations would eventually lead him. Daily life within the household of his Aunt Anne was comforting, but the sharp talons of reality could not be avoided forever.

Events began to unfurl well beyond Richard's little world, but they would impact upon him almost as much as any other in the kingdom. In January 1460, Warwick's experience in the Channel and the affection he was still held in both in Calais and the south-east of England paid dividends. As a fleet was being prepared to cross the sea and lay siege to the Yorkist lords' refuge, Warwick despatched a small force that managed to steal away all the ships, apart from the *Grace Dieu*, which was 'broke in the botome'. With the fleet was snatched the man ordered to lead it, Richard Woodville, Earl Rivers, and his oldest son Anthony.[2] By the end of the month, William Paston was writing to his brother John that Warwick, Salisbury and March had been ridiculing their newly acquired prisoners from the court party. Salisbury chided Rivers, 'callyng him knaves son, that he schuld be so rude to calle hym and these other Lords traytors'. Warwick chimed in to point out that Rivers' 'fader was but a squyer' and that he had only become a lord through his scandalous marriage to Jacquetta of Luxembourg, the widow of John, Duke of Bedford. Not to be left out, the young Earl of March 'reheted [berated] hym in lyke wyse'. Anthony received a similar dressing down in an awkward first meeting between March and his future in-laws.[3]

In the spring, Warwick managed to slip through the patrols in the Channel commanded by Henry Holland, Duke of Exeter, who had been appointed Lord High Admiral, and reach Ireland. Precisely what was discussed with his uncle York is unknown, but it would seem likely that this was the point at which their strategy to regain what they had lost was agreed. *An English Chronicle* notes that Warwick also collected his mother from York's protection, the attainted Alice having managed to flee there. Returning to Calais with his mother safe and a plan in hand, Warwick passed by Exeter's patrols, which 'durst nat sette opponne the erle'. In turn, Warwick declined to engage because of Exeter's position as Admiral and because he was 'of the kynges blood', but perhaps also because his mother was on board with him.[4] Once back in Calais, a set of articles were sent from the Yorkist lords in exile to the Archbishop of Canterbury, detailing their loyalty to the king and the unfair treatment they had received.[5] The Archbishop was Thomas Bourchier, a man promoted to the role by York during his first term as Protector. Thomas and his brothers were the sons of William Bourchier, Count of Eu, and Anne of Gloucester. Anne was a granddaughter of Edward III through his youngest son, her father, Thomas, Duke of Gloucester. The Bourchier family were close to York and the Archbishop provided a sympathetic ear at Henry's court, since the creation of an Archbishop of Canterbury was the one act the king had not undone following the Protectorate. Bourchier was also the half-brother of Humphrey, Duke of Buckingham, so could perhaps provide news or at least support for Cecily, who was still in the duke's care.

Support for the Yorkist lords was growing in London, where Henry was less popular and from whence he frequently retreated to the Midlands. Letters flooded into Calais assuring the lords of the people's support for them, 'besechyng thaym that they wolde in alle haste possible come and sucour thaym fro theyre enemyes'. Suspicious and by now naturally cautious, Warwick sent his younger brother William Neville, Lord Fauconberg, across the Channel to scout out the true situation. Fauconberg was a veteran of the wars in France and a respected soldier and on his arrival, 'the peple of Kent and of other shyres aboute resorted to the sayde lorde Fauconbrege in grete nombre'.[6] If any more encouragement were needed, it came in the form of a ballad nailed to the city gates of Canterbury, which screamed out for the Yorkist lords to come from Calais.

> Edwarde Erle of Marche, whos fame the erthe shalle sprede,
> Richard Erle of Salisbury named prudence,
> Wythe that noble knyghte and floure of manhode
> Richard erle of Warwick sheelde of our defence,
> Also lytelle Fauconbrege, a knyghte of grete reverence;
> Jhesu ham [them] restore to thayre honoure as thay had before,
> And ever shalle we syng to thyn Hyghe Excellence,
> *Gloria, laus et honor Tibi sit Rex Christe Redemptor!*[7]

It was clear who the people favoured. March might have been technically the most senior nobleman there, as the son and heir of a royal duke, imbuing him with fame. Salisbury must be placed above his own son and is almost fobbed of with prudence. The effusive superlatives are reserved for Warwick, a noble knight, the very flower of manhood and the nation's shield against all enemies. Then, 'lytelle' Fauconberg is able to squeeze in too. Such a public demonstration of support was the final piece of the jigsaw needed to activate Warwick's daring scheme.

On 26 June 1460, Warwick, Salisbury and March, accompanied by Fauconberg, landed at Sandwich on the south coast. Warwick appears to have been accepted by all as the military leader of the venture, and it is possible the daring plan was his own suggestion to York in Ireland. The duke had always been slow to act and unwilling to attack the king, but Warwick was a far more daring character, and the plan has the fingerprints of his personal flair all over it. His personal popularity would also be vital in gaining more support once they arrived in England. Also travelling with the Yorkist lords was a Papal Legate, Francesco Coppini. Coppini had been sent by Pope Pius II to obtain English support for a crusade against the Turks, but his patron the Duke of Milan had given him a secondary task of encouraging an English invasion of France that would distract Charles VII's attention from Italy. Henry's French wife had sent Coppini away with a flea in his ear, and the Legate's embarrassment had been soothed by Warwick's sympathetic ear and the promise of action if the Yorkist lords could only be restored. This was sufficient to secure Papal support for the exiled noblemen, and when Warwick landed in England, Coppini came with him, preaching the justice of their cause and writing to Henry to advise him to hear their case.

Having met little resistance at Sandwich, the small force moved through Kent, swelling its numbers as Warwick's reputation drew men to them. When they reached London, the city opened its gates willingly to the famous Warwick, the protector of merchants from the ruinous piracy in the Channel. Only the Tower held out under the command of Lord Scales, the same man who had, a decade earlier, fended off Cade's Rebellion as it gripped London. Scales ordered the Tower garrison to open fire as crowds pressed in around the walls. Cannon fired heavy, indiscriminate gun stones into the bodies below, but Scales gained the hatred of the mob when he unleashed wildfire to burn the crowd and spread panic with the pain. Once the initial furore had died down, a siege was set. Salisbury was left in command and Warwick, with March and Fauconberg, set out north to confront the king's forces. On 10 July, they clashed in the pouring rain at the Battle of Northampton. The royal army had dug a defensive position but was undone by the betrayal of Lord Grey of Ruthin, whose men helped March's outflank the defences, and Henry's men fled. The king himself was left behind and was captured by the Yorkists. On their return to London, they found the Tower in Salisbury's possession. Their victory was complete. Now, they only had to await the arrival of the Duke of York.

It was not until the second week in September that York eventually reached England, landing in Cheshire and travelling slowly, displaying the royal arms of England and France. To all intents and purposes, it was a royal progress to the capital. Christopher Hanson wrote to John Paston on 12 October to explain the sudden changes in London. Edward, Earl of March, had sent men to secure a place for Cecily, Margaret, George and Richard. From his letter it seems likely they were given permission to stay at Sir John Fastolf's home in Southwark. A few days later Cecily travelled to Hereford to meet her husband and make the rest of the journey with him, leaving her children in London. They were not alone, though, since Hanson wrote that 'the Lord of Marche comyth every day to se them.'[8] It was several days of peace in which Richard could grow more acquainted with his giant and previously distant oldest brother.

When York finally reached London, he marched into Westminster Hall, the space lined with the gathered nobility of England. Striding across the floor, he climbed the steps to the raised dais, reached out his hand and gently placed it onto a cushion on the seat of the king's throne. The meaning to those watching on in shock was as plain as it was disturbing and, judging by the reaction, unwanted. Embarrassed by the silence that met his bold claim, York was asked by the Chancellor whether he wished to see the king and replied in rage that there was no man in the kingdom who shouldn't rather come to him than York go to them. If this had been part of the plan settled on with Warwick, then it was a spectacular failure. Even Warwick seems to have kept silent. If York acted unilaterally, clearly even his allies did not expect nor welcome it. What ensued was a frantic but careful political bargaining game.

Parliament was in session, and one of its first items of business was the complete reversal of everything done at the Coventry sessions the previous year.[9] All of the attainders were lifted, and the Yorkist lords were entirely restored to their former positions. For young Richard, this meant a restoration too. No longer a comfortable prisoner in his aunt's household, he was back with his family, probably at their London home of Baynard's Castle. The Duke of Buckingham had been amongst those killed at the Battle of Northampton, and the release of Cecily and her children had been almost immediate. Baynard's Castle became a hub of business in London as the city awaited York's return and Richard was again at the heart of bustling and exciting events, though experience may already have left him twice shy after being bitten at Ludlow. With his father's return, he had become the son of a duke once more, no longer tainted by accusations of treason and stripped of any family prestige. Whether the young boy understood the implications of his father's claiming of Henry's crown is less clear.

The decision was taken that York should submit his written claim to the throne for scrutiny by Parliament. The importance of this step in the long-running struggle between the Crown and Parliament should not be underestimated. After the Conquest of 1066, the balance of power had been shifted entirely in favour of the Crown. The Great Charters that almost saw England handed to a French prince sought to redress that uneven distribution of authority. The word 'Parliament' emerged during Henry III's reign in the thirteenth century to describe what would previously have been a Council meeting. That century also saw the first appearance of elected representatives, though Simon de Montfort was not the first to implement this measure despite the tendency of history to bestow upon him the plaudits for inventing elected parliaments.[10] In the confusion and panic caused by York's challenge to the Lancastrian title, Parliament took the opportunity to gain further ground. Parliament had approved Henry IV's right to the crown in 1399, but only after the event and in recognition of the status quo. Now, the body was inveigling for itself the power to judge and rule on a royal title. This moved Parliament significantly closer to the position of the Anglo-Saxon Witan, which claimed the authority to appoint a king. This moment in the development of Parliament is highly significant and set a precedent for the decades that followed.

As the question of whose claim was to be deemed superior passed through Parliament, the comings and goings make almost comical reading.[11] The final arrangement was not funny in any way. The Act of Accord, passed into statute on 25 October 1460, recognised the senior claim of the House of York to the crown of England. However, the Lords could not bring themselves to cast Henry VI from the throne. He was not personally disliked in the way Richard II had been before his forced abdication. The Act confirmed that the Mortimer line of descent from Edward III's second son, although through a female line, had always been superior to the male line of the House of Lancaster from Edward's third son. Henry was to retain the crown until his death, at which point it would pass to York and his heirs. The duke was recognised as Prince of Wales in place of Henry's own son. The Lords may have considered it a suitable compromise to solve the problem, but in reality, it pleased no one. Henry was still king, Margaret of Anjou would not tolerate the disinheritance of her son, and York, a decade older than his cousin, might have a long wait and may never wear the crown. Whatever victory was achieved was perilously pyrrhic for both sides and might be undone by a further Act of Parliament as easily (if it was easy) as it had been created.

This episode appears to have little direct impact on Richard, but the events of 1460 can be seen as foreshadowing later years in which he would be a central figure. The way in which his father handled this situation, the settlement he achieved, the conviction that the House of York was the line holding a long-denied right to the throne and the mistakes York made would all feed into what followed. The immediate future would offer stark warnings to the young boy, too. Within a few months, he had gone from being the disinherited son of a traitor to being fifth in line to the throne of England.[12] The speed with which blind Fortune could give, take away and regrant was dizzying and entirely unpredictable. This was the terrifying merry-go-round Richard was forced to ride as a child, and these experiences began to shape the man he would become and his view of the world around him, the people inhabiting it and his own precarious position in it. If he needed the lessons of the past year brought home any more starkly, he would be left in no doubt by the end of the year.

Margaret of Anjou had escaped to Wales and then by ship to Scotland. The queen was in no way minded to accept her husband's capitulation to York and the handing away of their son's birthright. She busied herself in Scotland petitioning Mary of Guelders, the recently widowed queen consort of James II, for aid. Mary was trying to secure the future of her nine-year-old son James III, so Margaret was able to seize on the similarities in their positions to seek to obtain a sympathetic hearing. However keen Mary may have been to help, she had little money and enough problems of her own. She promised Margaret an army led by the Earl of Angus in return for which Margaret was to give the strategically sensitive town of Berwick-upon-Tweed to Scotland and her son Prince Edward was to be betrothed to of one of Mary's daughters. Margaret had little option if she wanted the help and though the terms were not favourable, she was compelled to accept them in a desperate bid to protect her son's inheritance. Margaret had her own problems too. She lacked the ready money to pay the Scottish army, so rashly, perhaps to punish her recalcitrant English subjects, she promised the Scots soldiers that they could take their pay in plunder once across the border. She either failed to realise the profoundly ingrained fear those in the north of England had of Scottish incursions, or she simply didn't care. Her real mistake would be in failing to appreciate the counter-productive terror her plan would draw out in the English. Those in the south were hardly less frightened by the Scots they viewed as barbaric than those in the north, who had seen centuries of border unrest. First, though, she had to get to London.

Those nobles still loyal to the House of Lancaster, including Henry Beaufort, Duke of Somerset, Henry Holland, Duke of Exeter, and Henry Percy, Earl of Northumberland, rallied to Margaret's cause. When news of the gathering of troops reached London, it came as something of a surprise. It was winter, and no sane commander raised an army and planned a campaign in winter when supplies were scarce and conditions treacherous. Nevertheless, York knew he could not ignore the threat to his freshly won grip on power. He had twice allowed it to slip through his fingers and having seen his family thrust to the very cusp of the highest power, he could not permit it to get away from him now. For once, he was in a position to fight for what he held with the full backing of Parliament and the law, which had made it treason to attack York.[13] Gathering what men he could, York headed north with his second son Edmund, Earl of Rutland, his brother-in-law Salisbury, and a handful of others. They left London on 9 December[14] but on entering Yorkshire, scouts were bringing back reports of a vast Lancastrian host that outnumbered York's own force. Taking sanctuary in his own fortress at Sandal Castle near Wakefield, York decided to await the reinforcements his oldest son Edward was raising in the Welsh Marches. Then, it all went wrong.

For reasons that have remained unclear ever since, York sallied out of Sandal Castle on 30 December and confronted the Lancastrian army. Anecdotes suggest he was taunted into leaving the safety of the walls by Lancastrians who branded him a coward, or that he went to the aid of a foraging party who were attacked during a Christmas truce. The most compelling version appears in *An English Chronicle* and is substantiated by the Burgundian Jean de Waurin. In this telling, Salisbury's half-brother John, Baron Neville, arrived at Sandal to ask York for a commission to raise men in his defence. John was from the side of the Neville family all but disinherited by their father in favour of Salisbury's branch, yet he was taken at his word and given a commission. He soon returned with 8,000 men, which may have tipped the numbers in York's favour. As soon as the duke's army set foot into the field to offer battle, Baron Neville's 8,000 turned on York's men as the Lancastrian army attacked.[15] Panic and chaos coursed through the Yorkist army, and Gregory reported around 2,500 Yorkist casualties compared to just 200 from amongst Queen Margaret's host.[16]

Amongst the dead was York himself. His son Edmund was reportedly captured by Lord Clifford whilst trying to flee the castle and killed in vengeance for Clifford's own father's death at the Battle of St Albans in 1455. The Earl of Salisbury was captured and imprisoned, only to be hauled out by an angry mob and beheaded. In an untypical act of battlefield brutality, York's corpse was beheaded, as was Edmund's. Their heads were sent to join that of Salisbury and others executed after the battle at York. The heads were set on spikes on Micklegate Bar, one of the main gates into the city of York. A paper crown was stuck onto York's lifeless head to mock his pretention to be king. It was not usual for the bodies of those who had fallen in battle to be subsequently mutilated, but the acts in the aftermath of the Battle of Wakefield mark the new levels of bitter hostility the sides were reaching as matters escalated. Richard's father and one of those big brothers he had admired at Ludlow were dead. The news must have been a crushing blow to Cecily after more than thirty years of apparently happy marriage, but she had more immediate problems than her own grief to deal with.

News of the defeat at Wakefield and the death of her husband, second son and oldest brother reached Cecily in London by 5 January 1461.[17] On 2 February, Edward, Earl of March, now also Duke of York as his father's heir, crushed a Lancastrian army trying to leave Wales at the Battle of Mortimer's Cross on the border, just south of Ludlow. The huge beast of an eighteen-year-old vented his rage at the loss of his father and brother Edmund, whom Gregory had described as 'one [of] the beste dysposyd lorde in thys londe.'[18] When a parhelion, or sun dog, a weather phenomenon in which ice crystals in the air create the appearance of three suns in the sky, terrified Edward's men as a bad omen, Edward rallied them with assurances that it represented the Holy Trinity and proved that Father, Son and Holy Spirit were on their side. It worked, as the force led by Jasper Tudor, Earl of Pembroke, was scattered. Jasper's father Owen Tudor, the grandfather of another small boy swamped by this conflict, was caught and beheaded at Hereford. Owen's other son Edmund had died of the plague but had left his thirteen-year-old wife Margaret Beaufort pregnant with a son, who was named Henry in honour of the king. Henry Tudor's story was destined to become inextricably linked with that of Richard's as two sides of the same coin.

A fortnight after Edward's victory, the Lancastrian army was pushing south, and Warwick placed his own force across their path at St Albans. Perhaps he felt it promised good fortune as the site of his previous glorious victory, but this time he was the one waiting for the attackers to fall on him. With the help of Andrew Trollope, the captain of the Calais garrison who had abandoned York at Ludlow, the Lancastrian army outflanked Warwick's position and dispersed his men with relative ease. With Edward still on his way from the Welsh border, nothing now blocked Margaret's path to London. Warwick fled west to try to meet Edward, leaving the capital dangerously exposed to their enemies, with

Cecily and her small children in the city. For some reason, perhaps to lend royal authority to his actions or to deter the Lancastrian army, Warwick had taken King Henry to St Albans with him. In the confusion, the king was left beneath a tree, guarded by two old knights, whose reward for refusing to abandon their bemused monarch as their own army fled was execution when Margaret regained custody of her husband.

None of this news can have reassured Cecily. Even Edward's victory solved nothing for her. London was prepared to resist the marauding Lancastrian army, full, as they were convinced it was, of savage northerners who could only be bent on plundering the city. At Ludlow, Cecily had been confident enough to trust in the king's grace to protect her and her young children. As the stream of bad news trickling into London became a torrent, her actions demonstrate how much the world had changed in a little over a year. Two years later, an annuity of 100 shillings would be given to a London widow named Alice Martyn by Edward for 'receivyng and keeping ... oure right entierli biloved Brethren The Dukes of Clarence and Gloucestre[19] from daungier and perill in thair troubles unto the tyme of thair departing out of this oure Reame into the parties of fflaundres.'[20] Cecily had clearly decided her two youngest sons were not safe either at Baynard's Castle or Fastolf's house in Southwark and had sent them into hiding in the city. Edmund's callous murder made the dangers all too clear, but it was York's success in having himself and his heirs declared rightful heirs to the throne that now caused such fear in his widowed duchess. With York and Edmund's death, George stood second in line to the throne behind Edward, and Richard was third in line. If Queen Margaret were to descend on London determined to be rid of all Yorkist threats to her son's position, then George and Richard could be in mortal danger. Certainly, Cecily was no longer willing to take any risks with their lives.

It is unclear when the boys were placed into the secret care of Alice Martyn, but by the spring Cecily had taken the even more drastic decision to send them across the sea for their own protection. Queen Margaret's host was still threatening London, and her vengeance seemed sure to be swift and brutal. The best Cecily could hope for if her sons were captured was a long imprisonment, far away from her. Whatever sureties she had offered to secure her position after Ludlow and to keep a path open for her husband to return to favour would inevitably be thrown back in her face by an enraged Margaret, should she gain entry to the city. Cecily would not get off so lightly again, and she clearly feared for her sons. Ireland and Calais remained safely under Yorkist control, though a long sea trip to Ireland might be perilous and risked capture. Calais might not remain loyal to the Yorkist cause for long if Queen Margaret regained the reins of government and set about driving out their party's influence from all corners of the kingdom. Instead of these options, Cecily took the radical step of packing her sons off to Burgundy. George, now eleven years old, and Richard, now eight, were sent away with minimal company to a foreign land. This time their sense of abandonment might have been even more heightened as their mother and sister did not travel with them. Bobbing across the Channel in a small ship, they now had only each other to cling to for support and comfort. It is possible a John Skelton accompanied them (could this be the father of the Tudor poet John Skelton?), since on 16 October 1461 he received 'the office of surveyor of the scrutiny in the port of London and places, ports and creeks adjacent' in payment for 'his good service to the king and his brothers'.[21]

Burgundy was by no means a certain safe haven for George and Richard. A significant reason for the English success in France during Henry V's reign had been the close alliance with Burgundy brought about by the assassination of the current duke's father in 1419. In the aftermath of Agincourt, French politics had two rival factions within the royal family, the House of Burgundy and the House of Armagnac. On 10 September 1419, under the cloak of a parley, John the Fearless, Duke of Burgundy, met with the French Dauphin, who was backed by the Armagnacs, on a bridge over the River Seine at Montereau. The bitter, long-running feud between the two sides, which the Dauphin appeared to be trying to end, caused the Armagnacs present to attack John, who was stabbed to death as the Dauphin watched. John's son, Philip the Good, succeeded his father and sought out an alliance with the English against the French he held responsible for his father's death. That coalition had swept Henry V to within touching distance of the French crown and made it his son's. The Dauphin had become King Charles VII, ensuring relations remained frosty with France, but those with England were soured in the mid-1430s. To what extent the faltering English effort in France caused Philip to reassess his options is unsure, but he was able to blame a personal insult for the fracture. The king's uncle, John, Duke of Bedford, had been married to Philip's sister Anne. When she died in 1432, Philip judged his brother-in-law's remarriage to Jacquetta of Luxembourg to have happened too soon and without proper consultation with England's Burgundian ally. A rapprochement with France was quickly underway as relations warmed at the expense of England's position. On top of that, whilst Lieutenant-General of France, York had tried to secure a marriage for his oldest son Edward to one of Charles VII's daughters and appears to have enjoyed a good relationship with the French king.[22]

However, Burgundy remained fiercely determined to protect its independence from a French Crown that nominally considered the territory part of its kingdom. Charles VII had endured a poor relationship with his own son, the Dauphin Louis, who had taken up residence in Burgundy under Philip's protection. The natural cordiality between a Lancastrian England with a French queen married to a peace-loving king meant that France was hostile to the Yorkist cause. Cecily's desperate assessment must have been as convoluted as hoping that the friend of her enemy's enemy might be her friend. Philip harboured Louis, who was Charles' enemy when Charles was, in turn, effectively, York's enemy. It was a huge risk, and the fact that Cecily was willing to chance two of her three remaining sons on such an apparently long shot is a testament to the frantic despair that must have gripped her in London as grief overwhelmed her and an enemy army threatened the city gates.

The quandary posed for Philip the Good with the arrival in his dominion of two such contentious, but defenceless, figures is clear from his reaction. Charles VII was displeased that Philip was giving succour to the recalcitrant Louis but aiding the enemies of an England presently on good terms with France was another matter. The boys had arrived precisely because the Yorkist cause appeared to be irrevocably floundering. A Lancastrian restoration would inevitably lead to an attempt to utterly destroy the House of York. If England turned a hostile eye toward Burgundy, France would need little incentive to join them and an assault by both could mean an end to Burgundian independence. The boys were hot coals, and Philip could not afford to get his fingers burned. The solution was easy to enact and obvious. Philip ruled over a sprawling strip of territories in Flanders, Artois, Hainaut, Holland, Zeeland and other regions of the Low Countries. The duke's court was peripatetic but kept to the larger cities of his dominion such as Brussels and Bruges. *The Chronicle of London* states that 'the Duchesse of York heryng the losse of that ffeeld sent over the See hir ii yong Sones George and Richard, which went unto Utryk'.[23] Utrecht was miles to the north and east of Philip's favoured haunts, so his solution was to do nothing. Philip allowed the boys to remain within his territories but did nothing to acknowledge their presence, to show them favour or to provide for them. In this way, he could not be accused of causing them harm by the Yorkists, but nor could the Lancastrians or the French find fault in him for making a fuss of the boys.

George and Richard had several weeks of seclusion, during which they were largely ignored by their absent host. How much they knew of the situation when they left England is uncertain, but George at least may well have been aware of the tension, fear and imminent peril that had caused them to be sent away. As they sat together whiling away the long hours, they must have wondered what was happening at home. Their mother and their sister Margaret had remained in London, relying on the protection of their sex, but were they still safe? What of Edward, the last adult to defend the House of York from those seeking to snuff it out? If everyone else was gone, what was to become of them? They can't have known whether they would see their family or their home ever again. For an eleven-year-old who might have begun to feel the weight of some responsibility for his eight-year-old little brother and, for Richard too, it must have been a frightening period of desperate uncertainty, hoping for news whilst praying it would not be more ill tidings.

Unbeknownst to the two boys in Utrecht, things in England had not quite reached the conclusion their mother had feared. London had kept its gates locked against Queen Margaret's army for fear of its intentions. Low on supplies, with Scots troops weighted down with plunder returning home, and realising the futility of trying to maintain a campaign in the winter months, Margaret and her force had retreated north. When Edward had arrived in London with Warwick, the reception had been rapturous. Gregory noted the revulsion felt in London when Henry left to travel north with his wife and their army, offering the couplet, 'He that had Londyn for sake, Wolde no more to them take'. He wrote that news of the arrival of Edward, Earl of March, was greeted with open delight as people called, 'Lette us walke in a newe wyne yerde, and lette us make us a gay gardon in the monythe of Marche with thys fayre whyte rose and herbe, the Erle of Marche.'[24]

George Neville, Bishop of Exeter and Warwick's younger brother, preached a passionate sermon at St John's Fields on 1 March asking the gathered host whether they believed Henry should continue as king, whether he 'were worthy to Reygne still'. The unanimous reply was 'Nay! Nay!'. When the bishop asked if they would have March as their king instead, they enthusiastically bellowed 'Ye! Ye!'.[25] On 3 March, Edward was petitioned at Baynard's Castle by the authorities of London and the nobility then present to take the throne from Henry.[26] The following day, 4 March 1461, Edward was proclaimed king 'by the Right of Enherytaunce as eldest Son unto the Duke of York'. After a solemn ceremony at St Paul's Cathedral, he sat in the king's seat at Westminster Hall as the gathered crowd again expressed their desire to have him as their king. King Edward IV, the first monarch of the House of York, accepted the crown and on the following day, a Te Deum Mass was celebrated at St Paul's, the king arriving in state along the river.[27]

The attitude of chroniclers to this development is interesting. *An English Chronicle* describes Edward being 'chosen kyng in the cyte of Londoun'.[28] *Hearne's Fragment* says that at the Council meeting at Baynard's Castle, Edward was 'by the sole assent and consent of all present, there elected and solemnly chosen for King of England'.[29] *Gregory's Chronicle* explicitly recorded that Edward 'toke upon hym the crowne of Inglond by the avysse of the lordys spyrytuall and temporalle, and by the elexyon of the comyns'.[30] The attitude in London was something similar to the Anglo-Saxon principles of the Witan. The nobility, through the use of Parliament in particular, had been carefully exerting and increasing control over the Crown, and this was reaching a new peak. The assiduous pressing back against royal authority was paying dividends and the nobility, but even more strikingly, the people, claimed and were perceived as having a role in choosing, electing, their king. Just as the chaos brought by King John had provided the opportunity for Magna Carta in 1215, so the chaos of the Wars of the Roses was seized upon as a chance to push the same aims forward again. Henry VI had not been a good king. York had been a popular figure, and his son was equally well-liked. His youth promised something new, which would always seem like something better. *The Crowland Chronicle* described Edward in 1461 as 'in the flower of his age, tall of stature, elegant in person, of unblemished character, valiant in arms' as well as a suitable descendant of Edward III.[31] In the jubilation of Edward's accession, the subtle shift in power that brought it about may have gone unnoticed, but once won, it would not be easily surrendered.

Edward refused to undergo a coronation ceremony while a Lancastrian army loyal to Henry remained in the field. Mustering a colossal force, he pressed north to meet the army led by Henry Beaufort, Duke of Somerset. One side would have their revenge and, one way or another, the matter would be settled. On Palm Sunday, 29 March 1461, the two hosts clashed at the Battle of Towton in Yorkshire. Estimates of the sizes of the armies, which are notoriously unreliable and hard to substantiate, suggest each side had about 30,000 men and heralds reported 28,000 casualties after fierce fighting in the blustering snow. Edward won the day. Somerset was killed, along with Henry Percy, Earl of Northumberland, and Andrew Trollope. Henry himself had not been at the battle and managed to flee north into Scotland, but the Lancastrian military opposition to Edward was crushed. Edward tarried in the north, trying to secure the region and also to make 'grete inquerens of the rebellyens a-gayne his fadyr',[32] before returning to London. His younger brothers had clearly been on his mind, though.

Francesco Coppini, obviously maintaining an interest in English affairs despite having left the country at some earlier point, received a letter dated 10 April from Nicholas O'Flanagan, Bishop of Elphin, bearing news from England. He confirmed that Edward was now king, before reporting news reaching Edward that 'the Duke of Burgundy is treating the brothers of the king with respect. This pleases them wonderfully, and they believe that there will be great friendship between the duke and the English by an indissoluble treaty, and that one of these brothers will marry the daughter of Charles.'[33] News of Edward's victory and confirmation in his crown reached Philip, solving the problem of what to do with the boys – or rather, forcing him into the decision he had tried to avoid. On 17 April, Coppini's physician wrote to the Legate with more updates from England, including the news that 'The brothers of King Edward are at Sluys, and are to come here to-morrow or Saturday after dinner.'[34] Sluis lies a short distance north-east of Bruges, where Philip's court was located. Either hoping to embrace a new Yorkist England, or fearful of being seen to continue to snub the new king's brothers, Philip had made the decision to have them brought to him and treated as honoured guests.

The timing of the boys' arrival at Philip's court was still uncertain the following day. The Milanese ambassador to France who was in Bruges at Philip's court, wrote on 18 April: 'To-morrow they say two younger brothers of March, son of the Duke of York, are coming here, and the Duke of Burgundy has given notice for great honours to be shown to them.'[35] Later the same day he was forced to update his master Francesco Sforza, Duke of Milan, with tidings that 'Since I wrote to-day the two brothers of King Edward have arrived,' adding that Philip, 'who is most kind in everything, has been to visit them at their lodgings, and showed them great reverence.'[36] It must have been dizzying, even bewildering, for the two boys. They might have heard rumours of events from England as they were hurried toward the most lavish and spectacular court in all of Europe. If anyone had managed to explain to them that their brother Edward was now King of England, the news must have seemed odd and unlikely. It made George next in line to the throne with Richard behind him. From the sons of a traitor, they had become members of a notional future ruling house, only to be cast out of the country under threats to their lives, and then summoned to the court of the Duke of Burgundy as genuine English princes. Only a return home could hope to make any sense of these tidings.

While they enjoyed the opulence of the Burgundian court and the feasting they were treated to, it is possible that George and Richard came into contact with an Englishman, then in Bruges, who would have a profound effect on later history and who might have left a personal mark on young Richard. Francesco Coppini's physician had mentioned in his dispatch that he was going to attend the feast as a representative of the Legate and many others must have wished for a place near to the new King of England's brothers. The governor of the Company of Merchant Adventurers of London in Bruges was a merchant named William Caxton. He would have been a suitable representative of English interests in Burgundy to attend the festivities and, a decade later, would transport the printing press from the Continent to England. It is tempting to imagine this well-travelled merchant extolling the virtues of books and manuscripts to the young princes as he excitedly described the new invention Johannes Gutenberg had unveiled in Germany more than twenty years earlier. Richard's later interest in books is well attested to, and might spring from this chance encounter in the midst of seemingly much weightier events.

As George and Richard were feasted by the Duke of Burgundy, celebrated as English princes, they must have wondered how long this new switch in their circumstances would last. Their brother wanted them home in time for his coronation, and that meant a journey to Calais before re-crossing the Channel, but the boys may have wondered what they would find when they reached England again. It had been a fickle and insecure home over the last eighteen months. Then, their future had relied on their father; now, it was in the huge hands of their brother Edward. He was a giant of a man, especially to two little boys, and his reputation as an unbeatable soldier and general was at its height after the Battle of Towton. This was the brother who had fought at Northampton to free them from their aunt's custody, who had secured lodgings for them in London and who had visited them every day without fail when their mother left to meet their father on his return from Ireland. There was the promise of security in his arms. Yet here too was the brother who had abandoned them at Ludlow. Perhaps that was in the more distant past than the glittering memories of kindness and the warmth of his protection. How long Edward could hold on to the throne he had won still remained to be seen. If he could, what would this dramatic upheaval mean for his two younger brothers? George and Richard were about to discover just that as their ship left Calais for English shores, ending their potentially dangerous exile.

4

To the King's Brother

*The like to the king's brother Richard, duke of Gloucester, of the office
of admiral of England, Ireland and Aquitaine, with all the accustomed
profits and powers, provided that he have no cognisance of affairs
within the counties or of wreck of sea. He is to have cognisance of
death and maiming however committed in great ships in the middle of
the great rivers, but only in the ports of those near the sea.*
Creation of Richard as Admiral, 12 October 1462, aged 10.[1]

With his foes crushed at Towton and resistance in the north broken by
his prolonged presence there, Edward was able to return to London and
prepare for the coronation he had earlier refused whilst the Lancastrian
army remained in the field. It suited the newly burnished Yorkist regime
to ignore the fact that King Henry, Queen Margaret and their son Prince
Edward, as well as many nobles whose sympathies lay firmly with the
displaced royal house, remained at large. After Towton, Henry had fled
to Scotland with his wife and son. Although an epic and crushing defeat
on the battlefield was fine and fitting propaganda atop which Edward
could be swept to the throne, Lancastrian resistance was not destroyed,
and Edward was aware of it.

After six decades of rule by three kings of the House of Lancaster,
England had grown comfortably accustomed to Lancastrian kingship.
Henry VI had been king for almost forty years and was the only monarch
most people had known in their lifetime. More critically for Edward, the
establishment and those knitted to it were, as demonstrated by York's
problems in Parliament in 1460, loyal to the inoffensive and incredibly
generous Henry VI. The Yorkist cause to date had attracted very little
noble support, relying heavily on the Neville family and to a lesser
extent on John Mowbray, Duke of Norfolk, and William, Lord Bonville
of Devon. Even these connections were simply fed by the rising tide of
unrestrained feuding during the 1450s. The Neville family set their cap

at York's feet after feuds with the Percy family and the Duke of Somerset alienated them from the court party. Lord Bonville was engaged in a long-standing dispute with the ancient Courtenay family, then Earls of Devon. Norfolk, whose late arrival at Towton had swung the battle in Edward's favour, was generally a political lightweight despite the high rank his birth had granted him. His Yorkist sympathies lay mainly in a regional battle for supremacy with the Duke of Suffolk, who had been murdered in 1450. After this, Norfolk found his anticipated superiority instead curtailed by Somerset. Edward would need to find a way to draw those clinging to Henry VI's cause to his own. First, though, he had a coronation to undergo.

On Friday 26 June, Edward travelled from Sheen to London to begin the spectacle of his coronation festivities. As he entered the city, the mayor and aldermen greeted him in their splendid scarlet robes to show the authorities' acceptance of their new monarch. They were flanked by 400 citizens, mounted and decked in green who accompanied the new king as he rode to the Tower of London.[2] On Saturday morning, Edward created twenty-eight[3] Knights of the Bath in preparation for his coronation the following day. The medieval Order of the Bath was entirely distinct from the order of the same name created by George I in 1725 and took both its name and ceremony from the symbolic purification in a bath of water of those to be invested with their knighthood. The two most prominent names amongst those who were bathed that evening and then required to spend the night in silent vigil to prepare for the ceremony were the king's two brothers. George, aged eleven, and Richard, aged eight, are unlikely to have been spared the requirement not only of a bath but also of a night-long waking vigil, which must have been simultaneously exciting and draining for both young boys.

Their reward came on the morning of the following day, Sunday 28 June 1461. Coronations were generally expected to take place on a Sunday or some high holy day to reflect the religious aspects of the temporal authority being bestowed on the new king. Processing ahead of the king were his newly invested Knights of the Bath, wearing new gowns and hoods with a badge of white silk across their shoulders that proclaimed their new status.[4] Edward was led to Westminster Abbey where the coronation ceremony was officiated over by Thomas Bourchier, Archbishop of Canterbury, who had been appointed by Edward's father during his first Protectorate. The event was lauded as a magnificent triumph, with 'greate Solempnyte of Bisshoppis and other temporall lordes' and 'as greate multitude of people in poules [St Paul's] as ever was seen afore in eny dayes'.[5] The fact that a portion of the nobility was absent due to their continued support for Henry VI is understandably glossed over, but it seems plausible that popular support was both widespread and fervent.

Edward had swept to power on at least the assumption that he represented his father's populist, reformist agenda. In the vital new monarch, London could see not only the hope of the end of corruption and misgovernment but the personification of everything that had been lamentably lacking in Henry VI. Finally, a warrior had emerged to pick up the dusty mantle last shouldered by Henry V and with the return of good government and fiscal responsibility came the promise of fresh glory in France. As Richard watched, the fruition of his father's work was reached, to popular acclaim and with the approval of God. He may have felt that it had all been worth it, that a new dawn had arrived and that his physically impressive brother was the rising sun. Nevertheless, to reach this point had cost Richard and his family dearly. His father and Edmund had been lost, along with their uncle Salisbury. A generation of the country's nobility had been decimated and what remained was polarised by the bitter nature of the toll taken by both sides. There was a new sanctuary from troubles presided over by Edward, who had cared for him, but recent experiences had taught Richard how fragile and fleeting security could be. It remained to be seen precisely what his own position would be in this brave new world.

The day following the coronation saw George created Duke of Clarence. Clarence had been the title held by Lionel, the second son of Edward III through whom the Yorkist dynasty claimed descent senior to the Lancastrian kings. It had also been granted to Thomas, the second son of Henry IV who had died during Henry V's campaigns in France. The choice of title was therefore hugely significant, not only in raising George to the highest rank of the peerage as Edward's heir, it also identified their father York as a man who should have been king, a rightful, deprived, monarch, whose second surviving son was entitled to the dukedom of Clarence. The promotion and endowment of George as King Edward's heir was proper and necessary. He was next in line to the throne until Edward found a wife and bore a son of his own, and in the unpredictable waters of English politics, that might never come to pass, and George might follow his brother onto the throne. What was conspicuous, from Richard's point of view, was the lack of provision made for him at that moment.

Edward had been provided with a birthright by their father and had grasped it in the heat of battle, making himself king. George immediately became a king in waiting as heir presumptive to their brother and a way was being forged for him in the world, presented to him on a platter. Richard, though still young, might have been left wondering what the future held for him, the junior brother, the spare. For most of the remainder of 1461, it might have appeared that he was to be left to find his own way in the world, unlike his brothers. The swift promotion of George was vital due to Edward's own lack of an heir; however, it became clear by the end of the year that Richard had not been entirely forgotten.

Edward summoned Parliament to meet on 4 November 1461 at Westminster and three days before it opened, on 1 November, the king created his youngest brother Duke of Gloucester.[6] It was another title loaded with royal significance. Edward III's youngest son had been Thomas, Duke of Gloucester, the most prominent of the Lords Appellant who had sought to curtail Richard II's tyranny during the 1380s. When Richard had regained sufficient control, he saw to their punishment, with his uncle, Thomas, arrested and sent to Calais where he soon died amid rumours (that were probably true) that Richard had ordered his murder. Henry IV had also created his youngest son Humphrey as Duke of Gloucester. Humphrey had been the last surviving brother of Henry V, and his championing of war in France had seen him marginalised as Henry VI's government moved closer to peace. Humphrey had been a popular champion of the people before his death in 1447, shortly after his arrest for treason. The charge was almost certainly a fabrication planted within the paranoid mind of the impressionable king, and although there were rumours of foul play, it is likely Humphry suffered a stroke brought on by the shock of his arrest. Humphrey had identified York closely with his own cause, and much of the widespread sentiment for the new ruling house sprang from this connection. The Duchy of Lancaster had been subsumed into the Crown estates since 1399 and was far too wealthy for Edward to part with. The Duchy of York also belonged to Edward personally and now formed part of the property of the king. The Duchy of Bedford had been used by Henry IV, but it was Gloucester that Edward selected, probably because of the associations with youngest sons of previous kings, which Edward was keen to foster. Identifying his father as a rightful king whose sons were entitled to dukedoms accordingly served to increase Edward's own legitimacy and strengthen his claim to the throne.

When Parliament opened, the presentation of the Yorkist title to the crown was one of the first pieces of business. The descent of the House of York from Lionel of Antwerp, Duke of Clarence, via the Mortimer line, was detailed – as it had been the previous year when York had claimed that his pedigree was superior to that of Henry VI's Lancastrian line. After rehearsing the usurpation perpetrated by Henry IV, the Commons took the decision to approve Edward as the new King of England. The Parliament Rolls record that 'The commyns beyng in this present parlement, havyng sufficient and evident knowlege of the seid unrightwise usurpacion and intrusion by the seid Henry late erle of Derby upon the seid coroune of Englond ... take, accept and repute, and woll for ever take, accepte and repute, the seid Edward the fourth, their soverayne and liege lord, and hym and his heirs to be kynges of Englond, and noon other.'[7] Parliament in 1399 had dealt with the deposition of Richard II and acceptance of Henry IV's claim, and it reached this pinnacle of its powers again in 1461 by approving Edward IV's title in place of Henry VI. If the aim of the lords spiritual and temporal, along with the Commons, gathered in the form of a Parliament, was to attain the authority previously exercised by the Anglo-Saxon Witan, they were now there. The Witan had held the power to appoint a king who was then beyond reproach, but now, for the second time in less than seventy years, Parliament oversaw the removal of one king and chose for itself another, albeit that in both cases it was approving a status quo.

Over the following twelve months, Edward received the recognition of foreign heads of state. In September 1461 he had received an embassy from Scotland. November saw Sir Robert Ogle handed a commission to conclude a peace with Scotland. In March 1462, Edward sealed a treaty with the Earl of Ross, who was to assist him in making war on Scotland. In the same month, Pope Pius II sent word that he 'congratulates the King on his accession to the throne' and in September peace with Burgundy was on the king's agenda.[8] Foreign powers might have been slow to offer the hand of peace to Edward because they needed to be certain that he was secure on his throne before they recognised him, thereby denouncing Henry VI. When it came, the propaganda coup was significant, but in reality, however safe European heads perceived Edward to be, he could be under little illusion that he still faced genuine problems at home that needed to be resolved quickly and finally.

Two days after the opening of Parliament, John Mowbray, Duke of Norfolk, died on 6 November. He was succeeded by his seventeen-year-old son and namesake as 4th Duke of Norfolk. Edward took the opportunity of the Parliament session to create other new peers to help bolster his regime. Henry Bourchier was created Earl of Essex in recognition of his family's support of the Yorkist cause. Henry was married to Edward and Richard's aunt, Isabel of York, and he held a French title, Count of Eu, which he had acquired from his father. Henry had served as a soldier in France for which he had been made Viscount Bourchier and his service to Edward at the Second Battle of St Albans and the Battle of Towton now earned him an earldom.

Henry's mother was Anne of Gloucester, the only child of Thomas of Woodstock, the Duke of Gloucester who had died suspiciously in Calais under Richard II, making Henry a great-grandson of King Edward III. William Neville, Lord Fauconberg, was also promoted to an earldom. William was a younger brother of Salisbury, and his military expertise, as well as his loyalty to the House of York, led Edward to create him Earl of Essex, though William would only enjoy the title for just over a year before he died peacefully in his bed in his late fifties.

Almost immediately, young Richard began to appear in the Patent Rolls and other governmental paperwork. Despite his young age, he was named on a commission of array for Cumberland on 13 November 1461 to help raise an army to defend against the Scots and the Lancastrians being harboured just across the border.[9] As in much of what followed, for some time, the appearance of Richard's name is little more than a formality and he was not expected to take an active part in such matters at his age. It was simply that his rank and position demanded his inclusion, however farcical it might seem. On 16 December, Edward granted confirmation of letters patent dating from Henry IV's reign that related to the establishment of the Guild of St George of Bishop's Lynn. It was perhaps a symptom of the uncertainty his accession and the delegitimization of the Lancastrian regime was causing that some felt the need to seek such reassurance. Edward took the opportunity to require the Guild to maintain one or two chaplains to pray for the wellbeing of the king, his two brothers, George Neville, Bishop of Exeter, and his older brother the Earl of Warwick. He also added that prayers should be offered for the souls of his father, his brother Edmund and his uncle Salisbury.

Edward seems to have balanced the problem of Richard's youth very carefully against the need to promote members of his own family to present not only a broad front but also to prepare his young siblings for the significant and vital roles they would need to play in his new regime. There was not a torrent of land and property flowing to Richard in the months that followed his creation as Duke of Gloucester. Given the positions of both George and Richard in the new order, this is perhaps surprising, since providing them with a solid block of power from which to project the king's authority would be of benefit to Edward. Their status as minors for a number of years to come would also provide the king with a deep well of patronage that would not require permanent alienation from the Crown. He could appoint men to administer those estates on behalf of his young brothers, offering a lucrative, if temporary, opportunity for some Edward might wish to reward. One reason the new king may have wanted to avoid this situation was the experiences of his own father, whose Duchy of York and Earldom of March estates had been subject to minority administration for years. The mismanagement and lack of care this led to had cost York a good deal of time and money to repair when he attained his majority; Edward perhaps sought to avoid the same dissatisfaction and expense for his brothers.

George, Richard and Margaret appear to have been installed at the Palace of Pleasaunce in Greenwich, a beautiful complex built by Humphrey, Duke of Gloucester, as Bella Court but acquired and renamed by Queen Margaret of Anjou.[10] Instead of endowing his brothers with too much property, Edward instead gave them offices of national importance, which, although they could not personally discharge them yet, made their status as national figures clear. George was given the post of Lord Lieutenant of Ireland, a role in which he followed his father. Connections to Ireland had been crucial to the House of York, and it made sense to keep them active. George had been born in Dublin, and York had appointed Edmund to the post before his death, so the importance and prestige of the position are easy to discern. On 12 October 1462, ten days after his tenth birthday, Richard was appointed Admiral of England, Ireland and Aquitaine.[11] It was another national appointment, meant to signal the importance of Edward's brothers but which Richard cannot have been expected to personally discharge yet. That is not to say that both siblings might not have taken their future responsibilities seriously and begun to prepare themselves for the day when these powers would be in their own hands.

Richard was not left entirely without property. On 12 August 1462 he 'and the heirs of his body' were given the castle of Gloucester and the fee farm of the town of Gloucester, both of which made sense given his position as duke. The same grant provided Richard with the constableship of Corfe Castle in Dorset, which had belonged to the Beaufort Dukes of Somerset, the manor of Kingston Lacy and 'the castle, county, honour and lordship of Richemond', which had belonged to Edmund Tudor and was subject to a claim by his son Henry Tudor. He also received the county, honour and lordship of Pembroke, which had belonged to Jasper Tudor, Edmund's brother, and small, dispersed packets of land in Oxfordshire, Cambridgeshire, Suffolk, Essex, Northamptonshire, Rutland and Kent, much of which was taken from the property of the attainted Earl of Oxford.[12] The disparate nature of these holdings might reflect what was available for Edward to give his brother as the beginnings of a provision meant to allow him to support himself, but it could also represent a deliberate effort to avoid building a substantial, single regional power block of which Richard would one day assume control. Property from the Duchy of Lancaster, valued at around £1,000 a year, was set aside to provide an income suitable to support Richard.[13] His grants remained shifting, though. The Lordship of Richmond was quickly taken back and granted instead to George.

After the death of the Duke of York, no guardian was officially appointed to care for George. Edward, along with Edmund, had been raised within their own household at Ludlow from a young age and George's new prominence, meteoric and doubtless bewildering as it was, meant that it was no longer appropriate for him to be out of Edward's personal control. For the moment, Richard was also kept close to the centre of power. It does seem that the boys either spent some time in the households of trusted men, or were placed under supervision when Edward was away from the capital or otherwise unable to take direct care of them. On 12 September 1462, Thomas, Lord Stanley, received an annuity in thanks for services to the king and his brothers.[14] In 1471, Edward would also make a grant to Thomas Bourchier, Archbishop of Canterbury, 'because in time past at the king's request he supported the king's brothers the dukes of Clarence and Gloucester for a long time at great charges,'[15] suggesting that the Archbishop had also played a role in caring for boys during this period of their adjustment to a new life.

On 23 June 1463, Richard witnessed a confirmation by the king at Westminster, with George, the Archbishop of Canterbury, the Bishop of Exeter, the Earls of Warwick and Worcester, Robert Stillington, William Hastings and John Wenlock.[16] In December, Richard received 'all castles, lordships, manors, lands, rents and services' which had belonged to Henry Beaufort, Duke of Somerset.[17] Following Towton, Somerset had fled across the border to Scotland with Henry VI, and Edward had taken control of his possessions. The grant was not entirely as substantial as all of the properties of a duke may sound. The Dukes of Somerset owed their position to their close family ties to the Lancastrian kings, and although their loyalty had brought them power and position, they remained poorly endowed. Nevertheless, the slow accumulation of property on a small scale was continuing for Richard. Significantly, this grant was made 'at pleasure', and Henry Beaufort would soon undergo a brief rapprochement with Edward that saw all of his property returned to him for a while.

In March 1464, Edward granted George and Richard 'that they may have all their charters, letters patent and writs in Chancery and all other courts of the king quit of fee or fine'.[18] That year also saw a final tilt of Lancastrian resistance to Edward during that decade. As John Neville, younger brother of the Earl of Warwick, travelled north to escort a Scottish embassy to meet Edward, he was ambushed at Hedgeley Moor in Northumberland on 25 April. A Lancastrian force led by Henry Beaufort, the Lords Roos and Hungerford, and Sir Ralph Percy, barred John Neville's way north, but as he advanced on the Lancastrian forces, the left flank commanded by Roos and Hungerford broke and fled. As the forces engaged, Somerset soon retreated too, leaving Sir Ralph Percy's contingent fighting alone until their leader was killed. The encounter ended in a comfortable victory for John Neville, who continued on his way. On his way back south with the Scottish ambassadors, John was ambushed again on 15 May at the Battle of Hexham. This encounter was brief and saw the deaths of Henry Beaufort, Duke of Somerset, and both Lords Roos and Hungerford. In response to the re-emergence of the Lancastrian threat, Richard was handed a commission of array on 3 May in the counties of Gloucestershire, Worcestershire, Warwickshire, Wiltshire, Somerset, Dorset, Devon, Cornwall and Shropshire.[19]

Although no army was required in the end, the commission may offer a suggestion of the region in which Edward was planning to install his brother as a regional magnate when he came of age. The Marcher region along the border with Wales was an area of great significance for the House of York. Edward had been Earl of March, and York had based himself at Ludlow in the Marches for every moment of uncertainty during his opposition to Henry VI. The traditional patrimony of the Duchy of York was not particularly rich, nor did it possess a geographical concentration of lands. When the Earldom of March came into the hands of Richard, Duke of York on the death of his uncle, it financially supported the duchy and gave it a solid power base, concentrated along the Welsh border from which to operate. It is possible that this was initially identified as a perfect area in which Richard might complete his training and eventually govern on Edward's behalf.

The precise point at which Richard's life underwent one of its most seismic and defining alterations is not entirely clear. At some time before the mid-1460s, Richard was placed into the care of his cousin Richard Neville, Earl of Warwick. There was nothing unusual about a noble boy being sent into the household of another aristocratic family to be trained and educated in preparation for adulthood. Nevertheless, it marked an end of Richard's time under the now familiar, nurturing wing of his brother Edward. It also served to demarcate his position from that of George, who, as heir presumptive, was not destined to be sent away from Edward's supervision. The earliest definitive reference to Richard Neville as his cousin's ward appears in *The Tellers' Rolls* in late 1465, when Edward gave Warwick £1,000 towards the costs incurred in caring for his youngest brother.[20] Although the timing and significant amount of the grant suggest that Richard was already under Warwick's care, and so costs had already been incurred, it is not impossible that the money travelled with Richard to Warwick's household to provide for future expenses. It is often assumed that Richard was placed under Warwick's supervision almost immediately after Edward's coronation in 1461, but the grants to those who cared for the king's brothers during this time, their installation at Greenwich and Richard's presence at Westminster to witness official documents in 1463, along with commissions of array in western and south-western counties, suggest he may have left London several years later.

As is typical when a boy becomes absorbed into a noble household for his education, even a boy as important as the king's brother, Richard disappears somewhat from the historical record. He made the long journey north that took him through the City of York, from which his family took its title, but the gates of that city had also displayed the gruesome sight of the severed heads of his father, brother and uncle. As he wound his way further north and west, Richard passed Harrogate, Ripon and Masham as he entered the rolling green hills and wide expanses of Wensleydale. His most likely final destination was Middleham Castle, an old stronghold that had formed the centre of the Earl of Salisbury's northern estates and now provided a focal point in the north for his son the Earl of Warwick.

Middleham Castle dominates the surrounding landscape for miles, making the imposing, palatial residence the perfect reflection of both the regional dominance and increasing wealth of the Neville family. A broad dry moat surrounded the thick, looming curtain walls as the young Richard would have entered through the fortified gatehouse in the north-east corner of the castle. Once inside, the walls utterly enclosed an outer bailey, similar to that Richard had seen at Ludlow, though not as large. Instead, it encircled the inner bailey with essential services given single storey buildings lining the outer wall, making the area a bustling and noisy centre of activity. The towering keep was one of largest in England, accessed at first-floor level by a stone staircase, which was in turn protected by a recessed guardhouse halfway up it. Inside the keep, the great hall provided a large public meeting space, while other rooms included a chapel and private accommodation probably reserved for the lord of the castle. From the walls, just to the south, the mound can still be seen today on which the original Norman motte and bailey castle had stood before its stone replacement had been begun during the twelfth century. Although still firmly advertising its control over the rolling dales for miles in all directions, Middleham Castle had also evolved into a comfortable home fit for one of England's most prosperous and now most powerful families. Richard could hardly help but have been impressed as his horse rode across the drawbridge and into the outer bailey of his new home.

Middleham was served by the Church of St Mary and St Akelda a short distance from the castle. Although chapels were located within the walls, the church nevertheless enjoyed strong links with the Neville family and was used for their worship. Richard would, therefore, have taken services at this small thirteenth-century church as part of his routine at Middleham. Sadly, with the exception of drawing on traditional texts for the education of noble and knightly boys, little is really known of Richard's time under the tutelage of the Earl of Warwick in his northern castles. It is likely that Warwick himself was not often to be found at Middleham in the mid-1460s as national politics kept him busy, and increasingly frustrated. It is also possible to speculate that although Middleham may have represented a central point during Richard's time in the north, he would have travelled around Warwick's other local possessions. This would have included Sheriff Hutton Castle some 40 miles east, just 10 miles north of York and therefore ideally suitable when business required a visit to the regional capital.

A boy's knightly training would consist of a balance of physical and academic disciplines, which would combine to create a late medieval ideal of a paragon of chivalry, properly prepared to take his place in the world and to contribute to improving it. The physical aspects of Richard's education aimed to prepare him to fight. He would train with sword, axe, mace and dagger, on foot, as well as mastering the lance and spear on horseback. Learning to hawk and hunt were integral parts of the regime as practice for combat, whilst skill on horseback could be honed during rides out across the Dales, perhaps to neighbouring Bolton Castle or the stunning monastery of Jervaulx Abbey. The fifteenth century had seen the growth in schools across England and a focus on the academic learning that ought to form part of a nobleman's education. Learning to read and write in English, Latin and French was vital. More abstract subjects such as law and theology were deemed essential, as was an understanding of history. A typical intersection of these two strands of education might be found in *De Re Militari*, a military treatise dating from the fifth century. The Roman writer Vegetius had compiled a survey of his nation's military history, standing at the crumbling end of its glory and looking back on what it had done well. *De Re Militari* was widely owned in manuscript form across Europe and was considered the definitive military text on tactics, organisation of an army and execution of battles a thousand years after it was written. These topics would have made up Richard's daily routine as his cousin Warwick prepared him for a senior role in the realm of his brother King Edward IV.

There are a few things that are known with certainty about this period. The first, as a result of the discovery of Richard's skeleton under a car park in Leicester in 2012, is that during his teenage years Richard developed scoliosis. Scientific analysis of the spine confirmed that the scoliosis was not present at birth but was of a type that becomes apparent in early teens, so Richard would have begun to develop symptom from around 1465 onwards. The lack of any widespread awareness of Richard's condition demonstrates that from this point onwards, until the end of his life, it remained a well-kept secret. For centuries, the Tudor image of Richard was dismissed as propaganda, and one of the greatest surprises for Ricardians was the revelation that the stories, though exaggerated and literally 'twisted', had a basis in fact. The disbelief was not unreasonable, since analysis of Tudor portraiture has demonstrated that it has been doctored and altered to add to or take away from the raised shoulder they often show, and the higher shoulder even switches sides. The discovery of scoliosis was, therefore, a genuine surprise to those aware of these physical distortions of Richard's appearance over the centuries. In the mid-1460s it must have been a terrifying shock to a young teenage boy.

Shakespeare would present his villainous Richard III with kyphosis (in Shakespeare's unkind parlance, a 'bunch-back'), a withered arm and a limp. None of these is accurate. Scoliosis causes a sideways curvature of the spine that can be seen when the back is bare and can result in one shoulder being raised higher than the other. In more severe cases, such as that displayed by Richard's skeleton, it can apply pressure to the lungs and restrict breathing during exertion. The condition would also cause pain in the back which, as ever-present in a time before clinical analgesia, would have been taxing in the extreme. The pain and a change in the appearance of his unclothed back were the first signals of the emerging condition. The impacts, psychological even more than physical, cannot be underestimated as Richard began to fearfully understand what was happening to his body. There was an association in the medieval psyche between physical disability and corruption of the soul. Although this might not reach the extreme of causing a person, particularly one of Richard's rank, to be overtly shunned or driven out of society, it was a connection and prejudice of which Richard would have been all too aware. For a boy in his delicate early teens, it was a source of self-consciousness and uncertain fear that would have been hard to shake, particularly in the household of another, where he might have been unsure who to turn to.

One of the greatest disappointments for Richard as the condition began to manifest itself would have been the loss of any hope that he would become a physical match for his oldest brother. From 1459 onwards, Edward cannot have failed to have made an impression on Richard. He was physically remarkable, as all who left comment agreed, but after his father's death, he had also been a paternal figure in Richard's life, visiting him regularly and providing him with security in the aftermath of his return from the Low Countries. For a small boy, it must have seemed that Edward was an heroic figure from Grecian myth and Richard could have harboured a legitimate hope of reaching the same striking stature and prowess as the king. The pain taking hold in his back would bring an end to any of those dreams and leave Edward as representing something unattainable that Richard had been denied by a twist of fate and a curve of his spine. It is not known whether any alterations were made to Richard's educational regime as a result of his condition or even how aware his tutors might have been of it. In the early stages, if the pain was bearable and the shame perceived by a young Richard less so, he may have managed to keep up with others during their training. The secret of his condition was largely kept from that time until the discovery of his remains over 500 years later (though probably revealed at his death).

Possibly around the time Richard came to Middleham, or after he had become comfortably installed, another addition to Warwick's household arrived who was destined to have a long-term impact on the Duke of Gloucester. At Michaelmas 1465, Warwick received, along with the payment towards Richard's care, the wardship and marriage rights to Francis, Lord Lovell.[21] Francis was about nine years old, four years younger than Richard, and his lands were in the king's hands during his minority because of his father's adherence to the Lancastrian cause. Francis was 9th Baron Lovell and 6th Baron Holand. On the death of his grandmother in 1474, he would also inherit the baronies of Deincourt, Grey of Rotherfield and Bedale, making him then the richest baron in England without an earldom. As adults, Richard and Francis were to become what can only be described as the best of friends. The connection that must have begun at Middleham during the mid-1460s was to endure for a lifetime. Given the age difference and its significance at nine and thirteen, it seems an unlikely comradery, but as two young boys in not dissimilar circumstances, particularly if they arrived together, the situation may have forged a bond that transcended the difference in their ages and development. As the youngest brother of his own family, who had benefitted from the protective arm of an older brother, Richard perhaps saw in Francis someone to whom he could offer the same comfort. It is interesting to wonder whether Francis might have been one of the few in whom Richard confided about the problems he was beginning to experience with his back.

The final indisputable fact that can be taken from Richard's time within the Earl of Warwick's household is his prominent attendance at the celebrations of George Neville's enthronement as Archbishop of York. George was the third son of Richard Neville, Earl of Salisbury, and younger brother to Warwick and John Neville. John's victories at Hedgeley Moor and Hexham had seen him promoted as Earl of Northumberland. The gifting of the prestigious and wealthy earldom of Northumberland to the Neville family was a significant victory in terms of prestige over their old rivals, the Percy family. George was the third influential element of what was now the most powerful noble family in England. Warwick was viewed on the Continent as the real ruler in England, as Edward's chief minister in all things.[22] However, the relationship that the two had appeared to enjoy had begun to tarnish for reasons that are not entirely clear. Warwick and his brother John, now Earl of Northumberland, had spent much of the time since Edward's accession in harness and fighting to keep the peace. John's victories in 1464 had won security and led to the capture of Henry VI the following year. Henry had been on the run in Lancashire since his cause had crumbled, sheltered first by the Pennington family at Muncaster Castle, and then the Pudsay family of Bolton Hall. After that, he spent almost a year at Waddington Hall before he was exposed and captured. Sir James Harrington received a grant of 100 marks from Edward IV for his prominent role in capturing the fugitive former king.[23] It is possible that this more thorough completion of his victories led Edward to allow his little brother to travel north. While Lancastrian commanders and their figurehead remained at large in Scotland, it would have been a dangerous region into which to place a prize as valuable as the Yorkist king's brother.

Warwick had been engaged in an embassy to France during 1464 to try to conclude a peace treaty that would also provide for Edward's marriage to Bona of Savoy, a sister of King Louis XI's wife Charlotte. As the matter became pressing and Edward's opinion on the idea of the marriage became unavoidably required, he dropped something of a political bombshell during a Council meeting at Reading in September.

Amid intensifying calls for his opinion and approval for the union with Bona, Edward disclosed to his gathered advisors that he had already married, in secret. Warwick was at the meeting, and his personal response was probably in line with the rest of those gathered and was perhaps muted in comparison to the more general prevailing opinion of the match. Edward's new wife was Elizabeth Woodville. Five years his senior, she was the widow of a Lancastrian knight, Sir John Grey of Groby, who had died at the Second Battle of St Albans, leaving Elizabeth with two young sons, Thomas and Richard. At the age of twenty-two, the new King of England, the most eligible bachelor in Europe, had married for love. The charge that Elizabeth Woodville was a commoner is not entirely correct. Her father was the son of John, Duke of Bedford's Chamberlain and her mother was Jacquetta of Luxembourg, the duke's widow. The two had married in a scandalously secret match after Bedford's death, and Richard Woodville had been created Baron Rivers in an attempt to balance the social disparity between them. Jacquetta was an English duchess, but she was also the daughter of Peter, Count of Saint-Pol, and sister to the current Count, Louis of Luxembourg.

Two weeks later, on 28 September, Elizabeth was presented in Reading Abbey as the new Queen of England. Suggesting that their outrage was neither as immediate nor as significant as would later be asserted, Elizabeth was led into the Abbey by George, Duke of Clarence, and Richard Neville, Earl of Warwick. There can be little doubt that the establishment was shocked by Edward's marriage, and that it meant Warwick's time in France had been wasted, though the lack of a marriage might not preclude the treaty he had really been working towards. Reports of the news began to reach the Continent and the disbelief there is almost tangible. A newsletter from Bruges to Milan dated 5 October reported that Venetian merchants returning from England 'say that the marriage of King Edward will be celebrated shortly, but without stating where. It seems that the espousals and benediction are already over, and thus he has determined to take the daughter of my Lord de Rivers, a widow with two children, having long loved her, it appears. The greater part of the lords and the people in general seem very much dissatisfied at this, and for the sake of finding means to annul it, all the nobles are holding great consultations in the town of Reading, where the king is.'[24] On the same day, the Milanese Ambassador in France noted that Louis XI's court had become aware 'that King Edward has married a widow of England, daughter of a sister of the Count of St. Pol' and that the marriage 'has greatly offended the people of England'.[25] By 10 October, the rumours had become firm reports, as the same Milanese ambassador at Louis's court wrote from Abbeville to the Duchess of Milan that: 'It is publicly announced here that the King of England has taken to wife an English lady, they say out of love. The king here and all the rest of us hoped and expected that he would be sending at this time to marry one of the sisters of the queen here as he had frequently caused his representatives to see them.'[26]

If Warwick was perturbed by this development, he was not alone. He does not appear to have been more upset than anybody else and certainly did not snub the new queen. The rumour mill across the Channel insisted that Edward's subjects were up in arms, but that did not really seem to be the case either. *The Chronicles of London* casually noted that 'in this yere the first day of May the kyng wedded Dame Elizabeth Gray.'[27] *Hearne's Fragment* is equally nonchalant, noting that Edward, 'being a lusty prince attempted the stability and constant modesty of divers ladies and gentlewomen' before deciding that he could find none as worthy as Dame Elizabeth. Edward, 'seeing the constant and stable mind of the said Dame Elizabeth, early in the morning the said King Edward wedded the foresaid Dame Elizabeth there [at the Manor of Grafton] on the first day of May.'[28] *Gregory's Chronicle* paints the news as in some ways welcome, complaining that 'men mervelyd that oure soverayne lorde was so longe with owte any wyffe, and were evyr ferde that he had be not chaste of hys levynge.' The writer claimed that Edward 'was wedded to the Lorde Ryvers doughter,' with no sense that the match was improper or scandalous, only noting that 'thys marriage was kepte fulle secretely longe and many a day' before Edward revealed it at Reading.[29] The Crowland Chronicler, writing in 1486, offered the typically prudish view that Edward had been 'prompted by the ardour of youth', adding that he had acted 'relying entirely on his own choice, without consulting the nobles of the kingdom'. This writer does suggest a degree of dissatisfaction. 'This the nobility and chief men of the kingdom took amiss, seeing that he had with such immoderate haste promoted a person sprung from a comparatively humble lineage.'[30]

There is little in the way of outrage or talk of revolt that was being touted in France. Certainly, the nobility were unlikely to be pleased that Edward had made such a crucial decision without consulting them, but that was perhaps the point. The more pressure they placed on Edward, the closer he came to wanting, or needing, to assert his own, independent authority. Henry VI had been steered by self-interested nobles, and Edward needed, at some point, to distinguish himself from what he had promised to sweep away. If the nobles, the people and foreign rulers held any firm opinion about Edward's marriage to Elizabeth Woodville, at least at the time it was revealed, it was most likely that Edward had been rash. His petulance had caused him to make a fool of himself by demeaning his own honour and passing up the chance for a politically advantageous marriage. If Warwick felt it harder than anyone else, he did little to show it, and it would only have been because he had believed himself closer to Edward than anyone else. That belief may well have caused Edward to consider reining in the creeping influence of the all-powerful Neville family.

All of this was happening away from Richard's increasingly familiar world amid the green hills and fields of the Yorkshire Dales. His lack of knowledge of the marriage and of participation in what was to follow might have caused him a pang of sadness, but he was learning his place in the Yorkist world. Edward now had two little stepsons, aged ten and eight, to consider in place of his youngest, faraway brother. George Neville acted as Steward of England at Elizabeth Woodville's coronation on 26 May 1465,[31] an event from which Warwick and Lord Hastings were absent due to diplomatic responsibilities in France rather than any note of petulant dissent. By September, the attention of the Neville family was firmly back upon itself and the celebrations of the most magnificent achievement of George Neville's career to date. George was a learned man who appears to have been genuinely concerned for his flock alongside his interests in national affairs. He was a patron of learning and was widely liked, seemingly possessed of the infectious Neville affability. As the temporal world was being kind to his two older brothers Richard and John, now both earls, so the Church took care of its Neville. The position of Archbishop of York gave George supremacy over all of the bishops of the north and made him second in authority only to the Archbishop of Canterbury. This was a moment for the family to celebrate, and they meant to do so in spectacular style.

It was this world, of Richard's cousins rather than his brothers, that was accessible for him to watch, learn from and enjoy. On 22 September 1465, just a fortnight before Richard's thirteenth birthday, the enthronement of the new Archbishop of York was celebrated at Cawood Castle, the palace of the Archbishops of York just to the south of the city. In fact, the feasting lasted several days and, bankrolled by Warwick, it was a spectacle to eclipse anything the king might have been able to put on. The Earl of Warwick acted as Steward for the feast, with his brother John taking the role of Treasurer. Other local lords and knights took prominent positions, ensuring that their ties to their Neville lords were kept tight and strong. George occupied the centre of the high table. On his right sat the Bishops of London, Durham and Ely while on his left, high-ranking temporal guests included Richard's brother-in-law the Duke of Suffolk and John Tiptoft, Earl of Worcester. Abbots and priors of local houses joined other prominent northern barons such as Lord Cromwell, Lord Scrope, Lord Dacre and Lord Ogle, along with officials from York and Calais, where Warwick was Captain, and justices of the law.

The significance to Richard came in his own prominent position as a guest in the chief chamber, just outside the main hall. Here, the Duke of Gloucester was listed at the head of the first table. It was an honoured position for a boy, albeit outside the main hall where the adult men were feasting. On Richard's right sat his sister Elizabeth, Duchess of Suffolk. Eight years Richard's elder, it is uncertain how well the two knew each other since Elizabeth had been married to John de la Pole at a young age. Nevertheless, this was a sibling coming to visit Richard, and he may well have been hungry for news from the south of his brothers, sisters and their mother. At Richard's left sat the Countess of Westmoreland, setting aside the internal Neville feud between the two branches of the family, and the Countess of Northumberland, John Neville's wife, Isabel Ingoldsthorpe. Isabel was not only the sole heiress of her father but also of her uncle John Tiptoft, Earl of Worcester, making her a valuable bride for a younger Neville son. Also listed at the same table were 'two of the Lorde of Warwickes daughters,' Isabel and Anne.[32] Anne was nearly four years younger than Richard but would become his wife. It is therefore significant that the two can be shown to have met on at least this one occasion before their union. It has long been suggested, anecdotally, that their match was based on love. Whilst that remains hard to prove, it is clear that the pair were known to each other and they may well have met on other occasions within Anne's father's household.

The feast enjoyed to celebrate George Neville's enthronement was immense, perhaps even obscenely so. The list of food prepared for the banquet includes an eye-watering 104 oxen, 6 wild bulls, 1,000 muttons, 400 swans, 304 veals, 2,000 pigs, 204 cranes, 400 herons, 2,000 chickens, 4,000 rabbits, 1,200 quails, 1,000 capons, 1,000 'egrits' (egrets), 200 pheasants, 500 partridges, 104 peacocks, 500 deer, 4,000 ducks, 308 pike and 12 porpoises and seals. Atop that, there were 4,000 cold pastries of venison, 1,500 hot pastries of venison, 4,000 jellies, 4,000 cold baked tarts, 3,000 cold baked custards and 2,000 hot custards. The list also describes 'spices, sugered delicates, and waifers, plenty'. Something would inevitably have been required to wash all that food down, and Warwick did not skimp on the drink he made available either. The 300 tuns of ale ordered totalled 75,600 gallons and the 100 tuns of wine equated to 25,200 gallons.[33] For good measure, a pipe of hippocras was available too, meaning there were 76 gallons of the spiced wine to be drunk.

The spectacle must have been enough to overwhelm Richard. There was unlikely to have ever been such extravagance before in his life, but he was in Warwick's household to learn how to be a lord. The enthronement feast of his cousin George Neville was a perfect opportunity to watch what was going on about him and how great men like Warwick projected their authority and inspired loyalty in their retainers. Open-handed generosity was an obvious tool to be used. The willingness to over-provide was probably in evidence as well. It mattered little how much might be thrown away, only that no one went without and that neither food nor drink ran out. Not only could Warwick display his hospitality, but also emphasise the vast wealth that ensured he cared little for how much it might cost to provide so much food and drink. What Richard may have missed beneath the surface was the thin crack in his cousin's relationship with his brother that was set to widen.

While it seems unlikely that Warwick would rail against Edward to the king's younger brother, the fractures may have begun to grow visible. Elizabeth may have brought news to her brother from court, and the extravagance of the Neville lords would become either a symptom or a cause of Warwick's worsening relationship with the king. Did Edward dislike Warwick's self-confidence and pre-eminence, which led to him throwing such immense celebrations? Or was Warwick putting on such a display in reaction to Edward's slow withdrawal of favour from the Neville family that had done so much to place him on his throne? Either way, Richard was about to get caught in the centre of one of the most epic spats in fifteenth-century history.

5

The Loyal Brother

The Count of St. Paul has gone as ambassador to the Duke of
Burgundy to keep him engaged in negotiations and not to let him
conclude a marriage alliance or league with King Edward of England,
until such time as the Earl of Warwick has arranged his affairs; if they
come to anything it will be contrary to the opinion of most people.
Milanese Ambassador to France to the Duke and
Duchess of Milan, 12 September 1467[1]

Richard's time in the household of his cousin Richard Neville, Earl of
Warwick, was likely to come to an end once the earl began to drift away
from the king. As their aims and intentions began to diverge, leaving the
king's brother in the earl's care began to make less and less sense. In 1466,
at the age of thirteen, Richard was invested as a companion of the Order
of the Garter, but was still living predominantly in Warwick's northern
castles centred on Middleham. He appears only irregularly and fleetingly
in official records over the next few years and locating him is therefore
difficult. Richard appeared in the *Calendar of Patent Rolls* as one of the
senior appointments on commissions of oyer and terminer – to investigate
and punish breaches of the law – and these possibly help, but it is far from
certain that he was personally attending to these commissions.

On 20 February 1466, Richard was appointed to a commission of
oyer and terminer with Warwick, his brother John Neville, Earl of
Northumberland, and a collection of nineteen other men, predominantly
local knights but also including John Marshall, the mayor of York.[2] The
commission was to operate 'within the county and city of York', and
although Richard was unlikely to have taken a lead role, his appointment
remains significant. The use of Richard's name as the most senior member
of the group is an extension of Edward's authority through the use of
his young brother. It provided the appearance of a farther-reaching royal
jurisdiction than might have been the case, particularly in the north where

families such as the Neville and Percy clans had traditionally expected a degree of freedom from the eyes and hands of the king commensurate to their distance from London. It is not entirely unreasonable to seek to locate Richard based on appointments such as this because, as well as serving a purpose for Edward, they would also have been ideal training arenas for Richard in which to hone the skills that would become indispensable when he came of age. Given that Edward was likely to reap the rewards of a well-trained younger brother who had refined his skills as an administrator under the watch of a man like Warwick, it would make sense for the king to expect a degree of involvement on his brother's part. Exposure to the machinery of local government and the mechanisms for the implementation of the king's national policy at a regional level would be invaluable for Richard and, in turn, for Edward.

During 1467, political shenanigans on the Continent would drive the aims of Edward and Warwick even further apart. The earl remained committed to finding a lasting peace with Louis XI in France, who in turn seemed to wish for the same. What Louis feared most was an alliance between England and Burgundy that would undoubtedly be aimed at threatening him. After all, it was just such an alliance that had seen Henry V appointed heir to Charles VI in 1421. The English Crown retained and continued to promote its claim to that of France as well, and Louis was understandably wary of such a threat. Throughout 1467 reports within the *Calendar of State Papers of Milan* track the development of Louis' scheme (assuming that what he reported was what he believed to be true). On 18 April, the Milanese ambassadors at Louis' court reported to the Duke of Milan that the French king was in secret negotiations with Edward. They wrote that 'his Majesty had and still has a secret understanding with King Edward of England by means of the Earl of Warwick.'[3] The tenor of this arrangement was that a permanent peace would be concluded between the two nations when 'King Edward and the King of France henceforth and for ever become brothers in arms, and will live as brothers together.'[4] This was no small undertaking. Brothers in arms were joined by insoluble pledges to support and protect each other. It was an undertaking frequently used to ensure that if one of the brothers in arms should die, the other would provide for his family and ensure any treasure found its way back to them. Implicit in the notion was the proscription of taking military actions against each other. Chaucer immortalised the chivalric idea of such a brotherhood in *The Canterbury Tales* between Arcite and Palamon, but it was not just a literary fancy.[5]

King Louis had become willing to share this deepest of secret arrangements with the Duke of Milan for reasons that remain unclear but were unlikely to be innocent. He was either trying to impress the Milanese or embarrass the English into finalising the agreement. Louis rarely acted without careful thought and at least one ulterior motive.

Strikingly, the ambassadors were advised that the negotiation included an understanding that 'King Edward will yield, quit and renounce all rights, actions and claims which belong to him, and which pertain or may pertain upon the kingdom of France'. This is a remarkable concession given the Yorkist commitment to initiating fresh hostilities with France as soon as possible. Yorkist rhetoric since 1450 had blamed the loss of France on the evil counsellors of Henry VI and in turn held these losses up as the cause of domestic problems in England. Henry VI had been faced with a bitter backlash when he had agreed to cede Maine and Anjou as part of the marriage treaty to wed Margaret of Anjou. Having settled English families there, Henry kept his arrangement with Charles VII secret until the French king would wait no longer, and then all but cut loose William de la Pole, Duke of Suffolk, to face the repercussions of a policy he had enacted, but not initiated.[6] Now, Louis claimed, Edward was ready to renounce the English claim in France altogether.

Richard had a part to play in these secret negotiations. Louis was to allow his second daughter, the two-year-old Joan, to marry 'the second brother of King Edward'.[7] The fact that this refers to Richard is made clear by the addition that this was 'because the first is married to the daughter of the Earl of Warwick.' This was untrue, but perhaps exposes the games Warwick was playing too. He coveted George, still heir to his brother's throne after six years, as husband to his own daughter Isabel. Edward was opposed to the match when the question was raised, but Warwick clearly took George off the negotiating table in France by claiming that the couple were already wed. For Richard, had he been consulted, a match with an infant as he approached fifteen would have held little appeal. It would have meant at least eleven years and probably more like thirteen before he could think about children, by which time he would have been almost thirty. To sweeten the deal, Louis was offering part of Burgundy and lands held by the duke's heir Charles, Count of Charolais, as dowry. The problem there was, of course, that these lands would have to be taken by force, which led to the part of the agreement that provided for 'a war of extermination' with Burgundy, the spoils to be divided.

Charles, Count of Charolais, was singled out for further attention. Louis was aware that Charles was trying to secure a marriage with Edward's last remaining unmarried sister, Margaret. In order to prevent this potentially dangerous union and 'to alienate him entirely',[8] plans were afoot to marry her to Philip of Savoy. Louis finally claimed that Edward had personally dedicated himself to this entire enterprise, having 'written him a letter in his own hand, a thing he had never done except upon this occasion.'[9] It is hard to be confident what was going on here. Louis had his reasons to lie, but Edward was probably not being entirely genuine either. Warwick championed the union with France, and although his hopes of a marriage for Edward to a French princess had been thwarted, he remained committed to a long-term peace with Louis. For his part, Edward would seek an alliance with Burgundy and had already broached the idea of marrying Margaret to Charles the previous year, though nothing had been settled.[10] Charles was clearly a figure who unnerved the French king, an attitude Warwick seems to have adopted too. The Crowland Chronicler would insist that Edward's decision to make an alliance with Charles was the real root of trouble between the two men, 'it being much against his wish, that the views of Charles, now Duke of Burgundy, should be in any way promoted by means of an alliance with England. The fact is, that he pursued that man with a most deadly hatred.'[11]

Philip the Good, Charles's father, died on 15 June 1467, making Charles Duke of Burgundy. At the time of his death, there was a large Burgundian embassy in England under cover of a tournament between Philip's illegitimate son Anthony, the Bastard of Burgundy, and Edward's brother-in-law Anthony Woodville. The two men were considered the leading tournament knights of their day, but the event, and the negotiations, were cut short when Anthony returned home to support his half-brother Charles. Why Warwick conceived such a hatred of Charles is unknown, unless it stemmed either from the prevailing opinion of him in France, where Warwick was spending so much time, or from Burgundy's efforts to thwart Warwick's own preferred policy. In a worrying development, on 19 May, just before Philip's death, the Milanese ambassadors were reporting that fresh negotiations to marry Margaret to Charles were underway, 'confirming once more the old league with the English'[12] that the French so feared. The response Louis was preparing to this threat was 'treating with the Earl of Warwick to restore King Henry in England, and the ambassador of the old queen of England is already here.'[13]

The doomed flirtation with a permanent resolution to relations with France ended in September 1467. The Milanese ambassadors informed their master on 12 September that Louis had been forced to give up on Warwick, having overestimated the earl's ability to deliver what he had promised. French ambassadors, who had been conspicuously ignored during their time in England, had returned to Louis in Paris with news that 'the Earl of Warwick met with many opponents to his plan' and that 'they found him unable to effect what he had promised on his departure.' Edward, they reported, 'seems very averse to France, and Warwick; they are constantly at strife,' adding 'King Louis complains bitterly that the Earl of Warwick has made so many promises without fulfilling anything. According to report, the earl has retired to his estates to raise troops.'[14] Whatever anyone in England thought, those at Louis' court in Paris clearly saw trouble ahead for England. Three days later, on 15 September, the Milanese ambassadors wrote that: 'In England things are upside down and in the air.'[15] Richard's marriage to a French princess was not to be, but this episode also emphasised the irreconcilable differences forcing Edward and Warwick apart. It made no sense, indeed it would be dangerous, to allow Edward's younger brother to remain under Warwick's care in such circumstances. The king must have feared the influence the earl might exert and the honeyed poison he might pour into Richard's young ears. As it turned out, Edward's concern was misdirected.

Although it cannot be shown for certain, it seems likely that Richard was extracted from the household of the Earl of Warwick in 1467. The earl continued to try to secure the French peace he championed, while Edward appeared willing to participate but showed far greater favour to Burgundy. As late as 31 August 1468, the Milanese ambassadors were still reporting the possibility of Richard marrying Louis' daughter, though it seems far more unlikely in 1468 than it had been the previous year. Nevertheless, the ambassador wrote that an embassy from England had arrived in Senlis to negotiate with Louis because 'they are content to have an understanding and friendship together.' The discussions apparently included 'the marriage of that sovereign's second daughter, although they say she is somewhat deformed in person, chiefly in one shoulder, to King Edward's brother', reprising the plan of the previous year in an attempt to create peace with France as well as Burgundy. The reference to a physical condition on the part of Louis' daughter that sounds suspiciously like scoliosis is interesting. Possibly the ambassadors identified the wrong party, but the way in which Richard's condition was kept so secret later suggests it was not a matter of public knowledge in 1468. Whatever the truth, Richard was not destined for a match with a French princess.

If commissions of oyer and terminer are to be accepted as reasonable evidence of where Richard was located, then the beginning of 1468 saw him in the Midlands. On 13 February, he was appointed to a commission based in Warwickshire, Worcestershire, Nottinghamshire, Derbyshire, Staffordshire, Shropshire and Herefordshire. George was named first in the list of officers, followed by Richard. George was eighteen now and had been managing his own household for a couple of years. He was based at Tutbury Castle in Staffordshire not far west of Derby, so his appointment was regionally appropriate. Richard's base is less clear but at fifteen he might have been hoping for a regional presence, somewhere to develop for himself over the coming years. The brothers were joined on the commission by Warwick, still too significant to be excluded from such operations even if Edward wished to push him aside; Edward's father-in-law Richard Woodville, now Earl Rivers in recognition of his new, lofty position; and River's oldest son, Anthony Woodville; as well as Edward's faithful friend, William Hastings. A significant number of local knights were also added to the commission, no doubt to do the real work on the ground and, if Richard were intimately involved in the commission, they would have provided vital tutelage and valuable connections for the young duke. The list included John Sutton of Dudley, a servant of Henry VI who had fought for the Lancastrian king at St Albans in 1455 and Blore Heath in 1459, though by Towton in 1461, he was fighting with Edward. Walter Devereux, Lord Ferrers, was in his mid-thirties and from an important Herefordshire family. His sister Anne was married to William Herbert, who would be created Earl of Pembroke in this year. Walter would die at Bosworth in 1485, fighting for Richard. These were networks the young duke would do well to foster and learn from.

The beginnings of a sense of regional power might have grown in Richard as the year went on. On 2 August, he, and the heirs of his body, were granted the manors of Alwerton and Tywarnayll Tees in Cornwall, seized from Eleanor, wife of Edmund Beaufort, Duke of Somerset, after the death of their son Henry.[16] The following day, Richard was appointed to another commission of oyer and terminer in Devon and Gloucestershire. Clarence was again the first name listed and Warwick, Rivers, Anthony Woodville and William Hastings were included. More local significant families added knowledge and experience, including Walter Devereux again. Humphrey Stafford was another who would remain loyal to Richard and fight for him at Bosworth. It is hard to say whether he made such an impression in these young years that men were immediately devoted to him, or whether these older men saw something they liked in the king's youngest brother; it is interesting, though, that men who had known him from this time were amongst those most loyal to him almost two decades later.

On 25 October 1468, just a few weeks after his sixteenth birthday, there was a further hint of the plan Edward might have been forming for his youngest brother. Richard was granted the castle, lordship and manor of Fareley in Somerset, and the lordships and manors of Haightesbury and Tefont in Wiltshire. These had been seised from Robert, Lord Hungerford, the Lancastrian loyalist attainted in Edward's first Parliament in 1461 and executed after the Battle of Hexham in 1464. With these named properties, Richard also received 'the other lordships, manors, lands, rents, reversions, services and possessions in the counties of Somerset, Wilts, Dorset, Devon, Gloucester and elsewhere in the realm of England' that had belonged to Hungerford. On top of this, the same grant gave him possession of Bedminster in Gloucestershire and all other properties in that county that had belonged to Eleanor, wife of Edmund Beaufort. There is a sense that Edward was attempting to provide a suitable income for his growing youngest brother and that he planned to do so by setting him up in the southern Marches, around Gloucester and Worcester, and the West Country, in Wiltshire, Somerset and Devon.[17] On 12 December, another commission of oyer and terminer saw Richard appointed to investigate lawlessness in Southampton, Wiltshire and

Devon, aided by some of the same nobles and knights and the mayors of Southampton and Salisbury.[18]

There is a great deal to be said for this plan. The Marches around Ludlow were loyal to the House of York and had been for decades. That influence waned further south, and the West Country was traditionally more sympathetic to the Lancastrian cause. The Courtenay Earls of Devon had been loyal to Henry VI and forfeited their title in 1461 following Towton, after which the last earl, Thomas Courtenay, had been executed. The Beaufort Dukes of Somerset were also dominant in the region, and Richard already had Corfe Castle and some of their other former possessions in Somerset and Devon. It was an area of the country where Edward lacked loyal nobility and where a vacuum of vanquished Lancastrian families needed to be filled. Richard, perhaps particularly with his dukedom located in the same region, was an ideal choice to fill this Yorkist void. If George was being provided with a power base in the northern Marcher area around Staffordshire and east in a line across the Midlands, and if Richard could be set up to control the south-west, then Edward would be surrounded and shielded by his brothers. George might even balance Warwick's influence in the Midlands and restrict him to his northern territories, where he was farther away. In theory, Warwick was still loyal to Edward, meaning that the north was also secured by a powerful cousin. If Edward could retain his popularity in the south-east and around London, then the country appeared subdued, divided between loyal men. It had the makings of a good plan, but little in the fifteenth century proceeding according to the schemes of kings.

Margaret had left England on 1 July 1468 to complete the contracted marriage Edward had agreed to with Charles, Duke of Burgundy. The union was officially celebrated in spectacular Burgundian style at Bruges on 10 July.[19] With the exception of increasingly strained relations with Warwick and his family, Edward might have felt settled, with his two younger brothers becoming reliable bulwarks and he looked forward to his second decade as King of England.

Edward and Elizabeth's third daughter, Cecily, was born on 20 March 1469, joining the three-year-old Elizabeth and eighteen-month-old Mary. The king was no doubt thinking that he could use a son to shore up his position sooner rather than later, but Elizabeth was proving as fertile as he must have known she was, since she already had two sons, and time was still on their side. The arrival of a son would bring to the fore the delicate matter of relegating George's position after eight years as heir to the throne, but it had always been only a matter of time before that came about. Whatever Edward believed he had built, and secured, over the last few years was about to come toppling down around him, and after the dust settled, or more appropriately, once it was all kicked up in the air, only one brother would still be at his side.

The fragile peace that had seemed to settle on England during the last few years was shattered as spring began to warm the air in England. As might be expected, events in the far north were poorly recorded farther south, where such regions were at best ignored and at worst held in nervous contempt. The scrappy evidence suggests there may have been a small uprising under a man taking the name Robin of Redesdale, in March. More certain is a swelling threat under the leadership of one using the name Robin of Holderness. Both men, if there were two, adopted the name of the increasingly popular hero of the common folk, Robin Hood, to emphasise the public and altruistic nature of their complaints against the regime. The leader of the uprising in May cannot be identified with any certainty, but it has been suggested that he was Robert Hillyard, a Percy retainer. Certainly, the stated aim of the revolt was to press for the restoration of Percy authority in the areas where the disgraced family had been ousted by their Neville rivals, particularly John, who also occupied their earldom. It was John who swiftly rode out to bring an end to the murmurings that might cost him his hard-won and prestigious title.

The flurry of activity in the south suggests that Edward was not taking this potential threat lightly. On 22 May, a general commission of oyer and terminer 'throughout the realm' was handed to Warwick, Henry Bourchier, Earl of Essex, the king's father-in-law Earl Rivers and William, Lord Hastings. A set of knights and administrators were appointed to assist them, but the national scope of the commission and the conspicuous absence of either George or Richard suggest that this was deemed a serious matter, not the sort of exercise to be used to give his young brothers experience. At the same time, George and Richard were added to a commission of oyer and terminer to cover York, Cumberland, Westmoreland and the city of York. In this, they were to be supported by a significant tranche of the nobility – their brother-in-law John de la Pole, Duke of Suffolk; and the earls of Warwick, Essex, Arundel, Shrewsbury, Rivers, Pembroke and Devon. Anthony Woodville also appeared in the commission, as did a long list of regional gentry including Henry, Lord Fitzhugh; John, Lord Audley; John, Lord Scrope of Bolton; and other men familiar to Richard such as John Sutton, Lord Dudley and Walter Devereux.[20]

At the start of May, Richard had been granted lands within Lancashire and Cheshire from the properties of the Duchy of Lancaster.[21] It seems likely that his income was not reaching the minimum felt appropriate to support him in his royal estate, which was probably around the £1,000 per annum mark. This was the figure provided by the Act of Accord in 1460 to support Edmund, Earl of Rutland, as third in line to the throne and may have offered a benchmark of a suitable income.[22] The grant gave Richard property within five of the six hundreds of Lancashire and a barony within Cheshire and was expressly made 'for the genuine and deep brotherly affection that we feel and have towards our dearest brother Richard, Duke of Gloucester, and in order that the same brother will be able to uphold the said estate and the costs and burdens incumbent on the same in accordance with the demands of his estate'.[23] It can hardly have been an accident, given the properties across the Marches and further south that Edward could, and had in the past, granted to his brother that these particular gifts placed Richard into the heart of a potential problem. Like a royal troubleshooter, Richard was being parachuted in to act as a block on someone else Edward may have nurtured growing concerns about.

It seems certain at this point that Edward became suspicious of the intentions of Thomas, Lord Stanley, for reasons that are unclear. Thomas was from a family beginning to dominate Lancashire, Cheshire and into North Wales. They held large swathes of land and were acquisitive in the extreme. Thomas's real power in the region was derived from the clutch of offices he held in the Duchy of Lancaster which, as a palatine county, could operate outside the royal writ. The offices brought Thomas wealth and astounding local authority, which was wide open to abuse. Perhaps, in May, this authority was enough to worry Edward. It is surprising that Warwick remained in such official favour and Thomas was married to Warwick's sister Eleanor. That connection would soon be enough to explain such wariness, so it is perhaps a signal that although he was not yet making a move against his most powerful subject, Edward was either planning to do so soon or was aware of Warwick's increasing disaffection. It is also true that Thomas had proven less than reliable in the past, having narrowly escaped a Commons petition to attaint him for treason for failing to heed a summons to arms from Henry VI in 1459.[24] Although his brother William had fought for the Earl of Shrewsbury at the Battle of Blore Heath, Thomas had committed to neither side, drawing the ire of the Lancastrian polity but perhaps also the suspicion of Yorkists.

As it happened, John Neville had swiftly crushed the unrest being raised in the Percy name. Such a revival would threaten him more than any other, and he was quick to restore the king's peace. That was not the end of trouble in the north, though. By late June, another popular revolt was underway led by another mysterious figure using, perhaps again, the sobriquet Robin of Redesdale. Guesses have been made at the identity of this shadowy character too, with Sir John Conyers being the most frequently offered. Conyers was a retainer of the Earl of Warwick and Neville men seem to have been prominent among the rebels. Warwick may have seen a template he could adapt to his own ends in the Percy uprising of May, or perhaps he simply needed to counteract a groundswell of renewed affection for a lost master, the grass always being greener in another noble family's fields. If the latter was the case, then it soon got out of hand. Edward was at the shrine of Walsingham in Norfolk around

21 June, and his brother Richard was with him. News arrived of what was becoming a significant threat from the north and that John Neville had not yet made any move against the rebels. The Neville connections and John's failure to act may have been the realisation of what Edward had feared, or even what he had planned by the carefully constructed exclusion of the Neville family. If this was what Edward had wanted, then he was playing a dangerous game with his most powerful subject.

Things must have moved quickly in East Anglia, as Edward began to gather men. Richard was sixteen and perhaps pestered his older brother to allow him to take part in the military effort. Richard had been training for years, working against his own body and the scoliosis that sought to restrict him. He had been sitting alongside men of experience to learn the craft of nobility and the exercise of the authority he possessed as the king's brother and a duke. Now came a chance to put all of that into operation, conspicuously so, at his brother's side – an opportunity to impress Edward. It seems that the king agreed. On 24 June, Richard wrote a letter from Castle Rising, 20 miles west of Walsingham. The castle was one of the Duchy of Cornwall's properties and boasted three baileys, each defended by raised earthworks, before the enormous central keep could be reached. Richard began his letter 'The Duc of Gloucestre' in his own hand before it continued,

> Right trusty and welbeloved. We grete you wele. And forasmuch as the Kings good Grace hathe appointed me to attende upon His Highnesse into the North parties of his lande, whiche wolbe to me gret cost and charge, whereunto I am soo sodenly called that I am not so wel purveide of money therfor as behoves me to be, and therfor pray you as my special trust is in you, to lend me an hundreth pounde of money unto Ester next commying, at whiche tyme I promise you ye shalbe truly therof content and paide agayn, as the berer herof shal enforme you: to whom I pray you to yeve credence therin, and showe me such frendlynesse in the same as I may doo for you herafter, wherinne ye shal find me redie.
> Writen at Risyng the xxiiij[th] day of Juyn.
> R. Gloucestr

A postscript was added to the letter, again in Richard's own hand as opposed to that of the writer of the main body of the message.

> Sir I pray you that ye fayle me not at this tyme in my grete need, as ye wule that I schewe yow my goode lordshype in that matter that ye labure to me for.[25]

The body of the letter is almost textbook and inevitably reflects the lessons Richard had learned both in the classroom and around more experienced men exercising authority on commissions, though a secretary would also have assisted with phrasing the request. Richard makes it clear that he has been suddenly ordered to perform his duty to the king and there is the hint in the emphasis here of an excited young boy seeking to become a man. The unexpected nature of the threat Edward was responding to is suggested by the fact that Richard found himself unprepared – 'not so wel purveide of money therfore as behoves me'. There is a sense here of not wishing to look like the poor relative. Richard could have asked Edward, or one of the other lords about them, for money, but chose instead to send away for a loan.

Richard committed to repaying the requested £100 by the following Easter, suggesting a degree of financial responsibility and care for his credit status that would be a feature of the remainder of his life. Richard cannot legitimately, at any point, be described as reckless with his money. The promise of good lordship in return for the favour of lending him the money is a standard form of currency in late medieval England. It paid to have a member of the nobility on your side to protect and promote your interests. In effect, Richard was offering to store up a favour in return for the loan. Good lordship was also to become a powerful and conspicuous aspect of the rest of Richard's life and would go a long way to explaining his success in years to come, and perhaps his ultimate failure too. Nevertheless, between a commitment to fiscal responsibility and the provision of good lordship, there is already a great deal of the adult Richard to be seen in this sixteen-year-old's letter.

The recipient of the request was Sir John Say, and with good reason. As Chancellor of the Duchy of Lancaster Sir John was aware of Richard's new acquisitions within the Duchy and the income he was due from them, making it easier for him to measure Richard's pledge to repay it in a timely fashion. The postscript suggests that the letter may have been of a form sent to several recipients, but makes it clear that Sir John was already seeking Richard's help and favour 'in that matter that ye labure to me for'. This would doubtless add to the reasons for selecting Sir John, particularly as Richard was in a hurry and needed the funds urgently. Not only could Sir John see a route to repayment through the duke's new acquisitions in a region he was intimately familiar with, but he was already petitioning Richard for something. There is no evidence of what the matter between the two men was, but it is tempting to wonder, with the dangerous magic of hindsight, whether it related to Thomas, Lord Stanley's stranglehold on the region. If so, it would add weight to the notion that Edward had provided his brother with land there to offer Stanley a gentle reminder that he was not omnipotent, and nor was he unwatched.

Edward began to move his forces west and north to confront the growing threat of Robin of Redesdale. The London Chronicler

John Warkworth credited the revolt with 20,000 men and names Sir William Conyers as the leader.[26] News of the extent of the challenge to his authority stopped Edward in his tracks at Nottingham, where he billeted his men and sent for reinforcements from Wales and the South West. William Herbert, Earl of Pembroke, had done the king sterling service in Wales and earned the earldom confiscated from Jasper Tudor in reward. Humphrey Stafford had only been created Earl of Devon in May but was the most prominent landowner in the south-west. It was to these two men that Edward sent his call for reinforcements, and he was to await their arrival at Nottingham. It is possible that intelligence from the north helped Edward make a connection to the Neville faction he had been conspicuously excluding because, on 9 July, Edward wrote to three of the most senior men absent from Nottingham and soon to be exposed as the real threat to his crown.

Sir Thomas Montgomery and Maurice Berkeley were sent with letters addressed to George, Duke of Clarence, Richard Neville, Earl of Warwick and George Neville, Archbishop of York instructing them to come before the king at Nottingham.[27] To Warwick, Edward wrote a letter that at least appeared to offer an olive branch, after making it clear that the king knew what he was up to. Edward told his cousin he refused to believe 'that ye should be of any such disposition towards us as ye Rumor here runneth considering the trust and affeccon we bere in yow'. He added at the end of the note 'ne thynk but ye shalbe to us welcome'. It is difficult to discern from this whether Edward sincerely offered the chance of a rapprochement or sought only to cause Warwick to come to him so that he could be more easily taken. George Neville was similarly summoned 'according to the promise ye made us' and assured that he would be 'to us welcome' on his arrival in Nottingham. If both men were exposed as being behind a major uprising in the heartlands of their family and involving their retainers, it would have been at least political if not personal suicide to go to the king now. It is more likely that Edward simply wanted them to know that he had uncovered their treachery. If he wasn't yet entirely confident of their parts in it, the letters would at least go some way to either bring them under his control or smoke them out as rebels.

The letter to George said little more than 'we trust ye will dispose you according to our pleasure and commandment; and ye shall be to us right welcome.' Whether his brother had been directly implicated is unclear, but is suggested by the nature of the letter, written, as the other two were, in Edward's own hand and to a similar end. Unless Edward had been aware of George's drift into the influence of Warwick, the news that he might be part of a rebellion must have come as a shock. Richard, if he was made privy to the reports, must have been surprised to find the brother he had grown up with embroiled in an attempt to dislodge their oldest brother from the throne. What Edward cannot have learned by

9 July was that the three men had left England's shores to defy him even more deeply.

On 6 July, George, Warwick and the Archbishop sailed from Sandwich to Calais. Richard's mother Cecily Neville had been at Sandwich to see them off, so there must have been some planning and communication involved. It is doubtful that Cecily was aware of the plan to rebel against Edward, but she was almost certainly there to give her blessing to her second son's planned nuptials. The men made for Calais, where Warwick was still Captain, to fulfil an ambition he had harboured for years. The earl had removed George from the table as a possible heir during negotiations with France two years earlier on the basis that the duke was already married to his own daughter. Edward had forbidden the match, but Warwick snatched at the chance to realise a union between his oldest daughter and the heir to the throne. On 11 July 1469, George and Isabel were married in a ceremony conducted by Isabel's uncle, George's cousin, the Archbishop of York. Warwick had secured a Papal dispensation for the marriage, due to the degree in which George and Isabel were related, on 14 March 1468[28] and he now used the distraction of revolt in the north to slip across the Channel and have the couple married. If Cecily did know of the plan to join them, she might not have sought to discourage it. Edward had made an impulsive love match to a penniless widow. How could she complain about George marrying the most valuable heiress in England? The effect of the marriage was also to make Richard the most eligible bachelor in the country in George's place.

The day after the wedding, Warwick issued a manifesto from Calais that all but mirrored the complaints of the northern rebels and offered an open threat to Edward's kingship, comparing him to Edward II, Richard II and Henry VI, three monarchs who had been forcibly removed from their thrones. Matters began to gather pace now. Edward's reinforcements were ambushed near Banbury on 26 July by Robin of Redesdale's men, who had slid past Nottingham in an attempt to join with Warwick on his return. William Herbert was executed after the battle, and Humphrey Stafford escaped, only to meet his end at the hands of an angry mob in Somerset the following month. Having triumphally re-crossed the Channel, Warwick set about making the most of this unexpected victory. The king's father-in-law Richard Woodville, Earl River, was apprehended on the Welsh border with his second son John, and both were beheaded after a perfunctory show trial. Whatever personal animosity had existed between Warwick and Rivers was vented while Warwick held the upper hand. It was the kind of ruthless act that had become almost acceptable during the troubles a decade earlier, but the earl can hardly have expected a warm welcome from the king in the wake of these executions. Two of the king's relatives by marriage and his key man in Wales were dead at Warwick's hand.

Seeing the way the wind was blowing, Edward took the decision not to fight Warwick. This is perhaps the best indication that Edward did not feel confident he could defeat the earl, deprived as he now was of any reinforcements. Instead, he sent those with him at Nottingham away. It was a tactical decision, certainly; it denied Warwick any form of justification for attacking Edward's position, but it was not without personal risk too. Warwick was not taking prisoners, and Edward must have felt confident he could prevent his own death at his cousin's hands. George Neville, learning that Edward was now alone at Nottingham, moved to take the king into his custody, and Edward acquiesced. The king was taken to Warwick Castle before being moved further north to Middleham amid supposed fear for his safety.[29] The earl sought now to rule in the king's name but found it harder than he had imagined. As with Henry VI's illness, the absence of a king exposed the utter reliance of medieval government on the person of the monarch.

Richard's whereabouts during this period are unclear. He is not recorded as having been taken with his brother, and it would have made sense for Edward to ensure that all the Yorkist eggs were not in one basket. George had betrayed them, and much might depend on Richard if Edward had misjudged Warwick's intentions at Nottingham. It is reasonable to surmise that, like other noblemen, Richard was ordered to escape the city and keep a watch for the right moment to act. Given the lands that he now held, it is likely that Richard went either to the West Country or, perhaps more likely, into Lancashire, which would keep him closer to Edward at Nottingham, Warwick and then Middleham. Without a real power base of his own, he did not have a natural, secure place to retreat to, a fact that may have worked in his favour during a period in which capturing him must have been something the rebels would have hoped for. It is not hard to imagine the sixteen-year-old duke protesting as his brother tried to send him away. It must have felt like cowardice, and Richard was never to display the kind of realpolitik that marked Edward's rule. Running from his brother George and his former patron Warwick was not the kind of chivalric bravery his tutors had taught him, but it was a sensible reaction to the mounting problems, and Richard must have, in the end, done as his brother and king instructed.

For Warwick, the problems came thick and fast. On 16 August, a letter to the Duke of Milan from London advised him that 'The Earl of Warwick, as astute a man as ever was Ulysses, is at the king's side, and from what they say the king is not at liberty to go where he wishes,' adding that 'they wish to arrange for a parliament to meet and in that they will arrange the government of this realm.' The writer also noted that: 'Every one is of opinion that it would be better not; God grant it so.'[30] Problems reached their peak in early September when a Lancastrian force led by Sir Humphrey Neville crossed the border from Scotland, seeking to take advantage of the chaos gripping Yorkist England. Warwick found himself unable to raise a force to defend the border without the king's direct authority. Crowland observed that 'the people, seeing their king detained as a prisoner, refused to take any notice of proclamations' summoning them to fight. Faced with stark reality, Warwick realised his seizure of the king was unsustainable and, despite what it may have meant for him personally, he set Edward free so that he could appear in York and the assault could be 'most valiantly routed'. Edward's gamble had paid off in short order. Crowland noted with a sense of amusement that 'beyond all expectation' the king 'did not so much make his escape, as find himself released by the express consent of the earl of Warwick himself.'[31]

By mid-October, the king, 'seizing the opportunity, in the full enjoyment of his liberty came to London'.[32] He was accompanied by those lords who had departed from him at Nottingham, including Richard. John Paston wrote that 'The Kynge is comyn to London, and ther came with hym, and roode ageyn hym, the Duke of Glowcestr, the Duke of Suffolke, the Erle of Aroundell, the Erle of Northumberland, the Erle of Essex'[33] and a host of lords and officials. They were greeted by the Mayor, twenty-two Aldermen dressed in scarlet and two hundred citizens clad all in blue.[34] John Paston also reported that the Archbishop of York and the Earl of Oxford were at the Archbishop's manor of Moor, having been denied permission to ride into the capital with the king and ordered to wait there until he summoned them. As for his wayward brother George and Warwick, 'the Kyng hymselffe hathe good langage of the Lords of Clarance, of Warwyk, and of my Lords of York [and] of Oxenford, seyng they be hys best frendys.' He added, ominously, that 'hys howselde men have other langage, so that what schall hastely falle I cannot seye.'[35] The king was apparently happy to sweep the matter under the carpet in public, but as the machinery of government swung back into action, it became clear that the rift was not going to be forgotten or healed quite so quickly.

Around the same day that Richard accompanied his brother into London, a letter was being written on the Continent that offers another glimpse of the marriage possibilities of the young Duke of Gloucester. Henry IV, King of Castile on the Iberian Peninsula, in an area that would become Spain, had no male heir. His half-sister Isabella was next in line to the throne, and with the likelihood of her succession, the question of her marriage and the urgency of procreation seems to have been a matter requiring immediate attention. On 12 October, Isabella wrote to her half-brother that,

> to remedy the danger and harm which could grow again if the said kingdoms and lordships did not have someone who could later

legitimately succeed to them, it was agreed by your Excellency and by the Grandees and Lords Spiritual and gentlemen of his court and by the high council that, according to the laws and regulations regarding such things, they would diligently explore which of four possible marriages – to the Prince of Aragon (King of Sicily), to the King of Portugal, to the Duke of Berri, or to the brother of the King of England – seemed more honourable to your Royal crown, and to offer a better chance of peace and growth in size to your said kingdoms.[36]

It is frustrating, or perhaps telling, that three suitors are listed by their title and the fourth only as a brother of the King of England. Isabella perhaps did not feel that an alliance with England was the correct choice, so listed this option last and almost dismissively. The list may be in the order of her own preference, given that Ferdinand of Aragon was the match eventually made. The wording leaves open the possibility that she was referring to George, but news of his marriage to Isabel Neville was well known by this date, even ignoring the fact that Warwick had been actively advertising George as off the market for years. Richard is almost certainly the brother referred to by Isabella, who was just eighteen months older than Richard and represented a prestigious match. For Edward, the union may have been less than desirable at that moment. He seems, maybe out of jealousy, to have resisted matches with foreign rulers for his brothers, despite regular connections of George to Burgundy and Richard to France. With all the unrest at home, it would not have been a fortuitous time to consider sending away a young man who was becoming a loyal pillar of Edward's government. Nevertheless, it demonstrates that Richard was now a key figure on the international marriage market, being talked about in the courts of the Iberian Peninsula.

Now seeking to ensure that he remained firmly in control, Edward further promoted his youngest and most loyal brother. The most significant office lying vacant was that of High Constable of England, which had been held by Richard Woodville, Earl Rivers, executed at Warwick's command. On 17 October, a fortnight after his seventeenth birthday, this nationally significant office of state was given to Richard for life 'in the same manner as Richard, late earl Rivers, had it'.[37] Anthony Woodville, now Earl Rivers in his father's place, appears to have relinquished his right to the office and it is possible that Richard sought it out for himself. The Constable effectively held responsibility for national security and military affairs but also had oversight of heralds and of coats of arms, a feature of the office that Richard would, in future, show himself keenly interested in. The Court of Chivalry was also under the jurisdiction of the Constable and offered draconian, inequitable powers for the delivery of justice against those suspected of treason in order to protect the Crown. This aspect of the office will come into sharper focus in due course, but either Richard coveted the post for the connection to heraldry it provided, or Edward wanted to indoctrinate his youngest brother into the role at a young age. It is feasible the appointment served both ends, but the willingness of the king to give it to Richard demonstrates the high esteem and trust the young duke was accruing.

Two days later, on 19 October, Richard was made Chief Steward of the queen's lands, also for life and with an income of £100 per year.[38] On 27 October, Edward's move to decisively dislodge the Neville family began in earnest. Richard was at Westminster[39] to act as one of the witnesses to the oath of allegiance offered to Edward by Henry Percy, son of the Earl of Northumberland who had died at Towton in 1461. Henry had been imprisoned in the Tower, his family disgraced and his inheritance placed into the hands of John Neville. Richard watched as Henry Percy now 'made corporal oath to the king within the palace of Westminster'. Percy swore that:

> I Henry Percy become your subject and liegeman and promise to God and to you that hereafter of faith and truth shall be as to you as to my sovereign liege lord and to your heirs kings of England, of life and limb and earthly worship for to live and die against all people, and to you and your commandment I shall be obeisant, as God me help and to his holy evangelists.[40]

Only Thomas Bourchier, Archbishop of Canterbury, appears before Richard in the list of witnesses to this oath. The Chancellor, Robert Stillington, Bishop of Bath and Wells, is listed after Richard and is a man whose significance would grow in years to come. Several other bishops and earls were present to watch the beginning of a rehabilitation that sounded a death knell for Neville authority. The uprising of Robin of Holderness had demonstrated lingering affection for the Percy family in a region now under Neville authority. John Neville, for all the valuable and unswerving service he had provided Edward, had moved quickly against this revolt, but all too slowly against that under Robin of Redesdale. This lethargy, along with his surname, was enough to wipe away a decade of loyalty for Edward and with Henry Percy released from the Tower on swearing this oath, John must have known it could only be a matter of time before his position was threatened. For now, though, Edward seems content to have put John on edge and did not act further.

In short order, on 29 October, Edward set up commissions of array across the country. Eighteen were given in total, and Richard was conspicuous in the Welsh Marches, leading three of the commissions. In Shropshire, he was assisted by the now familiar John Sutton of Dudley and Walter Devereux, Lord Ferrers. In Gloucestershire, Walter Devereux would again aid him along with William, Lord Berkeley, and Walter Devereux was to be his companion for the array in Worcestershire. This set of appointments raises again the possibility that Edward saw a permanent place for his brother on the family's traditional strongholds along the Marches. It is also feasible that Edward merely handpicked the safest, most loyal and fertile regions for raising troops in the Yorkist cause for his inexperienced brother. The appointments do fit with Edward's apparently erratic and varying plans for his brother that nevertheless seemed to focus on the Welsh Marches, Lancashire and the West Country. Part of this effort to find a place for Richard appears to have already been causing friction. In November, Edward wrote to Thomas, Lord Stanley, ordering him to pay Richard what he was owed from his Duchy of Lancaster lands.[41] It is likely that Richard remained short of ready money, but also that Lord Stanley was withholding funds because he was unhappy at the royal duke's insertion into territory he viewed as his own. Edward certainly had an interest in once more reminding Stanley who was in charge, given his unbridled power in such a critical region and his relationship to Warwick as the earl's brother-in-law. For the first time in Edward's reign, Neville names were utterly absent from all of the commissions.

On 7 November, Richard was appointed chief justice in North Wales with his wage to be paid by the Chamberlain,[42] reinforcing his increasing authority around the Marches but also giving him yet more power close to Stanley interests. On 14 November, Edward gave Richard the castle and manor of Sudeley in Gloucestershire, which he had himself only recently purchased from Sir Ralph Butler. Richard also received lands around Sudeley to the annual value of £20 at Toddington, Stanley, Greet, Gretton, Catesthorp and Newington, together with the advowson of Sudeley Church.[43] Sudeley was, and remains, a stunning property in eastern Gloucestershire that had been extensively rebuilt by Ralph Butler, Lord Sudeley, in 1442 from his proceeds of the wars in France. It would have made a logical and impressive centre for Richard's authority in the region. Further grants of land were made to Richard on 20 November from the forfeited Beaufort properties. In addition to confirming the previous gifts of Alwerton and Tywarnaylle Tess, Richard received property at Wilmington in Kent and associated lands nearby at Hucking and Dolly.

Offices continued to be added to land gains as Richard was appointed Chief Steward, Approver and Surveyor in Wales and the earldom of March's lands.[44] It brought further income to the duke, who was undoubtedly keeping one eye on the approaching prospect of a degree of independence that would require appropriate funding, but the appointments and grants also demonstrate Edward's increasing willingness to rely on young Richard. He had, in the space of a month, become a force to be reckoned with in Wales, acquired significant and prestigious property focussed on the Welsh Marches and been given the position of Constable, the most senior national office currently available to the king to grant.

Trouble in England tended to precipitate unrest in Wales, and on 16 December Richard's new authority in the region was put into direct action. He was granted

> ...full power and authority to reduce and subdue the king's castles of Carmardyn and Cardycan in South Wales, which Morgan ap Thomas ap Griffith, 'gentilman', and Henry ap Thomas ap Griffith, 'gentilman', with other rebels have entered into and from which they raid the adjacent parts, and to put them under safe custody and governance and to promise pardon to such rebels within them as shall be willing to submit and take an oath of fealty.[45]

It has the ring of a test to it. Richard may well have been keen to show his brother what he was capable of and here Edward found the perfect arena in which to test his brother's mettle. For the duke, it was a chance to be relished. He could prove himself to his martial brother, a man he respected and doubtless loved, and he was to get his first real military command, a campaign of his own, to lead at the age of seventeen. The castles of Carmarthen and Cardigan shared a constable in Warwick, and the brothers Morgan and Thomas had snatched them. Their father, Gruffydd ap Nicholas was a notorious local thug, pressing his own interests by bullying his neighbours and always able to rely on a failure of the distant government either to notice or to care. Another of Gruffydd's sons was Rhys ap Thomas, who would rise to significant power in Wales and would have a part to play later in Richard's story too. For the moment, it is interesting to note that Richard was sent to act against Rhys's brothers. That Richard was meant to personally oversee the endeavour is demonstrated by a gift from Edward of £100 ''er he departe hens'.[46] Finally, Richard's moment had arrived.

6

A Willing Exile

Here before God I make a vow – that I shall never marry a man for
wealth alone, and I will never take a man who is my inferior by
birth. Only if he has proved himself to be the best
knight in all the world shall I marry him
Ipomadon, *a 12th-century Anglo-Norman Romance*

When a young nobleman was developing an idea of himself, his place
in the world and the image that he wished to project, his motto was
a powerful and useful tool. The word motto is derived from the Latin
muttum, meaning to mutter. Unlike a coat of arms that is granted
formally to a recipient, a motto can be changed at will and offers some
notion of what a nobleman was either thinking, or what he wished the
world to think of him. The earliest known motto attributable to Richard
appears on a page within a copy of the twelfth-century romantic tale of
Ipomadon, who would become the perfect knight and win himself a bride
desired by all. The precise date on which the note was written is uncertain
but is likely to have been before 1470. The motto that appears beneath
Richard's name, in his own handwriting, is *'Tant Le Desiree'* – 'I have
longed for it so much.'[1] It is interesting that this motto should appear
within a tale of courtly love and knightly achievement. Another undated
motto which appears in a copy of the New Testament owned by Richard
as Duke of Gloucester reads *'A vo me ly'* and is signed 'Gloucestr'[2]. This
translates as 'I am bound to you', and begins to adopt the chivalric notion
of loyalty. In 1469, the idea that Richard longed to prove himself as a
great knight seems very fitting.

As Richard moved toward Wales and his first military appointment
on his brother's behalf, he seems to have travelled through the Marches
around his family's old stronghold at Ludlow. Richard borrowed £40
from John Carpenter, Bishop of Worcester, between Michaelmas (the
end of September) 1469 and Michaelmas 1470.[3] The date and purpose

of the loan are not recorded, but it may have been a further response to Richard's chronic lack of cash and his desire to make a good impression as he set about recovering the castles of Carmarthen and Cardigan for his brother. The possibility that Richard travelled through Ludlow is given credence by an entry for a similar period in the records of St Laurence's Church in the town, which records: 'Item rec'd for a horss of my lord of Glouc' yeffe, iiijs xd'.[4] Richard had presented the parish church with a horse valued at 4s 10d, which is suggestive both of a lack of ready money and of a sense of attachment to Ludlow since he would not pass through the town without making some offering.

Immediately before the entry recording Richard's gift, but similarly undated, is a record of 'Item rec'd of the Erle of Pembroke, xs'.[5] The fifteen-year-old William Herbert, son of the loyal servant of Edward IV executed after the Battle of Edgecote Moor, also made a gift to the church of 10s. It seems credible that the new Earl of Pembroke was accompanying Richard on his expedition into Wales. It would be good experience in a land he had to become familiar with for the young Herbert earl and a chance to forge links with Richard as he was being set up as a senior figure in Wales and the Marches. This apparent connection to William Herbert throws up two tantalising possibilities.

Firstly, Richard may have encountered at least the name of Henry Tudor for the first time at this point. By now Henry was twelve, a few years younger than William, but had been a ward of William's father and the two must have spent time together at Raglan Castle. Did idle chatter on the road fall to the son of the dead Earl of Richmond and Lady Margaret Beaufort who was somewhat in limbo within a Yorkist household?

The second intriguing potential of this connection is an explanation of something that has so far defied resolution. William had six sisters, and it is possible that one of them may have been the mother of Richard's illegitimate son. Richard had two acknowledged illegitimate children. Their dates of birth and the identities of their mothers are nowhere recorded, but they are generally accepted to have been the result of a relationship, or relationships, Richard had before he was married. His illegitimate daughter Katherine cannot have been the result of a relationship with one of William's sisters because she would go on to become William's second wife. In fact, one of William's sisters was named Katherine. The ages of William's sisters are not adequately recorded, but it seems likely that all were too young to be candidates as the mother of John, Richard's illegitimate son, at least in 1469. John would later be referred to as 'John de Pountfreit Bastard',[6] suggesting a connection to Pontefract. Richard would later make a grant of an annuity of £20 to Alice Burgh on 1 March 1474 whilst at Pontefract, leading to conjecture that she was John's mother.

The grant was made for 'certain special causes and considerations'[7] that are not expanded upon, so there can be no certainty in the matter. In a similar vein, Katherine Haute has been suggested as the mother of Katherine because she received an annuity of £5 in 1477.[8] As with so many aspects of Richard's life, the relationships that produced his two acknowledged illegitimate children remain frustratingly opaque. It has been posited that he had several other illegitimate children too, but in the absence of evidence, and with two openly acknowledged bastards, this seems like little more than attempts to smear Richard's moral reputation. John and Katherine may have shared a mother, or perhaps not. They may have been from before Richard was married, or not, though the former seems more likely. Their mother, or mothers, remain a mystery to us, perhaps because Richard sought to protect them in anonymity. He openly acknowledged and provided for these children, though, as will become apparent.

There is no real indication as to whether Richard did undertake a military operation in Wales in the winter of 1469. No record of an assault on either castle remains, and it is possible that the occupations were ended before Richard arrived. Interestingly, the Welsh bard Lewys Glyn Cothi claimed that there was an encounter between Gloucester's men and a Welsh force led by four brothers of Thomas and Henry, the men who had seized the castles. Welsh bardic tradition is a rich vein of material fraught with problems of reliability, but also too easily dismissed as entirely fiction. Although no battle is described, and it is likely that the encounter, if it took place, resolved the matter of the castle occupations peacefully, it raises the possibility that Richard's first contact with Rhys ap Thomas, who was a brother of Thomas and Henry, was less than friendly and the result of Richard's mission to assault his brothers. If that were the case, it would not be the last time a grudge was stored up against Richard that would later return to haunt him. By 18 June 1470, Richard was in Carmarthen presiding over a rare sitting of the great sessions to deliver justice to the region.

A commission of oyer and terminer on 6 January 1470 placed Richard at the head of its delivery in both north and south Wales, accompanied by William Herbert; John, Lord Strange; the familiar John Sutton and Walter Devereux, Sir James Harrington and others.[9] Lord Strange would remain close to Richard, and it seems likely that a connection originated from this period. A few years older than Richard, Lord Strange died in 1479, but the previous year he had shown confidence in the favour he still enjoyed with Richard. On 6 October 1478, he would write to Sir William Stonor of his financial problems, promising to repay money owed, but adding 'I woll do nothinge withowte my lorde of Gloucester, and I trust in all thinge he woll defend me and my tenauntes.'[10] Sir James Harrington was to become a fast friend to the young duke too, leading to Richard's entanglement in a dispute with Thomas, Lord Stanley, in the very near future.

The link between the young William Herbert and Richard was strengthened further when, on 7 February, Richard was appointed 'chief justice of South Wales, the king's chamberlain in South Wales and steward of the king's commote of Cantremaure and all the king's lordships, manors and commotes in the counties of Kardican and Kermerdyn in South Wales during the minority of William Herbert'.[11] Richard was effectively to hold authority in South Wales until the new Earl of Pembroke came of age, and there must have been some expectation both that Richard would protect William's interests and that he might act as a mentor for the authority William would soon inherit. It was a heavy responsibility for Richard, though he could rely on men like William's uncle and his own close associate Walter Devereux for practical assistance. It is clear that Edward was relying more and more heavily on his youngest brother in increasingly large parts of the country. It is equally clear that Richard was neither disappointing his king in the execution of these wide-ranging responsibilities nor baulking at a mounting workload.

Although Richard would be back in South Wales in June, the apparent end of immediate problems in the region that may have led to the grants he received in February afforded Richard time to visit his new acquisitions in the north-west from the Duchy of Lancaster. The trip may have been at the suggestion of Sir James Harrington, who had joined Richard on the commissions of oyer and terminer in January. The journey may also have been at Edward's request. Law and order were again beginning to disintegrate. Richard was not at the Battle of Losecoat Field on 12 March 1470, but with the defeat of that force under Lord Welles' son that began with Lord Welles' beheading on the battlefield, Edward exposed the plots set in motion by George and Warwick. This time, they meant to unseat him and place George on the throne in his place.[12]

It seems likely that Richard travelled back to the Marches, probably via Ludlow, and then up through the Ribble Valley to survey his new properties. If so, his route took in Halton in Cheshire before crossing into Lancashire to see Runcorn, Moore, Whitley and Congleton and Widnes.[13] In Halton and Widnes, Richard had replaced Thomas, Lord Stanley, as steward. He had also been given Stanley's office as master forester of Amounderness, where Sir James Harrington was steward. Stanley's toes had been trodden on from afar, but now Richard was coming to his front door to stamp on them in person. By 26 March, Richard was at the Harrington family's seat of Hornby Castle. In 1470, the castle had been the subject of a dispute for years. The reasons that Richard may have taken the action that he did are worthy of consideration. James's father Sir Thomas Harrington had been a Neville retainer and had fought for the Earl of Salisbury at Blore Heath in

1459, as had James. Father and son had been captured and imprisoned at Chester Castle before being released in mid-1460 when the Yorkist faction regained control of England.

Sir Thomas and his oldest son Sir John had marched north in December 1460 with Salisbury and Richard's father, York. Both men had taken part in the Battle of Wakefield on 30 December, when York had been killed. Although the precise details were disputed and formed part of James's case, it was reported that Sir Thomas died during the battle and Sir John shortly afterwards from wounds he had received. The timeline was important because if Sir Thomas died first, then however briefly, Sir John had inherited from his father. On John's death, his two daughters Anne and Elizabeth became co-heirs to the Harrington inheritance. James had tried to argue that the deaths occurred the other way around so that he inherited from his father rather than John, but it is likely this was clutching at straws in the vagaries of war reporting. Anne's custody and marriage rights were granted to another family by Edward, meaning that her husband would acquire the entire Harrington wealth. James and his brother Robert snatched their nieces and barricaded themselves in at Hornby Castle. In 1468, the brothers had been called before the Court of Chancery. Lord Stanley immediately applied for custody of both girls and Edward granted it to him. Anne and Elizabeth were swiftly married to Stanley husbands, Anne to Thomas's son Edward, and Stanley laid claim to Hornby, an excellent addition to his swelling portfolio. The Harrington brothers continued to refuse to vacate the castle. This story of seeming unfairness may have reached Richard when Sir James served with him in Wales, and it seems to have touched him.

In Norfolk, the Paston family were finding themselves besieged at Caister Castle by the Duke of Norfolk, who claimed the property for himself despite Sir John Fastolf having left it to the Pastons.[14] Stanley similarly decided to use the breakdown in law and order to resolve a matter in which the courts were being slow to offer satisfaction. He had a huge cannon named Mile Ende brought up from Bristol with the intention of blasting the Harrington brothers out of Hornby, just as Norfolk had bombarded Caister. No shot was fired at Hornby Castle though, and the explanation appears in a grant dated 26 March 1470. The gift itself is unremarkable. Richard provided Reginald Vaghan with an annuity of four marks from the income of the lordship of Chirk during the duke's pleasure. Reginald had obviously offered some valuable service to Richard, perhaps during the latter's recent time in Wales, that warranted recognition. What is striking about the document is that it is signed by Richard '*Datum sub signato nostro, apud castrum de Hornby*' – 'Given under our signet, at the castle of Hornby', dated 26 March.

Richard, aged seventeen, had placed himself in the stunning Hornby Castle, overlooking the valley of the River Lune, all but daring Stanley to fire a cannon at the king's brother. Although he may have been tempted, particularly in the rapidly deteriorating situation that threatened Edward, Stanley was never one for such rash commitment to a course of action. Stanley had avoided every major battle he could during the opening of the troubles, though his brother William had proved a far more devoted Yorkist and it seems likely that this was at least with Thomas's blessing, if not at his instruction. Conversely, the Harringtons had openly thrown in their lot with Salisbury in support of York's cause and never faltered. Sir James could boast that his grandfather had been Henry V's standard-bearer at Agincourt, where Richard's own great-uncle Edward, 2nd Duke of York, had died. They had both lost a father and a brother at Wakefield, and it had been Sir James who had delivered the fugitive Henry VI to Edward in London. There is little doubt that Richard was in the region to put Stanley's nose out, but he chose to do so by taking the side of the Harrington family. He backed men who had been utterly loyal to the House of York from the outset of troubles in England, against Thomas Stanley, who throughout had vacillated and avoided committing himself. Perhaps Richard thought his brother had acted unfairly, however legally, by failing to protect a family who had served them so well. Stanley's military might in the region doubtless influenced the pragmatic Edward, but Richard was young and still able to cling to chivalric ideals of loyalty and protection.

There is an apocryphal story in Stanley family legend, which is not supported in the contemporary record, though it can be by some circumstantial evidence. In the mid-sixteenth century, Thomas Stanley, Bishop of Sodor and Man, penned *The Stanley Poem*[15] that reports an armed encounter between Richard and Stanley which, although undated, would appear to refer to this period. The legend claims that Richard assembled a force to attack Stanley's manor at Lathom and that Stanley engaged with the duke at the Battle of Ribble Bridge to repel him. The poem claims that Stanley won the day and that Richard's standard was embarrassingly captured and put on display at a church in Wigan. If true, this episode may well have been Richard's first military action, and it ended in failure. Such an encounter may not sound like Stanley's style, but if he was backed into a corner and forced to take the field to protect his own property, it becomes more likely. Even if the incident itself is a later fabrication, it merely gives colour to what was demonstrably a feud, deliberately created by Edward, and may have been meant as a dramatic interpretation of rivalry between Richard and Stanley that was born at this time. Stanley can only have resented the insertion of Edward's young brother into lands and offices he had long considered his own by right. That very attitude was no doubt the cause of Edward's positioning of his brother.

Battle or no battle, the ill feeling was public and well attested to. On 16 March, the same day as Richard signed his warrant at Hornby Castle, Edward ordered proclamation to be made that he 'straightly commandeth that no man of whatsoever degree under colour of any wrong doing unto him for any matter of variance late fallen between his brother, the duke of Gloucester, and the lord Stanley, distress, rob or despoil any of his subjects.'[16] Was Edward pre-empting the trouble he planned his brother to cause and ensuring that no one misinterpreted the situation and rallied to Stanley's defence? Was he trying merely to contain a necessary resort to intimidation of a man who was getting too big for his boots, and a man who was Warwick's brother-in-law too? The reason for a possible escalation to armed confrontation is plain. A letter dated 27 March 1470 to John Paston relates details of the king's defeat of the rebels in Lincolnshire under Lord Welles' son. The writer also reports that 'the Duk of Clarence and the Erle of Warwik harde that the King was comyng to them warde, in contynent they departed and wente to Machestre in Lancashire, hopying to have hadde helpe and socour of the Lord Stanley butt in conclucion ther they hadde litill favor.'[17] Richard may have been sent word that George and Warwick were making for Stanley's territory for help and a raising of the stakes, possibly even to armed confrontation, may have been what deprived the rebel lords of a safe haven and reinforcements in Lancashire. Thomas Stanley would purchase a pardon from the king on 14 June covering all offences committed by him before 11 May.[18] That would include any plan to assist George and Warwick but might also cover an armed action or at least less than cordial relations between himself and the king's other brother, Richard.

On 28 March, Edward ordered the treason of George and Warwick to be proclaimed across the country. The king complained that despite his previous clemency to them, they had betrayed him again by plotting to put George on the throne, intending 'the king's destruction and the subversion of the realm'. Every person in the country was charged with capturing the two noble rebels and delivering them to Edward, for which a reward of land worth £100 a year or £1,000 in cash was offered.[19] Edward was at Nottingham, and with Richard blocking any help from the north-west, George and Warwick made for the earl's flagship *The Trinity* only to be met by a force under Anthony Woodville, now Earl Rivers and keen to avenge his father's and brother's executions. George and Warwick managed to slip onto a ship and made for Calais. Lord Wenlock, Warwick's deputy there, was sent orders to refuse the earl entry and despite their long association, he obeyed the king, firing cannon from the walls at their ship to keep them from approaching. Around 17

April, whilst still at sea, George's heavily pregnant wife Isabel gave birth to a daughter, who did not survive. Anne died almost immediately, and her father and grandfather were forced to land in French territory in their grief and desperation. Isabel and George had lost their first child; Warwick had seen his first grandchild perish.[20] Yet more bitter grudges thrived where little Anne had been unable to, and Warwick would never again be reconciled with the king he had helped to make.

Edward set about establishing commissions of array to assemble an army against the threat of revolt. On 26 March at York, he issued nine commissions 'for the defence against George, duke of Clarence, and Richard, earl of Warwick, rebels'. Richard headed efforts to raise men in Gloucestershire, aided by Thomas, Viscount Lisle, William, Lord Berkeley, and others. He was also appointed to lead the array in Herefordshire, where Walter Devereux was again to assist him. A further commission was given to Edmund Grey, Earl of Kent, on 15 April for Kent and on 17 April, the most likely day that George and Isabel were suffering the loss of their baby at sea, Richard was handed two more commissions of array in Devon and Cornwall.[21] Richard's troubleshooting now took him into these counties, where he met Edward at Wells on 11 April 1470 and moved to Exeter with the king by 14 April. This marked a return to the West Country authority Richard had been receiving piecemeal for years and the fact that he was being stretched so thin is evidence both of his ability and the narrow support on which Edward was able to rely. The Woodville family had remained unpopular in the country and lacked a landed patrimony from which to support the king, leaving Edward heavily reliant on his last remaining loyal brother.

It was perhaps in recognition of this increased workload and his lack of experience that Richard was replaced as Constable on 14 March by John Tiptoft, Earl of Worcester.[22] In the same month, Edward took the dangerous but predictable step of restoring Henry Percy to the Earldom of Northumberland. Doing so meant depriving John Neville of the title. In compensation, John was created Marquis Montagu, theoretically a promotion and his son George was made Duke of Bedford and promised a marriage to one of Edward's daughters. John Neville was a problematic figure for Edward to deal with. He had not been disloyal; in fact, he had given a decade of dependable service. Nevertheless, his hesitation the previous year when Warwick had inspired the northern uprising along with his name was probably enough to ensure that his grasp on the Percy earldom was untenable. Leaving John in possession kept a Neville in a position of immense authority in the north. Removing him would necessarily alienate a man who had done no wrong. The gift of a marquisate, sitting between an earldom and dukedom in terms of prestige and seniority, was meant to placate John, but depriving him of the rich

Northumberland lands and giving him a title with no associated lands left him unable to support himself. Of course, that may well have been the point. John was all but pushed into Warwick's arms. His son George would later have his dukedom revoked and would never marry one of Edward's daughters.[23]

When commissions of array were issued on 2 June 1470, Richard was the most senior figure appointed in Gloucestershire, Herefordshire and Somerset. Although Walter Devereux would assist him in Herefordshire, the other two appointments were alongside John Tiptoft. Richard may not have minded being replaced as Constable at this stage. He already had wide-ranging responsibilities and was working hard for his brother. In a crisis, Tiptoft was the more experienced option, having held the post between 1461 and 1467. He may have been better placed to leverage the powers of the office and he was certainly to prove ruthless in the execution of his duties. In May, Warkworth notes that 'Kynge Edwarde came to Southamptone, and commawndede the Erle of Worcetere to sitt and juge suche men as were taken in the schyppes' from Warwick's force as they tried to leave England. Twenty 'gentylmen and yomenne' were hanged, drawn and quartered after trial in the Constable's Court of Chivalry, essentially a military kangaroo court to try those suspected of treason. Tiptoft earned the lasting condemnation of his peers and of history for failing to leave the matter there. After their horrific deaths, the men were 'hanged uppe by the leggys, and a stake made scharpe at bothe endes, whereof one ende was putt in att bottokys, and the other end ether heddes were putt uppe one'. Tiptoft had the corpses impaled on wooden spikes and the heads set atop them, which Warkworth considered 'contrarye to the lawe of the londe' and the reason Tiptoft became 'behatede emonge the peple.'[24] It is worth considering the fact the Edward was there and did nothing to prevent this atrocity, which was doubtless meant to send a message to those considering further revolt. This was why Tiptoft was back in the office in place of Richard. This was what Edward expected from his Constable.

Richard was appointed to lead another commission of oyer and terminer on 11 July in the county and city of Lincoln, an entirely new sphere for him.[25] It is possible he did not personally act on this commission and was now being used by Edward as a rubber stamp of royal authority. The most striking thing about this commission is that it named both Henry Percy and John Neville to act together, which was either a signal to John that he was not out of favour or an attempt by Edward to push even more of his buttons. Richard's usefulness to his brother reached a peak in August when he was appointed to another commission of oyer and terminer, this time in York.[26] His new incursion into Neville territory was made more thorough when, on the same day, 26 August, Richard was appointed Warden of the Western March toward Scotland.[27] The office had previously been held by Warwick, and this is the first insertion of Richard directly into the earl's northern lands as his replacement. The position held responsibility for border security focussed around Carlisle and gave Richard lands, titles and offices that stretched from Cornwall, through the West Country, took in the whole of Wales and the Welsh Marches, encroached into Cheshire and ran through Lancashire all the way up to Carlisle in Cumbria. The young duke must have proven himself energetic and eminently capable during the crises of 1469 and 1470 for his brother to find himself reliant on Richard over such a swathe of the country.

Edward was in York for the second half of August when these appointments were made and Warwick, accompanied by George, took the opportunity to cross the Channel and land on the south coast at Plymouth, moving quickly north and gathering men to move against the king, who marched south against the threat. The earl had not been idle in France and had utilised the relationship he had enjoyed with Louis XI to conclude a new plan, sponsored by the French king. Louis had managed to bring together two implacable enemies by inviting Margaret of Anjou to join him and Warwick at court. The French king convinced both parties that the other represented their only hope of a return to power and although Margaret reportedly forced Warwick to remain on bended knee for more than fifteen minutes, she eventually agreed to a plan that would see her husband restored to the throne and her son married to Warwick's daughter Anne. By 7 August, Warwick was at sea with George without waiting for the marriage to be made official.[28] John Neville, Marquis Montagu, was finally disaffected enough to abandon Edward and raise Neville retainers in the north to march south. Warkworth reports that when John came within a mile of Lynn, he told his men, who had been raised using a commission of array from Edward, that they were in fact there to assault the king. He complained that he had been given 'a pyes nest to mayntene his astate withe', meaning a magpie's nest, empty and insufficient to support himself. One of John's 6,000 men slipped away and warned Edward to avoid a battle because 'he was not stronge enoghe to gyff batayle' to John, let alone Warwick and Clarence approaching from the south.[29] Taking the spy's advice, Edward found a ship at Lynn around Michaelmas according to Crowland,[30] but the date is usually taken as 2 October, Richard's eighteenth birthday.

For a long time, it was assumed that Richard was with Edward and took ship with his brother and other loyal lords on his birthday to sail into exile. Indeed, this writer has previously retold that story, which is almost certainly inaccurate. A record within the King's Lynn Hall Book left by the town clerk lists all of the nobles who arrived into the town and left with the king by sea, including Anthony Woodville and William,

Lord Hastings. Richard is not listed, and it seems impossible that the most senior noble present, the king's brother, should have been omitted from such a record.[31] The assumption is not unreasonable, though. Philip de Commines, a Burgundian commentator who would later defect to the French court, states that Richard arrived with Edward.[32] Commines was an eyewitness to some of the events on the Continent and met Edward IV, but he never travelled to England, so had to rely on what he could gather from those coming to Burgundy. At the outset of his explanation of these events, he also warns his readers that he does not plan to bore them with dates and such nonsense, so he tends to conflate the things he probably didn't remember so well.

According to Commines' embellished story, having left England 'without any clothes but what they were to have fought in, no money in their pockets, and not one of them knew whither they were going', Edward made for Holland, territory under the control of his brother-in-law Charles, Duke of Burgundy. Commines explains that the king's little fleet was chased by Easterlings, ships of the Hanse League in the Channel. With these, to Edward at least, pirates in pursuit, Edward missed his planned destination and tried to put ashore near to the small town of Alquemare in Friesland. He had arrived at low tide, though, and found himself unable to get his ships into the harbour. As the Easterling fleet approached, Edward was forced to run his ships aground near to the town.[33] Charles' governor in Holland, Louis de Gruuthuse, happened to be nearby and hurried to greet the English king. Sending notice to the Easterlings to keep back, he boarded Edward's ship 'and invited him on shore; whereupon the king landed, with his brother the Duke of Gloucester.'[34] Having no money with which to pay for his crossing, Edward gave the ship's captain a fine, fur-lined cloak and a promise to make good on the debt as soon as he was able. Commines commented that 'so poor a company was never seen before' and Louis de Gruuthuse made gifts to them all of clothes and paid all of their expenses until they left him to visit Charles.[35]

There is reason to doubt much of Commines' account, not least because of his own admission of a laxity in detail. Most other sources agree that Edward in fact arrived at Texel and no other source makes mention of a pursuing Hanse fleet, though Anthony Woodville's ship is noted as arriving at Wielingen,[36] further south than Texel, almost at The Hague, which may have been the planned objective. Local sources also record that Louis de Gruuthuse was actually in The Hague when Edward landed on 3 October. News reached the city on 5 October, and at that point, Louis set out north to help Edward.[37] Whatever the specific geography, in 1472 Edward would repay Louis' kindness in a time of need by making him hereditary Earl of Winchester, an unusual honour for a foreigner during this period, but doubtless a sign of the care Edward received.

When news of the landing reached Gruuthuse in The Hague on 5 October, he despatched Jan van Assendelft, the Treasurer of North Holland, to provide the English king with immediate assistance.[38] Three days later, on 8 October, a messenger was sent to Duke Charles at Hesdin to make him aware of the situation.[39] Edward and those with him began the journey south from Texel as Gruuthuse moved north to meet them at Alkmaar, where the fugitive king was finally greeted with some pomp and provided with suitable clothing.[40] The group then appear to have travelled from Alkmaar to de Blinken monastery at Heiloo, where they were able to venerate the relics of the English saint Willebrord. On the following day, they visited Egmond Benedictine Abbey, where the remains of another English saint, Adelbert, were housed. From here, Edward moved on to Leyden, with the city writing to Noordwijk that they 'await my lord the governor and to hear from him at what time the king of England would be at Leyden.'[41] The authorities were perhaps trying to gauge how long they had to make suitable preparations for the unexpected visitation of such dignitaries. It must have been no more than a flying visit because on the same day that letter was hurried off, 11 October, Edward finally arrived at The Hague too.

If Richard did not travel with his brother, then where was he? L. Viser-Fuchs has suggested that Richard was aboard the same ship as Anthony Woodville so as to avoid placing both York men together, lest some disaster befall one ship on the crossing.[42] This does not explain the gap in the recording of those leaving Lynn, from which a royal duke would have been a glaring omission. The first definite mention of him beyond Commines comes from a record at Veere, much further south than Edward's landing point in Friesland and south of The Hague where Edward had gone with Louis de Gruuthuse, so it was not really on a route Richard might have taken with his brother. The record refers to 'Item paid by order of my Lord of Boucham the bailiff of Veere which he had loaned when my lord of Gloucester travelled in Holland 3 pounds, 2 shillings, 3 pennies.'[43] The record appears for the second week in November 1470, and the implication must be that the bailiff had made the loan before the date of repayment.

There are several possible scenarios to explain Richard's absence from the official contemporary sources at this point. In England, John Tiptoft, Earl of Worcester, Edward's appointment to replace Richard as Constable when trouble erupted, was facing mob justice. Although Warwick was generally reasonably tolerant of those close to Edward's government who remained behind, he could not, or would not, save Tiptoft. The earl, who so recently oversaw the brutal impaling of men who had tried to support Warwick's insurgency, was apprehended in the Forest of Weybridge. This royal forest was almost 50 miles south-west of Kings Lynn, where Tiptoft had been with the king. Why such a controversial figure decided not to flee with the king is unclear, but in travelling south-west, he may have been making for London, perhaps to try and whisk the heavily pregnant queen out of the city to safety. He could alternatively have been aiming further west, towards his earldom and the Welsh Marches to lay down preparations for Edward's return. As a former Constable, probably hoping to recover the office, Richard may have undertaken a similar course, not unlike a captain refusing to abandon his sinking ship. If he felt some obligation to stay behind, either to help the queen or to begin raising and then maintaining resistance in the west, his previous grants and visits to the Marches and Wales may have made him the perfect representative of his brother to do so.

Tiptoft's fate would have been a stark warning of the dangers of such a course. The earl was taken to the Tower, where he was imprisoned on 7 October. On 15 October, he was tried for treason by the Earl of Oxford, made Constable for the purpose. Tiptoft had overseen, as Constable in 1462, the executions of Oxford's father and older brother, so can hardly have expected any leniency. Sentenced to die, on 17 October he was led to Temple Bar, from where the Sheriffs of London would take him to Tower Hill, but a great throng that had gathered to see Tiptoft beheaded prevented them from getting to their destination. After being forced to spend the night in Fleet Prison, he was finally taken to his execution the following morning, reportedly asking to be executed with three strokes of the axe in honour of the Holy Trinity.[44]

Richard may have been more successful, reaching the friends he had made in Herbert territories and up and down the Marches to bring word that Edward would return and that they should be ready. As we have seen, he had connections providing a channel of safe routes from Cumbria to Cornwall, in a strip that ran through the Yorkist heartlands around Ludlow and all down the Marches as well as extending into Wales. He was still Admiral of England, too, and held Corfe Castle on the south coast, which would have offered a perfect, secure departure point once his mission was completed and which might explain his arrival at Veere, in need of money, weeks after his brother had landed at Texel. Although Warwick was a dominant force in the Channel, he was preoccupied trying to secure London, and the government and Richard could conceivably have slipped past his patrols in the Channel to reach Holland. If Richard took this course of action, it was brave to the point of recklessness. Tiptoft, an experienced, older man, tried something similar and failed. Richard might have relied on a cordial relationship with both George and Warwick to keep his head if caught, but it was questionable how merciful a Lancastrian government might let them be to the Yorkist king's other brother. He cannot have ventured too far north in his ribbon of lands and offices for fear of Stanley treachery, but a dart west from

Lynn into the Marches and Wales to take messages of reassurance, and then south to Corfe Castle and across the sea is not impossible.

Frustratingly, the evidence is inconclusive so it remains possible that Richard did travel with his brother and was somehow overlooked in the notes made at Lynn of the dignitaries who accompanied the king. If Edward felt a little protective of his youngest brother, who, given George's treachery and Edward's lack of a son, might have represented the new Yorkist heir to the throne, it would be understandable. It would also explain keeping his whereabouts a secret, either keeping him close aboard Edward's ship, as Commines supposed, or sending him with Anthony Woodville to prevent the loss of both of them. Allowing Richard to charge off west as Edward departed would have been a signal that the king placed the utmost trust in Richard. He had, after all, grown up with George and been raised for a time under Warwick's wing. The earl was their cousin and also the kind of famous adventurer who could turn the head of a teenager confused about where his loyalties might lie. If Richard was allowed to undertake such a dangerous task for Edward, it showed courage on his part and utter faith on the king's. If he left with Edward on his 18th birthday, it also demonstrates that his loyalty was not in question and his devotion to Edward already unwaveringly ingrained within him.

There is another explanation for Richard's appearance in Veere that could allow him to have arrived in Duke Charles' territories with his brother, or which might have been coincidental to his later arrival at the port. Warwick's reputation as a sailor, or more accurately as a successful pirate, caused the Burgundian authorities to become immediately fearful of his new alliance with France, which involved a promise to help Louis XI wage war on Burgundy until it was utterly destroyed, for which Warwick would receive lordships in the region. So great was the fear of attack from the sea, led by Warwick, that the authorities at Veere set about fortifying their harbour by the construction of 'de Warwijkse poort' – Warwick's Gate.[45] Indeed, a road called Warwijcksestraat – Warwick Street – can still be found in Veere today, leading to the former site of Warwick's Gate on the island of Walcheren. The frantic preparations might serve to explain Richard's visit to Veere in late October or early November and, as we have seen, he was perennially short of cash during this period and perhaps borrowed some whilst he was away from his brother and from Gruuthuse's hospitality.

Richard's true movements and activities during this period remain uncertain. Edward and his band would stay with Gruuthuse, at their host's expense, until Christmas 1470. Duke Charles did forward 500 ecus a month toward their maintenance,[46] but this was, for the moment, the limit of his willingness to become entangled with Edward's problems. Burgundy was in an awkward situation. The brother-in-law relationship between Edward and Duke Charles has long been assumed to mean that Burgundy's favour would rest clearly with the Yorkist cause. In fact, just a few months before Edward's expulsion, Charles had granted Edward entry into the prestigious Order of the Golden Fleece. In recognition of this honour, Edward had quickly given his brother-in-law the highest honour he could bestow with a seat in St George's Chapel as a member of the Order of the Garter. Such bonds of chivalric brotherhood probably meant more to the two men than ties of marriage in a time of need, but even this was not enough to bring Charles to action on Edward's behalf. Duke Charles was unashamedly proud of his own Lancastrian heritage. Charles' mother, Isabella of Portugal, was a granddaughter of John of Gaunt through the marriage of Gaunt's daughter Philippa of Lancaster to King John I of Portugal. Charles was, therefore, a great-grandson of John of Gaunt and great-great-grandson of King Edward III. He had given refuge to arch-Lancastrian exiles Edmund Beaufort, Duke of Somerset, and Henry Holland, Duke of Exeter. They despised Warwick and were suspicious of the control he now had in England but did want the restoration of Henry VI. Doubtless, they urged Charles to look for a third way, an appealing prospect for a duke threatened by Warwick's aggressive alliance with France but with strong Lancastrian sympathies. Nevertheless, the Yorkist government had seen strong trade links developed between Burgundy and England that would necessarily be threatened by Warwick's current pre-eminence. The only antidote was either a more complete Lancastrian revival, such as that advocated by Somerset and Exeter, or Edward's restoration, no doubt equally advocated from The Hague.

On the surface, Charles stood to win either way, as long as Warwick lost, but things are rarely that clear. The duke seems to have preferred a Lancastrian alliance if one were possible and, much as he had done with George and Richard in 1461, he kept the Yorkist exiles at arm's length, hedging his bets as best he could. He could then afford to wait a while and see which side would offer him the best outcome against Warwick and France. He didn't have long to wait. In line with his agreement with Warwick, Louis XI declared all of Duke Charles' lands and titles forfeit on 3 December,[47] effectively opening hostilities with which Warwick was obliged to at least try to join in. Raiding parties began to harass the duke's lands from Calais while St Quentin and then Amiens, Somme towns currently in Burgundy's possession, declared for Louis XI. There can have been no firm plan of action coming from the Lancastrian lords at Charles's court, and Warwick's grip on England at least appeared solid. By 31 December 1470, Duke Charles had made up his mind. He ordered £20,000 to be provided to Edward 'for his and his brother Gloucester's expenses … and for their departure from my lord the duke's lands to return to England.'[48] It was an ideal solution for Charles. If Edward invaded, he would be out of Charles's lands and would be a distraction to Warwick. If Edward were victorious, Burgundy would resume a cordial relationship with Yorkist England. If Edward failed, Charles had a second roll of the dice available in Somerset and Exeter, who might be able to pounce on a weakened and distracted Warwick to effect a more complete Lancastrian revival. Either way, the fracas in England would buy Charles time to deal with France before it could fall upon him with English assistance.

Only on 2 January 1471 did Edward finally meet his brother-in-law face to face. Immediately after Christmas, Edward and Richard travelled to Gruuthuse's Oostcamp Castle, near Bruges. Here, they waited until Duke Charles arrived at Aires, where they finally discussed the forthcoming venture. As preparations got underway, Richard found time to travel to Lille between 12 and 14 February to visit his sister Margaret, Charles' wife.[49] As the two had grown up together, it was perhaps a source of comfort for the eighteen-year-old duke to spend a few days in the familiar company of his sister. He would soon face the dangers of returning to England to fight old friends, and the brother they had grown up together with, in an attempt to restore their family's fortunes. Richard could perhaps have reflected on his brother's reaction, inadequate and far too slow as it had been, to the threat in England. The fickle international politics of other rulers now guided their destiny, and their headlong dash back across the Channel might yet end in disaster and death for both himself and Edward. Margaret's own position was likely to become precarious in that event, whoever remained in power in England. Amid any thoughts of the disastrous collapse of Yorkist rule, the effect on the majesty of the crown of England and his opinion of his apparently indestructible big brother, who had abandoned him once before, Richard had these personal fears to deal with. His life, his brother's life and their sister's future all depended on the outcome of this dangerous enterprise.

On 19 February, Richard was back with Edward as they left Bruges for Arnemuiden, the harbour at Middelburg where ships supplied by Duke Charles or hastily secured with scant funds by the English were gathered. In a typical display of personal affability and comprehension of his own appeal, Edward decided to walk from Bruges to Damme before boarding a boat the rest of the way to show himself to the people.[50] That Edward displayed his appreciation by offering the opportunity to see him close up says a good deal about the man, but it also demonstrated the firm grasp that he had on the idea of personal majesty. He looked like a king, in stark contrast to Henry VI, and he was not afraid to show himself off. That Edward was a person immediately liked by anyone who met him is well attested to, but this mighty warrior king had allowed the crown to slip through his fingers, turning tail and running from his younger brother and one of his nobles.

Commentators, and so one might reasonably assume Richard too, seemed well aware of the main reasons for Edward's fall, and as he boarded ship at Middelburg, Richard could further reflect on them. Commines complained that Edward 'had indulged himself in ease and pleasures for twelve or thirteen years together, and enjoyed a larger share of them than any prince in his time. His thoughts were wholly employed upon the ladies (and far more than was reasonable), hunting, and adorning his person.' On Edward's physical appearance, Commines commented that 'his person was as well turned for love-intrigues as any man I ever saw in my life: for he was young, and the most handsome man of his time.' Commines qualified this by adding that he meant the physical plaudits to apply 'when he was in this adversity for afterwards he grew very corpulent.'[51] Although Commines reliability is open to question, he was in Calais for some of the time Edward was in exile, watching developments there, and seems to have met Edward at Charles' court, so in this, he can perhaps be trusted.

Support for this view can be found in the testimony of *Warkworth's Chronicle* too. Probably written by John Warkworth, it provides a robust and important account of events in England. Although it displays a Lancastrian bias, it nevertheless provides a sensible balance in its view of politics. Warkworth informs his reader that complaints against Henry VI had been justified. He added, though, that 'the common people said if they could have another king, he would regain all his lost possessions, and amend every corruption in the state, and bring the realm of England into prosperity and peace; nevertheless, when King Edward reigned, the people expected all the aforesaid prosperity and peace, but it came not; but one battle after another, and much trouble and loss among the common people.'[52] It was clear that the overwhelming sense was that Edward had squandered his gifts. He had been provided with a right to the crown by his father. He had the common touch in a way lacking in living memory in England. He had the physique of a warrior to go with all of these other attributes, yet after almost a decade he had been expelled from his own country. Warkworth believed the reason was clear: the Yorkist manifesto for change, supported by the common people, had not been delivered. Edward had squandered the mandate won in blood at Towton. His failure was a failure of the House of York. It made a mockery of their father's decade-long struggle for change, and it made the thousands of deaths at Towton and on other fields dotted around England seem meaningless. Sacrifices had been made for the sake of improvements, but many people could see none.

Richard could reflect on all of this as the ships sat in the harbour for nine days, waiting for the wind to change. They had embarked on 2 March and remained onboard so that they could seize the moment when the wind shifted.

The same poor conditions were keeping Queen Margaret of Anjou and her son Edward of Westminster, the Lancastrian Prince of Wales, in France too. She seems to have been reluctant to return, expecting Warwick personally to collect her when he could hardly be reasonably expected to turn his back on England for a moment – unless the plan had been to lure him out and cut him loose all along. The absence of Margaret and her son from England made Lancastrian loyalists edgy when the cause would have been better served by their confidence. Edward had failed to act quickly enough in October 1470. He wasn't going to make the same mistake. As the fleet of Englishmen, Flemish gunners and German and Danish mercenaries finally left port on 11 March 1471, Richard could reasonably have feared the outcome of the invasion, and even if they won, he might have wondered whether Edward could be relied upon not to make the same mistakes again. First, though, they had a country to win back.

7

The Trials of Battle

No great dependence is to be placed on the eagerness of young soldiers
for action, for fighting has something agreeable in the idea
to those who are strangers to it.

Vegetius, *De Re Militari*

'Here after folowethe the manner how the moaste noble and right victorious prince Edwarde, by the grace of God, Kinge of England and of Fraunce, and Lord of Irland, in the yere of grace 1471, in the monethe of Marche, departed out of Zeland; toke the sea; aryved in England; and by his force and valliannes, of newe redewced and reconqueryd the sayde realme'. This is the opening statement of a source known as the *Historie of the Arrivall of Edward IV*, usually referred to as *The Arrivall*. The writer identifies himself as 'a servaunt of the Kyngs, that presently saw in effect a great parte of his exploytes, and the resydewe knewe by true relation of them that were present at every tyme.'[1] *The Arrivall* claims to be an eyewitness account of Edward's campaign to retake his throne, with that which the writer did not personally see given as testimony from those he knew to have been witness to each event. It is overtly partisan, favouring Edward in every aspect against Henry VI and particularly Warwick, who is described as Edward's 'traytor and rebell', but it provides important information about the progress made on the campaign and does identify where Edward faced problems and resistance. Taking its inherent bias into account, it remains a hugely valuable and unrivalled source for this episode.

Edward and his ships left port on 11 March, and their plan was to land at Cromer in Norfolk.[2] There was little hope in many quarters for Edward and his small band. The Milanese ambassador in France commented to his duke: 'It is a difficult matter to go out by the door and then want to enter by the windows. They think he will leave his skin there.'[3] The region, not far from Edward's departure point, should have offered plenty of support from the Dukes of Norfolk and Suffolk. As it turned out, Warwick had taken several Yorkist lords into custody in London, including John Mowbray, Duke of Norfolk. John de la Pole, Duke of Suffolk, despite being Edward's brother-in-law was remarkable for keeping out of partisan episodes such as this. Edward had perhaps underestimated his opponent and the magnitude of the task before him. Warwick had sent men into Norfolk to protect against just such a landing. When Edward sent Sir Robert Chamberlain, Sir Gilbert Debenham and others ashore to find out the state of their support amongst the local gentry, they were rudely chased back out to sea. *The Arrivall* records that the men returned to report that 'thos parties wer right sore beset by th'Erle of Warwyke, and his adherents, and, in especiall, by th'Erle of Oxenforde, in such wyse that, of lyklyhood, it might not be for his wele to lande in the contrye; and a great cawse was, for the Duke of Norfolke was had owt of the contrye.'[4]

This account is corroborated by a letter from Oxford to his brother Thomas dated 14 March, two days after Edward's attempted landing. Oxford praises his brother's resistance to Edward and the 'faithful guiding and disposition of the Country to my great Comfort and Pleasure.' He goes on to reassure Thomas that he has been raising men in Essex, Suffolk and Cambridgeshire and intends to bring his force to Bury St Edmunds 'to the assistance of you and the Country, in case Edward with his Company had arrived there.' The earl's plan was still to go to Thomas in case Edward tried again, but also because if their fleet moved north, his men could shadow Edward along the coast and be prepared for their landing.[5] John de Vere, Earl of Oxford, appears to have been one of the few committed Lancastrians happy and willing to work with Warwick. Whilst others remained cautious and kept some distance from Warwick and George, doubtless suspicious of them, Oxford's real gripe was with Edward personally, probably a direct result of the execution of his father and brother and for which he had taken some measure of revenge against John Tiptoft. Had more Lancastrian lords been willing to find common cause with Warwick against Edward, events may have fallen out very differently.

As Edward's little fleet pushed north along the coast, brutal storms hit on Tuesday 13 and Wednesday 14 March and the days were spent being thrown about by wind and waves. The ships were scattered and forced to try to land. Edward's ship, all alone, finally struck solid ground at the now lost port of Ravenspur, the very spot on which Henry Bolingbroke had landed in 1399 when he took the throne from Richard II and began Lancastrian rule.[6] There can hardly have been deliberate symbolism in the choice of spot since the storm had cast them ashore there. It may have seemed like providence. Edward disembarked with his close friend

William, Lord Hasting, his Chamberlain, and the few others who had travelled in his ship, but the others were nowhere in sight.

Richard's ship was forced to land 4 miles away from Edward's location. He gathered the 300 men who were on board with him, and they set about finding the king, without knowing whether he was safe or not. Anthony Woodville, Earl Rivers, was in a third ship with 200 men that had run aground 14 miles away from their king.[7] Other ships dotted the coast, unaware of each other's fates and trying to work out how they might regroup before they were set upon in their small, defenceless groups and the war lost before it could be begun. Edward found lodgings for himself and his men in a nearby village, hardly somewhere suitable for a king, but it was somewhere to rest. During the night and the following morning, the bedraggled groups of his fledgeling army began to appear in the village as each found its way back to him. On 15 March, they were all together on English soil, and the campaign proper could begin. News of the landing had reached Oxford by 19 March, when he wrote to several men ordering them to raise as many troops as they could and meet him at Newark to resist Edward's advance.[8]

Edward's plans were being foiled at every turn. Despite being the head of the House of York, the north was traditionally Lancastrian in sympathy, and the south and west were where Edward could have expected more support. The writer of *The Arrivall* lamented that as Edward tried to rally men, 'there came but few to hym, or almost none.'[9] Instead, Edward's scouts could find only that people in 'greate nombre, and in dyvars placis, were gatheryd, and in harnes, redye to resiste hym.'[10] The countryside was taking up arms against Edward. Richard must have known that they were only a short distance south of York, a region in which one word from Warwick could bring thousands out baying for their blood. The writer of *The Arrivall* seems to have picked up a sense that the people in the north objected to Edward returning and laying claim to the throne, but had some sympathy, a residue of feeling for his father, for an attempt to reclaim his inheritance as Duke of York and to be reconciled with Henry.[11] Edward seized on the notion. The next objective of his army was to move into Lincolnshire, a region more sympathetic to their cause. There were two options to get there. Taking ship across the Humber would be quick and risk-free. The other option was to march around the river, towards York and Pontefract, heading west before plunging south. West meant deeper into Warwick's territories.

The choice was obvious, so Edward decided that they would march to York. He refused to take his men back on board any ships for fear that it would look like they were running away so soon after landing.[12] Instructions were given to all of his men that they 'shuld noyse, and say openly, where so evar they came, that his entent and purpos was only to clame to be Duke of Yorke, and to have and enjoy th'enheritaunce that he was borne unto, by the right of the full noble prince his fathar, and none othar.'[13] Edward sent word to the town of Beverley, which lay on his route, and to Kingston upon Hull, a stout, walled town, that they should open their gates to him, but they refused.[14] All was not going according to plan. Not to be deterred, Edward could draw confidence from the fact that despite the reported presence of armed forces all about him, no one had actually tried to engage him.[15] His army was only small, yet either the assurances about his intentions or the fearsome martial reputation he had won in previous years kept them all at bay. That was something, at least.

On Monday 18 March, Edward and Richard drew near to the city of York. When he was 3 miles away, the city's Recorder, Thomas Conyers, rode out to meet the king. Thomas warned the king that he would not receive a welcome in York. The city gates would be locked against him, and even if he managed to force his way in, he and all of his company would be destroyed. Richard, at least, must have known the truth of the words, given Warwick's strong connections to the city. The threat was very real. The safe course of action was plain but Edward marched straight on towards York. Undaunted, Edward had called Thomas Conyers' bluff and was rewarded as he neared the city when Robert Clifford and Richard Burgh came out to meet him with the news that York would support his claim to his dukedom, and that as long as that remained his goal, he would be allowed to pass through the city.[16] After resting and being refreshed at York, Edward moved on the next morning towards Tadcaster, a town 10 miles south of York that belonged to the Earl of Northumberland. From exile, Edward had written to Henry Percy, the man he had restored to the earldom shortly before losing his crown, and had received replies, which he showed now to win himself favour.[17] He still cannot have been confident of the response he would get from a man so long out in the cold and with an impeccably Lancastrian pedigree. Apparently well received at Tadcaster, and with Northumberland doing nothing to resist his movements, Edward's troops travelled the following day to Wakefield and Sandal, more firm ground that had belonged to his father and where both his father and brother Edmund had died at the Battle of Wakefield in 1460. The earl's inaction was perhaps the single greatest reason that Edward was able to travel through such hostile country without being assaulted. The slightly circuitous route not only brought them into Yorkist territory, but also skirted around John Neville, Marquis Montagu, who was at Pontefract Castle. Montagu's true allegiance and motives are hard to discern here. *The Arrivall* notes that he let Edward pass without trying to stop him, adding 'were it with good will or noo, men may juge at theyr pleaswre.'[18] Montagu had been slow to abandon Edward the previous year despite his shoddy treatment and was not keen to engage the deposed king now, even though he had only a handful of men with him. This is perhaps a testament to Edward's likeable personality, or else to the fragility of Warwick's position.

As they marched further south, appearing confident but undoubtedly still cautious, Richard could reflect on the sense of growing comfort. As they reached new areas, the inhabitants noted that no one before them had opposed Edward and so they did likewise, so that the Yorkists were allowed to pass unmolested, though still no more than a handful actually joined them.[19] Once Edward reached Nottingham on 25 March, things began to look brighter. Sir William Parr (the grandfather of Henry VIII's future sixth wife) and Sir James Harrington arrived with 600 men between them. Both men were associates of Richard, and James Harrington's arrival may have owed far more to the fast friendship he had forged with Richard in Wales and at Hornby Castle than a sense of duty to the king who had treated him less than favourably. As the man who had delivered Henry VI to Edward and the head of a staunchly Yorkist family, his loyalties belonged at Nottingham with Edward. Richard's support of his cause may well have served as the motivation to meet his responsibilities.

Edward, now on much safer ground, sent scouts out to find the Lancastrian forces. At Newark, they discovered the Duke of Exeter, returned from Burgundy, the Earl of Oxford, with Lord Bardolf and others, reported to number 4,000 men, raised from the south-eastern counties.[20] If *The Arrivall* is be believed, the sight of these outriders spooked the Lancastrian lords so that they fled out of Newark at 2 o'clock in the morning, dashing south to Coventry.[21] By the time Edward arrived at Warwick, his ranks swollen by 3,000 men who had come to him at Leicester, he had finally dropped the pretence that he sought only the restoration of his dukedom. He was welcomed into the city as king and began to again issue royal proclamations.[22] With his cause looking more promising, another long-term piece of Edward's work, or more properly the work of the whole House of York, paid rich dividends.

Commines had noted that during Warwick and George's exile in France, a lady-in-waiting to George's duchess, Warwick's daughter, Isabel, had passed through Calais carrying letters to George offering reconciliation.[23] It seems that throughout the ensuing troubles, the line of communication had been kept open and there had been a united effort to untangle George from Warwick's grasp. Cecily Neville had managed her position perfectly. As George's mother and Warwick's aunt, she escaped any repercussions for her oldest son's actions. George had, predictably, become marginalised by the new Lancastrian regime. Eyed with suspicion, losing lands to resurgent Lancastrian supporters and failing to receive offices he had been promised, he was wavering in the swirling wind and was ripe for the picking. Warwick had pledged to hand him the throne in 1469, but by 1470, the earl had put Henry VI back on it. Although the arrangement left George with a written guarantee that he would inherit the throne in the event that Henry's son Edward of Westminster died without an heir, it must have seemed far too distant a possibility to satisfy the duke. The author of *The Arrivall* confirms that Cecily Neville had been working constantly to bring George safely back into the fold. She had not been alone. Their oldest sister Anne, the Duchess of Exeter, who can only have been appalled to find her estranged husband back in the country and in power, had been working on George along with their other sister Elizabeth, Duchess of Suffolk. Thomas Bourchier, Archbishop of Canterbury, and Robert Stillington, Bishop of Bath and Wells, were also chipping away at the recalcitrant duke, aided by the Archbishop's brother Henry Bourchier, Earl of Essex. Although 'certayne priests, and other well disposyd parsouns' also contributed, special mention is reserved for Margaret in Burgundy, who had worked 'most specially' to convince George where his future lay.[24]

On 3 April, news arrived at Warwick that George was approaching from the south-west with several thousand men. Edward marched his own army out of the city, and the two forces faced off near Banbury. Edward set his men out in battle formation and raised his standards. He then stepped out from his army, accompanied by Richard, Anthony Woodville, Lord Hastings and a few others. George moved out in front of his own men, accompanied by a few lords, and halfway between the two armies, they met face to face. Edward and George made their peace in 'right kynde and lovynge langwage'. Richard then had conference with his brother too, no doubt offering him reassurances of Edward's goodwill and willingness to forgive him. Finally, to the immense pleasure of all, the brothers were reconciled, and George's men further swelled the ranks of Edward's growing army.[25] Richard's part in these talks was pivotal. The women of the family had fulfilled their role as peacemakers to perfection, but they could not offer George anything that he could hold onto and rely on. Edward would surely have said anything to prevent George's significant force joining up with Warwick and instead to add them to his own ranks. What was there to prevent Edward having him seized as soon as they left the field at Banbury together? Richard was the one able to close the deal. He had remained loyal to Edward, but he was well-known to George, and their previous trials must have forged some form of bond between them. It was Richard who was able to stand before George and assure him that Edward would honour his word and that all would work out well for George if he submitted to their older brother. In turn, George seems to have trusted in the assurances Richard gave. Now, after two years of fractured relations, the House of York was, through the effort of all of its members, reunified.

George immediately set about trying to bring Edward and Warwick to terms, hoping to avoid the bloodshed that was looking increasingly inevitable. Many nobles had sided with Warwick, and George also felt that peace with Warwick would allow them to be reconciled to Edward too, sapping support from Henry VI's Lancastrian government. Edward's offers to the earl were never good enough, and probably never could have been. In turn, Warwick's demands were beyond Edward's gift. The king could not allow his wayward subject too much power with which to threaten him in the future, and the earl could not so prostrate himself before the king as to be utterly embarrassed and unmanned, exposed to reprisals. As negotiations failed to make progress, Edward challenged Warwick to come out from behind the walls of Coventry and fight him. Warwick wisely declined. Eventually, Edward decided that retaking London had to be his priority and that a prolonged siege of Coventry would only play into Lancastrian hands. He marched out of Warwick to the walls of Coventry, where he once more challenged Warwick to come out and face him. Warwick had now been joined by Exeter, Oxford and Montagu and the presence of the former two at least must have made surrender or even negotiation all but impossible. When the challenge remained unanswered, Edward pressed on to London on 5 April. He had business, both political and personal, to take care of there. Warwick would have to wait.

On 6 April, the Yorkist army was at Daventry, where they stayed the night. The following morning was Palm Sunday, and the king with his men heard mass at the town's church, where one of those miracles that seemed to single out Edward and shine a divine light on the Yorkist cause was revealed to them. As decribed earlier, before the Battle of Mortimers Cross in 1461 three suns had appeared in the sky. It was a weather phenomenon known as a parhelion, but it seemed to Edward's men like a portent of doom. In a masterstroke of spin, Edward told them it represented the Holy Trinity and signified that the Father, Son and Holy Ghost were watching over them. His newly motivated men easily won the day. Now as Edward knelt before the rood screen, there was a loud cracking sound. Looking for its source, the congregation saw that the wooden boards hiding one of the statues in the church, as the rules for the Easter period demanded, had split open. The boards contracted again and then burst apart. Visible was an alabaster statue of Saint Anne, the mother of the Virgin Mary, and Edward was reminded that during his tumultuous sea voyage he had prayed to Saint Anne and promised to make an offering the next time he saw a statue of her. The king made his offering and those gathered, including the writer of *The Arrivall*, took the sign as 'a fayre miracle; a good pronositique of good aventure'.[26] Unlike the parhelion, Richard was able to witness this miracle, demonstrating

God's favour for the Yorkist cause. For a man whose personal piety was conspicuous and would become a powerful feature of his adult life, this represented a defining moment. Whatever his doubts and fears in Burgundy, and however inauspicious their landing and initial reception had been, he now had proof that what he was doing was right.

From Daventry, Edward moved to Northampton, writing letters from here to the queen, who was still in sanctuary at Westminster and who Edward must have known would have given birth by now. He also wrote to the officials in the capital to try to gauge the feeling within the city. The general populace in London tended to favour the Lancastrian cause whilst the merchants and aldermen had been made prosperous by Yorkist rule. On 9 April, in an attempt to galvanise the numerically superior populace, George Neville, Archbishop of York, had Henry VI paraded through the streets.[27] Warwick had asked his brother to hold the city until he could catch up with Edward even as the king was demanding admission through the sealed gates. The archbishop's stunt backfired spectacularly. The bedraggled and uninspiring Henry motivated no one, unless it was to consider the superior merits of King Edward, who had reached St Albans the same day. Although all pledged to support the Lancastrian king, they were already considering their options. On 11 April, the Recorder of London, Thomas Urswick, and some of the aldermen, ordered those who had been set to watch the city walls to go home for dinner, to take a break. Once they had all left, this small group opened the gates to Edward and allowed him to march into the city.[28] Warkworth here describes Edward taking both King Henry and George Neville into custody, but *The Arrivall* explains that the Archbishop of York understood the way the wind was blowing and had written to Edward to ask his forgiveness. Such secret negotiations were perhaps unknown to Warkworth and others, but when Edward entered the city, he went to St Paul's, to the Bishop of London's palace, where George Neville presented to him his prize prisoner: the bemused King Henry VI.[29]

From here, Edward went to Westminster Abbey, where he offered thanks for the success of his campaign so far and then hurried to his wife and daughters in sanctuary. Queen Elizabeth had indeed been delivered of a child, on 2 November. On 11 April, for the first time, King Edward met his first-born son and namesake. The birth of Prince Edward changed the shape of the Yorkist dynasty. No longer was Edward reliant on his brothers to offer the security of an identifiable male line succession. If Richard had briefly considered that he might replace George as their brother's heir, he was now disabused of the notion, returning to his more familiar role further down the line of succession. For George, though, who had spent a decade as heir to the throne, it would have been more of an adjustment. That Richard was willing to pass over his own chances of promotion is clear from his participation in bringing George back to their side and, in so doing, handing back the mantle of being Edward's heir, if Richard had ever considered it his. Whether George would take another relegation of his prospects so well remained to be seen. The Lancastrian efforts to strip him of position had pushed him back to his brothers' side. Now that he was there, he was to lose the prize he had held for ten years.

Philippe de Commines commented in his memoir about the reasons he had heard for London deciding to welcome King Edward rather than defend King Henry. The first consideration was the large number of Edward's supporters in sanctuaries dotted about the city, not to mention his wife at Westminster with their children. If they were to rise within the city walls, there was fear over the ability of the general populace to resist them. Secondly, Edward owed vast sums of money to merchants in the city and his creditors, for reasons that had little to do with dynastic politics, turned out in his favour. A Yorkist restoration was the only way they were ever likely to see their bills paid, and indeed to be able to continue a profitable relationship with the Yorkist regime. The third stream of support reported by Commines is scurrilous in its nature, but whether it is true or not, it is instructive as to the widely held reputation of this king. Commines understood that 'the ladies of quality, and rich citizens' wives with whom he had formerly intrigued, forced their husbands and relations to declare themselves on his side.'[30] The belief that Edward maintained a string of mistresses and conducted illicit affairs to such a wide extent is as hard to substantiate as it is to disprove, but the fact that such sordid behaviour could effortlessly and believably be attributed to Edward is a matter to be returned to in the future. If the king's licentious reputation did help him in 1471, it was to return with a vengeance after his death.

For Richard, it was an impressive move towards the end of a salutary episode. He had seen at first-hand how his brother was able to face dangers head-on and lessen their threat by such direct action. The young duke had helped to bring his wayward brother back into the fold and seen the mighty, famous Earl of Warwick cowed into avoiding a fight with Edward, a failure that had surely added to the impression that Edward was in the ascendant and was feared by enemies he sought to bring into the field. The miracle he had witnessed at Daventry was a sure signal that he was on the right side, doing the right thing. Richard had made himself indispensable to his brother and demonstrated an unwavering loyalty that was sure to bring some form of reward. More than anything else, he had seen that ultimate success was deemed to lie in taking and retaining control of London. Edward had left his enemies behind to achieve this end, and although they were still to be dealt with, his position had been greatly enhanced by his reception in London. It was in the political cauldron of the capital that kings were made and recognised and kept in the ascendancy. That was where the true power in England lay.

However, there was little respite to be had. Quickly refreshed and resupplied, Edward's army was prepared to leave the city again. Word arrived that Warwick was now marching south, *The Arrivall* claiming he thought he held the advantage in that if his brother the Archbishop had held London as instructed, he would have Edward trapped outside the walls between his own force and those protecting the capital. If Edward had managed to enter London, Warwick intended to arrive on Easter Sunday and fall upon his men as they observed this most sacred of holy days.[31] What Richard might have thought of this attempt to use the sacred event to win a military victory can only be guessed at, but he cannot have been impressed by Warwick's sacrilegious opportunism. On Saturday 13 April, Edward led his army out of the city, taking with him King Henry, doubtless to prevent him being used against Edward once he had departed. As they neared Barnet, 10 miles north of London, Edward's scouts encountered those of Warwick's force and drove them out of the town, chasing them half a mile down the road. As Edward and Richard neared Barnet, the king ordered that none of his army should take refuge within the town, but should make camp well outside its boundaries.[32] Two battles had taken place within the town of nearby St Albans, and both had been lost by those within, the first by Henry and the second by Warwick. Edward was far too accomplished a general to replicate those mistakes and instead drew his men closer to Warwick's force before ordering them to camp for the night in the fields.

In the deepening darkness of the evening, Edward had moved nearer to Warwick's camp than he intended. As it happened, fortune favoured Edward's party once more. Warwick had gathered far more artillery than the king and fired his guns all night at Edward's camp, but as they were closer than he estimated, they overshot the mark and fell harmlessly behind Edward's army. The king ordered his own guns to remain silent and kept his camp quiet to a man all night, so that Warwick would not realise his mistake and would waste ammunition and time to no avail.[33] Between four and five o'clock the next morning, Easter Sunday, 14 April, Edward stirred his army and formed them into ranks. The traditional method of arranging an army was still that laid down by the Roman commentator Vegetius in *De Re Militari*. The treatise was an examination of the previous good organisation of the Roman Empire that had led to so much success and where it had gone wrong. Attributed to Vegetius, a fourth-century writer, it is possibly an amalgamation of opinions and was almost certainly revised over the years, but it was still the accepted military textbook a thousand years later. An army would, where possible, be split into three battles. The vanguard, the most forward unit, would usually take the right wing if the battles was forming a straight line and would be expected to engage first. The centre would contain the main bulk of the army, and the rearguard would take the left flank, designed to provide reinforcements if required. It is therefore significant that as Edward's army took shape in the early morning darkness, Lord Hastings took the left wing, Edward himself held the centre, and it was Richard who was given command of the right wing, the vanguard. It was to be his first experience of battle, and he was handed a place of the utmost responsibility. Significantly, George was to stay in the centre with Edward, undoubtedly still not entirely trusted, but it was a snub to the older brother to see the younger given such a command.

Warkworth gives King Edward 7,000 men as he left London and credits Warwick, accompanied by the Duke of Exeter, Marquis Montagu and the Earl of Oxford with 10,000.[34] Warwick and Montagu held their centre. Oxford, an experienced soldier, took the right wing, the vanguard, and Exeter the left. Both Warkworth and *The Arrivall* agree that the early morning mist was to play a decisive role in the course of the fighting.[35] Sometime between four and five o'clock, with Edward's men in formation, he ordered trumpets to sound and his guns to begin firing. It seems Warwick was prepared, as the cannon fire was returned. After a brief period of exchanging shots, the combatants came to face-to-face blows, but the mist, 'whiche suffred neythar party to se other, but for a little space', had caused the two armies to line up off centre. Edward's right jutted out beyond Warwick's left. The fighting was intense and fierce, lasting until about ten o'clock, some five or six hours of gruelling, draining, hand-to-hand combat.[36] Warwick's force appeared on the brink of victory several times, only for the mighty Edward to rally his men and keep the fighting going.

The real problems lay on both flanks. At Edward's left, Lord Hastings was overlapped by Oxford's force, which quickly took advantage and flanked Hastings. Under the most severe pressure, the left broke and fled from the field towards the town of Barnet. Some ran so far that they reached London, taking with them the news that Edward had lost the battle. Unable to see the rest of the battlefield, or perhaps aware that Warwick was in the ascendant in the centre, Oxford's men pursued the fleeing Yorkists into Barnet and fell to plundering in premature celebration of their victory. On the other flank, Richard found little opposition from Exeter's force as he enveloped it, mirroring the problems at the other end of the lines. Nevertheless, the fighting was brutal and intense. Some men in Richard's retinue fell, as shall be seen later, and Exeter himself was so sorely wounded that he was left for dead on the battlefield. The tide seems to have turned when Oxford's men returned to the battlefield to find that their celebrations had been premature. As they reappeared from the fog on Warwick's right flank, Oxford's badge of a star and streamers was mistaken in the poor visibility for Edward's own insignia of the sun in splendour. As Warwick and Montagu's men unleashed arrows on what they assumed was a flanking manoeuvre by Edward's men, a cry of treason went up from Oxford's shocked, under-fire force and the seed of panic, so swift to take hold and spread, was sown. There had perhaps been some suspicion that Warwick, or at least Montagu, could not be relied on against Edward, so in attacking Oxford's men they had apparently revealed their treachery. Warwick's force collapsed and fled. In the ensuing pursuit, Warwick and Montagu were killed.

One newsletter sent to the Continent detailed the events of Edward's arrival in London and the Battle of Barnet. Written by Gerhard von Wesel, it listed the casualties of the battle, also noting that 'the duke of Gloucester and Lord Scales were severely wounded, but they had no [lasting] harm from it, God be praised.'[37] The implication seems to be that both men sustained wounds that appeared at first sight far worse than they actually were. It has been suggested that Richard lost the tip of the little finger on his right hand at some point in his life. His skeleton showed slight shortness of the bone at the tip of this finger compared to his other hand and a flattening of the bone surface. One of the surviving early portraits of Richard, held at the National Portrait Gallery, also shows him holding a ring over the tip of this finger as if to obscure it with the thumb of his left hand pressed against what appears to be a flat surface. The evidence of such a wound is not conclusive, nor is it clear when it might have happened, but he was injured at Barnet in a manner that seemed more severe at first glance than it later turned out to be. That report might be consistent with the loss of the tip of his finger, which would bleed significantly and doubtless be painful, but once treated, would not prove a significant hindrance.

On the following day, Edward ordered that the recovered bodies of Warwick and Montagu should be put on public display at St Paul's, 'open and naked'. It was not an unusual precaution after such a death and *The Arrivall* is clear that it was done because 'dowbtless ells the rumore shuld have bene sowne abowte, in all contries, that they bothe, or els, at leaste, th'Erle of Warwyke, was yet on lyve.'[38] It was vital that everyone knew Edward's victory over Warwick was complete and that Lancastrian or Neville sympathisers could not spread rumours that Warwick had escaped the field. The displaying of their bodies was made all the more necessary by the premature reports that had reached London of Edward's defeat, emboldening those who favoured Henry VI. With this gruesome spectacle, Edward drew a line under the matter. Here was another lesson for Richard in the art of securing power, when even the rumour of an opponent's success or continued existence could pose a threat. In a final act of respect and recognition of the bond that had once held the cousins close, Edward allowed their bodies to be taken to their family mausoleum at Bisham Abbey in Berkshire after the public exhibition. George Neville, the last remaining brother, was pardoned five days after the battle but remained in custody in the Tower until 5 June.[39] Henry VI was deposited in the Tower, still wearing the blue robe he had paraded around London in before Easter. He may even have been happy to return to a quiet seclusion that suited him far better than the confusing hurly-burly of the outside world.

Just two days after the Battle of Barnet, on 16 April, news arrived in London that Queen Margaret and her son Prince Edward had landed with Lord Wenlock, Warwick's deputy in Calais, and several other notables, including Warwick's now-widowed countess. They had arrived two days earlier, on the very day Edward had defeated Warwick. Edmund Beaufort, Duke of Somerset, and Thomas Courtenay, Earl of Devon, two Lancastrians who had been unwilling to work with Warwick, rushed to meet her. In this timing, Edward again had luck on his side. The absence of Margaret and Prince Edward was the key factor in Lancastrian hesitancy to support Warwick's attempts to control government. Prince Edward had been appointed Lieutenant of the King's Army on 27 March, a commission that was hurried to him when he landed.[40] If they had arrived just a few days earlier, Barnet might have been very different, and Edward would have found a more united bank of opponents, but Margaret's leisurely approach to leaving France left their faction in England divided and uncertain what was to be done. Still, that damage could not be undone, and many in the Lancastrian party would have been pleased to see Warwick eliminated. Quite how he would have fitted into a longer-term Lancastrian plan is unclear. Edward had been forced to give battle, tiring his men, and in this, there was an opportunity for the Lancastrians to strike.

At Exeter, Margaret spent two weeks watching men rally to her cause from throughout Devon and Cornwall before travelling through Taunton to Wells. In Wells, the now traditional unruliness of Margaret's armies, which had lost her support as her Scottish contingent pillaged their way south through England in 1460–1, was again on display. The Bishop's palace was looted, and the prison broken open. To the local populace, from whom Margaret might have hoped to add to her numbers, it was hardly a reassuring visit. By the end of April, her army had reached Bath. In London, Edward took stock of the casualties he had suffered at Barnet and set about replacing those lost or injured with fresh men, receiving regular updates of Margaret's movements and the state of her support. The king set a muster for Windsor, where he arrived on 19 April and celebrated St George's Day.

Edward's spies were busy. He prepared for what were deemed the most likely scenarios.[41] If Margaret moved directly eastward towards London, or south to the coast and then east through Kent and on to London, he meant to meet them as soon as possible and as far away from London as he could. The proximity to the city of Barnet and the confused reporting reaching the city had added to his problems. If they were not ready to meet him and moved north, towards the fertile regions of Cheshire and Lancashire, where they would find ready support, he would try to intercept them as far south as possible. If they were allowed to pass along the Welsh border there was a risk they would drum up support there and receive reinforcements from Jasper Tudor, the reinstated Earl of Pembroke. Margaret must have felt she needed more time and more men, and that Stanley territory was a good prospect because this was the path she took. Edward's plan to intercept her as quickly as possible demonstrates his own mistrust of Stanley at this point.

Whatever Richard's injury at Barnet had been, he was ready to fight for his brother again almost immediately. He joined the army that left Windsor on 24 April, heading west. On 27 April they lodged at Abingdon and moved on two days later, on Monday 29 April, to Cirencester. Word reached Edward here that Margaret's army would arrive in Bath the next day and planned to give battle the day after that, on Wednesday. Marching 3 miles outside Cirencester, Edward prepared his men to face the last Lancastrian army arrayed against them. When no word of their approach came, he moved forward to Malmesbury, where he learned that he had been tricked. Margaret's army had slid from Bath to Bristol and was making north, heading for the nearest crossing over the River Severn at Gloucester. Margaret now let it be known that she planned to move to Sodbury, where she really would give battle on 2 May, having been refreshed and reinforced at Bristol the previous day. A small skirmishing force met some of Edward's scout near Sodbury, and the king hurried to face the promised challenge, only to find that it was another trick, or that Margaret had thought better of the encounter. Instead, she had marched about 15 miles north to Berkeley.

On 3 May, the Lancastrians moved the same distance again to Gloucester, but the city and the bridge were closed to them on Edward's orders. The castle had belonged to Richard and lay in a region along the Marches and into the south-west where he had been active the previous year. Driven away in the mid-morning, they marched a further 10 miles to the next crossing at Tewkesbury. The writer of *The Arrivall* describes the early May weather as unusually hot and dry,[42] yet Edward's men, including Richard, made a forced march of more than 30 miles to keep up with the Lancastrian army and reach Cheltenham. From there, they pressed towards Tewkesbury as evening fell. The Lancastrian army was faced with an impossible dilemma. They were exhausted, hungry and thirsty. They could try to cross the river, but it would be slow and dangerous work in the darkness that risked Edward assaulting them part way through when they were divided and in disarray. If they stayed on this side of the river for the night, there would be no escaping Edward in the morning. A stand in the morning, after a rest and with their whole army together, must have seemed the lesser of the two unpalatable evils.

In the morning, a fight was inevitable. There was no way for the Lancastrians to escape with Edward so close and they took up what seemed like the strongest position available just to the south of the town. The precise location is lost, but the fields known as the Gastons, just beyond the Abbey, offer a long ridge that might have made a defensible position from which to face Edward's army. *The Arrivall* credits them with 'a marvaylows strong grownd' that seemed 'full difficult to be assayled'.[43] Margaret had taken the doubtless painful decision to allow her seventeen-year-old son to take up a position in the centre of the army while she herself retired a safe distance from the town. Prince Edward was old enough to fight – the same age as Edmund, Earl of Rutland, had been at Wakefield when he had been killed and older than Edward III's son the Black Prince when he had begun his notable military career. The entire future of the House of Lancaster rested on his young shoulders, and with a soldier like King Edward opposing them, it would hardly have given his army heart if the young prince had bid them good luck and farewell before the fighting began. Lancaster needed something different from the prince's father, but it must have been a wrench for his mother nevertheless. Somerset took command of the Lancastrian vanguard, with Lord Wenlock in the centre, where Prince Edward was also placed, and the Earl of Devon holding the rearguard.

Edward had divided his army into three battles in precisely the same way he had at Barnet. Richard had acquitted himself well enough to retain his brother's faith and confidence, despite any injury and the comparative ease of his assault on Exeter's flank. The duke again took command of the vanguard. Edward, accompanied again by George, held the centre of the army and Lord Hastings, with Edward's step-son Thomas Grey, Marquis of Dorset, was placed on the left. As he had done at Barnet, Edward ordered a blast of his trumpets and put his fortunes into the hands of God and the Virgin Mary.[44] Unlike at Barnet, but because of the experiences there, Edward appears to have avoided allowing Hastings to face Somerset, the most able of the Lancastrian commanders, because it was the two vanguards who moved first. The encounter began with artillery fire, but the Yorkists held far more guns, and Somerset soon realised that he could not simply wait to be undone by cannon fire. As Richard moved his vanguard up towards Somerset's position, his opponent spotted his approach and instead moved through the thickets on hidden paths they had discovered the previous evening. This brought them to Edward's flank, and Somerset attacked, taking the king by surprise.

Before the battle, Edward had placed a contingent of 200 footmen at the edge of a nearby wood to watch out for ambushes from that quarter. When Somerset attacked, they rushed to their king's aid and flanked Somerset, just as he had flanked Edward. The Lancastrian vanguard was slowly forced back towards Richard's vanguard and, caught in a trap about to spring shut on them, Somerset's men panicked. They began to flee, some drowning in the river under the weight of their armour and others running into the Abbey in the hope of finding safety there. Edward now fell upon the Lancastrian centre, causing some 2,000 casualties before the field was won. The Crowland Chronicler recorded that 'the result had long remained doubtful' before 'king Edward at last gained a glorious victory,'[45] hinting that it had been a close-run thing for a time, as Barnet was.

With the battle won, Edward turned his attention to those within the Abbey. He was reprimanded by a very brave priest when he stormed in bearing his sword in his hand. The priest demanded pardons for those who had taken refuge within the Abbey's walls, most notably the Duke of Somerset, and Edward, chastised, apparently agreed.[46] Despite this, the men were taken from the Abbey and tried for treason before a court of chivalry, convened under Richard as the reinstated Constable of England. Found guilty, they were beheaded in the town on 6 May. This moment represented Richard's first real exercise of the ultimate powers of the Constable, though it must have been at the king's direction. Edward would soon pay for the Abbey to be redecorated by way of an apology, though it was, and remains today, filled to bursting with Yorkist symbols, including Edward's sun in splendour badge.

One of the earliest acts of vicious murder later to be laid at Richard's feet resulted from the death at Tewkesbury of Prince Edward, whose remains were buried within the Abbey beneath a ceiling celebrating the Yorkist victory. The prince's death all but ended the House of Lancaster, with Henry VI in no fit state to bear the mantle of responsibility for its continuation, so it is perhaps a natural feature of the darkening of Richard's reputation after his own death that he should be blamed for such a calamity. This is one instance in which tracing the story back from later sources to the contemporary accounts can prove instructive. Shakespeare's Gloucester is present when the prince is captured and brought before them. The young prince berates his enemies until King Edward stabs him, at which Gloucester adds his dagger before George thrusts a third into the boy. Gloucester then offers to kill the distraught Queen Margaret before he is stopped by Edward.[47] Here, Shakespeare is laying the groundwork for his ultimate villain. He had already had his Gloucester kill a previous Duke of Somerset at the First Battle of St Albans in 1455 – when Richard was two-and-a-half years old.

Holinshed's Chronicle, published in 1577 and a source for Shakespeare, has King Edward striking the prince before George, Richard, Thomas Grey and Lord Hastings murder him. The account of England's history written by Polydore Vergil at the behest of Henry VII was completed around 1513 but not published until 1534 and has King Edward arguing with the prince and shoving him away. At that, 'those that wer present wer George duke of Clarence, Richard duke of Gloucester and William lord Hastings, crewelly murdered' the prince.[48] No contemporary source implicates Richard in the prince's death at all. *The Arrivall* states only that Prince Edward 'was taken, fleinge to the towne wards, and slayne, in the fielde,'[49] suggesting that he was a casualty of the battle and noting nothing special about his death. The equally contemporary Warkworth reported the George was implicated, though still maintains that he was 'slayne in the felde', adding that he had 'cryede for socoure to his brother-in-lawe the Duke of Clarence'.[50] Although George is not directly accused of involvement in Prince Edward's death, the connection between George, who in France was considered Prince Edward's ally, and was his brother-in-law by virtue of their marriages to Warwick's two daughters, may be significant. In a moment of panic, what name might Prince Edward invoke in the hope of succour but the only man he knew on the Yorkist side who was also related to him by marriage?

The politically well-informed writer of *The Crowland Chronicle* similarly offers no culprit. He notes cryptically that 'there were slain on the queen's side, either on the field or after the battle, by the avenging hands of certain persons, prince Edward, the only son of king Henry, the duke of Somerset, the earl of Devon, and all and every the other lords above-mentioned.'[51] The reference is frustratingly imprecise. Were the 'avenging hands' meant to apply only to Prince Edward, or to all the Lancastrian lords who had been thorns in various Yorkist sides? Who were the persons referred to? Horace Walpole, in later centuries, would suggest Richard is meant to be the owner of the avenging hands,[52] but this seems unlikely. This continuation of the chronicle was written in 1486, after Richard's death, and is not slow to pour disdain on him and his reign. Why, then, should the writer shy away from naming Richard as the culprit here? The avenging hands might equally have belonged to King Edward, to whom all of these men had been the cause of much trouble. Indeed, George had cause to hate Prince Edward. It was his and his father's restoration that had caused Warwick to relegate George from his plan to give him the throne. The Lancastrian faction in England had not warmed to George and had so ill-treated him, in his view, that he was easily drawn back to his brothers, where he was still, understandably, viewed with suspicion. Prince Edward represented all of that loss and failure. Again, though, it is to be wondered why George might not be named, since by the time the chronicle was written, he too was gone and his children without influence. The only figure the writer clearly admired and might seek to protect was King Edward, with possible consideration to be given to Lord Hastings. The chronicler was a fan of Edward and might have fudged this issue to save enshrining his former master's vengeance in writing. Then again, it might be a casually applied phrase that meant nothing to the writer more than these men died, either during the fighting or by execution after it, and that they deserved their fates for the trouble they had wrought. All that can be said conclusively is that, despite later claims of his guilt in the act, no contemporary commentator explicitly blamed Richard for the death of Prince Edward.

One aspect of the recovery of Edward's throne in 1471 that cannot be denied is the impression made by Richard on his brother and all contemporary observers. He had performed admirably in the encounters at Barnet and Tewkesbury, perhaps with some luck at Barnet and benefitting from the problems faced by Hastings there. Nevertheless, he had opened his martial account with a positive balance. A contemporary poem describing the campaign is effusive in its praise for the young duke.

> The duke of Glocetter, that nobill prynce,
> Yonge of age and victorius in batayle,
> To the honoure of Ectour [Hector] that he myghte comens,
> Grace hym folowith, fortune, and good spede.
> I suppose hes the same that clerkis of rede,
> Fortune hathe hym chosyn, and for the wyth hym will goo,
> Her husbonde to be, the wille of God is soo.[53]

Although the poem is in praise of the Yorkist victory, Richard is the only participant singled out for comparison to an ancient hero. Hector was the greatest warrior for the state of Troy when it was attacked by Greeks and the suggestion of Richard's leading role in winning back his brother's throne would not have been lost on those who heard it. For Richard, such recognition was the first step towards matching the enviable reputation of the brother he had, at least physically and martially, idolised for years. The achievements are made all the greater by the knowledge that he accomplished these feats with the pain and discomfort his scoliosis was causing him by this point.

Edward's victory was complete and made safe when news reached him a few days later on the road to Worcester that Queen Margaret had been located and taken into custody. With the former queen was Anne Neville, widow of Prince Edward. When he arrived at Worcester, less welcome news awaited him. A significant uprising had begun in the north. Determined not to repeat his mistakes of the previous year, Edward moved immediately to Coventry on 11 May, sending out commissions of array to replenish his army for a third trial. It proved unnecessary when news came on 13 May that the threat had evaporated, lacking any Neville leadership and with the Earl of Northumberland conspicuously allied to Edward now. It is an oddity of Edward's character that he was slow to act when decisive swiftness might save him trouble, yet once deep in adversity and under threat, he exploded with seemingly endless energy that made him a terror on the battlefield. The mere thought that he might move north had been enough to end opposition there.

In the king's absence, London had come under assault by a force out of Kent led by Thomas Neville, the Bastard of Fauconberg, an illegitimate son of Edward's ally William Neville, Earl of Kent and Lord Fauconberg. William, Warwick's uncle, had died at peace in 1463 before trouble between Edward and the Neville family had emerged. His illegitimate son Thomas, who was now in his forties, shared Warwick's reputation as a sailor and had been given the freedom of the city of London for his services in curbing piracy against English merchants in the Channel. Refused passage through London to lead an army against Edward, Fauconberg attacked the city, setting fire to several gates before a force from within, directed by Anthony Woodville, perhaps too severely injured to travel to Tewkesbury, drove him back, inflicting significant casualties and causing the attackers to retreat to the south coast.[54]

Edward returned to London on Tuesday 21 May. He knighted several of those involved in protecting the capital against the Bastard of Fauconberg, including the Recorder, Thomas Urswick, and the mayor, John Stokton, who had, wisely as it turned out, taken to his sick bed throughout the Lancastrian revival and taken no part in it. Edward spent only one day in London before he led his entire army back out towards the rebels at Sandwich on the south coast.[55] His approach was once again enough, and the Bastard of Fauconberg sent word that he wished to be forgiven by the king. Richard was sent on ahead, directly to Sandwich, to receive the Bastard's surrender on 26 May while Edward waited at Canterbury. Was his drive already beginning to evaporate and his willingness to rely on Richard, as he had done before his expulsion, allowing the re-emergence of the strong pull of his desire to get back to a life of hunting and feasting? Fauconberg was placed into Richard's custody and Warkworth notes with some disdain that Richard had the Bastard executed soon afterwards despite Edward's promised pardon. It seems unlikely that Richard acted without the king's instruction in this matter and certainly he was not censured for it. Nicholas Faunt, the mayor of Canterbury, was also executed by Edward for his part in the affair.[56] Fauconberg was declared a traitor, and when he was executed on 22 September 1471, Edward ordered his head to be sent to London where it was set on a spike, his hollow eyes looking into Kent, the scene of his earlier treachery. The Paston Letters refer to a brother of the Bastard who escaped into sanctuary at Beverley, though his identity is unclear.[57] Nevertheless, the suggestion is that once in the north, the Bastard involved himself in some new plot, which brought about his execution on Edward's orders, or at least with his approval.

Between Edward and Richard's arrival in London on 21 May and their departure south to resolve the revolt of the Bastard, which Richard seems to have moved on ahead of his brother to complete, there is an episode which should not be ignored. On the morning of 22 May 1471, the news ran through the streets of London like wildfire. King Henry VI was dead. His body, like those of Warwick and Montagu, was to be put on public display so that all might be certain of it. This is another moment with which Richard's name has become tightly embroiled, with most later commentators claiming that he plunged a knife into Henry himself, demonstrating the malice and lack of humanity with which they wished to imbue him. Shakespeare's Richard visits Henry in his room at the Tower, feigning hurt that the old king would think he was there to murder him: 'Think'st thou I am an executioner?' Henry's tongue is sharp, and Richard quickly responds by admitting that he has already murdered Henry's son: 'Thy son I kill'd for his presumption.' Yet we saw Edward strike the first blow, and George the last, so even here we are given a sense of the rumour and misinformation that quickly overtakes fact, even within the play. Henry rails at Richard for his deformity, and in rage, Richard thrusts his dagger into the last Lancastrian king, killing him.[58] This is the pinnacle of a story more than a century in the reforming and refining.

The Arrivall gives voice to the official version offered by the Yorkist regime. 'The certaintie of all whiche came to the knowledge of the sayd Henry, late called Kyng, being in the Tower of London; not havynge, afore that, knowledge, that, of pure displeasure, and melancholy, he dyed the xxiii day of the monithe of May.'[59] This account is the only one to date the death to 23 May, which would make other versions of the dates of death, display of the body and burial unfeasible. This version is dismissed out of hand as a cover story, its veracity negated by the convenience of Henry's death. Although this is probably correct, it does not deserve to be entirely ignored. By May 1471, Henry was forty-nine years old. He had been in poor health, certainly mentally and conceivably physically, for almost twenty years, since his first episode of illness in 1453. From his capture in 1465 until his release in 1470, he had been a prisoner in the Tower and on his re-emergence was a sorry, bedraggled and uninspiring figure who commentators suggested had been poorly looked after.[60] It is doubtful he enjoyed his readeption, the name created to describe the reinstatement of a deposed king. If he took a little comfort in a return to a quiet cell after all the stress of the previous six months, the arrival of news that his only son was dead and his wife a prisoner might have been enough of a shock to cause a fatal reaction such as a heart attack or stroke, perhaps. Despite his removal from the throne, Henry would have regarded himself as King of England, a position he had occupied for all but nine months of his forty-nine years. The primary dynastic responsibility of a king was the production of an heir, and in this, success had now been snatched away from him. With the death of his son, his only child, Henry would be responsible for the future of his dynasty, and that was the reality laid squarely at his cell door on the evening of 21 May 1471. That his death may have been convenient to the Yorkist regime does not preclude genuine natural causes brought on by ill health, stress and now a shock of the worst kind.

One contemporary, the London draper Robert Fabyan, writing a chronicle in the early sixteenth century and first published in 1516, recalled the event from the Tudor period. 'Of the deth of this pryncc dyuerse tales were tolde: but the moost comon fame wente, that he was stykked with a dagger, by the handes of the duke of Glouceter.'[61] The usefulness of Fabyan's testimony, like that of so many other writers, is hard to assess. He was almost certainly in London at the time, since he became an apprentice in about 1470, yet he wrote during the time of the man who had killed and replaced Richard. There can be little doubt that 'Richard bashing' became a fashionable exercise that was not discouraged by the fledgeling Tudor government, though it probably took a less active part as an institution than many might think. Still, Fabyan does not assert the truth of Richard's part in the murder. He informs his reader that many stories were in circulation so that he was only reporting rumours, selecting the most prominent as the one involving the ever-darkening character of Richard. He was probably compiling his work at around the same time as Vergil and Sir Thomas More, when Richard's culpability in all sorts of crimes was becoming increasingly accepted as fact. That is not to say, though, that the fashionable attacks on Richard bashing had no basis in fact. Disputes over the reliability of such sources remain lively today, but contemporary evidence should always be favoured over secondary sources, writing with hindsight and agendas, sometimes clear and other times more opaque.

Warkworth's Chronicle may be the seed of many of these later stories, or at least it reflects the working of the rumour mill. Also a contemporary, Warkworth was Lancastrian in his general sympathies, but seemed happy to praise and criticise both parties where he deemed

it necessary. For him, the death of Henry was the end of the faction
he had favoured. He noted that 'the same nyghte that Kynge Edwarde
came to Londone, Kynge Herry, beynge inwarde in presone in the Toure
of Londone, was putt to dethe, the xxi day of Maii, on the tywesday
nyght, betwyx xi and xii of the cloke, beynge thenne at the Toure the
Duke of Gloucetre, brothere to Kynge Edwarde, and many other.'⁶²
Warkworth places Henry's death between the hours of eleven o'clock
and midnight during the night of 21 May. He clearly states that a large
number of people were at the Tower during that night, but Richard is
the only one named. The suggestion, entirely reasonably, is that there is
some significance to this and the further implication is that Richard was
closely and personally involved in Henry's death. That may have been
Warkworth's intention. He may have meant to offer Richard's name as
the killer without expressly stating that the duke was guilty, but he may
equally have simply given the name of the most senior person known to
be there, a not unusual occurrence. The intended significance may have
lain in Edward's absence while such a momentous deed was carried
out. Doubtless, the association of a contemporary, of Richard with the
death, was later seized upon as proof of his culpability, but it offers no
more than the hint of a suggestion.

The writer of *The Crowland Chronicle* set down his version of the
event in 1486 and, as in so many areas, he is frustratingly cryptic despite
his anonymity and the fact that he wrote after Henry VII's accession. He
appears to lament the deed. 'I would pass over in silence the fact that at
this period king Henry was found dead in the Tower of London; may God
spare and grant time for repentance to the person, whoever he was, who
thus dared to lay sacrilegious hands upon the Lord's anointed! Hence it is
that he who perpetrated this has justly earned the title of tyrant, while he
who thus suffered has gained that of a glorious Martyr.'⁶³ This passage is
hard to dissect. It begins by describing Henry being found dead, suggesting
he had either died of natural causes or been killed by some lone assassin,
but then prays for forgiveness for the killer who laid hands on a king. The
writer hopes for time for the killer to repent, suggesting he is known and
still alive, yet follows this with a charge of tyranny against the killer. H.T.
Riley, in his notes to this edition, suggests that the use of the word tyrant
is meant as a hint at Edward's guilt, but that seems doubtful. The writer
seems to have served Henry and Edward and liked them both. The only
king he appears to disapprove of is Richard, who was being painted as a
tyrant so that Henry VII might be England's saviour. The reference seems,
therefore, directed toward Richard, since few others might qualify – few
have the status necessary to become a tyrant.

As in the death of Prince Edward, the writer here had no reason at
all to shy away from naming Richard if he believed him guilty. Richard
was dead, deposed and a figure who could be condemned for all kinds

of evil with the tacit approval of the new Tudor authorities. The author manages to firmly assert that he knew who had committed the deed, yet refrains from giving the name of the killer. If the crime was considered as heinous as it plainly seemed to the chronicler, why not condemn the killer by naming him? This anomaly gives some credence to H.T. Riley's observation that it might imply Edward's guilt. To the chronicler at Crowland, the killer had to be a tyrant as the victim was a martyr. In failing to name the murderer, he allows that Edward, for all he had liked about that king, erred in this act and ultimately brought about the downfall of his own dynasty by God's wrath.

The death of Henry VI is an event that requires separation into two constituent elements, the order and the act, about one of which there is certainty, and the other only rumour and conjecture. The instruction for Henry's death came, without any doubt at all, from King Edward IV. No one, not even one of his brothers, would have attempted such an action without the king's approval. If further assurance were needed, none were sanctioned by the king for undertaking such a drastic and constitutionally monumental act without permission or instruction. The understanding in Milan was that it was Edward who gained from the deed and he who ordered it. The Milanese ambassador to France wrote on 17 June that 'King Edward has not chosen to have the custody of King Henry any longer, although he was in some sense innocent, and there was no great fear about his proceedings, the prince his son and the Earl of Warwick being dead as well as those who were for him and had any vigour, as he has caused King Henry to be secretly assassinated in the Tower, where he was a prisoner. They say he has done the same to the queen, King Henry's wife ... He has, in short, chosen to crush the seed.'[64] There was little doubt the killing of King Henry had been undertaken at Edward's instruction, though the rumour that he had ordered Margaret put to death too is untrue. Ultimately, Edward must shoulder the blame, if any is due, for the death of King Henry VI.

Accepting Edward's responsibility excuses the actual killer from any real liability, at least in a political sense, if not a moral one. Of all the crimes Richard has been accused of, playing a part of some kind in the death of Henry VI is simultaneously the most likely and the least convincing of them all. It is unconvincing because any guilt belongs to Edward. It is likely both because of Richard's position and the troublingly unique nature of the assassination to be undertaken. Warkworth's comment that Richard was present at the Tower makes perfect sense because he was Constable of England, the office he had briefly held, relinquished to John Tiptoft and been restored to with Edward's resumption of the throne. The Constable was responsible for the delivery of the king's justice and would be a natural choice to carry the king's orders to the Tower and to ensure that the 'sentence' imposed was carried out. If Edward worried about the legality in the proceedings, Richard was able to convene a court of chivalry, or a court-martial, which could summarily try those accused of treason and impose a sentence of death. This was an important aspect of the Constable's office that will be more fully explored later, but such a legal nicety may explain his presence there. As the king's brother, the trusted one too, Richard was a natural choice to make sure Edward's wishes were carried out. Prior to the loss of the crown, Edward had been relying heavily on Richard to represent him and to see his will done in the west, from north to south, so he knew his brother was the right man for a responsible job. Richard's presence at the Tower of London when Henry VI was killed therefore seems both likely and reasonable. From the seed of this near certainty has grown a darker assertion that Richard was to blame for the vicious murder of the innocent, saintly Henry.

Richard's personal involvement in striking the fatal blow is possible.[65] Killing an anointed king, as Crowland's reaction reveals, was not an action to be taken lightly. It seems the most likely reason Edward himself would not have done it, and although that would translate to an unwillingness in Richard too (which would be true of any God-fearing medieval Englishman), when the king gave an order, it was not to be ignored. The killing might have been rationalised a little by the use of a Court of Chivalry, in which Henry would be considered an enemy combatant for his role in the Lancastrian restoration, even though he was hardly a combatant at any point in his life and played virtually no part, beyond that of a puppet, in the readeption. It could then be presented as a legal execution rather than an assassination. Kings, at their coronations, were anointed by God and became something sacred, hence the awful enormity of killing such a person. For Edward, once he had decided to have it done, he next had to resolve the question of who would undertake such an act. He was asking whoever it was to kill an anointed king. It was a dangerous precedent to set, one that might return to haunt Edward. Cheapening the murder of a king was, in itself, a hazardous thing. He could hardly allow a commoner to become a regicide, but who amongst the fickle nobility could he trust to commit the killing without fear that they might see in it a later authority to also murder him? Only one name would really stand at the forefront of Edward's mind. The king had to do it himself, which might have been the more noble course of action, or he had to entrust it to someone beyond suspicion. Warkworth may have been right to single Richard out, and later writers might have seized upon the correct rumour when they related that it was Richard who struck the blow that killed King Henry VI. Richard may not have been willing to do it, or he might have seen another opportunity to serve the brother he idolised and from whom he was about to seek rich rewards for his loyalty. He may have had few qualms about killing a man whose ineptitude had directly brought about the deaths of his father and brother Edmund, and caused years of strife for the country. If he did it, he had seen, aged eighteen, the necessity at critical moments of killing a king, committing an unpalatable deed for a greater good. It remains possible, though, that he had already left for Kent to deal with problems there by the time Henry died.

There is one more striking element of Richard's part in the story of Edward's restoration to the throne in 1471. In 1477, when granting the manor of Foulmire to Queen's College, Cambridge, Richard would request that prayers be said for his family, both living and deceased, which is entirely usual, but added that they should also be offered 'for the soules of Thomas Par, John Milewater, Christofre Wursley, Thomas Huddelston, John Harper and all other gentilmen and yomen servanders and lovers of the saide duke of Gloucef, the wiche were slayn in his service at the batelles of Bernett, Tukysbery or at any other feldes or jorneys, and for all cristen soulis.'[66] Richard clearly remembered those amongst his own retinue that had fought and died alongside him at Barnet and Tewkesbury to help win the Yorkist throne back again. This was more than the usual degree of gratitude expected from a lord for giving service and at least suggests that for Richard, the bonds that he created were important and personal. Beyond a traditional piety, he was considerate enough to include those he felt deserved his thanks, his remembrance and the shortening of their time in purgatory brought by such prayers. It is this attitude that would define the next decade or so of Richard's life and which explains the esteem he was held in by those who knew him well.

8

The Heir of Warwick

*The King entreateth my Lord of Clarence for my Lord of Gloucester;
and as it is said, he answereth, that he may well have my Lady his
Sister in law, but they shall part no Livelihood, as he
saith, so what will fall can I not say.*
Letter from Sir John Paston to John Paston
17 February 1472[1]

As the dust began to settle towards the end of May 1471, the Yorkist government started to try to re-establish a familiar rhythm so that the unpleasant upheaval of the previous months might be forgotten. It was never going to be as easy as Edward might have hoped. Although he had successfully destroyed the legitimate, male line of the House of Lancaster, that did not directly translate into a smooth, unopposed resumption of his authority. There was a tangle of legal problems to sort through, the depth and complexity of which is demonstrated by the first Parliament Edward called after his return in October 1472. It would sit for a total of forty-four weeks during the following two-and-a-half years, a record duration that would not be surpassed until Henry VIII's Reformation Parliament sat between 1529 and 1536.

For Duke Charles in Burgundy, the wager he had placed on Edward had paid off. He had managed to prevent English military assistance for Louis XI, and although he may have personally favoured a Lancastrian revival in England, he had succeeded in sapping Louis' support. Edward sent letters detailing his conclusive victory, including a cut-down version of *The Arrivall* known as *The Short Arrivall*.

For the French king, it was a setback amidst his grand scheming. It was he who had engineered the rapprochement between Warwick and Queen Margaret and both were in his debt. Louis had been dealing directly with the young Prince of Wales during his time in France to solidify the alliance Henry VI was never likely to be able to deliver on. It had almost

148

worked. It mattered little to Louis who was really pulling the strings of Lancastrian government. He was on the best of terms with Warwick, and Margaret was his wife's niece who owed him for supporting her through years of exile, financially at least. The only thorn in his side might be Edward, and Duke Charles had driven him hard into England, disrupting the latest French plan to subsume the Duchy of Burgundy. Now it was Charles who could expect England's favour and France who looked down the barrel of an alliance that had once cost the Valois kings their throne.[2]

Edward was keen for war with France, knowing, as Henry V had so cannily surmised, that foreign war was the natural antidote to domestic unrest. Parliament had to balance the resettlement of Yorkist rule and law and order with the king's desire to prepare the country for war. Inevitably, that meant taxation. A third, but no less pressing, matter distracted Edward and demanded his urgent and careful attention. Richard had expressed a desire to marry Anne Neville, the younger daughter of the Earl of Warwick and the widow of Prince Edward of Westminster. The match must have immediately appealed to Edward. The Warwick inheritance was vast and sprawling. If it were to fall to Warwick's daughters, it would have ended up in the hands of Isabel's husband, the untrustworthy George. The solution was to find a husband for Anne, but he would have to be someone Edward could trust implicitly, and someone capable of matching George, Duke of Clarence, the king's brother and member of the royal House of York. There were few men in the country who could satisfy all of those criteria. In fact, there was only one, and Edward needed something permanent and substantial with which to reward his conspicuously loyal youngest brother. It seemed like the perfect solution, but there were problems.

As Sir John Paston's letter above reveals, George was not willing to part with any portion of Warwick's inheritance, though he had no objection to his brother marrying his sister-in-law. Isabel and Anne were Warwick's co-heirs so any attempt to prevent Anne's husband acquiring an interest in Warwick's estate in right of his wife would require a subversion of the laws of inheritance. George was smarting from his courting, building up and then (it must have seemed to him)[3] abandonment by Warwick. The sting had been increased by his isolation during the readeption when he had lost land to returning Lancastrian nobles and had failed to receive offices he had been promised. Having successfully negotiated a return to the side of his brothers, which appears to have cost him nothing, the duke must nevertheless have been painfully aware that he was doomed to be eyed with a natural suspicion that threatened his position now that peace was returning. George's reaction to the suggestion that Richard might marry Anne Neville is superficially petulant, greedy and subversive, all traits widely applied to George himself. But the arrogant response was more likely to have been a defensive, frightened reaction to the realisation of his fears that he might be punished for his treachery once the war was won. In this, he overlooked Edward's capacity for forgiveness, something he indulged to a fault all too often. As the opening gambit in a negotiation, George's position is also entirely understandable.

George had reason to fear for his position. His actions suffered immensely in any comparison to his younger brother's behaviour and performance over the past months and years. George probably dwelt on the contrast more than anyone else. If he did, it could only have served to deepen his fears and entrench his sullen defiance. His hope lay in the apparent willingness of Edward to ignore the rules of inheritance.

On 18 May 1471, Richard was granted the office of Great Chamberlain of England[4] that had previously belonged to Warwick. The post sat above that of Constable, so it was a prestigious early reward for Richard's hard work and loyalty that provided him with much needed additional income. It is a signal of the length and complexity of the negotiations that followed that a year and two days later, Richard surrendered the office to George, as part of the attempts to reach a settlement agreeable to all.

The grant of a vacant office of state to Richard was neither striking nor unexpected in the months after Edward's return to the throne. Of more concern to George, and anyone else with a weather eye on the adherence to the laws of inheritance,[5] were other grants made to Richard. On 14 July 1471, Edward granted Richard and his heirs male 'the castles, manors and lordships of Midelham and Scyrefhoton, co. York, and the castle and lordship of Penreth, with their members and all other lordships, manors and lands in those counties which were entailed to Richard Neville, late earl of Warwick.'[6] Middleham and Sheriff Hutton formed the core of the Neville patrimony.

The primary problem with this grant, technical though it may have been, lay in the timing. Edward was pre-empting what at the time must have been the assumed impending attainder of Warwick and probably Montagu too. Once their lands were seised by such a legal mechanism, they would be available for the king to distribute as patronage to reward those he wished to acknowledge. When the grant was made, the lands were not subject to an attainder, and so Edward jumped the gun in granting them to Richard. This might have rung alarm bells to those concerned by the correct administration of such matters, but Edward lacked the time and security to observe such niceties. The loss of the senior Neville males, with the exception of George Neville, Archbishop of York, who was furiously trying to prove his readjusted loyalty, left the king with a huge power vacuum in the north.

The Earl of Northumberland might have felt entitled. He had, after all, kept the region from assaulting Edward on his return by his own inaction. Yet inaction was not encouragement enough, and this Henry Percy was from a Lancastrian family only very recently, and for the specific purpose of curtailing Neville influence in the north, reinstated to his earldom. Allowing the Percy family to add the swathes of Neville properties to their own risked recreating the same problem but wearing a different livery badge.

Edward had a fortnight earlier made a grant to Richard in similar terms of Middleham, Sheriff Hutton and Penrith,[7] which was replaced quickly by this fuller gift. The haste demonstrates that Edward was in a bind. He needed that vacuum in the north filled before Neville retainers began to cohere around someone else. In the worst case scenario, that would be Northumberland, who could set about collecting former Neville men to his own retinue. Before his expulsion from England, it was Richard who had been relied on by the king as a trouble-shooter, being parachuted into problematic areas to represent, restore and enforce royal authority. After his demonstrations of capability during the Barnet and Tewkesbury campaigns, Edward need look no further for a solution to the problem in the north, even if it was meant to be temporary. Richard's swift deployment there is demonstrated by the Bastard of Fauconberg's arrival in the region in Richard's custody. The Bastard had been well-liked in the south-east, he was a soldier, a leader and an able sailor in the Channel, but the fact that he was sent to the Neville heartlands when the Neville faction lacked an adult male leader betrays either a lack of thought or of options on the king's part. His swift involvement in some new treachery might have been expected, though not necessarily unwelcome as an excuse to be quickly rid of him.

This moment is often considered a defining one for Richard, setting him up for the rest of his life in lands he controlled, supported by men devoted to him, initially at least, because they were loyal to his wife, Anne. On the ground in the second half of 1471, that cannot have been the case. Richard had been sent to a region that had been in upheaval for two years and where the balance of power was shifting and teetering dangerously. He was not married to Anne Neville at this point, though he may have begun to see the benefit of such a match in bringing the Neville lands further under his control and establishing a more permanent claim to them. Richard had been pushed from pillar to post in his brother's cause, apparently entirely willingly, but he must now have hoped for something enduring to build a future on. The vacuum in Yorkshire created an opportunity for him in an area where the royal writ was notoriously weak. In that lay both freedom and the chance to better represent and serve his brother. For now, though, he was an interloper in territory that might be made hostile in a moment by an incursion into Neville authority or by an opportunistic action by Henry Percy, Earl of Northumberland.

Throughout the summer, rewards and honours continued to steadily build for Richard. On 8 July he was amongst those, including the queen; George; Robert Stillington, Bishop of Bath and Wells; Anthony Woodville,

Earl Rivers; and Lord Hastings, who were appointed administrators of the principality of Wales and the Duchy of Cornwall until the king's new son reached the age of fourteen.[8] Richard's associates were also put to work in Wales, where the young William Herbert, Earl of Pembroke, and his experienced uncle, Walter Devereux, were appointed to 'receive into the king's allegiance all rebels of South Wales and the marches'. Arch Lancastrians Henry Holland, Duke of Exeter, Jasper Tudor, former Earl of Pembroke, and several others were excluded from the offered pardon.[9] On 4 December, the lack of certainty in Richard's immediate future was accentuated by a grant of a clutch of estates and lordships in Essex, Kent, Hertfordshire, Cambridgeshire, Buckinghamshire, Oxfordshire and Cornwall that had been seized, though again not yet legally by the king, from John de Vere, Earl of Oxford, and other rebels in the regions.[10]

Amongst this uncertainty, Richard pursued the idea of marriage to Anne Neville. When the thought first occurred to Richard is unknown, and it remains unclear who initiated the contact between the two. This ambiguity has provided room for unsubstantiated guesswork that tends, predictably, to try to portray Richard as either an acquisitive monster or a romantic hero. The likelihood is that the truth lies somewhere in between. The champions of the black legend see only a ruthless, greedy nobleman keen to get his hands on the most valuable inheritance in England, whilst those who favour the white knight see him selflessly riding to the rescue of a damsel in distress. Neither of those is correct. It may have been Anne who first opened communications on the matter. Her concerns would have been almost precisely in line with those of Edward. If she were to take another husband and hope to prise her rightful share of the Warwick inheritance from George and Isabel, her new husband would have to be able to match George in standing and authority. Only one bachelor in all England offered such an opportunity. Anne had been taken after Tewkesbury with Queen Margaret, and could have been able to make contact with Richard, a boy she had known, even if only in passing, from his time in her father's household. We can place them seated at the same table during George Neville's enthronement feast in September 1465 and even if they had not been in each other's company beyond this, it was a moment Anne could cling to.

Alternatively, Richard may have broached the subject with the king first. If he did so, it might have been with an eye to Anne's inheritance, or to her personal safety. Perhaps he had his mind on both. Suggesting they had been genuinely in love since his time at Middleham as a child is probably stretching this a little too far, though it cannot be disproved. The most probable line is that Richard knew Anne represented his best hope of a substantial block of lands and influence. He knew that George might pose a threat to the peace of the realm and to the delicate, newly sown unity of the House of York if he was allowed to keep the entire Warwick inheritance. In this, he would surely have Edward's agreement. None of this need negate a degree of personal feeling for Anne, whether that might be a fledgeling form of love or even of responsibility. Despite Warwick's betrayal, he had been an important figure in Richard's life and a feeling that he ought to take care of Warwick's daughter could have affected his thinking. The truth is most likely to have been a tangled amalgamation of all of these considerations. Anne was Richard's best route to the acquisition of lands that would set him up for life. A union with her would help his brother reduce the potential threat George might pose, a problem that might be increased by holding all of Warwick's former power. She was also a young girl he had known as a child and one he may have liked enough to feel he could build a happy future with. Even if he had no personal affection for her, as mentioned in Chapter 6, his reading of texts such as the copy of *Ipomedon* that he owned and in which he had inscribed the personal motto '*Tant Le Desiree*', 'I have longed for it so much', demonstrates an awareness of chivalric expectations as to the rescue and protection of a damsel in distress. A copy of the New Testament owned by Richard, and now kept in the New York Public Library, bears the motto '*A Vous My Ly*', 'I am bound to you' in his own hand. It is undated, but it is interesting to consider whether it derives from this period when marriage was at the forefront of his mind, and he could satisfy chivalric requirements by positioning himself as Anne's protector, bound to her in some way that could, conceivably, have been love, at least of the courtly kind.

The notion that Richard did, in some way, rescue Anne is given credence by the *Crowland Chronicle*. It is another instance worthy of note because of the poor opinion the writer is believed to have held of Richard in later years. The chronicler, unable to resist a dig at Richard for the 'craftiness' he perceived, nevertheless reduces the protracted negotiations between all the parties to a romantic vignette. The writer acknowledges that George opposed the marriage because it threatened the inheritance he hoped to have for himself. To this end, 'he [George] caused the damsel to be concealed, in order that it might not be known by his brother where she was.'[11] The plan was foiled when 'the craftiness of the duke of Gloucester so far prevailed, that he discovered the young lady in the city of London disguised in the habit of a cookmaid; upon which he had her removed to the sanctuary of Saint Martin's.'[12] The ambiguity in this account is frustrating and lies in Richard taking Anne from George's custody into 'sanctuary'. It is possible that there was an element here of Anne being abducted from one state of confinement to another by brothers squabbling over a valuable commodity. That seems to be making too much effort to see malice in Richard's actions, since sanctuary at St Martin's, presumably St Martin's le Grand in London, was not the same as placing Anne into another place under his control. The implication at least is that she then had a degree of freedom greater than in her previous state of custody. Once more, this would have been in Edward's interests as well as any Richard had at this stage, since hiding her hinted at a jealous unwillingness to share the Warwick inheritance on George's part.

The Crowland Chronicle offers little more detail of the prolonged disputes that followed, saying only that 'such violent dissensions arose between the brothers' that Edward was forced to mediate. The writer, reputedly a doctor of canon law, shows a good deal of admiration for the legal arguments advanced by both parties in the course of clashes that he does not characterise as violent, but rather as debates on technical legal points. He reports that 'so many arguments were, with the greatest acuteness, put forward on either side, in the king's presence, who sat in judgment in the council-chamber, that all present, and the lawyers even, were quite surprised that these princes should find arguments in such abundance by means of which to support their respective causes.'[13] The protracted and in-depth wrangling seems to have been very real, and the issues involved are complex. The inability to resolve all of them in a manner satisfactory to all led Edward to a scruffy and ill-fitting solution. George was reluctant to let go of any lands and must have made demands in return as he conceded some parcels, including the office of Lord Chamberlain taken from Richard. But there were more abstract problems that proved far more intractable than the brothers. The first problem was that the portion of the Warwick inheritance Edward appeared to be eyeing for Richard, and which the duke may well have desired for himself, was entailed to the male line of the Neville family. This meant that legally, the inheritance of the Neville patrimony did not belong to Isabel and Anne Neville, but to their cousin George Neville, the young son of John Neville, Marquis Montagu. Warwick's brother's son was the next male heir and would therefore legally inherit the entire estate. It is doubtful that Edward was keen on the Neville faction retaining control of such a power base and equally certain that George and Richard would not accept the loss.

It has been widely argued that George and Richard pressed Edward not to attaint Warwick and Montagu in the wake of Barnet. The suggestion is that they preferred to inherit by right of their wives rather than receive the lands as gifts from the king. This had an attraction; a grant from the king might be taken back as easily as it was given, or by a further change of fortune or government, yet it posed problems too. Acquiring the properties by right of inheritance offered them protection from the winds of political change, but left them with the problem that legally, the legacy belonged to George Neville. The brothers, in fact, had a greater interest in receiving the forfeited lands of an attainted traitor directly from the king, since the acquisition would be clean and free from the possibility of challenge. It may have been that Edward was more interested in restricting his brothers, in particular George, but without being able to treat the two differently. It is clear that George was receiving no worse treatment than Richard despite their very different parts in recent events. In this, we see a rare consistency in Edward IV's approach, previously noted in his treatment of the Harrington family against the Stanley family. Even when preferential treatment was warranted or merited, it was not necessarily forthcoming.

Whatever legal wranglings and sibling bickering were indulged, a resolution was always going to be reached and it was likely to see half the inheritance given to each brother. All that was to be settled was precisely how this would be achieved.

The precise date at which Richard and Anne were finally married is not recorded, but it is believed to have been around May or June 1472. It must have been a low-key affair, perhaps to avoid irritating George with a public display. The issue of the inheritance had to be settled. The Neville entail needed to be dealt with, and it is here that a critical and frequently overlooked seed of future problems was sown. The Act of Parliament granting Richard his portion of the Neville inheritance was passed on 23 February 1473. It is here that we see the first reference to Edward having refrained from attainting John Neville 'at the humble request and prayer, aswell of his right dere brother Richard, duc of Gloucestr, and other lordes of his blode, as of other his lordes.'[14] The Act lists the castles, manors and estates Richard will receive as a result of the negotiations that had been going on for more than a year. Essentially, he acquired the northern part of the Warwick inheritance, the Neville lands, centred on Middleham and Sheriff Hutton in Wensleydale. Richard had already been working to establish himself there, and the fact that it was so isolated from royal authority and offered a degree of autonomy is the most likely reason that it went to Richard instead of George. The Neville title of Earl of Salisbury did not form part of this settlement, but it was an immense acquisition that was the culmination of years of Neville work, and it promised to provide Richard with a bright and prosperous future.

The devil was in the detail. Quite why Richard and George agreed to the same clauses being inserted is unfathomable. After all the intense negotiations, it was either an oversight, which is unlikely given the legal nature of the arguments provided, or a mechanism that Edward would not budge from. Edward built in safeguards that established the potential for a radical shift in the brothers' titles. The first hint appears early in Richard's grant, before the extensive list of his new properties. The Act stated that Richard was to 'have, hold, possese and enyoie to him and his heires of his body laufully begoten, also long as there be any heire mayle begoten of the body of the said marquys.'[15] In case the implications of the passing reference should be unclear, it was more fully explained at the end of the grant.

Also it is ordeyned by the said auctorite, that if the said issue male of the body of the said John Nevill, knyght, begoten or comyng, dye withoute issue mayle of their bodies comyng, lyfyng the said duc; that then the said duc to have and enyoie all the premisses for terme of his lyfe.[16]

The clause appears almost nonchalant, as though it was an afterthought, but it radically altered the nature of Richard's interests in the vast majority of his possessions over the following decade and played a critical part in the momentous events of 1473. This final statement was ostensibly designed to protect the Neville male heirs from any violent act of precaution on the part of Richard or George. It also gave lip service to the legal fact that the patrimony belonged, by right and in equity, to George Neville, the son of John Neville, because of the failure to attaint his father. The effect of this measure was that Richard only retained the ability to pass on his lands while there were heirs male of the body of John Neville, Marquis Montagu. In 1483, this rested entirely on the twelve-year-old shoulders of George Neville, Duke of Bedford. If George died without producing a male heir, Richard's interest in the Neville inheritance reverted to a life interest only. That would leave him with nothing to bequeath to any of his own children and give the reversion of the estate to the Crown.

When George's settlement was ratified in Parliament on the following day, 24 February 1473, it contained the same construct. George received only a small part of the Neville inheritance, including the earldom of Salisbury and some property in London and Essex. The northern block was given wholesale to Richard, so the effect of the clause on George was vastly reduced. Had our history, then their future, fallen differently, the provision may have meant nothing and been correctly forgotten. The lack of foresight from Edward in never doing anything to remove the Sword of Damocles he dangled over his youngest brother points to a fault in a man who seemed not to look beyond his own lifetime at any point. The fact that it was allowed to so directly affect his loyal brother but have little bearing on the treacherous George is an example of the consistent failure to reward good behaviour that marked Edward's reign.

The lesser interest of George in the Neville inheritance was due to the fact that Edward had settled on him the bulk of the Beauchamp and Despenser lands that belonged to Warwick's widow, Anne Beauchamp. Warwick had held the title by which he is remembered by right of his wife, and she had brought swathes of land in the Midlands and the West Country to their marriage. Anne Beauchamp was trapped in sanctuary at Beaulieu Abbey following her husband's death and the collapse of the Lancastrian faction. She was the rightful owner of lands now being dispensed by the king, and she had a right to a dower interest in the Neville patrimony of her husband too. Edward achieved his end with some murky legal trickery that allowed Anne Beauchamp's property to be distributed between her daughters as though she was dead. Legally, she was declared deceased by Parliament in 1474. The Act provided that George, Isabel, Richard and Anne were able to 'hensforth have, possese, enherit and enjoy, as in the right of their seid wyfes, all honours, lordships, castels, townes, maners, londes, tenementes, liberties, fraunchises, possessions and enheritaments, which were or be belongyng to the seid Anne, countes of Warwyk, or any other persone or persones to hir use; to have and to hold to the seid dukes, and their seid wyfes, and to the heires of their seid wyfes, in like maner and fourme, as yf the seid countes were nowe naturally dede.'[17] Perhaps of some concern to Anne was the additional provision that if Richard were to subsequently divorce her, this Act would remain in place as though no divorce had taken place, meaning that Richard would keep what he had gained, not her.[18]

For Anne Beauchamp, this was an horrendous violation of her rights. It left her destitute, deprived her of the significant wealth that was rightfully hers and created a situation in which she was legally dead. The countess was so terrified by the moves against her that she wrote to Parliament to plead her case from Beaulieu Abbey. Anne complained that she had been forced into sanctuary 'for none offence by her done,' though she appears to have been intimately involved in Warwick's machinations, but 'for surety of her person, to dispose for the weal and health of the soul of her said lord and husband, as right and conscience required her so to do.' Due to the 'absence of clerks' available to her, the countess had been forced to write in her own hand to the queen, the king's mother, the king's oldest daughter, Elizabeth, who was then about six or seven years old. She had written to the king's sisters, the queen's mother and other ladies as well as 'the king's brethren', presumably meaning her two sons-in-law. The appeal to women of power to help mediate with the king was entirely standard practice and might be expected to work, but Anne Beauchamp was managing to overlook the treachery her husband, and to some extent she, had been involved in. Her lands might have been seised under an act of attainder as Warwick's might, but she grasped at the fact that no attainder was forthcoming to try to get back what was hers. She asked Parliament 'to ponder and weigh in your consciences her right and true title of her inheritance, as the earldom of Warwick and Spencer's lands, to which she is rightfully born by lineal succession, and also her jointure and dower of the earldom of Salisbury.'[19]

It was a pitiful plea from a woman sorely treated, but it fell on deaf ears. Edward had no intention of allowing Anne Beauchamp to keep what had been hers any more than he would permit the Neville family to retain their northern lands. What Richard made of the business is not known, but he cannot have been too concerned since his own future was to be built from the ruins of Warwick and his wife's possessions. If he was callous in this, then it was to no greater extent than George, and it is Edward who was willing to ride roughshod over the rules of natural justice and the laws of inheritance to endow his brothers, an action that also served to reinforce his own position. Anne's pleas may have been little more than hopeful attempts to get some form of livelihood. If she were any kind of political realist, which, after so many years married to Warwick she could have become, then she would see the way the wind was blowing when the Neville inheritance was divided between her sons-in-law despite better claims to it. The countess may have felt that an appeal to the king's chivalric duty to protect women in need would give her a way out of her elective sanctuary at Beaulieu Abbey, but in this, she underestimated – or overestimated – Edward.

James Tyrell collected Anne Beauchamp from Beaulieu in June 1473, and she travelled north to join the household of her newly married son-in-law and daughter. George was apparently displeased by this development, perhaps fearing that his younger brother's influence might cost him some portion of the Beauchamp and Despenser lands.[20] What Richard made of having his mother-in-law to stay cannot be known, but she remained under their roof for the next ten years. When the countess travelled to join Richard's household, it seems to have given rise to rumours that she planned to give all of her lands to Richard, but she was no longer in a position to dispose of them at all. The Warwickshire antiquarian and historian of the Earls of Warwick, John Rous, would later claim that Anne Beauchamp had 'fled to him [Richard] as her chief refuge and he locked her up for the duration of her life.'[21] Given that his mother-in-law outlived Richard, the latter charge is impossible, and perhaps the embellishment of a man writing after 1485, when Anne Beauchamp was pursuing access to her former lands from Henry VII. The nature of the countess's stay with Richard and Anne cannot now be known, but simple imprisonment seems unlikely. Anne Neville may have been motivated by familial affection and a desire to protect her mother. Even Richard might have had some concern for the mistress of the household in which he had received his tutelage. Henry VII would later remember with fondness the care he had been given by the Countess of Pembroke in his own youth. Seeking out a sinister motive for providing a home to Anne Beauchamp is looking for base motive when it is not there. George is never criticised for failing to aid his mother-in-law, yet Richard, who even Rous suggested was viewed by Anne Beauchamp as 'her chief refuge' receives scorn in some quarters for taking care of a lady left destitute to his profit. If nothing else, in this he was able to fulfil a chivalric duty to protect those less fortunate than himself.

All did not go well in the wake of the settlement of the Neville inheritance. On 6 November 1473, Sir John Paston again wrote to his kinsman John Paston from London and informed him that 'the worlde semyth qweysye heer.'[22] The source of this queasiness was that all of the lords in London had sent for their armour and weapons, their harness, in preparation for what seemed like imminent trouble. Sir John names the instigator of these difficulties as George, writing that 'the Duke off Clarance makyth hym bygge.' It seems that George had decided to voice his disapproval at something by stomping around the capital with armed men telling anyone who would listen that he was going to 'dele with the Duke of Glowcester'. Edward was resolved to prove himself 'as bygge as they bothe' and have the matter resolved, but the fact that men were taking up arms suggests London was on the brink of erupting into violence. This moment came some nine months after the settlement of the Neville estates in the north on Richard, though such a delay was a characteristic of George's outrage that would reach a peak in a few years' time. Sir John hints that many thought there was some fresh treason behind the posturing, but ends the report with his typical, stoic sentiment that 'what shall falle, can I nott seye.'[23] George was in an increasingly uncomfortable position of lingering suspicion that was roused by his every action. If his annoyance at Richard's share in February did lie behind this incident, it might help to explain the rough dealing Anne Beauchamp was to receive in the following year to ensure George could enjoy access to her inheritance.

The threat of fresh violence on George's part may have been behind a commission sent by Edward to Richard on 10 September 1473 requiring him 'to array the king's lieges of the county of York and bring them to the king's presence with all speed when required.'[24] Edward seems to have been expecting trouble of some kind and preparing an armed response by Richard should it be realised. By 22 November, though, it seems this flash in the pan within the capital had blown over without any actual violence. When Sir John Paston wrote again on this date, there was no more mention of armed men in the streets. He commented only that 'I trust to God that the ii Dukes of Clarans and Glowcester shall be sette att one by the adward off the Kyng.'[25] Edward had gone some way to take the sting out of George's rage, suggesting that entire display had been a negotiating tactic on the duke's part, which had brought the result he had wanted. This letter contains another interesting report from Sir John. He notes, 'I hope by means of the Duke of Glowcester that my Lord Archebyshop shall come home.' George Neville, Archbishop of York, had been pardoned and released in the wake of Edward's return to the throne but was later sent to Guisnes Castle at Calais as a prisoner on suspicion of indulging in some new intrigue with the Earl of Oxford. Oxford was, at this moment, occupying St Michael's Mount off the Cornish coast, forcing Edward to send men to lay siege to the tidal island. Sir John suggests that Richard was providing support to secure the Archbishop's return.

As with so many of his actions, Richard's motives for involvement here are hard to fathom; not because there are none obvious, but because there are several competing possibilities. George Neville was his wife's uncle, and Richard perhaps felt that he had acquired a responsibility to champion the interests of a Neville clan bereft of secular adult males. Any broaching of the subject with Edward might have been at Anne's behest or at his own volition if he took such a burden seriously. It is a mark of his high favour with his brother that he felt comfortable to raise the issue of securing freedom for a man who had changed sides as often as George Neville had. Richard was already developing a reputation for conspicuous piety and may have felt uncomfortable at the prolonged imprisonment, which may have been on the basis of little real evidence, of a high-ranking churchman. A more cynical analysis might suggest that Richard was hoping to secure George Neville's release in order to strengthen his own position in his new home. Lingering sentiment for the Neville family of his new wife was something Richard had to rely on to establish himself as the new dominant force in their former lordships. Securing the release of George Neville would serve to prove himself as the champion of the family's waning fortunes. Furthermore, George was the region's Archbishop, the spiritual head of the community. He seems to have been well liked and well respected in this regard, and a genuinely dedicated shepherd to his flock as well as a campaigner for learning. In securing his return, Richard would improve his own standing in the local community and the region as a whole. Demonstrating his influence over the king could only improve the standing of the new Lord of the North.

It is unlikely that Richard's actions here were entirely altruistic. It is equally improbable that they were based solely on what he could gain from them. Like any other person, his motives and reasoning were most likely to be a complex mixture of the two that led him to arrive at a balanced decision. By petitioning his brother the king for the release of George Neville, Richard could fulfil his obligations to his wife and the broader Neville affinity. At the same time, it would do his reputation in the region no harm at all. There was a potential downside to associating himself with a suspected traitor in this way. Edward might be wary of Richard falling too deeply into the Neville nexus and going the same way as their brother George, so he took a risk in approaching the king with a request like this. If most of Richard's actions could be viewed in the same way as this – that his motives were neither purely selfless nor entirely evil – then the real man behind the veils of varying myths will begin to emerge: a man of his times making his way in a hard world.

Accusations that Richard mistreated the Countess of Warwick are unfair. At worst, he benefitted from the king's subversion of the law, and it was Richard who provided her with a home that allowed her to leave sanctuary. If, as Crowland asserts, George had already kidnapped

Anne Neville to secure himself a more substantial settlement, then her mother may have had reason to fear falling into his hands too. There is another countess who received Richard's close attention at this time, and his motives in this had less to recommend them. At the end of 1472, Richard was twenty years old. He was about to have the paperwork sealed on his Neville inheritance but remained, for now, short of ready cash and income. The previous year, he had received much of the lands of the attainted Earl of Oxford but the earl's mother, the elderly dowager countess, Elizabeth Howard, was then in her sixties and living within the nunnery at Stratford le Bow. Richard visited her there and ordered her to sign over all of her property to him. He had her moved to Stepney, where he was lodged at the time, and later on to Walbroke, all the time warning her that her only hope of release lay in signing over her property. She finally signed, and when Oxford later petitioned Henry VII for the return of her lands, he insisted that Richard had bullied his mother into handing over her dower share and any lands she held in her own right.[26] One of the countess feoffees, Henry Robson, would later claim that she had told him that Richard had threatened to send her next to Middleham, where she feared the cold would kill her.

The episode brought Richard twenty-eight manors worth around £600 per year.[27] It was one of the countess's manors at Foulmire that Richard would gift to Cambridge University to help fund the prayers for his comrades who had fallen at Barnet and Tewkesbury. The treatment of the elderly countess is an unpleasant smear on Richard's reputation, particularly in comparison to his apparent care for his mother-in-law and even George Neville. It is to be wondered how greatly the case before Parliament in 1485 was exaggerated. In 1474, after the countess's death, Richard claimed in Chancery that he had provided her with an annuity of £500, paid her debts to the tune of £240 and helped to promote one of her other sons at Cambridge University, which is perhaps why he felt it appropriate to use Foulmire as a gift. Whether Richard did, in fact, provide these benefits in return for the resignation of her right to her lands cannot be ascertained. If he did, then it was more than he needed to do, perhaps a salve to his conscience or a bribe to get the countess's signature, but possibly in line with his reasonable treatment of widows deprived of their property. In this instance, there is no evidence that Edward instigated the removal of the Countess of Oxford's lands as he had with those of the Countess of Warwick, but neither can he have disapproved. The Earl may have taken to piracy in the Channel, attempted his failed invasion of the south coast and subsequent occupation of St Michael's Mount because of the treatment of his elderly mother at Richard's hands. It is to be remembered, though, that the de Vere family were ardent Lancastrians who could not be reconciled to Edward IV's rule. The earl's father and older brother had been executed a decade earlier, and the present earl was an attainted traitor at large and trying to harrass Edward's borders. It is feasible that the countess was using her reasonably substantial income to support her son's activities and that this lay behind the desire to have her property removed. Richard may have had reasonable grounds, and the king's permission, to act in the way that he did, but he was nevertheless unkind to an elderly lady. Yet that elderly lady was a devoted enemy of the House of York, and that alone may have been enough to justify her treatment, in Richard's mind and the minds of his contemporaries. Edward would no longer tolerate threats to his crown, and it is likely that the desire for security motivated Richard too. If he provided the countess with the income and assistance he claimed he did, then he was more generous than he was required to be. Richard's treatment of the Countess of Oxford was an unpleasant episode that remains a stain on his character. All that can be offered in his defence is that he could have treated her an awful lot worse had he wished.

There is a small matter in relation to the marriage of Richard and Anne that casts a long shadow, particularly reaching into the darker corners of events in 1483. In 1468, Warwick had managed to obtain the papal dispensation for the marriage between George and Isabel required by the degree of their relationship to each other. George and Isabel were first cousins once removed and were related in the second and third degrees as well as in the third and fourth degrees. George's mother Cecily Neville was not only the sister of Isabel's grandfather Richard Neville, Earl of Salisbury, but she was also her great-niece's godmother. With the exception of that final consideration, Richard and Anne Neville were related in precisely the same degrees of relationships, with the added complication of relation by affinity, because Richard's brother was already married to Anne's sister. The relationships of in-laws were sometimes considered to create impediments similar to those of blood relations. It was a tangled business, but it was perfectly clear that Richard and Anne would require a papal dispensation for their marriage in order to make it legal and acceptable to the Church. For a long time, it has been asserted that no dispensation was ever obtained for Richard and Anne to marry and that their union was, therefore, unsanctioned by the Church, opening up the possibility that it, and any children they would have, were illegitimate. Strict and proper legitimacy was a preoccupation of the medieval nobility, and of Richard in particular, as would be demonstrated in 1483.

In 2006, a dispensation was, in fact, discovered amongst the newly available archives of the Papal Penitentiary.

Rome [at St. Peter's], 10 calends of May. Richard, Duke of Glouirestere, layman of the diocese of Lincoln, and Anne Neville, woman of the diocese of York, wish to contract matrimony between them, but because they are joined together in the third and fourth degrees of affinity therefore they asked to be dispensed with this. Also with declaratory [letter] upon third and fourth.[28]

The degrees of relationship are measured from a common ancestor. Prohibitions existed where a couple shared a common ancestor up to four generations into the past. They were therefore required to trace their lineage from their great-great-grandparents and find the points where they shared a direct relative. First cousins would be related in the second degree, since their shared ancestor, a grandparent, was two generations back. First cousins once removed would be related to each other in the second and third degree, because one would need to go back an additional generation to find the common link. Richard and Anne, like George and Isabel, were related in the second and third degrees because their shared ancestor was Ralph Neville, Earl of Westmorland. He was Richard's maternal grandfather, a second degree, and Anne's paternal great-grandfather, a third degree. Richard and Anne were also related in the third and fourth degrees because they shared descent from Edmund of Langley, 1st Duke of York. Edmund was Richard's great-grandfather and Anne's great-great-grandfather, falling just within the limits that required assessment. So this discovery solves the problem.

In fact, it does not. The dispensation is specifically to absolve the issue of *affinity* in the third and fourth degrees. Relationships by affinity are different to those of blood, consanguinity, and this dispensation removes explicitly an impediment of affinity that had been created by Anne Neville's previous marriage to Prince Edward. It does not remove any prohibition generated by the blood relationship between Richard and Anne. Marriage and the presumed sexual relations that accompanied it created an affinity between the widow and any relative of her dead spouse that stretched back four generations. In this case, Ricard was related to Prince Edward in the third and fourth degrees. Their shared ancestor was John of Gaunt, who was Richard's great-grandfather through the Beaufort line and Prince Edward's great-great-grandfather through the line of the House of Lancaster, thereby creating the affinity between Richard and Anne, as Prince Edward's widow, in the third and fourth degrees excused by this dispensation. It is also possible to argue that George's marriage to Isabel had created an impediment of affinity in the first degree, though this is less certain under canon law.[29]

We are lacking definitive evidence of a papal dispensation for the consanguinity between Richard and Anne. There are reasons to doubt the absence of such a provision, but they must be taken on faith and cannot be proven. Although no trace has been found amongst papal records of George and Isabel's dispensation, it was widely discussed and accepted that Warwick had secured it on 14 March 1468. There is reason, and room, to suspect that the earl may have at the same time obtained precisely the same permission for Richard to marry Anne in case it was required. When Richard had been placed into the care of Warwick, it is possible that marriage to Isabel was being considered. At the time, George was being suggested for foreign matches and Isabel, the greatest heiress in England, was free and just a year older than Richard. Warwick may have considered a union between Anne and Francis, Lord Lovell, who joined Richard in the earl's household, before deciding he could find a higher ranking husband for her and marrying Francis to Warwick's niece, Anne FitzHugh. As the earl's problems mounted, he might have seized on a previous, unrecorded agreement that he could have some involvement in Richard's marriage to seek two dispensations at the same time.

The possibility that this was, in fact, the case was hinted at by the Milanese ambassador in London in August 1469. He reported that Warwick 'has married his two daughters to the king's two brothers, and last St. John's day the Duke of Clarence married his wife at Calais across the water.'[30] The account is either very poorly constructed in mentioning marriage twice, or it refers in the first instance to the obtaining of a papal dispensation, which the ambassador might reasonably assume formed part of a planned or contracted union, and in the second to the actual ceremony undertaken by George and Isabel. This left the second marriage incomplete but is at least suggestive of the existence of a dispensation relating to Richard and Anne, obtained at the same time as George and Isabel's, and still available in 1472. The paperwork may have been in the possession of Anne Beauchamp, Warwick's widow, or at least she may have known where it had been deposited. If so, it was a lure that might explain Richard's desire to secure her person and treat her well so that she would hand over the critical document. The countess may have used her one bargaining chip to her best advantage.

The preoccupation of medieval nobility with legitimacy should not be underestimated in an examination of Richard and Anne's marriage, though reliance on it here offers problems in 1483. Few noblemen would have been willing to risk allegation of illegitimacy arising against their claim to any lands their wife brought to the marriage and also against their children. In the early 1470s that was particularly pertinent to Richard, who was attempting to marry Anne and gain an interest in her inheritance entirely against the wishes of his brother George. If he failed to secure a suitable dispensation, he risked handing George ample ammunition to undo at a stroke anything he had achieved. The complete and enduring silence of George on the matter of the validity of his brother's marriage to Anne is perhaps the most substantial evidence for accepting the existence of a dispensation. The negotiations for a settlement were protracted and unpleasant, ending in the threat of violence in London in 1473. If George had a mechanism as simple as a failure to obtain a papal dispensation at hand to undermine his brother's position, it is impossible to believe that he would not have used it.

Furthermore, it seems unlikely that Richard and Anne would go to the trouble of obtaining the papal dispensation that has been discovered and fail to secure one for the far more prohibitive relationship between them of blood. It is implausible to suggest that they would petition for and successfully obtain permission from Rome that excused the relationship of affinity created by Anne's marriage to Prince Edward whilst utterly failing to address the blood relationship between them. Sometimes, the absence of evidence to the contrary must be accepted, or at least considered, as proof of an obscured or lost fact. In few instances is this more pertinent than in the story of Richard. So, although there is no evidence to prove that there were the correct papal dispensations for a marriage between Richard and Anne Neville, there is ample reason to believe that it must have existed.[31]

As Richard travelled north with his new wife, it was into a promising but uncertain future. He had some security, but it relied still on others. He might now be able to have legitimate children to join the illegitimate son and daughter he had already fathered. But in the broad, rolling Yorkshire moors, he would have to bring former Neville families under his wing, or at least under his authority. There was no guarantee that he would be accepted in the instant that he arrived. He lacked the hindsight that would inform him of the warm regard the region would hold him in for the next 500 years and more. The threat or rejection was real and mortal. In the two years before Edward had lost his throne, Richard had acted as a troubleshooter, dispatched to uneasy areas to solve problems for the king and to step on toes when required. That had been his training. This would be the real test of what he had learned. He would need to bring powerful, disaffected affinities who had little regard for the distant authority of the Crown under his influence. As he had been a few years earlier, he was placed into direct and unavoidable opposition in the north-west to the interests of Thomas, Lord Stanley, whose position was unshaken despite several apparent oscillations in his loyalty. If the recently rehabilitated Henry Percy, Earl of Northumberland, hoped for an increase in his authority and autonomy in the region with Edward's aid – or absence of opposition – and the fall of the Neville family, then Richard's arrival was a blow to his aspirations too. The young Duke of Gloucester had all of this to consider as he made his way to his new home in the north.

The writer of *The Crowland Chronicle* looked back on this episode, as the three brothers of the House of York squabbled and fought over the inheritances of their wives and their mother-in-law, with a lament that warrants repetition. His admiration for the legal arguments put forward by Richard and George is outlined above, and coming from a lawyer, it is praise indeed. It is because of this that he expresses sadness that their efforts were arrayed against each other instead of building a unified polity that would have endured and defied all dangers. With Edward as king in the south-east, George overseeing the south-west and Midlands and Richard keeping the north safe and secure, nothing could have threatened the Yorkist grip on power. The enigmatic chronicler describes the problem perfectly.

> In fact, these three brothers, the king and the two dukes, were possessed of such surpassing talents, that, if they had been able to live without dissensions, such a threefold cord could never have been broken without the utmost difficulty.[32]

It was a solid edifice, but built on sand. It stood for a season, but it would not last forever.

9

The Lord of the North

... prudent, dignified but sympathetic, truthful, energetic, just but tempered with mercy, courageous but not rash, moderate in all things, magnanimous and munificent in his undertakings, a generous but careful rewarder of the deserving, he should love honour, be humble and friendly while commanding respect, have an equal as his wife with whom he shares secrets and above all love the common good and the welfare of the state.

Aegidius Colonna's qualities of a prince,
De Regimine Principum

There was a wealth of advice available to the medieval nobleman seeking to learn his craft. Books collectively known as *Mirrors for Princes* had become popular and widely available. As Richard looked for help in his new undertaking, he could turn to these pages for suggestions on the correct way for a successful prince to behave and the perils of greed and tyranny that must be avoided. The notion of 'good lordship', the exercise of power and authority for the benefit of a nobleman's retainers, clients and those unable to protect themselves, has become synonymous with Richard throughout his time in the north. As the structure of feudalism, already dragged into a bastard form and devolving into a purely financial arrangement, crumbled in England, Richard's approach was different. The chivalric ideal of protecting the weak against the strong can be seen running through many of Richard's interactions and hint at a sense of noblesse oblige, the obligations imposed by the privileged position of the nobility, which he shared with his father. Equity was important to him. He was successful because he was different, but in a volatile world, difference was not always welcome.

That such thinking was a prominent part of Richard's approach early in his career is demonstrable. The reasons for it are less so, though they may lie in his lifelong love of books. Chivalric romances harked back to a time of knightly purity when the bonds between men were based on notions such as loyalty, service and duty rather than the grubbier form of livery and maintenance that characterised Richard's society. Service was increasingly given in return for money, and money was given to avoid the fulfilment of duty. The explosion in retaining men had become a demonstration of authority granted by wealth rather than the inspiration of loyalty through the operation of equitable 'good lordship'. In Warwick's opulence and power, this had reached a pinnacle that had cost a king his crown. If Richard hankered for a bygone age, which may never have really existed, in which knights fought together, side by side, to protect the weak, and in which war was something waged against other nations, not neighbours, it would be hard to blame him. Almost as soon as he arrived in the north, he set about realising these ideals. It is here, too, that the national figure of the king's brother begins to fade and the regional magnate and administrator comes to the fore.

There are two intriguing cases from the early days of Richard's northern autonomy that can demonstrate his interests and commitment, and they are particularly striking because they occur at a time when building a robust and loyal affinity at any cost might have preoccupied most in his position. The first of these cases arose during the Long Parliament that sat after Edward's return to the throne. A petition was entered by the Commons, which may have been sponsored by Richard, but which relates to a murder case; an unusual local criminal matter for Parliament to be concerned with.[1] Katherine Williamson of Howden, near York, explained that her husband, Richard Williamson, had been brutally murdered on 1 October 1472. He had been returning from Riccall when he reached Hemingborough and was obliged to wait for the Barnaby Ferry to cross the water there. Suddenly, her husband had been assaulted by three brothers 'defensibly arrayed, that is to say, with jakkes and salettes, and with force and armes, that is to say, with bowes, arrowes, swerdes and speres, of malice afore thought.' The men appear to have been known to Richard Williamson and are named in the petition as Robert, Richard and John Farnell, the sons of Thomas Farnell from Newsholme near Howden. They were perhaps aware that Williamson had been away on business and might be returning with cash, and so they had prepared an ambush at the ferry.

There is a gory account of the brutal and cruel attack on Williamson. The brothers 'havyng noo mercy ne pite of hym, with their swordes smote of booth the handes of the same Richard Williamson, and oon of his armes above the elbowe, and hym houghsynued [hamstrung], and hym so dedely woonded and lefte hym there for dede, of which strokes and dedely woondes the said Richard Williamson within short tyme after dyed.' The elements of excess cruelty suggest either a personal vendetta or a sadistic enjoyment in killing a man. Williamson was stabbed with a spear, had both his hands cut off, then one arm further severed above the elbow before he was hamstrung and left to die of his wounds. All that the brothers managed to make away with was a bow, a dozen arrows, a sword, a buckler and 10 shillings' worth of other goods. It was hardly the haul they might have expected, and the torture may have been an effort to force Williamson to disclose where whatever the brothers had expected him to have was hidden. The brothers fled back to their father at Newsholme, where he reportedly sheltered them despite knowing what they had all done that day.

It is now that Richard appears in the story. Thomas Farnell, no doubt panicking about the justice that would come looking for his sons, approached 'the right high and myghty prynce and full honorable lord Richard, duk of Gloucestr, to take and accept hym and all his said myschevous sonnes to his service'. The plan worked, and the reason for pursuing that course is plain, Thomas, 'entendyng by the same that he and his said sonnes shuld have been supported in their horrible felonye, murther and robbery,' aimed to rely on the duke to protect them from the repurcussions of his sons' actions. His expectation was neither unreasonable nor unusual. When a nobleman retained a man during the fifteenth century, it was becoming less to do with knightly bonds of brotherhood and service and increasingly about money and power. Livery and maintenance meant that a man entering the service of a lord would be provided with that lord's livery – the badges and colours that would show his allegiance. Maintenance, which had, in its more chivalric origins, meant that a lord was then responsible for feeding and caring for his retained man, had come to mean the expectation that the lord would protect his retainer from physical and legal attacks. Corruption became inevitable. A nobleman could attract those needing legal protection by saving them from prosecution in local courts the lord controlled, thus swelling his numbers, his authority and his influence using men with little regard for the law.

Thomas Farnell and his sons relied on this widely accepted norm of English late-medieval society to protect them. Why Richard rejected the idea is not known. Perhaps his time troubleshooting for Edward in 1468–70 had left him with a romantic longing for a better England. He had travelled up and down the west of England mixing with other young men like the Earl of Pembroke, under the guidance of experienced hands like that of Walter Devereux. His frequent moves had meant that he never needed to worry about building long-term bonds that might have required the compromise of high ideals. He had been a fixer for his brother, righting wrongs and punishing crimes. It may have left him with an unrealistic, romanticised image of the world that he had not shaken off, or which he was determined not to lose. The Farnell family entered Richard's service expecting, entirely reasonably, his protection. They, and perhaps northern society, at least within the bounds of Richard's new authority, were in for a shock.

The petition described Thomas 'callyng hym self servaunt to the said duc, and weryng his clothyng uppon hym, goten and had by sotill and crafty meanes.' The implication is that Richard had been unaware of the reasons for the men seeking entry into his service. When the duke was notified of their crimes at a later date, he immediately 'commaunded that the said Thomas shuld be brought unto the gaole of York, there to abide unto the tyme that he of the felonye, murther and robery aforeseid were lawfully acquite or atteynted.' Richard defied the accepted norms of livery and maintenance, choosing instead to send Thomas Farnell to prison to face charges. Thomas and his three sons were then required to appear before the court of King's Bench, their failure to do so to lead to their immediate convictions for the murder. Why did Richard fail to protect Thomas Farnell and his sons? He had nothing material to gain by sending them to face justice, in fact, he stood to lose the potential strength of a substantial affinity bound to him in a variety of ways that might include a rank of thugs, protected by him from the law and available to him to do his dirty work. As he tried to take the reins of the Neville patrimony, he might have been excused for turning a blind eye to win loyalty, but he cannot have wanted loyalty from this type of person. Evidently, that was not how Richard intended to operate. He had shown himself willing to be ruthless in the case of the Countess of Oxford, though he had at least claimed to have provided for her in return. Is it possible to see an interest in justice and equity that was so unusual during this period that it can be dismissed as a Ricardian dream? His reasons for acting the way that he did suggest some noble aim because he gained nothing but the affection of those without power, whom he might now represent, helping to balance the uneven scales of justice. Sadly, the outcome of the case is unknown.

Another example of Richard's attitude in relation to his affinity can be seen in a complex land dispute that brought him into potential opposition to his own mother Cecily, Dowager Duchess of York.[2] John Prince, a servant of Cecily's, and his wife Lucy, owned the manor of Gregories in Theydon Bois, located within Epping Forest in Essex. Their ownership of the property was challenged by Thomas Wethiale, a London goldsmith who had entered Richard's service. Wethiale had included Richard amongst those benefitting from the enfeoffment of Gregories, and his subsequent action suggests that he, like Thomas Farnell, planned to rely on the backup this should have brought him from his master. On 19 September 1474, Wethiale and almost two dozen others, all wearing Richard's livery, burst into Gregories 'defensibly arrayed in maner of werre'. John Prince fled, and the men began collecting cattle they planned to take. An indomitable Lucy returned to the property with a male servant, three women and a writ from the sheriff instructing them to cease. She boldly warned Wethiale that her husband 'is a servaunt with my lady the Kyngs mother and my lady will not be wele pleased with you.' One of Wethiale's associates scoffed 'We be servaunts to my lord of Gloucester, and he woll mayntene his servaunts as well as my lady hirs.' The men left with the cattle, though Wethiale returned a few days later to try to apprehend John Prince. Finding that he was not at Gregories, he told one of the men there 'Now shalt thou see whether of my lords man, or of my ladies, shall have the better.' He clearly intended to pit his master directly against Prince's mistress in an effort to win the battle.

Cecily's biographer Joanna Laynesmith has characterised the settlement of this matter as something of a model of a polite, amicable search for justice. Mother and son were in contact by letter throughout the affair, and whilst Cecily maintained her conviction that John and Lucy Prince were in the right, Richard was willing to admit that his man Wethiale may have acted incorrectly. The two offered assurances that the matter would be resolved by lawyers alone so that there would be no more violence involved.

John Howard, Cecily's steward at the time, met Richard's council in London but was forced to return to Calais before the dispute was settled. Richard and Cecily subsequently met face to face at Syon Abbey to discuss the problem further. When John Prince appeared before Richard's council to provide evidence of his case, Sir Robert Chamberlayne, a knight of the king's body and steward of Richard's East Anglian estates, tried to force the man to 'ende his matier' with Wethiale. Cecily immediately wrote from her home at Berkhamsted to Richard, thanking him for his diligence in the affair but asking him to keep Chamberlayne out of it, in line with their agreement that only lawyers should settle the matter. The duchess also wrote directly to Chamberlayne, politely requesting that he refrain from interfering further. It is possible the knight thought that in seeking a swift end to the problem, he was serving Richard and Cecily, yet both seemed satisfied to await the correct, legal outcome.

Eventually, it was agreed that two lawyers appointed by Cecily and two appointed by Richard would arbitrate and be allowed to decide the matter. John Prince named John Catesby as one of his representatives, probably the uncle of William Catesby who would later become closely associated with Richard. John Catesby and his colleague Roger Townsend argued their side persuasively because the matter was eventually settled entirely in John and Lucy Prince's favour. Wethiale was ordered to appear before King Edward's council to answer for his 'right grete riotes and misgovernances'. It is striking that Richard had not used the incident as a chance to measure his authority against the position of his mother. He was striking out on his own but displayed a conspicuous willingness to see justice done, even if it was against his own men. Wethiale's confidence that he had begun a fight his master was going to win on his behalf was sorely misplaced. Richard had again shown that his interest lay in equity and justice, not in flexing his own muscles in order to strengthen his own position. It is possible to argue that he knew he could not win the case, or that his mother had an undue influence over him. The simple facts show that in the cases of Thomas Farnell and Thomas Wethiale, Richard was willing to defy the accepted expectations of societal structures, preferring to promote justice, even at the cost of his own authority. It was novel, but it was dangerous too.

Offices and royal favour continued to flow to Richard. On 18 February 1472, he was appointed Sheriff of Cumberland for life, 'rendering to the king 100l yearly at the Exchequer without any other account.[3] The role of a sheriff in the counties lay in collecting taxation. Much of the murky reputation they have been left with in popular mythology, most notably Robin Hood's nemesis the Sheriff of Nottingham, derives from their role as tax collectors. Each year, a sheriff would have an assessment made of his region, and a figure of expected taxation was set. The sheriff was then responsible for delivering that amount to the Exchequer and providing complete accounts for the county. The opportunity for abuse lay in the sheriff's right to keep anything above the agreed target that he could collect for himself. The profitability of the office was, therefore, dependant on the incumbent sheriff's willingness to drive up tax revenue one way or another. Richard's appointment to the post in Cumberland set the annual return at 100l, with no mechanism for reassessment, and did not require him to submit any accounts for the county at the Exchequer. His opportunity to abuse the post was thus greatly increased, signifying either Edward's willingness to allow his brother a free hand in generating income irrespective of the way he went about it or faith that such abuse was not in Richard's nature. Other evidence to date seems to suggest that the latter is the more likely.

On 18 May 1472, the nineteen-year-old Richard was also appointed Keeper of the Forests beyond the Trent,[4] another office that brought him a reliable income and significant authority in the north of England. On the same date, Richard was given the custody and marriage of William Walgrave, the young heir of Thomas Walgrave[5] to add to his grant on 1 April of the wardship and marriage of Henry Marney.[6] These were the sons of knights rather than significant noblemen, but it was the first steps towards the establishment of a fully functioning household for Richard. He would need to build up networks of retainers and clients who would be loyal to him and, aside from the income the careful administration of their estates could bring, the wardship of boys was a method of influence that could produce long-term benefits. These grants may also have served to compensate and reassure Richard for the removal two days later of the office of Great Chamberlain, which seems to have formed part of the ongoing negotiations between Richard, George and Edward.

The king's urgent desire for war with France was making little progress against the burden of settling matters at home. On 20 June 1472, Anthony Woodville, Earl Rivers, was given permission to take 1,000 men-at-arms and archers to Brittany 'at his own expense', with an order that 'proclamation be made that anyone wishing to go to him has licence to do so'.[7] Edward was short of funds for the war he wanted, and Parliament was preoccupied with the restoration of law and order. Little has been remarked on Edward's relationship with Parliament, but he seems to have resented the control it had over his finances. The Chamber system of finance was primarily devised by Edward to drive more cash into his personal coffers and increase his flexibility in raising funds. Parliament was responsible for granting direct taxation, but would frequently want concessions from the monarch in return that Edward was either unwilling to give or too impatient to negotiate. During his twenty-three year reign, Parliament was only summoned seven times and the time that lapsed between sittings increased throughout his reign. In 1472, he wanted money to go to war with France, but he wasn't getting it. Hence Rivers was launching a campaign he was funding himself and the rumours reported by the Milanese ambassador in November 1472 that either George or Richard was going to lead an army over the Channel soon came to nothing.[8] On a constitutional note, tensions between the monarch and Parliament rarely ended well for the country.[9]

In 1473, Edward was considering the position of his son and heir Edward, the Prince of Wales. Even before his third birthday, preparations were underway to establish a novel training mechanism for the infant for the time when he would be king. Edward planned to set his son up at Ludlow, the old Mortimer and Yorkist stronghold on the border with Wales. There, he would have his own household and council to rule Wales and the Marches as though it were a miniature kingdom. It was a training ground designed to deliver the next Yorkist king fully prepared for some of the challenges Edward must have realised he had been ill-equipped to face. No king had really been concerned with the preparation of an heir for more than a hundred years, since Edward III had overseen the Black Prince's development. When the Black Prince died shortly before his father, his son became Richard II, though he had once been the younger of two brothers and there must have been some sense that it would be a while before he became king. When Henry IV took the throne, the future Henry V was already a teenager and would die when his son, who became Henry VI, was just nine months old. Edward IV had become king aged eighteen, without any preparation to rule. Edward's solution was bold and elegant, providing a microcosm in which his son could learn to build and maintain the network of connections he would need as king and to operate the levers of power at a reduced level, and under supervision, before he was thrust into the role of king.

With this in mind, on 20 February 1473, Richard was amongst those appointed as tutors and councillors to his young nephew, Prince Edward. George was named too, as was the queen, her brother Earl Rivers, the Archbishop of Canterbury, Edward's friend Lord Hastings and the Earl of Shrewsbury, who would provide local authority. Some of Richard's connections in the area were to serve the Prince too, including the reliable Sir Walter Devereux. The appointment gave them the power to represent the Prince's interests in Wales, the Duchy of Cornwall and Earldom of Chester but only to make temporary grants or appointments while the Prince remained under the age of fourteen.[10] It is worthy of note as a matter of some importance to later events that fourteen was deemed by the king and his council to be the appropriate age for the boy to begin to take control of his own affairs.

In June 1473, Richard was placed in an awkward position. He was given a commission by the king to secure the removal of the Harrington brothers from Hornby Castle.[11] Richard had stoutly defended them in 1470 when he had visited Hornby Castle and placed himself between Thomas Stanley's cannon and the Harrington family. Now, with Richard's increased authority in the north, he was instructed to see the king's will done. Edward was clearly unmoved by James Harrington's arrival at Nottingham with a substantial force during the campaign to win back his throne. Richard was joined on the commission by Northumberland, Shrewsbury and Lord Hastings, but some more familiar contacts joined him too. Sir William Parr (the grandfather of Queen Catherine Parr), who had come to Edward's side with James Harrington in 1471, was prominent. Sir John Huddleston was a former Sheriff of Cumberland and served alongside Richard in the role in 1476. Sir Ralph Ashton was Sheriff of Yorkshire in 1472 and would remain a close associate of Richard in the north. A Sir John Ashton, who was probably one of Ralph's two sons to bear that name, also served, as did Sir Ralph's future son-in-law, Sir John Trafford. It is easy to see a core of northern support taking shape around Richard by 1473 that must have been pleasing both to him and to Edward.

The group were required to 'take into the king's hands, all of the lands formerly belonging to Sir Thomas Harrington', who had died at the Battle of Wakefield with Richard's father. The commission explained that these lands had passed to Sir John Harrington, who had also died at Wakefield, after his father, and so to John's two daughters, Anne and Elizabeth. They were 'to remove James Haryngton, knight, and Robert Haryngton, knight, and others who have taken possession' of the inheritance, which included Hornby Castle.[12] James's attempts to oppose the order of death of his father and brother, and even to prove that the inheritance was entailed to the male Harrington line, failed. Thomas Stanley had gained legal control of the young Harrington heiresses and married them into his own family, Anne to his fifth son Edward Stanley, who would reside at Hornby Castle, and Elizabeth to one of his nephews, John Stanley. Although James managed to negotiate the retention of their manors at Farleton and Brierley, he was forced to hand Hornby Castle over to his enemy Thomas Stanley. Richard cannot have been pleased with being forced to deliver this judgement to a man he probably considered a friend, but Edward may have sent his brother precisely because of their friendship. James Harrington did not fall out of favour with Edward, and if he gambled that Richard would be able to resolve the long-running dispute without resort to force, then he was proven correct. The inequity Richard saw in operation against someone who had been a loyal servant of the House of York and in favour of a man whose allegiance was constantly in doubt must have grated, but as he had with the dispute involving his mother, he achieved a peaceful conclusion.

Richard would need to create bonds with a range of other gentry families throughout his new territories in the north. As the heir to the Neville family in the region, with a prominent Neville bride on his arm, he hoped to secure the service of the majority of those who had held offices under Warwick and his father, Salisbury. In this, he appears to have been very successful. In 1473, thirty-six men drew fees from the lordship of Middleham and twenty-two of them had previously been in Warwick's service.[13] Prominent northern families are found either continuing in or entering into the service of Warwick's heir. The close association between Warwick and the Conyers family had led to William Conyers being widely identified as Robin of Redesdale, the populist leader of the northern revolt that fed into Warwick's own in 1469. Sir John Conyers had served Warwick as Steward of Richmondshire and continued in that post under Richard, with an increase in his wage.[14] Richard was able to add to this substantial, readymade affinity connections of his own and of the House of York in the region. Francis Lovell, whose family seat lay at Minster Lovell in Oxfordshire, was an outsider brought into northern society by his association with Richard. The Harrington family had long been connected to the House of York and as northerners, Richard, a proven friend, was a natural home for their loyalty. The Saville family were prominent around the Yorkist castle at Sandal near Wakefield. Having spent the entire fifteenth century to this point serving the House of York, Richard represented the best fit for their sympathies and interests too. Later, as Richard's reputation as a good lord spread, he added to this several families who had not previously been prominent in their attachment to Warwick or the House of York. The Mauleverer family, Sir Thomas Markenfeld and Sir Thomas Everingham, who held a reputation as a soldier during the later phases of the Hundred Years' War, gravitated to Richard. The most notable of these additions to Richard's circle was Sir Richard Ratcliffe, a younger son of a relatively obscure gentry family based in the Lake District. From this humble beginning, entirely through service to Richard, he went on to become one of the most prominent men in the kingdom. They saw something in an association with the duke that they liked, and he appears willing to reward good service as much as he was ready to punish those who flouted the law while believing he would provide them with impunity.

The balance of power, or at least of authority, in the north, remained an unspoken problem that demanded, ever louder, a final settlement. There is little evidence of real trouble, but there must have been some tension between Richard and Henry Percy, Earl of Northumberland. The friction may have been a result of a few of Northumberland's men transferring to, or perhaps being lured away by, Richard. Sir Hugh Hastings of Fenwick was an example of a relative of Northumberland who ended up a retainer of Richard. It is more likely that Northumberland had envisaged not only his own return to power but a chance for increased regional authority with the fall of the Neville family. With Richard's arrival in the north, a brother of the king who outranked him as a duke and now held by far the greater part of the Neville interest, those hopes had been dashed. It would have been reasonable for the earl's optimism to turn to fear of a collapse in his own authority. On 12 May 1473, both men appeared before the royal council at Nottingham to finally resolve the matter. Northumberland promised 'to the Duke to be his faithful servant', 'to do service to the Duke at all times lawful and convenient' whenever Richard required it, so long it didn't infringe upon his greater responsibility to the king and prince. In return, Richard swore 'to be the Earl's faithful Lord'. Specifically, Richard would refrain from laying claim to any office Northumberland had received from the king, hinting at his fear of a diminution in his position, and taking 'any servant retained by the Earl of fee, clothing or promise'.[15] What Northumberland made of the settlement can only be guessed at, but in removing the opportunity for increased authority, it must have been a setback to his ambitions. His formal submission to Richard's higher rank was a source of resentment that Northumberland would either have to come to terms with, or seethe over while it endured. He perhaps joined Thomas, Lord Stanley, who had been similarly cowed at Hornby, though who had eventually had his way, in conceiving an antipathy to Richard that would be hard to shake off. For now, though, the matter was settled. Edward had formerly recognised his little brother as the master of the north.

In August 1474, Richard was appointed to lead a commission to enquire into three valuable mines that had been reported in the north, one containing 27lbs of silver and another 4lbs of silver,[16] and in March of the following year he was amongst those, including the Earl of Northumberland, granted three mines.[17] They are presumably the same mines and the men were given them for a period of fifteen years on the condition that they paid an eighth of the mines' produce to the king. Richard was developing business interests in the region that would tie him more closely to the northern economy and to the men and merchants of the area. Richard also continued to acquire properties beyond the north. On 5 August 1474, the same day he was appointed to investigate the mines, he was granted a clutch of lordships and manors in Wiltshire, Somerset and Cornwall.[18] On 12 June 1475, he was further bolstered in the north with grants of the lordships and manors of Skipton and Marton in Yorkshire,[19] which had previously belonged to Lord Clifford, who was believed to have killed Edmund, Earl of Rutland, at Wakefield and had died fighting for Henry VI at Ferrybridge, the day before Towton. If further evidence of Richard's high favour were needed, on 20 July 1475, he and Anne were provided with a pardon from the king 'of all offences committed by them, all fines, issues, amercements, reliefs, scutages, debts, accounts and arrears due from them to the king and all alienations and perquisitions by them of lands held in chief without license'.[20]

When Edward began serious preparations for a campaign in France, the nettle was grasped with some enthusiasm. The king was finally getting what he wanted and was laying the pieces of his jigsaw down carefully, ensuring that he missed no part of the picture. Efforts to secure the requisite peace with Scotland had begun as early as August 1473,[21] and in November 1474 a treaty was ratified between the two nations, with an order on the same day for it to be proclaimed throughout England.[22] This left Edward free to focus his gaze south. As part of the agreement, Edward's daughter Cecily was betrothed to James's son and heir, the future James IV.[23] In January 1475, James III was providing safe conducts to Scotland, and Edward was arranging payment to be delivered of the first instalment of Cecily's dowry. On 3 February, James provided a receipt for 2,000 marks for this initial payment,[24] probably as much a bribe to secure the northern border as a pre-payment of a dowry.

Diplomatic efforts were in evidence on all fronts. On 1 May 1473, a treaty with Denmark was confirmed for a further two years. On 21 May, Edward promised to appoint ambassadors to resolve the ongoing disputes between England and the Hanse merchants and in July 1474 he was able to confirm that a settlement had been reached. In July 1474, there was a flurry of activity involving Burgundy, which was to be Edward's main ally in the effort to destroy Louis XI's kingdom. On 25 July, a treaty of perpetual friendship was agreed between Edward and Duke Charles, and on the following day, additional explanatory documentation was sealed. Edward promised Duke Charles the territories of Bar, Champagne, Nivernois, Rhetel, Eu, the properties of the Count of St Pol outside Normandy and Aquitaine and other parcels of land. On 27 July, an agreement was reached that Edward would be crowned King of France at Rheims, the traditional location of French coronations, even though it stood in Champagne, a region that would belong to Duke Charles. On the same day, a spart of the recompense for the favour, Edward agreed to pay the wages of a portion of Duke Charles' army. In addition to these treaties, Edward secured peace, and therefore freedom from concern about any involvement in France, from the King of Hungary, Frederick, the Holy Roman Emperor and Ferdinand of Castile, which saw the confirmation of a previous peace agreed with Ferdinand's predecessor Henry of Castile.[25]

Within England, preparations gathered pace too. On 3 December 1474, Edward issued a proclamation 'enjoining the manufacture of bows and arrows for the King's expedition to France'. Men such as Edward's stepson Thomas Grey on 18 November 1474 and Sir Richard Tunstall on 20 August were signing indentures to serve with the king. Men, ships, sailors and even goldsmiths were being requisitioned for use in the campaign and its preparations. On 1 February 1475, a proclamation was published 'summoning the lords and captains retained to serve in the army to be at Portsdown on May 26'. Thomas, Lord Stanley, seems to have used the increasingly frenetic preparations to obtain another victory for himself. On 1 May 1475, just weeks before the planned assault on France, Edward ordered John, Lord Scrope, a man closely connected with Richard, 'to abstain from wearing the arms of the earl of Man, which are also claimed by Thomas lord Stanley' during the French campaign.[26] The Isle of Mann was nominally a kingdom, ruled by the King of Mann, but as a vassal of the King of England. Both Thomas Stanley and John Scrope claimed a right to it and Scrope was obviously planning to add the claim to his banners to go to France, which was a chance for men to display their noble standing. Stanley objected, since he claimed a right to it as well, and his objection was upheld by Edward, no doubt his distraction with France and the need for Stanley to help raise men a more immediate concern than the rights or wrongs of the claim. The Stanley family would retain the title, so Thomas no doubt believed he was merely defending his own right and claim.

Edward's efforts to raise money for the expedition had not been satisfied by Parliament. The king invented a new method of raising money specifically designed to swell his war chest for the French campaign, but which proved so successful that he indulged in the practice for the rest of his reign. Edward asked his richer subjects to provide him with a benevolence. As they frowned at the unfamiliar term, they were displeased to find out that it amounted to a gift of money. Unlike a loan, it was not to be repaid. Unlike taxation, it was not approved by, nor the level set, by Parliament. John Morton was, at this time, Keeper of the Rolls of Chancery. He would go on to become Bishop of Ely and Henry VII's Archbishop of Canterbury. He became associated with a form of financial assessment known as Morton's Fork, which stated that if a lord lived a lavish lifestyle, then he could afford to pay more in taxation. For those nobles living a frugal life, the assessment determined that they must have plenty of money saved because of their prudence and so could afford to pay more to their king. It was unpopular because it was a no-win situation, and because it was successful. If Morton was not the mind behind the creation of Edward's benevolences, then it is easy to see how he developed it into what became known as Morton's Fork. As an emergency mechanism to raise money for war, Edward's wealthier subject may have let it slide in 1475, particularly with the promise of rich reward from a successful French campaign, but in continuing it in peacetime, Edward guaranteed its enduring unpopularity.

Richard and George both promised to attend the campaign, each bringing with them 120 men-at-arms (including themselves) and 1,000 archers.[27] Richard's call to arms must have been incredibly successful because he brought more men with him wearing his badge of the white boar, the blanc sanglier, than he had indented to provide.[28] It seems likely that Richard's was the biggest single contingent within Edward's army, which numbered about 13,000 and promised to be the largest English army ever to set foot in France.[29] It is tempting to see an element of sibling rivalry in outstripping George's provision for the army, or of a desire to impress his brother the king with his unfaltering and inexhaustible loyalty and energy. It is equally likely that after several years of Richard's good lordship, he was not short of men wishing to serve under him on a campaign that promised glory and riches.

Richard's adoption of the white boar as his personal badge is shrouded in mystery, at least as to its meaning. Precisely what it meant to Richard is not recorded, but there are several possible theories. The boar was an animal that was hunted in the forest, but unlike a deer, it was no timid animal prone to fleeing. A boar was a serious threat to the hunter, as likely to attack with its vicious tusks as it was to run away. It was also an animal renowned for protecting its young and disdaining escape to fight for its offspring. All of this may have begun to feed into Richard's search for a symbol that would project his presence into the world and onto the battlefield. The boar was small, but it was tenacious, and to be feared. There may have been a regional aspect to the adoption of the badge too. Eboracum, often shortened to Ebor, had been the Roman name for York and offers an anagram of *bore*, a spelling frequently used for boar in a time before such things were standardised. Richard could, therefore, allude to his connections to and affection for York, providing not only a symbol identifiable with him but with the region around York and Yorkshire that he was making his home. Ensuring that adherence to Richard personally became synonymous with loyalty to the north was a neat tactic that would initially ingratiate him to his new liegemen but in time would ensure all Yorkshiremen saw him as their natural lord and champion.

The boar had a place in early English mythology that offers another possible motive for Richard's adoption of the badge, and a hint at something mischievous too. The legend of Guy of Warwick boasts

> In Windsor forest I did kill a Bore of passing strength,
> Whose like in England never was for highness breadth, and length.
> Some of his bones in Warwicke yet, within the castle lie:
> One of his shields unto this daie doth hang in Conventrie.[30]

Guy of Warwick was a folk hero, another Arthur whose story is more myth than history and who may be an amalgamation of several Anglo-Saxon heroes. If there was a real Guy, he lived, according to events recorded in the poems that entered national folklore during the medieval period, during the reign of King Alfred's grandson King Athelstan (ruled 924–939). His story is largely forgotten now, despite interest in Arthur and Robin Hood remaining strong, but it is the stuff of medieval romances linked to epic Greek poetry. In short, Guy wishes to marry a daughter of the Earl of Warwick – a significant parallel for Richard – but is deemed too lowly born. To rectify this, he sets out on a quest to prove himself. He kills the Dun Cow, a huge beast of unknown origins, a bone from which was long claimed to be kept at Warwick Castle, though it turned out to be a whale bone. Next, he takes on a giant boar, which he also kills. He also claims to have killed a dragon in Northumberland before heading abroad to find more challenges. After a time, he returns to Felice, the earl's daughter, having righted wrongs and slain fell beasts wherever he went in Europe. The couple are married, but Guy, racked with guilt at his violent past, travels to Jerusalem on pilgrimage. He returns in disguise as a pilgrim, kills a giant named Colbrond the Danes have sent to attack Athelstan's England, and then, without revealing his identity, travels back to Warwick, where he ends up living as a hermit, only being reunited with his wife just before he dies.

Richard may have seen some appeal in Guy's story and adopted the boar as a symbol of his own power – 'Whose like in England never was' – whilst acknowledging that there was one superior to him; Edward was his Guy, holding the king up as a mythical hero. The desire to marry a daughter of the Earl of Warwick is a clear parallel from the story and Guy's feat of slaying an oppressive dragon in Northumberland might have been a swipe at Henry Percy, who had been forced to submit to Richard. An element of mischief might be seen in the selection of the boar as a badge in the poem's assertion that some of the bones of the boar remained in Warwick Castle. Given George's prickly attitude to the Warwick, Neville, Beauchamp and Despenser inheritances, Richard may have taken the opportunity to take a sly jab at his brother. The bones of the boar remaining within Warwick Castle could be a veiled suggestion that Richard had not entirely given up the Warwick inheritance that centred on the earldom and castle. It was, if it figured in Richard's thinking, perhaps meant to keep George on his toes, to stop him looking at what Richard had and make him keep one eye on his own possessions that Richard might seek to claim.

If piety played a part in the selection of Richard's badge, then this too can be traced to popular saintly devotion. St Anthony was an early Egyptian saint who had converted to Christianity and given all of his substantial wealth to the poor. He lived as a hermit for a time and then established a religious order incredibly similar to that St Benedict would found 200 years later, committing himself and his brothers to manual labour. During his time as a hermit, Anthony was tormented by demons who frequently attacked him, on one occasion beating him to death in a cave only for God to bring him back to life to face the demons again. When the demons appeared as wild animals, the boar was the only one who resisted doing the Devil's bidding and instead defended St Anthony. The boar, therefore, represented spiritual purity and the resistance of temptation and corruption as well as the defence of the weak against their enemies. Richard, whose scoliosis was now painfully certain to remain with him for the rest of his life, might have considered this a form of torment and been conscious of the widespread (though not universal) equating of physical disability with moral and spiritual corruption. In this sense, he could liken himself to Anthony, whose defender from his torment was a boar.

St Anthony was not the only religious figure with a connection to a boar. St Brigid, Patroness of Ireland was reportedly upset when a boar ran through the gates of her monastery in Kildare. It had been chased by hunters and seriously wounded so that it was nearly dead. The hunters stopped at the gates and waited for their quarry to be chased out, only for Brigid to announce that she had given it sanctuary. When the disgruntled hunters left, she set about tending to the boar, nursing it back to health and introducing it to her own pigs, where it lived happily for the rest of its life. The boar in St Brigid's story is a chased and hounded beast, just as Richard might have reasonably considered himself to have been after an uncertain childhood, two spells in exile and two pitched battles. The boar's comfortable integration with Brigid's own herd could have been an allusion to Richard's own arrival and welcome into the north, a place he planned to call home for the rest of his life.

For a medieval nobleman, the choice of his badge, along with his motto, were important matters deserving of serious contemplation. Men would take their livery badge away with them, and it would serve as their reminder of Richard; it was a message he could send with them to remind them of whatever it was he wanted them to think of him. On the battlefield, it was the symbol of his retinue around which his men could cohere and to which outstanding feats could be attributed. In an age before any kind of mass media or advertising, a lord's livery badge was as close as they could come to a brand. It is impossible to tell whether any of these considerations played into Richard's decision to adopt a badge of the white boar, or whether it was the product of several elements of the stories above. It would be unique at a time when dragons and lions were prevalent, so it would make Richard's men instantly identifiable. It could be a reference to his links with York, to the legendary warrior and folk hero Guy of Warwick, to saints Anthony and Brigid, and it might refer to his own personal battles with demons in the form of his physically restrictive scoliosis, the absence of which from almost any record until his skeleton was discovered is evidence that he felt the need to keep it secret during his lifetime.[31] Richard could look at the boar as a symbol of the resistance of temptation, something he had achieved in leaving England with Edward in 1470 rather than staying with George and Warwick. The subtle reference to the bones of the boar still being at Warwick Castle and the jibe at George might have been an added bonus. It is likely that several of these considerations, implications, personal relevance and public images combined to lead Richard to settle on the boar as his badge. It had a great deal to be said for it, and it was about to be seen snarling in the fields of France.

It is hard to gauge, but essential to consider without the benefit of hindsight, what the French campaign meant to those taking part during the build-up to their departure. The Hundred Years' War had brought sporadic successes, with huge gaps between them. Crécy and Poitiers in 1346 and 1356 respectively had not been recreated until Agincourt in 1415. Henry V's achievements in being declared legal heir to the French throne marked a high point, but his early death dashed the hopes he had built. The long-running feud had last seen a battlefield at Castillon in 1453, and the English had been decisively beaten there before being driven out of all France, with the exception of Calais, the last toehold of the English in France. For many, there was still a sour taste in their mouths after ending in such a defeat. Much of the Yorkist popular appeal during the 1450s had centred on complaints about the losses in France, which Richard, Duke of York, blamed on his nemesis Edmund Beaufort, Duke of Somerset. Having been ejected from his kingdom in 1470 in part for failing to deliver on the Yorkist manifesto, Edward felt obliged to make an effort to renew the English claim to France. He was a famous soldier and lacked the excuses of delicacy that had led to the deposition of Henry VI. If Edward had learned anything from the events of 1469–71, it was perhaps that war with France was his best hope of security at home.

Nothing distracted feuding nobles or vented the excessive energies of young lordlings quite like a good fight with the French on foreign soil.

Besides that, there was the opportunity for glory and riches that had been lacking for decades. At the height of the war, men had made their names and their fortunes in France. It was an opportunity for younger sons to carve out something for themselves and for those already wealthy to seek out the immortality of chivalric glory. Part of the domestic problems that had plagued England for decades, in the opinion of contemporary commentators, was the lack of this entirely reasonable outlet for energy and aggression that was instead pent up or directed into petty local squabbles. In short, the best thing for England was a good old-fashioned war with France. To few was this more apparent than to William Worcester, a servant of Sir John Fastolf, a soldier made wealthy by his successes in France only to be mocked by Shakespeare in the guise of Falstaff. Worcester originally wrote *The Book of Noblesse* in 1451 as a vehicle for his master's belief in the need to confidently reassert England's rights in France. It came to nothing then, but it reflected part of the Yorkist manifesto of the decade and in 1475 Worcester dug out his old manuscript, dusted it off and dedicated a new edition to Edward IV. It is incorrect to suggest that Worcester captured the spirit of the nation with his plea for a just war to defend the King of England's right to the crown of France. It was perhaps the death rattle of a bygone age, but it did make several points that tallied with the speech made by Bishop Alcock at the opening of Parliament in 1472.

Alcock's opening speech reminded those listening that 'tranquillite and assured peax' were the only route to 'abundance and richesse', and in contrast that 'bi discencion and discorde the grettest and mightiest reames and lordships have fallen to poverte and desolacion'. The bishop acknowledged that those in England needed no reminder of this since all had been affected by the recent wars and that, like a disease of the body, what afflicted one part of the kingdom soon infected the rest. The recent lawlessness that plagued the realm was still causing problems around the coast and men must be put from their 'idell lyvyng', which caused them to fall into crime and misrule, either by executions or some other means. If it were excutions, Alcock speculated that so many would have to be killed that England would appear ripe for invasion by the Scots, the French or the Danes. Defending England, he asserted, would be a far more difficult job than any offensive foreign war. Attention turned in particular to Louis in France and his frequent, always unfulfilled offers of peace and the return of the French crown to Edward, not to mention the trouble he had helped to stir up in England. Alcock turned the knife by adding that 'if Louis, for his owne imminent necessite or dainger, wold peradventure hereater offer or graunt the Kyng any recompence, it is to be douted whether, his unstablenesse known as it is, he wold kepe suche appointements as he maketh.' In short, Louis could not be trusted. The king's answer to both the internal problems of lawlessness and the external need to deal with Louis and reclaim France for England was simple: 'there can be founde noon so honourable, so necessarie, nor so expedient a werk, as to sette in occupation of the werre outward the foresaid idell and riotous people, undre the conducte of our Soveraigne Lord.' War with France, Alcock told Parliament, was the answer to all their problems.

A list of previous kings, Henry I, Henry II, Richard I, Henry III, Edward I, Edward III, Henry V and even Henry VI, before France was lost, was reeled off to prove that 'it is nat wele possible, nor hath been since the Conquest, that justice, peax, and prosperite hath contenued any while in this lande in any Kings dayes but in suche as have made were outward.'[32] Worcester's *Book of Noblesse* contained similar sentiments that perhaps caused the author to dust it off and dedicate it to the king for the campaign. The majority of the book is a study of the success and prosperity brought by various wars, and the fame won by the kings and rulers who pursued them. Worcester considered that 'every good man of armes shuld in the werre be resembled to the condicion of a lion.'[33] In line with Alcock's assertion that war brought unity of purpose to the realm and those within it expending their energies on causing problems, Worcester believed that in war, 'alle worshipfulle men, which oughte to be stedfast and holde togider, may be of one intencion, wille, and comon assent.'[34]

To Edward, the French campaign may have been something he felt unable to avoid rather than a genuine passion. All English kings made the required and expected overtures of war with France and spoke of themselves as the true King of France. In his late teens, driven to seek revenge, Edward had been an unmatched terror on the battlefield. He had been slow to see the depth of his troubles in 1469 and his failure to prepare had cost him the throne in 1470. That was perhaps the first signal that a more relaxed lifestyle had taken a firm grip on him that made war seem too much effort. Once forced to action, though, he had proven himself twice in 1471, and he remained undefeated on the field of battle, an enviable achievement in fifteenth-century England. It is possible some questioned his drive for an invasion of France, and likely, from their conduct even before leaving England, that a few familiars knew the king's mind. He had to attack, though. The failure to fulfil the Yorkist manifesto was part of the reason he had lost his crown, and he had now to correct that disappointment.

Richard may have been more enthusiastic about the adventure. He was still just twenty-two as he prepared for war on foreign soil. If great chivalric romances such as *Ipomedon* and the story of Guy of Warwick had formed part of his reading, he cannot help but have seen in this venture his opportunity to live up to those legendary figures, to prove to himself that his scoliosis did not make him less of a knight and to show his brother once more what he was made of. If he played a prominent part in the recapture of France, then his name would go down in the annals of history with great English warriors who had found fame and fortune there. The desire to deliver the Yorkist promise of a fairer England and the renewal of the English claim to France is likely to have weighed heavily on Richard's mind. He had lost his father and a brother to the cause, and just a few years earlier he had seen the backlash in the country for Edward's failure to bring it to fruition. He perhaps felt a duty to hold his brother's feet to the fire, to act as the Yorkist conscience and in the process, ensure his brother achieved the glory he was capable of and secure the Yorkist ruling dynasty.[35]

As he passed out his badge of the blanc sanglier, ordered banners stitched that would make him prominent on the battlefield, gathered men to him in numbers surpassing his brother's expectations, had his armour polished, his bright surcoat cleaned and his sword sharpened, Richard knew that glory awaited. He would take his leave of his wife and the home they were forging in the north of England, hoping, without knowing, that he would return alive and whole. If he did, he would bring a new, bright dawn of chivalric splendour to England, to the north and to his own hearth which no man could ever deprive him of. His eternal reputation would be forged in the reconquest of France. His father would be vindicated, and his oldest brother made even more glorious, with Richard able proudly to take his place alongside them.

To Dover, to France, to glory.

10

Tarnished Glory

And so shall we hunt through parts of France and there I will blow
my horn and release my hounds. I trust to God and to our Lady
that your mokke shall turn you to shame for ye wote of
right I am master of the game.
Edward IV of England to Louis XI of France[1]

After long, expensive preparations, Edward's vast army set sail from
Dover to Calais on 4 July 1475. The clergy and laity of England had
furnished their king with tax money for the campaign, and many of his
nobles had donated to Edward's newly created benevolences scheme,
willingly or otherwise. All had done so in the hope of a return on their
investment in money, security, peace and glory. Before leaving England,
Edward wrote to Louis to offer him the chance to avoid bloodshed by
handing over France immediately. Edward told Louis he was crossing
the sea with, amongst others, 'the Blak Bulle with the gilte hornes,' and
'the Bore', meaning George and Richard. Each of Edward's senior nobles
was represented by the animal of their badge and the war characterised
as a hunt: 'Thanne must I blow myn horne and folow my beestis and
my beestis must follow the chase and so shalwe hunte throughe the
parties of Fraunce and there wol I blowe myn horne and releve myn
howndes.'[2] Philip de Commines offered the barbed compliment that the
'letter of defiance' was 'written in such an elegant style, and in such polite
language, that I can scarcely believe any Englishman wrote it.'[3] When
the English began to land at Calais and fill the town, which had been
prepared for their arrival, it was not long before the shine started to fade
from the whole expedition.

On 6 July, Margaret arrived to greet her three brothers at Calais.
Richard and George may well have been pleased to see their sister once
more, but Edward was not happy with the news she brought. Instead
of the planned rendezvous at Calais, Duke Charles had allowed himself

to be lured into assaulting the town of Neuss, far to the east, with all of his military might. Neuss was powerfully protected and was proving impossible to breach so that Philip de Commines believed it was a sign of God's favour sitting with France. He could hardly fathom that after Duke Charles had worked so long and hard to get the English to invade France, he had immediately been distracted from involving himself in the completion of the task now that Edward was there.[4] After lingering in Calais for a few days, Margaret left for St Omer, escorted by George and Richard.[5] When Duke Charles finally arrived himself on 14 July, it was to announce that he had let his army loose in Lorraine to pillage and refresh themselves. He tried to dampen the English army's indignant rage by flattering them that they hardly needed his input, having brought such a large and impressive contingent themselves. The duke suggested that Edward should descend on Normandy with the Duke of Brittany and the Count of St Pol and then move into Champagne, where Duke Charles would join the offensive from the east. He would then meet Edward at Rheims for the coronation they had planned.[6]

The Count of St Pol, who was the Constable of France, was also Edward's wife's uncle, Louis de Luxembourg. The connection may have been behind St Pol's promise to hand over the town of St Quentin as soon as Edward arrived there, and when he reiterated the offer, Edward decided to travel through Doullens and Peronne to take possession of St Quentin. On 18 July, the English army moved out of Calais. Duke Charles stayed with them as far as Guisnes before taking his leave and joining his wife and his two other brothers-in-law at St Omer. Edward made a lumbering march through Boulogne, his enthusiasm for the endeavour perhaps already sapped completely. By 24 July, Duke Charles had rejoined the army, apparently still accompanied by George and Richard, who may have enjoyed some time in Margaret's company. The army camped for several nights at Fauquembergues before spending two nights in the fields of Agincourt, drinking in the earth's memory of the glory the English had won there sixty years earlier.

Louis XI was not idle. He seems to have struggled to gain intelligence on the English movements and was uncertain even when they had landed, a testament to English dominance in the Channel, but by 27 July he was at Beauvais with a large and growing army. On 29 July, as the English army neared Doullens, Duke Charles once again graced them with his presence. If Edward still held out any hope for the enterprise, it must have been finally dashed when they reached Peronne on 6 August. Duke Charles entered the town, only to close the gates on Edward and his army and force them to camp in the fields. Edward's patience was wearing thin, and the discipline of his men was beginning to fray too. Some fell to foraging, and one group travelled as far as Noyon, almost 30 miles south, where they encountered some of Louis XI's men. Around fifty Englishmen were killed before they fled back to their army. Duke Charles became increasingly concerned by the behaviour of the English army, which threatened to cost them support in the area, and suggested pushing on to St Quentin. Edward agreed but as some of his enthusiastic men neared the town on 11 August, the guns opened fire on them, and a mounted force rode out to attack. A few Englishmen were killed and several more captured before the rest scrambled back to their king in the pouring rain to complain bitterly about St Pol, 'calling him a traitor'.[7] It should be considered whether this betrayal of English hopes in France at the hands of the queen's uncle added to the suspicion, mistrust and hatred in some quarters of her and her Woodville family.

On the following day, Duke Charles again took his leave to go to his own army, though Commines reported that the English 'began to entertain an ill opinion of their ally, and could not believe he had any army at all.'[8] Edward moved to Lihons-en-Santerre and, as soon as the duke was gone, opened negotiations with Louis XI. Edward sent a captured Frenchman with a message for Louis. Before the man left, he was also approached by Lords Howard and Stanley, who each gave him a gold noble and asked him 'to present their most humble service to the king his master, when he had the opportunity of speaking to him.'[9] Louis sent back a servant, dressed as a herald, to relay his own message to Edward. The man relayed that 'the King of France for a long time had had a desire to be at amity with him, that both their kingdoms might be at ease, and enjoy the blessings of peace; that since his accession to the crown of France, he never made war, or attempted anything against him or his kingdom; and as for having entertained the Earl of Warwick formerly, he said he had done that more in opposition to the Duke of Burgundy than out of any quarrel with King Edward. Then he went on to state that the Duke of Burgundy had invited him over, only in order to make his own terms the better with the King of France.'[10] Louis also observed that the lateness of the season was not favourable for campaigning and that it was costing Edward a fortune to keep his army in the field. All this, the French king suggested, could be easily solved if Edward would just name his terms. In trying to drive a wedge between those allied against him, Louis hit the right nerve as English confidence in Duke Charles evaporated.

Louis' confidence in Edward's desire to make peace was not unreasonable. When Garter Herald had travelled to France with Edward's bellicose letter of defiance, it had not been the only message he had delivered. On receiving the letter from the English king, Louis had recited reasons similar to those he now gave again for seeking peace rather than war. He was, he had told Garter, 'very sensible that his master had not made this descent upon any disposition of his own, but at the importunity of the Duke of Burgundy and of the Commons of England.'[11] Louis encouraged the herald to return and suggest peace negotiations, giving him 300 crowns and offering 1,000 more when a peace was concluded. Garter responded by telling Louis that Edward could not possibly be expected to discuss peace before his army had landed in France since honour must be satisfied in that regard, but assured Louis that 'he believed his master would not be averse to it.' He continued that the French should 'address letters to the Lords Howard and Stanley, and also to himself', which explains both men's gift to the French prisoner sent back to Louis and the French king's willingness to accept that the overtures were genuine. Whether Warwick had filled Louis in on Edward's increasing lack of drive and vigour a few years earlier or not, the French king seems to have had the measure of his English counterpart from the outset. In entertaining the idea of peace before the campaign even began and by providing a mechanism for opening negotiations, through Howard and Stanley, Edward had confirmed Louis' suspicions and doomed the expedition before an English soldier had even set foot in France. Louis believed Edward had been pressurised into attacking France and would prefer peace. He was probably right.

If Richard had been unaware of his brother's preparation of an escape route from the war before leaving England, it became suddenly clear now. He was going to lose the opportunity for the glory that this invasion had represented. There would be no booty for him, his men or any other Englishman. After the financial exactions in England, returning without having met the French even once in battle would risk angry revolt and return the Yorkist regime to the position it had previously been in; failing to deliver its promises. Richard would soon take a stand that suggests these considerations were genuine and for which it is hard to discern a cynical subplot. He may have had private audiences with his brother to try to dissuade him from this course of action, pointing out all of the problems it risked bringing down on the king's head. Richard's life had been thrown about on the choppy seas of civil war. Now he was to be denied a chance to fight in France, but the ease with which Edward was being brought to the table risked more trouble when they returned home, which Richard must have hoped had been put behind him with the end of the Lancastrian line in 1471. Honour could have been satisfied, and better terms extracted if they had fought just one battle to bring Louis to the table, but Edward's mind was made up, perhaps long before Richard tried to change it.

Edward sent back his demands on 13 August with Lord Howard, John Morton, William Dudley, dean of the king's chapel, and Thomas St Ledger, a knight who had only recently married Richard's oldest sister Anne after her separation from the dedicated Lancastrian Henry Holland, Duke of Exeter. The English king asked for 75,000 crowns to be paid immediately so that he and his army would leave France, with hostages to be provided to prove his goodwill. After that, 50,000 crowns were to be paid each year, half at Easter and half at Michaelmas, as long as both kings lived.[12] Louis' oldest son was to be married to one of Edward's two oldest daughters at Louis' expense, and the French king was to provide her with an income of £60,000 a year. Edward also wanted a personal agreement of mutual military support between himself and Louis to last seven years with a trade agreement for the same period.[13] On 15 August, the English and French ambassadors met face to face. Howard, Morton, Dudley and St Ledger began with a traditional and anticipated demand that Louis hand over the crown of France to Edward, which was politely refused. They then moved on to insisting on the return of Normandy and Guienne, which was once more adroitly argued against by the French. Finally, they requested that when the Dauphin married Edward's daughter, they should be given Guienne, or 50,000 crowns a year for nine years and then the entire revenue of that region.[14] It was a formality, a display for the sake of honour that had already been bought and sold. It was a negotiation in ever decreasing circles toward an agreement already made. Some of Louis' councillors were still suspicious of Edward's motives, fearing that he would attack at any moment, but Louis was confident because 'he was perfectly acquainted with the King of England's temper, and that he loved to indulge himself in ease and pleasure.'[15] Louis had been proven right.

On 18 August, Duke Charles reappeared at Peronne in a hurry and a rage. Edward asked the duke whether he wished to speak in private rather than in front of the court, but Duke Charles simply asked whether it was true that Edward had agreed terms with Louis. Edward said that he had and that both Duke Charles and the Duke of Brittany were able to join the accord if they wished, which Edward hoped they both would. Still furious, Duke Charles addressed the king loudly in English so that everyone gathered could understand. He listed the brave achievements of previous English kings in France 'and how they had spared no pains, nor declined any danger, that might render them famous, and gain them immortal honour and renown abroad.'[16] The implication that Edward was not fit to join their illustrious company was plain to all. Duke Charles refuted the claim that he had only brought Edward into France to improve his own negotiating position with Louis. To prove what he said, and that he could look after himself, he swore not to make a treaty with France for at least three months after Edward left. It was too late, Edward told his unreliable ally. It was all agreed. As Duke Charles stormed away, Edward and his council 'were extremely displeased with his language', no doubt citing the duke's failure to fulfil his side of the bargain for the collapse of the campaign, 'but others who were averse to the peace highly extolled it.'[17] It is not hard to imagine Richard amongst those who sympathised with Duke Charles' display of frustration. His opposition to the peace was to become clear soon.

Louis offered to host the English army at Amiens, where both kings arrived on 25 August with their troops in battle array, still trying to maintain the semblance of being enemies. Louis sent between 80–100 carts of wine[18] to the English and threw open the gates of the town for any who wished to visit. Two tables laden with food and wine sat either side of the open gates and the town's taverns were ordered to give their wares freely to the English and assured that Louis would meet all the costs. Perhaps as Louis hoped, the English soon lost their discipline, aided by the fact that 'not a drop of water was drunk.'[19] When Edward became aware of the unruly behaviour of his men, he asked Louis to eject them from the town, but the French king insisted that he could not, having offered them his hospitality, but that Edward was welcome to send a few men to remove them. Louis once more played his hand to perfection. The English had been rendered insensible by his hospitality and had to be forcibly removed by their own king, much to the embarrassment of the English. Although Louis might have feared sparking a confrontation if his own men had tried to drive the English out, it served a purpose to force Edward to do it himself.

During all of this merriment-gone-astray, a bridge was being built over the Somme near the village of Picquigny where the kings were to meet and seal their agreements. Louis was wary of past history, so the bridge was blocked across the middle by a wicket fence with a small opening to speak through. In 1419, Louis' father had been involved in the assassination of John the Fearless, Duke of Burgundy, Duke Charles' grandfather, during a parlay on a bridge at Montereau. The fallout from that event had seen Burgundy allied to England and Henry V's subsequent crushing success. There would be no repeat of that at Picquigny. The two sides met on 29 August with the kings bringing their closest advisors. Edward brought George, the Earl of Northumberland, Lord Hastings, Bishop Rotherham and a few others with him. Amongst Louis' retinue was Philip de Commines, who gave a description of the English king he had last seen in Burgundy five years earlier, 'he was a prince of a noble and majestic presence, but a little inclining to corpulence. I had seen him before when the Earl of Warwick drove him out of his kingdom; then I thought him much handsomer, and to the best of my remembrance, my eyes had never beheld a more handsome person.'[20] The ease and pleasure that Louis was so confident Edward enjoyed were apparently beginning to show on the English king. Edward was just thirty-three years old, but Commines felt he was already losing his looks and spreading a little at the waist, though he had once been the most handsome of men. In this, and in other respects, there are similarities to be seen between Edward and his grandson, Henry VIII. Edward and Louis signed and sealed their agreements before indulging in some light-hearted conversation, during which Louis invited Edward to Paris to enjoy the women there and offered the services of Cardinal Bourbon, who was present, to absolve him of any sins he might indulge in. Louis regretted it when Edward joked that he might accept the offer, suddenly wary that English kings had previously spent too much time in Paris, and that if Edward were to go once, he might wish to return a second time, with an army.[21] It was all settled, and Lord Howard and Sir John Cheney would remain as hostages until the English army was back across the Channel.

Where was Richard throughout all of this? He was conspicuous by his absence. For Edward, meeting the King of France was a moment to display prestige, to surround himself with as many high-ranking nobles as he could and even to demonstrate unity within the House of York. George's presence would serve as a reminder to Louis that his efforts in 1470 had not caused a rift between the brothers. Why, then, would Richard, the king's brother and a duke, be missing from the bridge at Picquigny? George may have desired it as a sign of his own pre-eminence, but that would not mean Edward would forgo the kudos of another prince at his side. Commines is clear that 'the Duke of Gloucester, the King of England's brother, and some other persons of quality, were not present at this interview, as being averse to the treaty.'[22] If he is correct, then it can hardly have been a secret and Richard was not alone in thinking his brother erred in making the swift peace, however financially rewarding it was. Commines does add that 'they recollected themselves afterwards, and the Duke of Gloucester waited on the king our master at Amiens, where he was splendidly entertained, and nobly presented both with plate and fine horses.'[23] Richard did have an audience with Louis at Amiens after everything was agreed, though this does not necessarily mean that his opposition to the peace had passed. It was a separate matter, and it seems likely that Louis was keen to get the measure of Edward's youngest brother. He evidently had Edward sized up. George had been in France with Warwick, and his temperament was not hard to discern. In Richard, he saw something of more concern. He appeared committed to war in France and unwilling to be satisfied with a swift settlement. If Edward was easily bought off and George too fickle to be of real concern (in fact, he was capable of being turned against Edward), what of this youngest son of the House of York? Louis prided himself on knowing his enemies. In Richard, he saw someone worthy of treating with caution, a man to keep a close eye on. This was the brother on whom Edward increasingly relied. If there was ever another English invasion, it was possible Edward would not take part at all and that Richard may be at the head of an army, far less willing to forgo honour for gold than other English nobles.

That Richard could not be bought off is evident from the pensions paid by the French king to other Englishmen. John Morton received 600 crowns a year, Bishop Rotherham, the Chancellor, 1,000 crowns. Lord Howard was given 1,200 crowns annually and Lord Hastings, for his part in securing the peace, 2,000 crowns a year. Richard did not take any pension from Louis, although it is not certain that he was actually offered one, it is likely from the subsequent cordiality at Amiens that Louis would have tried to secure Richard as a pensioner. Lord Hastings' behaviour regarding his pension is interesting and can help to explain Richard's opposition to the peace. Commines makes a passing reference to Hastings receiving his pension amount, adding 'who would never give an acquittance for it'.[24] Hastings had become a willing pensioner of the Duke of Burgundy in 1471, who was paying him 1,000 crowns a year for which he happily provided receipts. When his pension from Louis was delivered for the first time, and a receipt was requested, he refused to provide one and is reported to have replied 'this present proceeds from your master's generosity, not from any request of mine; if you have a mind I should receive it, you may put it into my sleeve, but neither letter nor acquittance will you have from me; for it shall never be said of me, that the High Chamberlain of England was pensioner to the King of France, nor shall my receipt be ever produced in his chamber accounts.'[25] Louis was displeased at the response, but respected Hastings all the more for his refusal because Hastings was right; Louis was collected receipts to show just how many great English lords were in his pocket. If Louis admired Lord Hastings' stance, he must have been more impressed still, or else very worried, by Richard's.

Hastings was unwilling to be recorded as Louis' pensioner because there was an element of dishonour in being bought off by an enemy. His pension from Duke Charles was from a friend and ally, but accepting Louis' payment must have left a bitter taste in the mouth of a man whose Book of Hours and personal record demonstrate a commitment to the ideals of chivalry. Yet he had allowed himself to be bought. Richard refused to partake in the affair even though it might have made him wealthy and brought some return on his investment in the expedition. It is difficult to discern any reason for Richard's actions other than a genuine distaste for his brother's course of action and an unwillingness to be associated with it. Hastings felt his honour was satisfied by gaining the money but providing no record for the French king to gloat over. For Richard, only refusal would suffice. To him, the campaign had been a resounding failure for which some backlash might be expected. Edward had no such qualms. When he chose an image to be carved onto his misericord in St George's Chapel, Windsor, he selected for this most private of icons the depiction of his meeting on the bridge at Picquigny with Louis XI. Edward may have got more than he had hoped from the business with no battle and a fat pension, which he was keen to present as a tribute from France to keep him at bay. He apparently viewed it as a victory, one that would help secure his kingship. Richard, it seems, profoundly disagreed with his brother.

The feeling within England seems to have mirrored that of Richard's far more closely than Edward's view of the situation. The sentiment of many, including Richard, was ably articulated by Louis de Brettelles. Commines records a conversation with the Gascon member of Edward's court.

> He was very much displeased at this peace; and having been an old acquaintance of mine, he told me privately, that we did but laugh at the King of England. Among the rest of our discourse, I asked him how many battles the King of England had won. He told me nine, and that he had been in every one of them in person. I demanded next how many he had lost? He replied, never but one, and that was the one in which we had outwitted him now, for he was of opinion that the ignominy of his returning so soon, after such vast preparations, would be a greater disgrace and stain to his arms than all the honour he had gained in the nine former victories.[26]

Foreign war focussed men on their obvious loyalties so that they set aside petty squabbles. The lack of it left them with time and energy to consider what else they might do, which inevitably led to the taking up of those trivial, local feuds. If Brettelles thought the French were laughing at the English, he was right. Nevertheless, Edward, satisfied with his work, set out with his army on receipt of Louis' payment back to Calais and across the Channel to England. On the voyage home, Henry Holland, Duke of Exeter, mysteriously fell overboard and was drowned. He had been Edward's brother-in-law before the annulment of his marriage to Anne, but was a devoted Lancastrian. There were rumours, reported as far away as Milan, that Edward had ordered Exeter drowned to be free from potential trouble at home.[27] He was soon able to rid himself of another niggling problem by ransoming Henry VI's widow, Margaret of Anjou, to the French king. In November, Sir Thomas Montgomery was tasked with delivering the former queen and receiving an initial payment of 10,000 crowns as well as Louis' bond for a further 40,000.[28] Margaret renounced any right to the English crown and lived out the final years of her life in seclusion. She died in 1482, just missing the delight she may have taken at the beginning of the implosion of the House of York the following year.

On the Continent, there had been talk of trouble for Edward on his return home. The Governor of Nice asserted that Edward 'would be torn to pieces the moment he returned to England' if news of the peace treaties was made public.[29] Duke Charles declared gleefully that he had intelligence from England 'that the people there are extremely irritated at this accord, cowardly as it is, because they paid large sums of money without any result.' The report continued that 'King Edward did not want his brothers to proceed to England before him, as he feared some disturbance, especially as the Duke of Clarence, on a previous occasion, aspired to make himself king,' before the ambassador added that 'I gather that some revolution would give secret satisfaction to the duke here.'[30] Even the Crowland Chronicler commented that Edward 'was by no means ignorant of the condition of his people, and how readily they might be betrayed, in case they should find a leader, to enter into rebellious plans, and conceive a thirst for change.'[31] Edward was so cautious on his return that he kept the details of the Treaty of Picquigny secret for a time and bought favour by cancelling the majority of the final tax due to be collected towards the war effort.[32] That seemed to sap enough ire from the people that they overlooked the disappointment of the king's much-vaunted trade agreement, which brought seven years of benefit for merchants but none of the wealth and glory that had been promised.

Something caused a threat within England in March 1476. For reasons that are nowhere made clear, Richard and the Earl of Northumberland were sent to Yorkshire with a powerful force, numbering as many as 5,000 men according to the York House Books. The two great regional magnates arrived in the city on 13 March 1476, 'sent by the king to support the rule of law and peace'.[33] Once the city officials had offered their greetings, Richard addressed them inside Bootham Bar, one of York's four main gatehouses, and instructed that a proclamation should be written and published throughout York. The proclamation ordered every man to 'ne cause to be made any affray or any othir thing attempt to doo, wherthrough the pease of the king our saide sovereine lorde shulde be broken'. No man was to carry any weapon, unless authorised to do so by virtue of his office, on pain of imprisonment, confiscation of his weapons, and payment of a fine. Above this, Richard and Northumberland 'straitely chargeith and commaundith that every man observe, kepe and obeye all the premises upon the peyne abovesaide.'[34] There must have been trouble, or the serious threat of it, for such a force to be sent. The respect in which Richard was already held by the region, and his desire to assert his own authority there, can be seen in the addition of a personal plea, made alongside Northumberland, that the city keep the peace and help ensure those breaking the law were not encouraged, but brought to order.

There were rumours around England and on the Continent that Duke Charles was planning to make a bid for Edward's throne in revenge for his willingness to be bought off by Louis. In October 1475, the Milanese ambassador at the Burgundian court, Panicharolla, reported that 2,000 Englishmen had entered the duke's service after Edward agreed peace with France. Duke Charles had welcomed them because 'he well knows they will be cutting one another's throats in England, and it will be better for them to fight against the French,' but the ambassador was certain 'there is likely to be disturbance in England, because the king exacted a great treasure and did nothing.' He also informed his master the Duke of Milan that 'The duke here foments this all he can.'[35] It is possible that Duke Charles was stirring up trouble, driven by his resentment at gaining nothing from the assault on France that he had been trying to set in motion for so long. Edward's unwillingness to fight might have caused Duke Charles to consider his own Lancastrian pedigree and view England as a ripe target, though he was already engaged in war with the Swiss and must have been conscious of the threat from France now too.

Crowland knew that Edward felt the threat keenly enough, whether it came from Burgundy or within the kingdom. As Duke Charles was predicting, those returning with the army who had been whipped up by the promise of war and plunder and dragged back without sating themselves in France were taking to 'theft and rapine, so that no road throughout England was left in a state of safety for either merchants or pilgrims.' Edward, wary of a repeat of his previous ejection, used the energy he might have expended in France at home instead. The king set about delivering hard justice so that 'no one, not even his own domestic, did he spare, but instantly had him hanged, if he was found guilty of theft or murder.' The hard-line response worked, and law and order was restored 'for a considerable time'. The writer does not deem Edward's actions unreasonable but instead praises the swift crackdown. If, he thought, Edward had not acted so hard and so fast, the problems would have run out of hand 'to such a degree that no one could have said whose head, among the king's advisers, was in safety.'[36] Next, Edward set about maximising his own revenue, resuming grants wholesale, tasking customs inspectors with ever more diligence and involving himself in trading in wool, cloth, tin and other resources of England, growing wealthy by commerce, 'like a private individual', with Italians and Greeks.[37] The measures were not popular with English merchants, either who found themselves taxed more at English ports or now having to compete with the king.

Edward also sought to resurrect more archaic streams of income. He set men to work sifting through the Chancery rolls and imposing fines on those found to have taken possession of an inheritance without observing ancient and largely ignored rules. By these means, 'and more of a similar nature than can possibly be conceived by a man who is inexperienced in such matters,' Edward grew rich.[38] A large part of the reason for such diversification and the development of the Chamber system of finance was Edward's desire to be free of Parliament. Taxation there always came at a cost, either of reform or concession to the Commons and Edward had no desire to be beholden to any man or institution. Louis XI had insisted that the Commons had driven Edward to undertake a war in France that the king himself had not wished for, and he might well have been right. Parliament met only twice after Edward's return from France until his death eight years later, and the final meeting was only in response to a crisis. The first, in 1478, was to facilitate the resumption of grants that Edward wanted. One of the casualties of that sitting was George Neville, Duke of Bedford. The son of John Neville, Warwick's brother, it was in George Neville that the male succession of the Neville inheritance ought to have been vested, and it was on George Neville's life and male line that both George's and, more so, Richard's title to that inheritance rested. George Neville was stripped of his dukedom, and any other title he might claim. Parliament declared that this was because he lacked a sufficient income or landed estate to support the rank, but he was only deficient in these because Edward had bypassed the law to give former Neville possessions to his two brothers.[39] He seems to have entered Richard's household, joining his aunt, Warwick's widow, as one of the fallen Neville family given sanctuary by Richard, though perhaps not for entirely altruistic reasons.[40]

For Richard, watching all this, there were some lessons to be learned and some warnings to be heeded. He was amongst those disappointed by the conclusion of the French expedition, as his opposition to the treaty demonstrates. On returning home, he saw the lawlessness such a failure and the return of thousands of disappointed and angry soldiers could bring. Duke Charles had gone from ally to enemy in a stroke and was threatening to foment rebellion in England, as well as, embarrassingly to some, using Edward's soldiers to do what Edward had not. Richard had been forced to lead a sizeable armed force north, into his own home region, in an action that could only have been related to disquiet after the return from France. He had seen his brother deliver swift, harsh justice in a way that was successful and, according to the well-placed writer of the *Crowland Chronicle*, avoided more significant problems. Worryingly, Edward had still failed to deliver on the Yorkist manifesto. War with France was now off the table and lawlessness at home had been reignited, even if it was quickly quashed. It was the Commons in Parliament who had been their father's greatest support, and which was becoming an increasingly influential force in English politics, but Edward was now seeking methods to suppress that authority and restrict its influence by seeking ways to raise income without parliamentary assistance. Richard might legitimately wonder whether Edward had really learned any lesson from the events of 1470, or was simply being pushed closer to tyranny by his preference for an easy life.

The realm was disquieted throughout much of 1476. The Milanese ambassador in Burgundy continued to report to his master that Duke Charles was eyeing the English crown. On 9 February, he wrote that Duke Charles 'gathers in Englishmen for his service, taking as many as come, so that recently he has enlisted more than 2,000 of them, in order to win popularity in that kingdom, in which he says he has a strong party and is much beloved. Once he has that kingdom he need only lift his other shoulder and forthwith he would be King of France.'[41] It may have been idle posturing, but this was just weeks before Richard had cause to visit York. On 16 May, John Howard, John Morton, William Dudley and Thomas St Ledger received an exemplification from the king explaining that they had been asked by Edward to make the offer of terms that became the content of the Treaty of Picquigny.[42] All four were most likely becoming agitated becuase of the obvious unpopularity of Edward's chosen policy and feared a backlash similar to that which had followed Henry VI's marriage to Margaret of Anjou and the ceding of large swathes of France. In October, Richard was at Westminster a week after his birthday to witness the charter that granted Evesham two fairs a year, but as late as November he was handed a commission of oyer and terminer to investigate offences in Essex by a group of named individuals. The involvement of the king's brother, the Earls of Essex and Rivers, Lords Stanley, Howard and Audley, and a host of knights, suggests that it was a serious matter touching the king's security.

One of Edward's antidotes to this well of ill feeling in the wake of the French campaign was to stage a lavish and pointed ceremony to reinter the bodies of his father Richard, Duke of York, and his brother, Edmund, Earl of Rutland. York and Edmund had been killed at the Battle of Wakefield on 30 December 1460, and after the Battle of Towton on 29 March 1461, Edward had ordered their heads removed from Micklegate Bar at York and reunited with their bodies. It is not recorded where they were then buried, but it is likely to have been at the Priory of St John the Evangelist near Pontefract Castle. Richard was appointed to act as chief mourner for the procession from Pontefract to their final resting place within the Yorkist mausoleum at Fotheringhay. There is no record as to whether Richard requested this honour, but as the greatest lord in the north as well as one of York's sons he was an appropriate candidate. His role in the proceedings does at least suggest a genuine affection for his lost father and brother, or at least for the familial bonds and personal heritage they represented, though there is nothing to confirm his feelings about the event.[43] On Sunday 21 July 1476, the two bodies were exhumed, and their coffins placed beneath cloth of gold coverings bearing a white satin cross. The structure surrounding the caskets was huge, burning with thousands of candles that made the church so hot the doors had to be kept open and some windows removed.

An effigy of York, life-sized and with his eyes open as though he was living still, knelt above his coffin, his hands clasped together in prayer and his eyes gazing upward at an image of Christ. York's effigy was dressed in dark blue gowns trimmed with ermine, the mourning clothes of a king, and an angel held a golden crown just above his head to signify that, according to Yorkist ideology, he had been King by Right of England and France. That evening, masses for the dead were said by the bishops and clergymen in attendance.

On Monday, the funeral procession left Pontefract, leaving behind the valuable structure and adornments as a gift to the church. Richard rode at the head of the spectacle, followed by the Earl of Northumberland and other lords, including Lord Stanley. The coffins were pulled by seven horses trapped all in black, and all of the mourners wore black gowns with black hoods. The only splash of colour was provided by the heralds and kings of arms, who wore their surcoats over their black attire. The carriage was draped in black cloth, pulled back only enough to allow onlookers to see the effigy of York. Throughout the journey, each morning the bishops would ride ahead to prepare the next church in which the coffins would spend the night and each evening requiem masses were held. It took eight days for the funeral to reach Fotheringhay in Northamptonshire on 29 July. The dean of the college at the Church of St Mary and All Saints in Fotheringhay, a Yorkist foundation of York's uncle Edward, met the coffins outside the church with ten bishops and the Archbishop of York. Here Edward joined the funeral, dressed, as the effigy of his father was, in royal mourning robes of dark blue, furred with ermine, reportedly weeping and treating the bodies with reverence. York's coffin was placed before the altar inside a church filled with women in mourning clothes, including Queen Elizabeth and two of her daughters. Edmund's body was placed in the Chapel of Our Lady nearby, and that night, former servants of York guarded both the bodies.

The following day, 30 July, the funeral proper was held, and three masses were said for York and Edmund. Edward offered the mass penny, meant to pay for wine, bread and candles for the ceremony, and offered his respects again, followed by the queen, their daughters, Richard and a line of dignitaries.

After the bodies were placed into their new tombs, Edward hosted a feast at Fotheringhay Castle; it cost at least £331. Thousands of people were provided with the king's hospitality, with several thousand given a penny in alms by the king. The accounts record forty barrels of wine, thirty-one kegs of ale, 139 cows, 210 sheep, 200 pigs and plenty of chickens, capons, cygnets, salmon, pike, bread, honey, milk and eggs amongst the purchases for the feast. It was a poignant moment for the Yorkist family. Their father and brother were now within familiar surroundings and had received the respect their bodies had been denied sixteen years earlier. It was also a propaganda stunt on an epic scale.

The notion that York had been King by Right was designed to give added weight and credibility to Edward's rule, as though he was the second Yorkist king rather than the first. The fact that Henry VI was the third in his dynasty had been a significant factor in the unwillingness of the establishment to abandon him in favour of York. Now, Edward sought the protection of at least the perception of being established, so that his son would be the third monarch of their dynasty, with all the extra authority that should bring him. It was also a reminder to anyone who continued to doubt, in the wake of the French campaign, that Edward was here to stay. Edward's failure to deliver his father's manifesto for change and war with France had caused him problems for years. This funeral not only served to reconnect Edward with his father in the public mind but also to symbolise the final placing at rest of his father and what he had stood for. Yorkism could no longer seek to reform the establishment because Edward now *was* the establishment. This is perhaps a cynical interpretation of the event and does not preclude Edward's genuine desire to honour the man who had presented him with his throne. The extravaganza of Yorkist pageantry, religious conformity, the end of his father's work and the lavish display of largesse were at least equally important to a king who could not appear to be as nervous as Edward was. For York's youngest son, it was a chance to demonstrate again his position at the very centre of Yorkist power, but also an opportunity to connect with and mourn a father whose name he bore and who had not lived to see his youngest son's achievements.

Throughout the kingdom's troubles, Richard continued to foster his links with northern families. An example of this at work can be found in January 1476 when Elizabeth Scrope signed an indenture with Richard to secure the duke's care for her sixteen-year-old son. Elizabeth's husband, the 5th Baron Scrope of Masham, had died a few months earlier and whether to protect her son's inheritance from aggressors, from the king's increasingly reckless disregard for the laws of inheritance or simply to foster strong ties with the most powerful man in the region, she looked to Richard for help. Thomas, 6th Baron Scrope of Masham could trace his family as northern landholders back to the days of Edward the Confessor. His father and grandfather had been loyal servants of the House of Lancaster before accepting its fall and being reconciled to Yorkist rule. Elizabeth waived the fee usually associated with a lord taking control of a minor heir and promised that all her servants would also enter Richard's service, suggesting that she was concerned for her future as a widow and looked to Richard for some form of protection and support. Thomas, Lord Scrope, entered Richard's household and was married to one of John Neville's daughters, a match almost certainly arranged by Richard which brought Lord Scrope closer by marrying him to Richard's wife's cousin. All of this demonstrates that despite problems in England at a national level, Richard continued to shore up his own local and regional authority, building the network of connections that would help him retain power in the area for the rest of his life. In doing so, he seems to have followed the example of Warwick, positioning himself as the natural protector of the region and its people, winning rather than demanding their loyalty and gaining their affection along the way. Richard is often characterised as lacking the easy, affable nature of his oldest brother, but those who knew him during these years developed loyalties to the man that would prove impossible to break.

Richard and Anne became parents at some point during this period too. They were blessed with a son, named Edward for his uncle, perhaps another signal of the esteem in which Richard still held his brother. Born at Middleham Castle, he was known as Edward of Middleham, but even the year in which he was born is not recorded. His birth has been placed as early as December 1473 but is likely to have been as late as 1476.[44] He would spend much of his childhood at Middleham Castle. His governess was Anne Idley, whose husband Peter wrote *Instructions to his Son*, an instructional text on raising boys, so it is likely that no effort or expense was spared in his education and care. Nevertheless, he remains a character shaded from view, a shadow made all the more impenetrable by the light that has been shone continually on the life of his father. Like many children in medieval England, he simply does not appear in detail in the historical record, and when something as fundamental as his year of birth cannot be known, the hopes of finding the real boy in the fog of history are all but lost.

Personal disaster would strike the family of the House of York before the end of 1476, perhaps just as Richard and Anne were celebrating the birth of their son. Anne's sister Isabel, Duchess of Clarence, died on 22 December 1476, around ten weeks after giving birth to a son who would only outlive her by a matter of ten days. George and Isabel had lost their firstborn, a daughter, at sea off Calais in 1470. Since then, they had become parents to a girl, Margaret, born on 14 August 1473, and a son named Edward, born on 25 February 1475. Their second, short-lived son was named Richard, either for George's father or his brother, but the choice of name suggests no irreparable rift between George and Richard after the fallout of the division of Warwick's estates. Isabel possibly died from complications following the baby's delivery. Infections were a common danger and no pregnancy during this period could ever be considered safe for the mother or the baby. In an age before proper hygiene, detailed understanding of the female body, germ theory or medication, whether for pain relief or to treat infections, complications during pregnancy or after birth were no respecters of rank, and noble women were in as much danger as even the poorest wife. Within a fortnight, George had been given a son, only to have his wife and then the baby snatched away from him by the cold fingers of fate. For any man, it was a bitter blow that might trigger rage and resentment. For George, who seems always to have felt resentment at his position,[45] as lofty as it was, it was a dangerous disaster too, which would soon cost him dearly.

Not many would have shed fewer tears than Edward in early 1477 when news reached England that Duke Charles had been killed at the

Battle of Nancy on 5 January. Having engaged himself in quarrels almost the length and breadth of Europe, Charles took an army to Nancy in the dead of a bitterly cold winter to fight men of Lorraine and Switzerland. He lost, and it cost him his life. He was found days after the battle frozen into the water of a river, his face split open by a halberd, his body stripped naked and cut open. His face had reportedly been so chewed by wild animals that his physician had to identify the body from his long fingernails and old scars. It ended one problem for Edward, since Duke Charles was suspected of sponsoring trouble in England and coveting Edward's crown, but it created another set of issues that had to be addressed. The Burgundian inheritance devolved entirely on Charles' only legitimate child, his daughter Mary, an unmarried nineteen-year-old. Suddenly, she was the focus of intense attention. Louis XI seized the opportunity to snatch most of the Burgundian territories and try to secure a marriage between Mary and his own heir, the future Charles VIII, who was thirteen years Mary's junior. Richard's sister Margaret, now Dowager Duchess of Burgundy, was left trying to protect her stepdaughter's inheritance and secure a marriage that would keep Burgundy independent from France.

Naturally, Margaret turned almost immediately to her brother, the King of England, for support. An embassy arrived at Edward's court from Burgundy at the end of January and tried to appeal to Edward's chivalric imperative to defend his sister and the isolated Mary of Burgundy. Edward was little affected by such notions, and Margaret was perhaps relying on stirring feeling within the court or the country rather than hoping Edward would spring to her defence of his own volition. To Edward, the French pension and promised marriage between one of his daughters and the Dauphin were of far more importance. Sir John Donne was dispatched to Louis XI's court to raise concerns about the French king's plan to now marry the Dauphin to Mary. Somehow, Louis reassured Edward whilst continuing to try to marry his son to the new Duchess of Burgundy.[46] The Crowland Chronicler noted that Margaret altered her approach slightly when Edward proved unwilling to send help. The writer recorded that 'the duchess, lady Margaret, whose affections were fixed on her brother Clarence beyond any of the rest of her kindred, exerted all her strength and energies that Mary ... might be united in marriage to that duke.'[47] Margaret, it seemed, was understood to have a soft spot for George. If it were true, it was doubtless the result of their shared upbringing and similar ages. Margaret was to show herself a pursuer of lost causes throughout the rest of her life, and she immediately hit a wall of opposition in Edward.

If George really was Margaret's favourite sibling, then there is no evidence of such favouritism outside Crowland's assertion. It is more likely that Margaret was, in fact, using George's bad reputation to drive some action, but not from Edward. Before his death, Duke Charles had been trying to secure an alliance with Frederick III, the Holy Roman Emperor, and a marriage for Mary to Frederick's son and heir Maximilian. Touting a potential match between George and Mary rang alarm bells across Europe. Edward simply could not allow his brother to make such a powerful alliance with an heiress who had also inherited Duke Charles' Lancastrian blood, serving to strengthen any assault George may seek to launch against Edward. In France, Louis was concerned by the threat of a renewed Anglo-Burgundian alliance and the arrival of extra soldiers at Calais under the command of Lord Hastings, who had been averse to the peace of 1475 despite taking a pension,[48] can only have served to heighten his anxiety. On 13 February a Great Council met to discuss the fallout from the death of Duke Charles. Sir John Paston was convinced that either George, Richard, or both of them, would imminently take an army to Burgundy to help their sister. Paston himself was heading to Calais with Lord Hastings and was certain there would be war: 'It seemeth that the World is all quavering, it will reboil somewhere, so that I deem young men shall be cherished,' a reference to a need for soldiers.[49]

The truth was almost certainly very different. Edward would never risk his prized pension, nor the marriage of his daughter, to help Mary, nor even to support his sister Margaret. It was even less likely that he would allow George to become ruler of one of Europe's richest nations. Equally, Margaret cannot have thought George was really the right option for her stepdaughter even if she was fond of her brother. Burgundy needed power at its back, an army capable of fending off Louis XI and defending its independence. George could not offer that, particularly when Edward remained unwilling to involve England and fearful of his brother's intentions. The only real hope lay in the union with Maximilian that would wrap the protective arms of the Holy Roman Empire and the Habsburgs around Burgundy. Margaret had a good deal of influence over her young stepdaughter so that her reported desire to marry Mary to George was immediately viewed as something she could achieve. It was just the spur that Frederick needed to finalise details of a marriage to Maximilian, which took place on 16 August 1477. George had been used. Again. Perhaps he was guilty of allowing his vanity to draw him into such plots, and it is striking that Richard never suffered, or allowed himself to suffer, the same treatment, but it was yet another setback for George.

The same year, the King of Scotland wrote to Edward suggesting a marriage between one of James III's sisters and George, as well as one of his brothers, the Duke of Albany, to Margaret. Edward politely replied that although he knew the idea sprang from James' affection for Edward, both George and Margaret were still within the first year of the death of their spouses and so, in line with traditions of mourning, could not yet remarry.[50] Edward was cutting George off at every pass, adding insult to injury. George was never a patient man, ever mindful of his exalted position, and the culmination of his losses and setbacks was to prove explosive, tearing apart the unity of the House of York that Edward had worked so hard, and been so forgiving, to project.

11

After E., G. Should Reign

And because there was a certain prophesy that after E. (that is, Edward IV), G. should reign, for this ambiguity George Duke of Clarence, who was the middle brother between Edward and Richard, was killed on account of his name George

John Rous[1]

Rous's story of prophecy, which implicates Richard, as 'G' for Gloucester, would be immortalised by Shakespeare, but the events of 1478 it refers to were far from a simple case of fear on Edward's part. If Richard did feel any disappointment or resentment at the way the French campaign had fallen out, he kept such feelings to himself. It seems likely that he had wanted Edward to help Margaret in her distress, even if it was exaggerated, or to take an army back across the Channel himself to defend his sister. The later view of Richard as a schemer who kept his designs secret for a long time was born of his smooth acceptance of setbacks such as these. It is presumed that he must have allowed his annoyance to fester until he reached the point of waiting for a chance to avenge himself. The application of hindsight is always dangerous, and there is nothing in Richard's behaviour in the immediate aftermath of these events, or even later, to suggest he nurtured a grudge. The acceptance of setbacks was a feature of Richard's life from childhood. He had been left to face an enemy army aged nine, fled the country twice into an unknown future, fought in battles with all the risk they brought and stepped into a region belonging to a former mentor whose death his brother had brought about. Richard was a man who made the best of what he had rather than fixating on what he did not have or thought he ought to have. The same was never true of George.

One of the rumbling, fractious disputes in which Richard involved himself, and which is reasonably well documented, relates to fishgarths around York. A fishgarth was a manmade dam or weir in a river or along the coast that was designed to trap fish in large numbers. For landowners or wealthy merchants who installed them, they offered an efficient method of increasing the number of fish caught, but for others, they hampered navigation of waterways and reduced the available catch downriver. Fishgarths were unpopular, but their operators were usually those who did not need to concern themselves with the problems of others. On 22 March 1476, just nine days after Richard's visit to York with Northumberland and their 5,000 men, the city officials wrote to the Bishop of Durham to advise him that the king had ordered all new fishgarths to be removed on pain of a 100 mark fine. The bishop, and presumably other local landowners who received similar letters, were given three months to remove any such blockages. After that, they were to be fined and would continue to be penalised at a rate of 100 marks per months for as long as they defied the ruling. Edward was entering his phase of maximising royal revenue, and it is telling that he chose to offer a fine rather than any more direct action against those who defied him, but the amount was significant and would have been a deterrent. The city also added, aware of the increased impact that it would have, that Richard had been shown the king's commission 'and after the sight therof it hath pleased his goode lordeship to graunt to us therin his gracious aide and assistence.' More than that, Richard had promised 'to directe his ful honourable lettres unto his baillies and tenauntz', so that he was willing to begin the process on his own lands.[2]

Enclosed with the letter was the transcript of the message Richard sent to his own tenants in which he ordered them to 'ammove, take up and withdrawe all suche forsaide fishe garthes, piles, stakes, hays, scarves, and kidelles aswell to us belongeing as to any of you.'[3] Richard was planning to set an example on his own lands that he expected others, like the Bishop of Durham, to follow. Such willingness to accept the rule of law even to his own detriment was probably striking to most in the north, but Richard was there to see his brother's will done in the region. His own sense of equity may have been at play too. It is impossible to discern his true motives, but Richard won nothing material by the example he set. In fact, he would lose money and a steady supply of fish. All he stood to gain was the affection of the city of York and its people who could see in him a lord willing to champion their complaints against the most powerful interests in the region.

Eighteen months later, the issue remained unresolved. On 21 October 1477, York's officials wrote to Richard to explain that they hoped to write to the king about the failure to remove many fishgarths. There is no reference to any remaining on Richard's own lands, suggesting he had fulfilled his promise, but the mayor and aldermen asked Richard if he would 'impende your favorable gude grace concernyng the reformacion of certan ffisshegarthez as yit standyng in certain ryvers.' If the duke would continue to support the city in the matter, they promised to 'evermore pray to the almyfluent God for your prosperus estate.'[4] Soon after, they wrote to the king about one fishgarth in particular, which was causing a hazardous blockage to river traffic on the River Aire. The obstruction, called Goldalegarth, lay within one of the king's Duchy of Lancaster holdings at Snaith, on the East Riding of Yorkshire. The city therefore desired direction from the king concerning its removal, since it was something 'your sade besechours durst not ne will attempt, your plesour not knawen to theym in that behalfe.'[5]

Richard replied to the city from London on 15 November 1477 to advise them that he had 'moved the kynges grace in the same and therapon his said grace hathe commaunded us at our next home commyng to take a vewe and oversight of the said garthes and weeres.' He was obviously keen for them to be made aware that he had intervened directly with the king as they had requested. He advised the mayor and aldermen that he had been given authority to have any fishgarth or weir erected without the permission of the Justices of the Ayre 'pulled doune'. Richard ended the letter by assuring them that 'the which or eny other thing that we may do to the wele of your said cite we shall put us in our uttermoste devour and gode will by Godes grace.'[6] As late as October 1482, there was a fracas at Snaith when men were arrested for breaking up the fishgarth there. York intervened on their behalf, since it was done with the king's permission, but the strength of feeling of those protecting fishgarths is clear to see.[7]

If Richard felt a concern for the common man who lacked a voice in a world run by a handful of landowning gentry and nobility, one can cynically dismiss his interest, but it is hard to find another explanation for some of his actions. A willingness to upset vested interests in favour of those who were rendered incapable of securing justice for themselves is a developing feature of Richard's public life. He gained no wealth or office by these actions. He risked making enemies amongst the higher strata of society so, in fact, it came with a cost. His willingness to be governed himself, as in the case of Catherine Williamson and her husband's murderers as well as fishgarths, suggests that this is not some posturing to force the obedience of the region. In one dispute, Richard's increasingly personal relationship with the city officials can again be seen at work, as can his willingness to upset other powerful interests. During the summer of 1476, the city sought to dismiss its clerk, Thomas Yotton, because of 'diverse and many offences, excessive takynges of money, misguiding of our bookes, accomptes and other evidences.'[8] Essentially, Yotton was accused of fiddling the city's finances and pocketing money himself.

Henry Percy, Earl of Northumberland, intervened on Yotton's behalf and tried to prevent the dismissal in an action that would have been considered typical of a nobleman's use of his authority to sidestep the law and protect those he wished to preserve in their posts.[9] Richard was asked by the mayor and aldermen to intervene, not because his authority might overrule that of Northumberland (though it would), but rather to protect their right to select their own officers. On 8 July, Richard wrote from Middleham Castle to Lords Hastings and Stanley to ask them to press his case to the king. The route to Edward's ear is here made clear, as is Richard's willingness to work with those who could influence his brother, even Lord Stanley, with whom Richard had frequently butted heads years earlier. After reciting Yotton's offences, Richard tells the lords that the mayor and aldermen 'have instaunced me to shew unto theyme therin my goode lordeship'. He asked Hastings and Stanley 'at this myne instaunce and praier to move the kinges goode grace on my behaulf' to allow the city to appoint their own choice of clerk 'accordeing to thayre liberties, grauntes, privileges, laudable custumes and olde ordinances'. Richard stressed the personal nature of the appeal to the king, asking Hastings and Stanley to request that Edward 'be unto theyme therin the more singler goode and gracious sovereine lorde for my sake.' To further encourage the recipients of the letter, Richard added that 'in this your so dooing ye shall not oonely have merite of God but doo unto me right singler pleaser and to thayme thing right thankefull.'[10] From this episode, Richard gained nothing beyond the increased affection of York's officials and a reputation for ensuring that the correct, legal outcome was achieved. For Northumberland, it was a slap on the wrist, a reminder of his subservient place in the north and a warning that the old levers of livery and maintenance were jammed and a lord's ability to ride roughshod over the law for his own gain would be blocked under Richard's jurisdiction. It can only have left a bitter taste in the earl's mouth that he would spend a decade trying to wash away.

The city of York was willing to show its appreciation to its new champion. When Richard visited in early 1477, he was given a gift of six swans and six pike 'for his grete labours of nojw late made unto the kings goode grace for the conservacion of the liberties of this citie,'[11] a reference to the success in the Thomas Yotton matter. The visit came within weeks of the sad death of Richard's sister-in-law Isabel Neville, aged just twenty-five. George would soon become the centre of rumours about a marriage to Mary of Burgundy or the King of Scotland's sister, but Edward would do all within his considerable power to block both matches. For the seemingly unstable George, there was always a breaking point, and 1477 would see a final, sad and divisive resolution to the matter.

Isabel probably succumbed to tuberculosis, perhaps exacerbated by her recent pregnancy and labour. Although childbearing remained a grave threat to life, George was unable to accept what had happened. The delay in his reaction may have several explanations. It is usually acknowledged that Isabel's death sent George into apoplexy and certainly it would fit his character to view the loss as a personal affront from a world out to get him, but the fact that he fell silent for some months must be explained. Such a delay removes credibility from the notion that it was a fit of pique brought on by a sense of injustice. There would soon be a charge that George had plotted to have his son and heir Edward, later Earl of Warwick, removed from the kingdom either to Ireland or Burgundy and that this had taken him time to set in motion before he acted as he did.[12] The alternative reading is that it was not Isabel's death, or at least not solely that loss, which drove George into a self-destructive series of actions. It may have been the subsequent efforts by Edward to prevent him from remarrying any lady who would give him a significant position in the world. The king might, entirely reasonably, have judged that his brother was too unpredictable and had shown himself too fond of rebellion to allow him any match that would facilitate a threat to Edward's throne. To George, it was abundantly clear that his brother's generous forgiveness was not genuine and that he would never be free of the taint of his former dalliances with revolt. Something had to give.

George sprang into action on Saturday 12 April 1477, more than four months after his wife's death. Ankarette Twynyho, who had been a lady-in-waiting to Isabel Neville, was at her manor of Cayford in Somerset, her mistress's household having been disbanded. Her peace was rudely interrupted by Richard Hyde, a man from Warwick, and a local man named Roger Strugge who burst into her home with eighty or more men 'equipped and assembled in manner of war and insurrection'.[13] Ankarette was seized and dragged to Bath. On the next day, she was moved 'under similar duress' to Cirencester in Gloucestershire, and by eight o'clock on Monday evening, she found herself in Warwick, a journey of some 70 miles in three days. She was apparently under some form of arrest but 'without a writ, warrant or any other lawful authority'. Ankarette was thrown into a cell for the night, though it is unclear whether she yet understood the nature of the charges against her. Her daughter and son-in-law, who had tried to keep up with the soldiers who had snatched her, were ordered to leave Warwick and forced to find lodgings at Stratford-upon-Avon, 10 miles away. On Tuesday 15 April at nine o'clock in the morning, the bewildered Ankarette found herself at Warwick's Guildhall standing before George, Duke of Clarence. To her shock, George accused her of killing his wife by poison. She was indicted for having given Isabel 'a venomous drink of ale mixed with poison' on 10 October 1476, which had caused her to slowly sicken until her death on 22 December. A jury was produced and found her guilty, later claiming that they 'for fear and dread of great threats, and fearful of losing their lives and goods, reached the said verdict against their own wishes, truth and conscience.' By midday, Ankarette had been charged, tried, found guilty and sentenced to death. The sheriff of Warwick was ordered to have her immediately drawn to the gallows at Myton, and she was hanged. Her family later secured a reversal of the conviction and a return of her property and good name, but for Ankarette, vindication came too late.

Did George really believe this lady-in-waiting had poisoned his wife with a draught that took more than two months to kill her? It seems unlikely unless his petulant rage against the world he considered cruel to him had disconnected him from reason. The sorry truth for Ankarette is that her death was an elaborate message aimed primarily at the man George saw at the centre of the plots to deny him a fair place in the world; his brother the king. George had exercised regal powers in his shoddy assumption of authority to act in such a high-handed way. It was sharply at odds with a response that might have been expected from Richard in such circumstance and the startling contrast between his brothers was something Edward could no longer ignore. George had probably acted in a deliberately clumsy and provocative way to attract Edward's attention, but if he thought this was the way to get what he wanted, he had, on this occasion, overestimated his brother's capacity to forgive. Richard might have been able to justify such an act as Constable, if he could give it the colour of treason against a member of the royal family, but George had no such powers with which to justify his actions. *The Crowland Chronicle* records that a whispering campaign broke out at court, with 'flatterers' carrying messages to Edward and George spreading gossip about what the other was saying and threatening.[14]

The crunch came in May 1477 when an astronomer named John Stacy was arrested. Crowland describes Stacy as 'a great sorcerer' who was arrested, 'among numerous charges', for making lead images of Richard, Lord Beauchamp, in order to bring about his death at the request of his 'adulterous wife'. When Stacy was questioned 'in a very severe examination', he implicated Thomas Burdet, a member of George's household, who was also arrested. The pair were sentenced to death and hanged at Tyburn, where each was permitted to make a final speech. Though Stacy spoke 'but faintly', Burdet launched into a long, loud and defiant soliloquy which ended with an exclamation of 'Behold! I must die; whereas I never did such things as these.'[15] The day after their executions, George burst into a Council meeting at Westminster with Doctor William Goddard, a man with close Lancastrian links. Goddard was instructed by George to read aloud the speech made by Burdet to the Council, which he did and then left the room. Edward was enraged. It was the final straw in George's field of betrayals that Edward had indulged up until now. George was summoned to appear before his brother at Westminster on 10 June and, after a dressing down from the king, he was arrested and thrown into the Tower, where he would languish for six months.

In January 1478, Parliament was summoned, and part of the reason for the assembly was to try George, Duke of Clarence, brother of the king, on a charge of high treason. Edward conducted the case himself, and George offered his own defence. As Crowland commented, the brothers had shown their keen grasp of legal argument several years earlier when Richard and George had disputed the Warwick inheritance and Edward had arbitrated. In this case, George cannot have laboured under any illusion that he had a chance of escaping from this crisis of his own making. The king did not open proceedings in Parliament to attaint the most senior nobleman in the land without being certain that he would get the outcome he wanted. The attainder of George, Duke of Clarence, began with a recollection of 'the manifold grete Conspiracies, malicious and heinous Tresons'[16] that Edward had previously suffered at the hands of his 'unnaturall Subgetts, Rebelles and Traytoures'. In a thinly veiled reference to George, the attainder claims that Edward, having crushed all these threats and punished most of those involved, yet 'not oonly he hath spared the multitudes in theire feldes and assemblies overcomen, but thaym and certeyn other, the grete movers, sturers and executours of suche haynous Tresons.'

There was a new threat now, 'agaynst his mooste Royall persone, and against the persones of the blessed Princesse oure alther Soveraigen and Liege Lady the Quene, of my Lorde the Prince theire Son and Heire, and of all the other of thaire most noble issue.' The plot extended, it was said, to encompass the 'grete parte of the Noble of this Lande' and was 'a moch higher, moch more malicious, more unnaturell and lothely Treason, than atte eny tyme hertoforn hath been compassed, purposed and conspired.' All of this build-up was a combination of Edward's anger at the betrayal and the position it placed him in, his disappointment that his forgiveness had been thrown back in his face and the need to explain why he would take such an extreme action as demanding the death of his own brother. It exposed a crack at the heart of the House of York that Edward cannot have wished to make visible to all. The perpetrator, not yet named, was 'the person that of all erthely creatures, beside the dutie of ligeaunce, by nature, by benefette, by gratitude, and by geftes and grauntes of Goodes and Possessions, hath been moost bounden and behalden to have dradde, loved, honoured, and evere thanked the Kyng.' The need to ensure that the dire nature of the treason was understood is expressed in the length of this introduction.

Finally, with the faux suspense ramped up and Edward's reticence trumpeted loudly enough, there is the final, dramatic reveal: 'He sheweth you therfore, that all this hath been entended by his Brother George the Duke of Clarence.' Edward's generous treatment of his brother who was 'not borne to have any lifelode, but oonly of the Kynges grace' was recited and added to by the assertion that no 'Kyng of Englande hertoforn within his Royaulme gave soo largely to eny his Brothers.' George's betrayal was not, in fact, anything new, as the Act next acknowledges before reminding those gathered to try the duke 'whiche all the Kyng, by nature and love moeved, utterly forgave, entendyng to have putte all in perpetuell oblivion'. Despite this, George had indulged in 'newe Treasons, more haynous and lothely than ever aforn' by plotting to destroy not only Edward but all of his children, with foreign assistance as well as the domestic rebels he hoped to stir up. An example of the trouble George was causing was given in his use of servants to spread the word that Thomas Burdet had been wrongly convicted, giving money to any who would listen and feasting groups of them with venison the duke provided.

In an appeal to the superstitious folk of the country, George, it was claimed, had accused Edward of using necromancy and of poisoning his subjects 'to th'entent to deslaundre the Kyng in the moost haynous wise he couth.'[17] These scandalous charges might have been meant to cover the really dangerous matters that Edward had to charge George with, but on which he might have preferred to keep silent. If he was going to justify the execution of his own brother, though, he needed every bit of dirt he could get to stick. George was charged with embarking on 'the falsest and moost unnaturall coloured pretense that man might imagine, falsely and untruely noysed, published and saide, that the Kyng oure Sovereigne Lorde was a Bastard, and not begottone to reigne uppon us.' This particular charge will be discussed in greater detail later, but it was in circulation on the Continent during Edward's lifetime and before George was charged with promulgating it. Warwick may have come into contact with the accusation at Louis XI's court and possibly passed it on to George as part of his efforts to separate him from his brother. If Edward were illegitimate, then George would be the rightful heir of Richard, Duke of York, and a belief in the story he had been told might go some way to explaining his ructious behaviour throughout the preceding years.

The real problem that Edward faced was laid bare next, the one that he probably felt threatened him the most and played on his mind for as long as George lived. His brother had secured 'an exemplificacion undre the Grete Seall of Herry the Sexte' which included a provision that 'if the said Herry, and Edward his first begoton Son, died withoute Issue Male of theire Body, that the seid Duke and his Heires, shulde be Kyng of this Lande'. Henry VI and his son Prince Edward had died without producing any male heirs, so the exemplification made George legal heir to the throne, a possible Lancastrian alternative hiding within the House of York. The document had been kept secret by George, perhaps only uncovered when his property was searched, though Edward may well have been aware of its existence for some time. The records of the Parliament that had been held during the brief readeption of Henry VI were destroyed when Edward IV returned, but the Acts it passed were never expressly repealed. It is reasonable to assume that Parliament had reasserted Henry's right to the throne and re-established the succession on his son, possibly with reference to the agreement with George too. This would mean that although Edward was ruling *de facto* – in fact – George was king *de jure* – in law. Edward had tolerated Lancastrian threats before but had lost patience with their plots after his return from exile. Henry VI and his son were dead, even Henry Holland was no longer a problem, but George remained a man in a position to harness Lancastrian sympathy against his brother. He had been given a lot of rope by Edward and had chosen to fashion it into a noose.

The delay in George's response to his wife's death might be explained by the next portion of the attainder, in which it is claimed George used the time to try and have his son spirited away to safety so that he could remain a threat to Edward if George failed. The Abbot of Tewkesbury, a clerk named John Tapton and a Roger Harewell had been enlisted 'to cause a straunge Childe to have be brought into his Castell of Warwyk, and there to have be putte and kept in likelinesse of his Sonne and Heire.' The plan was to replace George's son Edward with an imposter and have the real boy sent 'into Ireland, or into Flaundres, oute of this Lande'. If George travelled to Ireland, or to his sister Margaret in Flanders, that would explain the inability to locate him during the months after Isabel's death. It would also be a point of concern for a future Tudor regime who believed they had that son, then Earl of Warwick, under lock and key in the Tower. Tapton and Harewell denied having found a boy to impersonate Warwick, though strikingly there is no denial that the real Edward had been taken away, so it remains possible that George managed to get his son away and that Tapton and Harewell either lied, or a boy was found from elsewhere.

The king might, the attainder continued, have forgiven George his efforts to raise revolt if he had not already shown himself 'to be incorrigible' by his previous betrayals. Furthermore, Edward hoped to avoid the 'effusion of Christian blode' that would be caused by a fresh outbreak of civil war and was responsible to God for the preservation of his own heirs, the peace of the Church and the good governance of the nation. He could not ignore George's actions any longer. Parliament enacted that 'George Duke of Clarence, be convicte and atteyntit of Heigh Treason, commyttet and doon agaynst the Kynges moost Royall persone; and that the same Duke, by the said auctorite, forfett from hym and his heyres for ever, the Honoure, Estate, Dignite and name of Duke.' All of George's lands and properties were seised too with no right for his heirs to claim them later. With the words of assent – 'Le Roy le voet'[18] – the fall of George, Duke of Clarence, was complete. On 18 February, at the age of twenty-eight, George was executed in private, as his rank required. A legend sprang up that he had been given the honour of selecting the method of his execution himself and that, in a last act of petulant defiance, he chose to be drowned in a vat of Edward's favourite malmsey wine. There is no record of this, though it does not seem beyond the realms of George's rebelliousness.

For Edward, another threat had been removed. Whether he was genuinely reluctant to move against his brother or glad of an excuse to be rid of his troublemaking cannot be known, but his previous willingness to forgive George's every wrong suggests that he had no real desire to act against him. There can be no doubt that George was the architect of his own destruction. Shakespeare would have Richard plotting to achieve it, but that is storytelling for dramatic purposes.

Dominic Mancini would write at the end of 1483 that 'Richard duke of Gloucester was so overcome with grief for his brother, that he could not dissimulate so well, but that he was overheard to say that he would one day avenge his brother's death.'[19] Mancini was reporting gossip that had stewed for five years by this point and was passed to him by those who disliked Richard and sought, with hindsight, some impetus behind his actions. The surest sign of Richard's feelings about the matter is found in a letter he wrote in September 1484 to give instructions to an envoy, Thomas Barrett, Bishop of Annaghdown, for a visit to James Fitzgerald, Earl of Desmond. Barrett was to make a direct comparison between the execution of the earl's father by John Tiptoft, Earl of Worcester, and the death of George.

> Also, he shalle shewe that albe it the fadre of the said earl, the king than being of young age, was extorciously slayne and murdred by colour of the lawes within Irland by certain persones than havyng the governaunce and rule there, ayenst alle manhode, reason, and good conscience; yet, notwithstanding that the semblable chaunce was and hapned sithen within this royaume of Eingland, as wele of his brother the duc of Clarence as other his nigh kynnesmen and gret frendes, the kinges grace alweys contynueth and hathe inward compassion of the dethe of his said fadre, and is content that his said cousyn now erle by alle ordinate meanes and due course of the lawes, when it shalle lust him at any tyme herafter to sue or attempt for the punysshement therof.[20]

Richard sympathised with the death of the earl's father and made a direct comparison to George's execution and the deaths of other 'nigh kynnesmen and gret frendes'. The Fitzgeralds had believed that the Woodville family of the queen had been behind the death of the earl's father and it is possible to infer that Richard felt the same way about George's execution. It is worth bearing in mind not only that Richard was seeking support from the Earl of Kildare at this point but also that he was zealously pursuing justice on several fronts, as will appear later. Mancini had noted the rumour that Queen Elizabeth had been the real drive behind Edward's determination to be rid of George by 1478. 'The queen then remembered the insults to her family and the calumnies with which she was reproached, namely that according to established usage she was not the legitimate wife of the king.'[21] Again, this may be the application of hindsight, rumour and the story in circulation in 1483 to earlier events, or it may tell us that the story of the illegitimacy of Edward's marriage to Elizabeth Woodville was in the public's ear in 1478. Was the impetus to deal with George a threat to reveal information about Edward's marriage that would be hugely damaging? We cannot know, though the arrest and imprisonment of Robert Stillington, Bishop of Bath and Wells, at the same time as George is worthy of note. Whatever may be guessed, the suggestion in Richard's letter that George's death had been contrary to his own wishes is clear. How he might have rationalised this and expected Edward to continue to indulge George's treachery is hard to imagine. Richard and George seem to have been close, whatever disputes they took up against each other, and it seems reasonable that Richard would not be happy to see one brother killing another. However necessary it might be, it rocked the unity of the House of York and deprived him of a brother he had grown up alongside. It is possible he blamed the queen and her family, but impossible to show with any certainty amidst the later assertions that he was bent on revenge.

The execution of George, Duke of Clarence, again exposed Edward's own insecurities to the country. Just as he had done in the wake of the French campaign with the reburial of his father and brother, the king sought to distract the nation from his personal problems and failings. On 14 January 1478, the five-year-old Anne Mowbray was led into the king's great chamber at Westminster and proclaimed the Princess of the Feast that was held to celebrate her forthcoming marriage. The feast was attended by a large number of the nobility, including Richard, and Anne Mowbray was escorted by the queen's brother Anthony Woodville, Earl Rivers. On the following morning, 15 January, Anne emerged from the queen's apartments at Westminster, her right hand held by John de la Pole, Earl of Lincoln, a nephew of Edward and Richard, and her left by Earl Rivers. They passed through the king's great chamber and into the vast Great Hall of Westminster Palace before reaching St Stephen's Chapel. The chapel was decorated with azure blue carpets worked with golden fleur-de-lis and just inside the door stood a canopy of estate made from dazzling cloth of gold. Beneath the canopy sat the king, the queen, the Prince of Wales, the king's mother Cecily Neville, referred to as 'the right high and excellent Princesse and Queene of right'[22] in reference to her husband's position as King by Right. They were also joined by King Edward's daughters Elizabeth, Mary and Cecily.

James Goldwell, Bishop of Norwich, received the little girl at the chapel door and moved to begin the ceremony of marriage between the little girl and her groom, the four-year-old Richard, Duke of York, King

Edward's second son. Suddenly, a voice was raised in complaint. Doctor Cook objected to the match because the bride and groom were related in the third and fourth degrees and a papal dispensation was required to excuse the relationship. Doctor Gunthorpe, Dean of the King's Chapel, immediately produced the Bull that permitted the marriage, and the staged legal objection was demonstrated to be overcome. The king gave away the little girl, and they proceeded to the high altar to hear mass. Before the wedding ceremony, golden basons filled with gold and silver coins were produced by Richard, 'the high and mighty Prince the Duke of Glouc',[23] and he distributed these amongst the 'comone people' gathered there. After the marriage ceremony had been conducted, the little princess Anne was led from the chapel with Richard holding her right hand and Henry Stafford, Duke of Buckingham on her left. They strolled back to the king's great chamber where a lavish feast was laid on for the occasion. Minstrels played, and heralds proudly proclaimed titles and honours as all those filling Saint Edward's chamber ate and enjoyed the spectacle.[24]

The joust that followed was dominated by the Woodville family of the queen. Her brother Anthony, Earl Rivers, was a famed tournament knight and was joined by his brother Sir John and the queen's sons from her first marriage Thomas Grey, Marquis of Dorset, and Sir Richard Grey. The Duke of Buckingham carried Thomas Grey's helm for the joust, which can hardly have pleased him. Sir James Tyrell and Sir John Cheney, a giant knight believed to have been 6 foot 8 inches in height and who was an Esquire of the King's Body and Master of his Horse also took part with other knights.[25] It was a lavish display of the largesse and unity of the House of York, just as the king was having to proceed to the execution of one of his own brothers.

This splendid occasion had a shabbier motive behind it. Edward's willingness to set aside the laws of inheritance to shore up his own position was a dangerous indulgence that frightened the landed nobility who had the most to lose. Parliament would soon enact the promotion of Edward's second son as Duke of Norfolk, Earl Marshal, Earl Warenne and Earl of Nottingham by virtue of his marriage to Anne Mowbray.[26] Anne was the sole heiress of John Mowbray, Duke of Norfolk, who had died in January 1476. It was not unusual that Prince Richard might hold her lands and titles *de jure uxoris*, in right of his wife – but Edward indulged in some legal chicanery to keep the considerable inheritance in his own family. Prince Richard would only gain legal control of his wife's lands in his own right when the couple had a child, at which point Prince Richard could hold the inheritance on behalf of that child. Edward, perhaps concerned by the youth of the bride and groom and seeing how far off the appearance of an heir would be, subverted this established legal position. An act of Parliament ensured that 'if the said Anne happens to die before she and the same duke of York and Norfolk have had any children together, which God forbid, that then the same duke shall have, hold and enjoy to him, for term of his life'[27] the lands that were hers. Furthermore, property held by Anne Mowbray's mother for her lifetime would devolve upon Prince Richard after her death. This placed Prince Richard into the same position he might be if the couple had a child, whether they in fact had heirs or not.

Tinkering with the laws of inheritance had cost Richard II his crown in 1399. The writer of *The Crowland Chronicle* noted that in the aftermath of this and George's execution 'many persons left king Edward, fully persuaded that he would be able to lord it over the whole kingdom at his will and pleasure.'[28] The seizure of George's lands and the provision for his second son using the Norfolk inheritance achieved one of Edward's goals. Finally, the Crown became solvent, and Edward was able to live off his own means with the help of his new trading ventures. He would no longer be beholden to Parliament to grant taxation, nor required to meet their demands for reform. It was a step towards an absolute monarchy that would ring alarm bells amongst the nobility and those concerned with protecting and promoting the influence of Parliament. Throughout Yorkist opposition and rule, Parliament had seen its power increased, becoming the arbiter of royal titles, but now Edward was seeking to step back from a position that diminished his personal authority. He felt safe from all threats and financially secure. He also took a step closer to the tyranny Crowland may have alluded to when describing the death of Edward of Westminster at Tewkesbury.

Richard had taken a leading role in the marriage of his nephew to Anne Mowbray, but he did not approve of the legal mechanism Edward used to keep the little girl's inheritance within his own family at all costs.[29] It is likely that he disapproved of George's execution, though he might have conceded that Edward had little choice and that George had brought judgement down upon himself. Richard seems to have remained in London and used the time, and perhaps even the circumstances, to obtain favours from the king. It is a demonstration of the lack of suspicion with which Edward viewed his last remaining brother that he was so willing to grant what he requested. On 15 February, at Westminster, Richard witnessed a grant to his son of the earldom of Salisbury, part of the Neville inheritance that had fallen to George. Described as 'the king's nephew Edward Plantagenet', he was created Earl of Salisbury, 'with remainder to the heirs of his body' and a grant of £20 a year from the income of Wiltshire.[30] On 21 February, Richard was given the office of Great Chamberlain, which he had previously held but surrendered to George as part of their negotiations to settle the Neville inheritance. The office gave Richard authority over the Palace of Westminster and a position at coronations. It also meant that Richard, as Lord High Admiral, Lord High Constable and now Lord Great Chamberlain, held three of the nine great offices of State, making him a truly national figure with broad-ranging influence.

On the same day, Richard was given licence to found a college at Barnard Castle consisting of a dean, twelve chaplains, ten clerks, six choristers and a clerk sacristan. The college was to be endowed with lands and other income to the value of 400 marks per year.[31] At the same time, he was also granted licence to establish a similar college at Middleham Castle consisting of a dean, six chaplains, four clerks, six choristers and a clerk sacristan and with an income of 200 marks per year. The establishment of a college within the Church of St Mary and All Saints had been considered a significant achievement of Edward, Duke of York, the great-uncle of Richard, and had been chosen as the place for the reburial of their father and brother in 1476. Founding colleges would serve to demonstrate not only Richard's orthodox and undoubtedly genuine piety but also his indissoluble links to the north, an area he considered home and the place where he envisaged his son and the dynasty that followed him holding influence and providing good lordship. When Richard returned to the north, he was able to set about establishing these lasting edifices of his piety, which would pray for him and his wife Anne, the king and queen and for their souls after death along with the souls of their father and siblings, a list of losses that now included George.

Richard exchanged some properties with the king whilst he was in London too. Presumably, with his estates so far from the capital, it was necessary to cram much business into any visit to the court. Parliament enacted the exchange of the lordship of Elfael in Wales, held by Richard in right of his wife, for that of Ogmore, also in Wales.[32] The purpose was perhaps to solidify the areas of influence within which the young Prince of Wales was to operate, since Elfael lay on the border with England, not far from Ludlow, while Ogmore is in the south. On 5 March, Richard also exchanged Sudeley Castle in Gloucestershire, which he had held since his brother had granted it to him in 1469, as well as Farleigh Hungerford Castle in Wiltshire and Corfe Castle in Dorset for Richmond Castle in Yorkshire.[33] This too represents an adjusting of landholdings that made sense, swapping dispersed southern properties for one closer to Richard's main block of estates. In September, Richard was appointed to lead a commission of oyer and terminer to investigate unspecified offences in York. The other commissioners would be a notable assembly of key players during 1483, with Thomas Grey, Marquis of Dorset; Henry Percy, Earl of Northumberland; Thomas, Lord Stanley; and William, Lord Hastings, all serving with Richard.[34] In the same month, Richard was granted £50 per year from the fee farm of the city of York to pay part of the money he was owed as Warden of the West Marches towards Scotland, which suggests that the importance of the office was recognised by the king and the city of York but that Richard's wages for the role were slipping into arrears.

Statutes for Richard's ambitious project for a college at Middleham were drawn up on 4 July 1478, seemingly with the close involvement of the founder himself. The focus of Richard's piety, which is in many ways both conventional and northern, can be seen from the words he chose for the statutes. Referring to his comparatively humble beginnings as a fourth son of a duke, Richard described how 'it haith pleased Almighty God, Creatour and Redemer of all mankind, of His bounteuouse and manifold graces to enhabile, enhaunce and exalt me His most simple creature, nakidly borne into this wretched world, destitute of possessions, goods and enheretaments, to the grete astate, honor and dignite that He haith called me now unto, to be named, knowed, reputed and called Richard Duc of Gloucestre.'[35] Richard thanked God for his efforts to 'preserve, kep and deliver me of many grete jeoperd, parells and hurts' before describing the structure and workings of 'a Collage within my Town of Middelham at the parrishe church there', Saint Akelda's.

As agreed with Edward, there was to be a dean, six priests, four clerks, six choristers and a clerk sacristan. It is perhaps striking that Richard chose to place the smaller of the two colleges he was founding at Middleham, a place traditionally associated with him as a favourite property, or a home, though these might be concepts that Richard would not easily recognise. Middleham seems to have been used as his seat of power and the centre of his administration, though the Neville structures made the continuation of such a setup practicable and desirable. Whether Richard felt a particular affection for this one of his many properties beyond the fondness he developed for the region cannot be known without attempting to project some degree of emotion that has no basis in any evidence, but to more modern sensibilities at least, Richard may well have considered Middleham home. The college was to pray for the health of the king and queen, 'my lady and moder Duchesse of York' and 'me, my wiff, my son of Salesbury, and such other issue as shal pleas God to send me' for as long as they lived and for their souls after death. Cecily's appearance here is worthy of note as she had been omitted from the list of those to be prayed for in the original grant by Edward, though there is no signal anywhere else of a breakdown in the relationship between mother and either son, unless Edward had felt some unrecorded backlash to George's trial and execution. Certainly, Richard included her in his statutes, suggesting no serious rift between him and his mother. The college was also to offer prayers for the souls of Richard's father and his siblings, his ancestors and descendants and 'all Christen soules'. The college was to be 'named for ever the College of Richard Duc of Gloucestre, of Middleham.'

An initial set of appointments were made by the statutes. William Beverley, previously the procurator of the Archdeacon of Richmond, was the first dean of the college. The first six chaplains were Laurence Squier,

William Simpson, Richard Cutler, William Bunting, Hugh Leverhede and John Bell. The clerks were Thomas Patrik, Alexander Bank, William Brown, and Richard Walker and the six choristers were named as John Part, Thomas Sexten, William Sturton, William Griffith, Henry Farefax, and John Essam. The first clerk sacristan was to be William Nanson.[36]

The list of statutes that follows contains several that are worthy of note. No dean could be appointed who was not already a priest, ensuring that secular officials or favourites could not secure the office and devalue the religious purpose of the foundation. The six chaplains too must have 'taken thordure of presthode' and the right to appoint the dean and chaplains was reserved for Richard and his heirs. The layout of the stalls for each of the members of the college was prescribed very specifically, and each one linked with a particular saint. The dean was to have the first stall on the right-hand side of the high altar, and this was to be known as Our Lady Stall in honour of the Virgin Mary. The first stall on the left was to be reserved for the first chaplain and was to be named St George's Stall. St George was a national saint by now, particularly revered by Edward, who had expanded St George's Chapel at Windsor as a mausoleum for his Yorkist dynasty. It is tempting to see a little mischief in the naming too if Richard was remembering his recently lost brother. The second stall on the right, next to the dean, was for the second chaplain and would be named for Saint Catherine. The most likely Catherine for this to refer to was Catherine of Alexandria, reputedly a princess and a virgin martyr. Catherine was one of the Fourteen Holy Helpers, particularly worshipped in the Rhineland, who was invoked to protect against sudden death. Given Richard's problems with his scoliosis and the delicate grasp he still had of the Neville inheritance, relying as it did on the male line of George Neville, a preoccupation with protection from sudden death is understandable. He needed time to build in security for his son.

The second stall on the left was to be dedicated to Saint Ninian, and it is here that a more northern flavour begins to emerge. St Ninian was strongly associated with the north and Scotland. He was, according to some stories, a Briton who was educated in Rome and returned to convert the Picts of southern Scotland, though he had a robust following in Northumbria too. The next stall on the right was to be named for Saint Cuthbert, a figure widely regarded as the patron saint of northern England and sharing Ninian's connection to Northumbria. St Cuthbert was said to have appeared to King Alfred the Great during his efforts to drive out the Danes, becoming closely linked afterwards to the House of Wessex. He perhaps held a certain appeal along the Scottish borders because of his association with driving out invaders too. The third stall left of the altar was dedicated to Saint Anthony, a figure perhaps more personal to Richard and his selection of the boar as his badge. St Anthony was one of the Four Holy Marshals, again popular in the Rhineland by this time and his intervention was believed to be particularly effective against plague. The fourth stall on the right of the choir was for the sixth priest and would be dedicated to Saint Barbara, another of the Fourteen Holy Helpers. Barbara's father had been killed by lightning, and so she became a patron saint of armourers and gunners, was invoked to protect against thunder and lightning and was believed to offer protection against sudden death and fevers. Richard's concern for the preservation of his health against unforeseen threats seems evident in the choice of saints he chose for his college to offer special prayers to. It is perhaps a natural side effect of an uncertain childhood and a precarious grasp of his livelihood that he had been unable to shake off. If his son was to have anything, it relied on Richard making it happen, and for that he needed time.

Absenteeism was strictly prohibited since it would serve to reduce the effectiveness and integrity of the religious foundation. The dean was required to be 'resident and continually abiding upon the same', and the six chaplains, four clerks and the clerk sacrist were required to lodge with the dean too.[37] None of these officers was permitted to 'in eny wise [to] be absent frome my said College'. The college was required to offer divine service every day 'after the use of Salesbury',[38] rather than that of York. This is a striking departure from his northern piety that can only have been a personal preference on Richard's part for the rule of Salisbury Cathedral. It demonstrates that he was conventional and conservative, as the Use of Sarum was widely used in England during the fifteenth century, but that he was also perfectly able to be his own man in the north and that he did not feel the need to conform in every way to northern religious life. This serves to make his position more impressive in the region, since he did not rely on placating local interests to secure loyalty and service. He was willing to adopt southern ideas in the heart of Yorkshire when he thought them the best solution. The departure gives more credence to his selection of northern saints too, since he obviously felt no obligation or compulsion to strictly conform to win his place in the hearts of the northern community.

The statutes make it clear that discipline within the college was of paramount importance too. None of the members of the college was to 'hawnt tavern or oder unhonest place or persone at eny tyme, or lye out of the College eny nyght, withoute especiall licence of the saide deane'.[39] If any of the priests or clerks 'use at eny tyme in ire eny inhonest or slaunerous words ayenst his fellow, his superior or inferior, of the same College', he would be required to pay two pence from his wages for each such occurrence.[40] Drawing a knife on a colleague would result in a fine of four pence for each infraction, and if one of them drew blood from another, his fine was to be set by the dean and one of the other priests at a suitable level. The notion that the dean could not unilaterally decide such matters and that violence or bad language was to be punished whether it was directed at a superior or inferior are hints that impartial, equitable justice were genuine concerns for Richard. He felt the need to specify these matters in the statutes of his college, so he must have been aware of the problems the absence of such provisions might allow, and perhaps did allow in other religious orders. In such a personal foundation, it is a sign that this issue was of personal importance to Richard.

He also specified a list of saints who were to be venerated within his college and provided for 'as double feast' saints.[41] Some were required by the 'ordinal of Sarum', but others were appointed by Richard as his own choices and some offer insights into his view of himself and the world about him. St Jude was one of the apostles and was widely known as the Brother of Jesus in the Catholic Church, though other accounts refer to him as a brother of James, and may speak to Richard's place as the dutiful brother and follower of the king. The inclusions of St Anne, the mother of the Virgin Mary, and St Elizabeth, the mother of John the Baptist offer a nod to the importance of mothers and motherhood. It may have been referring to his own mother, who had protected him in his younger years, or to Anne, the mother of his heir with whom he hoped to have more children. St Sebastian was another name invoked for protection against plague, but he was also a man shot full of arrows for his faith, left for dead, but who survived. He confronted Emperor Diocletian who had ordered his execution and was clubbed to death at the instruction of the shocked emperor. Did Richard perhaps see himself as a conscience for his brother, telling him where he believed the king was wrong even if it cost him a (verbal) battering? In the wake of France and with Edward executing George, it is possible Richard found himself feeling a responsibility to protect his brother and the House of York from the dangers of tyranny.

Several of the saints, including St Sebastian, St Alban, St Eustace and St Blaise are connected with relief from torture or were martyred by being beaten to death. Richard's pain in his back would undoubtedly have felt like a form of torture from which he sought relief, and he might have considered that his body had suffered a beating at the hands of God so that invoking these saints had a very personal element to it. A local connection was offered by the veneration of St William of York, a former Archbishop whose cult was focussed on the city of York, and St Wilfrid of Rippon, a seventh-century Northumbrian noble who became a bishop. St Winifred was a Welsh saint whose shrine was at Shrewsbury and is perhaps a figure Richard became aware of during his time on the Marches and in Wales in the late 1460s. St Ursula is another Welsh figure who was a patron saint of archers. St Dorothy was the patron of midwives and newlyweds and may have been a figure Richard or Anne had appealed to on their marriage or during the birth of their son and is a sensible inclusion for a couple looking to have more children. St Agnes and St Agatha both have connections to ideas of preserving virginity and assisting rape survivors, which could conceivably be a reference to Anne's first marriage to the Lancastrian Prince Edward if the couple had resolved to characterise that union as being against her will.

There was a broad mixture of saints listed, thirty-nine in total. Though it may have been no more than conventional piety and a hotchpotch of available saints, it was Richard, and probably Anne by his side, who drew up the list of those to be treated with special reverence, so it is not unreasonable to see meaning in some of the selections. There were a small number of particularly northern saints, but they did not dominate the devotions to suggest cynical reasoning in the preferences. There were some saints primarily appealed to by women, which hints at Anne's involvement, though she remains frustratingly obscure as a personality, even by the standards of medieval women. One of the notable preoccupations continued to be the need for protection against deadly diseases and sudden death, which might offer an insight into the mind of an insecure younger brother trying to shore up a place in the world for himself, his wife and their son. In the absence of reasoning for the nominations provided by Richard, his deeper-rooted fears and convictions remain a matter for conjecture.

With the death of George behind them, the last two brothers of the House of York might have believed their troubles were finally ended. Edward, in his mid-thirties, was more secure than ever, both financially and in his freedom from domestic threats. Richard, at twenty-five in mid-1478, was deeply embedded in northern political life and was proving a fine deputy for his brother in the region. He and Anne had joined the prestigious Corpus Christi Guild in York in 1477, just as Richard's parents had done before him. It is possible the family connection was important to him, but it also shows that he was keen to involve his family in a civic guild of the city he was working so closely with. Their sisters seemed settled too. Although Anne, the eldest sibling had died in 1476, Elizabeth was Duchess of Suffolk and gave birth to the seventh of her eight surviving children in 1478 and Margaret, although a childless thirty-two-year-old widow at present, retained immense influence in Burgundy. The future looked brighter than ever for the remaining children of York, but their time in the gentle sun of spring would be brief, and the most destructive storm of all was yet to break over them.

12

War in the North

Thank God, the giver of all good gifts, for the support received from our most loving brother, whose success is so proven that he alone would suffice to chastise the whole kingdom of Scotland.

Edward IV to Pope Sixtus,
25 August 1482[1]

The later suspicion that Richard stayed away from Edward and his court because he was aggrieved by the decision to execute George is unlikely.[2] He was at Westminster Palace on 13 January 1479 to witness a charter given by the king to St Peter's monastery, Westminster, giving them land at the queen's request.[3] On 8 April the same year, Richard received a grant from Edward to hold two fairs at Middleham, one for three days from the Thursday of Whitsun week and the other for three days from the feast of Saint Simon and Saint Jude on 28 October.[4] Although it was stipulated that the fairs should not be 'to the harm of neighbouring fairs', the grant would significantly increase the local prestige of Middleham and, by extension, of Richard's lordship. In November, Richard received an exemplification of his previous grant that he should not be required to pay for charters and the like because the original had been lost.[5] There is little to suggest a rupture between King Edward and his most powerful noble. Indeed, as external and internal politics began to run away from Edward, it was to Richard that he turned for support, and it was in no way slow to come.

Part of the reason that Richard may have appeared less and less in the records relating to the court in the south is that he was kept busy on his northern lands, performing the role his brother needed of him. There are continuing examples of Richard's good lordship, both in the active relationship he was enjoying with the city of York and local gentry families, but perhaps most significant are the examples of his persistent interest in equity and justice for those less powerful people within his sphere of influence. As early as 1472, when he had ordered the arrest of Katherine Williamson's husband's murderers, Richard had demonstrated a keen appreciation of equity and its application to those unable to gain it for themselves in spite of the tangential established norms of livery, maintenance and retaining. It is easy to dismiss a single case, particularly when it occurred at a time when Richard was himself harassing the widowed Countess of Oxford, but continued examples should offer evidence that his concern, or even preoccupation, was both genuine and shocking to contemporaries.

On 12 April 1478, Richard gave his judgement in the arbitration of a dispute between two local families.[6] Neither Richard Clervaux nor Roland Place were retainers of the duke, but some quarrel over lands and rights had brought about Richard's intervention. The settlement provided by Richard is striking for the even-handed and common sense nature of the provisions. Neither party was punished in any way nor was either man favoured. Richard had offered to act as arbitrator not only 'tendiryng the peas and welle of the contre where the saide parties doue inhabite,' but also 'gladly willyng gode concorde, rest and frendly unite to be hadde.' Before giving his judgement, Richard made it clear that he wished the violence that is implied between the two men and their parties to be ended by it. He instructed that 'as welle the sayde Richard as the sayd Roland at all tymes after shall be of gude beryng and demenynit aither enens other and that nowder of thame shall brake nor cause to be broken the peas of the kyng.'

Richard instructed both parties to enclose their lands with a boundary of whatever kind they wished to prevent their cattle from straying onto each other's properties. It was made clear that should any animal wander either whilst the boundaries were being made good or afterwards because of damage, neither man was entitled to 'take amends for the hurte'. Instead, they were required to 'esely dryffe thame of hys grownde'. Effectively, stray cattle were to be driven back to their owner's property rather than harmed or taken as some form of compensation. An exchange of land between the two men was provided as evidence and upheld by Richard with the instruction that both men should be 'content for ever with such land' as the document provided specified, suggesting that even something as simple as this was causing squabbling between Clervaux and Place. The sides of the aisle in the parish church on which the two families were to sit was settled by Richard. Clervaux, his wife and their family would take the south side 'in such places as he and hys ancestres and theire wyffes heretofore have allways used to sitte'. No other person was to be permitted to sit in their places, suggesting that Sunday services had recently been disturbed by the petty placing of men into each other's seats to cause trouble. Place and his family were to keep to the north side of the aisle as his ancestors had done. There is a strong element of chastising naughty children about the matters in dispute that the duke had been asked to settle.

Neither man was to take into service any retainer of the other and they were to refrain from hunting of any kind on each other's lands without licence from the other. If, whilst hunting on their own lands, their dogs should chase prey onto the property of the other, they were not to follow their dogs but only call them back, unless they had express permission to enter the other's lands. In such a case, the man finding dogs belonging to his neighbour on his property was to 'rebuke thame and no noder hurt ne damage do thame'; they were to be shouted away, but not harmed. In each case, with each provision, the same requirement was imposed equally on both men. Richard set up a panel of four men who would meet whenever required to settle any more disputes that arose between Clervaux and Place, but he also reserved the option to get involved again personally if the matter was serious enough. 'And if the sayde greffe be of such weight that thai in no wysse can nor may appease the same, than thai show unto us the cause why they ne so can do to the intent and effecte that we thereupon may determine the same.'

A similar example of Richard's personal and equitable intervention as an arbitrator can be found on 12 August 1480, when he wrote to Sir Robert Claxton of Horden regarding a dispute.[7] A John Randson had appealed to Richard that Sir Robert had deprived him of land that rightfully belonged to him. That a lowly husbandman felt able to make such an appeal and must have felt confident that he could obtain justice through that route is a powerful testament to the local opinion of Richard as a fair mediator. Sir Robert was John's social superior, which he seems to have believed gave him the right to bully Randson off his lands. Furthermore, Sir Robert had a son and a son-in-law in Richard's service, which he might reasonably have expected to ensure his case was championed by the duke, but that was not Richard's way in these matters. On 12 August, Richard personally wrote to Sir Robert to rebuke him and demand his immediate correction of the offence. Richard had been caused to 'marveille gretly' that Sir Robert had not 'peasibly suffered' John Randson to 'occupie suche lyvelode to him of right appertaining' as Richard had instructed in previous letters. Sir Robert had apparently been offered the opportunity to provide evidence of his own case at Raby Castle but had failed to attend or send any proofs. Sir Robert was offered a final chance to put his case at the next court session at Durham, or to give up his claim. Furthermore, Sir Robert was warned to 'so demeane you herin that we have no cause to provide his lawfull rememdy in this behalve,' amounting to the medieval equivalent of a warning not to force Richard to come down there and sort the matter out himself.

A further example of Richard's willingness to act against his own men where the law would demand him to do so but the social norms of his day would allow him to do otherwise can be found as late in his career in the north as 12 April 1482. On that date, the city of York recorded that Sir Ralph Assheton had arrived on Richard's instructions to deliver a servant of the duke's treasurer to the mayor to receive justice for an offence he was accused of within the city.[8] Thomas Redhead, 'of old rancour and evilwill', had committed some unspecified crime against a Roland Pudsey, a citizen of York, and so Richard had sent Redhead to the mayor 'to corect and punyssh hym for the said offence and uppon that commit to prison'. It was clear that being a member of Richard's affinity did not protect anyone from justice. During the decade from the Williamson case of 1472 to Redhead's surrender in 1482, a willingness to take action against his retainers in favour of the law is clear, as is Richard's inclination to stand up for those of lower social standing who could not force justice for themselves. What did Richard gain from this?

A cynical view might suggest that he deliberately courted the favour of the city and the local populace to solidify his position, but it is plain that he he did not need their support, nor was he averse to upsetting more powerful vested interests in the region that he would have been better served courting. What Richard was doing might have been popular with the lower echelons of society, but it upset those with power and authority who had previously relied on bullying and the strong arm of a Neville lord to protect them from justice. A sense of natural justice out of balance with the times in which he lived might have been fostered by Richard's early reading and education, particularly if this youngest son of a duke had initially been intended to build a career in the Church. The sense of injustice he might personally have felt at the scoliosis that twisted his spine, caused him pain and had to be hidden from public view could have contributed to a desire to champion those the world considered weak and incapable. He may have felt a sense of noblesse oblige – the obligations of nobility – that seems to have formed part of his father's belief system and was steeped in the chivalry by which Richard was affected.[9] From tearing down fishgarths to imprisoning his own servants, Richard consistently operated in the same manner. It is to be remembered that in 1483, this was the sort of information those in London had about Richard, Duke of Gloucester; that he was unpredictable, did not adhere to strict social norms and was willing to abdicate his own personal authority to that of the law. For some in London in 1483, that would be a terrifying thought, but for now, it remains one for the not-too-distant future. Richard's present was becoming increasingly absorbed by open war with Scotland.

Edward had enjoyed his French pension since 1475. It had made him financially secure, and Louis XI had proved as good as his word. Two payments of 25,000 crowns each per year had been arriving as regular as clockwork. Margaret had been unable to induce her brother to come to the rescue of her, or Duchess Mary, or England's former ally Burgundy and the loss of this pension was the most potent leverage Louis XI possessed to keep the old alliance of England, Burgundy and Brittany that France had always feared at bay. The French king's investment had paid dividends when Edward had shied away even from helping his sister when she personally visited him to plead for his intervention. Maximilian, after marrying Mary of Burgundy, found himself short of cash to defend the region and increasingly losing control of areas of Burgundy to Louis XI. The diplomatic effort to entice Edward back across the Channel was stepped up.[10] In 1480, Margaret revisited England to try to convince Edward not to renew his truce with France but instead to join with Burgundy and Brittany. At the very least she hoped to obtain a promise of several thousand archers. Edward's priorities are betrayed by his insistence that Maximilian should replace the pension he would lose from Louis if they were to invade and eventually Maximilian agreed, at least until Edward had secured France. Unbeknownst to Margaret, Maximilian or Mary, Edward had in fact already renewed his truce with Louis and, unless it would serve to make him better off with minimal effort, was unlikely to be moved from his current comfortable position. He kept all parties dangling in a manner not dissimilar to that employed later by Henry VII, though Henry achieved a far more accomplished balance than Edward, who had already tied his hands with France and shown himself to prefer easy cash to war.

The impact of this diplomatic juggling act on Richard lay in the eruption of hostilities with Scotland. It would not be unreasonable to assume that a concerned Louis XI saw the resurrection of the Auld Alliance as a chance to draw Edward's attention north rather than south and across the Channel, keeping him distracted from any thoughts of a second invasion of France. James III of Scotland had displayed a lack of interest in war with England that had culminated in 1474, just before Edward's invasion of France, with a truce and an agreement to marry James's heir to Cecily, one of Edward's daughters. For this agreement, Edward had begun paying annual instalments of 2,000 marks towards Cecily's dowry in a scaled-down version of his own agreement with France.[11] An alliance with England that precluded one with France was necessarily unpopular in Scotland, but James persisted in his policy of peace with his nearest neighbour for the rest of the decade. Something altered in 1480 and the Crowland Chronicler is clear in his belief that Scotland was 'encouraged by the

French' to 'imprudently' break the thirty-year truce.[12] At the same time, something frustratingly hard to pin down was happening in parallel in England.

On 18 February 1480, Richard was appointed to a commission of oyer and terminer with Thomas Grey, Marquis of Dorset, Lords Hastings and Howard, his old friend Walter Devereux, Bartholomew James, the Mayor of London and several others. They were tasked with investigating unspecified offences committed within London by a goldsmith, a barber, a baker and a physician.[13] The need for the commission with such high-ranking members is suggestive of unrest in the capital, but trouble was soon to follow from the northern border. On 12 May 1480, Richard was appointed 'king's lieutenant-general to fight against James, king of Scotland, who has violated the truce lately concluded with the king.'[14] The following month, on 20 June, Richard headed commissions of array in the East Riding of York, the North Riding, Westmoreland, the West Riding, Cumberland and Northumberland. Henry Percy, Earl of Northumberland, appeared on each commission alongside Richard, and this was clearly envisioned as an endeavour in which these two northern powerhouses were to work together. The commissions were sent out 'for defence against certain men of Scotland who, notwithstanding the treaty between the king and his kinsmen James, king of Scotland, have burnt townships and dwellings in the marches and imprisoned and slain the king's lieges.'[15]

York set about making preparations to raise a force, providing all of those riding against the Scots with a jacket of white and red at the city's expense. Each parish was also to be required to double their previous assessment of tax toward the cost of the effort.[16] The effort came to very little. As was traditional, the English crossed into Scotland, the Scots refused to engage the invaders, and once supplies were exhausted, the English were forced to withdraw south of the border again.[17]

Richard was paid £6 13s 4d from the Exchequer 'for the safe custody of the Marches'[18] and was given an extra 50 marks, on top of the 100 marks he had already received, for repairing the walls at Carlisle, which had either been damaged by the Scots or were to be strengthened against the threat of an attack.[19] Although John, Lord Howard, had executed an effective raid by sea, capturing ships in the Firth of Forth and burning Blackness, by mid-October Richard was back at his castle of Sherrif Hutton.[20] It is possible Richard travelled south to meet Edward at Nottingham, where a grey gelding was given to the king as a gift from his brother.[21] Richard's personal attendance is not certain, but he must have at least sent word to his brother of what had happened and perhaps raised concerns that Edward had not reached them to bring the matter to a fuller conclusion.

For the moment, the war had stalled, and the year was getting late for campaigning into Scotland. A fresh attempt to bring James back into line would have to be made when the new year brought suitable weather, and Edward was personally determined to see it reach success. In August 1481, Richard was given an instruction by his brother to 'give assurances to all Scotsmen wishing to come into England, and treat with them in the King's name – promising them lands, lordships, and other gifts for their services.'[22] Letters of denizenship were later issued to several men,[23] though it seems doubtful that the plan to lure support away from James worked as well as hoped. It was James himself who was doing a fine job of driving away his own natural support.

The notion that Edward felt a renewal of an internal threat to his crown is suggested in the letters he wrote to Pope Sixtus IV during the troubles with Scotland. In May 1481, the king had told the pope although he would have liked to involve himself in the plans for a crusade in the east, he was unable to because of 'this stormy period'. Edward then separates the issues into two parts; 'to provide for the future events of our kingdom, and to complain that we are thwarted ... on account of the fickle movements of the Scots.' It seems possible that some domestic unrest was causing Edward concern as well as the aggression of Scotland, which was causing him to 'lead in person into Scotland'.[24] The fact that Edward did not lead his army himself is frequently put down to laziness, but it is possible internal unrest made him unwilling to leave the south-east. Richard's first campaign in sole command may have been as a result not of Edward's lethargy and indulgent lifestyle, but rather a necessity created by Edward's fear of losing his kingdom again.

As early as 24 February 1482, Richard was given licence to buy 2,000 quarters of wheat, 1,000 quarters of barley, rye, oats and other supplies 'in any places of the realm or Wales or Ireland'. This measure was necessary because 'on account of the war with the Scots the king has been occasioned to fortify the west and east marches' so that 'there is a great scarcity there of victuals and especially corn.'[25] Finding himself struggling to raise the huge sums necessary to raise an army by indentures, Edward turned not only to the benevolences that were by now the bane of any Englishman with money, but he also determined in 1481 to enforce the part of his last parliamentary grant of taxation that he had remitted in 1475 on his return from France.[26] That he refrained from calling Parliament and sought all and any other means to secure funding suggests he had a reason for not wanting Parliament to sit at this time, perhaps hinting yet again at internal insecurity or the threat of unrest. More evidence of this can be found in the establishment of a commission of oyer and terminer, led by Richard, in York on 5 March 1482, which included Northumberland and many of Richard's close associates, including Francis Lovell, John Scrope of Bolton, Sir William

Parr and Sir James Harrington.[27] Further west, the turmoil within the Duchy of Lancaster's territories, described as 'great strifes, variances, controversies, debates', were so out of hand that they could be resolved 'by no person but only the King himself'.[28] Just as Edward had feared Duke Charles had stirred up trouble within England a few years earlier, it is not unreasonable to believe the king now saw Louis XI at work to destabilise his kingship by a combination of domestic unrest and Scottish aggression.

Even in York, things were on edge. The mayor and aldermen were compelled to deal with instances of citizens ringing the Common Bell, an alarm or a call to arms that, beyond some mischief, points to some turbulence within the great northern city. On 20 March it was 'agreid that the offenders in the ringyng of the common bell shalbe puniysshed by way of imprisonment according to the kynges high comaundment and the duc of Gloucestr.'[29] Such a heavy-handed response suggests that this was no mere drunken merrymaking gone too far. Neither did the matter end there. On the following day, the city decided to send to Richard for more instructions for the 'forther correccion of certan persones prisoned for ringyng of the comon bell.'[30] Richard wrote back to them on 29 March ordering 'ther delyvere', which seems to suggest that they were freed without further action. Tolerance may have won the day as the threat of imminent and large-scale war with Scotland loomed closer. On the south coast, Edward's problems in other directions were mounting. On 23 May, Richard Cely wrote from London to his brother William at Calais that 'howr mother longys sor for yow' because 'whe be lyke to hawhe whar with Frawns and that makys hyr ferde.'[31] Richard had clearly heard rumours that Calais was about to be attacked and that war with France was likely enough to cause their mother to fear for William in Calais. Fighting on two fronts would prove disastrous for Edward and more than ever, he needed to rely on Richard to keep the north safe for him.

Edward saw leverage in May in the arrival in England of the Duke of Albany, James III's exiled brother. Albany had come from France, and it seems impossible that Louis was not the cause of the gift that came to Edward's shores. After all, the French king cared little about England or Scotland, who had made peace with England despite his overtures. He only cared at this point that Edward was kept away from Burgundy and Brittany. Edward had agreed to marry his daughter Anne to Maximilian's son and was seeking a similar marriage alliance with Spain, none of which is likely to have escaped Louis' web. As strands began to quiver, Louis set about focussing Edward's mind on Scotland with the hope of an easy victory and overlordship of that country.

In May, the city of York prepared men to go with Richard and a large army as he 'intendeth brivelie in hys owen person to entre Scotland upon

Wedhenisday next commyng.'[32] When Richard did cross the border, it was to make a lightning strike on Dumfries, leaving it in flames behind him as he retired south. The raid may have been intended to infuriate the Scots and draw an army into the field or to reconnoitre the defences north of the border, though it is equally possible that the assault was ended by news of the Duke of Albany's arrival and an adjustment in Edward's plan. As June blazed into life, Richard found himself at his old home, Fotheringhay Castle, where he met his brother and Albany. On 10 June, Albany, now described by Edward as Alexander, King of Scotland, promised to break all alliances with France, to cede the border town of Berwick to England and, perhaps most significantly, to do homage to Edward for the kingdom of Scotland as soon as he had won it. On the following day, a marriage alliance was added by which Albany would marry Cecily, the king's daughter who had been pledged to James III's heir, without any dowry, and on 12 June Richard was appointed the commander of the army that would be taken into Scotland.[33] For Edward and Richard, it was almost too good to be true. They had a readymade replacement for James in his more popular brother and not only a guarantee of peace in the north, but also of the recognition of lordship over the Crown of Scotland that England had sought since the late thirteenth century under Edward I. Paul Murray Kendal has described Albany as 'a Clarence in a kilt',[34] suggesting his unreliability was a match for George's, and in this Edward and Richard allowed their excitement and desire to settle the war with Scotland to blind them. Albany was sent by Louis, and that should have been warning enough, but Edward seems to have blindly taken the bait. Either Louis must have been aware of Albany's fickle failings and known that his involvement would never win Edward the swift victory he hoped for, or Louis encouraged Albany to win Edward's confidence and then betray it, for money, for a return to favour in Scotland, or for both. Whatever the truth, Louis seems to have read Edward just right once again. The lure of an easy win and possession of Scotland was too much for him to resist.

Preparations mounted excitedly for this new direction in the campaign. Edward paid £433 6s 8d for arrows and ordnance for Richard's mission to Scotland.[35] Richard was handed a staggering £4,504 11s 8½d as part payment of 20,000 men under his command as well as 2,000 marks in payment of an indenture Richard had personally taken out with the king.[36] From Fotheringhay, Richard and Albany travelled north to York, where the city made extensive preparations for a lavish reception. The aldermen were to meet the two dukes in their scarlet robes, with every craftsman required to turn out in his 'best aray'. Any alderman who failed to attend was to be fined 12d, and any citizen found missing would have to forfeit 6d. The city would greet the illustrious guests at Micklegate Bar and provide them with gifts of bread, four gallons of red wine, four gallons of white wine and claret, two gallons of sweet wine, two large pike and two tenches, or breams.[37] Richard must have arrived shortly after these preparations were agreed on 17 June and Northumberland soon followed, the city making a gift to him of bread, five gallons of red and claret wine and a gallon of sweet wine. By the middle of July, Richard led an army out of York towards Berwick that was more numerous and threatening than any that had been seen at the border in more than eighty years.

The town of Berwick-upon-Tweed surrendered quickly in the face such a vast army, but the citadel within the castle refused to give up and was defiantly held against the assault. Richard decided not to allow the siege to delay him from his real aim and, leaving Thomas, Lord Stanley, in command of the blockade at Berwick, he marched his men directly towards Edinburgh. James III had not been idle as news of the English approach flew through Scotland. He ordered a muster at Lauder, 25 miles south-east of Edinburgh and just more than 30 miles directly west of Berwick and had assembled an impressive force to resist the English. At this moment, James's domestic problems came home to roost. He had a group of favourites who were despised by the Scottish nobility and their appearance at Lauder seems to have been the final straw. James was taken into custody, several of his favourites were hung from Lauder Bridge, and the king was taken back to Edinburgh where he was locked up in the castle. Perhaps inadvertently, this action was to save Scotland and James, though he doubtless failed to see the benefit at the time.

As Richard and his army burnt their way north,[38] trying to provoke the Scottish army into a pitched battle, they found no resistance and in short order arrived at Edinburgh, where they found the city undefended and open to them. James and his noble captors had withdrawn within a castle that would easily withstand a lengthy siege. The queen and her sons were at Stirling Castle, another stout fortress some 30 miles away. The new month had begun, and Richard's men were only paid until 11 August, so further manoeuvres or a long siege were beyond his current means. Given Edward's troubles in raising the funds he had given his brother and the growing threats elsewhere, Richard cannot have known that he would be able to keep the army in the field for long. He could not depose a king he could not gain access to, and the city seemed less than warm to the idea of Albany as their new king. Some resolution had to be found.

It is unclear whether Albany now acted as he had always intended, in violation of his agreement with Edward IV, or whether Richard sanctioned, or even encouraged, his course of action. As early as 2 August, Albany was in open negotiations with the several bishops and the authorities of Edinburgh – the only people available to negotiate with – to renew his allegiance to James III and to secure a pardon and the full restitution of his lands and titles. The pardon was even to cover 'aspiring and tending to the Trone of Scotland'.[39] If Richard had not been the prime mover behind this rapprochement, he quickly saw the way the wind was blowing. He caused Garter King of Arms to read out a proclamation at the high cross in Edinburgh's marketplace which made no mention of Albany's claim to the throne. He insisted that James should fall back into line with his treaties with Edward, provide compensation for the breaches at the borders and the damage his men had caused in England and restore Albany to all of his possessions. The demands were followed by a warning that if James should refuse, Richard 'was redy at hand to destroy him, his people and contrey with slaughter, flame and famyn.'[40]

Also on 2 August, Richard received word from the Scottish army that had withdrawn to Haddington, 20 miles east of the city. If he had considered marching there to confront them, the sting was taken from his desire by their request for peace terms. They asked for a renewal of the truce with England and confirmation of the planned marriage between their prince and Edward's daughter Cecily. Richard, who may not have had instructions from his brother for the eventuality of the complete capitulation of an absent enemy, had to think on his feet. He told the Scottish lords that he could not speak for his brother's mind on the marriage, but that if they wanted peace they must agree to it taking place as soon as possible if that was Edward's wish, or to return all of the dowry paid to date if Edward no longer wished to make the match. Furthermore, they were to surrender Berwick Castle if they could do so and if not, they were to abstain from helping those within the castle.[41] The Scots swiftly agreed and on 4 August, Walter Bartrahame, the Provost of the city, personally agreed terms with Richard. The marriage was to take place as soon as possible if Edward still wished it. If not, 'We, Walter Provest, Burgess, Merchandes and Commons of the above nemit Toune of Edinburgh, or ony of Ws, sall Pay and Content unto the King of Ingland forsaid, all the said Soumes of Money that was Payt for the said Mariage.'[42] Edward was asked to give them notice of his decision by All Hallows on 1 November. With the written proofs under his arm, Richard took his army out of Edinburgh and marched back south towards Berwick.

The people of Edinburgh were doubtless delighted to get the English out of their city and heading out of their country, whatever the cost. It was perhaps to their surprise that the price had been set so low. Richard did not demand James' abdication in favour of Albany, which had been the aim of the expedition, nor were his terms for withdrawal too onerous. He had brought the largest English army into Scotland in generations and was in possession of the capital city. The discipline of his army had been impeccable whilst they remained. There had been no pillaging, brawling or even provocation from the English, a sure testament to Richard's control over his men. That may not have lasted indefinitely, so speed was of the essence for the city, and it was little trouble to agree to the small things Richard demanded. They can only have wondered why, with the country's capital in the palm of his hand and its king a prisoner of his own nobles, he had failed to extract harsher terms from them.

Richard's position was problematical. James' imprisonment had not been done for the king's own benefit, yet his unavailability to fight, negotiate or even be taken captive by the English probably saved his crown. It certainly made Richard's job more complicated. He could not unseat a king who was not currently on his throne, nor could he seek terms from a prisoner he had no access to. By the time of the agreement on 4 August, Richard only had wages to keep the army in the field for one more week, and there was still the capture of Berwick to be completed. His men might be set loose, but that would only serve to galvanise the currently splintered Scottish political body against them. If he gave consideration to the real purpose of his mission, it was to end the threat of war with Scotland so that Edward was free to focus on internal issues and the perhaps more significant problems of France and Burgundy. It was clear that Scotland had its own internal problems and leaving Albany there would help to prolong them. Either he would gain control of the government and be bound by his promise to be Edward's ally and liegeman, or he would further destabilise the country and keep them gazing inward. Either way, the aim was achieved, within time and within budget, if Berwick would fall within the week. There was little more success to be had and nothing to be gained by staying longer. Peace was what Edward had wanted, and peace was what he was getting.

By 11 August, Richard was back at Berwick, where the castle was still holding out but was now deprived of any hope of assistance from Scotland. There, he disbanded the vast majority of his army on the day that their pay ended. For soldiers in fifteenth-century England to be paid for all of the days they had been in service and not asked to extend their term without certainty of when wages would follow was no mean feat. Richard distributed rewards amongst the men to the tune of £350 provided by Edward, with almost £95 sent for Northumberland's retinue.[43] A force of 1,700 men was kept on a little longer to secure Berwick's fall,[44] but the remainder were released. Almost immediately, the Scots felt encouraged and sent out their forces to help Berwick, but even with a much smaller army, Richard's presence seems to have kept them at bay. They sent word that they would destroy the castle walls if Richard would flatten those around the town. They would even allow an English garrison in the town if a Scottish one could remain within the castle. They were chancing their arm, and Richard would have no truck with them, and so the Scots withdrew again.[45] It had perhaps been a gesture to show some defiance in the face of their embarrassment at Edinburgh, but it had not worked.

The castle at Berwick fell by 24 August. Although this date is usually cited as the date it surrendered, Edward had knowledge of it on 25 August, when he wrote to Pope Sixtus. The news, even with the relay of couriers Edward had provided for the expediting of intelligence, would probably have taken three days to reach London, so unless Edward was pre-empting the tidings or confusing the fall of the castle with that of the town, it seems likely it happened around 21 August. This suggestion is supported by the fact that on 22 August, Richard created several knights and knights banneret, which would suit the celebrations for the end of a campaign. Francis, Lord Lovell, Richard's close friend, was knighted, as were other northern connections of the duke such as Thomas, Lord Scrope. In total, Richard dubbed twenty-seven men that day, and Northumberland created eighteen more knights.[46] These were added to those created in Edinburgh, where Richard had made thirty-four knights banneret and fourteen knights. Amongst these, the names of James Tyrell, Edward Woodville, the queen's brother, Ralph Asheton, John Savage and Robert Harrington are prominent figures for one reason or another. Some would soon become forever tied to Richard's name, and others would become his enemies.[47] It was a fitting closure to a largely successful campaign, though the direction had been changed more than once as events overtook Richard and his plans.

Views of the campaign appear, at least on the surface, to have differed widely. Richard could take pleasure in having marched into and occupied Edinburgh and recovered Berwick, lost to England since the Lancastrians had given it to Scotland in return for an army in 1460, all without the loss of a single man. Furthermore, he had achieved the aim of reducing the threat from Scotland within the timescale set by the wages of the army and without additional time or expense. If Edward wanted quick results, he had them. When the king sat down to write to Pope Sixtus IV on 25 August, he was effusive in his praise for his younger brother. 'Thank God,' he wrote, 'the giver of all good gifts, for the support received from our most loving brother, whose success is so proven that he alone would suffice to chastise the whole kingdom of Scotland.'[48] Further support is given to the notion that internal problems, or those further south at least, had prevented Edward taking part by his confession that Richard had commanded the army 'we ourselves intended to have led last year, had not adverse turmoil hindered us.' The 'turmoil' is unspecified, but it cannot have been an easy admission for a king that he had troubles to face more important than his national security at the northern border, and an embarrassing one to cover a lack of good health when simple illness could have been cited. The king explained that in Edinburgh, his men, 'had not their compassion exceeded all human cupidity, would have instantly doomed the same to plunder and the flames.' Richard and his 'noble band of victors, however, spared the supplicant and prostrate citizens, the churches, and not only the widows, orphans, and minors, but all persons found there unarmed.'

Edward referred to the recapture of Berwick as the 'chief advantage of the whole expedition', but in this, the Crowland Chronicler disagreed, perhaps believing Edward put a brave face on the disappointment of the campaign for the pope's benefit. The writer lays the blame at the feet of Richard, who was given 'entire command of the expedition' but 'uselessly squandered away' all of the taxes and benevolences Edward had extracted.[49] He explains that the 'trifling, I really know not whether to call it "gain" or "loss", (for the safe keeping of Berwick each year swallows up ten thousand marks), at this period diminished the resources of the king and kingdom by more than a hundred thousand pounds.' Quite what the writer would have preferred Richard to do in the circumstances he does not venture to offer, and his claim that 'King Edward was vexed at this frivolous outlay of so much money' is at variance with Edward's own words of joy. It is perhaps here that the Crowland Chronicler begins to look for hints of what was soon to follow and to seek to lay the blame at the feet of one other than Edward. Richard's reception when he reached London and his continued high favour suggest that Edward was not irritated at his brother's conduct, but was in fact very pleased. A few days before All Hallows, Garter King of Arms arrived in Edinburgh to relay the news that Edward no longer wished to marry his daughter Cecily to the King of Scotland's son, and so wanted his dowry payments returned as agreed, so that cash became another benefit of the campaign, as well as the reduction of funds available to James.[50]

It is ironic that 1482 might seem like the last year of peace that Richard would enjoy since it had been consumed by a war, albeit one without any battles. His place in national politics was solid and secure. He was the senior nobleman in the land, Constable, Admiral and now a victorious military leader, if the Scottish episode is judged a success in achieving its aims. At a local level, he was deeply embedded in northern politics and society. His circle of influence was expanding and drawing loyalty by his examples of good lordship. The city of York counted him a friend and honoured him whenever they could. In February 1482 they sent proof of the election of a new mayor for Richard's approval.[51] When he visited the city in March before heading to Scotland, the mayor and aldermen met him at the Austen Friars to give 'a laudable thanke for his gude and benevolent lordship that he at all tymez have had unto this cite, desirying his grace of gude contynuaunce.'[52] When fishgarths caused problems or troublemakers rang the Common Bell, it was to Richard that the city turned for help and guidance and in return, Richard had shown himself willing to send his own servants for punishment where they had broken the law. His foundations at Middleham and Sheriff Hutton were underway so that in every aspect his reputation could hardly have been higher.

The king certainly felt buoyed enough by Richard's achievements to call Parliament for the first time in five years. Writs were sent out on 15 November 1482 for a session to open on 20 January 1483 at Westminster. Perhaps the most significant piece of business was the recognition and reward of Richard for his exploits the previous summer, again confirming that Edward was far from outraged or disappointed by the results. Parliament was informed that Richard, as Warden of the West Marches, 'late by his manyfold and diligent labours and devoirs, hath subdued grete part of the West bordures of Scotlande, adjoyning to Englond, by the space of xxx (30) miles and more.'[53] The king insisted that there was more to come against Scotland from his brother and that 'moche more therof he entendith, and with Goddis grace is like to gete and subdue herafter'. The office of Warden of the West Marches was granted to Richard to 'have to hym and to his heires males', and offices, with their associated income, that Richard held in his own right and could pass to his heir unshackled by other considerations, were significant and important to his future, since the Neville inheritance was still conditional on the production of a son by George Neville at some point.

Included in this grant were the castle and lordship of Carlisle, the castle, manor and lordship of Bewcastle and other 'possessions and hereditaments whatsoever they be' in Cumberland. Richard was to have control over the appointment of the sheriff and escheator of · Cumberland too. Richard was being given a County Palatine with powers similar to those enjoyed by the Bishop of Durham in the one there, or by the Duchy of Lancaster that had rested with the Crown for almost a century. It was a startling development that risked storing up problems for Edward and his successors since although the County Palatine would fall under the authority of the Crown, it would enjoy substantial freedom and autonomy in an area carved from north-west England. That was not to be the limit of Richard's scope, though. He was also permitted to add to his territories any lands in Liddesdale, Eskdale, Ewesdale, Annandale, Wachopedale, Clydesdale and anywhere else in the West Marches of Scotland that he was able to conquer. The effect was that Richard and his heirs would be the hereditary barrier between England and Scotland in perpetuity. They were to have the power to offer any Scot who wished to submit to England citizenship and a full pardon, and were to receive all monies from fines in the region.[54] Any of Richard's heirs who might inherit whilst underage were to be taken into the wardship of the Crown and their lands and offices protected by the monarch until they reached majority. Finally, Richard and his heirs were to have 10,000 marks per year from the king as payment for their service as Warden of the West Marches.

The creation of a County Palatine for Richard was a recognition of more than a decade of service, but also an opportunity to provide more valuable service in the future with direct and tangible rewards for success. The reason for Edward's willingness to give away so much power and authority to Richard and his heirs has been suggested as demonstrating his failing health and inability to resist the striding ambition of his brother,[55] but the provision benefitted the king too. Scotland had, for centuries, been a thorn in England's side, a distraction from conquest in France and often a pawn of the French kings who needed English attention diverted. Richard had, for ten years, proven an effective foil to Scottish aggression and now they had reason to fear him. At that moment, Edward's problems were mounting exponentially. During Christmas, word had arrived that Edward's foreign policy had catastrophically collapsed. Louis XI had signed the Treaty of Arras with Archduke Maximilian and this created a crisis for England. Mary of Burgundy had died after a riding accident in March 1482 and left Burgundy to her son Philip, under Maximilian's protection, but Louis' aggression was proving too much to resist. With Edward refusing to help for fear of losing his pension from Louis, but keeping Maximilian in hope of assistance, Burgundy had eventually been forced to capitulate to Louis. The Dauphin was to wed Maximilian's daughter Margaret, and Burgundy was to be her dowry. Edward's pension, due at Michaelmas, had failed to arrive and his worst fears were confirmed. Louis had won and might soon be looking to invade England in revenge for 1475. At the very least, Calais was in imminent peril. What Richard had provided, and could offer in the future, was the restraint of Scotland, encouraged by France, as a threat in the north. If Edward could entrust this task to his brother, he was free to concentrate on defending Calais and the south coast, or even attempting a new invasion of France. This measure was not forced upon Edward by Richard, but rather by circumstances. The Scots had been a problem for centuries. This was Edward's long-term solution.

Edward was looking to the future, however bleak it may have been. He had lost the primary source of his financial security, and French aggression was a genuine threat for the first time in decades. The suggestion that ill health was overtaking him is at odds with his failure to make preparations at this moment for his own death or the protection of his son. It is likely he was frightened by developments and that stress was unhelpful as he passed forty and was increasingly obese and unfit, but he showed no signs of flagging. Louis had played the English king and had won the battle, but the war was only just about to begin.

It requires an effort of cynicism and the unreasonable application of hindsight to see Richard by this point as any kind of a threat to his brother's throne. He was looking to build a secure future for himself, but there is nothing sinister or unnatural in that. By the beginning of 1483, he had achieved this aim through solid and reliable service to his king and was set to reap the rewards. His final insecurity, the nature of his hold on the Neville inheritance, was being corrected, or at least compensated for, and he undoubtedly believed he would be in a position to resolve that issue with his brother. England was under threat, but had a united royal house poised to be her shield against the coming storm of swords. Edward had never lost a fight, and that was an achievement during this period that was worth clinging to, a chink of light in the growing darkness to show the way.

Although 1483 promised to be a trying year, no one can have expected the shockwaves that pulsed through England that year. It would mean a return to an old uncertainty for Richard after more than a decade of settled maturity. The question was whether he would respond to its challenges as an accomplished adult, or as a frightened, insecure child.

13

The King Is Dead, Long Live the King

You might have seen, in those days, the royal court presenting no
other appearance than such as fully befits a most mighty kingdom,
filled with riches and with people of almost all nations, and (a point in
which it excelled all others) boasting of those most sweet and beautiful
children, the issue of his marriage, which has been
previously mentioned, with queen Elizabeth.

The Crowland Chronicle
Christmas 1482[1]

On the surface, all appeared well at Edward IV's court during Christmas 1482. The king showed himself in lavish, flowing robes with full sleeves that resembled a monk's habit, lined with expensive furs.[2] England looked solid, secure and prosperous, but beneath the ostentatious surface, Edward was faced with the most challenging set of political problems in a decade. Few can have been fooled by his display of opulence, though the royal family presented an attractive and promising proposition for Yorkist rule. The bright horizon would soon be eclipsed by a gathering darkness, a crisis none had foreseen that would rock the foundations of the House of York and leave them cracked and fragile.

Edward IV died on 9 April 1483, just as foreign policy disasters threatened to overtake the country. The cause of death is uncertain, but a chill caught whilst fishing is the most cited origin of the sudden demise of the forty-year-old king. The continuator of *The Crowland Chronicle* seems to have been unaware of any long-term illness or degeneration in the king; 'the king, neither worn out with old age nor yet seized with any known kind of malady, the cure of which would not have appeared easy in the case of a person of more humble rank, took to his bed.'[3] A sudden illness, which should not have claimed the life of a man of the king's age, rank and physical stature, even if he was carrying too much weight by this point, struck Edward down.

Rumours of foul play have, almost inevitably, clung to the king's death, doubtless because it was so sudden and unexpected. There is no evidence to substantiate any of these accusations, least of all that the Woodville family of the queen had poisoned him, but the existence of such stories should be included in the mix of rumour and misinformation that cloaks the events of the rest of the year 1483. If there was uncertainty and suspicion, even if it were without foundation or could not be proved, it would influence the thoughts, fears and actions of those left behind to ensure Edward's heir succeeded his father. The first uncertainty appears in the York House Books, showing that a report arrived in the city on 7 April that the king had died the previous day. The dean (presumably of York Minster) had sent Sir John Hart to relay the message to the mayor and to summon the city's officials to a dirge at the Minster on 7 April to commemorate the dead king.[4] The report was premature, particularly if Edward's death was to prove a shock. The message may have been sent early or in the expectation that the king would not last beyond 6 April, but the arrival of news that Edward was dead three days before his actual passing might have been enough to furrow the brows of those wondering what was happening and what might come next.

Developments in the authority of the queen's Woodville family during the weeks preceding Edward's death may have been a cause for concern to some. Towards the end of February, Edward had issued a new set of ordinances for the Prince of Wales's household at Ludlow Castle, confirming Anthony Woodville, Earl Rivers, and John Alcock, Bishop of Worcester, in their responsibility for the prince's person, his education and reserving for them the authority to move the heir to the throne from one location to another.[5] Sir Richard Grey, the younger of Elizabeth Woodville's sons from her first marriage, was also given extensive authority in the prince's household by these new ordinances. The three men together were to keep the prince from 'any unprincely demeaninge' and to correct him where necessary, referring the matter to Edward or Elizabeth if his behaviour was not immediately rectified.[6] The next king was going to be a product of Woodville influence.

In March, Rivers had written to his attorney in London, Andrew Dymmock, to explain that he had arranged for his other nephew, Thomas Grey, Marquis of Dorset, to be given Rivers' office as Deputy Constable of the Tower of London. Rivers asked Dymmock to approach the Constable of the Tower, Lord Dudley, 'in that matter in all haste and send me word of their disposition.'[7] It was to this letter than a postscript was added which would add fuel to any suspicion about Woodville motives. Rivers asked Dymmock to retrieve documents from the earl's paperwork and to send a proof of his powers. 'Send me by some sure man the patent of mine authority about the lord prince, and also a patent that the king gave me touching power to raise people if need be in the march of Wales.'[8]

Rivers clearly felt a need to have demonstrable proof of his position as head of the Prince of Wales's household, and his power over the person of the king, to be close at hand in March 1483. A desire to be prepared to raise troops in the Marches might have indicated the tension a rupture with France was causing. It is possible Rivers was planning to cross the Channel to lead the defence of Calais against Louis XI, or to begin a fresh offensive in France, but it is doubtful a small force from the Marches would have been enough to constitute an army capable of invasion. In the atmosphere that was about to erupt spectacularly in England, it might have been enough for the Woodville faction to be eyed with renewed suspicion. At best, they had manoeuvred themselves into an unassailable position, at worst, they were plotting a coup of some kind. If Edward's illness had been a long time in taking him, their positioning, given their general unpopularity, would seem natural, if unwanted. If Edward had died as suddenly as Crowland suggests, their actions would become those of guilty folk with a plan. The fact that the truth of this matter, like so much else in the weeks that followed, cannot be established even now leaves room to expect uncertainty in April 1483.

All of this was a potential problem to some who disliked the breadth and depth of Woodville authority, most notably William, Lord Hastings. Dominic Mancini, an Italian visitor to England during the explosive events of 1483, had heard gossip that Hastings was 'hostile to the entire kin of the queen on account of the marquess' (Dorset).[9] The main problem with Dominic Mancini's testimony, which is relied on to a fault by many commentators on this brief period, is that he spoke no English, had no prior knowledge of England's politics or personalities and was not involved in some of the activities he reported. Mancini was reliant on Italian merchants and collected gossip, the more licentious the better, before declaring it as fact, or else identifying it as reports he had heard, without guessing at the truth of them, which have later been read as facts. Thus Edward is 'of a gentle nature and cheerful aspect', 'an angry countenance', 'immoderate' in food and drink, 'fat in the loins' and 'licentious in the extreme', led astray by 'relatives of the queen, her two sons and one of her brothers'.[10] Mancini had never met Edward, so was reporting gossip from the streets of London, since it was all he could access. Perhaps he had no reason to doubt what he was told, but that does not make any of it accurate. Mancini may have been an honest reporter of what he saw and heard, but he lacked the depth of information or the insight to get at the real truth. For this reason, his testimony should be handled carefully and with suspicion, without discounting it altogether.

The rift between Hastings and Dorset seems to have been real. The Tudor antiquary Richard Grafton crafted a deathbed scene for the king which epitomises the later acceptance of the rift Mancini had heard rumour of. Typically placing words into the mouth of long-dead figures,

Grafton has Edward pulling Hastings and Dorset to his side and causing them to swear to end their feud for the sake of his son. Edward pleads 'in these last wordes that ever I looke to speake to you or with you, I exhort and require you all for the love that ye have ever borne to me, for the love I have ever borne to you, and for the love that our Lorde and saviour Christ beareth us all, from this time forward, all griefes forgotten, eche of you love other.' If the king ever thought to save his kingdom at this last moment, he must have known he was grasping at thin air. Grafton, with a heavy application of hindsight, tells his reader that 'eche forgave other, and joyned their hands together, when (as it after appered by their deedes) their hartes were farre a sunder.'[11]

Later chroniclers do not seem to make much effort to hide the fact that they believed Hastings and the Woodville family were openly feuding and plotting against each other. A minority, which Edward V was going to have to endure on his father's death and for several years afterwards, was fraught with problems. The last minor king had been Henry VI, ejected from his throne by Edward IV for incompetence. Edward had at least taken the precaution of having his son trained in a miniature kingdom of his own at Ludlow, but his security would rely on the unity of his noble support and his advisors. It is perhaps the jostling for position in his last days that caused Edward suddenly to alter the course of his policy. The Woodville family had been accruing offices and authority over the previous months, which Edward seems happy to have granted them. His policy would suggest that the queen and her brothers would lead the minority government of his son, yet that was not what happened. Lord Hastings was perhaps disturbed, and threatened, enough by the stranglehold his enemies were gaining on power to try to convince his old comrade that it was not the correct direction to take. A Woodville regency would likely see Hastings expelled from the centre of government, for the new king had no great ties to or affection for him except as his father's friend. The battle for self-preservation was beginning even before the king had breathed his last. The importance of understanding this situation lies in the later belief that it was Richard's arrival that caused trouble and shockwaves, when in fact he arrived precisely because this was already going on.

What happened next is far from certain. It is asserted that Edward IV added a codicil to his will, just before he died, appointing his brother Richard to act as Protector, but no documentary evidence of this survives. It is feasible, given the events that followed, that this was Edward's plan, but it would be a significant shift from the focus on Woodville authority that had been building. There are several significant factors relating to the English manner of dealing with minorities. The first is that those of the dead monarch's Council who remained in power could change the wishes of the king after his death. As Henry V lay dying at Vincennes in France, he added codicils to his will to provide for the long minority of his nine-month-old heir. It is perhaps this that has fuelled the assumption that Edward did something similar. What Henry envisioned, though, was not what was put into effect after his death.[12] Henry V wanted his son's education and upbringing overseen by Thomas Beaufort, Duke of Exeter, with a group of men made responsible for attending on the young king and Exeter's role one of formal oversight. With Henry's senior brother John, Duke of Bedford, tied up with the effort in France, where he was to act as Regent for the infant king, Henry left control of England to his youngest brother Humphrey, Duke of Gloucester. Humphrey was to be Henry VI's 'tutor', though in a Latin legal sense rather than an educational one, meaning that he had responsibility for all the new king's possessions and finances during his minority. Effectively, Humphrey was to act as Regent in England, mirroring John in France.

Objecting to this arrangement, the Council blocked and altered these provisions, mainly as they related to Humphrey. They retained the arrangements for the personal care of the person of the new king but asserted the right of the Council to govern the kingdom. Humphrey was instead given the entirely invented role of Defender of the Realm, a title that would later be referred to as Protector without any alteration in meaning or powers. What the Council envisioned and enacted was a division of power into three parts; the care of the person of the king, the military protection of the kingdom and the day-to-day operation of government. It was understood that Humphrey would be a prominent member of the Council, but would not hold the authority of a Regent, and he was required to relinquish the position to his older brother John whenever he returned to England. This was an entirely novel invention, designed to restrict Humphrey, who was seen by many (though significantly, not by his brother Henry V) as reckless and untrustworthy, and to keep power in the hands of members of the Council, some of whom, most significantly Henry Beaufort, Bishop of Winchester, would prove not to be on good terms with Humphrey. The separation of powers might sound attractive, but it left no single hand on the tiller of the nation and created space for uncertainty, argument and jostling for position.

Edward and Richard's father, Richard, Duke of York, had acted as Protector on two occasions, from 1454–5 and 1455–6, being ejected from office relatively quickly in both instances and left in political isolation. If Edward gave thought to what would happen after his death, he must have been conflicted. On the one hand, the Council and the broader ruling classes would accept the division of power that had become the norm by the late fifteenth century without baulking. There was value in that, but the system had not worked well in the past. Henry VI had become an incompetent king in a faction-riven country by the time he came of age, though Edward V would perhaps have a much shorter minority. His father had suffered for trying to take on the mantle of Protector, and he must have worried that he was condemning Richard to the same fate. Humphrey had fallen so far from favour that he had ended up arrested then dead (most likely caused by a stroke, though rumours of poisoning and foul play were quick to follow). York had been driven so far from power and favour that a bitter civil war had ensued. Richard was incredibly powerful by now and risking his alienation or opposition would not bode well. If Edward considered this accepted structure, then Woodville control of Edward V's person and education would be natural, Richard as Protector with military responsibility was reasonable, and Council operating government would be broadly welcomed. Given the state of relations with France and the increasing threat, drawing Richard's martial expertise down from the north was more or less a necessity, even if it left the Scottish border more exposed.

Alternatively, Edward may have considered a more traditional, Continental-style Regency, with Richard, as the last adult male heir of the House of York, given entire control of the country until Edward V came of age. In 1473, when Richard was amongst those appointed tutors and councillors to Prince Edward, it had been envisaged that he might require oversight of his possession until he was fourteen.[13] That might have been extended if he was king, subject perhaps to his development in the meantime, his personality and the emerging treacherous foreign situation, but he was, at the time of his father's death, eighteen months away from this initial potential milestone. If the Woodville family and Hastings were at loggerheads, it would inevitably create more problems for his son to leave either one of the factions in control with the other alienated, or to expect them to work together in harmony when that appeared impossible. In the absence of proof of what Edward intended, it is as likely that he envisaged a Regency under his brother Richard as that he sought to recreate the model of the unsuccessful Henry VI. What, if anything, of Edward's real plans was ever revealed is impossible to know, but if he had favoured a Regency, precedent would suggest that Council would reject and modify the arrangements and appoint Richard as Protector. It remains possible that the tripartite solution was Edward's favoured course because it would be acceptable to the establishment that he needed to support his son, but if Richard had been intended to act as Regent, he may never have known it, or may have moved on that basis if he did have news to that effect.

The idea that Edward planned for a Regency under Richard is given substance by the rumours reaching Mancini. He claimed that two opposing notions were debated in London on the king's death, while Richard was still far in the north. 'One was that the duke of Gloucester should govern, because Edward in his will had so directed, and because the government ought to devolve on him.'[14] Mancini may have been reporting the prejudices of a man from the Continent, where a regency would have been the natural result of Edward IV's death whilst his son was underage. He cannot have been aware of the complexities of the English system established sixty years earlier, yet he asserts that Edward's will, rather than appointing Richard Protector, intended him to be in control of the whole government. He continues that 'this was the losing resolution; the winning was that the government should be carried on by many persons among whom the duke, far from being excluded, should be accounted the chief.'[15] The fear, Mancini's gossip concluded, was that 'no regent ever laid down his office, save reluctantly, and from armed compulsion, whence civil wars had often arisen,'[16] but this ignores instances of successful regencies, particularly on the Continent. If a regency always ended in civil war, why was it still the system of choice in all countries but England?

It is generally accepted too that Richard was not informed of his brother's death by the queen. There is no evidence to substantiate or refute this assertion, but it, like many other suppositions, has endured. Certainly, Mancini had heard that 'Hastings reported all these deliberations by letter and messenger to the duke of Gloucester'[17] as the queen and Council sought to undo Edward's will. The rumours in the streets and merchants' haunts were that Hastings 'advised the duke to hasten to the capital with a strong force, and avenge the insult done him by his enemies. He might easily obtain his revenge if, before reaching the city, he took the young King Edward under his protection and authority, while seizing before they were alive to the danger those of the king's followers, who were not in agreement with this policy.'[18] For a source generally considered hostile to Richard in the events that followed, it is striking what Mancini had heard of Hastings; mercantile contacts might have been aware of his complaints and fears about Woodville authority, telling Richard that Edward had planned a regency and that he should take control of Edward V. Hindsight may have influenced Mancini's recollection, but if his negative testimony about Richard must be believed, then this cannot be ignored either. The word in London was that Richard had been made Regent in his brother's will, that the Woodville family of the queen were working to prevent it, and that Hastings had informed Richard of all of this. Polydore Vergil would later concur in both aspects with Mancini that 'William Hastings his chamberlaine sent from London trusty messengers in post to certify him of his brothers death, and from himself to signify, that the king at his death had commyted to him onely, wyfe, chyldren, goodes, and all that ever he had, and therfor to exhort him, that he would with all convenient spede repare unto prince Edward in Wales, and coom with him to London to undertake the government.'[19] This would appear to support the belief, at least in Richard's mind, based on the news reaching him, in both the Woodville family's efforts to exclude him for their own benefit and in his brother's decision that a

Regency was required under Richard. He had spent more than a decade doing all that his brother wanted of him, repaying the care Edward had given a frightened little boy and trying to impress the man who impressed him most in the world. He was not going to stop now.

In the swirling confusion of the spring of 1483, with the absence of much real evidence of anything, it is the human actions and their potential causes that we are left to examine. We cannot prove Richard's intentions (nor, for that matter, those of his contemporaries), but we can build an idea of what he might have understood, or been told (true or otherwise, he was not necessarily to know), even before he left Yorkshire for London. If there is any substance to Mancini's story and the similar accounts of later Tudor writers, then he would have been on his guard against Woodville schemes and would have understood that his brother had wanted him to act as Regent, with control both of the person of the new king and the government. Given the precarious state of England's relationship with France, it might seem natural both to vest entire authority in one person, free from the factional politics of court, and that the man to choose was Richard. He was a capable military leader, political governer in his region and the senior adult male of the House of York.

Mancini had heard that Richard had written to the Council expressing his concern that 'nothing contrary to law and his brother's desire could be decreed without harm.'[20] There is the sense of a threat about this warning, or else the application of hindsight by Mancini as he sat at his writing desks several months later. Richard needed time, not least to arrange and attend the requiem mass for his brother, to extract fresh oaths of loyalty to the new king from the northern polity and to travel to London. The Council had sent word to Ludlow, where the new king was still resident, that he should hurry to London and that his coronation would take place three days after his arrival. There is nothing inherently unseemly in the rush. Government effectively ceased without a king on the throne and in the interests of national security and stability, establishing the new king and his regime was of paramount importance. Even Mancini, though, had heard that some disapproved of the haste, fearing that it was being done precisely to prevent the involvement of the young king's paternal uncle in any decisions. The rapidly diverging interests in London are perhaps best captured by the words Mancini puts into the mouth of Thomas Grey, Marquis of Dorset. 'We are so important, that even without the king's uncle we can make and enforce these decisions.'[21] For the Woodvilles and their associates, it was time to stake their claim to remain at the centre of power. They were unpopular and had lost the protection from the effects of this dislike provided for them by Edward IV. The new king, with half-Woodville blood in his veins, was their best hope of resisting efforts they must have feared were coming to eject them from authority.

Richard must have written to the household at Ludlow to arrange to meet Edward, either before he left as Hastings had advised, or en route, but in any event, before he reached the capital. In Ludlow, things seemed to move surprisingly slowly. Edward IV's funeral, with his nephew John de la Pole, Earl of Lincoln as chief mourner, took place from 16 to 18 April before the old king's body was buried at the mausoleum he had prepared for himself and his dynasty at St George's Chapel, Windsor. Edward V remained stationary. His household, led by his uncle Anthony Woodville, Earl Rivers, celebrated St George's Day at Ludlow on 23 April, perhaps to satisfy Rivers's chivalric ardour, or else as an act of remembrance for the new king's father, whose funeral at the home of the Order of the Garter had been missed. The following day, 24 April, the household rode out of Ludlow to make for the capital. The delay is not consistent with a Woodville desire for haste, but the eventual departure may have been caused by word from Richard that he planned to come and take custody of the new king, as his brother had wished; alternatively, news may have arrived from the queen in London that events were getting away from her and only the arrival of Edward V might prevent their fall.

The Crowland Chronicler details intense discussions in Council and an increasing uncertainty and fear in London that was to no one's benefit. Although the queen had been striving for a swift coronation, there was frantic debate about the size of retinue the new king should travel with. 'Some were for limiting a greater, some a smaller number,' though all agreed that 'this prince should succeed his father in all his glory.'[22] The Woodville faction was losing its grip on events as the opinion was voiced louder and louder that 'the guardianship of so youthful a person, until he should reach the years of maturity, ought to be utterly forbidden to his uncles and brothers by the mother's side.'[23] Hastings' position, diametrically opposed from the queen's family, was made abundantly plain to all when he threatened to flee to Calais if the new king was permitted to arrive with a large Woodville escort. 'For he was afraid lest, if the supreme power should fall into the hands of the queen's relations, they would exact a most signal vengeance for the injuries which had been formerly inflicted on them by that same lord; in consequence of which there had long existed extreme ill-will between the said lord Hastings and them.'[24] It was becoming a dangerous, tangled mess.

Eventually, it was agreed between the factions that Edward V should travel with an escort of 2,000 men, Crowland believing that Hastings agreed to this number on the basis that Richard would hopefully bring at least the same. The date for Edward's coronation was set in Council as 4 May 1483. It was traditional for a monarch to be crowned on a Sunday, the Lord's day, reflecting the inherent spirituality of the ceremony and involvement of God in appointing a king. This was ten days after Edward and his household left Ludlow and probably the earliest Sunday he could make it to London with a large entourage. There were preparations to be made too, both to receive him in the capital and to provide for a suitably lavish coronation. The great and the good needed to reach London as well in order to attend the event, though there seems to have been at least one nobleman in the far away north who it might have been hoped would not reach London in time to contest the plans being set in motion.

Richard wrote letters to London and to the queen in particular assuring everyone of his 'duty, fealty, and due obedience to his king and lord Edward the Fifth'.[25] If Hastings' warnings were ringing in Richard's ears, then his response was not to fall on London as quickly as possible with a large armed retinue, as Hastings might have hoped or as a man spying an opportunity to snatch the throne might. Instead, he sent reassurances that he had no intention other than to support his nephew and work to secure his safe succession. Richard arrived at York with 'a becoming retinue'[26] rather than an army. A funeral mass was said for his brother, after which Richard caused all of the nobility and gentry gathered in the city to take an oath of fealty to Edward V as their new king. Richard himself did not shirk the pledge, but 'was the first of all to take the oath'.[27] The significance of this moment in dismissing any belief that Richard planned to take his nephew's throne cannot be overestimated. In a deeply religious age, a solemn oath of loyalty to a king appointed by God was not something to be taken lightly and was a powerful weapon in the political arsenal of a king. In particular, it had posed a problem for the House of York in the recent past. When Richard's father had eventually laid claim to Henry VI's crown in late 1460, part of the reason that Parliament, while recognising his superior right by descent, had objected to deposing Henry was that so many oaths of allegiance had been given him that men were entirely bound by them. They had renewed these oaths just a year earlier at Parliament in Coventry. York had tried to remind them that oaths made to a man holding office by fraud should not be considered binding, but it had been one of the reasons cited for making York Henry's heir rather than his replacement. If Richard had any hope or desire to see himself made king, causing these oaths to be sworn worked entirely against that end. The only reasonable conclusion is that, at this point, as he prepared to leave York, Richard intended to see his nephew crowned.

What Richard knew at this point, as far as can be determined from the remaining commentaries, is that London was in chaos. Hastings was frantically writing to warn him the queen and her family were working to subvert Edward IV's wishes so that they could retain power for themselves using their influence over the new king, who had grown up in the bosom of his Woodville family. Richard would understand that his brother had meant for him to act as Regent, if Hastings was to be believed on the matter. His mind would surely be immediately set swirling with problems of security in Calais and the threat from France to the south coast, not to mention the possibility of the Scots stepping back out of line as soon as he was away from the northern borders. It was going to be a mammoth task. The news from London suggested to him that those outside the queen's immediate circle were all in agreement that the Woodville family should not be allowed to retain control of the person of the king and that as Regent, that responsibility fell to Richard. Indeed, Hastings was advocating a swift descent on Ludlow by Richard to take custody of young Edward. One other thing would have become evident as the news arrived by Hastings' messengers. William, Lord Hastings, was in dread fear for his own position. He had, according to Crowland, threatened to flee to Calais and barricade himself in if the queen and her family got their way. Hastings' authority and influence had derived directly from his relationship with Edward IV; he had estates in the Midlands and was Captain of Calais, but had never managed to gain an earldom from Edward, who was cautious in the creation of nobles during his second reign. Hastings clearly feared losing everything, and whilst his apparent loyalty to the House of York was admirable and useful, it was born from dread and self-preservation. Hastings had his own agenda in encouraging Richard.

The next portion of the shadowy events of spring 1483 is as shrouded in myth as the rest. Crowland and Mancini differ in some details but agree on the general course of events; that Richard arranged to meet his nephew before arriving in London and that Edward assented. The king moved beyond their meeting point, but his maternal uncle, Earl Rivers, travelled back to meet Richard and Henry Stafford, Duke of Buckingham, who was also to meet them at the same location. After a night spent in convivial company, the men retired to bed only for Rivers to find himself arrested in the morning. Richard and Buckingham travelled on to meet the king, where they seized others of his household, dismissed the 2,000-strong retinue and took control of the boy. Rivers, Sir Richard Grey (the queen's younger son from her first marriage – Edward V's half-brother) and Thomas Vaughan, the long-serving Chamberlain to Edward, were sent north as prisoners and Richard, Buckingham and Edward continued their journey to London.[28]

There is no other record of the details agreed by Richard and Rivers for the journey. A legend has taken hold that they decided to meet at Northampton, that Rivers travelled on with the king to Stony Stratford and that he then returned to Northampton to meet Richard and Buckingham. It is by no means certain that those were the arrangements made, though they seem to have become the accepted facts. Stony Stratford was Woodville territory, and it is possible the plan was always for Edward to wait there. It lay about 60 miles north-north-west of the capital, maybe three days' travel, so that the approach to London might be made together. If the agreement had been to meet at Northampton and Rivers had overshot the town by 15 miles, it was sure to begin to confirm what Richard was already wary of. Even if Rivers explained that they had moved on to ensure that there was enough lodging in the town for Richard, Buckingham and their retinues, Hastings had made Richard suspicious enough to question the truth of this. Rivers's return is odd in almost all circumstances without understanding the man and his relationship with Richard. If the plan was to hurtle headlong to London, then why go back and meet Richard, unless it was to assuage any suspicion? It would be more prudent to keep going, half a day or so ahead of the others, unless Richard and Buckingham had made better time than the ponderous progress of a household and 2,000 escorts, and Rivers was in danger of being caught up. It is equally likely that Rivers had no ulterior motive, had genuinely sought to leave room for the retinue of two dukes, and had travelled back to begin making arrangements to enter London together. The truth of his motives cannot be known beyond a doubt, but we can be confident that Richard, already watching for treachery, might reasonably have interpreted this as a development that confirmed Hastings' warnings.

Another myth at play in this incident is the bitter hatred between Richard and the Woodville family. It just did not exist, at least not overtly or in any record before 1483. As gossip did its work, it was easy to look back and see Richard blaming the queen for George's downfall, despite the wealth of evidence that George had brought it about entirely on his own. The nobility and much of the country had been somewhat scandalised by Edward's marriage in 1464, but there is no evidence Richard felt any special outrage. After George's execution, Richard had not made efforts to stay away from court, though business kept him often in the north. Rivers particularly seems to have been on good terms with his sister's brother-in-law. The reputation of the two men was not dissimilar. Rivers shared Richard's interest in books and literature and had, in 1477, commissioned what was probably the first book printed in England by William Caxton on his new printing press. It was Rivers's own translation from French of *The Dictes and Sayings of the Philosophers*, a compendium of inspirational phrases originally gathered by the Syrian scholar al-Mubashshir ibn Fatik. It drew on religious texts and ancient wisdom and reveals Rivers's interest in such matters. Militarily, the men also enjoyed similar, though subtly different, reputations. Rivers was an internationally famous tournament knight. In 1467, he had fought a two-day duel with Anthony, the Bastard of Burgundy, an equally renowned knight, during a tournament hosted by Edward IV designed to display the alliance between the two nations. As had been the case at the wedding of Richard, Duke of York, and Anne Mowbray, Rivers was always prominent in the lists. Richard did not partake of these spectacles, never, as far as is known, having entered a tournament. His martial reputation rested on the field of battle, whereas Rivers's contribution in these arenas was not remarked upon by anyone. He fought at Towton for Henry VI and was injured at Barnet, as Richard was, though remained in London when the king left for Tewkesbury, mounting an impressive defence against the Bastard of Fauconberg. On 12 October 1471, Edward had granted Rivers a safe conduct to travel to Spain to fight against the Moors there, supposedly in fulfilment of an oath to do so, though the king had been outraged that Rivers planned to leave the kingdom within months of its reconquest.[29] It seems Rivers never left, perhaps hoping to regain Edward's favour instead, though in 1472 he was helping Brittany fend off the attentions of France. So Rivers was the leading tournament knight in England to Richard's leading military reputation. Both men shared a love of books and a deep piety, as was soon to become clear on Rivers's part. They were perhaps more similar than they were different.

Richard had worked on commissions with Rivers, Dorset and other members of the Woodville family, and had personally made another of the queen's brothers, Sir Edward Woodville, a knight banneret just months earlier during the Scottish campaign. Only a few months before Edward IV's death, Rivers had submitted a land dispute that he was involved in to Richard for arbitration, suggesting both that the men were on good terms and that Anthony was not afraid to be judged by a man who preferred justice to entitlement. So what was happening at Northampton on the evening of 29 and the morning of 30 April? Rivers must have been aware of his sister's plans to rush the coronation and to try to exclude Richard from acting as Regent. Did he disagree with the course of action? Perhaps he felt a Regency under Richard was the correct course of action, both because Edward IV had wished it and circumstances favoured it. Rivers may not have shared his sister's fear of exclusion if he was on cordial terms with Richard and may have seen more danger in trying to oppose the duke than working with him. Rivers may have disclosed his sister's concerns and plans, hoping that his honesty would win Richard over, or the men may have fallen into a quarrel about custody of the new king's person, which both may have wished to secure. If Richard had been set on edge by Hastings' news, Rivers might inadvertently have heightened, if not confirmed, the duke's concerns.

The only thing that is certain is that on the morning of 30 April, Rivers, Grey, Vaughan and Sir Richard Haute, Edward V's comptroller, were arrested and spirited north, dispersed amongst Richard's castles there. Rivers was imprisoned at Sheriff Hutton, Grey at Middleham and Vaughan at Pontefract. Haute was apparently pardoned at some point and released. The shock of these events was felt the following day in London when the queen took her daughters, her younger son with Edward IV, Richard, Duke of York, and Thomas Grey, Marquis of Dorset, into sanctuary at Westminster Abbey. She had been forced to take a similar course of action in 1470 when her husband had lost his crown, but then she could rely on the imposing and reinvigorated Edward to rescue her. Her future now was far less certain. Two things remain unexplained in this sharp action by Richard. If his intention was always to kill Rivers, Grey and Vaughan, why did he not dispose of them at the roadside in Northampton or Stony Stratford? As Constable, he had only to claim some treason against the new king on their part, and he would have legal authority to summarily execute them. It would matter little whether the treason was real or not, nor whether anyone believed in it. The executions would have been a clear statement of intent. The fact that Richard chose not to do this is evidence that their deaths were not on his mind at that moment. His intention may have been both to remove them from the fractured political scene in London and to use them as hostages to secure the queen's co-operation. At this point, Richard had not arrived in London himself and had no real idea of the situation he would find. If Rivers tried to block a Regency or refused to hand over custody of the king, then Hastings' warnings would have sounded even more convincing. If the Woodville faction was plotting, or at least if Richard had increasing reason to suspect that they were, the arrest of Rivers and the others would have been a sensible precaution.

When Elizabeth Woodville fled into sanctuary, it must have appeared the terrified retreat of a guilty conscience. What more evidence might Richard need that something was indeed amiss? Mancini claims that the flight of the queen came only after she had tried to raise an army in the capital using funds from the royal treasury to oppose Richard. She 'had exhorted certain nobles who had come to the city, and others, to take up arms' only to discover 'that men's minds were not only irresolute, but altogether hostile to themselves.'[30] If news of this reached Richard, his suspicions could only have been increased. Elizabeth Woodville hid at Westminster Abbey not just because she feared Richard, but because she saw that she and her family lacked any support to keep them in any kind of authority. All of London was opposed to them. Her gamble, her attempt to retain power by excluding Richard, had failed spectacularly. Crowland also confirms the mounting tensions as Richard and the new king drew closer. 'In the morning you might have seen there the adherents of both parties, some sincerely, others treacherously, on account of the uncertainty of events, siding with one party or the other. For some collected their forces at Westminster in the queen's name, others at London under the shadow of the lord Hastings, and took up their positions there.'[31] It was a mess within London. That Hastings is cast as a shadowy, looming figure in this may not be an accident. In an atmosphere of uncertainty, when each person is carefully watching every other for some sign of their intentions, the smallest actions can become magnified. Richard did not know what he was walking into as he headed towards the capital and

Elizabeth Woodville could not tell how he might react to news that she had tried all in her power to subvert a Regency led by him. The pasts of both would have taught them to act quickly, before their lives could be lost to barely distinguishable threats from unexpected quarters. The real legacy of the Wars of the Roses was only now being realised. Suspicion and pre-emptive self-preservation were a way of life into which most were indoctrinated from a young age.

Back at Northampton, Richard deliberately slowed matters down, giving time for the dust to settle and intending not to rush, as the queen had planned to do. The royal party did not leave Northampton until 2 May, when it travelled as far as St Albans, 25 miles north of London and the site of two recent battles, a victory for Richard's father in 1455 and a loss for Warwick in 1461. What young Edward made of these events is by no means certain, but Mancini's rumour mill had churned out a story that the young king had been dismayed at the arrest of those who had been responsible for his upbringing for years, though there was no hint of any real resistance.[32] Crowland overlooks any mention of Edward's reaction, but claims that Richard 'did not omit or refuse to pay every mark of respect to the king, his nephew, in the way of uncovering the head, bending the knee or other posture of the body required in a subject.'[33] There was no arrogance or sense of victory in the way Richard addressed his king. At some point before their arrival in London, the new king, his uncle Richard and their cousin Henry Stafford, Duke of Buckingham, scribbled their signatures and mottos on a scrap of paper that has survived.[34] This was perhaps the playful jottings of men trying to reassure and win the confidence of a young king suddenly deprived of the company that had been his constant for most of his life. Edward's signature appears at the top, in a stiff hand using block capitals to declare EDWARDUS QUINTUS. After a space, Richard has signed himself 'Richard Gloucestre' and above his signature, bracketed with it, appears the phrase *Loyaulte Me Lie* – Loyalty Binds Me, the final evolution of Richard's personal mottos appearing for the first time in surviving records. Loyalty was an all-encompassing chivalric ideal that had featured in previous mottos used by Richard. It meant not only personal loyalty to a king, but to those in a lord's care and to more abstract ideals of service and knightly behaviour, to the code of chivalry itself. Perhaps it was designed to reassure the unsettled king that his uncle meant him no harm, but it is also an iteration of long-held ideals espoused by Richard throughout his adult life.

Beneath Richard's signature is that of Buckingham. He wrote his motto *Souvent Me Souvene* above a flourish that denotes 'Harre Bockingham'. The motto translates as 'Remember Me Often', a striking message from a man for so long out in the cold. Buckingham had been in the political wilderness during Edward IV's rule. At the age of eleven, he had been married to Catherine Woodville, one of the queen's younger sisters, who was around seven at the time. Many chroniclers claim that Buckingham despised the queen and her Woodville family because he resented having such a low-born wife foisted upon him, though there is no real evidence to suggest that the marriage was an unhappy one. The couple had two sons and two daughters and may have got on well, even if Buckingham felt he had deserved a higher ranking prize. The eruption of this twenty-nine-year-old duke onto the political scene is something of a mystery. He had held no office nor made any contribution to government under Edward IV. His patrimony lay in Wales, where resentment may have grown from his exclusion due to Woodville and Stanley influence there, sponsored by the king. During the French campaign, Buckingham had travelled with the king but left to return home before the Treaty of Picquigny had been signed. Did Richard mistake a bored, sulking malcontent for a man with a similar mind on the matter to Edward's swift resort to peace there? Possibly Richard saw a nobleman, a duke of the blood royal (Buckingham was a great-great-great grandson of Edward III through Thomas of Woodstock, Duke of Gloucester) and a cousin (Buckingham's paternal grandmother was Anne Neville, a sister of Richard's mother Cecily) who might be an ally. Years of apparent removal from politics made him the closest thing to a neutral that was available and, if he did dislike his Woodville in-laws, it might be harnessed by Richard, using a senior nobleman to help him neutralise the threat he had been warned awaited him in London. If any of this was the case, it was to prove a serious miscalculation; an inability to judge character that was a fault in Richard's own makeup, and one he shared with his father. Buckingham was a smooth character and doubtless turned on the charm, but Edward on this occasion had seen something there that he had kept at arm's length for years. Richard instead embraced it, to his own peril, but perhaps as a sign of his own desperate uncertainty and need for allies. The court was unfamiliar to him, at least compared to those he was heading to face, and he perhaps felt comfort in having someone in a similar position at his side, just as George had accompanied and reassured him in captivity and exile.

Whilst at St Albans on the evening of 3 May, Edward V, under the guidance of his uncle, gave effect to the very first act of his government. He started off with something simple and personal. This was probably the first time he had exercised power in his own right anywhere, since his household at Ludlow had been strictly supervised and effectively run by Rivers. Edward wrote under his signet to the keeper of the seal of the Earldom of March to instruct him to make up letters patent addressed to the Bishop of Hereford exercising the new king's right to appoint a new rector to the vacancy at Pembrigge. Edward chose John Geffrey, a chaplain who seems to have been a favourite of Edward's at Ludlow.[35] Was Richard discovering that young Edward had not been allowed to

Fotheringhay Castle, Northamptonshire. Formerly the seat of the House of York and later the site of the execution of Mary, Queen of Scots, it was the birthplace of Richard III on 2 October 1452. All that remains now is a mound and one piece of stone. (Author's Collection)

The Church of St Mary and All Saints, Fotheringhay. Richard may have been baptised here, or in a chapel at the castle, but he did attend services at the church in his early years. He would also see his father and older brother Edmund reinterred there in 1476. (Author's Collection)

The outer bailey of Ludlow Castle, Shropshire. Richard moved here briefly in 1459 when his father raised an army in protest against his treatment at the hands of Henry VI. Richard would have watched as men poured into the town and castle, practised with their weapons and prepared to march to battle. (Author's Collection)

The inner bailey of Ludlow Castle, where Richard lodged. Much of the accommodation was refurbished ready for Henry VII's son Prince Arthur after his marriage to Catherine of Aragon. The circular Chapel of St Mary Magdalene was built in the 12th century. (Author's Collection)

Ludlow town from the top of the castle keep. When Richard's father and his brothers Edward and Edmund fled the town, they left Richard behind with his mother, brother George and sister Margaret. The town was plundered by royal troops and the castle ransacked, and all the goods removed. Richard was just nine when he witnessed it. (Author's Collection)

The three brothers of York. This depiction of Edward IV (centre), George, Duke of Clarence (right) and Richard, then Duke of Gloucester (left) was taken at the re-enactment of the Battle of Tewkesbury, which is held in July each year. (Author's Collection)

Above left: **Edward IV's Court.** Edward receives a book from Jean Wavrin. It has been suggested that one of the figures standing nearby might be Richard, though it is not clear whether it is, or which one he might be. (British Library Illuminated Manuscripts)

Above right: **King Edward IV of England.** He was Richard's oldest brother. (Wikimedia Commons)

Elizabeth Woodville, Queen Consort to Edward IV. Elizabeth is often viewed as an implacable enemy of Richard, yet the two were reconciled in March 1484. The motives and intentions of the Woodville family during the spring of 1483 remain hotly debated. (Wikimedia Commons)

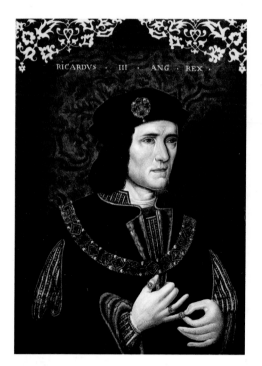

Above left : **King Richard III.** The image is a later one, probably copied from a contemporary likeness. The way in which he holds the little finger of his right hand may suggest an injury received at the Battle of Barnet. (Wikimedia Commons)

Above right: **Margaret of York, Duchess of Burgundy, kneeling before the resurrected Christ.** Margaret worked hard to promote Burgundy's interests in England, and to oppose Henry VII after 1485. She had grown up with George and Richard at Fotheringhay. (British Library Illuminated Manuscripts)

The arms of Anne Neville, wife of Richard and later his queen consort. As the daughter of Warwick the Kingmaker, Anne had a proud heritage and brought Richard much-needed respect and credibility in the north of England. (British Library Illuminated Manuscripts)

Middleham Castle, Yorkshire. This imposing building was centre of the vast Neville estates and probably Richard's main seat of power during his time in the north. It is often considered to have been Richard's 'home', though he may not have thought of properties in the same way we do now. Nevertheless, he was quick to return to the north after he became king. (Author's Collection)

The Church of St Mary and St Akelda, Middleham. It was used as a place of worship by the Neville family and by Richard during his time in the north. Richard's college at Middleham was to be based in the church. (Author's Collection)

The Great Hall at Middleham Castle. Richard and Anne would have entertained local magnates and dignitaries here. Richard also spent time in the castle as a teenager in the household of his cousin the Earl of Warwick, Anne's father. (Author's Collection)

Interior of the Church of St Mary and St Akelda, Middleham. (Author's Collection)

A genealogy of Edward IV. During the C15th, legitimacy became more important than ever as competing lines of the royal family vied for the throne. (British Library Manuscripts)

Right: **The tomb of Richard, Duke of York and Cecily Neville, Duchess of York at St Mary and All Saints, Fotheringhay**. Richard acted as chief mourner when the bodies of his father and brother Edmund were moved to Fotheringhay in 1476. The original tombs were in the College, which was destroyed during the Reformation. Elizabeth I ordered the erection of a new monument and the moving of the bodies of her great-great-grandparents when she visited the town. (Author's Collection)

Below: The Falcon and Fetterlock badge of the House of York on the ceiling of the Church of St Mary and All Saints, Fotheringhay. (Author's Collection)

Left: **Richard, Duke of York and his oldest son Edward IV.** This stained-glass window is at St Laurence's Church, Ludlow. The Victorian window shows the descent of Marcher lordship. (Author's Collection)

Below: **The remains of the banqueting hall at Sudeley Castle, Gloucestershire.** This addition was built during Richard's ownership of the castle. It is possible Edward originally envisaged Sudeley as a base for Richard in the west, before he finally moved to the north. (Author's Collection)

The signature of Richard, Duke of Gloucester on a page within *Chroniques de France ou St Denis, France* (Royal MS 20 C. vii, f. 134r). (British Library Illuminated Manuscripts)

Edwin Austin Abbey's 1890's depiction of Richard, Duke of Gloucester and Lady Anne Neville, very much following the Shakespearean view of Richard still prevalent during the Victorian age and beyond. (Wikimedia Commons)

A scrap of paper on which Richard, Henry Stafford, Duke of Buckingham and Edward V wrote their names. Richard and Buckingham added their mottos, the first known use of *Loyaulte Me Lie* by Richard. It would appear again in the document incorporating the Wax Chandlers' Company of London in February 1484. The signatures were written between Richard taking custody of Edward V at Stony Stratford and their arrival in London. (British Library BL, MS Cotton Vesp. F xiii, f. 123)

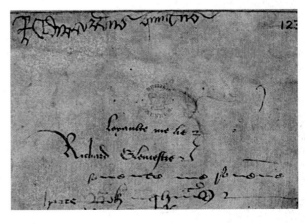

Left: Edward V, oldest son of Edward IV and nephew of Richard, depicted in stained glass at St Laurence's Church, Ludlow. Edward was proclaimed king, but never crowned, disappearing along with his younger brother Richard, Duke of York. As the Princes in the Tower, their fate remains a mystery to this day. (Author's Collection)

Below: **The Tower of London.** Edward V was installed here shortly after arriving in London. The Tower was the traditional place in which monarchs prepared for their coronation. When Richard took the throne, Edward and his brother were moved out of the royal apartments, perhaps to the Garden Tower. Subsequently, they were moved again, their servants changed, and they were seen less and less, finally disappearing from sight by September 1483. (Author's Collection)

Above left: Richard III, his wife Anne Neville and their son Edward of Middleham from the Rous Roll. (Author's Collection)

Above right: Plaster copies of the seal of Richard III kept at The Church of St Mary and St Akelda, Middleham. Seals were the main instrument of medieval government. (Author's Collection)

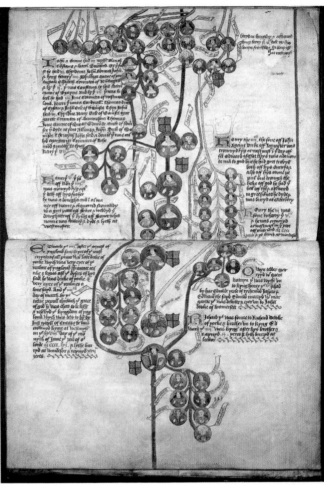

A manuscript genealogy of the kings of England, with a close-up (left) showing Richard III between his brother Edward IV and Henry VII. (British Library Illuminated Manuscripts)

ELIZABETHA · VXOR
HENRICI · VII ·

Elizabeth of York, the oldest child of Edward IV and Elizabeth Woodville. Rumour abounded in London during 1485 that Richard was planning to murder his wife Anne in order to marry his niece Elizabeth, but this is probably a corruption of the true plan for Richard to marry a Portuguese princess with Lancastrian blood and to marry Elizabeth to a Portuguese prince at the same time. (Wikimedia Commons)

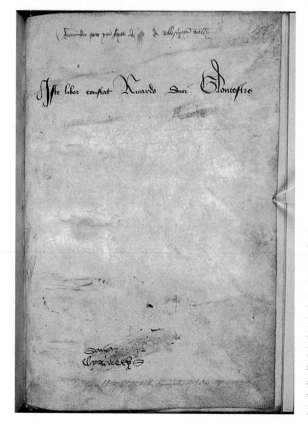

Ownership inscriptions in a book. The top entry reads *Iste liber constat Ricardo Duci Gloucestre*. At the bottom of the page is another that reads *sans remevyr Elyzabeth* in the handwriting of Richard's niece Elizabeth of York. It is odd if he was the murderer of her brothers, and he tried to force himself on her, that she would keep one of his books and add her signature to the page with his. (British Library Illuminated Manuscripts)

Above: Richard III and his household knights prepare for their ill-fated charge at the re-enactment of the Battle of Bosworth, staged every August. (Author's Collection)

Below: Richard is struck down, the crown falling from his head at the Battle of Bosworth re-enactment. (Author's Collection)

Above: **A Yorkist stained glass window at the Church of St Mary and All Saints, Fotheringhay.** The window was donated by the Richard III Society in 1975. (Author's Collection)

Below: **The White Boar, Blanc Sanglier, from the Yorkist window at Fotheringhay.** Richard adopted the boar as his personal badge for reasons that are uncertain, but probably complex. (Author's Collection)

The statue of Richard III now located outside Leicester Cathedral, opposite the Richard III Visitor Centre. (Author's Collection)

Loyaulte me lie

Above: **The tomb of Richard III.** Following the discovery of his remains, they were placed within a coffin constructed by one of Richard's collateral descendants, cabinet maker Mr Michael Ibsen. The stone of the tomb contains fossils, shows Richard's coat of arms and his motto, Loyaulte Me Lie – Loyalty Binds Me. (Author's Collection)

Below: **Part of a prayer found in Richard's personal prayer book, now engraved on a wall at the Richard III Visitor Centre, Leicester.** The extract reads: 'Lord Jesus Christ, deign to free me, your servant King Richard, from every tribulation, sorrow and trouble in which I am placed.' (Author's Collection)

LORD JESUS CHRIST, DEIGN TO FREE ME YOUR SERVANT KING RICHARD, FROM EVERY TRIBULATION, SORROW AND TROUBLE IN WHICH I AM PLACED...

stretch his wings at Ludlow because of the tight restrictions his father had imposed on his household and the close watch of the Woodville faction there? If so, he set about putting the matter right immediately, reassuring the king in the process that Richard meant only to support him and teach him how to use the power he had so suddenly inherited. It was a small matter, but it must have been thrilling to the twelve-year-old king.

On the morning of 4 May, the party made its final approach to the capital. It can be no accident that this was the date a Woodville-influenced Council had set for the king's coronation. Richard's message was clear; he was in charge now and things would be done at a pace he set. The route from St Albans to London took the royal procession through Barnet, where Richard was able to provide a first-hand account of the battle he had fought at the king's father's side more than a decade earlier, when they had vanquished the mighty Warwick together. It would have been another reminder of Richard's steadfast loyalty to the Yorkist regime now embodied in his nephew. Richard had written letters of reassurance to the Council, which had been read out in the capital's streets, and the guarantee that Richard, far from imprisoning the king, had rescued him and that they would soon be in the city together to begin his nephew's reign had procured the desired, calming effect.[36] As they neared London, the mayor and aldermen greeted them at Hornsey Park, dressed in their finest scarlet and surrounded by citizens in violet, eager to catch a glimpse of their new monarch. With only a small guard, perhaps around 500 men drawn from Richard's and Buckingham's retinue, the cavalcade rumbled into the city to be greeted by more noisy, excited crowds. Edward was dressed in deep blue velvet, the colour of royal mourning, and all of those accompanying him were in black cloth, providing a sombre contrast to the bright colours of the city officials.[37] The king was flanked by his uncle Richard on one side and Buckingham on the other, but as much of a spectacle, and a far more controversial one, clattered along the street in front of them.

Four wagons, loaded with arms and armour and displaying Woodville coats of arms, was pulled through the streets as Richard's officials proclaimed along their route that these had been discovered as part of a Woodville plot to ambush and assassinate Richard.[38] Mancini seems to have known, or at least those who fed him his information claimed to know, that these armaments had been laid down a long time before in preparation for the war with Scotland. This apparent deception on Richard's part caused suspicion of his motives, Mancini claimed, yet he is the same writer who believed the queen had been trying to raise an army in London against Richard. Sir Richard Grey's whereabouts are uncertain during early 1483. He had been added to those with authority in the household at Ludlow, but it is not certain that he was yet lodged there. Is it possible that he had ridden out of London at his mother's behest with men and arms to meet Rivers and confront Richard? Grey's arrival with wagons of arms might have been the spark that set events in motion at Northampton and Stony Stratford. It is far from unreasonable that Richard, who had been warned to be on his guard against Woodville plots, might see one, even if he were mistaken. Hindsight has caused the wagons of weapons to be seen as a ruse by Richard to incite the crowds against the queen, yet she was already so hated that she had been driven into sanctuary, and she was still the new king's mother. What Richard might hope to gain by fabricating this incident, except to confirm what the populace already thought of the queen and her family, is unclear. The road from Northampton to London wound through Woodville heartlands, and it is by no means impossible that Richard really did find wagons of weapons hidden somewhere, perhaps where Rivers had forewarned him if his resolve had wavered at the last moment. To be confronted by such a stash within the territories of a family working against him could only have been the final straw for Richard. Perhaps there was an innocent explanation, but there was no room to take a risk now. Possibly, Sir Richard Grey had come to ensure his uncle Rivers followed the plan through and in doing so, doomed them all to failure.

Edward was installed at the Bishop of London's Palace, next to St Paul's Cathedral. Richard set himself up at his London home, Crosby Place on Bishopsgate Street, a mile north-east. Mancini asserts that Richard guarded the king 'lest he should escape or be forcibly delivered', yet he was willing to leave Edward in a suitable place and travel to his own home. Richard, as he had done in York, caused all of the noblemen and prelates then in the city to swear a personal oath of fealty to Edward V, which 'was done by all with the greatest pleasure and delight'.[39] If Richard had begun to harbour some scheme to seize the throne for himself, reinforcing the problem of asking men to break solemn oaths was an odd course of action. The oath taken by Richard himself, along with his promise to protect the queen if she would emerge from sanctuary, was read before the Common Council, again to the delight of all.[40] Her continued stay in sanctuary was made to look increasingly unreasonable, unless she was actually guilty of something.

The year 1483 had begun under the shadow of a threat from abroad. Unexpectedly, power in the kingdom had splintered by April. Instead of the experienced King Edward IV holding all the reins, there was an interim government in London, a new boy king in Ludlow under the control of his maternal family and the senior male of the royal house in the distant north. Edward's rule had been, in many ways, a success. He was an early Renaissance figure before such a thing was fashionable everywhere, his tastes heavily influenced by the Burgundian court, and he had become a solvent king, albeit late in his rule, by harnessing the flourishing power of trade and the unpopular resort to benevolences. He had freed himself from a Parliament that expected him to do things he didn't want to do. Yet in other ways, he had been a dangerously poor king. He had subverted the laws of inheritance, which was a dangerous game to play, though he had not created an unassailable position for the Crown by his manoeuvres. Patrimonies seized in 1461 were quickly granted to reward loyal Yorkists and Warwick had never been attainted, so the vast Neville lands had never reached Crown hands. The failure to provide the Woodville family with an independent power may well have been the result of having nothing with which to endow them. Hastings may have missed out on an earldom for similar reasons, since it is hard to understand the omission otherwise. The Woodville family had become something akin to a Yorkist version of the Beaufort family under Lancastrian rule; utterly dependent on the king's patronage and terrified at the loss of the influence their proximity brought.

A failure to pursue a foreign war had left a gaping, aching hole in Edward's reign, made worse by the promise of the invasion of France in 1475. England had undergone years of sporadic civil war that had been brought to an end in 1471, but nothing united a medieval nation like a war on foreign soil, particularly if it would avenge the embarrassments of the last encounters of the Hundred Years' War. That Edward had been cajoled into it in 1475 by the Commons and his lords demonstrates the ample appetite, but it was not one Edward shared. He perhaps felt he had done his fighting and that England was enough of a problem without trying to rule France too, but Henry V had understood the unifying benefits of war in France that Edward had ignored in favour of a large pension. Bored nobles indulged in local quarrels when they had no focus for their martial energies. Louis XI spent much of his reign terrified of a united effort against him by England, Burgundy and Brittany precisely because it had a good chance of success, but the French king had the measure of his English counterpart, paying him off long enough to deal with Burgundy and Brittany before turning on England.

Edward had been the glue that had held England together. He was well-liked and could manage the factions and squabbling, even from those close to him such as Hastings and the queen's family. Both sides stayed reasonably within the bounds of acceptable behaviour because of Edward, either because they feared him or loved him, or maybe both. With his larger-than-life presence, both his physical size and the strength of his personality, gone, there was nothing to hold the factions together. He may not have expected his death, but if the chief aim of a monarch is to secure the succession of an heir, then he failed; a deathbed plea was too little too late. Seeing the peril in which his kingdom stood, not only from across the Channel but from within, Edward turned to the most dependable constant of the royal family: Richard. He could not leave power to the Woodville family without alienating Hastings and other nobles, nor could he exclude them when they were closest to his heir and the relations of his other children, having no way to protect themselves without Edward. Richard, free from association with either side in particular and with the foremost military reputation in the country, was the perfect solution, but Edward was placing his brother's head into the lion's mouth, risking the future of the House of York on the hope that Richard could balance or restrain these fractious, arguably irreconcilable groups.

From his home in the far north, the news reaching Richard was designed to set him on edge against a Woodville plot, and it must have worked. The truth of the queen's intentions and those of her family are hard to ascertain. They may have been plotting against Richard, or for their own survival, or they may have been running scared of what was happening in London, but there was enough to raise already heightened suspicions. Each step seemed to further confirm the possibility of a Woodville plot, and if Richard acted to pre-empt a threat, that was precisely what his brother had wished him to do; prevent problems. If Richard believed he had been appointed to serve as Regent by his brother, then it was clear the queen was working to avoid this. Custody of Edward V would have been Richard's responsibility in that case, and if Rivers tried to deny it to him, or confessed that the queen, in fear, was plotting against his arrival, then the actions at Stony Stratford make sense and are sensible. Keeping the men alive demonstrates a lack of an immediate imperative to kill them. Richard arrived in London to find a city bristling, nervous and with armed factions in the streets. He almost immediately put an end to the discord and was welcomed. What followed is further steeped in mystery, uncertainty and myth, but on his arrival in London, nothing appeared amiss to the establishment in Richard's actions.

As for Edward IV, the tallest monarch in English or British history, he is perhaps best summed up by Philippe de Commines. 'King Edward was not a man of any great management or foresight, but he was of invincible courage, and the handsomest prince my eyes ever beheld.'[41]

14

Protector

*The feast of the Nativity of Saint John the Baptist being appointed as
the day the coronation would take place without fail, all both
hoped and expected a season of prosperity for the kingdom.'*
The Crowland Chronicle[1]

On the day that Richard entered London with his nephew, his world was
becoming more precarious and uncertain in the far north. The news would
have taken a few days, perhaps two at the absolute minimum, to reach the
capital, a messenger thudding down the road south as his mount huffed
and snorted in protest beneath him. Richard installed the new king at the
Bishop of London's palace and could reflect that things seemed much as
Hastings had warned him in the city, but that he had delivered the king
safely and removed the immediate threat of any Woodville plot, real, or
imagined. When the courier arrived, the news was of the worst kind,
and something Richard had probably not expected amongst all his other
troubles. On 4 May 1483, George Neville, son of John Neville, Marquis
Montagu, died. He was about twenty-two years old, and worryingly for
Richard, unmarried and childless. The clause in the decade-old grant of
the Neville inheritance to Richard was instantly triggered. His interests in
the vast northern territories that had become his home reverted to a life
interest only, all of it going to the Crown on his death and none available
for his own son, Edward of Middleham.

The impact of this shock should be considered as influencing Richard
in the weeks that followed, some of the most turbulent of his tumultuous
life. At the very point he needed to be at his strongest, his position was
significantly weakened, and everyone would be aware of it. It was blood
in the water, and London was never short of hungry sharks. He must
have considered it a boon now to have decided to take action against the
Woodville faction, for it was one less corner from which to worry about
an attack. The immediate impact of this shift in fortunes should not be

ignored, but neither should it be overestimated. Richard himself was no worse off in the short term than he had been. He was unaffected by the loss, the cost of which would only be realised by his son when Richard eventually died. It made physical survival an immediate imperative if he was to resolve the problem but his power, authority and wealth were not diminished in the slightest. He had time to seek the new king's approval for an amendment to the original grant and his excellent service, as with everything else in his life, was the best route to attaining it. He also still had an hereditary right to the County Palatine his brother had created for him and which had been ratified by Parliament. It would mean a loss for his son if it could not be corrected, but it did not leave him facing destitution, merely having to shift focus. Undoubtedly, this was news Richard could have done without, one more care atop so many others, but it was not immediately devastating nor was there a lack of potential to put it right over the coming months. Edward IV had seen Richard and his heirs as protectors of the northern border for generations to come. Would Edward V really wish to risk reversing that policy, particularly with France offering a new threat? It was a worry, certainly, but not a catastrophe.

On 7 May, Richard was at his mother's London residence, Baynard's Castle, which for years had been the base within the capital of the House of York. Nestled against the Thames and close to St Paul's Cathedral, it was a beautiful mansion arranged in a trapezoid around a central courtyard, rebuilt by Humphrey, Duke of Gloucester, before passing, via the Crown, to Richard's father, York. It was strategically well placed within the city for business and had been the location of Edward IV's acceptance of the throne at the behest of the city officials in 1461. Buckingham joined Richard, nine bishops and as many of the executors of Edward IV's will as could be gathered to prove the document. Although that will does not survive, a copy of an earlier version is extant and demonstrates the problem that caused the executors to delay their work indefinitely.[2] Elizabeth Woodville was given significant authority as an executor by the older will and is likely to have held the same role in the final document. Her absence, as well as the fact that the rest of Edward's children, beneficiaries of his will, were in sanctuary made it impossible to administer the will.[3] It is unclear whether Cecily was in London during this period, but it seems plausible since her oldest son had died, her grandson was due to be crowned, and her youngest son was being thrust into the political turmoil to weave order from chaos. Cecily's concern was for the future of the House of York and she would surely have been available to offer the guidance and advice that her experience meant she had at her fingertips. At the very least, she permitted Baynard's Castle, her personal property, to be used throughout the weeks that followed, which suggests no opposition to what was happening.

Thomas Rotherham, Archbishop of York, had been Chancellor to Edward IV but found himself swiftly removed from office. Sir Thomas More later asserted that Rotherham had taken the Great Seal, the ultimate mechanism of government, to the queen at Westminster to try to preserve her authority. Contemporaries do not make this accusation, though Mancini understood that the archbishop had been the most vocal champion of the Woodville faction in Council.[4] His removal might then have been a natural consequence of the failure of the queen's plans, whatever they had been. John Russell, Bishop of Lincoln, was appointed Chancellor instead, a man widely respected as one of the most learned men of his age.

When Council met on 10 May, there was much to discuss, and the session lasted several days.[5] The majority of Edward IV's councillors were retained, including Lords Hastings and Stanley, Archbishop Rotherham, despite being deprived of the office of Chancellor, and Bishops Stillington of Bath and Wells and Morton of Ely. John Alcock, Bishop of Rochester and a tutor to Edward V, was amongst those added to the Council, demonstrating that this was not a body designed to work for Richard against the new king. One of the matters broached was where the new king should be lodged. The Hospital of St John was suggested, as was the Palace of Westminster but, at Buckingham's suggestion, it was decided to move him to the Tower of London.[6] Something sinister is meant to be understood by Buckingham suggesting this, but that is to ignore the fact that the Tower was the traditional place for a monarch to prepare for their coronation at Westminster Abbey. There was evidently a desire to move Edward from the Bishop of London's palace for some reason, so it made sense to install him at the Tower rather than at one of the other locations, only to have to be relocated to the Tower at a later date anyway. Besides, if London was unsettled and the queen might try to organise an attempt to gain custody of the king, the Tower was the ideal location within which to keep him safe and secure. For some, though, there are only dark motives at work in these days. Crowland's assertion that some were bitterly opposed to what seems an obvious and sensible measure is perhaps the application of hindsight from 1486 onto what would become one of the most significant decisions of the medieval period. Anyone writing during Henry VII's reign would surely wish to distance themselves and others still alive from decisions made by that king's predecessor, this decision in particular becoming the cause of centuries of consternation.

The date for the coronation of Edward V was set for Sunday 22 June, with Parliament to be summoned to open three days later on 25 June. Crowland understood that it was to take place then 'without fail',[7] doubtless to reassure those concerned that 4 May had been, almost certainly deliberately, missed. With all of this resolved, Council set about approving Richard's position and authority during the minority of the new king. Richard may well have been expecting to be appointed Regent and may have worked to this point in the belief that this had been his brother's intention. It has always been assumed that he was only ever intended to fill the role of Protector previously fulfilled by Humphrey, Duke of Gloucester, which would give him military authority for the defence of the nation and a place on the ruling Council, but no more authority than that. The evidence of the language used in the aftermath of Edward's death points towards a Regency, with full powers invested in Richard. Crowland seems to contradict his own version here, as well as throwing in the word 'Parliament' to describe the meeting of the Council. It is perhaps deliberately abstruse. He states that 'the duke of Gloucester received the same high office of Protector of the kingdom, which had been formerly given to Humphrey, duke of Gloucester, during the minority of king Henry.'[8] This would leave Council to run the government, but nowhere is there any mention of the third separation of power by a nomination of a person to be responsible for the person of the king. The Woodville family were clearly in no position to fulfil this role any longer, but no replacement was identified. The reason for this may lie in Crowland's next, seemingly contradictory, statement.

Richard was, according to Crowland, 'invested with this authority, with the consent and good-will of all the lords, with power to order and forbid in every matter, just like another king, and according as the necessity of the case should demand.'[9] These were not powers enjoyed by Humphrey, Duke of Gloucester, as Protector, nor even by Richard's father, who is an odd omission as a precedent for the powers of a Protector from far more recent, and Yorkist, history. The writer, who identifies himself as a lawyer, cannot have been unmindful of the realities of the office of Protector as Humphrey had performed it, nor of the original intention of Henry V that his brother should have been Regent. The confusion may not have been accidental. At a point when words had to be chosen carefully, particularly regarding the previous regime, Crowland may have left a clue that Richard was, in fact, appointed Regent, even if the more English style of Protector was used to denote the office. York had been granted the same powers that Humphrey had actually acquired as Protector; he was responsible for military affairs and a prominent member of the Council, which governed, as the king was placed into the care of the queen. That example is passed over in favour of a reference to Humphrey, which is immediately followed by the description of the powers of a Regent, which Humphrey had been meant to hold by his brother's will, but had been denied. The implication is that Richard was appointed *de facto* Regent, even if under a different title, as Humphrey had been intended to be by Henry V. Either way, the powers Crowland describes were not those of the previous holders of the office of Protector in England, but those Henry V had planned in 1422.

The distinction is crucial because it has been asserted that Richard acted more and more as though he was the centre of all power, yet clearly he was, and was meant to be. His seizure of the person of the king has been painted in a sinister light, yet as Regent, it was his responsibility. The Woodville faction seems to have favoured something closer to the system put in place after Henry V's death, no doubt hoping and believing the Council would share their vision and Richard's powers could be marginalised with their influence over the king maintained. Crowland, recalling events in the spring of 1486 under the rule of Henry VII, had reason to be careful in what he said. He was at the centre of political power during this period. If the Woodville family were excluded and Richard welcomed as an all-powerful Regent, it was not something to be broadcast now that Elizabeth Woodville was free and her daughter was queen. It could be obscured by clouding the issue, pleading reluctance on the part of many and schemes hidden by Richard. The reference to powers is brief, but strikingly important as a hint that all in 1483 was not as it has been recorded in later years.

One more piece of business from this meeting of the Council has entered into legend with little supporting evidence. Mancini reported that Richard worked to get the Council's approval to convict Rivers, Grey and Vaughan of trying to set ambushes for him and of treason. He was unable to achieve his aim, which would presumably have been followed by their executions, 'because there appeared no certain case as regards to ambushes, and even had the crime been manifest, it would not have been treason, for at the time of the alleged ambushes he was neither regent nor did he hold any other public office.'[10] This story was picked up by later writers and provides colour for the accusation that Richard planned their downfall and his own accession from the earliest days after his brother's death. As with all that Mancini reported, it was gossip. His sources were exclusively Italian merchants or those close to the Woodville family, as is plain from much of the information, or misinformation, he seemed to have, which is almost entirely from a Woodville perspective.[11] Doubtless, they were the keenest to speak to those hungry for information and to look to spread damning rumours about Richard, removed from power as they suddenly found themselves. Much of Mancini's report is their agenda of slander. Nowhere else does a contemporary commentator record this accusation; that Richard, around 10 May, was seeking the convictions and executions of Rivers, Grey and Vaughan. It has the ring of malicious gossip designed to draw sympathy for the Woodville family and encourage outrage and mistrust of Richard and his motives. Crowland makes no mention of it in his account of the meetings. Fabyan did not know of a scheme to have them convicted at that point.[12] Grafton entirely fails to mention any request at Council that the men be dealt with.[13] Vergil makes no mention of it,[14] so Mancini appears to be the sole source of the story, yet it has taken a firm hold. That the Italian heard this story from his sources is a demonstration that the Woodville faction was still at work, trying to destabilise Richard and the government he now led. The passage in Mancini is also instructive in establishing how poorly informed he was. He claims that Richard 'held no public office', ignoring his long tenure as Constable, Admiral and Chamberlain. The bald claim that he was of no national importance has the dismissive ring of Woodville prejudice about it. It is typical of any attempt to study Richard's life in general and this episode in particular that rumour with no corroboration or substance clings to him as though it was well-attested fact. Wash all of this mud away, and the man will become a little clearer. It cannot be claimed with any confidence that in mid-May 1483, Richard was trying to have Rivers, Grey and Vaughan executed.

Another widely accepted myth is that the Woodville family emptied the royal treasury and that the queen's brother Sir Edward Woodville took half of it to sea. This myth also derives from Mancini alone. He claimed that before Richard arrived in London 'it was commonly believed that the late king's treasure, which had taken such years and such pains to gather, was divided between the queen, the marquess, and Edward.'[15] This must have come from the circles of gossips rather than Woodville sources, but once more Mancini is the only person to report such a thing at the time. Firstly, and importantly to the rest of Richard's story, it is certain that Edward IV did not leave some vast horde of treasure and cash. Two years of war with Scotland, preparations for defence against the French and the loss of his French pension had depleted any reserves before his death.[16] Moreover, Sir Edward had been sent to sea by the Council on 30 April in response to a genuine French threat, led at the time by Lord Cordes. By mid-May, Sir Edward's fleet was around Southampton and it is here that the story of him acquiring a huge sum of money probably originated. On 14 May, Sir Edward seized £10,250 from a ship that was forfeit to the Crown, giving the merchant it was taken from an indenture that he would personally repay it if it was seized incorrectly.[17] Again, Crowland makes no mention of an event as significant as the theft of royal funds by the Woodville family. Mancini's account seems to condemn the Woodville family in this as much as it damns Richard, and with as little evidence. Given the fragility of the Woodville position, it is not unreasonable that they would do all in their power to keep a grip on their authority. It was their position that was under threat, not Richard's, who was enjoying Council's favour, yet it is Richard who is condemned as the schemer in all of this on the evidence of one ill-informed visitor.

That Richard was held in high opinion is attested to by Crowland, who notes that Hastings, the enemy of the Woodville family, 'was extremely elated'. He saw nothing more than 'the transferring of the government of the kingdom from two of the queen's blood to two more powerful persons of the king's'. He was all the more impressed that it had been brought about 'without any slaughter, or indeed causing as much blood to be shed as would be produced by a cut finger'.[18] The single criticism offered by Crowland is that the Council felt Richard did not 'with a sufficient degree of considerateness, take measures for the preservation of the dignity and safety of the queen'.[19] This is hard to reconcile with the events. Elizabeth Woodville had taken herself into sanctuary with her children. Surely no one advocated breaching sanctuary to force the queen out in order to preserve her dignity. Richard had apparently offered an oath to protect the queen if she emerged, but she had chosen not to. What more was expected? Once more, Crowland's context may be important. In 1486, Elizabeth of York, one of the children with the queen at Westminster Abbey, was consort to Henry VII and there was perhaps a need to create the appearance that those still hoping for a role in government, or at least to keep their heads, had tried to mitigate the situation. In fact, almost every piece of evidence suggests that the Woodville family were out of favour, feared and mistrusted and that the queen's 'dignity' was on no one's mind.

Edward V's government ground into action amidst all the tumults. As early as 9 May, commissions were sent around the south coast and to the Isle of Wight to secure those areas against the French threat. William Berkeley was given custody of Carisbrooke Castle on the Isle of Wight, and the inhabitants were instructed to assist him. Porchester, Portsmouth, Pembroke and Jersey were all dealt with, and the mayor of Plymouth was ordered to deliver two French ships that had been taken.[20] On 10 May, Sir Thomas Fulford and another named Halliwell were sent to sea so that they could travel to the Downs 'among Ser Edward [Woodville] and his company', though they were not instructed to take any action and were probably sent with a watching brief to report back.[21] Something had changed by 14 May, when Edward Brampton, John Wells and Thomas Grey were sent to sea 'to take Ser Edward Wodevile.'[22] All but two ships returned, one of those failing to do so being Sir Edward's.

On 11 May, one of Edward IV's chaplains, Thomas Langton, was recommended to the Pope and the Dean and Chapter of St David's for the vacant bishopric there,[23] and it was in Wales that the most striking transfer of authority began. On 15 May, Hugh Bulkeley, Deputy Constable of Conwy Castle and Deputy Mayor of the town, was ordered 'to avoide from the possession therof, and to suffer the Duc of Bukingham to occupie the keping of the said castell', with a letter sent to Hugh's father William to ensure Hugh's compliance.[24] A similar instruction went to Carnarvon, ordering the inhabitants to 'obey and assiste' Buckingham as the new Sheriff of the county.[25] Ludlow Castle, the key strategic stronghold on the Marches and the centre of government of Wales, was to be handed to Buckingham, and the keeper of Bewdley Manor was ordered to provide Buckingham with whatever weapons were there at the duke's demand. The grants to Buckingham flowed throughout the month. On 21 May, Buckingham was made Justiciar and Chamberlain of South Wales, Constable and Captain of Aberystwyth Castle and other, unnamed towns in South Wales, Constable of all royal castles in Shropshire and Herefordshire and Steward of South Wales. Furthermore, he was given the control and incomes from all castles, manors and towns in North Wales, South Wales and the Marches of Wales that formed part of the Duchy of Lancaster.[26] On 26 May, possession of all of the lordships in Gower in South Wales were given to Buckingham, and those previously holding the properties were warned their instructions 'be not failed upon the feith and alliegeaunce ye bere unto us.'[27]

The power that flowed swiftly to Buckingham's inexperienced hands has been viewed as a form of payment for his support of Richard, and doubtless it was a reward. Buckingham was a charismatic figure and an eloquent orator, perhaps filling gaps Richard recognised in his own personality that would be of assistance when he arrived in London, before he knew for certain what he might face. As a political neutral who apparently had no love for the Woodville family, he had been a natural ally, even if Richard had misjudged, or ignored, his character. The other reality behind the propulsion of Buckingham to high authority in Wales and the Marches was that a vacuum had been left by the translation of the Prince of Wales to the throne and the removal of Woodville influence in the region. It was a vacuum that needed to be filled quickly to prevent unrest, either stirred by Woodville interests there, or by the Tudor exiles in Brittany. Jasper Tudor had been a popular Earl of Pembroke and might spy in the upheavals a chance to return with his nephew, Henry Tudor. That is perhaps the reason that Pembroke Castle in Wales received special attention amidst the shoring up of the vulnerable south coast of England. It was a suitable reward too; Buckingham was based at Brecon in Wales and had seen any hope of authority there squeezed by Woodville and Stanley influence, no doubt at the deliberate behest of Edward IV, who evidently considered Buckingham either ineffectual or dangerous. The duke was getting what he wanted in return for helping Richard secure what he needed. Buckingham was even given custody of the Duchess of Exeter, Richard's niece.[28] Richard's sister, Anne, Duchess of Exeter, had died in 1476. Her first marriage to Henry Holland, Duke of Exeter, had been dissolved, and she had remarried, to a knight named Thomas St Ledger. They had a daughter named Anne who had been permitted to gain the Exeter inheritance of her mother's first husband by more of Edward IV's legal chicanery. This matter was soon to receive closer scrutiny from Richard, but for now, his niece was placed into the care of Buckingham, perhaps with the intention of marrying her to one of Buckingham's sons.

Francis, Viscount Lovell, also received favours as a result of his close friend's new position of authority. Richard and Francis seem to have become close when they were both within Warwick's household at Middleham and Francis built a life around being near to Richard rather than returning to his family's lands in the south. In January 1483, he had been created a viscount and was a wealthy baron prior to that, perhaps the richest in England. On 27 May, Lovell was given the Honour of Wallingford, an ancient title based at Wallingford Castle in Oxfordshire and then a parcel of the Duchy of Cornwall.[29] Lovell was also handed the office of Chief Butler of England on 19 May. It gave Lovell duties at the coronation that was to come, and a new appointment was required because the office had previously belonged to Rivers. Richard needed men he knew and could trust, and few fitted that bill as well as Francis, Viscount Lovell.

There was not a clean sweep of Richard's enemies in favour of his friends, as might at first appear. In fact, it is hard to say that Richard had enemies at this point. Circumstance had placed him and the queen's family at odds, but it was not because of an old vendetta, but a new uncertainty. Sir William Stanley, younger brother of Thomas, Lord Stanley, was commissioned as Chamberlain of the County Palatine of Chester to obtain a new seal. It was to weigh 25 ounces, with each ounce to be worth 3s 2d with 20s 4d set aside for its engraving. The instruction was given 'by our commaundment, and advise of our derrest uncle the Duc of Gloucestre protectour and defendour of this our royalme during our yong age'.[30] Richard had previous experience with the Stanley family that might have given him cause to be suspicious of them, though he had worked with them in recent years, most notably during the Scottish campaign of 1482. In the prevailing uncertainty, it might have been desirable, or at least advisable, to have divested himself of Stanley assistance and restrained their power, but he chose not to do so, demonstrating that his intentions and fears were not self-absorbed. On 10 May, the new king had made an indenture with Henry Percy, Earl of Northumberland, confirming the earl as warden of the East and Middle Marches, in return for which Northumberland pledged to do all that was within his power to defend the border. He was clearly being set up to protect the north during Richard's absence, suggesting both that the threat there was real and that Richard realised business would keep him in the south for some time. It is likely that Northumberland had resented his own family's loss of authority in the north at Richard's hands and was now being presented with an opportunity to prove himself. It was a necessity, but another dangerous one, since expecting him to surrender his power after he had grown used to it might become a problem for Richard. The threat in the north from Scotland was further acknowledged on 25 May when the king, on his uncle's advice, authorised George Porter, a master carpenter, to source wood from as far away as Essex and 'other places whereon ye shal thinke is best tymbre' for the repairing and strengthening of Berwick town and castle. All of Richard's knowledge and experience was being brought into play within a month of his arrival in London to help secure the kingdom in the name of his nephew.

Richard even found an opportunity to provide something for his sister Margaret, Duchess of Burgundy. Her position had become precarious as a result of Edward's foreign policy, when he had failed to support her, and even more so when France took possession of the duchy's lands. She had retained a place at Mechelen in Flanders where she still held authority and was well liked, but that might change at any moment as France went on the offensive. It was only a small thing; a licence to export 200 quarts of oats from Kingston-upon-Hull, but it meant that Margaret was in the thoughts of her brother and nephew, which might have been both a reassurance to her and a warning to France.

On 5 June, letters were sent to fifty men instructing them to prepare to be knighted at the king's coronation. The men were ordered to appear at the Tower by 18 June, four days before the coronation, 'to have commynycacion with oure commissioners cencernyng the mater'.[31] This was a normal piece of the business of preparing for a coronation. Those selected were considered appropriate company for the new king, possibly predominantly because of their age, but this was a dangerous move if Richard's motives had changed by this point. Inviting fifty young men charged with chivalric pride to the capital for the express purpose of supporting and protecting Edward V would create a problem if Richard was already planning to overthrow his nephew. It would have been better to delay the matter, put it off or divert the letters. It seems that as the June sun blazed across the sky, Richard remained committed to securing the succession of his brother's son. By 6 June, instructions had reached York that four citizens were to be sent from the city to attend the Parliament at Westminster on 25 June. A week later it was decided that the four representatives should have additional funds to leave six days earlier so that they could be in London for the coronation to represent the city at that event.[32] Only two days later, things had changed dramatically.

By 2 June, Richard, through Edward V, was disposing of Rivers's property, suggesting that there was already no immediate route back to power for the queen's family.[33] In fact, seizures of Woodville property had been going on for some weeks by this point, as Richard tried to restrain their ability to fight back. On 10 June, Richard wrote from the London to the mayor, John Newton, and aldermen of York. He described himself as 'The Duc of Glocestr, Broder and Uncle of Kyngs, Protector, Defender, gret Chamberleyn, Constabill and Admirall of England'. He continued that he

...hertely pray you to come unto us to London in all the diligence ye can possible aftir the sight herof, with as mony as ye can make defensibly arrayed, their to eide and assiste us ayanst the Quiene, hir blode adherents and affinitie, which have entended, and daly doith intend, to murder and utterly destroy us and our cousin the duc of Bukkyngham, and the old royall blode of this realm, and as it is now openly knowen, by their subtill and dampnabill wais forcasted the same, and also the final distruction and disheryson of you and all odir thenheritors and men of honer, as weile of the north parties as odir contrees, that belongen us.[34]

By 15 June the letter had reached York, and on that day, the city's council arranged for 200 mounted men to be mustered at Pontefract, where they would join Northumberland in travelling to London to assist Richard. The next day they arranged for money to be collected to pay each of the soldiers 12*d* a day, though they were required to provide their own jackets. A traditional reading of this moment would conclude that Richard had now decided to take the crown for himself and was summoning help from York to implement his designs. There are several problems with this view and there is a more plausible explanation available. York was not given to raising great hordes of armed men in a hurry. The city had provided just a few hundred men for the Scottish campaign, not enough to make a substantial impact and too few to try to mount an attack on London. Richard sent a similar letter to Lord Neville of Raby in the north and Northumberland was clearly planning by now to move south, though this may only have been for the coronation and the opening of Parliament that were approaching. This was no large-scale muster of forces, nor would this force arrive swiftly to execute some sudden plan. Traditionally, it is seen as Richard crying wolf, justifying later actions by pleading that there were plots on his life, that of Buckingham and several others, but it is questionable what such a message to the far north of the kingdom, which already knew Richard well and would seek to support him where possible, would really achieve.

The overlooked possibility is that Richard was still concerned about Woodville power. It would not be long until Elizabeth Woodville was plotting with new conspirators. She had far from given up, and there was perhaps some last-ditch attempt to regain their hold on power, to force a role for themselves. Possibly there was a genuine threat, or the very real fear at least, that they were plotting against Richard's person. The queen was well connected in London and might have been able to find a willing assassin. By this point, Richard may have simply felt embattled and surrounded by the unfamiliar and uncomfortable machinations of court life and London politics. He might have written to York out of genuine fear or panic, or from a need to touch base with a more comfortable, secure part of his life. Richard seems to have seen Woodville plots from before he had left Middleham and this apparently hadn't stopped, whether the threats were real, imagined or whispered into his ear by men like Hastings with a vested interest in keeping the Woodville family at bay. Richard's wife Anne arrived in London on 5 June, and it is possible she brought news that changed Richard's outlook, of a threat, or even the possibility of some suspicious circumstances surrounding the sudden death of George Neville. There need be no switch in direction in this moment, but rather the continuation of the threats that had been swirling about Richard for weeks and either a determination to deal with them once and for all, or a growing sense of panic at living with the fears.

The news emanating from London during this period is scant and uncertain. Simon Stallworth, a member of the household of John Russell, Bishop of Lincoln and newly appointed Chancellor, wrote to William Stonor in Oxfordshire with news of recent events. On 9 June, he was able to offer few new tidings. The queen, her youngest son the Duke of York, and her brother Lionel Woodville, Bishop of Salisbury, were still in sanctuary at Westminster and 'wyll nott departe as yytte'. The Prior of Westminster was reported to be in some trouble on account of some goods he had received from the Marquis of Dorset, who had fled and escaped attempts to catch him,[35] eventually reaching Brittany. Council met for four hours, but no one made efforts to speak to the queen. Stallworth reported that frantic preparations for the coronation were continuing and hoped that Stonor would be in London on the day to see it for himself. Aside from the king's continued residence at the Tower and the arrival of Anne Neville, Duchess of Gloucester, in the capital, he had little else to report.[36] It might have been Dorset's flight and evasion of efforts to find him that convinced Richard of the persistence of a threat from the Woodville faction. If Dorset could make it to sympathetic territory, he might be able to stir men to an attack on London. Uncertainty alone might have been enough to drive Richard to seek aid from the north, where he knew that he could trust the men sent to him. If he had been using Rivers, Grey and Vaughan as hostages to leverage some co-operation from the queen and the rest of her faction, then it was not working.

The next moment of crisis came hard on the heels of Richard's appeal to York for support, and it is one of the most controversial moments in all of this contentious episode. On 13 June 1483, some of the members of the Council gathered at the Tower of London. Richard and Buckingham were there and amongst the others present were the Lords Hastings and Stanley, Archbishop Rotherham of York and John Morton, Bishop of Ely. Morton was a man who had been a faithful servant of the Lancastrian regime and had only made his peace with Edward IV when that cause had been wholly lost. He was a figure worthy of some suspicion who would prove himself deserving of far more than was held. At some point in the meeting, there was uproar, Lord Hastings was accused of treason, dragged outside and summarily executed on a makeshift block. For many later historians, this was an unforgivable act of tyranny that can only be explained by Richard's desire to plough a clean furrow to the throne. Once more, if the grime of centuries of caked-on rumour is washed away, the truth appears very different, even in the stories of the later architects of Richard's poor reputation.[37]

Mancini asserts that Richard 'rushed headlong into crime, for fear that the ability and authority of these men might be detrimental to him'. Mancini had heard that Richard had been secretly sounding out people who he thought might support the bid for the throne he was planning to make and found these men unreceptive. His account of the rest of the events is brief.

> One day these three and several others came to the Tower about ten o'clock to salute the protector, as was their custom. When they had been admitted to the innermost quarters, the protector, as prearranged, cried out that an ambush had been prepared for him, and they had come with hidden arms, that they might be first to open the attack. Thereupon the soldiers, who had been stationed there by their lord, rushed in with the duke of Buckingham, and cut down Hastings on the false pretext of treason; they arrested the others, whose life, it was presumed, was spared out of respect for religion and holy orders. Thus fell Hastings, killed not by those enemies he had always feared, but by a friend whom he had never doubted.[38]

Mancini's account is the only one in which Hastings is 'cut down' in the Council chamber. He seems unaware that it was a meeting in progress and not just a visit to say hello and makes no reference to Lord Stanley's presence there. Mancini cannot have known that any cry of treason was 'prearranged' either, so if opinion is stripped from the facts that he seeks to report, then during a Council meeting, Richard raised the alarm that Hastings was armed and threatening him. Soldiers burst into the room and Hastings was killed in the ensuing commotion.

A second contemporary account of the events appears in a note from an anonymous London citizen, who wrote:

> the Lord Hastings was takyn in the Towur and byhedyd forthwith, the xiii day of June Anno 1483. And the archbeschope of Yorke, the bischop of Ele, and Olever King the secoudare *(secretary)*, with other moo, was arestyd the same day and put in preson in the Tower.[39]

In this account, Hastings is beheaded, which suggests a more formal execution than the melee Mancini describes. Stanley is not mentioned here either, but Oliver King, Edward IV's secretary, principally in the

French language, was added to the list of those arrested with Rotherham and Morton.

The final version of Friday 13 June 1483 come from Crowland. After describing Hastings' joy at the bloodless success of Richard's removal of the Woodville family, the writer dryly notes:

> In the course, however, of a very few days after the utterance of these words, this extreme joy of his was supplanted by sorrow. For, the day previously, the Protector had, with singular adroitness, divided the council, so that one part met at Westminster, and the other at the Tower of London, where the king was. The lord Hastings, on the thirteenth day of the month of June, being the sixth day of the week, on coming to the Tower to join the council, was, by order of the Protector, beheaded. Two distinguished prelates, also, Thomas, archbishop of York, and John, Bishop of Ely, being, out of respect for their order, held exempt from capital punishment, were carried prisoners to different castles in Wales. The three strongest supporters of the new king being thus removed without judgement or justice, and all the rest of his faithful subjects fearing the like treatment, the two dukes did thenceforth just as they pleased.[40]

Crowland joins the other contemporaries in failing to place Stanley at the meeting. It is possible that later accounts involve him because he was alive after 1485 and perhaps boasted of his involvement. By then, this incident had become about Richard's scheme to deal with those considered the most ardent supporters of Edward V, so Stanley, with Edward's sister Elizabeth as queen, had reason to place himself there to establish credentials contemporaries do not credit him with. Crowland similarly had cause to be careful what he said about Rotherham and Morton, both of whom were also still alive when he wrote, Morton becoming a key pillar of the early Tudor regime.

There is one more aspect covered by the accounts of Mancini and the anonymous citizen that are worthy of consideration. Mancini begins his account of the events by saying that Richard had been made aware 'that sometimes they forgathered in each other's houses,'[41] the suggestion being that Hastings, Rotherham and Morton were indeed up to something, though precisely what is not known. If they were widely rumoured to be meeting in secret away from the Council, is it unreasonable, in the atmosphere cloying the London air, for Richard to see a threat there? Not only is it reasonable, but it is also possible that they were in fact plotting. The anonymous citizen is even more certain that something sinister was going on, writing that 'ther was dyvers imagenyd the deyth of the duke of Gloceter, and hit was asspiyd and the Lord Hastings was takyn in the Towur and byhedyd.'[42] The assertion here is clearly that there were plots swirling around in London, that Hastings' involvement in one to kill Richard was exposed, and that he was executed for it.

At the end of his explanation, Mancini, no doubt hearing from his gossips in the street, explains:

> After this execution had been done in the citadel, the townsmen, who had heard the uproar but were uncertain of the cause, became panic-stricken, and each one seized his weapons. But, to calm the multitude, the duke instantly sent a herald to proclaim that a plot had been detected in the citadel, and Hastings, the originator of the plot, had paid the penalty; wherefore he bade them all be reassured. At first the ignorant crowd believed, although the real truth was on the lips of many, namely that the plot had been feigned by the duke so as to escape the odium of such a crime.

It is hard to fathom how Mancini might have known the truth or otherwise of what was going on. If his opinion is again separated from the facts, there was some uproar in London caused by a lack of understanding of what was occuring, but it was immediately quieted when Richard sent a herald into the streets to explain what was happening. Obviously, Mancini has to cast those who believed as 'ignorant', because from his secluded position with a narrow stream of information, he knew much better. Whether any evidence was produced at this stage is uncertain, though later accounts embellish the story with written proof that was presented so quickly it must have been prepared before the staged incident. This ignores the possibility that the break in the meeting these writers always refer to might have been the moment that written proof from Hastings' home or elsewhere had reached the Tower.

It is striking that these three contemporary accounts seem to concur that Lord Stanley was not amongst those present or arrested. Two of the reports refer to actual plots, or at least secret meetings between Hastings, Rotherham and Morton. One also asserts that Londoners immediately believed Richard's explanation of Hastings' treason. The lack of further outrage is perhaps telling. Hastings was a popular figure in London so it might have been reasonable to expect some backlash from his death, either from the nobility or the populace, but none was forthcoming after Richard provided his description of events. There was no army in London to back Richard at this point; the men in York were yet to set out. Why was the death of a well-liked friend of the former king and a supporter of the new monarch accepted so quickly and quietly? It makes perfect sense if he had been embroiled in plots against Richard, but is otherwise hard to fathom.

The execution of Hastings has traditionally been viewed not only as an unjustified act of terror, which it seems not to have been, but also as an illegal killing, a murder, which it certainly was not. The summary nature of the sentence delivered upon Hastings has been cited as evidence that it was a rushed action outside the law, but that ignores Richard's previous and current positions. As Constable of England, he was entitled to summarily try acts of treason based on evidence that he had seen and to deliver a death sentence with no right of appeal.[43] We may not recognise this as a desirable method of administering justice, but it had been created for precisely the type of crisis that seems to have faced Richard on 13 June 1483. If a plot was exposed, he was able to convene an *ad hoc* Court of Chivalry to try the matter and deliver the sentence. If that was what happened, then he had done nothing illegal at all. He had followed the law as his brother had previously instructed him, using powers he had held for fourteen years. Richard was intimately familiar with the Constable's office and would have known what he was legally able to do to protect the king and himself. If the Council had really objected to a desire to try Rivers, Grey and Vaughan because Richard was not Protector when they supposedly tried to ambush him, he was in that office now. Not only that, but as Regent, an attack on him was treason. As Crowland said, Richard was 'just like another king',[44] and plotting to murder a king was treason, as was plotting to kill his Regent. If it is still accepted that Richard fabricated the charge against Hastings to be rid of him, the act might be judged immoral, but it was not, technically, illegal.

The possibility that Hastings was working against Richard by this point is a theme of most accounts of the event, even those that appear entirely hostile to Richard. Crowland is exceptional in making no reference to it beyond the report that Hastings was in arms in London before Richard's arrival and threatened to flee to Calais if the queen remained in power. Polydore Vergil asserts that after Richard took control of the king at Stony Stratford, a course Hastings himself had advocated, he had a change of heart. Hastings,

> ...when he saw all in uprore and that matters fell owt otherwyse than he had wenyd, repenting therfor that whiche he had done, caulyd together unto Powles churche suche frindes as he knew to be right carefull for the lyfe, dygnytye and estate of prince Edward, and conferryd with tham what best was to be doone.[45]

Vergil is clearly trying to demonstrate that Richard's actions made those most concerned for the new king nervous even before he arrived in London. If his ample application of hindsight can be believed, he is actually conceding that Hastings was plotting against Richard even before the Protector reached London, and despite advising Richard to take the course of action he had followed. Vergil includes Lord Stanley amongst those arrested at the Tower and imprisoned, though why Stanley was spared execution is not guessed at. Sir Thomas More's account is even more outrageous and further from contemporary records. Here, Stanley is not only present but is wounded in the melee within the Council chamber, avoiding decapitation narrowly by ducking under a table, a near miss surely worthy of mention by contemporaries.[46] More's account is replete with demonstrable errors and was never completed by Sir Thomas. It would be More's nephew who wrote the end of the story and published it after his uncle's death.

In More's account of the incident at the Tower on 13 June, Richard bares a withered arm that he claims is the result of witchcraft used by the queen and Jane Shore, one of Edward IV's reputed mistresses. Richard, it is entirely certain, had no withered arm to display. Earlier in the imagined scene, Richard asks Bishop Morton if they might send for some strawberries from the bishop's gardens in Holborn, a request that is readily agreed to.[47] The introduction of strawberries into the scene is of interest because of their meaning in a Catholic context, particularly since no other source mentions them. Strawberries are used in Catholic imagery to denote righteousness, the fruits of which are good works. It may be a coincidence, but More might also be pointing to the deliberate effort to besmirch the reputation of a righteous man. As a student of Morton's, he may also be referring to his mentor's garden, plentiful with the greatest works of a righteous man, and it is More's connection to Morton that should give rise to the greatest concern as to his motives in writing his account.[48]

It is the addition of later writers that gives us the dramatised scene that includes Lord Stanley, perhaps taking a blow to the head for the sake of Edward V, but at least being imprisoned. No contemporary mentions him even being at the meeting. There seems to be some consensus from contemporaries and later writers that Hastings was busy in London with his own agenda, fuelled by a desire to remain at the heart of power even though his link – his friend Edward IV – was gone. There are plenty of suggestions, without firm evidence, that the Woodville faction was plotting to further their own cause, so it is possible that Hastings was working to preserve his own position too. None of the plots can be proven, but neither can they be discounted. It is worth remembering that Richard was entering unfamiliar territory and that even the appearance of a threat, especially with Hastings' warnings, would have warranted action.

These need not be the only sources of scheming in London in the spring of 1483. The transfer of power had always been a point of ruction and threat. When Henry IV took the crown from Richard II, he spent the rest of his reign fending off plots. Henry V faced the Southampton Plot to kill him just as he prepared for the Agincourt Campaign and Henry VI's minority was rife with faction fighting, not to mention the execution of at least one Mortimer male who might have represented a threat. Edward IV had won the throne only to spend a decade watching for Lancastrian revivals and lost his crown for six months before regaining it and dealing ruthlessly with remaining threats, even, eventually, his own brother George. It is reasonable to conclude that the Woodville faction and Hastings had their own agendas in 1483 that caused them to scheme against Richard's Regency. Both were excluded from their former prominence by Richard's supremacy, and Richard was far less prone to the indulgences that made Edward easy to persuade and control.

One person who it is possible to see at the heart of these events is Sir William Catesby, a lawyer who had been in the service of Lord Hastings but also had connections to Richard and Lord Stanley. Sir Thomas More directly implicates Catesby in revealing the story of Hastings' plot to kill Richard in the hope of gaining Hastings' influence in the Midlands for himself.[49] The part played by this lawyer may not yet be over, but there are others who were far more certainly plotting Richard's downfall. In the confusion that seeped through the streets of London in the spring of 1483, there was one party who definitely saw an opportunity to use the troubled succession of a minor king to great advantage.

Within six months of Edward IV's death, an invasion of England took place led by Henry Tudor, the exiled Earl of Richmond, whom Edward IV had tried to get his hands on. Just before Edward's death, talks had been underway to bring Henry back to England and to marry him to one of Edward's daughters, but they were stalled by the king's death. Whether Edward was genuinely willing to be reconciled is uncertain. He had been at pains to kill every other threat to his throne, but Henry Tudor had evaded him. These negotiations had brought his return near, though Edward might have meant to trick Henry and, in turn, Henry seems unlikely to have blindly accepted Edward's outstretched hand. Henry's uncle Jasper Tudor, formerly Earl of Pembroke, was also in Brittany, but Henry had a powerful foothold in England. Margaret Beaufort, his mother, was a wealthy and influential woman. She had been conducting the negotiations with Edward for her son's return to England and must have been disappointed when they came to an abrupt end. A minor king was never going to tolerate the import of such a threat so, having come so close, she had lost her chance.

For an invasion to be launched in October 1483, planning must have been underway for some time. It is therefore feasible that as early as May and June, Margaret Beaufort spied a chance to win something grander for her son than a return to his earldom. Margaret was the great-great-granddaughter of Edward III through John of Gaunt, the founder of the royal House of Lancaster. The Beaufort family, initially the result of Gaunt's affair with his mistress, was later legitimised and, despite constant belief to the contrary, was never barred from the royal succession.[50]

Margaret had been married at a young age to Edmund Tudor, Earl of Richmond, a maternal half-brother of King Henry VI. Henry Tudor's grandmother was, therefore, Katherine of Valois, a daughter of King Charles VI of France, giving him at least a theoretical, if tenuous, claim to the thrones of both France and England.

In the chaos of 1483, at some point it is proven that Margaret Beaufort saw an opportunity for her son to become king because he invaded England with that aim in October that year. The question is how early her scheme was born. As London's political classes splintered and eyed each other with suspicion, Margaret may have seen her moment. After the death of Edmund Tudor whilst she was still pregnant, Margaret had given birth, aged thirteen, to her only child. She had married again, to Sir Henry Stafford, a seemingly happy union with the second son of Humphrey Stafford, Duke of Buckingham, that made her an aunt to Henry, the current Duke of Buckingham, who appeared at Richard's side. After Sir Henry Stafford's death, she had married for a final time, to Thomas, Lord Stanley, giving her even more influence and bringing her closer to Yorkist power. The rumours flowing around London that the Woodville family were plotting and that Hastings' faction was scheming, may have been deliberate plans to destabilise the new regime and to create the space for her ultimate project – a Lancastrian revival and a crown for her son. There was almost certainly no life-long plan to see Henry on the throne, but the idea may have been sparked into life in 1483.

15

A Question of Legitimacy

Thus far, though all the evidence looked as if he coveted the crown, yet there remained some hope, because he was not yet claiming the throne, inasmuch as he still professed to do all these things as an avenger of treason and old wrongs, and because all private deeds and official documents bore the titles and name of King Edward V.

Dominic Mancini[1]

There are three versions of Richard that exist. There is the traditional Ruthless Richard, who plots for the throne perhaps from before his brother's death and kills those who get in his way. A Romantic Richard is viewed as a victim of the events of 1483, dragged to his own doom by a sense of duty. The final persona is a Reactive Richard, lurching from one enforced decision to the next as crises swallow him. Each of these can be placed on a sliding scale between moderation and extremity with intersections at various points that do not rule out any two or all three of these personas making an appearance. It is probably somewhere in these intersections that the heart of the real man beats; neither victim nor evil mastermind, but a man remembered incorrectly by history from the later tales of storytellers keen to harness the imagery of the wicked uncle driven to heinous acts by a lust for power. Many of the later accounts jumble the details to fit their narrative. Most place the extraction of Richard, Duke of York, from his mother's side before the execution of Lord Hastings to create the appearance that Richard hoarded his brother's sons before acting. This is untrue.

The events within the Tower of London on Friday 13 June 1483 were undoubtedly shocking, but the initial uncertainty quickly gave way to an acceptance of Richard's explanation that most subsequent historians cannot give credence to. The ultimate example of this dichotomy was about to erupt and fracture the House of York even as it tried desperately to survive. With Hastings' plot exposed, or the troublesomely loyal lord removed, the fact that his brother's younger son remained with the queen, beyond his control and a potential focus for further threats, must have vexed Richard. Unlike the versions bequeathed by later writers, it was only after Hastings' execution that Richard turned his attention to his other nephew, Richard, Duke of York. It must have been abundantly clear that the queen had no intention of leaving sanctuary even for her son's coronation, yet it would send a message of disunity that might prove dangerous if the new king's only brother failed to attend the event.

It was on Monday 16 June that Crowland recalled 'a great multitude' taking the river to Westminster 'armed with swords and staves'. Here, they 'compelled' Thomas Bourchier, Archbishop of Canterbury, to go to Elizabeth Woodville inside the sanctuary 'to appeal to the good feelings of the queen and prompt her to allow her son Richard, duke of York, to come forth and proceed to the Tower, that he might comfort the king his brother.'[2] Mancini disagrees, placing the boy's removal from Westminster just before Hastings' execution. The Italian had heard that Richard had 'submitted to the council how improper it seemed that the king should be crowned in the absence of his brother'.[3] Both writers concur that the queen agreed to let her son go with the archbishop to attend the coronation. Crowland characteristically absolves the still-living Thomas Bourchier from any fault by asserting that he was 'compelled' to do it. Mancini similarly explains that 'the cardinal was suspecting no guile, and had persuaded the queen to do this, seeking as much to prevent a violation of the sanctuary as to mitigate by his good services the fierce resolve of the duke.'[4]

The nine-year-old Richard, Duke of York, left sanctuary with no violence to join his brother in the Tower and prepare for a role during the coronation. Despite the arrest of her brother and son Richard Grey, despite her own continued refusal to leave sanctuary, and despite reports by some writers that by now Richard was bent on taking the throne, even if he concealed his plans, Elizabeth Woodville let her son go. It is hard to find a reasonable explanation for this. Elizabeth might have feared that armed men would breach the Abbey, yet surely it would have been better to dare them to do so and condemn their souls than to give up one of her children. Indeed, young Richard was the most valuable person in her possession and was of far more importance than his sisters. She relinquished her best bargaining chip, apparently willingly. The only way that it can be reconciled to the care a mother must have had for her small son is if she knew Richard meant both his nephews no harm. Her guilty conscience might have been at play in her decision if she had gambled on defeating Richard and had lost. It might have been the first step towards the emergence of her and her daughters in time for the coronation if Richard, having neutralised both obvious threats, felt confident enough to allow them to do so. Without some deep and absolute confidence in

Richard, it is hard to see why Elizabeth would have so weakly relinquished her son as though he were a lamb to the slaughter.

Up to this point, no one seems to have spotted any foul play or dark motive on Richard's part. His brother had apparently appointed him to hold the powers of a regent during Edward V's minority, and his reasons for doing so were twofold. Firstly, there was a genuine and immediate threat to England's security and Richard was the best placed and most experienced man available to deal with that danger. Secondly, the factions that Edward had restrained during his lifetime would, he knew, explode into open opposition when he was no longer there. Richard was drafted in because he was outside of these blocs and part of his task was to stop them ruining the accession by their squabbling. If Richard found both the Woodville family and Lord Hastings to be irreconcilable and caught in an endless cycle of plotting, then it is to be wondered whether arresting Rivers and executing Hastings for treason was really an overreaction. He had cut the heads from the two snakes threatening the House of York. That was what Edward had wanted of him. If the old king had seen the price of his son's accession as the death of Hastings and the arrest of Rivers for their plots, he might not have baulked at paying it. The fear of their schemes had led him to bring Richard into the picture, and they had been neutralised.

John Russell, the new Chancellor, had been busy drafting his speech for the opening of Parliament. It was traditional for the Chancellor, who was generally a clergyman, to give an oration on a relevant and poignant topic. It would usually incorporate scripture and take on the air of a sermon, but would draw from secular sources where it helped to make the desired point. Russell's draft has survived to offer an insight into what he felt needed to be said to the nation's Lords and Commons.[5] The speech was to open with a quotation from Isaiah 49:1: '*Audite insulae, Et attendite populi de longe, Domins ab utero vocavit me*' – 'Listen to me islands, and people from afar, the Lord has called me from the womb.' Russell planned to begin by speaking of triumvirates, since nations were comprised of three parts; the prince, the nobility and the people. Some attention is given to the notion of islands as the best lands available on earth, making England a special region of God's creation. In asserting that '*Nobelesse is vertu and auncienne Richesse*', Russell gave support to Richard's position that the old nobility, rather than the newly created family of the queen, were the right people to rule. A more direct attack is found in the question 'who can make eny infallibille or certene suerte amonges gret waters and tempestuous Rivers, but that by brechys and inundacions the ferme londe and isles may be oft tymes lost and aneintised, or at the leste gretly diminisshed'. This is an open assault on the authority of Rivers and his family, who had caused the safe land of England to be flooded and diminished. Russell must have been aware that plenty in the chamber at Westminster would agree with his words, and it was an attack he was willing to launch.

Russell's draft continued to remind his audience that the nobility should be above petty squabbling and 'ought more to be persuadid to accord, and eche amyabilly to herken apon other.' The order of things is that 'princes and lordes have the fyrst and principlalle understondynge and knowledge of every gret thynge necessarye to be redressed, the lower people and commens herkene and attende uppon them.' He planned next to compare the realm to a human body. 'The bodye ys hole and stronge whois stomake and bowels is ministred by the utward membres'. The working of a nation was to be likened to the functioning of a body, 'for if the fete and hondes, whyche seme to doo most paynefulle labour for mannys lyvyng' decide to withhold food from the womb, then the whole stomach would collapse and the entire body, hands and feet included, would fail and die. The common folk were to be understood to be England's hands and feet, working hardest to keep it fed and healthy. The nobility were the stomach and intestines, meant to digest what the hands and feet put before them. The womb represented the prince, who might seem to perform no role, but who is, in fact, the cradle of life and the assurance of the realm's continuation.

At the conclusion of the speech, Russell would make a direct reference to Richard. He would assert that 'of the tutele and oversight of the kynges most roialle persone durynge hys yeres of tendirnesse my sayd lorde protector wylle acquite hym self lyke to Marcus Emilius Lepidus twyes consul of Rome.' Perhaps interestingly, Lepidus had supposedly bumped into Ceasar's assassins as he went to gather some soldiers before then encountering Caesar's corpse.[6] There is perhaps a nod here to Woodville plots against Edward and their efforts to intercept Richard on the road to London. What Russell planned explicitly to refer to was a story that Lepidus had been appointed tutele to the young heir of Ptolemy of Egypt. Lepidus, after being appointed by the senate (for which we are to read England's Parliament), performed 'as welle in thedication and conduite of the persone of that yonge prince as in administration of alle grete thynges concernynge his Reme.' So good a job did he do that when the prince came of age, none knew whether to place the credit for his 'noblesse and prosperitie' with his father or his tutor. Edward V stood similarly between his father and his uncle Richard. Edward IV had 'by the over hastely course of nature' been taken away, but Richard 'ys ordeigned as next yn perfyt age of the blod Ryalle, to be his tutor and protector.' Richard's 'marcialle kunnyng, felecite and experience' were the promise of a bright future for the king. Russell concluded his draft by reminding those gathered of the importance of the appointment of the Protector. 'In the meane tyme, tylle rypenesse of yeres and personelle rule be, as by Godys grace they must onys be, concurrente togedyr, The power and auctorite of my lord protector is so of reason to be assented and established by the auctoritie of thys hyghe courte, that amonges alle the causes of the assemblynge of the parliamente yn thys tyme of the yere, thys ys the grettest and most necessarye furst to be affermed.'

Confirmation of the extent of Richard's authority is provided by this draft, at least as Russell understood it to be. In comparing him to Lepidus, he says that Richard will have both 'thedication and conduite of the persone of that yonge prince' – the education and custody of Edward V – and the 'administration of alle grete thynges concernynge his Reme'. This was not to be the office of Protector held by Humphrey, Duke of Gloucester, or by Richard's father, York. These were the powers of a Regent by a more English name, with control of the person and education of the king and complete authority in government. It is clear that whatever peril the Council saw in 1422 that caused them to alter Henry V's plans and prevent Humphrey amassing too much authority was not felt in 1483. An even more explicit confirmation of this situation was to be made by the use of the word *tutele* – tutor. This referred not to a role as an educator, but to a Roman legal construct. The *tutele* in Rome was an individual with control over the person and estates of a minor.[7] Richard was not to be appointed Protector of the Realm in the recently formulated manner that separated power into three. He was to be a Regent, using the English denotation Protector. In taking custody of Edward V at Stony Stratford, he had, assuming that this was what Edward IV had provided for, performed the requirement of his office, and in opposing him, Rivers and the Woodville family had tried to usurp his authority. Their arrest and marginalisation was therefore entirely proper.

The willing acceptance of all that had gone before and all that would follow within London is overlooked but is key to getting a feel for the city's sense of what was going on. There had been no resistance to Richard either in Council or in the streets. When Rivers was arrested, the queen fled into sanctuary with her royal children, Hastings executed and little York moved from sanctuary to the Tower, there was no reaction. Richard, we are told, produced evidence of Hastings' plotting, which does not survive but which was accepted by those who saw it. Indeed, on 28 June, Richard would write to Hastings' brother Ralph in pleasant terms, requesting him to give credence to what four men were to show him. Robert Bradbury, Robert Allerton, Hugh Bag and Tristan Hatfield were to show Ralph 'suche things and newes as we have commanded thaym to shewe unto you on our behalve'.[8] Was this the evidence of his brother William's guilt? Whatever it was, Ralph did not seek reprisals and William's other brother Richard Hastings, Baron Welles, would soon attend Richard's coronation. These are hardly the actions of a family unjustly robbed of their head, suggesting that even they accepted Lord Hastings' guilt and that he deserved his fate.

London was never averse to opposing a monarch, let alone a duke, and was never afraid of locking out an army or fighting a mob within its walls. In living memory, the city had delivered Lord Saye and Sele to Jack Cade for execution, fought Cade's men on London Bridge when they became unruly, locked its gates against Margaret of Anjou, opened them to Edward IV despite Henry VI's presence in the city, murdered Lord Scales for firing artillery at them and fended off the Bastard of Fauconberg's attack. The examples of the city's resolve and willingness to protect its own interests are legion. The fact that they accepted, at every step, and without murmur, Richard's actions is worthy of note. They were not scared. Richard had no army. Crowland wrote that soldiers were expected 'in fearful and unheard-of numbers, from the north, Wales and all other parts', but that sounds like scaremongering or excuse-building for failing to take action. Either way, the troops were still a long way off on 16 June, and London might have locked its gates had it wished. Plenty of lords and prelates were gathering by this point as the coronation date drew near, yet none of them tried to prevent Richard's actions either. That he was too cunning for them makes a good excuse to offer to his successor for their collaboration. Richard was not a subtle man.[9] People accepted the proofs he provided, and although those documents do not survive, that does not mean they did not exist – indeed, they are reported in chronicles, albeit in hindsight as fabrications. This is true of the Woodville plot, of Hastings' guilt and of all the shocking revelations about to break with a deafening crash on the rocky shores of the House of York.

Something had now changed, though. On 16 June, the same day his young nephew had left Westminster for the Tower, Richard issued writs to postpone the coronation until 9 November and cancel the opening of Parliament due on 25 June. Mancini looked back on this as the moment Richard 'took off the mourning clothes that he had worn since his brother's death, and putting on purple raiment he often rode through the capital surrounded by a thousand attendants.'[10] Having never seen Richard, it is clear Mancini did not witness either this transformation nor the entourage clogging the streets. The postponement was very late in the day. The city of York only received word of the cancellation of the Parliament on 21 June, the day before the coronation was due to take place, and it seems to have reached several regions after the representatives had left. Thomas Wrangwish and William Wells, two of the city's four representatives, were still to be sent to London as Captains of the force Richard had requested on a wage of 4s a day.[11] The lack of urgency in the preparations to move south can only suggest that Richard had not made any desperate appeal for thousands of men to hurry to him. A week after his letter, there was still a muster lazily moving along at Pontefract.

The reason for the delay can only have been the development of a story that has defined Richard's life. On 21 June, Simon Stallworth completed another newsletter to Sir William Stonor summing up what he knew of events in the capital on the eve of a massive shift in direction.[12] He refers to Hastings' execution and the events on Monday, when 'gret plenty of harnest mene' accompanied the Archbishop of Canterbury, several bishops and a delegation of nobles to receive the little Duke of York from sanctuary. The boy had been taken to Westminster Hall, where Buckingham had received him, and then he had been met at the door to the Star Chamber by his uncle Richard 'with many lovynge wordys' before being escorted by the archbishop to the Tower to join his brother the king. He comments on the boy's arrival at the Tower that he is still there, 'blessid be Jhesu Mery', as though there was some relief that he was parted from the influence of the queen. Lord Lisle 'is come to my Lorde Protectour and awates apone hyme', a significant development because this Lord Lisle was Edward Grey, the brother of Elizabeth Woodville's first husband. He was married to Elizabeth Talbot, a granddaughter of John Talbot, 1st Earl of Shrewsbury, and his daughter Elizabeth would later marry Arthur Plantagenet, an acknowledged illegitimate son of Edward IV.

Stallworth had also heard that some 20,000 men of Richard's and Buckingham's were to descend on the capital at any moment, a gross overestimation of the muster in the north that mirror's Crowland's fears and probably the runaway rumours increasing the number at each circuit around London's streets. Russell, Stallworth's boss, was apparently complaining that he had too much work to do and he reported that Rotherham, Morton and Oliver King were still in the Tower. There was evidently no concern for their lives since he supposed 'they schall come oute Nevertheless.' In the meantime, there were men 'in ther placese for sure kepynge' and a rumour that Richard was likely to send more men to their homes in the country. It is likely the search for more evidence to establish the truth and extent of any plot was taking up valuable manpower, and this may have been the reason Richard sought help from men he trusted in York, and why a relatively small number would have sufficed rather than an army. Certainly, Stallworth believed the three men 'ar not lyke to come oute off warde yytt'.

Jane Shore was in prison at Ludgate Gaol, having been forced to perform a public penance in the streets of London for harlotry. Jane Shore is believed to have been a mistress of Edward IV who had looked to William Hastings for protection after the king's death. She may have become involved, or at least suspected of becoming involved, in some plot by passing messages for Hastings. She is also suspected of having an affair with Dorset, the queen's son. She had been forced to walk through the streets of London around St Paul's wearing only her underskirts and holding a lit taper before being placed in Ludgate to await any further charges, or to keep her off the streets and out of any ongoing plots.

Stallworth ends his news there with the excuse that he is too ill to hold his pen and write further.

Still, nothing seemed too far out of place to Stallworth, who must have known what his master Russell, the Chancellor, was aware of. He saw no need to panic, even believing that the troops heading to London were meant only 'to kep the peas'. Something changed dramatically though, and it exploded across the stunned streets of London the day after Stallworth wrote his letter. For some, the story is an unbelievable fabrication created to be Richard's excuse for taking the throne, yet the great and the good within London in June 1483 believed what they were told. Once more, there is evidence that they were shown proofs and accepted them, but because they do not survive, and given what followed, they should not be expected to have survived, the story is dismissed as a fantasy. Given that it was the very crux of the culmination of the events of 1483, it lies at the very heart of understanding what happened, whilst also remaining deeply obscured in the mists of a poorly recorded episode. Even the precise nature of the charge is either confused or was altered during the days that followed.

On 22 June, the day the coronation had been planned for before its postponement, it was proclaimed in a sermon by Dr Ralph Shaa, brother of the mayor of London, at St Paul's Cross, that the sons of Edward IV could not legally inherit the throne. The crowd must have been stunned. Mancini gives his version of Richard's actions as follows.

> After that he took a special opportunity of publicly showing his hand; since he so corrupted preachers of the divine word, that in their sermons to the people they did not blush to say, in the face of decency and all religion, that the progeny of King Edward should be instantly eradicated, for neither had he been a legitimate king, nor could his issue be so. Edward, said they, was conceived in adultery and in every way was unlike the late duke of York, whose son he was falsely said to be, but Richard, duke of Gloucester, who altogether resembled his father, was to come to the throne as the legitimate successor.[13]

Mancini understood that there had been a number of sermons preached rather than one at St Paul's Cross. This seems likely given the need to spread news and have it relayed accurately rather than muddled by rumour. He had also heard that the sermons had announced that Edward IV had been an illegitimate son, born of Cecily, Duchess of York, and a lover. This illegitimacy made Edward's children similarly illegitimate and unable to inherit. As with much of what Mancini relays, there is reason to doubt its accuracy without doubting his belief in what he wrote. Firstly, the sermons would have been given in English because they were designed for the multitudes to understand. Mancini spoke no English, so even if he had attended one of the sermons, which he does not claim to have done, he would have relied on someone else to translate the contents for him.

There may have been some genuine confusion in Mancini's understanding or, perhaps more likely, he never really knew the precise contents of the sermons, but guessed at it from the subsequent events. Mancini's patron, Angelo Cato, was based in France as the king's physician and there had been a running joke at Louis XI's court that Edward IV was a result of his mother having an affair with an English archer named Bleybourne. The archer was a giant of a man, and supposedly that is where Edward acquired his build. The predisposition to great size was held in the Plantagenet genes, though. Edward I, the Longshanks, was notably tall. In particular, Lionel of Antwerp, Duke of Clarence, the second surviving son of Edward III and the root of the Mortimer claim to the throne inherited by the House of York, was almost 7 feet tall. He was Edward IV's great-great-great grandfather, so may well have been the source of his height and build. With a better diet than most, Edward had the tools to meet the potential of his genetic makeup.

During the French campaign of 1475, Philip de Commines had been caused by Louis to stand behind a screen with an envoy of the Duke of Burgundy. Louis had then received a representative of the Count of St Pol, the Constable of France and Elizabeth Woodville's uncle, who had betrayed the English efforts. Commines explained that 'Louis de Creville, in imitation of the Duke of Burgundy, stamped with his foot, swore by St George, called the King of England Blancborgne, the son of an archer who bore his name.'[14] It is entirely likely that Mancini either already knew this story, or heard it on his return to France as he tried to piece together what had happened in England, and assumed this had been the charge Richard lay before the people. It almost certainly was not. There is no other contemporary suggestion that Richard claimed his brother had been a bastard. It would have been an outrageous charge to lay before his mother, who may well have been in London. Even if she wasn't, Richard was using her home at Baynard's Castle for his business and would continue to do so, suggesting that she was not dishonoured by such an accusation.

The truth of the content of the sermon is far more likely to have been that noted by Crowland, which would go on to form the core of the Parliamentary Act giving it legal effect.

The colour for this act of usurpation, and his thus taking possession of the throne, was the following: It was set forth, by way of prayer, in an address in a certain roll of parchment, that the sons of King Edward were bastards, on the ground that he had contracted a marriage with one lady Eleanor Boteler, before his marriage to queen Elizabeth; added to which, the blood of his other brother, George, duke of

Clarence, had been attainted; so that, at the present time, no certain or uncorrupted lineal blood could be found of Richard duke of York, except in the person of the said Richard, duke of Gloucester. For which reason, he was entreated, at the end of the said roll, on part of the lords and commons of the realm, to assume his lawful rights. However, it was at the time rumoured that this address had been got up in the north, whence such vast numbers were flocking to London; although, at the same time, there was not a person but what very well knew who was the sole mover at London of such seditious and disgraceful proceedings.[15]

Crowland returns once more to pleading fear of a northern army vastly overestimated in number and not yet departed from Pontefract to explain the general acceptance. By the time Crowland wrote his account, Henry VII had reversed the legal illegitimacy of Edward IV's children, demanded the return of all copies of the Act on pain of imprisonment, removed it from the statute book without having it read in Parliament and married Elizabeth of York, one of those affected by it. He had to be careful to position it as a falsehood, carried forward on a wave of fear, but the truth is that it was widely and almost immediately accepted. Notions that the story changed rest on allowing Mancini's flawed version alone. No contemporary speaks of the crowd resisting or failing to be impressed. That is the embellishment of later writers during the reign of Henry VIII.

There is no contemporary evidence, but unanimous later claims, that two days later, on 24 June, Midsummer's Day, Buckingham addressed the city officials and those of the nobility in the city for the coronation and Parliament that had been delayed at the Guildhall. He is supposed to have eloquently elucidated the case and offered evidence, all of which was readily accepted by the men there. Fear of an impending northern army alone cannot explain the willingness to depose the new king in favour of his uncle. There is an argument that a child king would have been disastrous in the prevailing circumstances of French aggression, but Richard had proven himself willing to act as Regent and to defend the realm for his nephew. The most simple explanation for the acceptance of the old king's bigamy is that it was sufficiently proven to those asked to weigh the evidence.

The emergence of a story reaching Richard's ears around 16 June or a few days earlier might explain both his sudden desire to secure the person of the Duke of York from sanctuary and to postpone the coronation. It was, in medieval terms, the most serious of accusations and if there were a *prima facie* case, it would need to be examined, most properly in an ecclesiastical court, to determine the truth of the charge and the legal position that resulted from it. In the first instance, it would surely not have been an accusation considered to stand beyond the realm of possibility. Rightly or wrongly, Edward IV had a reputation as a carnal man who kept many mistresses. When he was retaking his throne in 1471, Philip de Commines had noted three main reasons that London had welcomed him back, and one had been 'that the ladies of quality, and rich citizens' wives with whom he had formerly intrigued, forced their husbands and relations to declare themselves on his side.'[16] Whether it was true or just salacious gossip, it demonstrates the extent of Edward's reputation as a seducer of women. People would have believed Edward capable of contracting a secret marriage to a lady. After all, that was precisely how he had become married to Elizabeth Woodville; a wedding in May, kept secret for months. Elizabeth, legend tells us, had refused to sleep with Edward until they were married. Was she the first to win a promise of a royal union before allowing the king into her bed? To an audience in 1483, it must have seemed plausible at least and perhaps even likely.

The lady in question, Lady Eleanor Butler, had been married to Sir Thomas Butler but had been born Lady Eleanor Talbot, a daughter of John Talbot, Earl of Shrewsbury, and had died in 1468. Her social status was not dissimilar to that of Elizabeth Woodville, and she had been in her mid-twenties when Edward had won the crown. If the king found himself drawn to Elizabeth Woodville, Eleanor Talbot may have captured his interest too. No noble lady of good standing would willingly surrender her virginity and risk her future marriage prospects without something to gain from it. A marriage contract could be created during this period by a simple promise to marry someone. 'I will marry you' was considered sufficient to establish a legally binding contract of marriage, enough to satisfy any maiden who did not know that the king might regularly use this tactic. It is possible that Elizabeth Woodville fell for the same trick and that is why the match remained a secret. There is a sense that Edward blurted it out in Council later in 1464 in exasperation at Warwick's badgering about a marriage to a French princess. Perhaps Elizabeth Woodville had been the most recent victim of his manoeuvres and the first name to spring from his lips. It is equally possible that she was simply the one who, unlike the others, refused to shrink away in embarrassment that they had been duped, keeping silent to protect their future marriage prospects. An experienced lady and mother, she may have forced Edward to recognise their union. She had already been married and had sons. She was not a virgin who needed to protect her reputation and so could threaten to expose the marriage herself if Edward did not. These are matters of speculation, but the possibility that Edward had been indiscreet in his youth would have been believable in London in 1483.

Tradition asserts that Richard fabricated the story of bigamy to make space for himself to take the throne. His actions up to the middle of June do not point to some grand scheme to become king. He defended his right to be Regent, which seems to have been what his brother had wanted and it was also something readily accepted by Council and the nobility.

By 16 June, when the coronation was postponed, something had changed. If the story was invented, it is here that Richard is most likely to have decided that Regency was not enough for him, or that the only way to stop the plotting swirling about him was to take the crown himself. In both cases, it was out of character and an odd response, to counter plots by uniting the disparate enemies in horror at his actions. The frequent charge is that the sudden emergence of the story of the precontract, which created bigamy, was simply too convenient to be true. It was, in fact, anything but convenient. Richard had been preparing for his nephew's coronation and governing in his name. He must have known that a sudden departure from that steady course, which had been applauded by Council, would result in fresh turmoil, particularly if he just made something up.

It is hard to see a point prior to 1483 at which a previous contract of marriage could have been safely revealed. Edward IV was unlikely to take kindly to anyone bringing it to public attention. If the precontract was real, it most likely required Edward IV's death in order for it to come into the light. Revealing it whilst he was still alive was akin to requesting a death sentence. The attainder of George, Duke of Clarence, in 1478, offers tantalising hints that this was not the first time the story had threatened to emerge. Edward asserted that George had plotted 'agaynst his mooste Royall persone, and against the persones of the blessed Princesse oure Soveraigne and Liege Lady the Quene, of my Lorde the Prince theire Son and Heire, and of all the other of thaire moost noble issue.'[17] The charge of questioning Edward IV's legitimacy is made openly by claiming that George 'falsely and untruely noysed, published and saide, that the Kyng oure Sovereigne Lorde was a Bastard, and not begottone to reigne upon us.'[18] George had perhaps acquired this story from Warwick or during his time in France with the earl, but the Act also accused George of telling people that Edward 'ne lived ne dealid with his Subgettes as a Christian Prince'.[19] This, along with the inclusion of plotting against the queen and their children, may well have been an allusion to bigamy, which Edward could not overtly mention if it were true. The charge of his own bastardy was one he plainly felt comfortable confronting and denying, but it seems there was something else going on too. The charge in 1483 may not have been new or original, but the revival of one that had rocked the House of York before. Richard could see the damage it had wrought then, so it would be dangerous to try the same tactic again. Yes, Edward was dead, but the fate of the whole House was at stake. It was anything but a convenient charge to lay at that moment. It brought into question the entire nature and legitimacy of two decades of Yorkist rule, hardly something that was in Richard's best interests.

The source of the news that reached Richard is not known with any certainty, but there are several possibilities. Philip de Commines, from his position at the side of Louis XI, had heard that Robert Stillington,

Bishop of Bath and Wells, 'affirmed, that King Edward being in love with a certain lady whom he named, and otherwise unable to have his desires of her, had promised her marriage; and caused the bishop to marry them, upon which he enjoyed her person, though his promise was only made to delude her; but such games are dangerous, as the effects frequently demonstrate. I have known many a courtier who would not have lost such a fair lady for want of promises.'[20] Commines apparently did not feel that the charge was implausible. Stillington is an intriguing character whose career hints at the possibility of the truth of this story without ever confirming it beyond a doubt. When Edward announced his marriage to Elizabeth Woodville in 1464, Stillington was an archdeacon, Keeper of the Privy Seal, and in his mid-forties. The following year, he became Bishop of Bath and Wells and in June 1467 was appointed Chancellor, the highest office in government. With the exception of the period of the readeption, he remained as Chancellor until he was dismissed in 1473. This may simply be the trajectory of a capable churchman, but it is striking that the sudden propulsion upward of his career followed hard on the heels of the king's marriage. The appointments may have been designed to reward Stillington for keeping secret what he knew about the king's previous marriage, or marriages. After his removal from office, Stillington seems to have gravitated toward George, and when the duke was arrested in 1478, Stillington was also thrown into the Tower.

On 20 June 1478, Stillington was given a royal pardon for unspecified offences.[21] They perhaps remained unnamed because they could not safely be detailed. Stillington may have gone to one of Edward's brothers with the story of bigamy once before. It is entirely feasible that, seeing the imminent succession of an illegitimate boy, the bishop felt compelled to show his hand once more. He was nearing his mid-sixties by this point and, with Edward just forty, had perhaps hoped never to be faced with the moral dilemma of what to do, but illegitimacy was a serious matter, and his conscience may have demanded that he acted. The story might have been a fabrication, taken to George and then Richard and believed by both, or Stillington could have been co-opted to give Richard's story the air of authenticity, but it remains possible that the tale that had doomed George in 1478 now found its reluctant way to Richard's ear. Even Mancini, who does not make reference to the precontract with Eleanor Talbot in 1483, only to the charge that Edward IV was a bastard, knew that this rumour had been in circulation in 1478. He wrote that Elizabeth Woodville had been terrified of George due to 'the insults to her family and the calumnies with which she was reproached, namely that according to established usage, she was not the legitimate wife of the king.'[22]

Stallworth's comment that Lord Lisle had come to the king and was now attending on him may be significant.[23] Lisle, Edward Grey, was married to Elizabeth Talbot, a niece of Eleanor Talbot, the lady around whom the scandal was focussed. It is possible that on hearing Stillington's news, Richard summoned one of the few remaining relatives of Eleanor to discover whether the family knew whether there was any truth in the story. John Talbot, Earl of Shrewsbury, had died at the Battle of Castillon in France in 1453, and of his eleven children from two marriages, only two were still alive in 1483. We do not know whether they were questioned, but it is certain that Lord Lisle came to Richard in June 1483 and stayed with him. Did he confirm what Stillington had said, or was he the origin of the story, passing on a Talbot family legend that his wife knew? It may be coincidence, or if the precontract was a fabrication, he could have been contacted to ensure there would be no denial of it from the Talbot family, which there was not in 1483, but again, it seems plausible that the story was being built around Richard by others.

A third potential source of the story, of its corroboration or its invention, is the lawyer William Catesby. Catesby's step-mother was the daughter of Eleanor's paternal aunt, Alice Talbot, who married Sir Thomas Barre. Their daughter Jane was the second wife of Sir William Catesby Snr, providing a connection between the Talbot family and Catesby's.[24] On 4 June 1468, Eleanor had made a gift of land to her sister Elizabeth, Duchess of Norfolk, the mother of Anne Mowbray, the unfortunate little bride of Richard, Duke of York. One of the witnesses to the deed was William Catesby Snr, so it is clear that there was an active business relationship between Eleanor Talbot and the lawyers of the Catesby family.[25] Like Lord Lisle, Elizabeth would soon attend Richard's coronation without any sign of being upset by the story he had told the world about her sister. Perhaps she knew her sister had felt betrayed by Edward, robbed of a crown, and that now she was receiving restitution of some kind. The Catesby family may have held vital documents or at least been privy to their client's secret, stored for her ready one day to see the light.

Any one, or all three, of these figures might have provided increasingly alarming testimony that Edward had allowed himself to become a bigamist. Each may have been summoned to substantiate what had been alleged, and by 22 June, the evidence must have been overwhelming. This is true whether the accusation is believed to be fabricated or not, because evidence was placed before the establishment by Dr Shaa and then by Buckingham, and perhaps in other closed sessions examining the men and any documents they had, and it was accepted. This was not a result of fear, for Richard had no army in London and even if one came, as previously noted the capital was well versed in closing its gates and seeing off such threats to its freedoms. Although all of the evidence remains circumstantial, it is entirely plausible, and makes sense of subsequent events, if news reached Richard of the story some time during mid-June, perhaps from the ageing lips of Bishop Stillington. He then called Lord Lisle to inquire about what the Talbot family knew and was also able to draw on Catesby's family connections to delve deeper. When the facts were sufficiently plain, he placed the dreadful truth he had discovered before others for judgement. Their adjudication was unanimous and unequivocal. Edward had married bigamously, and his children were therefore illegitimate and incapable of inheriting the throne. There is no way in which Richard could have forced this decision on reluctant nobles and officials. There remains the possibility that he fabricated it, but he risked destabilising a situation he had only just set on an even keel, and he may not have achieved the outcome that one view believes he desired so desperately.

To a modern ear, the charge of illegitimacy as a bar to holding land or office sounds incongruous, but in 1483 it was a serious and absolute matter.[26] The inquiry into whether there was a legal case for illegitimacy if the pre-contract is accepted, as it had been in 1483, is split into four discrete questions.[27] Firstly, was only the first child of the marriage illegitimate? That would have affected Elizabeth of York, but not Edward V and Richard, Duke of York. Secondly, did the clandestine nature of Edward's marriage to Elizabeth, without banns being read and with minimal witnesses, affect the legitimacy of the union? Thirdly, should the long length and recognition in the highest echelons of Church and State preclude a charge of illegitimacy in the marriage? The fourth point is whether or not Parliament is the appropriate judge of a question fundamentally based in canon law.

It has been asserted by Levine that Eleanor Talbot's death in 1468 ended any impediment affecting Edward IV's marriage to Elizabeth Woodville. This would be correct under modern legal constructs, but medieval canon law was more severe. A couple polluted by adultery were barred from subsequently marrying each other.[28] Efforts were made in some cases to mitigate the harsh effect of this impediment, particularly where the second husband or wife had been unaware of the first and so had acted in good faith. It is unclear whether or not Elizabeth Woodville might have known about any previous dalliances by Edward, though Mancini claimed that by 1478 she knew of rumours that she was not Edward's legitimate wife. The matter would be unclear and would require proof, but in this respect could not be dismissed out of hand. The second point is not dissimilar. The clandestine nature of Edward and Elizabeth's marriage did not make the marriage invalid in itself, but it did remove from the children protections relating to illegitimacy that were available when parents had been married openly before the Church.[29] It is, therefore, another element that plays upon this case, whatever the facts were because it placed under suspicion the good faith of those taking part in the marriage. The presumption was that if they wished to avoid publicity and the reading of banns, they had something to hide. If Eleanor Talbot felt that she was already married to Edward, she was denied the opportunity to bring her claim before the Church by the secrecy of his wedding to Elizabeth Woodville.

On the third issue, it is correct that canon law provided for an assumption of a valid marriage and therefore the legitimacy of children based on long outward appearance. However, Helmholz offers three pillars of objection in this particular case. As previously stated, presumptions of legitimacy were not available to those whose parents had married in secret, as Edward and Elizabeth had done. Secondly, decrees of Pope Gregory IX explicitly allowed for the investigation of legitimacy after the death of one or both of the parties so it would be proper to permit an inquiry into the succession to the Crown. Thirdly, canon law was clear that long practice of a sin did not make it acceptable; rather, it magnified the sin. Prolonged adultery did not excuse the crime, it only exacerbated it.[30] The final argument against a case lies in the jurisdiction to try it. The illegitimacy of Edward V and his siblings was not placed before any court to be examined in 1483 and was never put before an ecclesiastical court. It was eventually, in 1484, dealt with by Parliament, but as a secular body, it is questionable whether Parliament had the jurisdiction to rule on this matter. Pope Alexander III had established clearly that matters of inheritance were entirely secular and that if a question of illegitimacy arose, the secular trial might be stopped in order to get an opinion from an ecclesiastical court on the narrow issue of bastardy before the case was concluded by the secular authority. There are, at least on the surface, efforts in the Act of Parliament that appear to deal directly with this jurisdictional conflict and to circumvent a time-consuming referral to the ecclesiastical courts, which would hardly be conducive in a question of succession to the throne during a time of impending war. *Titulus Regius*, the Act approving Richard's title to the throne, explained that the marriage was not legal 'as the comon opinion of the people, and the piblique voice and fame is throughout the land'.[31] The introduction of notoriety may have had the effect of placing the burden to disprove it on the children of the marriage, though obviously, they were in no position to mount such a defence by 1484. One decree on canon law specifically provides that 'If the crime is so public that it might rightly be called notorious, in that case neither witness nor accuser is necessary.'[32] The introduction of this specific element might have been meant to subvert the need to refer the matter to an ecclesiastical court for examination. It is perhaps telling that no attempt was made to deny the potential for ecclesiastical jurisdiction by reference to the entirely secular matter at stake, but that rather, the possible clash was side-stepped. Although Continental states were beginning to move away from recognising canonical authority in secular cases, England was still applying older rules that gave the Church a greater interest in the common law.

The issue of the technical legitimacy or otherwise of Edward IV's children can still be argued either way. There are holes in it that might be exploited, including the failure ever to obtain the opinion of a canon law court, but it is equally true that, assuming the pre-contract was established and accepted, it had merit and made efforts to mitigate the shortfall in ecclesiastical opinion. It is likely that the entire issue should also be considered in the light of Parliament's continued accrual of power, particularly in relation to the appointment of monarchs. Since Henry IV had sought to confirm his right to the throne in statute after deposing Richard II, Parliament had seen a window through which its authority and influence might be greatly increased. In 1460, it was to Parliament that Richard, Duke of York, had turned for judgement of the merits of his claim against that of Henry VI. When Edward IV took power, he provided a similar parliamentary approval of his right to the crown and Richard was simply to do the same. There was no accepted legal mechanism for the removal and replacement of a monarch, but Richard seems at least to have relied on the available precedent that was always the basis of English common law. Already established as having a keen legal mind and surrounded by men like Catesby, well versed in the law, it is unlikely that Richard would risk a shoddy presentation of his title that would be wide open to long and potentially successful challenge. Crowland, in his typically apologetic fashion, described the efforts to address the matter in Parliament. 'Parliament confirmed the title, by which the king had in the preceding summer, ascended the throne; and although that Lay Court found itself [at first] unable to give a definition of his rights, when the question of the marriage was discussed, still, in consequence of the fears entertained of the most persevering [of his adversaries], it presumed to do so, and did do so.'[33] Crowland pleads fear once more to excuse the actions of those now seeking a livelihood under the new king, Henry VII. The new queen consort, Elizabeth of York, had been made illegitimate by their actions in 1483 and in Parliament in 1484, making the position of anyone involved in Richard III's government uncomfortable. Ultimately, Crowland is forced to admit, though, that they did approve Richard's claim.

The question of the validity of Edward IV's marriage to Elizabeth Woodville, of the existence of a previous contract of marriage to Lady Eleanor Butler and the effects on the legitimacy of the king's children as a result, remains unanswerable. Evidence does not survive to confirm or deny it, with circumstantial proofs all that remain to both sides of the argument. In the absence of evidence that we can examine, which would surely have been destroyed in late 1485 when *Titulus Regius* was obliterated, it is reasonable to fall back on the actions and omissions of those involved in the events. Nowhere is there a record of any resistance – armed, launched from a pulpit, or by any secular source – to Richard's claims. Later sources describe a disbelieving audience cowed by fear to obey, but those later writers, and even their sources, had good reason to paint those days as dark and fearful, in which no man acted as he wished, but only as his dread allowed him. The simple fact is that in 1483, the bigamy of Edward IV and subsequent bastardy of his children was accepted, as was the bar of attainder affecting George's son and daughter.

On 26 June 1483, a delegation from the city and gathered nobility visited Richard at Baynard's Castle, his mother's London home, and petitioned him to take the throne. It was a precise, no doubt deliberately so, recreation of Edward IV's accession in 1461 when he had been asked to take the throne at Baynard's Castle. The requirement to follow precedent in the absence of legal mechanisms was paramount. Richard agreed to the request made of him and moved to Westminster Hall, where he sat on the marble throne in King's Bench and formally began his reign as King Richard III. There is one word that is frequently used to describe Richard's assumption of the throne in 1483 that has stuck, for various reasons, but which deserves a closer examination. It pollutes any view of the events and affects opinion, as it is no doubt meant to do. The standard title for Mancini's commentary on the period is the perfect example of the use, or perhaps misuse, of the word 'usurpation'.

The short Latin title of Mancini's work is *De Occupatione Regni Anglie Per Riccardum Tercium*. This was translated by Armstrong as *On Richard the Third's Usurpation of the Realm of England*, more commonly referred to as *The Usurpation of Richard III*. This translation fits with the narrative and what it seeks to establish but was a conscious choice on the part of the only person yet to translate Mancini's report into English. There is a Latin word for usurpation – the verb *usurpo*. Mancini's original title more accurately translates as *The Occupation of the Kingdom of England by Richard III*. It makes no mention, or judgement, that it was a usurpation; perhaps because the writer could not establish the facts well enough to comment on its legality. The difficulty with the word 'usurpation' derived from different definitions that can be found. The most widespread and satisfactory definition is either 'to take control of a position of power, especially without having the right to,'[34] or 'to take a position of power or importance illegally or by force.'[35] Some definitions exist that remove the need for force, illegality or lack of right, but these would serve to make any appropriation – including getting a job – a usurpation. Given what can be discerned of the events of June 1483, can Richard's ascent to the throne be legitimately described as a usurpation?

Taking the three requirements of these definitions, it should demonstrate illegality, force or a lack of right. The question of illegality has been dealt with to some extent above. There was no legal mechanism to remove and replace a monarch, but it is clear that Richard acted according to established precedent, a valid use of the principles of common law, and that his actions, albeit retrospectively, were given parliamentary approval. During the events too, there is no sign of a legal challenge of any kind to Richard's claims either regarding his nephews or his right to succeed. He operated within what framework existed, was not legally challenged and subsequently had his actions ratified by Parliament. It is clear that, whether they are judged morally correct and fair, Richard's activities were not illegal and were not viewed as illegitimate by his contemporaries.

It is even more demonstrable that no force was used. There were armed men in the streets of London when Richard arrived, and the atmosphere was tense. He and Buckingham brought a small retinue with them, and despite Crowland's fear of tens of thousands of northern men descending on the city, that is an exaggeration, and no soldier, never mind army, ever arrived. There were reports of armed men going to Westminster when Richard, Duke of York, emerged from sanctuary, but no hint that they were there with menace. This reception of a royal duke, at that moment the heir to his brother's throne, in the centre of a city placed on edge by recent events, seems a sensible precaution. The fear that Richard planned to violate the sanctuary has no basis in fact and is most likely the excuse-making of men who did not later wish to appear complicit.

Even the looser requirement of acting without authority is not one that stands up to examination. Richard was Regent, with powers confirmed by Council. He held authority to act in any way and a responsibility to uphold the law, which meant that if the charge was laid before him, he was required to examine and act upon it. The acceptance of Richard's authority is clear in the establishment that asked him to take the throne, and it is crucial that Richard did not claim the crown as his father had done, but was petitioned to become king. If anyone acted without authority, it was the officials of London, the prelates of the Church and the nobility of England. The events that culminated in Richard becoming king do not satisfy the definitions of a usurpation.

It is odd, even if one chooses to continue to view it as a usurpation, that Richard is singled out amongst his peers for this undesirable title. Henry IV certainly usurped the throne from Richard II. There was never any pretence that Richard was not the legitimate king by lineal descent from his grandfather Edward III. Edward IV had won the crown at the Battle of Towton in 1461, where tens of thousands witnessed the violence with which he deposed Henry VI. In a little over two year's time, Richard would face an invader who would win the battle and take Richard's crown, a clear usurpation by military force. Henry IV, Edward IV and Henry VII fit the definition of a usurper perfectly, yet are rarely, if ever, tarred with that brush. Instead, it is reserved for Richard, the case in which it is at least far less clear-cut and perhaps, in the final analysis, does not really stand up to scrutiny.

To the people of England in 1483, the events of June were undoubtedly surprising and shocking. Yet that need not make them untrue or a fabrication. The truth of what was alleged was accepted by those able to examine evidence that has not been permitted to survive. This fact alone should cause credence to be given to the notion that there was belief in the existence of bigamy on the part of Edward IV, that the truth of it made his children illegitimate, that their bastardy legally barred them from the succession and that Richard was viewed by those who asked him to become king as the only viable alternative. The evidence of the pre-contract may have been fabricated, we cannot tell. It might have been invented at Richard's behest, or it may have been presented to him and accepted by him in good faith so that he was amongst those fooled. There were forces with an interest in destabilising the House of York that would soon show their hand and may have spied their opportunity in the chaos consuming the capital in the spring of 1483. It is equally likely, perhaps more so on the evidence available, that the charges were true. At the very least, they were generally accepted as proven sufficiently to remove Edward IV's children from the line of succession and offer the crown instead to their uncle as King Richard III.

16

King Richard III

*Ascertaining you that, among other our lesinesses and cures, our
principal intent and fervent desire is to see virtue and cleanness of
living to be advanced, increased and multiplied, and vices and all other
things repugnant to virtue, provoking the high indignation and fearful
displeasure of God to be repressed and annulled*

King Richard III to the Bishops
10 March 1484[1]

For many, Richard III remains a usurping tyrant, despite evidence that
neither charge can successfully be levelled against him. Tyranny is the
operation of government in favour of the ruler at the expense of justice
for the populace. The opposite is true of the reign of Richard III, a factor
that almost certainly contributed to his eventual downfall. As Duke
of Gloucester, Richard had demonstrated not only martial competence
but also the ability to build a broad and loyal support base through his
delivery of equitable justice and good lordship. The translation of his
previous regional success to the national stage would be the greatest test
of his life.

The day before Richard had been asked to become king, the executions
of Anthony Woodville, Earl Rivers, and Sir Richard Grey had taken place.
The order for them must have been sent from London two or three days
earlier, probably on 22 June, just as the sermons were being preached in
London. By this point, the decision was made that Edward V would not
continue as king and although the postponement a week earlier of the
coronation might have suggested that a longer enquiry was anticipated,
by 22 June the decision was made. At that point, Rivers became a threat
more dangerous than he might have been earlier. If Richard had been using
Rivers and Grey as hostages to try and bring the queen into line, then it
had failed. If he had threatened to execute them if she continued to work
against him, then he was left with a choice between displaying weakness

by failing to fulfil his threat or going through with the executions. As the senior male of the Woodville family, Rivers was the most likely source of an attempt to revive the kingship of Edward V.

Crowland describes the executions as 'the second innocent blood which was shed'. He wrote that 'on their arrival at the town of Pomfret, by command of the said Richard Ratcliffe, and without any form of trial being observed, Antony, earl of Rivers, Richard Grey, his nephew, and Thomas Vaughan, an aged knight, were, in presence of these people, beheaded.'[2] Mancini similarly reported that 'so as to leave no source of danger to himself from any quarter, when by means of the council the duke could not compass the execution of Lord Rivers and Richard Grey, who, as we have said, were confined at a place in the country, of his own authority as protector he ordered dependable officers to put them to death.'[3] The lack of a trial, implying that these were illegal acts of murder, is contradicted by other sources and by the facts.

John Rous, later no friend to Richard's memory, recorded the incident differently. 'Shortly after, the lords previously described were cruelly put to death at Pontefract, being lamented by nearly everyone, and innocent of the deed with which they were charged. The Earl of Northumberland, their chief judge, then proceeded to London.'[4] Rous seems to believe that some form of trial took place at Pontefract and the Northumberland acted as judge. Richard, as Constable, was entitled to appoint deputies who were empowered to convene courts-martial and try cases with the same draconian, but entirely legal, powers of the Constable. When Ratcliffe, a close associate of Richard's from the north, took the instruction for Rivers and Grey to be executed to Northumberland at Pontefract, it is entirely plausible that Richard also sent authority for Northumberland to try them as a deputy of the Constable. This would explain Rous's apparent acceptance that a trial had taken place with Northumberland as judge. The other consideration that is suggestive of some form of hearing is that the men were gathered at Pontefract Castle. After their arrest, Rivers had been sent to Sheriff Hutton and Grey to Middleham. If they were simply to be murdered, Richard had men in those places to do the deed for him. Instead, they were gathered at Pontefract Castle before being beheaded. This would seem like an unnecessary move unless it was to facilitate some form of legal proceedings in line with Rous' description. Richard was a man deeply attached to notions of justice, legality and legitimacy, as recent and future events demonstrate, so it would be entirely out of character to rashly order the murder of these men, particularly when powers to achieve the same end by legal means were within easy reach.

The execution of Sir Thomas Vaughan, Edward V's Chamberlain, is generally included with that of Rivers and Grey. Crowland and Mancini, from their position in the south, appear to disagree. Crowland lists Vaughan as being executed, but Mancini only names Rivers and Grey.

The Warwickshire antiquarian Rous, with a slightly more northerly location and connection to old Neville men (he predominantly wrote a history of the Earls of Warwick), does not mention Vaughan specifically, only lords, which would be an incorrect description of Vaughan, a knight. Further confusion arises from the fact that Sir Thomas Vaughan's tomb can be found at Westminster Abbey, which would be an odd honour for a man executed as a traitor by the reigning king. The Purbeck marble chest in St John the Baptist's Chapel may be a later memorial rather than the actual location of Vaughan's burial, perhaps erected by his daughter, but there is cause to question whether Vaughan was executed alongside Rivers and Grey or not. He may, like Haute, have been released only to die soon afterwards. He was, by 1483, in his seventies.

Anthony Woodville, Earl Rivers, had sat down to write his final will and testament on 23 June, two days before his execution.[5] Whether or not there had been a plot by the queen to exclude Richard, whether Rivers had tried to prevent Richard taking custody of the king, whether he had revealed the scheme, or whether he was entirely innocent of any involvement in any plot, remains a matter for debate. Whatever the truth, he was facing his end now. The will has the air of a stream of consciousness rather than a legal document, probably because Rivers had little or no legal support in preparing it. Perhaps hopefully, Rivers willed the Woodville patrimony to his father's next male heir. 'I will that all such land as was my lord my faders, remayne holy to his right heyres; with my cupp of gold of columbyne, which was lefte me by bequest to that entent it shuld remayne to the right heires of my seid lord my faders.'[6] The medieval mind was deeply concerned with paying debts, since they were believed to lengthen a soul's time in purgatory. Sitting within his captor's fortress, stripped of his 'boke' of debts, which he wrote would be found 'in my closett in London', he racked his brain for the payments he would need to make. He owed money to the Bishop of Worcester, the Mayor of Lynn, a London mercer named Lomner, a goldsmith called Ocles Mayce and a draper in Norwich.[7]

Rivers bequeathed his 'gowne of tawnet cloth of gold' to the Prior of Royston and a 'trapper of blakk cloth of gold' to the Shrine of Our Lady at Walsingham. He requested that the rest of his clothes, his tournament armour and horse harness be sold 'and with the money therof be bought shyrtes and smokkes to pouer folkes'. He also asked that his lands held in fee simple be sold to pay for a hospital in Rochester to provide for thirteen poor folk and 'other dedes of charite'.[8] Rivers made other bequests of gilt basons and cash to St Mary's in York 'to pray for my soule' and money to Bewdley to 'pray for the sowles of my seid lord my fadre, my lady my modre, my brother Sir John, me, and all Christen sowles.'[9] He then requested that he be buried 'before an image of out blissid Lady Mary, with my lord Richard, in Pomfrete'.[10] He clearly expected both his own and his nephew Richard Grey's deaths and recognised that a local burial was likely. Rivers listed those he wished to act as executors and asked that Richard be their supervisor. This may have been little more than the acceptance of political reality; if his will were to be proved, it would need Richard's support to achieve it, but there may also be an element of guilt in the gesture. If nothing else, Rivers may still have believed that he could trust in Richard's probity as he had done just a few months earlier with his land dispute. When he was executed, Rivers was found to be wearing a hair shirt next to his skin, a sign of religious devotion through discomfort. He had perhaps been more like Richard than history has allowed, fate placing them on opposite sides of an irreconcilable dispute.

Richard was now King of England. Preparations began for his coronation, which could be achieved quickly due the part-completed state of that planned for Edward V. The date was set for 6 July and efforts were made to explain the situation at the farthest reaches of the kingdom. Instructions were sent to Calais that detailed a requirement to set aside oaths of allegiance made to Edward V and to swear new ones to Richard III. Every man was 'bounde upon knowlag had of the said verray true title, to depart from the first othe so ignorantly given to him to whome it apperteyned not and thereupon to make his outhe of newe.'[11] The letter asserted that Richard's 'sure & true title is evidently shewed & declared in a bille of peticione whiche the lords spirituelx & temporelx and the commons of this land solemplye porrected unto the kinges highnes at London the xxvi[ti] day of Juyne.' A copy of this bill was sent to Calais to be read aloud so that the people there had heard the same version of events as those in London.

Back in England, Northumberland, the Earl of Westmoreland and the northern troops finally arrived outside London in early July. Richard rode out to a field between the city and Halywell to inspect the arrayed men and to thank them all for coming to attend upon him. Mancini numbered them at 6,000[12] while the Mercers reckoned 10,000 or more,[13] but both are probably an exaggeration. Richard led the men through Bishopsgate and to St Paul's Cathedral to join him at a service held there.[14] As the day of the coronation drew close, London was packed with nobles, bishops, knights, merchants and citizens keen to be involved in the pageant. There was no sense in any report of unease, apprehension or uncertainty about what was about to take place. Some may have doubted Richard's claim, but others might have been relieved to be spared the trials of a minority. None, though, openly opposed what was happening.

Mancini explained that Richard left the Tower on 5 July and rode to Westminster 'attended by the entire nobility and a display of royal honours, with bared head he greeted all onlookers, who stood along the streets, and himself received their acclamations.'[15] He continued that on the next day, 'the cardinal of Canterbury, albeit unwillingly, anointed and crowned him king of England.'[16] Mancini could not have known Archbishop Bourchier's state of mind. It would be strange for a man who had apparently given his word to keep Richard, Duke of York, safe when he left sanctuary to participate in the crowning of a man he suspected of any foul play, either in deposing the boys or in their physical fates.

Details of the coronation of Richard III and his wife, Queen Anne, remain amongst the records of English royal events.[17] On 5 July, Richard rode through London from the Tower to Westminster accompanied by an array of the nobility 'with great pompe'.[18] With Richard rode his son, Edward of Middleham, now Prince of Wales, though not yet invested. The Dukes of Norfolk, Suffolk and Buckingham came next. Norfolk was John, Lord Howard, to whom Richard had given the Mowbray inheritance. Howard had a legal claim to the dukedom barred by Edward IV's legal manoeuvres to keep it in the royal family. Richard, with his typical commitment to equity and concern for legitimacy, took it from his nephew and gave it to Howard. Suffolk was Richard's brother-in-law, John de la Pole, and Buckingham was a constant at Richard's side. These were the only three dukes in the country at the time of the coronation. Edward IV's sons were no longer dukes, though Edward was able to keep the earldom of Chester, which he held in his own right rather than as Prince of Wales. The only marquess in England was Thomas Grey, Marquess of Dorset, who was a fugitive at the time of the coronation.

The earls present at the coronation were those of Northumberland, Arundell, Kent, Surrey, Wiltshire, Huntingdon, Nottingham, Warwick and Lincoln. The only absentees were the earls of Westmoreland, who was eighty, in the grip of dementia and would not live much longer; the five-year-old Edward Stafford, Earl of Stafford, Buckingham's son and heir; and the fifteen-year-old George Talbot, Earl of Shrewsbury. Edward Tiptoft, the Earl of Worcester, son of John Tiptoft and a man who remains an elusive figure, did not attend for reasons that are unclear, but he would pass away within two years of the coronation. Two men who failed to participate probably due to ill health and two underage earls were the only absentees from this rank of the English nobility. Louis de Gruuthuse was not in attendance and held the title Earl of Winchester as a reward from Edward, but he was not in England during any of these events.

Viscounts Lovell and Lisle were listed as attendees, as were the Lords Stanley, Audeley, Dacres, Ferrers of Cherlie, Powis, Scrope of Upsall, Scrope of Bolton, Grey of Codnor, Grey of Wilton, Stourton, Cobham, Morley, Abergavenie, Zouch, Ferrers of Groby, Wells, Maltravers, Herbert and Beecham. The names of seventy-seven knights are listed next, with some interesting inclusions. There were men who came from Richard's affinity and had been associated with him for many years, such as Sir James Harrington, Sir Ralph Assheton, Sir John Conyers and Sir James Tyrell. Other names had been prominent in Edward IV's household, yet were willing to attend Richard's coronation. Sir William Brandon would later carry Henry Tudor's standard at the Battle of Bosworth, and Sir John Cheney would similarly fight at Tudor's side. Sir William Norris was from a staunchly Lancastrian family, had been an Esquire of the Body to Edward IV, but would soon oppose Richard. On 6 July, there was a dazzling display not only of pageantry but also of unity as virtually all of the available lords of England celebrated Richard III's coronation.

The streets of London were lined with bustling, cheering citizens waiting for a glimpse of their new monarchs as Richard and Anne processed from the White Hall of Westminster into the Great Hall and on to King's Bench. From there, they walked barefooted on brightly striped ray cloth across to Westminster Abbey. The crowd had some reason to be excited by the spectacle of the royal couple. The joint coronation of Richard and Anne was the first in 175 years, and it had only happened three other times since the Conquest in 1066.[19] The absence of a couple being crowned together at a mature age was a testament to a century-and-a-half of upheavals and minority rules. Edward III had replaced his father at fourteen years of age. Richard II was just ten when he succeeded his grandfather, and Henry IV was a widower when he took the crown from Richard. Henry V was unmarried when his father died, Henry VI had been just nine months old when he became king, and Edward IV had been an unmarried eighteen-year-old when he replaced Henry as king. Richard was thirty years old, his wife Anne was twenty-seven, and they had a seven-year-old son and heir. It must have felt like a promise of a more settled future, harkening back to a different age before civil war had torn the country apart.

As the procession entered Westminster Abbey, there was a blaring of trumpets and perhaps a blast of organ music too. The trumpeters were followed by Heralds of Arms, a group under Richard's jurisdiction as Constable for many years and soon to receive his further favour, suggesting his particular care or interest in this area. They wore the vibrant, colourful coats of their office in a dazzling display of pomp and pageantry as they walked behind the trumpets. Next, a large cross was carried behind which came rows of priests in their finest surplices, a bank of sober white after the colour of the heralds. The priests were followed by abbots and bishops, returning to a dazzling splash of colour in their robes, each carrying their ornate crozier, the adorned staff of their office. The Bishop of Rochester walked behind his colleagues, holding another cross aloft before elderly Cardinal Thomas Bourchier, Archbishop of Canterbury. Immediately behind the archbishop strode William Herbert, Earl of Huntingdon, who had known Richard from their teenage years together in Wales and the Marches.[20] He carried a pair of shining gilt spurs to symbolise knighthood and chivalry. Next in the procession came St Edward's Staff, a relic reputed to have belonged to Edward the Confessor[21] to further emphasise the religious and ancient nature of the ceremony.

Henry Percy, Earl of Northumberland, came next, bareheaded and holding the unsheathed Pointless Sword, which represented mercy. Thomas, Lord Stanley, provided with a prominent position that defies his rank, his previous friction with Richard and the later claim that he was arrested on 13 June at the Tower, carried the Mace of the Constable. This can only have been a nod, as Edward IV had been forced to offer, to Stanley's unassailable position in the north-west and his military weight. On the right of the next pair, Edmund Grey, Earl of Kent, carried the sword that represented temporal justice, and on the left Francis, Viscount Lovell, bore the sword that symbolised ecclesiastical justice. Richard's brother-in-law John de la Pole, Duke of Suffolk, walked next holding the golden sceptre in his hand to signify peace.[22] Suffolk's son, Richard oldest nephew, carried the fourth sword of the procession, sheathed within a rich scabbard, known as the Sword of Estate. The next three figures, walking side by side, were the Mayor of London, Sir Edmund Shaa, on the right, carrying his mace of office; Garter King of Arms, John Wrythe, in the centre in his splendidly colourful coat; and on the left, the Gentleman Usher of the Privy Chamber. John Howard, the newly created Duke of Norfolk, came next with the royal crown held in his hands.

Then Richard finally entered the vast space of Westminster Abbey, wearing sumptuous robes of purple velvet and still barefoot. The four Barons of the Cinque Ports each carried a pole at the corner of a canopy of estate, which was held above his head. The king was flanked by Robert Stillington, Bishop of Bath and Wells, and possible origin of the story that had made Richard king; and William Dudley, Bishop of Durham, who had supported Richard's claim and may have been a long-term acquaintance from the north. Henry Stafford, Duke of Buckingham, the most prominent of Richard's supporters in the previous weeks, carried the king's train, also managing to grasp the white staff that displayed his office of High Steward of England. Precisely what Richard was thinking as he slowly stepped closer to being crowned and anointed king cannot be known, but the moment was either the culmination of impulsive plotting to win this very prize, or the putting on of a heavy mantle he had not looked for just weeks earlier. Even in the latter case, it must have been an exciting moment to be recognised by the nation and by God as king. There was, perhaps, some divine solace offered for the problems that had caused Richard's spine to curve, a fact he had hidden with some success all of his life. If it had ever concerned him that twisting of the body was sometimes considered a sign of a corrupted soul, his final confirmation that it was not true lay at the altar he walked towards. God was about to approve him in the highest possible fashion.

A bank of the lords of England followed next before there was a shift of focus to the queen, who was to be consecrated at Richard's side. The Earl of Huntingdon is listed again, having previously appeared at the very front of the line, carrying the Queen's Sceptre; one or the other must be an error. Viscount Lisle bore another rod, the Sceptre with a Dove, representing peace and the Holy Spirit, before Edward Stafford, Earl of Wiltshire, a cousin of Buckingham's, entered the Abbey carrying the queen's crown. Anne Neville herself followed the crown that would make her queen, wearing purple velvet robes to match her husband and with a coronet of gems and pearls atop her head, similarly flanked by bishops with a canopy of estate held above her.

Another significant appearance directly behind the queen, carrying her train, was Lady Margaret Beaufort, wife of Lord Stanley and mother of Henry Tudor. After her came women who ought to have outranked her: Richard's sister Elizabeth, Duchess of Suffolk, and the widowed Duchess of Norfolk, Elizabeth Talbot, older sister of the Eleanor Talbot upon whom the pre-contract revelations had rested.

Lady Margaret's station, like that of her husband, is remarkable, particularly in light of the stalling of recent negotiations for her son to return to England. The honour was perhaps meant to reassure her that neither she, nor, by extension, her son, were out in the cold and that hope remained for a reunion. The fact that Elizabeth Talbot attended may also hae been a significant signal that there was no ill feeling between the Talbot family and Richard after the disclosures of the previous fortnight.

This entire procession, brought to a close by the remaining countesses, baronesses and gentlewomen who had been invited, had moved from Westminster Hall to the Abbey and entered through the west door. From this entrance, the nave spread out before the nobility of England as the high ceilings rang with trumpet blasts. Moving through the quire towards Henry III's Cosmati pavement, the king and queen finally reached their thrones, placed before the High Altar. Religious music filled the space as they climbed the steps to kneel on the spot where their lives would be transformed forever. The Archbishop of Canterbury addressed the crowd packed within the Abbey, finally asking them: 'Will ye Syrs at this tyme give your willes and assentes to the same consecration, Inunction and Coronacion'? The Abbey was filled with calls of 'Yea! Yea! Yea! So be it! King Richard! King Richard! King Richard!'[23] Next, Richard was required to make his coronation oath, a promise that had been largely unchanged since Henry I offered his in 1100.

To each question, Richard was required to give affirmation of acceptance of the responsibility.

'Will ye graunt and keepe to the people of Englande the Lawes and customes to them as olde rightfull and devoute kinges graunted, and the same ratifie, and confirm by your oath?'

'And specially lawes customes and Liberties graunted to the Clergie, and people by your Precdecessors, and glorious Saynct Edwarde?'

'Ye shall keepe after your strength and power the church of god to the Clergie. And the people hoole peace and godlie concorde.'[24]

With these requirements confirmed, the purple velvet robes were removed from both Richard and Anne before they were anointed with the holy oil of St Thomas Becket from an ampulla, which is one of the few pieces of the royal regalia to survive Cromwell's purge during the seventeenth century. The front and back of their shoulders, as well as their elbows, were amongst the places carefully anointed with this most precious and holy of oils. After this most significant of moments, Richard and Anne were re-dressed in cloth of gold and finally took their seats on their thrones. Here, Archbishop Bourchier lowered St Edward's crown onto Richard's head and then the queen's crown onto Anne's. Richard was given the sceptre in his left hand, the sign of a king's pastoral duty to maintain discipline but also to keep his flock close and together. Into his right hand was placed the golden ball topped with a cross that symbolised his responsibility to uphold Christ's dominion on earth. Anne was given the queen's sceptre to hold in her right hand, and the rod topped with the dove of the Holy Spirit was placed into her left.

Archbishop Bourchier sang a Mass as two dukes flanked Richard, the Earl of Surrey stood before him holding a sword, and the queen sat with a bishop and a kneeling lady at either side. After the archbishop had then said the *Pax* to bring peace to all those gathered, Richard and Anne rose from their thrones and descended the steps to make an offering at St Edward's Shrine. Here, Richard also removed and set down St Edward's crown and put on his own in its place. When all of the weighty and profoundly sacred ceremonies had been completed the participants began to move back out through Westminster Abbey's Great West Door in the same order they had entered. That was not the end of the day, though. The coronation had taken place, running smoothly and without incident under the careful watch of the Duke of Buckingham. It was now time to celebrate.

As Richard and Anne retired to their chambers for a brief rest, John Howard, Duke of Norfolk and Earl Marshall, rode into the vast space of Westminster Hall on a horse trapped in shimmering cloth of gold and drove away any anyone lingering there in a staged display. At 4 o'clock in the afternoon, the new king and queen entered. Richard sat at the centre of the table on the raised dais. The queen sat to his left with countesses standing gathered behind her ready to serve her drinks as required.

At the king's right hand sat the aged Archbishop of Canterbury, no doubt wearied by a long day of ceremonial work. As each man entered, he was required to give an oath of loyalty to the new king:

> I become true and feithfulle liegeman unto my soverain lord Richard iii[de] by the grace of god king of England etc and to his heires kinges of England & to him and theim my feithe and trouthe shal bere during my lif naturalle and with him and in his cause and quarelle at alle tymes shal take his parte and be redy to leve and dy ayenst alle erthly creatures and utterly endevor me to the Resistence of and subpressing of his ennemyes Rebelles and traytors if I shal any knowe to the uttermost of my power and no thing courte that in any wise may be hurting to his noble & royal persone so god me helpe and thise holy evaungeliers.[25]

Along the middle of the Hall, the ladies sat on one side and the Chancellor and the lords opposite them. The Mayor, the Lords of the Ports and the remaining barons filled more tables. When everyone was seated, Norfolk, his son Surrey as Constable for the day, Lord Stanley as Lord Steward, Sir William Hopton, the Treasurer, and Sir Thomas Percy, the Comptroller, entered the Hall and mounted the steps to the dais. There, they offered Richard one dish filled with gold and another full of silver before setting before the queen a gilt cup.

The feast and festivities then began in earnest, with no shortage of food or drink. As the second course was being served, there was more traditional theatre that formed part of the ritual of coronation. The King's Champion, Sir Robert Dimmock, dramatically entered the Hall riding a huge destrier trapped in red and white silk, his own armour a polished, gleaming white. He issued his traditional challenge to anyone who doubted Richard's right to be king, throwing his gauntlet down and offering to fight to the death any man who opposed King Richard. When no challenge was forthcoming, the room was filled with loud voices proclaiming 'King Richard!' His challenge remained unmet at two more offerings in different parts of the Hall. His work completed, a golden cup of wine was carried to him. Taking a sip and casting the rest onto the floor, Sir Robert left with the cup as a wage for his service. When all the food had been served and every guest was satisfied, the Mayor of London served the king and queen sweet wine and received from them a golden cup set with pearls as a gift to be used at the Guildhall during public entertainments.[26] By the time the festivities of the coronation banquet were over it was late in the night, 'so the King returned to his Chamber and every man to his lodging.'

Richard, almost immediately, made the first significant mistake of his reign.[27] By 13 July, a week after the coronation, he was at Greenwich, and a week later he arrived at Windsor. On 21 July he reached Reading and continued to Oxford on the 24th of the month. Here, the king 'by popular request', according to John Rous, disafforested a large area, which Edward IV had removed from public use, and annexed to the Forest of Wychwood 'against conscience and to the public damage'.[28] Richard and Anne stayed at Magdalen College in Oxford, where they attended disputations on philosophy and were given a tour of the university. After two days drinking in the academic atmosphere, they travelled on to Woodstock for three nights. On Tuesday 29 July, they arrived at Minster Lovell, a stunning property that was the seat of Francis, Viscount Lovell. The manor had been extensively rebuilt by Francis's grandfather William in the 1430s, funded by the proceeds of his success in France during the Hundred Years' War. The north approach brought visitors to a porch before entering the Great Hall that dominated the apartments. Wings ran from the east and west down to the banks of the River Windrush, where a wall served to enclose a large central courtyard. Francis was there to greet his friend, but the manor probably held little sentimental value to him. Francis's father John had fought for Henry VI and had died when Francis was a small child, leaving him a ward of the Crown. After his time in Warwick's household at Middleham, where he seems to have struck up a lifelong friendship with Richard, Francis had remained largely in the north, rarely visiting his ancestral home. Now, it was probably just a suitable and private place to relax.

The mistake that Richard had made was to leave London so soon after his coronation. It is undoubtedly desirable for a new monarch to show himself to his people but there is a balance to be found against more pressing needs, including security, which might have kept him in the capital. Richard was not well known by the political elite of London and had not given them time to become familiar with him, his ways and the kinds of policies he might seek to pursue. Richard is unique in English history as being capable of consideration as a northern king. He had been born in Northamptonshire and was a visitor to the south when business required it, but for more than a decade he had immersed himself in northern life, something still viewed as fundamentally different from southern society, a more barbaric place and a region worthy of suspicion.[29] For the southern polity, used to Edward IV's rule, it was a change that was probably unwelcome. For Richard to vacate London with unseemly haste and follow a progress that would take him back north can have done nothing to assuage any fears and played directly into the hands of anyone seeking an opportunity to undo the new king. For Richard, though, the appeal was obvious. After three months of unexpected upheaval and trials, whether he had schemed to win the crown or found it pushed into his lap by circumstance, he surely welcomed a return to something more familiar, where he was well known, well loved and in complete control. Had Richard plotted and lied his way to the throne, it seems likely he would have wanted to remain in London to tighten his grip on power and avoid any backlash. His apparently overrriding desire to return to Yorkshire may suggest that he had not wanted or enjoyed what had befallen him in London.

On 2 August, Richard was at Gloucester, where he granted the city with which he had for so long been connected in name a charter of liberties,[30] and two days later he arrived in Tewkesbury, the scene of the battle he had fought for his brother a dozen years before. He could reflect there on how much his world had changed since the day he fought the last of the Lancastrians in the baking heat within sight of the Abbey. The royal couple remained there only one night, suggesting the visit was personal and sentimental, before visiting Worcester on 5 August and staying three nights in the city. On 8 August, Anne was able to return to her birthplace, her father's old castle at Warwick. A week was spent there before they moved to Coventry and via Leicester to Nottingham, where they lodged at the castle from 20 August for several nights. Richard wrote to seventy-one knights and gentlemen when he stopped at Leicester on 18 August, instructing them to meet him at Pontefract Castle on 27 August without fail.[31]

The reception that the king and queen had received at each stop so far appears to have been warm and entirely positive. John Rous noted that he had endowed Queen's College, Cambridge, to the tune to 500 marks in annual rent, and that during his progress 'money which was offered to him by the peoples of London, Gloucester, and Worcester he declined with thanks, affirming that he would rather have their love than their treasure.'[32] In this, Richard was offering a clear distinction between himself and his brother, whose benevolences and extra-parliamentary methods of raising funds had become increasingly unpopular with those shaken down. There may also have been some recognition by Richard that he needed to make positive efforts to win people over, at least those outside the north, because they did not know him well and because of the nature of his arrival on the throne. Whatever the truth, history has proven that the worst would be assumed by most.

Thomas Langton, Bishop of St David's, wrote to the Prior of Christ Church of his very favourable impression of the new king during his progress. 'I trust to God sune, by Michelmasse, the Kyng shalbe in London. He contents the people wher he goys best that ever did prince; for many a poor man that hath suffred wrong many days have been relevyd and helpyd by hym and his commands in his progresse. And in many grete citeis and townis wer grete summis of mony gif hym which he hath refused. On my trouth I lykyd never the condicions of ony prince so wel as his; God hath sent hym to us for the wele of us al.'[33] The beginning of the letter explains to the Prior that he should be able to ship wine from France even though 'the Kyng wil for no thyng graunte licence to you, ne to non other' to use foreign ships. A prohibition was probably a reaction to the threat of French aggression, but it also displays a concern for protecting English merchants that would solidify over the coming months. Langton assured the Prior that he should be able to find an English ship, asking if he would order some wine for the bishop at the same time, or if not, to use a foreign vessel. The chief justices had ruled that no licence from the king was required for such purchases and transportation and the apparent implication from Langton is that Richard was sure to be bound by the law rather than seek retribution.[34]

He paints a picture of Richard's progress as an unmitigated triumph, confirming the stories of refusing gifts of money and pointing also to his fair application of justice as he travelled. Richard had never been afraid to upset vested interests as Duke of Gloucester and seems to have been keen to continue that theme as king. The difference from before was twofold and significant; earlier, he had his brother to protect him and his quirky attitude only affected those in the north. Now, he had to be his own shield and try to impose his vision across the whole country. To those already wary of a northern king, the odd willingness that Richard displayed to favour justice where it might otherwise have been denied those of lower social standing against their superiors represented a threat. As feudalism has become a bastardised form of itself, those at the top had become used to getting what they wanted despite the law, and the injustices only flowed downwards. It was a tide Richard seemed willing to try to turn, but he would make enemies in doing so. If 'many a poor man that hath suffred wrong many days' had found comfort in Richard's justice, then as many powerful men were being upset.

Richard may have planned to operate a more peripatetic court than Edward had. He had seen the neglect the north often suffered and, in his younger years, spent time in the west. He perhaps saw the absence of an enforceable royal writ in such places as a contributory factor in the civil strife that had dogged England for decades. Maintaining such mobility would be another way to demonstrate clear space between his and Edward's style of government. His brother had remained more and more within the friendly confines of London and Windsor, failing to travel north to face Scottish aggression even when he had stated that he would do so. If this had caused rumblings of dissatisfaction that had reached Richard's ears, he had an easy way to offer a favourable alternative. Almost as soon as possible after his coronation, he had travelled in a zig zag from east to west as he moved ever further north.

Business was not being neglected during the king's travels, suggesting that he had established mechanisms to facilitate the necessary work of government during his progress. On 21 July, Louis XI had written to the new king of England:

My lord and cousin, I have seen the letters that you have written to me
by your herald Blanc Sanglier, and thank you for the news of which you
have apprised me. And if I can do you any service I will do it with very
good will, for I desire to have your friendship. And farewell, my lord
and cousin. Written at Montilz lez Tours, the 21st day of July.

LEWIS.
Villechartre[35]

The letter was part of an exchange that rumbled on with the ailing
Louis, who would die on 30 August, just four months after Edward IV,
in which Richard seemed to lay down a much firmer stance with France
than his brother had employed. On 18 August at Leicester, Richard wrote
to reassure Louis 'I do not mean to break such truces as have hitherto
been concluded between the late king of most noble memory, my brother
deceased.' He also took Louis' offer of service by asking the French king
to insist on improved security for English merchants in France.

Nevertheless, the merchants of this my kingdom of England, seeing
the great occasions given them by your subjects by taking vessels and
merchandise and otherwise, doubt greatly to adventure themselves to
go to Bordeaux and elsewhere in your obeisance, until they be assured
on your part that they may surely and safely exercise the feat of their
said merchandise in all parts of your said obeisance, according to the
right of the said truces. Upon which matter, in order that my said
subjects and merchants be not deceived under the shadow of the same,
I pray you that by my servant, this bearer, one of the grooms of my
stable, you will let me know by writing your full intention, and at the
same time if you desire anything that I can do for you, that I may do
it with good will.[36]

This letter was far more direct than Edward tended to be. The English
king's pension had, as Louis had hoped, kept him compliant and afraid
to rock the boat. Richard, who had refused to become Louis' pensioner
almost a decade earlier, was freer to hammer markers into the ground. In
assuring Louis that he did not mean to break the truce between the two
nations, he left the door open not only to do just that but to blame Louis
for the breaches that might bring about renewed hostilities. Ever since the
English invasion of France in 1475, Louis, known as the Universal Spider
for his far-reaching webs of intrigue and the knowledge of his enemies he
gathered and sifted, must have kept an eye on Richard. He had neutralised
the half-hearted threat Edward had represented with cash. Richard had
proven himself less amenable to being bought off and more inclined to a
martial approach. Scotland had felt the sting of his campaign the previous
year, and the threads of Louis' web must have begun to vibrate as soon

as he heard that Richard had become King of England. Richard did not ask for indulgence for his subjects to increase his own glory or for his sake. He demanded Louis' personal promise that the matter should be resolved to prevent harm to his merchants. This was no ambassadorial mission by high ranking barons, which Edward had been prone to send, usually including Lord Howard amongst others, but rather Richard sent a groom of his stable. What the King of France chose to read into that was for Louis to decide.

Just two days later, on 20 August, Richard wrote again from Nottingham to explain that he had placed an order with his herald, Blanc Sanglier, who was currently with Louis, 'to make provision of certain wines of the growth of Burgundy and la Haute France, for myself and the queen my consort'. Richard again insisted on Louis' personal intervention to 'give order to your officers and subjects to suffer him to procure the said wines, and freely conduct them.'[37] Richard may have been testing the waters with Louis to see how he responded to a more forceful tone than he was used to from England, sending a warning shot across Louis' bow that the wind was changing.

Richard may have been emboldened by receipt of an embassy from Queen Isabella of Castile. Her ambassador explained Isabella had been 'turned in hur hart fro England in tyme past for the unkyndeness the which she toke against the king last deceased, whom God pardon, for his refusing of her and taking to his wiff a wedowe of England'. Coupled with the close friendship she had enjoyed with Warwick, the snub had caused her to become allied 'against hur natur', to the King of France. Isabella now hoped for a reconciliation, 'she now retournyng to hur natural kinde and disposicion'. Not only that, but she offered to move against Louis as Richard wished, citing four breaches of their truce of which he was guilty including his refusal to approve of a marriage she hoped to arrange for her son to the daughter of the Queen of Navarre. Isabella offered Richard 10,000 spearmen and 30,000 foot soldiers to be 'at his pleasure'.[38] After Louis' ascendancy, it seems the powers that surrounded him were on the brink of coming together to oppose him.

A desperate plea and thinly veiled blackmail attempt arrived from the Duke of Brittany as Richard moved north.[39] George de Mainbier, Duke Francis' ambassador, was given instructions to thank King Richard for 'the good will and affection which he exhibits towards him.' He was to 'assure the said king that the duke has not less love and affection for him, in which he intends to persevere from good to better.' Francis asked to be excused for failing to send a proper embassy, but explained that it was the time of his annual equivalent of a Parliament, requiring all his advisors to remain in Brittany, and that he would send men as soon as that was concluded. Next, the matter of the English naval threat was raised because 'a great number of vessels of the said kingdom of England put themselves in warlike array upon the sea, and have threatened to take and plunder the subjects of the duke.' Francis therefore asked Richard to forbid his subjects from acts of piracy against Breton ships, offering a promise to deliver the same message to his own sailors.

With these matters covered, George de Mainbier was to move to the real meat of Francis's missive. The duke claimed that Louis, 'since the decease of the late prince of good memory king Edward last deceased, has several times sent to the duke to pray and request him to deliver to him the lord of Richmond his cousin.' The French king had, Richard was to be told, 'made the duke great offers' but Francis had resisted, 'fearing that the said king Lewis would thereby create annoyance and injury to some of the friends and well-willers of the duke.' It was easy enough to understand what Francis meant. There was a price for Francis' continued resilience, mainly because of 'the great power of men of war, artillery, and finances, which the said king of France has.' The independence of Brittany was, Francis warned Richard, inextricably linked to keeping Henry Tudor, Earl of Richmond, out of French hands. The implication both that Louis would use Henry to destabilise England and that Francis knew as much suggests that he was already being viewed as a potential claimant to the English throne in August 1483. Francis may have got wind of a plan by Louis, born of his fear of a more aggressive England under Richard, to try something similar to his setting of Warwick and Henry VI's queen together against Edward IV. Possibly, communications were already escaping England, trying to reach Henry, from his mother that there was an opportunity for much more than a simple homecoming in the confusion that had erupted in May and June. Francis already understood Henry Tudor to be a possible threat to Richard's crown.

The duke's price for keeping Henry safely out of Louis' reach was 4,000 English archers, paid for by Richard, with good captains and an able commander. They were to be put at Brittany's disposal for six months within one month of the duke's request. Francis also requested an additional 3–4,000 archers to be made available, their wages met by Francis, if he should need them. 'And so doing the duke will await the fortune of war, such as it shall please God to send him, rather than deliver into the hand of the said king Lewis the said lord of Richmond, or do anything prejudicial to the said king or kingdom of England.' The growing desperation in Brittany can be felt in George de Mainbier's instructions to remain no more than three or four days in England and to report back to Francis as quickly as possible 'to apprise the duke of everything'. An alliance against Louis was looking like an increasingly viable aggressive step from Richard that would, not unlike it had done for Henry V, prove the righteousness of his kingship in the eyes of God. Louis, as his health failed and he faced the reality of leaving a thirteen-year-old son to take the throne after him, cannot have missed the turning of the tables of his own foreign policy as enemies gathered and France was looking down the barrel of a minority government.

Richard made provisions for Ireland during the summer, appointing his son Edward of Middleham as Lieutenant of Ireland.[40] He also sent William Lacy to the Earl of Kildare, the prominent nobleman in Ireland, to confirm the earl as deputy because 'the king our soverayne lord hathe the said Erle for his gret merites in special favor & tendrenesse.'[41] This flurry of activity also included instructions sent to the Bishop of Annaghdown, who was to visit the Earl of Desmond. Desmond was the next most senior nobleman in Ireland after Kildare, though his authority at this point nowhere rivalled that of Kildare. Part of these instructions has proved cryptic and may reveal Richard's urgent need to be confident that Ireland accepted him and offered no challenge.

> Also he shalle shewe that albeit the Fadre of the said Erle, the king then being of yong Age, was extorciously slayne & murdered by colour of the lawes within Irland by certain persones than having the goveraunce and Rule there, ayenst alle manhode Reason & good conscience, Yet notwithstanding that the semblable chaunce was & hapned sithen within this Royaulme of England, aswele of his Brother the duc of Clarence, As other his nighe kynnesmen and gret Frendes, the kinges grace alweys contynuethe and hathe inward compassion of the dethe of his said Fadre, And is content that his said Cousyne, now Erle, by alle ordinate meanes and due course of the lawes when it shalle lust him at any tyme hereafter to sue or attempt for the punysshement therof.[42]

The tone and content of this instruction is hard to pick apart, not least because it differs in key ways from any previous or subsequent statement Richard ever made, whilst retaining other strands of his policy. His commitment to properly pursued and applied justice is evident in his offer that Desmond was free to seek a legal remedy at any time he wished for the death of his father. The story of the execution of Thomas Fitzgerald, 7th Earl of Desmond is a complex and disputed one.[43] Desmond was accused by some of levying illegal taxation and by others of telling Edward IV that he should never have married Elizabeth Woodville, that he should have the union dissolved and make a better match for himself. This view may have led Desmond into some harmony with Warwick as he edged closer to rebellion, but it would, if true, certainly have earned him the suspicion of the queen. Desmond had been Deputy Lieutenant of Ireland at a time when the House of York, through its Mortimer heritage and the time Richard, Duke of York, had spent there as Lieutenant, was well loved. Something eventually led to Desmond's removal and, in February 1468, his execution at the hands of his replacement, John Tiptoft, Earl of Worcester, later known as the Butcher of England for his gruesome round of killings during Warwick's rebellion. There have been suggestions that Tiptoft hoped to resolve a land dispute with the earl in his own favour by killing him, but none of the motives can be clearly established, and it may be that a combination of reasons caused Desmond's execution.

Richard's letter seems to hint at some contemporary substance to the belief that Elizabeth Woodville had taken umbrage against Desmond for some reason and brought about his downfall. The language used in describing 'certain persones' who have brought about the deaths of Richard's 'nighe kynnesmen and gret Frendes' is similar to the letter Richard wrote to York accusing the queen and her affinity of plotting to destroy him and others of the old blood. It is hard to see who else Richard might refer to. Tiptoft was long dead, yet Richard clearly refers to someone living who can be brought to justice for the execution. The comment about the death of his own brother George is particularly significant if Richard is referring to the Woodville family. Having offered no signal five years earlier of especial blame or hatred for anyone, Richard would appear to be blaming Elizabeth Woodville, if that is who he is really speaking about, for George's downfall. At the very least, he is claiming to blame *someone*, other than George, for it. If a signal that Richard was capable of hiding such deep feelings for a long time were looked for, then this letter may well offer proof.

An alternative interpretation would be that Richard, keen to secure support from Ireland, sought to woo Desmond with empathy. For it to work, he must have known the earl still resented his father's death and wanted justice for it, but he must also have been aware of the rumour that he blamed the queen for George's execution. Mancini had heard just such a story during his time in England. That does not necessarily make it true, but if he was aware of it, it was something Richard could harness to paint a likeness between himself and the earl. George was well-loved in Ireland, even amongst the favoured House of York, because he had been born in Dublin. By explaining his horror at that, he might better win Desmond over and, at the same time, make more of the threat he was telling the nation the Woodville family posed where there seems to have been little love for them anyway. He never made any similar comments on his brother's death elsewhere, only to Desmond, where they would have a particular effect. The question remains: was he telling a long-hidden truth that lay behind his actions in 1483, or playing a part that would bring him swift security in Ireland?

York had been preparing for the return of a lord who had worked so closely with the city for years, but who would now be visiting as king. The connection offered hope of even more favour for the region, and as much as that caused consternation further south, it was only positive for York. As early as 12 July, the city had begun sending gifts to Prince Edward, the new heir to the throne, at Middleham Castle. Fostering the goodwill of the next king was sensible in procuring long-term benefits for York and the surrounding area. Within a week of his father's coronation in London, Prince Edward was to receive six cygnets, twenty-four rabbits, a number of herons (that was not quite settled in the council meeting), two barrels of wine and some bread.[44] A week later, Thomas Asper was paid 14s 4d for his time riding to Middleham with the mayor to offer respects to the prince.[45]

The next month was taken up in giving exceptional care to the reception to be provided for the king. York was aware that Richard was on his way by the end of July at the latest, when it was decided that the mayor and aldermen would dress in scarlet for the occasion and be accompanied by twenty-four horsemen to greet King Richard at Breckles Mills.[46] The plans continued to take shape over the weeks that followed, and on 4 August, further details were settled. Along with the mayor, aldermen and twenty-four horsemen, anyone who held or had ever held office in the city was to be present in red gowns and on horseback. Anyone failing to attend turned out in suitable attire was to be fined 20s by the mayor, and if the fines were not collected, the mayor himself was liable to pay the city 40s to help ensure everyone knew that the fine would be enforced. The entire population of the city was to await the king's arrival near St James's Church in a dazzling array of blue, violet and grey.[47] On 11 August, the city's chamber was tasked with funding the 'syght' – the show – to be put on for the king when he arrived, and the chamberlain was tasked with keeping a record of what it cost.[48] Five days later, a set of gifts for the Earl of Northumberland were agreed, and the need for the mayor and aldermen to be ready in their scarlet gowns was reiterated.[49] A spanner was thrown into the works on 26 August when Thomas Peirson, one of the sheriffs appointed to ride to Tadcaster to meet the king before he drew close to York, was struck down with a sickness that made his participation impossible. William White was ordered to take his place and carry the rod before the approaching king that Peirson should have borne.

The day before Richard arrived, details were still being frantically settled. All foreign butchers, fishmongers and anyone else bringing goods into the city for the king's visit were to be permitted to sell their wares without the usual tolls to ensure that there was plenty available to eat. Richard was to be offered 500 marks in gold in a pair of silver basins, or a gold cup, the vessel had apparently not been procured even at this late hour, and the queen would have a gift of 100 marks. The names of all of those who contributed were proudly recorded.[50] Richard and Anne finally arrived on Friday 29 August. They were met at Tadcaster by the sheriffs and escorted to Breckles Mills to be greeted by the mayor and aldermen in their bright scarlet robes. The swelling entourage then moved through the city, being received by virtually all of the population in a sea of colour and finery, before reaching York Minster.[51] Here, Richard, Anne,

Prince Edward, many noblemen, including Northumberland, Surrey, Lincoln, Lovell, Stanley, Lisle and Greystoke, and the bishops of Durham, Worcester, St Asaph, Carlisle and St David's, participated in a celebratory service. The king was welcomed at the west door by the Dean and Canons, where he was sprinkled with holy water and wafted with incense. Before the font, on a specially supplied footstool, Richard said a Paternoster before moving before the High Altar. Here, prayers were said for the new king before organ music filled the space and then a Te Deum.[52]

On 7 September, the Creed Play was performed in York for Richard and Anne's benefit, and the royal couple lingered in the city until 21 September, when they moved to Pontefract until early October. Richard took the opportunity to honour the city as the location of his son's investiture as Prince of Wales. The official appointment had been made at Nottingham Castle on 24 August with a poetic introduction that explained: 'The clarity and charity of the sun's light is so great that when it is poured on the other heavenly bodies the sun shines with no less light and splendour, nor does it suffer any diminution of its strength, rather it is pleased to be seen, to shine as a king in the midst of his nobles and to adorn the greater and lesser stars in the whole court of heaven with his outstanding light.' Edward of Middleham had been created Prince of Wales and Earl of Chester (a title now removed from the former Edward V) in part because 'amongst the provinces subject to us none requires separate and immediate rule under us as much as the principality of Wales' and the county of Chester that bordered it. The prince was invsted 'as the custom is by the girding on of the sword, the handing over and setting of the garland on his head, and of the gold ring on his finger, and of the gold staff in his hand.'[53] Once in York, Richard seems to have made a spur of the moment decision to hold a public ceremony of investiture, probably to thank the city for its support and hospitality.

On 31 August, the king sent letters to London requesting a raft of clothing from the Royal Wardrobe for his son's investiture. The fact that the items had not travelled with them suggest that the celebration had not been planned. Sir James Tyrell, a knight with a long-standing connection to Richard, was despatched to reach London and return again as fast as he could with the purple satin-lined doublet, the tawny satin-lined one, crimson cloth of gold gowns and a myriad other articles required for the investiture.[54] It has been suggested this hurried trip by Tyrell had a dark ulterior motive, using the retrieval of clothing as a cover for murdering the two sons of Edward IV at the beginning of September and swiftly returning north to confirm to Richard that it had been done. There is insufficient evidence to confirm or deny this. If Richard had decided that his nephews must die, he would be cynical enough to use the investiture of his son as cover, but there is no evidence that he ever made such a decision, only speculation as to his state of mind. To the outside world at least, he presented himself as the sun, fearing no dimming of his own power by the light he cast upon others in his kingdom. The investiture took place on 8 September, the day after the Creed Play, and was a chance for York to take centre stage in national politics as well as for Richard to thank them. The king's illegitimate son, John of Gloucester, was also knighted during his half-brother's investiture.[55]

Richard and Anne both attended the ceremony at York Minster wearing their crowns, which may have given rise to the understanding in some quarters that their own coronation was repeated. The Minster was again packed with lords and bishops as the Bishop of Durham stood before the High Altar, which was decorated with twelve gilt statues of the Apostles and several relics that Richard had provided for the solemn occasion. After celebrating Mass, they returned to the Archbishop of York's palace at Bishopthorpe, just south of the city. There, Prince Edward was formally invested in front of all of the guests before a feast was enjoyed, during the four hours of which the king, queen and prince sat wearing their crowns.[56]

The idea that a king could roam his realm holding court from north to south and east to west was not new, but it was old-fashioned by 1483. Then again, Richard seems in many ways to have been an old-fashioned man who harkened back to what looked, from his position at the end of a long civil war, like a brighter, shimmering, golden age of chivalry and brotherhood. It had benefits. Richard himself had seen what the north was like and had spent time before that in the Welsh Marches where the royal writ was equally shaky. He was perfectly able to deal with matters from France, Brittany and Spain as well as domestic issues and he would be able to show himself in regions traditionally distant from the person of the king. In Burgundy, he had watched Edward walk to his ships in order to show himself to people, to great effect. After a few months in London, with the plotting, back-biting, chaos and reversal of events that had led him to the throne, it seems likely he hankered for a return to something familiar, settled and secure, even if only to steel himself to be ready to dive back into London politics. It was a chance to take stock. All seemed well, and he was enthusiastically received wherever he went. It was not to last. His mistake was turning away from London too soon, before the scheming had ended.

17

The October Rebellions

For asmoche as the King our sovrayn lord Richard the therd, by the
grace of God King of England and of Fraunce, and lord of Ireland,
understandeth for certan, that the duc of Bukingham traitoursly is
turned upon hym, contrarie the duetie of hysliegeaunce, and entendeth
the utter distruccion of our said sovrayn lord, the subversion of hys
roylme, and thutter disheriting of all his true liege peple, oure said
sovrayn lord therefore considering the wele and suerte of hys roiall
persone, the tranquillite and peas of hys said roylme and subgettes,
taketh and reputeth the said Duc as hys rebell and traitor, and
chargeth and commaundeth all hys true subiegettes so to take hym

Proclamation by Richard III
16 October 1483[1]

Anyone claiming to know either that Richard III definitely killed or
definitely did not kill the sons of King Edward IV, remembered as the
Princes in the Tower, is wrong. Even after more than five centuries, the
matter is as clouded by lack of evidence and heightening of emotion
as it was in 1483 and the years that immediately followed. It was the
ultimate medieval watercooler debate. Their fates were the subject of
gossip and rumour then as they frequently are on social media today.
It is not a question that can be answered definitively, but an opinion
on the likelihood of any given action will rest almost entirely on a view
of Richard, his state of mind, his immediate fears and aims and the
temperature of the blood in his veins.

Edward V and Richard, Duke of York, had been declared illegitimate,
though the matter had not yet been confirmed by Parliament and might
be subject to a challenge in an ecclesiastical or secular court. Even if their
illegitimacy is considered settled by the events of late June 1483, it could
be reversed as easily as it had been agreed upon and Edward V would
immediately become a threat to Richard once more. Crowland looked

back on this time, as summer turned to autumn, as one in which the boys' fate was still being widely discussed, with the assumption of course that they were alive. 'In order to deliver them from this captivity, the people of the southern and western parts of the kingdom began to murmur greatly, and to form meetings and confederacies. It soon became known that many things were going on in secret, and some in the face of the world, for the purpose of promoting this object.'[2] The princes – as they had been known, were no longer, but would later become again – had not ceased to be a threat to Richard. Crowland describes the conspirators as 'those who, through fear, had availed themselves of the privileges of sanctuary and franchise,'[3] suggesting that they belonged to the suppressed Woodville faction. The boys now represented their only certain hope of a return to authority.

The outbreak of the first organised threat to Richard's reign would come in October, after he had been absent from the capital for four months. It may be significant that Crowland's men of the south and west saw something they did not like in a northern king who had returned to those far-flung, barbaric parts. The uprising is traditionally viewed as one co-ordinated assault on Richard, with a single aim, but this may be a later construct that owes as much to Richard's own propaganda in dealing with its aftermath as the dangers and difficulties of pulling the tangled web apart. There may have been at least two, if not three, disparate schemes that would have become gradually moulded together, though some cohesion between them may well have grown out of a common overarching distrust of Richard. A return to a more comfortable set of known parameters would have appealed to anyone worried about this little-known king.

Richard had been aware of problems in London during his absence. One anonymous citizen noted that there had been 'a resistance made in the parlement tyme' for which four servants of the king had been hanged at Tower Hill.[4] It is possible that the 'parlement tyme' was around the point in June when Richard was taking the throne and Parliament had originally been summoned to sit after the coronation of Edward V. By the time Richard reached Minster Lovell on 29 July, there was already news of more trouble from the capital. The king wrote to his Chancellor, John Russell, regarding 'certaine personnes of such as of late had taken upon thaym the fact of an enterpruise, as We doubte nat ye have herd, bee attached, and in warde. We desire and wol you that ye doo make our lettres of commission to such personnes as by you and our counsaill shalbee advised forto sitt upon thaym and to procede to the due execucion of our lawes in that behalve.'[5] There is no mention of what the 'enterpruise' might be, but men had been arrested. Something was going on in the capital that required the attention of the Chancellor and the Council, yet at the same time, Richard did not feel compelled to hurry back to London to deal with it himself. The matter must have been serious, but not so threatening that the king's presence was needed, not least because those involved were already in custody. If Richard had launched a bid for the throne based on lies and was in desperate fear of a plot to free his nephews, it might be reasonable to expect a more panicked reaction and a dash to the capital to ensure the threat was over. His relaxed approach and delegation is not the response of a man on the brink of murdering his brother's sons out of fear that he might lose his crown.

Crowland was convinced that plots were forming during the king's absence that summer. He had also heard rumblings of plans to extricate Edward IV's daughters from sanctuary and spirit them away to safety 'in order that, if any fatal mishap should befall the said male children of the late king in the Tower, the kingdom might still, in consequence of the safety of the daughters, some day fall again into the hands of the rightful heirs.'[6] This is a telling piece of gossip, since by the time Crowland wrote, Elizabeth of York was Henry VII's queen consort amidst much feeling, resisted by Henry, that he was king because he had married her, and that she was the rightful heir to the throne. Nevertheless, these rumours seem to have reached Richard on his travels, because suddenly 'Westminster, and all its neighbouring parts, assumed the appearance of a castle and fortress, while men of the greatest austerity were appointed by king Richard to act as the keepers thereof. The captain and head of these was one John Nesfield, Esquire, who set a watch upon all the inlets and outlets of the monastery, so that not one of the persons there shut up could go forth, and no one could enter, without his permission.'[7] If Richard was really considering murdering his nephews to protect himself, it was becoming clear that Edward IV's daughters would replace them as threats and he would inevitably have been compelled to deal similarly with them too. He never did. In addition to Edward V and Richard, Duke of York, Richard had seventeen more nephews and nieces and of them, five were daughters of Edward IV, alive at Richard's accession, and not one failed to survive until the end of his reign. This is hardly the haphazard approach of a man driven to child murder by a desperation to retain power – killing two, but sparing seventeen.

John Stowe, a Tudor antiquarian writing about a century later, claimed to have the names of four men executed shortly after Richard's coronation. Robert Russ, a sergeant of London; William Davy, a pardoner from Hounslow; John Smith, a Groom of the Stirrup to Edward IV; and Stephen Ireland, who worked in the Wardrobe in the Tower of London, are names no one else seems to have picked up. Stowe notes that they were convicted of 'having sent writings into the parts of Britaine to the earles of Richmond and Penbrook, and the otherlords'. has been suggested [8] Their plan, he wrote, had been to set fire to parts of London and while the city panicked and tried to put out the flames, they would liberate the sons of

Edward IV from the Tower. The conjectured contact with Henry Tudor, Earl of Richmond, and his uncle Jasper Tudor, Earl of Pembroke, may be significant in adding weight to the suggestion that plots swirled around this young exile from almost immediately after Richard's coronation. If his prospects were being championed within England, then the campaign would almost certainly have been led by his mother, Lady Margaret Beaufort.

If the writer of the continuation of *The Crowland Chronicle* covering this period is accepted as being a well-informed member of the government, even if he cannot be established as being John Russell, the Chancellor himself, then his commentary on the uprising is interesting. It is most intriguing on the subject of the Princes in the Tower, and that is because he remains so vague.

> At last, it was determined by the people in the vicinity of the city of London, throughout the counties of Kent, Essex, Sussex, Hampshire, Dorsetshire, Devonshire, Somersetshire, Wiltshire, and Berkshire, as well as some other of the southern counties of the kingdom, to avenge their grievances beforestated; upon which, public proclamation was made, that Henry, duke of Buckingham, who at this time was living at Brecknock in Wales, had repented his former conduct, and would be the chief mover in this attempt, while a rumour was spread that the sons of king Edward before-named had died a violent death, but it was uncertain how.[9]

The writer offers no motive for Buckingham's sudden decision to abandon Richard. He later asserts that the duke wrote to Henry Tudor at the urging of John Morton, Bishop of Ely. Morton had been placed in Buckingham's custody after his arrest at the Council meeting on 13 June and was at Brecknock Castle with the duke. Morton, a former servant of the Lancastrian Henry VI, may have nurtured Buckingham's own family's Lancastrian sympathies and heritage to prise him away from Richard. Henry Tudor was a great-great-grandson of John of Gaunt through the Beaufort line, but so was Henry Stafford, Duke of Buckingham, twice over. His maternal grandfather was Edmund Beaufort, Duke of Somerset, who had been killed at the First Battle of St Albans in 1455. Buckingham's father was also descended from John of Gaunt's daughter Joan Beaufort, wife of Ralph Neville, through their daughter Anne Neville. Anne was a sister of Richard's mother, Cecily. Atop that, Buckingham was also the great-great-grandson of Edward III's youngest son, Thomas of Woodstock, Duke of Gloucester. Buckingham's claim to the throne was at least as good as Henry Tudor's, if not significantly better. Why he would abandon his own right in favour of an earl living in exile, who he had probably never met, is unfathomable. He was already the second most powerful man in the country. The only better seat available to him was the throne itself, and it is possible that this is the mischief Morton planted and cultivated at Brecknock.

The second critical element of the account provided by Crowland is that he mentions a rumour being spread that Edward IV's sons had been killed in order to further the aims of the rebellion. He does not offer any attempt at confirmation of the story, nor does he deny it. Possibly the most politically astute commentator available elected to remain silent on the fate of the sons of Edward IV, a prime charge to level at Richard III that would have worked in Henry VII's favour, meaning that there was little reason not to report their murders if he knew that Richard had ordered them. Mancini had heard the same rumours about the boys' fate, saying that he had 'seen many men burst forth into tears and lamentations when mention was made of him [Edward V] after his removal from men's sight; and already there was a suspicion that he had been done away with.'[10] Mancini left England soon after Richard's coronation, and it seems unlikely that he witnessed such displays of grief in England before he left. His sources, once he returned to the Continent, were exclusively those utterly hostile to Richard who had been involved in spreading the rumour of the deaths in the autumn. In the end, the Italian had to concede that 'Whether, however, he had been done away with, and by what manner of death, so far I have not at all discovered.'[11]

What happened to Edward V and his brother Richard, Duke of York, must, for now at least, remain an unsolved mystery. It is fraught with contradictory evidence, wide open to interpretation and continues to heighten emotions on both sides of the debate. If Richard had not done away with the boys, why did he not show them in public when rumours began to sprout into open rebellion? For some who see his guilt, it is a sure sign that he did not have them alive to display. To others, it would have been folly to wheel them out on demand and keep their cause alive. Better to hide them somewhere and let them be forgotten. If people believed they were dead, they wouldn't search for them anymore. Personally, I remain sceptical that Richard would have resorted to murdering family members, children to boot, though the notion cannot be dismissed. If he did it, it was to keep his throne safe from the threat they had posed. That threat was only removed if everyone knew they were dead and could no longer threaten him. If Richard had them murdered, he needed to display bodies to prove that they were dead. He might blame natural causes, a botched attempt to free them or any manner of assassin. It mattered little whether people believed his story, only that they understood beyond any doubt that they were dead. Failing to publicise their deaths left wide open the potential for continued threats in their names, as Henry VII was to discover for the first decade-and-a-half of his reign. Killing them and remaining silent achieved nothing and made the terrible act pointless.

There was a near contemporary parallel that Richard might look to if he sought a way to deal efficiently with his nephews that did not require two murders. Almost 300 years earlier, King John had been faced with a rival claim from his nephew, Arthur of Brittany, who had subsequently disappeared and is widely believed to have died at John's hands. King John's was hardly an example any subsequent monarch would seek to follow. On the other hand, when Henry IV had taken the crown, Richard II's heir presumptive had been Edmund Mortimer, 5th Earl of March, from whom the House of York traced their own claim to the throne. Edmund, at eight years old, and his younger brother Roger were taken into custody. Soon after, a member of the House of York had tried to kidnap them and deliver them to Wales so that Edmund could be proclaimed king, but they had quickly been recovered. After that, they were hidden in a series of royal castles, and their locations kept a secret. On Henry's death in 1413, his son, Henry V, almost immediately freed the Mortimer brothers. Edmund, then twenty-one and at the age of majority, was given his earldom and although Roger died shortly after his release, Edmund outlived Henry, dying in 1425. In 1415, there was another plot by the House of York to put Edmund on the throne, the Southampton Plot, led by Richard's grandfather, but this attempt failed because Edmund himself went to Henry to expose the scheme. His treatment had bred in him a degree of loyalty. If Richard sought a template that would keep his nephews safe from harm and prevent them from being used as a threat against him, the Lancastrian treatment of the Mortimer brothers was a perfect model. The story of the Princes in the Tower is the subject of entire books, which examine theories and try to reach conclusions that cannot be proven. As far as the remainder of Richard's story is concerned, it was a mystery then as it is still. It will crop up during, but not dominate, the rest of his days.

It is possible, perhaps even likely, that news of the potential uprising in the south reached Richard around Sunday 21 September. On that date, he moved from York to Pontefract Castle and begun a flurry of activity. On 22 September, Robert Morton, a nephew of Bishop John Morton, was removed from his post as Master of the Rolls of Chancery,[12] a key administrative position he had secured in succession to his uncle when John had become Bishop of Ely. On the same day, Richard wrote to Southampton, and possibly other towns on the south coast, instructing the mayor to prevent the wearing of livery badges within the town. This was, he said, because 'it is fulle according and righte welethy that the commonaltee of every Citee or Towne be hoole and of one wille and agrement in alle causes.' The possibility that Richard was aware of something particular in motion lies in his concern about 'taking and using lyveres at the desires of foreyne persones' which 'hathe caused oftentymes gret divisione & goperdie.'[13] He was, perhaps, concerned about Southampton and other ports receiving incitements to rebel from across the sea, in particular from Brittany, where Henry Tudor continued to enjoy the protection of Duke Francis.

One of Elizabeth Woodville's brothers, Lionel, Bishop of Salisbury, had all of his possessions seized on the following day.[14] This sudden move to a more business-like posture after enjoying his time in York may be coincidental; Richard had been away from the capital for several months and, even if he planned to operate a more mobile style of government, he must have known he would have to show his face there again soon. Nevertheless, the assault on Morton's nephew and the queen's brother suggests that he had received intelligence that something more serious was brewing. The fact that information might have reached him from men primed to look for plots may be another reason Richard had elected to go so far north and stay there so long. His experiences in Scotland had taught him that an enemy that cannot be seen cannot be fought. He had, just a year earlier, marched all the way into Edinburgh without facing a single battle. That had left him in an awkward position. It was far easier when the enemy was out in the open and prepared to be confronted. In making his northern progress so quickly after his coronation, Richard may have hoped to draw out the remaining plotters in the south, luring them into the light so that they could be challenged and defeated. If this were the case, then it would seem that 21 September brought the news that he was waiting for, and that Robert Morton, the Woodville family and a threat from across the Channel were all coalescing.

The scale of the threat must have been finally uncovered around 9 or 10 October, for in those days Richard travelled some 40 miles south to Gainsborough, before covering a further 20 miles south to Lincoln on Saturday 11 October. It was here that he probably received confirmation of the most unexpected and unwelcome feature of the unrest that was brewing. Henry Stafford, Duke of Buckingham, the man who had helped Richard onto the throne and been rewarded with virtual control of Wales, money and offices, had turned his coat and meant to rebel. It has been suggested that Buckingham was dissatisfied with the speed at which he was being given access to a valuable part of the de Bohun inheritance he had previously been denied, but it appears that Richard was simply waiting for Parliament to sit in order to legally ratify the transfer. In any case, it seems a petty thing for which to launch into rebellion when so many other rewards were already in Buckingham's hands.

From Lincoln on 12 October Richard dictated a letter to the Chancellor, John Russell, requesting that he send the Great Seal to the king immediately. This marks a change of pace and a recognition of the increased level of threat, since the Great Seal was the mechanism for all of government under the king and for raising troops. Richard's sudden need to have it close demonstrates a more urgent focus on the revolt. The king told his Chancellor that 'we, by Godds grace entende briefly to avaunce Us towards our rebelle and traytour the Duc of Bukingham to resiste and withstande his maliciouse purpose' before asking for the Seal. Russell was excused from coming in person due to 'such infirmitees and diseases as ye susteyne',[15] though it is also possible that Richard, shaken by the news of Buckingham abandonment of him, was uncertain who he could trust any more.

To this letter, Richard added a postscript in his own hand that demonstrates the outrage he felt at Buckingham's betrayal. For a man steeped in chivalric ideals and with a martial focus that fostered a belief in brotherhood and honour, it was an unfathomable act of treachery. Richard had grown used to the tightly knit band of knights and gentry he drew around him in the north and who had served him so well in Scotland, never seeing this duplicity and disloyalty coming. Edward IV had excluded Buckingham, but Richard seems to have missed something that Edward saw clearly, perhaps that Buckingham was a weak reed in the strong currents of the political waterways, and too changeable to be trusted or of use. Either because he panicked in April 1483 and felt he needed support close at hand from outside the London political classes, or because he thought his brother was wrong, Richard allowed a wolf into his flock, duped by the smooth sheep's clothing it wore. It was a character flaw that Richard shared with his father; an inability to judge the true motives of those around him, which left him wide open to being duped and betrayed. Richard's handwritten note drips with a sense of disgust and disbelief.

> We wolde most glady ye came yourself yf that ye may, and yf ye may not, we pray you not to fayle, but to accomplyshe in all dyllygence our sayde comawndement to sende our Seale incontent upon the syght heroff, as we trust you, with suche as ye trust, and the Offycers pertenying, to attend with hyt; praying you to assertayne us of your Newes. Here, loved by God, ys all well and trewly determyned, and for to resyste the malysse of hym that hadde best cawse to be trewe, th'Duc of Bokyngham, the most untrewe creatur lyvyng, whom with Gods grace we shall not be long tyll that we wyll be in that partyes, and subdewe hy malys. We assure you there was never false traytor better purvayde for, as this berrer Gloucestr shall sheue you.[16]

Richard seemed to change his mind from what was in the dictated part of the letter and admit he would prefer Russell to come with the seal, if his health allowed. The vitriol poured on Buckingham is, if anything, intensified by the contrast between the more businesslike part of letter and this personal comment. Richard rails against the malice of one who has been so well rewarded, exposing his own sensitivity to personal betrayal by those he expects to have more honour, before famously lambasting him as 'the most untrewe creatur lyvyng'. What brought about Buckingham's dramatic and unexpected volte-face is impossible to determine. It may have been Morton's honeyed words, though it is hard to see what he might have promised the duke under Henry Tudor that would make him more powerful than he already was. Morton's plan might have been to splinter Richard's support by encouraging Buckingham to believe that there would be support for his own Lancastrian-based claim to the throne. In that way, Richard would be forced to fight on two fronts, and whether Buckingham or Tudor won, Morton had as close to a Lancastrian revival as could be looked for in those days. It is possible that the fate of Edward IV's son played a part in the rupture, but that could equally involve Buckingham having them done away with to launch his own bid for the throne as a discovery that Richard had ordered an act Buckingham considered beyond the pale. Richard's outrage might have its roots in the discovery that Buckingham had murdered his nephews, or it might have been because Buckingham had advised and encouraged Richard to do it.

The letter was taken to Russell by Richard's own Herald, Gloucester King of Arms, which further underlines the sensitivity of the business and the narrowing of the field of those who could be trusted. Gloucester was clearly meant to show Russell some evidence that related to Buckingham's betrayal, though nowhere is there a record of what that was or what it related to: the Princes, Morton, Henry Tudor? Russell, despite having been prominent in Edward IV's government, seems to have retained Richard's trust, and would send the Great Seal to the king as requested, suggesting that in the case of the Chancellor, the king's faith was not misplaced.

Crowland recalled that Richard acted 'in no drowsy manner, but with the greatest activity and vigilance', sending orders for forces to be raised in Wales. Thomas Vaughan was set to watch Brecknock and the surrounding countryside, and Humphrey Stafford was set to work breaking some of the bridges over the River Severn and guarding the rest with 'a strong force'[17] to keep Buckingham in Wales. The king set about raising an army at Leicester to counter the threat. On 11 October, his close friend Francis Lovell wrote to Sir William Stonor to ask 'youe and all other to attende upon his grace', bringing as many men as possible to Leicester by 20 October.[18] Lovell was at Lincoln with his friend the king and was involved in drawing on the connections that helped a monarch raise an army. In this case, Stonor would elect to side with Buckingham and would later be attainted for treason.

On the same day that Lovell penned his letter, Richard sent one to York, and probably to other cities and lords he believed remained loyal. He advised the city of Buckingham's 'traiterous entent' and asked them to send as many armed men as they could to reach Leicester no later than 21 October[19]. This was not the only front on which Richard was resisting the swelling tide of unrest. John Howard, Duke of Norfolk, had remained in London to keep the south secure during the king's absence. He had been sending men into Kent, most likely to gather intelligence, and by 10 October was writing to John Paston to warn him that 'the Kentysshmen be up in the weld [Weald], and sey they wol come and robbe the cite, which I shall let [prevent] yf I may.'[20] Howard's presence in London and his experience meant that he was capable of dealing with the uprisings in the south, freeing Richard to focus on the potentially more threatening actions of Buckingham in Wales.

By 19 October, Richard had reached Grantham, where the Great Seal was delivered to him. Russell had handed the critical instrument of government to Robert Blakwall, a clerk of Chancery, in the presence of four other men. The seal was enclosed in a white bag and sealed with Russell's own signet to prove that it had not been tampered with during its journey. The similarly structured handover to the king took place at noon in The Angel Inn, Grantham. The Bishops of Worcester, Durham, Menevia and St Asaph, the Earls of Northumberland and Huntingdon, Lord Stanley and Thomas Barowe, Keeper of the Chancery Rolls, witnessed the deliberately stage-managed moment.[21] On 22 October, Richard was at Leicester for the muster he had ordered, and on the following day, he issued a proclamation from the city. The opening paragraph displays a belief that his commitment to equitable justice ought to have brought him the love of the general populace and an almost puritanical religious zeal that motivated him. The king had, 'in his owne Person, as is well knowen, hath dressed himself to divers Parties of this his Reame for the indifferent Admynystracion of Justice to every Persone.'[22] He expressed a certainty that 'all Oppressours and Extortioners of his Subjectes, orible Adultres and Bawdes, provokyng the high Indignation and Displeasure of God, shuld have be reconsiled and reduced to the wey of Trouth and Ventue.'[23] Richard almost seems to have been amazed that some would react to his policies by revolting against his rule in spite of his good lordship, which was now available throughout the nation, reinforcing the notion that he struggled to see complex motives in the actions of those around him.

There is more religiously driven language in the condemnation of particular individuals. Thomas Grey, Marquis of Dorset, was singled out for particular attention for 'not feryng God, nor the Perille of his soule'. Dorset had, Richard claimed, 'many and sundry Maydes, Wydowes, and Wifes dampnably and without Shame Devoured, Defloured, and Defouled' and, in particular, Richard denounced him for 'holding the unshampfull and myschevous Woman called Shores Wife in Adultry.'[24] Jane Shore had clearly not been exorcised from Richard's mind as being in some way responsible for Edward IV's troubles and subsequent plotting in London. The other men directly accused were Sir William Norris, Sir William Knyvett, Sir Thomas Bourchier, Sir George Brown, John Cheyne, John Norris, Walter Hungerford, John Rush, and John Harcourt. Several of them would go on to fight for Henry Tudor at Bosworth, most notably John Cheney and Walter Hungerford. William Knyvett was married to Buckingham's aunt, Joan Stafford. The uprising was being led, Richard proclaimed, by the 'grete Rebell and Traytour the late Duc of Bukyngham, and Busshoppes of Ely and Salesbury'. The king offered succour to any of their followers who would immediately leave the revolt, assuring them that 'shall not be hurte in their Bodies ne Goodes if they withdrawe theym self fro their False Company, and medell no ferther with theym.'[25] A bounty of £1,000 or £100 a year worth of land was placed on Buckingham's head, with 500 marks on offer for Dorset and the Bishops of Ely and Salisbury. The king must have felt hopeful that he could draw support away from the leaders of the revolt and even turn their men against them with cold, hard cash.

As Richard marched out of Leicester heading south-west, it became abundantly clear that the revolution had stalled and collapsed. Between the broken or guarded bridges and the torrential rain, Buckingham was kept in Wales and failed to make any contribution before his disillusioned men began to drift away home. In the south, no real attack ever materialised. Buckingham, Crowland wrote, changed into the clothes of a common man and 'secretly left his people', only to hide in the cottage of a poor man and be discovered. Led to Salisbury, he was executed as a traitor in the marketplace on 2 November 1483, his brief flirtation with national authority abruptly ended. Much of the evidence for the chronology and organisation of the uprising comes from the parliamentary attainder of those involved. This represents the official version of events and works hard to paint a picture of a single, cohesive rebellion led by Buckingham.[26] This may have been deliberately misleading. The revolt in the southern counties that aimed to target London appears in many ways discrete from whatever Buckingham was planning from Wales. Those in the south, perhaps encouraged in their mistrust of Richard by his return to the north immediately after his coronation, initially sought to restore Edward V, thereby returning to a more familiar, southern-based government. The Woodville connection to this aim is telling, and they probably worked on communities to nurture their fears and offer an alternative that would bring about their own restoration.

Buckingham's part and his precise motives remain a mystery, but it seems improbable that, as claimed, Morton convinced the duke to write to Henry Tudor and encourage him to invade. Close to the heart of Richard's government, Buckingham must have felt that his scheme had a high probability of success or he would not have made the attempt. He was unlikely to have looked beyond his own claim to the throne if he considered unseating Richard, his preference for an exiled earl he had never met making little sense. Whether the duke was driven by regret at having supported Richard, or had lent his aid in the hope of destabilising the Crown enough to launch his own bid, backed by latent Lancastrian feeling, or whether the fate of Edward IV's son played into the decision to abandon Richard can only be guessed at. News of Buckingham's betrayal seems to have reached Richard later than intelligence about a southern, Woodville-led plot, suggesting both that Buckingham was not the leader of a national, coherent scheme and that he came to the affair late, perhaps spotting a chance to grab something for himself in the fallout. Richard was keen, using the attainders of those involved, to create the impression of one unified threat that had ultimately failed to get off the ground, which had been led by the most senior figure who had rebelled, and who also happened to have been captured and executed. As Dorset, Morton, Lionel Woodville and Henry Tudor remained at large, an impression needed to be created that they were bit players who caused Richard no concern. That was not the truth.

If there was a link between parts of the plots, it must have been John Morton, Bishop of Ely. He was with Buckingham but would become inextricably attached to Henry Tudor's cause. Buckingham's wife, Catherine Woodville, may also have played a part in co-ordinating efforts, but nowhere was her involvement suggested. Buckingham's Beaufort ancestry also gave him a blood tie to Margaret Beaufort, Henry Tudor's mother., who had been married to Buckingham's uncle Sir Henry Stafford. It is therefore plausible that the uprising was a single affair, but perhaps more likely that the Woodville family stirred trouble in the southern counties, Buckingham was convinced, either by Morton or his own ambition, to chance his arm, and Henry Tudor's small but burgeoning faction saw an opportunity to inveigle itself into internal, national proceedings. It was better for Richard to claim that he had seen off one threat and executed its leader than to admit three separate fronts, the leaders of two of which remained beyond his grasp.

Tudor's sudden appearance as an unexpected and unlikely claimant to the throne is fascinating and hard to disentangle from other events. Polydore Vergil, writing towards the end of Henry VII's reign, seems to have been under the impression that something other than a single uprising led by Buckingham was going in in the summer and autumn of 1483:

> before the duke all in a rage had begun to alienate in mynde from king Richard, the same very time a plot of new conspiracy was layd at London betwixt Elyzabeth the queen, wife to king Edward, and Margaret mother to erle Henry, in this sort: This Margaret for want of health used thadvyse of a physition namyd Lewys, a Welsheman born, who, because he was a grave man and of no smaule experience, she was

wont oftentimes to conferre frely with all, and with him famylyarly to lament her adversitie. And she, being a wyse woman, after the slaughter of king Edwardes children was knowen, began to hope well of hir soones fortune, supposing that that dede wold withowt dowt proove for the profyt of the commonwelth, yf yt might chaunce the bloode of king Henry the Sixth and of king Edward to be intermenglyd by affynytie, and so two most pernicious factions should be at once, by conjoynyng of both howses, utterly taken away. Wherfor furthwith not neglecting so great oportunytie, as they wer consulting togythers, she uttered to Lewys that the time was now coom when as king Edwardes eldest dowghter might be geaven in maryage to hir soon Henry, and the king Rycherd, accountyd of all men enemy to his countree, might easyly be dejected from all honor and bereft the realme, and therfor prayd him to deale secretly with the quene of suche affayre.

This passage is long, yet only describes half of the affair. It is worth consideration in full because Vergil is frequently relied upon as a witness when Richard's bad reputation is espoused. He may well have had access to some people who had lived through these events, though their testimony would have been provided through Tudor Rose-tinted spectacles and they would have been conscious of not disturbing the new regime. Vergil understood that Margaret had, before Buckingham turned from Richard, been plotting to get her son Henry Tudor onto the throne. This alone offers substance to the notion that a Tudor scheme was in progress early in Richard's reign. The logistics of communicating with Henry in Brittany, the queen in the well-protected sanctuary at Westminster and of co-ordinating other likely participants mean that it could not have been accomplished quickly. Margaret also acknowledges, in Vergil's retelling, that the death of the sons of Edward IV ought to be sufficient to propel her son to the throne through marriage to Elizabeth of York. Vergil is adamant that Richard ordered their deaths, though no contemporary is so certain. Crowland would admit only that a *rumour* of the boys' deaths was in circulation, but that this was enough to achieve Margaret's aim. The insistence in some quarters that Margaret lacked a motive for killing the princes is specifically denied by Vergil, who claims that she saw precisely that as her son's route to the throne. Perhaps even just spreading the rumour of it was enough to draw support.

Dr Lewis Caerleon went on to visit Elizabeth Woodville in sanctuary and negotiate with her for her oldest daughter to marry Henry Tudor so that they could win the throne together. The fact that the queen was willing to go along with this scheme is cited, reasonably, as evidence that she believed her sons by Edward IV were dead and their cause lost. The question that must be answered is how she might have come to know such a fact when it has never otherwise been proven. The answer is simple.

Her primary source of news must have been Dr Lewis Caerleon. The physician may have negotiated for the marriage without divulging that the plan included placing Henry on the throne, only that it would buy an ally to help restore Edward V, and by extension Woodville authority. Alternatively, he may have brought her in her seclusion news that her sons were dead, confirming her worst fears as she languished cut off from the world. This would not require Dr Caerleon to know that it was true, or necessarily that Margaret Beaufort had been able to tell him it was true. If they hoped for the queen's promise of a match and her backing for Henry to take the throne, she only needed to believe it for now. The rest would need to be sorted out later, maybe, but that was a problem for another time. The point is that the plan to make Henry king may not have been precisely what Elizabeth Woodville agreed to, and if it was, it could have been predicated on assuring her of something no one knew with any certainty; that her sons with Edward IV were dead.

Tudor left Brittany with a small fleet provided by Duke Francis and aimed for the south coast. His flotilla was scattered by the same storms that kept Buckingham bogged down in Wales, and when his own ship drew near to the English coast, he was beckoned ashore by soldiers who told him of the success of the revolt. Unconvinced, showing a trademark shrewdness that would never desert him, Henry turned his vessel around and returned to Brittany. His cause had failed, but in mid-October 1483, Henry Tudor had launched an invasion of England with the aim of taking the crown, based on a promise to marry Elizabeth of York and a rumour that her brothers were dead. The Tudor plot had almost worked, and enough hope was retained to keep it alive. The precise date that the idea was conceived cannot be pinpointed; it may have been as early as June or July when confusion and shock gripped London, or as late as September, but by October 1483 the conspiracy had sprung into life.

The revolt had been far more threatening to Richard than history has allowed, or than Richard was keen to project. The abject failure of all fronts, whether co-ordinated or not, facilitated attempts at its consignment to footnotes, offering little more than a confirmation of Richard's authority and military skill. In fact, the number of counties involved and the nature of some of the men – a duke, two bishops, a marquess and several men with either previous Lancastrian sympathies or an attachment to Edward IV that had not successfully been transferred to Richard – demonstrate the gaping holes in Richard's authority. History would have taught him that those who came to power following a deposition rarely sat comfortably on their thrones. Neither did they suffer just one abortive attempt to unseat them. If Richard gave any thought to it, and the moulding of the attainder to present the revolt in the fashion of a unified affair doomed to failure suggests that he did, he must have known more was coming. Henry Tudor had given notice that could not easily be withdrawn that he would replace Richard. Despite Vergil's insistence that Henry was of Henry VI's blood, he was not. His grandmother was Henry VI's mother, Catherine de Valois. His father had been Henry VI's half-brother, but in the female line rather than by the all-important paternal descent. His Lancastrian blood, distant as it may have been, was real though, running through his mother's line back to John of Gaunt. His promise to marry Elizabeth of York caught the imagination of those who would not be reconciled to Richard's kingship and offered a natural, welcoming home to their disaffection.

During the summer, on 30 August, Louis XI of France had died at the age of sixty. He left his thirteen-year-old son to rule as Charles VIII, creating a minority in France that worryingly mirrored the one in England months earlier. Returning to Brittany was a man who had an eye on a crown. The concern for France was that Henry, as a great-grandson of Charles VI, might have considered his claim to the French throne a brighter and more obtainable prize than the one in England, occupied by a military man of thirty-one. Louis had been keen to get his hands on Henry Tudor as a means to disrupt England. Now, France had reason to keep Henry's eye focused on that side of the Channel, and not on the French throne.

Richard spent much of the first fortnight of November, after dealing with Buckingham at Salisbury, deep in the south-west. He travelled to Dorchester before spending a week in Exeter. He returned east via Salisbury to Winchester, spending the night of 24 November at Guildford as he prepared to re-enter his capital for the first time in more than four months. On Tuesday 25 November, Richard was welcomed into the city by the mayor and more than 400 members of various companies who rode out to greet the king in their gowns of murrey. A proclamation was sent into Kent decrying the rebels there, but also thanking the population who had abandoned the instigators when their treachery became clear. It is unclear whether this was a piece of spin meant to further degrade the uprising, or whether it provides a genuine insight into the rebellion's failure. Norfolk had been in contact with men in Kent, and there was no assault on London made from that quarter, so it is possible that Richard was not as unpopular as is generally believed, at least not amongst those below the gentry. For these people, Richard reiterated his promise 'to see due administracione of Justice thoughe out this his Realme'. He encouraged all men with a complaint to place it before him when he arrived in the county, promising 'he shalbe herd and without delay have suche convenient remydye as shalle accorde with his lawes.'[27]

Finally, on 9 December, Richard felt able to send out writs summoning Parliament to sit at Westminster on 23 January. One of those summoned was Richard's seven-year-old son, Edward of Middleham, a courtesy for his rank. He was called to attend as Prince of Wales, Duke of Cornwall and Earl of Chester.[28] Parliament could not reasonably have been called any earlier, and Richard may have hoped to see it sit sooner. His title remained to be confirmed and, with Edward IV's coffers depleted by war in Scotland, the French pension gone and taxation halted by Edward's death in April 1483, finances must have been on his mind too. France might have posed less of a threat as they looked inward at their own tricky minority, but Richard had been made aware of disgruntlement in the south of England and a new threat from across the sea had been exposed. On Christmas Day 1483, Henry and those who had now joined him in Brittany gathered at Rennes Cathedral, where they confirmed their pact. The fugitives would lend their support to Henry if he would pledge to marry Elizabeth of York when they had won the throne.[29] This Henry did gladly, though the notion of holding the crown by right of his wife was never to sit well with him.

The uprising in the southern counties had been largely middle-class in its nature. Buckingham was the only nobleman involved, though Dorset was cited too, and Richard had thanked the commons of Kent for remaining loyal to him. There was something about Richard that the southern gentry could not warm to. It is tempting to see it as their previous flourishing under the 'lax regime' of Edward IV, as Richard was soon to describe it formally, which meant that when Richard arrived with a driving commitment to impartial justice, they saw their prospects curtailed. If they knew much about Richard, they had perhaps heard stories of the duke who handed his own retained men and servants over to be tried and who found in favour of husbandmen against their social superiors. Those who relied on a blind eye being turned to corruption and bullying had much to fear from such a man, and that may offer some explanation. Alternatively, something substantial was known regarding the fabrication of the pre-contract story, or of the murder of the sons of Edward IV, which caused such disgust that these men were rendered utterly unwilling to work with Richard. As with so many aspects of this story, either is possible and can be equally successfully argued for or against.

Whatever the truth of their motives, the evacuation of numbers of office-holding gentry from the southern counties and the feeling that others could probably not be trusted created a problem. The empty spaces needed to be filled and more than ever, Richard needed to be able to trust the people occupying them. This dilemma perhaps had no easy answer, but the king's solution only further alienated a cautious and suspicious south. Crowland voiced the southern outrage at Richard's response. 'What immense estates and patrimonies were collected into this king's treasury in consequence of this measure! all of which he distributed among his northern adherents, whom he planted in every spot throughout his dominions, to the disgrace and lasting and loudly expressed sorrow of all the people in the south, who daily longed more and more for the hoped-for return of their ancient rulers, rather than the present tyranny of these people.'[30]

The 'plantation' of the south with members of Richard's northern affinity was both a smaller and more serious affair than Crowland's complaint suggests. There was no wholesale replacement of any nobility or even the senior gentry in areas. The men who had joined the rebellion and fled, forfeiting their offices by the loss of royal favour and their lands by a later act of attainder in Parliament, were predominantly Edward IV's old household members who exercised a degree of local authority. These connections helped information to flow from the regions to the king and back again and provided a mechanism by which local worthies could become known to the king and secure progression.[31] Richard looked to men he had known and trusted in the north but in an effort to avoid unsettling that region, he frequently selected younger sons, or heirs yet to inherit, to travel south. Marmaduke Constable was an oldest son, but his father was still alive and heading the family at Flamborough in Yorkshire. George Neville was an illegitimate son, and John Musgrave and Thomas Stafford were younger sons who were brought south. Perhaps the most prominent of these men was Sir Robert Brackenbury. Brackenbury was the second son of Thomas Brackenbury of Denton in County Durham. He became Richard's Constable of the Tower of London and would develop a landed interest in Kent as well as accruing other offices ultimately valued at about £500 a year.[32]

The pattern, if one existed, seems to have been the parachuting of northern men into areas where the household connections had been lost, a grant of land and some small offices and a place on commissions of the peace. It was not an invasion in the sense that a new polity was imposed on entire regions. Small pockets were filled by men Richard knew he could trust in an attempt to rebuild his influence in areas where it had been severely damaged. There was an effort to develop these men into new insiders rather than to forcibly insert men who were to remain overtly outsiders. The higher ranks of society were unaffected, but those lower down the gentry with hopes of moving up through the ranks to royal service found their previously smooth path made rocky by the introduction of strangers. This break, and the imposition of unknown men into local life, and perhaps the fact that they were not only northern but second sons, was enough to cause the kind of consternation Crowland expressed. It was a novel solution. When Edward IV had suffered problems with the Neville powerbase in the north, his answer had never been to send southern men there to fill a hole. The single most notable exception to that was Richard himself. He had acquired the Neville lands with a degree of local acceptance because he was married to Warwick's daughter, but he may have seen first-hand that a younger son could build a future in a new region, becoming accepted by good lordship and hard work. If he had become as deeply integrated into northern society as he was by 1482, then his transplanting of men had every chance of working, with the added advantage that they already knew Richard and how he liked to operate. Ultimately, it was a mistake that would contribute to Richard's eventual downfall. It is likely that this fracturing of the court's links with southern society represents the critical disruption of the rule of the House of York rather than the fact of Richard becoming king.

William Colyngbourne was one of the men disaffected by Richard. He has been remembered as the author of the verse 'The Catte, the Ratte and Lovell our dogge rulyth all England under the hogge.' It is cited as a measure of Richard's ruthless desire to keep control of his realm that Colyngbourne was executed for pinning the rhyme to the door of St Paul's Cathedral. The lines are instructive as to the attitude of Richard's opponents by 1484. The Catte was William Catesby, the lawyer who had become a very close advisor to the king during 1483. The Ratte was Sir Richard Ratcliffe, a northern knight and landowner who followed Richard south and became one of his most trusted ministers. Francis Lovell, Richard's close friend, was referred to as 'our dogge' in reference to his family's badge of a silver wolf, and the hogge they served was Richard, denoted by his own personal symbol. The inference was clear and a perfect microcosm of the sense that northern men now dominated the southern king. He was controlled and directed by northerners, lawyers and friends.

Colyngbourne was no parochial outsider. He was frequently on Commissions of the Peace in Wiltshire, but that county had been hit hard by suspicion after the rebellion of 1483. He had also been Cecily Neville's steward of her lands in that county and had lost his post. On 3 June 1484, Richard wrote to his mother to offer the services of Francis Lovell in Colyngbourne's place, a reasonable offer as Lovell already had lands in Wiltshire, but it was in the wake of these losses that Colyngbourne made his attack.[33] He seems to have been at least suspected of involvement with some aspect of the October uprising, and it is possible Richard had asked his mother to dispense with Colyngbourne's services. By 1484, Colyngbourne was in contact with Henry Tudor and was encouraging him to launch another invasion.[34] It was for this treason, not merely a cheeky piece of satire, that Colyngbourne was arrested. He was tried before a commission of oyer and terminer by the Dukes of Suffolk and Norfolk; the Earls of Nottingham and Surrey; Francis, Viscount Lovell; Edward, Viscount Lisle; Lords Audley, Stanley, Grey, Beauchamp and Scrope, and others including Walter Devereux, Richard Hastings and the mayor of London. He was convicted, along with John Turberville, and sentenced to death, though Turberville, who must have been accused of a lesser crime, was only imprisoned.

The Tudor chronicler Edward Hall would lament that Colyngbourne's fate was a demonstration of Richard's pettiness and tyranny. He wrote that 'the wilde worme of vengeance waverynge in his hed could not be contented with the death of diverse gentlemen suspected of treason, but also he muste extends his bloudy furye agaynste a poore gentleman named Collyngborne for making a small ryme of thre of his unfortunate councelers.'[35] Hall's story took hold and became accepted in its repeating, yet it is demonstrably untrue. Colyngbourne was executed as a traitor for encouraging Henry Tudor to invade. If anything, he had been given two chances. In late 1483, he had lost his offices in Wiltshire owing to his involvement in the rebellion, but was otherwise unmolested. It was only when he continued to spend the next twelve months fomenting further rebellion that he was arrested, tried and executed. He had been given a second chance, perhaps because his involvement was low-level or only suspected rather than proven, but he elected to use it to continue in opposition. Colyngbourne's story is in many aspects typical of much of the incorrect information utilised to paint Richard as a petty, cruel man that has become deeply implanted by its recitation. William Colyngbourne was not a 'poore gentleman' executed 'for making a small ryme'. He was a member of the Wiltshire gentry who rebelled in 1483 and persisted in treasonable activity for another year, at which point he was caught and punished. The truth may be less shocking and lurid, but it remains the truth and belies the image of a desperate, heavy-handed tyrant.

Nevertheless, the problem for Richard was not diminished. He had to rebuild royal authority, and, in 1484, Parliament met to begin that process more formally.

18

The King in Parliament

He was a good lawmaker for the ease and solace of the common people

Sir Francis Bacon,
Lord Chancellor 1617–21

Richard III's reign saw only one Parliament. Initially planned for November 1483, the outbreak of revolts in the south had caused it to be postponed. Parliament opened at Westminster on 23 January 1484 and sat for one session of twenty-nine days, closing on 20 February. As with almost every other aspect of Richard's life, the actions of his Parliament divide opinion. The one thing that most commentators can agree on is that Parliament passed many good and valuable laws in 1484, which did not require repeal. The question has arisen as to how much credit Richard might deserve for these positive steps. The acid test will be whether they can be demonstrated to be in line with his attitude and policies as Duke of Gloucester in the north, and as king.

Parliament was a body that had been evolving, often against the wishes of the monarch, for centuries. Before the Norman invasion, a role similar to Parliament's later position as a body to advise the king was performed by the Anglo-Saxon Witenagemot, a council of leading noblemen and churchmen who offered the king advice, guidance and support. The Witenagemot, or Witan, had powers that set it apart and doomed it when William the Conqueror arrived. Aelfric of Eynsham summed up the important authority by noting that 'No man may make himself a king; for the people have the option to choose him for king who is agreeable to them; but after that he has been hallowed as king, he has power over the people, and they may not shake his yoke from their necks.'[1] The Witan had the authority to elect a new king rather than relying on direct, male-line succession. In the aftermath of the Battle of Hastings, the Witan hurriedly appointed the teenage Edgar the Aetheling as their new king. Edgar was the grandson of Edmund Ironside and great-grandson of Aethelred the Unready, and in the panic of the loss of King Harold, the Witan elected the last male of the House of Wessex to rule. Their problem was that William the Conqueror was hardly going to agree.

In August 1086, William formally broke the power of the Witan and drastically restructured English society when he caused the Oath of Sarum to be sworn to him at Old Sarum, now Salisbury. William's 'council came to him there, and all the landholding men of any account throughout England, whosesoever men they were. And they all bowed to him and became his men, and swore oaths of fealty to him, that they would remain faithful to him against all other men.' The Norman king not only demanded this oath of his 170 tenants-in-chief, but of anyone who owned land. The effect of this was not only to give each landowner a direct link to the king, but also to tie them to him in service. If a lord rebelled, landowners in his sphere of influence no longer doubted where their obligations lay; they owed their allegiance directly to the Crown.

The word 'parliament' first appears in 1236, used to describe a meeting of the barons and senior clergy; 1254 saw the first instance of elected members attending to represent towns and burghs, drawn from the knightly classes. Simon de Montfort's reputation as the father of democracy is almost wholly unwarranted. He was the first to summon Parliament without the desire of the king, Henry III then being his prisoner, and he used elected officials, but this was not the first instance of elections, and they were used to broaden Simon's support, which he lacked from the nobility and the Church. The reign of Edward I saw an effort to codify and unify the laws of England, which had always varied at local level. Edward has been called an English Justinian for his efforts to bring harmony and clarity to the law, though it served the needs of a centralised government too.

The Magna Carta in 1215 represented an attempt to rebalance the relationship between the Crown and the barons. Parliament, as its role developed throughout the rest of the century, became a vehicle for the maintenance of that relationship; the king would request a grant of taxation, but in return, Parliament would expect reforms of behaviour it viewed as breaches of the Charters. The period of the Wars of the Roses saw a new high-water mark in the power Parliament had been slowly accruing. When Richard, Duke of York, had laid claim to the throne in 1460, he had placed his bid and his evidence before Parliament for their adjudication. The following year, his son Edward IV took the throne and ratified his *de facto* kingship in Parliament. The Lords and the Commons had come closer than ever to the role of the Witan, and their approval was viewed as the only legitimate means of establishing a dynasty. Edward had also used Parliament to give legality to some of his more dubious tinkering with the laws of inheritance. By 1484, Parliament was a vehicle for legal permanence, a route to legitimacy for a king and a way for the nation to continue gathering power from the Crown.

The precise composition of Richard's Parliament is unclear, quite possibly deliberately obscured by those wishing to deny involvement with the confirmation of Richard's title. This piece of business came first and involved the illegitimacy of Edward IV's children, something Henry VII later had to swiftly reverse to marry one of them, but which no one was likely to own up to approving in 1484. William Catesby was elected Speaker, Dr Thomas Huton was Clerk of the Parliament, and Thomas Barowe was Master of the Rolls, but no other officers of the session are recorded. Bishop Russell, as Chancellor, had begun a draft of his opening speech in preparation for the abandoned Parliament in November, as he had done for Edward V's cancelled meeting. The difference between the themes of this draft and the final speech offers an insight into the shifting political landscape. The first draft for Richard's abandoned Parliament no longer focusses on the responsibilities of the nobility during a minority and the powers of a *tutele*, since both were now redundant.[2] Russell retains his analogy of the country as a human body, requiring sustenance and the co-operation of all parts to function properly. The notion that 'no membre, be he never so nobille, that may sey to the leste or to the vileest of them all, I have no nede of thee'[3] has a strong ring of Richard's own oft-demonstrated belief that those at the top of society do not have a right to abuse those lower down simply by virtue of their station.

Continuing the analogy, Russell planned to refer to the blindness that might cause a nation's downfall but also to the threat posed by those who would lead a blind man into obstacles. This begins a more open attack on Edward IV's foreign policy, berating the liars who had sworn oaths of peace with England only to abandon them before Edward's death.[4] The possibility of renewed war with France was one that would appeal to Parliament as the body that had driven Edward to cross the Channel in 1475. For Richard, it offered a much-needed distraction from internal politics that might unify the country behind him, but Russell's words were also a warning about not only outward enemies but internal ones, the advisors of Edward IV who had led the blind king into obstacles over which he stumbled. For a brother whose career and subsequent reputation has, in attempts to examine it in a more positive light, been predicated on his loyalty to his brother, it is a brutal attack. Some of this must have been what Richard was feeling, and his willingness to work for his brother nonetheless a signal of his dedication, but it is clear that he wished to be understood as having disapproved. This was not news, of course. He had openly opposed peace with France in 1475 and, almost a decade later, had not changed his mind. Russell planned to ask about Edward 'was not hys pensissous sikenesse encreced by dayly remembraunce of the derke weys, that hys subtille feythe frendes had lede hym in?'

In searching for something that is lost, Russell was to tell his audience that light was the key requirement. He referred to the Parable of the Lost Coin, in which a woman has ten coins and loses one. Her reaction is to search desperately for the lost coin and when it is found, to call together all her friends and neighbours to celebrate.[5] The story sits alongside the Parable of the Lost Sheep and of the Prodigal Son to illustrate God's attitude to sinners, and Russell considers that the source of a body's light is its eyes. So it is with the country. If it is blinded and led by false men, the lost coin can never be found, and the nation can never be whole and complete. Parliament, Russell considered, was the place for things to be corrected and decided. 'We be yn the place where thys shuld be tretyd. Thys tyme ys prefixed for the same entente.'[6]

A second draft was prepared by Russell for the Parliament in January. The document that remains is sadly fragmentary and appears to have been only the beginning of the speech.[7] No record of the full content remains. It seems to be the rough content of the address that was delivered and perhaps subsequently destroyed because of some dangerously inflammatory passages kept from the eyes of Henry VII. The theme of the opening speech was *In uno corpre multa membra habemus* – In one body there are many members – drawing on the ideas of the previous drafts. The notion that no person of high degree can do without those of the lowest degree is retained in the same form, perhaps because it pleased the king's sense of equity. Russell added the conclusion that 'every estate, be he hye, be he lowe, ys ordeyned to support othyr.'[8] An odd, perhaps telling but perhaps meaningless, reference tells the audience 'There be many children, many menne of divers condicions and estates, yn thys Reame of England whoyse body muste be preservyd.'[9] The comment is preceded by the Latin phrase *Filiae tibi sunt serva corpus illarum* – 'If you have daughters, keep them.' It was perhaps a comment on the protection generally of daughters within the kingdom, but it could have meant more. Richard could not have been oblivious to the contribution of rumours of his nephews' deaths to the rebellion against him. Was there an effort here to reassure the Lords and Commons that the queen could keep her daughters, who were in no danger, and the children – Edward V and Richard, Duke of York – were to be 'preservyd' in Richard's England?

As king, he is frequently criticised for failing to explain what happened to his nephews if he had nothing to hide. Given that the full text of this speech did not survive, but a fragmentary draft did, it is possible that obscure references were made to the continued safekeeping of the boys and those references were similarly eradicated. The speech goes on to compare those who rebel to rotten parts of the body that threaten to bring the whole down.[10] The notion of blindness remains, as does the need for light to guide the nation. The Parable of the Lost Coin is also retained, suggesting that the desire to refer to searching for something lost and of sweeping the house clean and setting it in order had not lessened. The rest of the speech is lost, but the themes remain the unification of the nation, the restoration of order and the addressing of both external and internal threats.

The first piece of business Parliament addressed was taxation.[11] Richard was granted tonnage of 3s import duty on every tun of wine, with 6s from foreign merchants, including Hanse and German merchants. Parliament also gave poundage of 12d duty on every 20s of goods for English and denizened merchants and 2s on every 20s for foreign merchants. The protectionist policy of favouring English merchants was of course very popular amongst the merchant classes who disliked the competition from their foreign counterparts. Exclusions from the duty were made for the export of woollen cloth, wool, woolfells (hides with the fleece still attached), hides and ale or victuals sent to Calais. Imports of corn, flour, fresh fish, meat and wine were also exempted. Anyone caught trying to avoid paying duty was to be fined double the amount they would have owed if they had paid the tax. The king was given a subsidy of 33s 4d on every sack of wool and 66s 8d on each sack exported by a foreign merchant. For woolfells, the tax was 33s 4d on every 240 items from English merchants and 66s 8d from foreigners and for hides, 66s 8d for English merchants and 73s 4d from foreigners was payable on each last (a standardised shipload) of hides.[12] Much taxation granted to Edward IV had ceased on his death almost a year earlier, so the Crown was missing out on significant amounts of income. A willing grant of taxation was usually a signal of Parliament's confidence in the government of the realm by the king and a preference for war. There was no immediate concern about Richard's government on display at Westminster.

The main body of Parliament's work was divided into Private Bills, that affected individuals, and Public Bills that were to provide law for the country as a whole. In the case of both, Richard's Parliament is interesting. The first Private Bill was known as *Titulus Regius* and detailed Richard's title to the crown.[13] The Bill claimed to be a recitation of 'a Rolle of Perchement, conteignyng in writeing certeine Articles of the tenour undre writen, on the behalve and in the name of the thre Estates of this Reame of Englond'. The implication is that *Titulus Regius* was a reproduction of the petition presented to Richard at Baynard's Castle in June 1483 requesting him to take the throne, and there is little reason to doubt that it would be the same. The need to reiterate the details is explained as 'forasmoch as neither the said three Estats, neither the said personnes, which in thair name presented and delivered, the said Rolle unto oure said Souverain Lord the King, were assembled in fourme of Parliament; by occasion wherof, diverse doubts, questions and ambiguitees, been moved and engendred in the myndes of diverse personnes.'[14] The requirement for parliamentary approval of a king's title more likely came from that body than Richard, though the desire to solidify his right was made obvious by the events of a few months earlier.

The Act then launches into a stinging assault on Edward IV and his reign, during which 'such as had the rule and governaunce of this Land, delitying in adulation and flattery, and lede by sensuality and concupiscence, followed the counsaill of personnes insolent, vicious, and of inordinate avarice.'[15] The primary charge related to Edward's 'ungracious pretensed Marriage' to Elizabeth Woodville, because the king 'was and stode maryed and trouth plight to oone Dame Elianor Butteler, Doughter of the old Earl of Shrewesbury.'[16] This impediment meant that Edward's children were illegitimate, and because George's children were still barred from succession by their father's attainder, the crown fell naturally to Richard. There remains some question of the validity of Parliament's jurisdiction, but this method of accession was supported by precedent and Parliament itself, keen to build on the power it had been accruing, was happy to act as arbiter of the title of kings.

Next, Parliament addressed the lands and estates of the Duchy of Exeter. Here, it is possible to see Richard's preoccupation with the idea of legitimacy and the rule of law, particularly the rectifying of Edward's tampering. He had already made John Howard Duke of Norfolk, to undo the removal of that inheritance from the correct line of succession. The Exeter case related to Richard's oldest sister Anne, who had died in 1476. Anne had been married at a young age to Henry Holland, Duke of Exeter, a recalcitrant Lancastrian who had opposed the House of York from the earliest stages of the Wars of the Roses despite York being his father-in-law, and would die on the voyage back from France in 1475. The couple became estranged in 1464, and after the readeption, their marriage was annulled. Around 1474, Anne married again, to Sir Thomas St Ledger, a knight with close ties to Edward IV. St Ledger took part in the October uprisings against Richard, and when they failed, he was captured and executed. St Ledger was amongst those household men of Edward IV who chose not to work with Richard III, and his betrayal might well have been deemed by the king as more serious and personal as the widower of Richard's sister.

The Act detailed how St Ledger had married Anne 'by sediciouse meanes'[17] and gone on to secure interests in the Exeter lands for their daughter, Anne St Ledger, to which she was not entitled. Thomas had petitioned Edward IV in a previous Parliament to grant lands, titles and incomes from the Duchy of Exeter to his daughter Anne, and Edward had agreed. This was done, the Act insisted, despite the fact that Anne St Ledger 'was not enheritable, nor for other greate causes and consideriations entitled in right nor in conscience'. In Edward IV's last Parliament in early 1483, Thomas had petitioned the king again to allow part of the Exeter inheritance to be assigned to Sir Richard Grey, the king's stepson.

Edward had agreed once more. These acts were undone, and the Duchy of Exeter lands were taken into Crown hands. Richard effectively took away the lands and titles of his niece Anne St Ledger on the basis that she had no legal right to them. In this, he was, technically, correct. None of the Exeter inheritance was Richard's sister's, so she could not legitimately pass it on to her daughter. Richard's real aims in this are obscured, but critical to understanding what he was trying to achieve.

There was no need to worry about Sir Richard Grey's interests in any lands. He had been executed in June 1483. Anne and Thomas were dead, and Anne St Ledger was a child of eight. Much of Richard's rhetoric around Edward's performance as king focussed on not only the illegitimacy of his marriage and children but also of his actions. It is possible to see a desperate power grab in the south-west by Richard, except that legitimacy and justice had always been primary amongst his concerns. In 1484, a cynical nod to other illegal actions of Edward's would serve an agenda, but long before that, as Duke of Gloucester, Richard had exhibited time and again a deep and apparently genuine concern for justice and equity. It was this that perhaps made the revelations of 1483, if he had not invented them himself, so shocking, decisively breaking Edward's dynasty with no hope of recovery. Legitimacy was an incontrovertible absolute: either one was, or one was not. Richard was now in a position to unpick all the wrongs he had watched his brother sew together, as though they had gnawed at him for years. These were not the false concerns and actions for public consumption of a desperate usurper. Richard had been working for years to prevent the kinds of injustices his brother had been perpetrating.

Parliament next turned its attention to the attainting of the principal figures of the October 1483 uprisings.[18] Henry Stafford, Duke of Buckingham, was at the head of the line, even though he was already dead. His son was now disinherited by attainder. It is here that the construct of Buckingham as leader of a single, unified conspiracy is enshrined in law, much as Guy Fawkes would become the public face of the Gunpowder Plot more than a century later. Fawkes was captured and made a spectacle of. Buckingham was caught and executed while others who might, in reality, have posed more of a threat, or at least a different strand of opposition, had evaded capture. Their diminished part gave the appearance that they were negligible threats.

Three bishops were amongst the list of traitors.[19] John Morton, Bishop of Ely, is no surprise. He was credited with turning Buckingham and had escaped to the Continent. Lionel Woodville, Bishop of Salisbury, had been identified early in the affair when his lands had been forfeited. Peter Courtenay, Bishop of Exeter, was also included for his part in stirring up rebellion in the south-west. The three prelates were stripped of all their temporal offices and estates, but the Act appeared to be lenient with them, 'howbeit that the said Bishopps, for their greate and haynous Offenses before remembred, have deserved to lose Lyfe, Land, and Goodes.'[20] Despite the sentences due, because they were bishops, 'set in greate Estate in the Church of God' they were to be spared 'rigorouse punysshement'. The apparent compassion was due to 'the Kyng preferryng mercy and pitee before rigour', but Richard could certainly afford to appear generous in this case, even if he did not want to be. Bishops were protected by benefit of clergy, a right to be tried by an ecclesiastical court rather than a secular one. The benefit lay in the lax justice and punishments that could be expected, and the right meant that the three bishops lay beyond Richard's jurisdiction. That is not to say that action by the monarch was impossible; Thomas Becket may have been killed on Henry II's orders in 1170, though he denied it, and Henry IV had Richard Scrope, Archbishop of York, executed in 1405 after his part in a northern uprising. It would have been exceptional if Richard had laid a death sentence on the heads of these men, but he is often portrayed as an exceptionally vicious and vengeful man. The truth is that in this case, he could appear merciful when, in fact, he had little option. Apart from the benefit of clergy, none of the bishops was in his custody.

An entire Act of Attainder was then presented for a single person, one of the primary conspirators in the events of 1483; Lady Margaret Beaufort.[21] In contrast to the general effort to portray Buckingham as the prime mover, Richard could not entirely ignore Henry Tudor's part or the threat that he continued to pose. Margaret was described as 'Countesse of Richmond, Mother to the Kyngs greate Rebell and Traytour, Herry Erle of Richemond' and was accused of having 'conspired, considered, and committed high Treason'. Margaret's guilt was asserted 'in especiall in sendyng messages, writyngs and tokens to the said Henry, desiryng, procuryng and stirryng hym by the same, to come into this Roialme, and make Were ayenst oure said Soveraigne Lorde.'[22] The prescribed punishment for treason of being hung, drawn and quartered applied only to men, but there was a punishment in place for women who committed this crime; burning at the stake. Attainders were brought in the safe knowledge of a conviction, just as Edward had brought his against George. All of the rebels were convicted without question, and the Bishops only escaped because they were men of the Church. It seems likely that Margaret had been co-ordinating the effort to bring about her son's invasion and claim to the throne in England. Her Beaufort inheritance made her wealthy and influential, and her husband, Thomas Stanley, was the engine of a north-western powerhouse that could bring thousands of men to a battlefield. Henry had pledged to marry Elizabeth of York and take the crown at Rennes on Christmas Day, reiterating rather than abandoning his plan. It would be madness to show leniency to the plot's critical English connection.

The attainder against Margaret was denied by the king. This was rare, shocking and dangerous. Her guilt was not in doubt, yet Richard chose to refrain from punishing her for her actions. This, the Act stated, was 'of his grace especiall, remembryng the good and feithfull service that Thomas Lord Stanley hath doon, and entendeth to doo'.[23] The king exercised his right to be merciful to the one high-ranking participant in the revolt who was still alive and within his reach. It was an astonishing act of political self-harm that is hard to explain. Lord Stanley was in favour, as his role at the coronation demonstrates, but it seems impossible that he was not at least suspected of involvement in his wife's schemes. The reasoning offered by the Act implies that Thomas had petitioned the king for mercy and promised either specific or general demonstrations of his own continued loyalty, and Richard had accepted his pledges without reservation. Given Thomas's personal track record over the course of the civil war, it is hard to see why this would have been appealing to Richard. The two men had butted heads in the north-west fifteen years earlier, though most recently they had worked together successfully during the Scottish campaign. Richard's willingness to blindly trust the words of those he had reason to suspect is a serious flaw in his character. He seemed prepared to believe them and wait for them to disprove his faith, which is a dangerous game for a king to play.

Nevertheless, Richard 'remitteth and woll forbere the greate punysshement of atteynder of the said Countesse', primarily he said for the sake of Lord Stanley. Instead, it was enacted that Margaret would be 'dissabled in the lawe from hensforth to have, enherite or enjoye … Manours, Londs or Tenements' as well as 'to bere or have any name of estate or dignite'. Despite his earlier softness, Richard was still taking all of Margaret's lands and titles from her as if she had been attainted. He might have considered the measure in line with the way his brother had dealt with the Warwick inheritance, though this approach was out of step with his previously expressed concerns for justice and the laws of inheritance. It was something of a compromise that prevented the uncomfortable and novel situation of executing a noble lady. It is perhaps ironic that it was Margaret's grandson who would make that shocking possibility seem almost normal. Having seized all of Margaret's property, Richard did not add it to the Crown's estates for his own enrichment. Instead, he gave them all to her husband, Lord Stanley, for his lifetime, after which they would revert to the Crown.[24] The effect was to leave Margaret in much the same situation as she had been previously, but to disinherit her son, giving him no access to her wealth and influence to threaten Richard further. It was a deeply inelegant and unsatisfactory solution. It left Margaret able to carry on her schemes as before and made Thomas Stanley even more powerful in his own right. The only explanation is that it might have represented a direct challenge to Stanley, forcing him to pick a side and either support Richard or expose his own treachery by allowing his wife to use Stanley's resources to continue her treason. If so, the possibility that Stanley might smile to Richard's face while passing Margaret a knife with which to stab him in the back seems to have eluded the trusting Richard.

The remainder of the Private Bills dealt with matters such as the return of lands to the Archbishop of Canterbury, wrongly taken by a William Calleway.[25] Two of Richard's most loyal supporters were able to make use of their new connection to royal authority. Francis, Viscount Lovell, was granted the correction of a fine against his family that dated back more than a century to the reign of Edward II.[26] James Tyrell was successful in gaining the return of lands that he claimed belonged to his wife Anne but had previously been granted to William de la Pole, the Duke of Suffolk, murdered in 1450. The other Private Bill was a reward for an associate of Richard's, but it was to prove another misjudgement. Henry Percy, Earl of Northumberland, was granted the return of all Percy lands that had been forfeited during the family's rebellion against Henry IV and not yet returned.[27] The rehabilitation of the Percy family begun by Edward IV when he gave the earldom to Henry was completed. There was some sense in this. If Percy loyalty to the House of York was to be maintained, then a steady drip of rewards was the way to do it. There was a whiff of a Lancastrian scent to Henry Tudor's plans and the Percy family had, throughout the Wars of the Roses, remained staunchly Lancastrian. Richard had worked with the earl during his time in the north too, so there was a personal connection to be maintained that would help Richard retain influence in the farthest reached of his kingdom.

The miscalculation, in this case, was believing Northumberland would see nothing more in the gift. The Percy family had rebelled against Henry IV, but remained loyal to Henry VI, a fact that owed more to their regional feud with the Neville family who became associated with the House of York than a blind devotion to the Lancastrian cause. The growth in Neville influence in the north, culminating in John Neville taking the Percy title of Earl of Northumberland, had pressed the Percy family down. As Neville favour slipped and floundered, they had been given a second chance, providing Edward with a regional balance to Neville power. After Warwick and his family were gone, Northumberland probably expected the return to regional dominance that he felt his family deserved and had previously enjoyed, only to find his toes firmly stepped on by Richard's arrival. With Richard now forced to base himself further south, or at least to be away from the north more than he was there if he planned a mobile court, Northumberland finally saw the chance to take back his birthright as the senior nobleman in the region. The restoration of the remainder of his inheritance can only have fuelled that expectation. Richard would soon demonstrate that this was not his intention, and having built up Northumberland's hopes, they would be dashed by the creation of the Council of the North.

Public Bills provided the meat of the work of Parliament that would affect the populace. History is generally unanimous in acclaiming them as positive and well-founded but is divided as to where the credit should be placed. Some of the Acts directly benefitted the Chancellor by lightening the workload passing across his desk, but each should be considered in the light of Richard's previous commitments. In no other medieval Parliament is the input of the monarch questioned as much as it is of the 1484 sitting. No one doubts who was behind the Reformation Parliament and the split with Rome fifty years later, and there is perhaps a lingering unwillingness in some quarters to allow Richard any credit for anything on the basis that he *may* have been evil in other aspects of his life.

One of the most famous Acts of this Parliament was the abolition of benevolences, the system of forced gifts that Edward IV had exploited since 1475 to help him avoid taxation via Parliament. The impositions were described as 'new and unlawful inventions' born of 'inordinate covetise' that had caused the country to be 'put to great thraldom'.[28] The invention had forced donations from subjects 'against their wills and freedoms' to their 'almost utter destruction'. The Act went on to forbid the imposition of benevolences or any similar, arbitrary tax.

> Therefore the King will it be ordained, by the advice and assent of the lords spiritual and temporal, and the commons, of this present parliament assembled, and by authority of the same, That his subjects, and the commonalty of his realm, from henceforth in no wise be charged by none such charge, exaction, or imposition, called a benevolence, nor by any such like charge; and that such exactions, called benevolences, before this time taken, be taken for no example to make such or any like charge of any of his said subjects of this realm hereafter, but it shall be damned and adnulled for ever.[29]

This measure would undoubtedly be popular with Parliament and anyone in the country with money to be exacted. It was the equivalent of H.M.R.C. being able to appear on your doorstep and demand thousands of pounds with no explanation or assessment and no choice but to pay or be ruined. There are reasons to believe that Richard was involved in the abolition of benevolences. They were inequitable and indiscriminate, and these are things he had worked against during his time in the north, promoting justice. The move would also serve to demonstrate to Parliament that Richard meant to live within his means, to be financially responsible in a way that his brother had shunned, a commitment that would play well with Parliament. A return to structured taxation also gave Parliament back its power to insist on reforms in return for grants, a rebalancing of a relationship that Edward had not been interested in. Taxation was the traditional carrot used to bring about reforms from a monarch, and Richard was not only reinstating that agreement but also demonstrating that he was willing to operate within that framework. The long-term impact can be seen during Henry VIII's reign when Wolsey reportedly tried to exact a benevolence for the king and was reminded that Richard III had abolished them.[30] The willingness to bolster parliamentary authority at the expense of his own independence is diametrically opposed to accusations that Richard was a tyrant.

The bulk of other Public Bills can broadly be divided into those that deal with matters of trade and those that address issues of justice. There was an Act to deal with the length and breadth of cloth and the dying thereof. A petition to the king complained that products were 'imperfect and decyvably wrought', failing to keep the proper sizes.[31] This substandard cloth, made cheaper by skimping on the process and sizing, was endangering genuine merchants and the entire industry. The response was to alter the law so that it could no longer be sold 'unless the same cloth be before fully watered' and met strict size requirements, being 'in length twenty four yards, and to every yard an inch, containing the breadth of a man's thumb.'[32] The rest of the Act laid down strict guidelines relating to treatment and sale of cloth that were welcomed by merchants who felt they were being undercut by shoddy, low-quality merchandise.

Restrictions on the activities of foreign merchants were equally popular, and draconian measures were taken in support of English trades and traders. A ban introduced by Edward IV on the import of lace and silk was confirmed and extended for a further ten years.[33] A whole list of produce was banned from import by foreign merchants too, further protecting domestic trades. These were 'girdlers, pointmakers, pinners, pursers, glovers, cutlers, bladesmiths, blacksmiths, spurriers, goldbeaters, painters, saddlers, lorimers, founders, cardmakers, capmakers, wiremongers, weavers, horners, bottlemakers and coppersmiths.'[34]

Italian merchants were singled out for particular attention, probably due to their increasing success. They 'keep houses, as well in the city of London, as in other cities and boroughs.'[35] Outrageously, they filled warehouses with their goods and dared to go on to sell them, often at high prices. The response was to financially cripple Italian merchants operating within England. They were required to sell all of their goods at wholesale rather than retail price to English citizens before 1 May 1485. With the proceeds of these sales, they were to be forced to buy English goods at English ports or forfeit their money.[36] Italians were to be strictly forbidden from involvement in the wool or cloth trades within England[37] and barred from taking on any employee who was not an English subject.[38]

These measures are shocking, isolationist and xenophobic, but they were precisely what the Commons asked for on behalf of English merchants to inject growth into their businesses. One significant exclusion was made to all of the restrictions placed on foreign merchants.

> Provided always that this act, or any part therof, or any other act made or to be made in this said parliament shall not extend or be in prejudice, disturbance, damage, or impediment to any artificer, or merchant stranger, of what nation or country he be or shall be of, for bringing into this realm or selling be retail or otherwise, any books written or printered, or for inhabiting within this said realm or the same intent, or any scrivener, alluminor, reader, or printer of such books, which he hath or shall have to sell by way of merchandise, or for their dwelling within this said realm for the exercise of the said occupations.[39]

The book trade was explicitly and completely excluded from the restrictions placed on foreign merchants, suggesting that it was to be fostered and encouraged instead. Caxton was, by now, well established in London with his printing press, but there was no protection offered to English subjects within this sphere. Richard was a bookish man. He maintained an extensive library, which might simply have been a display of wealth, but several of them show signs of use or writing in Richard's own hand, implying at least that this was of personal interest to him as king. A desire to spread books and writing is not something a tyrant would willingly support, since the spread of ideas and news was the enemy of such rulers.

The Lombards of northern Italy were singled out even more for the attentions of Parliament. Another petition from the Commons described how 'the seditious confederacy of the Lombards'[40] had led to the import of bow staves at vastly inflated prices, costing £8 per 100 instead of the old cost of 40s. Not only were the prices being driven up, but the Lombards, it was claimed, mixed in inferior quality staves with their wares so that 'by likelihood in short time this realm is like to fail as well of stuff of artillery, as of workmen therof'.[41] This, the Commons insisted, was a matter of national security. For centuries, English armies had relied on longbowmen, and they had become feared and envied across Europe. Imports of low-quality goods threatened the country's ability to put an effective force in the field and endangered the skills involved in producing these fearsome weapons. Security was of prime importance, and as an experienced military man, Richard would have plainly understood the value of archers with good, strong bows. Parliament countered this threat by insisting that for every butt of malmsey or tyre imported, a merchant must bring ten bowstaves of suitable quality. Failure to do so would result in a fine of 13s 4d for every unaccompanied barrel of wine.

Another petition sought to address the issue of incorrect measures, and Richard allowed that no barrel of wine was to be imported unless it was assessed and met the old measure of 1 butt, being 126 gallons.[42] All these trade measures were highly preferential to English merchants and would have been very popular in the wider country, protecting trades and tradesmen as well. There is some evidence that the steps were in line with Richard's attitude as Duke of Gloucester when he had secured tax concessions for the region and tried to establish a Continental presence that would allow northern merchants to rival those of London in Europe. Edward had blocked that proposal for fear of upsetting the southern mercantile community, but Richard had shown previous concern for tradesmen and merchants.

There is a possibility that these measures expose a grander plan on Richard's part. It is striking that he made no new creations of nobility during his reign apart from his son and heir. Howard had become Duke of Norfolk, but that was more about correcting an abuse of the laws of inheritance. Edward IV's second reign had seen a dramatic slow-down in the creation of earls that Richard seems happy to have continued. Despite his own lack of regional influence in the south and west, and even the Midlands, he did not set up any loyal supporter as a representative. This policy was largely followed by Henry VII too, with a few exceptions and there may have been a realisation after thirty years of civil strife that the nobility and their capacity to gather vast and threatening wealth and landed interests lay at the core of the problem. Richard had always shown an interest in bolstering and supporting the lower levels of society, and he had perhaps developed a distaste for the attitudes of most noble families that was only reinforced by his painful and potentially disastrous experience with Buckingham. If the nobility were to be stripped of their authority, the vacuum would need to be filled, and Richard may have seen the merchant class as the perfect foil. Hard-working, self-made men who got as far as their talents could take them might serve the country better than those deposited there by an accident of birth, whatever their abilities, or lack thereof, might have warranted. Time for any such plan was cut short, but when Henry VII came to the throne, there was no wholesale rejuvenation of the ranks of the nobility. He, perhaps, took up the baton dropped by Richard and shared the view that the old nobility's time was up.

The remainder of Parliament's significant Acts dealt with justice, a matter that had always been close to Richard's heart and at the forefront of his mind. Secret enfeoffments were a widespread problem exploited by unscrupulous sellers of land. A buyer could purchase a piece of land or property in good faith, believing they held full title to it, only to discover later that there were restrictions or other claims on the land. The buyer had paid a price to buy the land outright, but could then find themselves owning only a small interest in the property. This led to 'great unsurety, trouble, costs, and grievous vexations' in the country that Parliament now sought to address. A buyer's title was to be 'good and effectual' in the event of deception, and the burden of disclosure was placed onto the seller.[43] This measure would help reduce the flood of complaints clogging up the Chancellor's office, but it is also in line with Richard's previous attitude toward equity, suggesting that he was heavily involved in ensuring these matters were directly and effectively addressed.

The rooting out of corruption lay at the heart of another legal reform relating to bail. Richard III did not, as is sometimes claimed, invent bail. The system that allowed prisoners to be released if they provided surety that they would not abscond before their trial was mentioned as early as 1275 in the Statute of Westminster. Since then, the system had been addressed and reformed several times, and would continue to be refined and corruption tackled after Richard's reign. However, the specific reforms enacted by Richard's Parliament were significant, particularly for those most likely to be victims of abuse of the system; the common man.

Forasmuch as divers persons have been daily arrested and imprisoned for suspicion of felony, sometime of malice, and sometime of a light suspicion, and so kept in prison without bail or mainprise, to their great vexation and trouble: Be it ordained and established by authority of this present parliament, That every justice of peace in every shire, city, or town, shall have authority and power, by his or their discretion, to let such prisoners and persons so arrested, to bail or mainprise, in like form as though the same prisoners or persons were indicted thereof of record before the same justices in their sessions; and that justices of the peace have authority to enquire in their sessions of all manner escapes of every person arrested and imprisoned for felony. And that no sheriff, under-sheriff, nor eschaetor, bailiff of franchise, nor any other person, take or seise the goods of any person arrested or imprisoned for suspicion of felony, before that same person, so arrested and imprisoned, be convicted or attainted of such felony according to the law, or else the same goods otherwise lawfully forfeited; upon pain to forfeit the double value of the goods so taken, to him that is so hurt in that behalf.[44]

This reform is in two distinct parts. The first deals with cases in which local officials were arresting those accused of a crime, on evidence that was often very flimsy, and denying them bail. The implication was that corrupt officials were willing to use trumped-up charges to keep someone in prison on behalf of another party who offered a bribe. This was something fundamentally at odds with Richard's idea of the application of justice, and his Parliament took steps to prevent it by empowering justices to provide bail where it had been improperly denied.

The second portion of the amendment to bail law is equally significant. The seizure of property was no longer to be permitted until an accused person was convicted of a crime. It would appear that goods and property were being taken at the time of arrest and possibly never returned, depending on the level of corruption in operation. These might be the tools of a trade or everything a poor man had in the world, so a false charge might lead to his ruin even if he wasn't convicted. Corruption and bribery were a part of this problem too and Richard tackled it head-on. Anyone who seized the goods of an accused person before they were convicted was now liable for a fine of double the value of the things they had illegally taken. This reform is something taken entirely for granted ever since, but it was an essential contribution to the provision of equality of justice for ordinary people.

One measure that might sound unjust and inequitable to a modern ear is the rules established by Richard's Parliament relating to jury composition. The preamble to this Act explained that 'great inconveniencies and perjuries do daily happen in divers shires of England by untrue verdicts given in inquisitions and enquiries before sheriffs in their turns, by persons of no substance nor behaviour, not dreading God nor the world's shame.'[45] Those who sat on juries were prone to bribery and intimidation where they lacked any money of their own or found themselves sitting on a case in which a local worthy had an interest. The result of this was the returning of faulty verdicts that defied the evidence, another issue that would ring clear in Richard's mind. From this Parliament onwards, jurors were to hold freehold land within the same county as the court was sitting worth at least 20s a year, or copyhold worth 26s 8d per year. Those appointing jurors would be fined 40s for each unqualified person that sat on a jury. Today, it is the right of all citizens to qualify for jury duty, but clearly, in 1484, it was considered a problem that undermined justice. Richard's response was a practical and effective one, since those who were financially stable were far less likely to be bribed or easily frightened.

Another Act dealt with the regulation of the powers of the Court of Piepowders, those sessions attached to local fairs.[46] New restrictions were placed on the authority of these courts, which frequently sat beyond the times of the fair and unjustly exacted fines. Anyone failing to abide by the rules was subject to a penalty of 100s. One Act sought to reinstate the announcement of those subject to fines that had taken place in the time of Edward I but since been allowed to slip. The Church received some practical backing from Richard's Parliament, too, when it was pointed out that the provinces of Canterbury and York were frequently tricked and bullied into making payments to the Exchequer that were not due.[47] They insisted that whenever they granted a tax to the Crown, the representatives of the provinces would appear before the Barons of the Exchequer to make payment only to be charged with other fees and claims. It was enacted that from that point forward when a dismes tax was delivered by either province, the Barons of the Exchequer were forbidden to bring unrelated matters before them.

The final entry in the statute book was brief: 'A resumption of all grants, and estates of land, etc made to Elizabeth Grey late Queen of England.'[48] The fact of Edward IV's bigamy was legally established and enshrined in law. The jurisdictional issue was not raised, and the decision was widely accepted, passing through Parliament unchallenged. Edward V and his siblings were illegitimate, and Richard was the rightful King of England. For a man concerned by the meaning of the scoliosis that had been given him by God, it can only have been a blessed relief to find himself at the pinnacle of the temporal world, appointed by God to rule over England. This also marks the closest the House of York would come to delivering the promises made by Richard's father and largely ignored by his brother. Yorkist popularity in the 1450s had grown from a belief that it offered reformation, equity and even a return to a more aggressive policy against France. By the time Parliament closed, Richard had promised to live within his means, to work with the Lords and Commons in Parliament, brought about legal reforms that benefitted those at the bottom of society's ladder and corrected abuses of the laws of inheritance. Although many would, of necessity, plead later that they had never liked or supported Richard III, it is hard to see evidence of that in early 1484. Richard had begun to address problems that had cost Edward his throne in 1470 and distanced the Crown from Parliament as the representatives of the people of the nation. If Richard's measures were unpopular, it was surely only with the higher nobility and corrupt officials who found themselves losing power and authority. As it began to drip down to the lower rungs, it was necessarily diminished at the top. It was perhaps a realisation of this that helped those household officers of Edward IV who rebelled in the autumn of 1483 to make up their mind. If they profited from loose regulation, and it was about to be tightened, their interests were suddenly at odds with the Crown's. The problem remained whether enough reform could be implemented before the nobility and those deprived officials reacted.

Almost as soon as Parliament wound up, Richard achieved another stunning victory that has defied satisfactory explanation for centuries. On 1 March, Elizabeth Woodville sent her daughters out of sanctuary and into the care of their uncle, Richard. It is not recorded whether Elizabeth herself emerged at the same moment, but there is no further reference to her remaining in sanctuary, so it seems likely that she did. Crowland insisted that the former queen had done this only after 'frequent entreaties as well as threats had been made use of' and because she was 'strongly solicited to do so'.[49] The traditional belief has been that Elizabeth was forced to confront the reality of her indefinite status in sanctuary, with no hope of rehabilitation, particularly if her sons by Edward IV were dead. Even if this was the case, or at least she still believed they were dead based on the rumours of the 1483 uprising relayed by Dr Caerleon, it is a hard decision to understand. Elizabeth would be in no doubt that Richard was capable of killing her children – he had ordered the execution of her second son, Sir Richard Grey, the previous summer. If she also believed he had killed his own nephews, how could she possibly justify sending her daughters to him, even if the only option was to remain in sanctuary? It is incorrect that she lacked hope. Henry Tudor was still pledged to Elizabeth of York and was planning another bid for Richard's throne.

Something must have changed, but Elizabeth Woodville would not release her daughters before she obtained a public oath from Richard to care for them. On 1 March 1484, the king stood and gave his promise before the gathered crowd.

Memorandum that I Richard by the grace of god king of England and of Fraunce and lord of Irland in the presens of you my lords spirituelle & temporelle and you Maire & Aldermen of my Cite of London promitte & swere verbo Regio & upon these holy evangelies of god by me personelly touched that if the doughters of dam Elizabeth Gray late calling he self Quene of England that is to wit Elizabeth Cecile Anne Kateryn and Briggitte wolle come unto me out of the Saintwarie of Westminstre and be guyded Ruled & demeaned after me than I shalle see that they shalbe in suertie of their lyffes and also not suffre any maner hurt by any maner persone or persones to theim or any of theim in their bodies and persones to be done by wey of Ravisshement or defouling contrarie their willes nor theim or any of them emprisone within the Toure of London or other prisone but that I shalle put theim in honest places of good name & fame and theim honestly & curtesly shalle see to be foundene & entreated and to have alle thinges requisite & necessarye for their exibicione and findinges as my kynneswomen. And that I shalle do marie suche of theim as now bene mariable to gentilmen borne and everiche of theim geve in mariage landes & tenementes to the yerely valewe of CC marc for terme of their lyves and in like wise to the other doughters when they come to lawfulle Age of mariage if they lyff and such gentilmen as shalle happe to marie with theim I shalle straitly charge from tyme to tyme lovyngly to love and entreate theim as their wiffes & my kynneswomen As they wolle advoid and ashue my displeaure. And over this that I shalle yerely fromhensfurthe content & pay or cause to be contented & paied for thexibicione & finding of the said dame Elizabeth Gray during her naturelle liff at iiii termes of the yere that is to wit at pasche Midsomer Michilmesse & Christenmesse to

John Nesfilde one of the quires for my body for his finding to attende upon her the summe of DCC marc of lawfulle money of England by even porcions. And moreover I promitte to theim by any persone or persones that than I shalle not geve therunto faithe ne credence nor therefore put theim to any maner ponysshement before that they or any of theim so accused may be at their lawfulle defence and answere. In witnesse wherof to this writing of my othe & promise aforsaid in your said presences made I have set my signemanuelle the first day of Marche the first yere of my Reigne.[50]

The fact that Richard was compelled to make this public statement has been cited as evidence that he must have murdered his nephews because Elizabeth was so terrified of giving him custody of her daughters. The fact that she was willing to release them suggests that she cannot have believed he did it, because if he would kill two of her sons in cold blood, no oath would prevent him from slaughtering her daughters too. It seems far more plausible that negotiations had been going on for some time and that the statement reflects Elizabeth's legitimate fears from the seclusion of her sanctuary. The emergence of her daughters would make far more sense if Richard had been able to provide her with proof of his innocence. That may mean that they were dead, but Elizabeth was satisfied that it was not by the king's hand, or that they were still alive. If the stories reaching her at Westminster Abbey had been exposed as tricks to get her agreement to Tudor marrying her oldest daughter, or if she had believed the uprising was still in favour of her sons, then she may finally have been given access to the truth. Certainly, something changed and convinced her that her daughters were not under any serious threat from their uncle.

If Richard was looking to give Elizabeth proof, the date of 1 March makes perfect sense. The autumn uprisings had been successfully crushed, and Parliament had just closed after legalising Richard's title and the attainder of the rebels. Only now was Richard legally (as far as precedent allows legality to be established) king and equally his nephews rendered incapable of inheritance. The one threat that remained beyond Richard's grasp was Henry Tudor, who was still promising to marry Elizabeth's oldest daughter and take the throne. There could be no better propaganda coup to whip the rug from under that plot than getting Edward IV's daughters back to court, publicly displaying their reconciliation with Richard. If Richard remained fearful or even paranoid, then his nieces were a menace. One of them was the focus of a worrying plot to unseat him. By this point, Elizabeth of York was just as much of a threat as her brothers had been, so if Richard felt obligated to kill his nephews, that compulsion would have transferred directly to their sister. The need for such an explicit oath may also owe much to Elizabeth Woodville's own experiences during the Wars of the Roses. Her father and one of her brothers had been executed by Warwick, her marriage had been declared bigamous, her oldest brother and second son had been beheaded, her oldest son was on the run, and the fates of her two princes were unknown. Her caution is natural.

An old Tyrell family story tells how Sir James Tyrell hosted Elizabeth Woodville and her children at Gipping Hall after she emerged from sanctuary. It holds that Richard arranged regular contact between them and that Sir James later became embroiled in their story as their murderer because of the kernel of truth the association could be built around.[51] Unless some certain proof had been given to Elizabeth of the safety of Edward and Richard, her dispatches of messages to Thomas Grey, Marquis of Dorset, her oldest son in exile with Henry Tudor, defy belief. Elizabeth urged her son to abandon Henry and return to England, where she assured him the king would treat him well and forgive him. What could possibly have compelled a mother to write such a letter if not the realisation that Richard had never been a threat to his nieces or his nephews? For Richard, his position could now be enhanced by Dorset's return, a defection that might open the floodgates, hurrying along the restoration of his authority and the diminution of Tudor's threat. As it was, Dorset tried to leave, only to find himself stopped and returned to Henry's faux court, which grew in size and confidence as time passed.

This point marks a pinnacle of Richard's rule. He had seen off an attempt to depose him, used Parliament to confirm the legitimacy of his reign, provided laws that benefitted the populace and brought about the reconciliation of the former queen and her daughters. The future looked bright to the thirty-one-year-old Richard, but clouds began to gather above him that would leave the rest of his life in shadow.

19

The Cords of Death

I ask you, most gentle Lord Jesus Christ to keep me, thy servant King Richard, and defend me from all evil, from the devil and from all perils, past and to come, and deliver me from all tribulation, sorrows and troubles in which I am placed

A personal prayer of Richard III[1]

The first few months of 1484 were proving triumphant for Richard as he set about putting his agenda for government into operation. He was as secure, legally, as he could hope to be, internal unrest appeared to have subsided, and although Henry Tudor was attracting support in Brittany, it was not in the numbers or quality of men to pose a real threat. It was something that would need to be dealt with, but there were diplomatic levers that might yet be arranged carefully to end that problem. Richard saw much work to be done at home that kept him busy.

The king called together all of his justices in the Star Chamber at Westminster and set before them three real legal issues. They were sophisticated matters that asked what constituted a violation of the law and hinted at the part justices had to play in making sure the law was not circumvented or misused. One of the cases was reviewed in light of a statute of 1429, and the justices were asked in each case what the correct outcome should have been. Where it did not match the original result, they were set to work putting it right. The third case related to the incorrect deletion of convictions against John Barret, who claimed that the real villain was, in fact, a William Barret. John Barret found himself outlawed, as he should have been, and four men involved in the erasure of the records in Middlesex were hauled before King's Bench, where Richard sat in person to hear them confess and receive a fine and a sentence of imprisonment until the fine was paid. The man responsible for the London end of the legal mess was tried at the Guildhall and found guilty of misprision, the wilful concealment of a felony.[2]

Why Richard decided to undertake this detailed review of three specific cases before all of his justices can only be inferred. The correct application of the law had been an obsession of Richard's for years, and he appears keen to apply that commitment to the national stage. His own legal acumen had been commented upon, but by extracting three specific cases, he was able to make it plain to the justices that he was, at the minutest level, watching what they were doing and that he expected them to apply the law fairly and rigorously. If they understood that he was capable of pulling them up on the most complex questions of law, they might be discouraged from the kind of petty crookedness or turning of blind eyes that facilitated unfairness. Furthermore, they would see that in setting it right, those involved, if they had acted corruptly, could expect the full weight of the law to bear down on them, in Richard's person, where warranted. The matter was concluded by the king telling his justices 'this is the King's will to wit, to say "by his justices" and "by his law" is one and the same thing.'[3] Corruption was no longer acceptable, the law was the law, and Richard would see it correctly enforced by his justices.

On 2 March 1484, Richard's interest in legitimacy was on display once more, either cynically, to reinforce his own trickery, or because it was a genuinely held fascination. As Constable of England for fourteen years, part of Richard's duty had been oversight of the heralds. The role of these officers had begun on the frontline of war, where they were responsible for agreeing and declaring to which side victory fell. Over time, they became ambassadors, and as tournaments erupted across Europe, their experience on the battlefield made them ideal arbiters of legitimacy and standing. They had become intimately familiar with family crests and banners to allow them to record and judge encounters, so when it came to establishing a pedigree for tournament entry, they were the natural officers to fulfil that function. As such, they had, over the decades and centuries, become experts in the family histories of the nobility and a resource for anyone attempting to establish their legitimacy as a knight or lord. Now, after his long association with them, Richard created the College of Arms that still survives today. On 2 March, he granted them letters patent that they 'shall form one corporate body and shall have perpetual succession and a common seal'. They were given lands worth £20 per year and a home at Cold Harbour on Upper Thames Street.[4]

Religious concerns marked the third strand of Richard's immediate policy, joining justice and legitimacy. On 10 March, the king wrote to all his bishops to explain what he expected of them in his new England. Richard wrote that amongst his plans to improve the state of the nation, 'our principal intent and fervent desire is to see virtue and cleanness of living to be advanced, increased and multiplied.' Alongside that, he wished 'vices and all other things repugnant to virtue, provoking the high indignation and fearful displeasure of God to be repressed and annulled'.

The bishops were the right place to begin because if it were 'put in execution by persons of high estate, pre-eminence and dignity', it 'not only induceth persons of lower degree to take therof example', but caused God to be 'placable and graciously inclined to the exaudition of petitions and prayers'. The letter continued

> We therefore will and desire you, and on God's behalf inwardly exhort and require you that, according to the charge of your profession, ye will see within the authority of your jurisdiction all such persons, as set apart virtue and promote the damnable execution of crime and vices, to be reformed, repressed, and punished condignly after their demerits; not sparing for any love, favour, dread, or affection, whether the offenders be spiritual or temporal. Wherein ye may be assured we shall give unto you our favour, aid, and assistance, (if the case shall so require) and see to the sharp punishment of the repugnators and interrupters hereof, if any such be. And, if ye will diligently apply you to the execution and performing of this matter, ye shall not only do unto God right acceptable pleasure; but, over that, we shall see such persons spiritual as been under your pastoral care none otherwise to be entreated or punished for their offences, but according to the ordinances and laws of Holy Church.[5]

There is something very straight-laced and sober in Richard's attitude to the religious life of his nation, but it was a demand for a return to the way his people should live. He had expected no less during the establishment of his college at Middleham several years earlier and was in a position now to extrapolate that same interest across the entire country. The bishops were reminded that their role was not only to nurture the good amongst their flock, but to reform, or punish if they would not be corrected, those who had wandered from the path. These people were to be sought out and confronted whatever protection their standing in society or their connections might have previously offered; 'not sparing for any love, favour, dread, or affection'. In return for this activity amongst both the clergy and their temporal flock, Richard constrained himself by promising to keep out of matters of ecclesiastical justice. He was offering to uphold the Right of Clergy and stay out of Church business in a way that would, just a few decades later, be utterly lost. For a man accused of tyranny, exempting a large section of society from his authority would be a strange decision.

Richard's pious attitude was at work when his own solicitor, Thomas Lynom, decided to try to marry Jane Shore, the former mistress of Edward IV, Hastings and Dorset and who was in Ludgate prison after her penance for harlotry. The king wrote to the Chancellor that Thomas was 'marvellously blinded and abused' by Mistress Shore. Richard told

Russell he was 'very sorry that he should be so disposed', asking the Chancellor to 'exhort and stir him to the contrary'. Despite his obvious displeasure that his solicitor should seek to marry a woman suspected of involvement in plots against the king, Richard did not block the wedding. He told Russell that if Lynom could not be dissuaded, and 'if it may stand with the law of the church, we be content.' He asked that the marriage wait until he was back in London and that Lynom find suitable security for Jane's release from prison, but otherwise, he did not stand in their way.[6] Richard was neither puritanical enough to refuse the marriage on the grounds of his own distaste nor sufficiently nervous of his own position to deny the request. In fact, the reference to a 'contract of matrimony' between the pair might be something Richard considered had to be binding, especially in light of his own accession the throne. Either way, he left the matter to the Church to decide rather than imposing his own authority where it did not belong. Richard cannot be accused of insisting others do as he says, whilst he does as he pleases.

These three examples demonstrate an approach to government in line with Richard's previous concerns. Legitimacy was a critical factor in all that he planned to do, and his policies were to be delivered by two prongs; the justices and the bishops. Between them, they were to root out evil and corruption, whether spiritual or juridical, and deal with it. There was no obvious space made for the role of the nobility in this worldview. If Richard considered them and the corruption their authority cultivated to be the source of the nation's problems, then his answer was to exclude them, to never rebuild their influence and to apply fairer principles. The justices were to answer directly to him, and the clergy would be left to their own devices for as long as they played their part. Parliament had bolstered the position in society of English merchants, and these were perhaps the three pillars upon which Richard looked to build a new England, free of corruption and based on fair access to justice for all. The bishops were encouraged to intervene with their temporal flock. The justices were warned to apply the law regardless of rank and influence. Merchants, if they flourished and prospered, would be the new financial powerhouse of the country so that the king would no longer be at the mercy of unreliable nobles to try to raise men and money. The balance Parliament expected between king and country was to be restored, and the nobility's influence would be allowed to wither and die. If Richard pursued this kind of policy, it was radical and progressive. He had never shied away from affronting those with a vested interest, but the problem remained that these were still powerful men, and they would not like the direction of travel of Richard's government.

Foreign policy continued to offer opportunities for Richard, particularly when Maximilian approached the king with a fresh idea for an offensive against France. Maximilian had lost control of Flanders and Burgundy after his wife's death but had been trying to regain it. In his lengthy instructions to his ambassador, he was careful not to characterise these setbacks as failures, only that he had withdrawn to save harming the population. Maximilian's envoy began by explaining his master's desire for an alliance with Richard. It was 'for the very great virtue and excellent virtues which are in his person, he is that prince of all Christian princes to whom my said lord has most love and affections, and with whom he desires most to ally and confederate himself.'[7] Richard seems to have let Maximilian know that he would be interested in resurrecting the old alliance against France, and including Brittany, if Duke Francis would surrender the English exiles within his territories. Maximilian was happy to negotiate such an arrangement if it would secure Richard's help.[8] England was asked for 6,000 archers to help in the recapture of Burgundy,[9] but in return, Maximilian would provide Richard with 14,000 men for two years and 6,000 after that for an invasion of France.[10]

It is against this backdrop, and that of France's own minority crisis and the threat that the Duke of Orleans would launch a bid for the throne that the speech made by Guillaume de Rochefort to the French States-General was given. Rochefort told the gathering in January 1484 the King Edward's 'children, already big and courageous, have been slaughtered with impunity, and their murderer, with the support of the people, has received the crown.'[11] The remainder of the speech detailed the horrific and barbaric history of England since the Conquest in an effort to inspire the French to resist the threat from England now that Richard was king. Mancini himself seems the likely source of the story since he and Rochefort were friends and were in the same place when Mancini wrote his account.[12] The Chancellor of France simply took the rumours and turned them into a compelling, stirring indictment of English brutality that would act as a warning to France, both about England and the Duke of Orleans. It is unlikely that the French Chancellor knew for certain what has eluded every enquiry for over 500 years and entirely plausible that it made a good scare story for him to use.

Early in 1484, Richard also concerned himself with providing for those close to him and who had supported him without fail. The king arranged a marriage between his illegitimate daughter Katherine and his friend William Herbert, Earl of Huntingdon. Herbert had been harshly treated by Edward IV and left all but impoverished by his move from the earldom of Pembroke to Huntingdon. In arranging the marriage, Richard doubled Herbert's annual income with an annuity of 1,000 marks and bound him closer to the Crown.[13] Men like Sir Richard Ratcliffe, Sir William Catesby, Sir Robert Brackenbury and Sir Edward Brampton continued to reap the rewards of their service in grants of land and income.[14]

More evidence of a commitment to the delivery of access to justice for the poor can be interpreted from Richard's appointment in December

1483 of James Harrington to act as a clerk responsible for the applications of the poor. Whether or not Richard began a system that would go on to be the Court of Requests, or whether he took something his brother had initiated and expanded it is unclear, but he certainly saw it as important. The Court would provide what would equate to an early form of legal aid, providing access to courts that would otherwise be beyond the reach of people who could not afford it.[15] His favour for this system is understandable, given his concern for this issue in the north.

It was not only those closely associated with Richard who were enjoying favour and rewards. Two of Lord Hastings' younger brothers were still in favour, Richard receiving an annuity of 100 marks on 22 May and Ralph the confirmation of his right to several offices in Northamptonshire that he had shared with his brother William on 10 August.[16] On 20 June, Katherine Woodville, the widowed Duchess of Buckingham, was given an annuity from the king of 200 marks. As a Woodville sister of the former queen and the wife of Henry Stafford, Richard had reason to shun her but chose instead to ensure that she was well provided for, which suggests no bitterness or vindictiveness on his part. Attempts to keep these individuals within the fold indicate a recognition of the need to rebuild royal influence and to stop more support leaking away to Henry Tudor in Brittany, but also that Richard did not hold a grudge against them for the actions of their family members.

One of Richard's enduring contributions during this year was the re-establishment of the Council of the North as an extension of his ducal council and a mechanism to ensure a robust royal presence. Edward IV had first created the institution in 1472, appointing Richard as its first Lord President. The Council would be continued by Henry VII and recreated by Henry VIII in the 1530s, lasting until 1641 when the Long Parliament ordered it to be disbanded. Richard, as was becoming his trademark, took care to personally draw up a constitution for the Council that doubtless drew on his own extensive knowledge of the region and its problems. The Council was to provide administration, security and justice throughout the area. The Council was to be made up of impartial men, not appointed 'for favor, affeccione, hate, malace or mede' and was to ensure that the king's law was maintained at all times. To avoid conflicts of interest, any member of the Council affected by a matter under discussion, or a case brought before it, was to leave the chamber during the investigation. There were to be gatherings of the whole Council at least four times a year 'and oftyner if the case require' at which any bills or complaints could be presented and deliberated upon. Whenever there was a disturbance of the peace, the Council was to act immediately to end the unrest, committing anyone involved to the nearest royal castle as their prison, only using a 'common gaole' if no castle was close, to await trial. A register was to be maintained of the Council's activities and decisions, signed and sealed by the most senior member of it, and Richard reserved the right to appoint 'certen lierned men' to attend the meetings to help ensure the law was being properly applied.

The Council was not an innovation of Richard's, but he doubtless knew the benefits that it offered. The region would have a steady source of reliable justice and administration, backed by the king, and providing it with a sense of unity with the rest of the realm that had always been lacking. At the same time, the Council gave the king a clear oversight of what was happening and how his designs and influence were being represented in the region. It was no less than the north would have hoped for from the first king considered to be a man of the region. After all of the tumult of 1483, the new year was panning out nicely for the king. Just as his plans got underway and he appeared to be rebuilding royal authority, personal and dynastic, disaster struck.

Around 9 April 1484, Edward of Middleham, Prince of Wales, and sole legitimate heir of Richard III and Anne Neville, died. He was aged around eight, and his state of health is uncertain, but this loss came as a shock to his distraught parents, suggesting there had been nothing bad enough to cause them to expect this. Richard had moved to Nottingham Castle in mid-March, probably a strategic decision in expectation of an invasion by Henry Tudor at the beginning of campaigning season. It may have been the beginning of another progress north to celebrate the success with which the year had begun, but whatever the plan, it was interrupted in the most heart-breaking way. Crowland, who shows little sympathy for the king, explains that Richard and Anne, 'hearing the news of this, at Nottingham, where they were residing, you might have seen his father and mother in a state almost bordering on madness, by reason of their sudden grief.'[17] It was a hammer blow, made all the more painful by the personal loss and the political catastrophe it represented. The grief of the couple was considered genuine, Crowland dropping all politics for a moment to simply refer to them as a father and a mother; in that moment they were not a king and queen, but parents whose child had been torn from them. Dynastically, it opened up a new set of wounds for Richard. He and Anne had only one child, and as the years had passed since Edward's birth, it must have become clear that there would be no more.

A primary responsibility of a king was to ensure the success of his dynasty, and Richard found himself suddenly without an heir. He had an illegitimate son and daughter, but given his obsession with legitimacy it is unlikely that he considered John or Katherine as his successors, and if he did, he would be forced to quickly discount it, given his insistence that Edward V was barred by illegitimacy. The Warwickshire antiquarian John Rous would insist that 'the young Earl of Warwick, Edward, eldest son of George Duke of Clarence, was proclaimed heir apparent in the royal court, and in ceremonies at table and chamber he was served first after the king and queen. Later he was placed in custody and the Earl of Lincoln was preferred to him.'[18] This is a difficult claim to unpick. Nowhere does any official document refer to Warwick being made Richard's heir, nor to Lincoln. John de la Pole, Earl of Lincoln, was Richard's oldest nephew, the son of his sister Elizabeth, Duchess of Suffolk. Warwick was the last of the male line of the House of York, but he remained barred by his father's attainder, which would need to be undone before he could be made heir.

The fact that Rous has the appointments made as 'heir apparent' would be incorrect, unless Richard was admitting that he never intended to have any more legitimate children of his own. The heir apparent was the indisputable heir, usually the oldest legitimate son. A person who fulfilled that role but could be displaced by the arrival of an heir apparent was the heir presumptive. Kings would not usually expressly appoint an heir presumptive; the entire purpose of their position was that they would be recognised in law if there was no heir apparent. Aside from Rous's claim, there is no record that Richard ever addressed the issue of who would be his successor if he died without another legitimate child. Primogeniture would favour Warwick, but his father's attainder still barred him. Lincoln was the next in legal order, his descent through a female line being no bar in England. Rous's assertions may have reflected the confusion and debate in the country as to who would now follow Richard, but there is no other evidence that Richard addressed the matter, publicly or privately. Grief aside, it would be more desirable to remain silent, especially while some hope of a new heir apparent remained.

As pressing once the grief subsided was the impact the loss of his heir would have on Richard's security and authority. One of the benefits of his kingship was being a settled, older couple with a growing young son to follow them. With that torn away, Richard had to cope with his and his wife's grief whilst dealing with the realisation that this would only bring concern to his supporters and encouragement to his enemies. The couple left Nottingham on 27 April to travel north, spending time at York, Middleham and Barnard Castle[19] as they tried to come to terms with their loss. The location of their son's burial is not recorded. For many years, a crumbling tomb at Sheriff Hutton Church was believed to have been Edward's, but it is now strongly suspected that this is an earlier tomb, perhaps of a Neville child.

The king remained in the north again throughout May, June and July.[20] It is in this context that Richard wrote to his mother about replacing Colyngbourne with Francis Lovell. Aside from the business, the emotion of a newly bereaved father appealing to his own mother for comfort rings loudly from the pages. Richard wrote to Cecily 'Beseching you in my most humble and effectuouse wise of youre daly blissing to my Synguler comfort & defence in my nede And madam I hertely beseche you that I may often here from you to my Comfort'. He ends the letter 'Written at Pountfreit the iii[de] day of Juyne with the hande of Youre most humble Son Ricardus Rex.'[21] There is a strong sense of a youngest son retreating into the comfort of his mother's arms in a time of dire and desperate grief.

John de la Pole, Earl of Lincoln, was given the position of Lord President of the Council of the North after the death of the Prince of Wales and a new set of ordinances were set up for the household. The details, drawn up on 24 July 1484, recognise Lincoln as the new senior figure on the Council but have also thrown up a potential clue about the sons of Edward IV. The comment has survived because it is so vague that it cannot be proof of their continued existence. The line in question provides for eating arrangements and instructs 'My lord of Lincolne and my lord Morley top be at oon brekefast, the Children togeder at oon brekefast' and the rest of the Council at another.[22] It is clear from this arrangement and a later reference to Lincoln and 'the Children' being the only ones able to take extra food and drink, that there were high-status youngsters within the household of the Council of the North, entrusted to Lincoln's care. It is possible that Richard's illegitimate son John was there, and shortly after these ordinances were drawn up, Edward, Earl of Warwick, and Elizabeth of York would move to the household, so it is feasible that the preparations were for their arrival. It is also reasonable to suggest that if Edward IV's sons were still alive, the north, in the care of another of Richard's nephews, was a reasonable place for them to be taken.

Whether this was the Princes in the Tower, now the Bastards in the North, cannot be discerned from the meagre evidence, but even if they were Warwick and Elizabeth, it demonstrates that Richard was treating his nephews and nieces well, with honour, rather than as a threat. A few scattered, equally tantalising references can be found elsewhere. On 9 March 1485, a warrant was sent to Henry Davy to deliver to John Goddeslande for 'the lord Bastard two doublettes of silk oon jaket of silk oone gowne of gloth twfo shirtes and two bonetes'[23]. It is possible this was a reference to John again, though he was not a lord. The title may have been applied as a courtesy since he was the king's son, but it might equally have been used to describe the illegitimate Edward V or Richard, Duke of York. A similar reference appears around the time that John was appointed Captain of Calais in March 1485, when money was paid for 'leavened bread allopwed for the Lord Bastard riding to 12*d*, and paid for a pike given to Master Brackenbury Constable of the Tower who at that time returned from Calais frome the Lord Bastard 3s 4d'.[24] It is assumed that this refers to John, who is by then addressed as Lord Bastard, but it may still be a reference to one of the sons of Edward IV. No evidence as yet exists to verify the fates of the boys, but some of the snippets are interesting. As has been widely asserted, the absence of evidence is not the evidence of absence. Of course, the same logic can be applied to corpses,[25] and so the debate wheels round and round.

The increasing uncertainty in the realm was evident by August when Richard issued a proclamation commanding that no man was to take a ship to sea without first reciting an oath of allegiance to Richard and offering a surety for his good behaviour.[26] During the same month, the City of London agreed to provide Richard with a loan of £2,400, made up of £100 from each of the aldermen.[27] Also in August, Richard arranged for the body of Henry VI to be moved from Chertsey Abbey to the Chapel of St George at Windsor, directly opposite the spot on which Edward IV had been laid to rest. The newly designated mausoleum of the House of York was made home to their enemy, albeit a wretched one. The College of Windsor records the king spending £5 10s 2d on the exhumation and translation of Henry's body, which was placed into a lead casket before being sealed in a wooden coffin.[28] In marking St George's Chapel as a burial place for kings, Westminster Abbey being all but full, Richard may have signalled his own eventual intention to be buried there. Henry VI had been attracting pilgrims, and a saintly cult was developing around his tomb, fuelled by stories he had appeared and of miracles performed since his death. One man claimed that he had been saved from hanging when the ghost of Henry thrust his hand between his neck and the noose to prevent him from being strangled.

Richard may have sought to harness this growing devotion, not only to bring pilgrims and money to Windsor but to increase the holiness of the chapel where he himself might have planned to rest. The precise circumstances of Henry's death more than a decade earlier remain unclear, as do Richard's involvement in and feelings about it. Regret may have played a part in the relocation of Henry's body. If Richard was directly involved at his brother's command, he may have felt guilty and sought to put the matter right as best he could. If he was not part of the act, it is possible that it was another of his brother's actions of which he had disapproved. In that instance, there was a degree of mischief in placing Henry directly opposite Edward for all eternity, forcing his brother to forever look at what he had done. Richard was at Windsor on 19 August,[29] possibly to inspect and pay his respects at the new tomb, if not to attend the reinterment in person.

October saw more activity that may mean nothing of import, but which might give a further clue about the fate of the Princes in the Tower. Once more, there is no direct evidence to confirm the supposition outlined, but nor can it be disproved, and so it bears a moment of consideration. On 15 October, Richard wrote to the newly appointed Pope Innocent VIII. He began by congratulating the Pope and expressing his pleasure 'that the Church of God has been provided with so worthy a pastor.'[30] Richard explained that he would soon be sending ambassadors, to be led by the Bishop of Durham, who was already in Rome. John Sherwood was a former Archdeacon of Richmond who had been nominated Bishop of

Durham by Richard in March 1484. He was a northern man and now held one of the most prominent ecclesiastical posts in the region, but he also had an association with the Princes in the Tower through their physician, John Argentine. On 16 December, Richard wrote again to explain that his embassy was on its way and brought their business in letters patent.[31]

Given that Richard was faced with an immense dilemma now that he had no heir, he was undoubtedly exploring possibilities. Warwick was a boy with no support in the country after being orphaned and off the political scene for years. Lincoln, similarly, did not have broad support in the country and there might be a query of his descent in the female line that could be enough to cause attempts on the throne. If the sons of Edward IV were alive, Edward had spent his entire life being trained and prepared to be king. It is possible that Richard considered harnessing that experience, along with the undoubted support within the country, by exploring the idea of making Edward his heir. He would need to think about how his illegitimacy might be corrected, and Rome would be the perfect place to do that. It would also need to be balanced against a question of the strengths of their respective claims, but Richard was now the anointed king, and Edward could be legitimised and appointed his heir. To a religious man like Richard, the Pope was the perfect authority to resolve the situation. Of course, the business may well have been something far more trivial and mundane.

On 7 December 1484, Richard was forced to finally acknowledge the lingering threat across the sea, in part because it had taken on several new aspects. The king issued a proclamation, warning his people of the danger Henry Tudor posed and the damage he and his followers were sure to inflict on England and her people if they should succeed. Having expected an invasion throughout 1484, it had not materialised, but the concern had intensified for the coming year.

Forasmoche as the King oure Soverain Lorde hathe certaine knowledge that Piers Bisshop of Excestre, Jasper Tidder sone of Owen Tidder calling himself Erle of Pembroke, John late Erle of Oxon, and Sir Edward Widevile, with other diverse his rebells and traitours disabled and attaynted by authoritie of high Courte of Parliament, of whom many been knowen for open murdrers, advowters, and extortioners, contrarie to the pleasure of God and against all treuthe, honour, and nature, have forsaken thair naturall countrey, taking theim furst to be under the obeissaunce of the Duc of Britaigne, and to him promised certain things which by hym and his Counseill were thought thinges to gretly unnaturall and abominable for theim to graunte, observe, kepe, and perfourme; and therfor the same utterly refused, The said Traitours seeing that the said Duc and his Counseill would not aide and succour theim, nor folow their weyes, prively departed out of his countrey into Fraunce, there taking theim to be undre th'obbeisance of the Kings auncient ennemie Charles, calling himself King of Fraunce; and to abuse and blynde the Commones of this said Royaume, the said Rebeles and Traitours have chosen to be their Capitayne oon HENRY TIDDER son of Edmond Tidder son of Owen Tidder, whiche of his ambitious and insatiable covetise and usurpeth upon hym the name and title of royal estate of this Roialme of Englande, wherunto he hath no maner interest, right, title, or colour, as every man wel knoweth ; for he is descended of bastard blode both of the fader side and moder side ; for the said Owen, the grandfader, was a bastard borne, and his moder was doughter unto John Duc of Somerset, sone unto John Erle of Somerset, son unto dame Kateryne Swynford, and of her in double advoutrow goten; wherby it evidently appereth that noo title can or may be in hym, whiche fulley entendeth to entre this Royaume purposing a conquest: and if he should atcheve this false entent and purpose, every mannys lif, livelood, and goods shuld be in his hands, and disposition: wherby shuld ensue the disheriting and distruction of all the noble and worshipfull blode of this Royalme for ever. And to the resistence and withstanding wherof, every true and naturall Englisheman born must lay to his handes for his own suertie, and well, and to the entent that the said Henry Tidder might the rather eschewe his said fals entent and pourpous by the aide, supporte, and assistence of the Kings said auncient ennemye of Fraunce, hath covenaunted and bargayned with hym and with all the Counseill of Fraunce to geve, and relesse in perpetuyte alle the right, title, and clayme that the Kings of England have had and mighte to have to the Corone and Royaume of Fraunce, togidder with the Duchies of Normandye, Angeoye and Maygne, Gascoygne and Guyenne, the Castelles and Townes of Caleys, Guisnes, Hammes, with the merches apperteignyng to the same, and to dessever and exclude the armes of Fraunce out of the armes of England for ever. And in more prove and sheweing of his said pourpose of conquest, the said Henry Tidder hath geven aswele to divers of the Kings said enemyes as to his said rebelles and traitoures, the Archbisshoprekes, Bisshopriches, and other dignities spirituel, and also the Duchies, Earledomes, Baronies, and othre possessions and inheritaunces of Knights, Esquires, Gentlemen, and othre the Kings true subgets within this Roialme; and entendeth also to chaunge and subvert the lawes of the same, and to enduce and establisshe newe lawes and ordinaunces amongs the Kings said subjiettes, And over this and besids the alienations of all the premisses into the possession of the Kings said ancient enemyes, to the gretest augeutisement, shame, and rebuke that ever might falle to this lande, the said Henry Tider and othre the Kings rebells and traietours aforesaid, have entended at thair cummyng, if theye can be of powair, to doo the moost cruell murdres, slaghters, robberies, and disherisons that ever wer seen in any Cristen Royaume, For the whiche and othre inestimable daungieres to be eschewed, and to the entent that the Kings said rebells, traitours, and enemyes may be utterly putt from their said malicious and fals pourpose, and soon disconfited of their enforce to lande, the King oure soverayn Lorde desireth, willeth, and commaundeth all and everych of the naturel and true subgiets of this his Royaume, to call the premisses into their myndes, and like good and true Englisshemen to thaym self with all their powairs for the defense of theim, thair wifs, children, goodes, and hereditaments, agenst the said malicious purposes and conspirations whiche the said auncient ennemyes have made with the Kings said rebelles and traitours for the fynal destruction of this lande as is aforesaid. And oure sayde soverayn Lord, as welewilled, diligent, and couragious Prince wol put his royal persone to all and payne necessarie in this behalve for the resistence and subdueing of his said ennemyes, rebelles and traitours to the moost comfort, wele, and esuertie of all his true and feithfull liegemen and subgiettes; and over this oure said soverayn Lorde willeth and comaundeth all his said subgietts to be redy in their defensible arraye, to do his Highnesse service of Werre, whan they by open proclamation or other, wise shall be commanded so to do for the resistence of the Kings said rebells, traitours, and enemyes. [32]

The most startling thing about the details of this proclamation is that Henry Tudor was now in France, not Brittany. On 8 June, Richard had concluded a treaty with Brittany to commence on 1 July.[33] As part of the agreement, Richard was to provide 1,000 archers for the defence of Brittany, in return for which Henry Tudor and other rebels would be handed over. Duke Francis was, by now, very ill and his Chancellor Pierre Landais was in effective control. Francis had protected the Englishmen in his care, as much because he had pledged on his honour to do so as because they were a valuable counter in the struggle to retain the duchy's independence.[34] It was Landais who agreed the policy with England, but Henry got wind of the scheme to return him to England, perhaps from John Morton, Bishop of Ely, who had found his way to Flanders, and he managed to slip across the border into France. Nervous of English aggression during their own minority, France's regent, the king's sister Anne of Beaujeu, saw in Henry's arrival an opportunity to do as her father had done and destabilise England enough to keep her attention focused on her own problems.

The next point of concern within the proclamation was that John de Vere, Earl of Oxford, was now with Henry too. Oxford had been a prisoner at Hammes Castle since his capture a decade earlier when he had occupied the fortress on St Michael's Mount for a time. Within weeks of George, Duke of Clarence's execution, Oxford had jumped from the walls of his prison, and it remains a mystery whether he was trying desperately to escape or to end his life. There is evidence to suggest that Oxford's gripe was with Edward, who had executed his father and older brother, rather than the broader House of York. The loss of George might have stimulated a pang of hopelessness. If so, it was erased in 1484. Oxford managed to convince some members of the garrison at Hammes not only to let him go, but to flee with him to Henry Tudor. Most of those men returned shortly after, securing a royal pardon and resuming the comfort of a regular wage from the Crown.[35] Oxford was the most experienced military commander left amongst the English nobility. His arrival in Henry Tudor's band placed a ram amongst the sheep, a leader who could organise an army and turn an irritation into a terrifying threat.

Henry Tudor was accused of being illegitimate in both lines of his descent, and of planning to destroy England, change the laws of the land and deprive the people of everything they owned. With the prospect of French support, their cause became a more substantial threat, but also easier to characterise as a French invasion, an image sure to galvanise the country behind Richard. It is odd to find that just four days after this vitriolic proclamation was issued, a general pardon was given to none other than John Morton, Bishop of Ely.[36] The king can only have been trying desperately to reconcile with Morton, who was infinitely capable of stirring trouble, and so of helping Richard, but it should have been clear that the bishop had no intention of working with Richard. At best, he was covering himself in case Tudor's cause collapsed and he needed to consider how he would return to England, but once more, Richard seems to have been unable to see the real motives of men who schemed around him, taking their words entirely at face value.

With the grief at the loss of his son still raw, the business of running a country, trying to establish what would happen after his own death and now the increased likelihood of an invasion when campaigning season arrived, Richard was hit by more personal tragedy. Christmas was celebrated at Westminster in lavish style, to the traditional disgust of the monkishly-minded Crowland. He lamented all of the disgraceful things that he felt obliged not to write about Richard, but considered that this Christmas warranted inclusion. The writer complained that 'far too much attention was given to dancing and gaiety, and vain changes of apparel presented to queen Anne and the lady Elizabeth, the eldest daughter of the late king, being of similar colour and shape.'[37] He went on to explain that many lords and bishops were shocked and disgusted by the display and in particular the part of the king's niece, Elizabeth of York. Crowland wrote that 'it was said by many that the king was bent, either on the anticipated death of the queen taking place, or else, by means of a divorce, for which he supposed he had quite sufficient grounds, on contracting marriage with the said Elizabeth.'[38]

There are several charges laid there. That Richard hoped his queen would die soon is not substantiated anywhere else. The possibility of a divorce from Anne is worthy of consideration. There is no evidence that Richard and Anne's long marriage was anything but happy, though there is little to suggest that they were madly in love either. Richard kept no mistress that is known of, but that may have owed more to his personal morality than passionate love of his wife. A medieval marriage between nobles was a business transaction more than anything else, and the union of Richard and Anne had been incredibly good business for both of them. If they loved each other after more than a decade, then it would be no surprise. The principal object of that commercial arrangement, though, was always, and was always understood to be, the production of heirs. It was, by now, plain to see that Anne would bear the king no more children. Those missives to the Pope which might have related to the sons of Edward IV could just as easily have been to investigate a divorce for the king on some grounds. It was a practical solution that would not necessarily mean Richard did not love Anne; he could design for her a suitable package of compensation if she would allow him to remarry and try to produce an heir to his throne.

The accusation that Richard planned to marry his own niece has stuck like thrown mud. Matters changed early in 1485 as Anne fell ill, apparently with the same tuberculosis that had taken her sister Isabel almost ten years earlier. The grief of the loss of her only child and possibly the stress of being set aside, even if she understood the need for it and was willing to co-operate, might have allowed the illness to take hold of her. She passed away on 16 March 1485, a solar eclipse marking the day, an ill omen for her husband's reign. The youngest daughter of Warwick the Kingmaker, Anne had ruled the north alongside her husband and become a Queen of England, with a son destined to rule the nation. Her father would surely have been proud, but just like him, she saw it all fall down about her before her death, losing everything. Crowland's cruel accusation that 'her illness was supposed to have increased still more and more, because the king entirely shunned her bed'[39] is unfair. If she had contracted tuberculosis, it would be extremely contagious, and Richard would not have been able to share her bed. The insinuation that he stopped having a sexual relationship with her is equally unfair, unless it is meant to be understood as part of a move towards a divorce that has become conflated with her illness. Anne was buried in Westminster Abbey, a fitting place for a queen to rest. Wherever Richard planned to be interred now, it would be with his new wife if she gave him a son, but Anne was hardly shunned and hidden in an obscure, out-of-the-way place.

Two things are interesting and odd about the accusation that Richard planned to marry his niece, Elizabeth of York. Firstly, it was no later invention of Crowland and others looking back and trying to darken Richard's name. It was current in 1485. The claim that Richard poisoned his wife was also in circulation, but the second fascinating element is how poorly recorded Richard's public denial of these matters was. The Mercers' Company noted their attendance at the rejection of the rumours, but no one else seemed to note it in 1485.

> Where as longe saying and muche symple Comunycacion amonge the peple by euyll disposed parsones contryved & sowne to verrey grete displesure of the Kyng shewyng how that the quene as by concent & will of the Kyng was poysoned for & to thentent that he myght than marry and have to wyfe lady Elizabeth, eldest doughter of his broder, late Kyng of Englond decessed, whom god pardon etc for the whiche & other the Kyng sende fore & had tofor hym at sent Johnes as yesterdaye the Mayre & Aldermen where as he in the grete Hall there in the presens of many of his lordes & of muche other peple shewde his grefe and displeasure aforsaid & said it never came in his thought or mynde to marry in suche maner wise nor willyng or glad of the dethe of his quene but as sorye & in hert as hevye as man myght be, with muche more in the premysses spoken, for whiche he than monysshed & charged every parson to ceas of suche untrue talkyng on parell of his indignacion. And what parson that from hensford tellith or reporteth and of thes forsaid untrewe surmysed talkyng, that the said parson therfore be had to preson unto the auctor be brought furth of whom the said parson harde the said untrue surmysed tale etc. And in this maner the Kyng hath given comaundment & Charge unto the Mayre so far to punysshe and that he for the same to call tofore hym the Wardens of all craftes, Constables & other & to shewe unto them the mater of his displesure etc.[40]

Richard's authority was reaching a new low ebb, and his state of mind can only be guessed at after such personal tragedy, but to stand before the city officials and deny such heinous charges is remarkable. Despite the novelty of the moment, the Mercers' Company is alone in noting it. Crowland wrote a year later that 'the king was obliged, having called a council together, to excuse himself with many words and to assert that such a thing had never once entered his mind,'[41] but no other contemporary civic chronicler noted the incident. They must surely have been aware of such a denial but neglected to record it, perhaps deliberately because the story was well sponsored and more interesting than Richard's denial of it.

If the October rebellions of 1483 had been aided by the rumour that the Princes in the Tower were murdered by Richard, then fresh stories that he had killed his wife and planned to marry his niece represent an extension of this pattern. The Tudor faction, still represented in England by Henry's mother Margaret Beaufort, had seen the power of the rumour in 1483 and may well have adopted the same approach in 1485: undermine the king with gossip that cannot be easily denied as the groundwork for an invasion.

The kernel of truth from which the rumour of 1483 emerged was the disappearance of the boys, used to assert their murders. Now, the death of Richard's wife was turned against him, and there was once more an element of truth that was exploded into the story of marriage to his niece. The very fact that a plan to marry his own niece was such a feast for Richard's enemies ought to suggest that it was a terrible idea that he is unlikely to have entertained. Not only that, but Richard would have to admit Elizabeth's legitimacy as a princess and therefore the illegitimacy of his own kingship in order to marry her, something he cannot have intended to do. Sir George Buck, an early seventeenth-century examiner of Richard's reputation, recorded a letter he had seen, but which has since been destroyed, that has been used as evidence of the plan to marry uncle and niece. Buck recorded the letter in a manuscript that has been damaged, and the original message was never seen again. The content of the letter, apparently written by Elizabeth herself to the Duke of Norfolk, has been rendered thus:

> First she thanked him for his many courtesies and friendly [offices, an] d then she prayed him as before to be a mediator for her in the cause of [the marriage] to the k[i]ng, who, as she wrote, was her only joy and maker in [this] world, and that she was his in heart and thoughts, in [body] and in all. And then she intimated that the better half of Fe[bruary] was past, and that she feared the queen would ne[ver die]. And these be her own words, written with her own hand, and this is the sum of her letter.[42]

The manuscript was badly damaged by fire, and the words in square brackets have been surmised from the surrounding contents and remains of the pages. This letter has been used to support the idea that a planned marriage was real, but that argument is flawed. Firstly, even if it did relate to a marriage to her uncle, this was Elizabeth hoping for it, not Richard. If she was still hoping to marry Henry Tudor and rumours were being started, then Elizabeth writing letters to Richard's key supporters, such as Norfolk, would simply be part of the scheme to undermine him. It says nothing of Richard's role in any plans.

The far more likely backdrop to this letter is the embassy that left for Portugal within days of the Queen Anne's death. It must have been planned before Anne died, so Elizabeth writing in late February would have been aware of its purpose since it involved her. Richard sent ambassadors to King John II of Portugal to negotiate a marriage between himself and John's older sister Joanna of Portugal. Joanna was a great-granddaughter of John of Gaunt through Philippa of Lancaster, so Richard planned to unite the Houses of York and Lancaster, negating a portion of Henry Tudor's appeal in the process. The other side of the negotiations, exceeding his promise in March 1484, was a match between Elizabeth of York and King John's second cousin Manuel, Duke of Beja. Manuel would go on to become King of Portugal, but even as a duke, it surpassed Richard's pledge to marry his nieces to gentlemen. The added bonus of this union was that it prevented Henry Tudor from marrying her, thus draining more support from his cause.

Read in this context, the letter demonstrates Elizabeth's excitement at the prospect of marriage to a Portuguese duke, suggesting that at this point the match with Henry Tudor held significantly less appeal. The letter is then an appeal to Norfolk to help ensure that Richard continued to include a match for her to Manuel in his plans. Rather than wanting Norfolk to be a mediator for a marriage between her and the king, she hopes he will be a mediator with the king for her marriage to Manuel. The complaint that the queen seemed likely to never die seems callous whatever the letter meant, but rather than being an impediment to her marriage to Richard, it was rather the delay in an embassy leaving for Portugal, reflecting the inappropriate exuberance of youthful hope. It is also clear from the letter that Elizabeth held no ill will against her uncle, the supposed murderer of ther brothers, who was 'her only joy'.

For Richard, having lost his son and his wife, the rumours that he had murdered Anne and planned to marry his own niece would have been incredibly hurtful. Unless he was monstrous enough to have been behind these things, they were cruel stories used to undermine his support, and his public denial demonstrates a degree of exasperation which suggests his control was slipping. For a pious man obsessed with legitimacy, a story that he murdered his wife to marry his niece would have been disgusting. That people believed it in London in 1485 would have been hurtful and the fact that many continue to think it is true today would defy belief.

Marriage negotiations and plans would ultimately come to nothing. Tudor's invasion, perhaps brought on by the king's plan to try to negate two threads of his support, was coming. A battle for the crown of England was not far away, and only one king could leave that field alive.

20

The Battle of Bosworth Field

Well beloved Friend, I commend me to you, letting you to understand
that the King's Enemies be a-land, and that the King would have set
forth as upon Monday, but only for our Lady day; but for
certain he goeth forward as upon Tuesday

John Howard, Duke of Norfolk to
John Paston, August 1485[1]

In February 1485, Richard began taking out loans to fund the likely military needs of the year. These arrangements have often been characterised by Richard's decriers as benevolences, the system of forced gifts that he had outlawed in Parliament but now returned to in desperation. The evidence is clear and to the contrary. Each of the requests is a loan with a structured method and timescale for repayment.[2] Henry Tudor was writing to his supporters within England as though he was already king, coming soon 'to advance me to the furtherance of my rightful claim, due and lineal inheritance of that crown, and for the just depriving of that homicide and unnatural tyrant', Richard III.[3] The use of the word tyrant is another charge that has clung to Richard. A tyrant is a leader who focusses on his own needs at the expense of those he rules and gives no regard to the law. Richard had demonstrated throughout his life that he was the very antithesis of a tyrant; willing to be governed by the law and to legislate for the benefit of his people.

On 5 April, a letter from Richard to the city of York against 'diverse sedicious and evil disposed personnes both in our citie of London and elleswher' was read out.[4] He must have been aware that the threat was at its highest point. Crowland noted the rising tension in the summer of 1485. Rumours were 'increasing daily that those who were in arms against the king were hastening to make a descent upon England', though Richard could not uncover at which port they planned to land.[5] He sent his friend Francis Lovell to Southampton to keep the fleet in good order, but also perhaps because Milford had been brought to him by his spies as a possible landing spot. There was a Milford just a little east of Southampton, and Richard may have thought to have Lovell keep the coast safe there. The king himself moved to Kenilworth and then Nottingham,[6] taking up a traditional central spot within the kingdom from which to prepare to defend his crown.

The king ordered the Great Seal to be sent to him at Nottingham, as he had done during the uprisings of 1483, demonstrating that by now he was confident the threat was imminent. He asked Bishop Russell on 24 July to send the device, and on 29 July, it was handed to Thomas Barowe in a careful ceremony at the Old Temple, witnessed by five men. A few days later, on 1 August, Barowe arrived to transfer the Great Seal into Richard's hands in the chapel of Nottingham Castle. This end of the process was witnessed by the Archbishop of York; the Earl of Lincoln; Lord Scrope of Upsall; George, Lord Strange, the oldest son of Thomas, Lord Stanley; and the king's secretary John Kendall.

It was not until 1 August, the same day that Richard received the Great Seal, that Henry Tudor, with a fleet of thirty ships, left Harfleur to chance his fortunes once more in England. His force, no more than a few thousand, was made up of disaffected Englishmen and French mercenaries supplied by Charles VIII. They crossed the Channel and swung west, rounding Land's End and sailing across the mouth of the Bristol Channel to reach Mill Bay and Milford Haven, south-west Wales. It was 7 August when the invaders nosed around the last outcrop of land before laying anchor and sending boats onto the narrow beach fringed by steep cliffs. Touching the sand of his homeland for the first time in fourteen years, Henry Tudor fell to his knees and recited Psalm 43: 'Judge me, O God, and distinguish my cause.'

As Tudor began a slow march north along the Welsh coast, support was slower to come than he might have liked. His course suggests he was heading for the Stanley territory of his step-father in north Wales and Cheshire, but he eventually turned east and crossed into England. He was shadowed by Sir Rhys ap Thomas, who Richard had promoted in South Wales after Buckingham's fall. A story developed that Sir Rhys had sworn to protect the coast and that any man entering the king's domains would be forced to do so over his belly. In order to fulfil the oath, it was claimed that Sir Rhys stood beneath a bridge at Dale as Tudor and his men crossed over it. The story is a later addition that cannot be traced back to any contemporary record, but it is certain that Sir Rhys did not oppose Tudor's landing and so betrayed the responsibilities of his office.

Crowland notes that around this time, Lord Stanley asked the king for permission to leave and go to his lands in Lancashire.[7] Richard agreed on the condition that Stanley left his son Lord Strange in his place, but this was a shocking misjudgement on the king's part. If Tudor was heading north toward his step-father's lands and Stanley was being permitted to return there at the same time, it presented them with the perfect opportunity to communicate and form an alliance. The fact that Richard failed to see this threat demonstrates the lack of suspicion Stanley was under at this time and the gaping flaw in Richard's character that prevented him from seeing the motives of others behind their words.

Richard was at the royal hunting lodge of Bestwood, near Nottingham, when news finally arrived of the landing of his long-expected opponent. Crowland believed that Richard was enthusiastic to face this rival claimant and end the matter, writing that 'the king rejoiced, or at least seemed to rejoice' because 'the long wished-for day had arrived.'[8] From Bestwood, Richard wrote to Henry Vernon, one of the squires of his body, to tell him to prepare to face the enemy.

> Trusty and welbeloved we grete you wele. And forasmuche as our rebelles and traitours accompanyed with our auncient enemyes of Fraunce and othre straunge nacions departed out of the water of Sayn the furst day of this present moneth making their cours westwardes ben landed at Nangle besides Mylford Haven in Wales on Soneday last passed, as we be credibly enfourmed, entending our uttre destruccion, thextreme subversion of this oure realme and disheriting of ouretrue subgiettes of the same, towardes whoes recountring, God being our guyde, we be utterly determined in our owne persone to remeove in all hast goodly that we can or may. Wherfor we wol and straitely charge you that in your persone with suche nombre as ye have promysed unto us sufficiently horssed and herneised be with us in all hast to you possible, to yeve unto us your attendaunce without failling, al manere excuses sette apart, upon peyne of forfaicture unto us of all that ye may forfait and loose. Yeven undre our signet at oure logge of Beskewode the xi day of August.[9]

Richard made it clear to Vernon, and undoubtedly others, that they were to be with him or be treated as rebels themselves. The need to threaten forfeiture demonstrates how uncertain Richard must have been of his own support and the depth of the Tudor plot within England. John Howard, Duke of Norfolk, was writing to John Paston at the same time to explain that Tudor had landed and a muster was to take place at Bury, where Paston was to bring 'seche company of tall men as ye may godly make at my cost and charge.'[10] Letters were also sent to cities requesting support for the king, York receiving theirs on 19 August. It requested eighty men be sent 'defensible araiyed' under the captaincy of John Hastings.[11]

The king mustered his forces at Leicester, where he arrived on 19 August. The speed with which he now moved to confront Tudor suggests either confidence or desperation, and it denied time for some, even those who wanted to, to get to the king's side. York's men never reached Richard. Tudor had cut east into England and made for Watling Street, the ancient Roman road that thrust north-west from London. At Nottingham, that path would allow Tudor to pass south of Richard and head directly for London, where it would become infinitely more possible for the pretender to claim power. Richard may have been forced to lurch into Tudor's path before he was fully prepared, but he also had a significant force gathered at Leicester before he marched out of the city on 21 August.

The king camped his army that night near to Sutton Cheney, close to Tudor's reported position and to where Lord Stanley was placing his army, ominously, according to many versions, precisely halfway between the two other forces. No battle plan of either army remains from Bosworth and domestic and foreign commentators during the immediate aftermath and the decades that followed have all muddied the waters as to precisely how the battle was fought. Military historians today continue to debate the nature and tactics of each army, where portions of the battle were fought and how artillery was used. Archaeological finds around the battlefield continue to refine and adjust our understandings and interpretations of that morning, but some of the facts are more readily agreed upon.[12] The size of each force is also uncertain, but the most likely estimates give Richard around 10,000 men, perhaps more. Tudor had gathered about 5,000 men to his cause, and Stanley watched on, for once at the scene of a battle before it happened, with about 6,000 men.

Many accounts report that Richard slept poorly on the night of 21 August, a tale that Shakespeare would turn into a haunted nightmare of all of Richard's supposed crimes. There is evidence to suggest that Richard rose early and threw the camp into momentary disarray by calling for Mass to be said. Crowland claimed that 'there were no chaplains present to perform Divine service on behalf of king Richard, nor any breakfast prepared to refresh the flagging spirits of the king.'[13] The king's always austere and ashen face was, that morning, more drawn and pale than usual. All of these things are meant to foreshadow a bad day in the making.

Richard probably arranged his army along the ridge of Ambion Hill. Stringing out such a vast host would make an imposing statement along the skyline as polearms prodded the air and cannon were wheeled into position. At this moment, before the battle began, Crowland asserts that Richard ordered the immediate execution of George Stanley, Lord Strange, Thomas's son, but the fact that George survived the day suggests there is little substance to this claim of desperate callousness.[14] John Howard, Duke of Norfolk, seems to have been given control of the vanguard of Richard's army, leading the first troops to engage and perhaps assisted by Sir Robert Brackenbury. Sir Thomas More would later identify Brackenbury as a man so disgusted with Richard's order to murder the Princes in the Tower that he refused to have it done, yet he joined his king at Bosworth Field. It would have been an odd decision for a man convinced his master was so evil, and an even more odd one for a supposed tyrant to keep men near him who flagrantly disobeyed his orders. Northumberland was placed in charge of the rearguard, tasked with providing reinforcements when needed. Richard himself seems to have decided to remain with the centre of his army, as Edward had always done.

Tudor's army was much smaller and probably abandoned the traditional three battle blocks, favouring a single compact unit under the command of Oxford, the most experienced military commander in their ranks. Stanley, we are generally assured, watched on from as neutral a position as he could manage. Their opponents had far more artillery and superior archers, so remaining still to be picked apart was not a tactic that would favour them. Instead, they advanced towards Ambion Hill. With uncharacteristic rashness, Richard seems to have allowed Norfolk's vanguard to charge down the hill, abandoning their superior position in favour of a swift victory. If Stanley was looming like a dark, undecided shadow over the field, it favoured Richard to end it quickly with his greater numbers.

Richard is said to have placed the crown of St Edward atop his helmet. If he did, it was an action loaded with significance. The last king to conspicuously wear his crown into battle was Henry V at Agincourt. Richard perhaps hoped to draw on parallels to that victory, though he seems unlikely to have considered himself the outnumbered underdog unless his poor sleep was born of a growing fear that he was becoming increasingly isolated amidst traitors. The result of a battle was considered a judgement made by God, victory handed to the Lord's favoured side. In wearing his crown, Richard was asking for God's judgement of him as king. As Norfolk engaged with Oxford, he found he was not getting the answer he desired.

John Howard was killed, and his son the Earl of Surrey was severely wounded. Sir Robert Brackenbury was hacked down in the melee as it began to spread out over the countryside. Northumberland's part remains even more of a mystery than most of the morning's events. In some accounts, he was sent to prevent Stanley from intervening on Tudor's side only to find his way blocked by marshy ground. Alternatively, when ordered to reinforce Norfolk's flagging vanguard, he could not reach them through the marsh, both of which would point to abysmal planning on Richard's part, or smart thinking by his opponents. Still other accounts claim that Northumberland elected not to follow Richard's orders and sat out the battle. His arrest afterwards suggests this was not agreed beforehand, though his assassination in the north a few years later, reputedly for abandoning Richard III, might support the idea that people at least thought that was what he had done. Northumberland had travelled a long way to watch events and do nothing if that had been his plan, though his attendance at least hedged his bets a little. He had never received the authority in the north that he had hoped for and believed he deserved. It was plain that he would never get it while Richard lived, so he perhaps saw some benefit in a change of regime, particularly to one with no ties to the north that would need a representative there. Without a record of his personal motives, it remains a matter for debate whether Northumberland actively abandoned Richard at Bosworth by deliberate inaction, or was restricted by the terrain from providing the support that might have won the day.

There was no record of any abandonment of Richard on the battlefield by the rank and file, but as Norfolk's banner toppled to the churned-up earth, the day was already going badly. It is now that most accounts assert that Richard saw Henry himself, accompanied by a small band of men behind his banner of the red dragon of Cadwaladr, riding toward Lord Stanley's position. It would appear that even Henry was uncertain of his step-father's intentions and had to go in person to encourage him to intervene. Spying a chance to end the day decisively, Richard and a contingent of his household knights set off atop their huge destriers, couching their lances and watching the small band of their enemies closing in through the slit in their visors. Tudor's bodyguard may have arranged themselves in a defensive formation known as the *hedgehog* around their leader, bristling spears protecting him from the thundering approach of mounted knights. The encounter that followed was sharp. Richard himself faced and wounded Sir John Cheney, a giant of a man who stood 6' 8" tall, an impressive feat for a small man restricted by scoliosis that lessened his lung capacity. Richard came so close to Tudor that he personally killed the invader's standard bearer, Sir William Brandon.

At this moment, with Richard's closest friends fighting around him, he must have felt a rush of chivalric pride, but it did not mean the battle was going his way. As the result stood on a knife edge, a decisive intervention could be made by the masters of that art, the Stanley family. Sir William Stanley, almost certainly at the instruction of his older brother Thomas, led his contingent of about 3,000 men down the hill and fell on what remained of Richard's household knights. The king himself was hacked to death as he fought in the midst of his enemies, reportedly bellowing 'Treason! Treason! Treason!' as he was beaten to the ground and sliced by many weapons. The killing blow was probably a slice to the back of his head by a halberd or similar heavy chopping weapon, which sheared a piece of bone away and damaged his exposed brain.[15] Sir William had been a firm Yorkist from the very outset of the Wars of the Roses, fighting for the Earl of Salisbury at the Battle of Blore Heath in 1459. Twenty-six years later, for reasons that remain unclear, he abandoned that cause. Perhaps the rumour that Richard had killed the princes had turned him away from the new House of York, though if so, he must have feared that he had been tricked. A decade later, in 1495, Sir William would be executed by Henry VII for his involvement in the Perkin Warbeck affair, an attempt to place a man on the throne who claimed to be Richard, Duke of York. If William thought he knew on that morning in 1485 that the boys were dead, he clearly doubted it ten years later.

For Thomas, Lord Stanley, it perhaps gave him a measure of satisfaction to see the boy he had had trouble with fifteen years earlier fall under the weight of his decision. Whether the Hornby incident and the circumstances that surrounded it figured in Stanley's thinking, or whether he simply saw a brighter future for himself with his wife's son on the throne, cannot be known for certain. His reward for his intervention that day would be the Earldom of Derby that his family still holds today.

On 22 August 1485, at the age of thirty-two and just over two years after becoming king, Richard III lay dead in a field near Market Bosworth in Leicestershire. He was stripped naked and his corpse thrown over the back of a horse. His remains show the marks of postmortem humiliation wounds, including a dagger driven into his buttocks as he slumped over the saddle. His scoliosis was laid bare for the world to see now, a secret kept for so long but revealed by his death. The victor, now King Henry VII, issued a proclamation about the old king's body.

> And moreover, the king ascertaineth you that Richard duke of Gloucester, late called King Richard, was slain at a place called Sandeford, within the shire of Leicester, and brought dead off the field unto the town of Leicester, and there was laid openly, that every man might see and look upon him. And also there was slain upon the same field, John late duke of Norfolk, John late earl of Lincoln, Thomas, late earl of Surrey, Francis Viscount Lovell, Sir Walter Devereux, Lord Ferrers, Richard Radcliffe, knight, Robert Brackenbury, knight, with many other knights, squires and gentlemen, of whose souls God have mercy.[16]

Some of the early reports of the battle were flawed. Francis Lovell was certainly not dead and may not have made it to Bosworth from

Southampton in time for the fight. It was probably, quite understandably, assumed that he had fallen with his old friend. Surrey was injured, but survived. Sir Richard Ratcliffe was amongst the dead, as were many of Richard's closest associates, such as Sir James Harrington. The lawyer William Catesby was arrested and executed at Leicester a couple of days after the battle. After a few days on display, the Greyfriars asked Henry for permission to bury the body. They must have been given short shrift because it was a hastily dug, shallow pit in the choir of their church into which they placed his broken body.

Shakespeare's famous depiction of the battle is sometimes viewed as an indictment of Richard's personal cowardice. Not only is that at odds with all of the contemporary evidence, but it is also a misreading of the text. The famous 'A horse! a horse!' line is often asserted to demonstrate that Richard tried to flee the battle, but that is simply not true.

KING RICHARD III
A horse! a horse! my kingdom for a horse!
CATESBY
Withdraw, my lord; I'll help you to a horse.
KING RICHARD III
Slave, I have set my life upon a cast,
And I will stand the hazard of the die:
I think there be six Richmonds in the field;
Five have I slain to-day, instead of him.
A horse! a horse! my kingdom for a horse![17]

Here, Richard enters calling for a horse. Catesby assumes he means to escape the battle, but Richard rebukes him, explaining that he has thrown the dice and will stand or fall by the result. He believes there are multiple Henrys on the field, because he has already killed five men he thought were Tudor and calls again for a horse, but it is to return to the battle, not to run away from it. It is an irony that even when Shakespeare credits Richard with personal bravery, it is misinterpreted as cowardice.

Contemporary and even near-contemporary writers were utterly unanimous in their praise for Richard at the moment of his death. Even those otherwise hostile to him cannot help but concede that he fought bravely and well.

Crowland wrote:

For while fighting, and not in the act of flight, the said king Richard was pierced with numerous deadly wounds, and fell in the field like a brave and most valiant prince.[18]

John Rous recorded, after cataloguing Richard's evil acts and comparing him to the Antichrist:

> For all that, let me say the truth to his credit: that he bore himself like a noble soldier and despite his little body and feeble strength, honourably defended himself to his last breath, shouting again and again that he was betrayed, and crying 'Treason! Treason! Treason!'[19]

The Spanish ambassador Diego de Valera noted that:

> Now when Salazar, your little vassal, who was there in King Richard's service, saw the treason of the king's people, he went up to him and said: 'Sire, take steps to put your person in safety, without expecting to have the victory in today's battle, owing to the manifest treason in your following.' But the king replied: 'Salazar, God forbid I yield one step. This day I will die as king or win.' Then he placed over his head-armour the crown royal, which they declare be worth 120,000 crowns, and having donned his coat-of-arms began to fight with much vigour, putting heart into those that remained loyal, so that by his sole effort he upheld the battle for a long time.[20]

Jean Molinet considered that:

> The king bore himself valiantly according to his destiny, and wore the crown on his head.[21]

Polydore Vergil conceded in his account that:

> king Richard alone was killyd fighting manfully in the thickest presse of his enemyes.[22]

When news reached the City of York of the result of the battle on the following day, they bravely, given that a new king was holding the crown now, recorded in the civic records:

> Wer assembled in the counsaill chambre where and when it was shewed by diverse personnes and especially by John Sponer send unto the feld of Redemore to bring tidings frome the same to the citie, that King Richard late mercifully reigning over us was thrugh grete treason of the duc of Northfolk, and many othre that turned ayenst hyme, with many othre lords and nobilles of this north parties, was piteously slane and murdred to the grete hevynesse of this citie, the names of whome foloweth herafter.[23]

York would soon be reconciled to the rule of Henry VII. Pragmatism demanded that it must be in order to continue in safety, but the sense that Richard was a good lord and a fair king has lingered in the north ever since, as though they saw something that the rest of the country and all of history has missed. Their Richard was not a murdering, usurping, cruel tyrant.

The question that has remained ever since is as simple as it is impossible to answer: was the first thirty years of Richard's life a lie, or have the last two been obscured to create a monster from which England had to be saved by the valiant King Henry VII, the first Tudor king?

Epilogue

Henry VII found the business of ruling was not as easy as it might look. His first Parliament saw him date his reign from the 21 August 1485, the day before the Battle of Bosworth. This allowed him to attaint all of those who fought against him, but within a few years, he was forced to rectify this sleight of hand when men became hesitant to follow him when his defeat might make them traitors. He would eventually pay to erect a tomb over Richard III's grave in recognition of his predecessor's position. Much of Henry's reign was consumed by caution and fear that, after personal loss, slipped into miserly paranoia. By the end of his life, he perhaps understood even better than his adversary at Bosworth the toll becoming king could take on a man.

History has characterised Richard III and Henry VII as mortal enemies who hated each other. In truth, before they came a sword's breath from each other at Bosworth, they had never met. Their lives have far more in common than distinguishes them. Both men lost their fathers, Henry before he was even born. Both had spells in exile, Henry's much longer, and both saw their lives tossed and turned on the rolling seas of the Wars of the Roses. Fate happened to place them on opposing sides, but they were men trying to make their way in the world the best they could. Bosworth was not the culmination of some Hollywood-style goodie versus baddie epic struggle. It was, despite the nature of it, utterly impersonal. Admiration for Richard does not and should not require equal and opposite emotions to be applied to Henry, and vice versa. Henry was not the architect of Richard's later bad reputation. It began during Richard's lifetime and was expanded by gossip in the absence of information and later writers. Henry had no need to criticise Richard. It was happening organically all around him.

Richard III has been the cause of much spilt ink, and many readers of this book will no doubt have wondered at the outset of this book whether there was space on the shelf for another. If you still feel that way, then I am sorry. My intention has been to examine Richard's life as a whole, not two years of it in isolation. Understanding what happened in 1483 can only be helped by considering the kind of childhood Richard had, the type of man he grew into and the people and country that surrounded him. I am a Ricardian, as I do not doubt is by now plain. I make no apology for this but offer in explanation that this does not mean I believe Richard was a saintly figure incapable of doing wrong, only that he was a human being making his way in a complex and brutal world. I think the facts of his life, stripped of later addition and embellishment, do not tally with the cruel tyrant of the traditional histories. In the north, he was a man devoted to providing good lordship, equitable access to justice and opportunity for all. There is no reason to doubt that he meant to continue in this vein as king.

The events of 1483 remain shrouded in enough mystery and uncertainty to sustain life in the 'bad King Richard', but I think it takes an effort to create this image against the facts. It is apparent that he was meant to be Regent for his nephew, not Protector in the more limited English sense of previous decades. That the Woodville family did not want that is equally sure, though they can hardly be blamed either for seeking to preserve their position against mounting threats. Lord Hastings may well have been plotting against Richard as his own authority weakened. At least, arriving in London in May 1483, it is not unreasonable that Richard was wary of plots and poised to act decisively against them. It is striking that some of the most learned men of the Church of their age offered no condemnation of Richard and what he did, actively accepting the evidence of a pre-contract and Richard's right to rule. Thomas Bourchier, Archbishop of Canterbury, was happy to anoint and crown Richard. John Russell, considered by Thomas More to have been a great mind, worked with the new king, as did John Alcock after his initial arrest. It is hard to accept that none of these men would have raised a concern about a man who had murdered his nephews and illegally taken the throne.

What became of Richard's nephews must also remain a matter as yet unsolved. For many, their murder was a requirement of Richard's accession, but his silence, and therefore failure to negate their threat, does not tally with this need. Nor does the ruthless murder of his nephews fit with the profile of the man who came south in 1483 after more than a decade in the north. No other case like it has ever been uncovered against Richard, yet for many his guilt is beyond contest. That none of his other nieces and nephews failed to reach the end of his reign alive and well is surely instructive, even when his brother's daughter was the figurehead of the plot that eventually brought him down. It is striking that Richard is all too frequently convicted in the court of history for murdering his nephews based on rumour, hearsay and no firm evidence, yet given no credit in this account for sparing the life of someone like Lady Margaret Beaufort. She was convicted of High Treason in Parliament, yet remarkably escaped a death sentence. Ironically, it would be her grandson who would normalise the killing of noble ladies, but if Richard is to be deemed so desperate and power-crazed that he would murder two children, how can that man be reconciled with the one willing to spare the life of a woman convicted of treason?

The approach adopted by the writer of *The Crowland Chronicle* is fascinating in this regard. He is considered no fan of Richard's, yet, in parts, has good things to say about him, and it is often what he doesn't say, the matters on which he chooses to remain silent or cryptic that can be the most telling. Nowhere is this truer than in his treatment of the fate of Edward IV's sons. He reports a rumour that they were dead, but neither states his belief or disbelief in it, and never mentions it again. Odd, for one of the most politically well-informed commentators of the entire period. When Henry VII ordered all copies of *Titulus Regius* to be returned on pain of imprisonment and had them destroyed, striking the Act from the Rolls of Parliament without having it read in Parliament, as protocol demanded, it is clear that he was expunging inconvenient truths. It may be no coincidence that the only copy ever located turned up in the library of Crowland Abbey, hidden amongst its books. Was the elusive writer of the 1486 account of the Wars of the Roses the first Ricardian, preserving evidence he knew would be destroyed forever, and going as far as he dared to suggest that Richard was not guilty of the crimes being levelled against him? If a purge of documents began, was the gathering of influential churchmen at Crowland Abbey in early 1486 an effort to subvert that, to keep information alive? Does *The Crowland Chronicle* represent the downloading of a hive mind that, when these old men died, would be lost forever?

Richard's character has been smeared for centuries and for some, it is not even worth considering how much of it is true. Re-approaching the facts of his life with an open mind can be rewarding, and expose the possibility that he was not a man of pure evil. If he acted wrongly in 1483, it was a reaction to the almost impossible situation bequeathed to him, the fear of which was precisely what had caused his brother to call upon him. After his coronation, there is plenty of evidence that his rule aimed to continue the policies he had pursued in the north. There was no radical change of direction. Richard's ideas were threatening to those who had thrived on corruption and connection, but are surely to be applauded by a modern audience. They were not simple bids for popularity from a floundering king because they demonstrably followed the pattern of his time in the north. In fact, it was probably these very ideals and policies that brought about his downfall and death. His accession shows no signs of illegality. He was not a usurper, or at least he fits that bill less well than other kings of that century. His rule offers no examples of tyranny, yet for some, he remains a murdering, usurping tyrant despite evidence to the contrary.

The nobility suffered, and their time was coming to an end as the fifteenth century dragged toward a tired close. Their ability to insulate themselves from and even challenge royal authority had burned down the structures upon which society had been built for centuries, and something needed to be done to re-balance society. Edward IV created only a handful of nobles. Richard III created none, and Henry VII would largely continue in the same direction. The Duchy of Lancaster, the Duchy of York, the Duchy of Exeter, the Earldom of March, the lands of the Marquis of Dorset and of the mighty Neville family were all in Crown hands. Richard, I think, recognised that the merchant classes might be the best hope to replace the untrustworthy nobility, but in showing his hand too quickly, he alienated the people he would need to support him on a battlefield and suffered the consequences at Bosworth.

Richard was a man. He made mistakes and misjudgements. He had his flaws, as we all do, but beneath the grime of centuries of slander and gossip, the facts can be uncovered and polished up to provide a far more rounded and interesting man, with novel ideas that seem ahead of his time. Undoubtedly he was willing to do that which was within his power to protect his position and that of his family. He was a fifteenth-century nobleman when they were a brutal and acquisitive breed. That does not mean that he was incapable of less selfish acts than many of his contemporaries, or of hankering for a bygone age in which men, at least in the stories he read, had been honourable and lived by codes. Any time a person from history is viewed as one-dimensional, as simply good or bad, that should be cause to look again and question more deeply, because they were people, just like you and I. They had hopes and fears, dreams and insecurities that fused together to make them. When Richard charged at the Battle of Bosworth, did he blindly believe he could kill Henry Tudor and that would be the end of it? Was he, perhaps, afflicted by the loss of his son and wife? Did he wonder what the purpose of carrying on might be? Did he hope that God would help him win the day and once more approve of him? We cannot know for certain. Arguably, what makes him unique amongst medieval monarchs and nobles was the antithesis of what history has remembered him for. He was no petty tyrant bent on murdering all in his way. He was a forward-thinking reformer who tried to tackle the real problems he saw in English medieval society, and paid the price for thinking he could resolve them.

I hope that this book has proven a worthy addition to your library. If you came to it as a Ricardian, it is my hope that you enjoyed it, recognised some of the elements of Richard that have appealed to you and perhaps garnered some information that was new to you. For neutral readers, I hope that the book has been informative and given you a flavour of what we 'loony Ricardians' see in the generally accepted story of a man that is so far removed from the facts of his life. To those 'traditionalists' who picked it up, if you made it this far, I am pleased. I do not doubt that some of my opinions or interpretations have been hard to swallow, but

I think they are well supported by evidence. It is my opinion that clinging to More's and Shakespeare's versions of Richard requires an effort to ignore facts and hopefully, there is enough evidence in these pages to at least soften your view. If you maintain that Richard was a monster, then I wholeheartedly support your right to do so. Like the whole Richard III versus Henry VII thing, Revisionists versus Traditionalists does not need to be a bitter feud. The truth does not belong to one side or the other. It most likely lies somewhere in the middle, in the murky grey areas that define each and every one of us.

Discuss Richard and his life, please. But do not allow the discussion to fall from debate into nasty arguments. Somewhere along that road, everyone loses, including history. The study of history is the asking of questions. In an age of fake news and dangerous agendas, it is a skill that must never be lost.

Selected Bibliography

Primary Sources

Acts of the Court of the Mercers' Company 1453–1527, Cambridge University Press, 1936

ed C.A.J. Armstrong, *The Usurpation of Richard III* by Dominic Mancini, Alan Sutton Publishing, 1984

L.C. Attreed, *The York House Books, Vol I*, Alan Sutton Publishing, 1991

ed J. Bain, *Calendar of Documents Relating to Scotland, Vol IV*, Edinburgh, 1888

J. Bohn, *The Chronicles of the White Rose*, London, 1845

ed F.W.D. Brie, *The Brut*, Early English Text Society, 1906

ed R. Brown, *Calendar of State Papers of Venice*, London, 1864

ed J. Bruce, *Historie of the Arrivall of Edward IV*, The Camden Society, 1838

Calendar of the Patent Rolls, Edward IV, 1461–1467, Public Record Office, 1897

Calendar of Patent Rolls, Edward IV, 1467–77, Public Record Office, 1900

Rev J.S. Davies, *An English Chronicle*, The Camden Society, 1856

F. Devon, *Issues of the Exchequer*, London, 1837

R. Edwards, *The Itinerary of King Richard III 1483–1485*, The Richard III Society, 1983

ed H. Ellis, *Three Books of Polydore Vergil's English History*, London, 1844

Robert Fabyan, *The New Chronicles of England and France*, London, 1811

R. Grafton, *Grafton's Chronicle, Vol I*, Johnson et al, 1809

ed J. Halliwell, *A Chronicle of the First Thirteen Years of the Reign of King Edward IV by John Warkworth*, London, 1839

J. Halliwell, *Letters of the Kings of England, Vol I*, London, 1848

P.W. Hammond & A.F. Sutton, *Richard III: The Road to Bosworth*, Guild Publishing, 1985

T.D. Hardy, *Rymer's Foedera, Vol II*, Longman and Co, 1873

ed R. Horrox & P.W. Hammond, BL Harleian *MS 433, Volume 1*, The Richard III Society, 1979

ed R. Horrox & P.W. Hammond, BL Harleian *MS 433, Volume 2*, The Richard III Society, 1980

ed R. Horrox & P.W. Hammond, BL Harleian *MS 433, Volume 3*, The Richard III Society, 1982

Leland's Collectanea, Vol VI, London, 1770

C. Lethbridge Kingsford, *The Stonor Letters and Papers, Vol II*, London, 1919

ed H.E. Malden, *The Cely Papers*, Longman, Green and Co, 1900

J.G. Nichols, Grants etc *From the Crown During the Reign of Edward the Fifth*, The Camden Society, 1854

D. Pickering, *The Statutes at Large, Vol IV,* Cambridge, 1763

H.T. Riley, *Ingulph's Chronicle of the Abbey of Croyland*, George Bell and Sons, 1908

Rotuli Parliamentorum, Vol VI, London, 1777

ed A.R. Scoble, *The Memoirs of Philip de Commines, Vol I*, George Bell & Sons, 1906

ed A.R. Scoble, *The Memoirs of Philip de Commines, Lord of Argenton, Vol II*, London, 1856

Secondary Sources

N. Amin, *House of Beaufort*, Amberley, 2017

A. Carson, *Richard Duke of Gloucester as Lord Protector and High Constable of England*, Imprimis Imprimatur, 2015

Sir William Dugdale, *Monasticon Anglicanum Volume IV, Part III*, 1846

H. Ellis, *Original Letters Illustrative of English History, Vol I*, Harding and Lepard, 1827

J. Fenn, *Original Letters Written During the Reigns of Henry VI, Edward IV and Richard III, Vol II*, London, 1787

J. Gairdner, *History of the Life and Reign of Richard the Third*, Cambridge University Press, 1898

ed J. Gairdner, *Letters and Papers Illustrative of the Reigns of Richard III and Henry VII, Vol I*, London, 1861

J. Gairdner, *The Collections of A Citizen of London*, The Camden Society, 1876

J. Gairdner, *The Paston Letters, Vol I, 1872*

J. Gairdner, *The Paston Letters, Vol II, 1910*

ed P.W Hammond, *Richard III: Loyalty, Lordship and Law*, Richard III and Yorkist History Trust, 1986

P.W. Hammond, *The Battles of Barnet and Tewkesbury*, Alan Sutton Publishing, 1990

A. Hanham, *Richard III and His Early Historians 1483–1535*, Clarendon Press, 1975

ed. C.L. Kingsford, *Chronicles of London*, Clarendon Press, 1905

J.L. Laynesmith, *Cecily Duchess of York*, Bloomsbury, 2017

William Shakespeare, *Richard III, Act 1, Scene 1*

C. Scofield, *The Life and Reign of Edward the Fourth, Vol II*, Fonthill, 2016

R.R. Sharpe, *London and the Kingdom*, London, 1894

A.F. Sutton & L. Visser-Fuchs, *The Hours of Richard III*, Stroud, 1990

Online Sources

British History Online

Abbreviations

The Arrivall	ed J. Bruce, *Historie of the Arrivall of Edward IV*, The Camden Society, 1838
CPR	*Calendar of the Patent Rolls, Edward IV*
Crowland	H.T. Riley, *Ingulph's Chronicle of the Abbey of Croyland*, George Bell and Sons, 1908
Grants etc	J.G. Nichols, Grants etc *From the Crown During the Reign of Edward the Fifth*, The Camden Society, 1854
Itinerary	R. Edwards, *The Itinerary of King Richard III 1483–1485*, The Richard III Society, 1983
Mancini	ed C.A.J. Armstrong, *The Usurpation of Richard III by Dominic Mancini*, Alan Sutton Publishing, 1984
MSS433 Vol I	ed R. Horrox & P.W. Hammond, BL Harleian *MS 433, Volume 1*, The Richard III Society, 1979
MSS433 Vol II	ed R. Horrox & P.W. Hammond, BL Harleian *MS 433, Volume 2*, The Richard III Society, 1980
MSS433 Vol III	ed R. Horrox & P.W. Hammond, BL Harleian *MS 433, Volume 3*, The Richard III Society, 1982
Scofield	C. Scofield, *The Life and Reign of Edward the Fourth, Vol II*, Fonthill, 2016
York Books	L.C. Attreed, *The York House Books, Vol I*, Alan Sutton Publishing, 1991

Notes

A Note on Sources

1 Mancini, p57
2 Crowland, p510

Prologue

1 'Henry VI: November 1450', in *Parliament Rolls of Medieval England*, ed. Chris Given-Wilson, Paul Brand, Seymour Phillips, Mark Ormrod, Geoffrey Martin, Anne Curry and Rosemary Horrox (Woodbridge, 2005), British History Online http://www.british-history.ac.uk/no-series/parliament-rolls-medieval/november-1450 [accessed 27/11/2017]. An Act of Resumption at Item 17 states that Henry VI's debts stood at an eye-watering £372,000 whilst his annual income was just £5,000.
2 'Henry VI: November 1449', in *Parliament Rolls of Medieval England*, ed. Chris Given-Wilson, Paul Brand, Seymour Phillips, Mark Ormrod, Geoffrey Martin, Anne Curry and Rosemary Horrox (Woodbridge, 2005), British History Online http://www.british-history.ac.uk/no-series/parliament-rolls-medieval/november-1449 [accessed 27/11/2017]. The charge relating to Lady Margaret Beaufort is found in Item 19.
3 *RP, v, 337*; PRO SC8/28/1387
4 For the full text of Richard, Duke of York's oath at St Paul's see *The Paston Letters Vol I*, New Complete Library Edition, James Gairdner pp101–2

Richard Liveth Yet

1 Rev H.K. Bonney, *Historic Notices in Reference to Fotheringhay, 1821*, p1
2 Ibid, p4–5

3 Ibid p22

4 T.B. Pugh, *Revolution and Consumption in Medieval England*, Edited by M. Hicks pp71–88. This article provides in-depth detail of Duke Richard's financial circumstances. Although his incomes appear to have fallen in later years, the couple clearly had a huge amount of disposable income in their younger years.

5 Ralph's father John Neville, 3rd Baron Neville was married to Maud Percy, a daughter of Henry Percy, 2nd Baron Percy of Alnwick. This Henry's grandson and namesake would become 1st Earl of Northumberland.

6 N. Amin, *House of Beaufort*, Amberley, 2017 pp36–8 for details of Richard II's legitimising of the children of his uncle John of Gaunt. pp82–3 provides a discussion of the insertion by Henry IV later of the clause *excepta dignitate regali* – 'except to the royal dignity' which appears to have no legal effect on the original act of legitimisation.

7 William Shakespeare, *Richard III, Act 1, Scene 1*

8 J. Gairdner, *History of the Life and Reign of Richard the Third*, Cambridge University Press, 1898, p5

9 Ibid, from S. Turner, *History of England During the Middle Ages, 1830*

10 J. Gairdner, *History of the Life and Reign of Richard the Third*, Cambridge University Press, 1898, p5

11 Sir William Dugdale, *Monasticon Anglicanum Volume IV, Part III, 1846*, p1602

12 J. Gairdner, *History of the Life and Reign of Richard the Third*, Cambridge University Press, 1898, p5

13 J.L. Laynesmith, *Cecily Duchess of York*, Bloomsbury, 2017 p60

14 Ibid

15 A.F. Sutton & L. Visser-Fuchs, *The Hours of Richard III*, Stroud, 1990, pp44–6

16 Aidan Kavanagh, *The Shape of Baptism: The Rite of Christian Initiation*, The Liturgical Press, 1992 page 59

17 Chrism is consecrated oil, also known as myrrh.

18 B.D. Spinks, *Early and Medieval Rituals and Theologies of Baptism*, Ashgate, 2006 pp138–9 for details of the York Manual 1509 baptism order of ceremony.

19 A. Dalby, *The Treatise of Walter of Bibbesworth*, Prospect Books, 2012, p41. Walter's treatise is aimed at helping to teach children French in order to learn the language of the Norman aristocracy.

20 Rev J.S. Davies, *An English Chronicle*, The Camden Society, 1856, p70

21 J. Gairdner, *The Paston Letters, Vol I*, 1872, pp263–8 (p265 for the Queen's articles)

22 Ibid

23 'Henry VI: July 1455', in *Parliament Rolls of Medieval England*, ed. Chris Given-Wilson, Paul Brand, Seymour Phillips, Mark Ormrod, Geoffrey Martin, Anne Curry and Rosemary Horrox (Woodbridge, 2005), British History Online http://www.british-history.ac.uk/ no-series/parliament-rolls-medieval/july-1455 [accessed 01/12/17]. Item 19 contains the text written to the Archbishop of Canterbury from Royston on 20 May 1455. Item 20 details the letter sent to King Henry on 21 May 1455 from Ware.
24 Rev J.S. Davies, *An English Chronicle*, The Camden Society, 1856, p71
25 CPR, *Henry VI, Vol II, 1452–1461*, Public Record Office, p424
26 *A Chronicle of London*, Longman, Rees, Orme, Brown and Green, 1827, p251
27 R. Grafton, *Grafton's Chronicle, Vol I*, Johnson et al, 1809, p59

Caught in the Wheel

1 G. Chaucer, *The Canterbury Tales*, J.M. Dent & Sons Ltd, 1908, p203
2 Rev J.S. Davies, *An English Chronicle*, The Camden Society, 1856, p79
3 Ibid
4 Ibid
5 ed F.W.D. Brie, *The Brut*, Early English Text Society, 1906, p526
6 Rev J.S. Davies, *An English Chronicle*, The Camden Socety, 1856, p79
7 Ibid
8 Ibid
9 Ibid, p80
10 Ibid. The writer describes many of those in Audley's army as 'notable knyghtes and squyers of Chesshyre that had resceved the livery of the swannes'.
11 J. Schofield and A.G. Vince, *Medeival Towns*, Equinox Publishing, 2003
12 ed F.W.D. Brie, *The Brut*, Early English Text Society, 1906, p527. The writer asserts that none would disobey the queen's summons so that 'every man come, in suche wise that the king was stronger, & had moche more peple than the Duke of York & therles or Warrewik & of Salesbury.'
13 Ibid
14 Ibid
15 p689. October 9 1459 – *Power for Henry duke of Somerset as captain of Calais to appoint officers and grant letters of safe conduct. Westm. O. xi. 436 H v. p. ii. 90.*
16 Rev J.S. Davies, *An English Chronicle*, The Camden Socety, 1856, p81–3 for a transcript of the letter written on 10 October.

17 'Henry VI: November 1459', in *Parliament Rolls of Medieval England*, ed. Chris Given-Wilson, Paul Brand, Seymour Phillips, Mark Ormrod, Geoffrey Martin, Anne Curry and Rosemary Horrox (Woodbridge, 2005), British History Online http://www.british-history.ac.uk/no-series/parliament-rolls-medieval/november-1459 [accessed 02/12/17]. Item 16 details this charge and is part of the list of grievances brought against York and his allies.

18 Ibid, Item 18

19 ed F.W.D. Brie, *The Brut*, Early English Text Society, 1906, p527: 'the Duke of York, with the other lords, seyng tham so descevyd, toke A councel shortly that same night, & departed fro the felde, levyng behynde thame the moste parte of ther peple to kepe the feld til on the morne.'

20 'Henry VI: November 1459', in *Parliament Rolls of Medieval England*, ed. Chris Given-Wilson, Paul Brand, Seymour Phillips, Mark Ormrod, Geoffrey Martin, Anne Curry and Rosemary Horrox (Woodbridge, 2005), British History Online http://www.british-history.ac.uk/no-series/parliament-rolls-medieval/november-1459 [accessed 04/12/2017]. Item 15 details the events at Blore Heath and the pardon Henry offered to those who were not involved.

21 Ibid

22 Ibid

23 Ibid

24 J. Gairdner, *The Collections of A Citizen of London*, The Camden Society, 1876, p207. Pipes (pypys) and Hogsheads (hoggys hedys) were measures of wine. The removal of bedding and clothe attests to the value and portability of such items. The defouling of women is understood to refer to acts of rape committed during the looting of Ludlow.

25 *The Chronicles of the White Rose*, James Bohn, 1845, p5. 'After the which departing King Harry rode into Ludlow, and spoiled the Town and Castle, where-at he found the Duchess of York with her two young sons'.

26 ed F.W.D. Brie, *The Brut*, Early English Text Society, 1906, p528

27 *The Chronicles of the White Rose*, James Bohn, 1845, p5–6

28 Rev J.S. Davies, *An English Chronicle*, The Camden Socety, 1856, p83

29 ed F.W.D. Brie, *The Brut*, Early English Text Society, 1906, p528

30 J. Gairdner, *The Collections of A Citizen of London*, The Camden Society, 1876, p207

31 J.L. Laynesmith, *Cecily Duchess of York*, Bloomsbury, 2017, p71

32 'Henry VI: November 1459', in *Parliament Rolls of Medieval England*, ed. Chris Given-Wilson, Paul Brand, Seymour Phillips, Mark Ormrod, Geoffrey Martin, Anne Curry and Rosemary Horrox

(Woodbridge, 2005), British History Online http://www.british-history.ac.uk/no-series/parliament-rolls-medieval/november-1459 [accessed 05/12/2017]. Item 22 details those attainted at Coventry.

33 Gregory's *Chronicle* lists the executions in the aftermath of Cade's Rebellion in 1450, concluding with the note that 'Men calle hyt in Kente the harvyste of hedys'. These executions were in spite of pardons given at the conclusion of the revolt to all those involved if they returned home. J. Gairdner, *The Collections of A Citizen of London*, The Camden Society, 1876, p197

34 'Henry VI: November 1459', in *Parliament Rolls of Medieval England*, ed. Chris Given-Wilson, Paul Brand, Seymour Phillips, Mark Ormrod, Geoffrey Martin, Anne Curry and Rosemary Horrox (Woodbridge, 2005), British History Online http://www.british-history.ac.uk/no-series/parliament-rolls-medieval/november-1459 [accessed 05/12/2017]. Item 21 details Alice's part in prompting the treason of her husband, son and brother-in-law.

35 ed J. Gairdner, *The Paston Letters*, Bloomsbury, 1872, p499

36 J.L. Laynesmith, *Cecily Duchess of York*, Bloomsbury, 2017, p71–2

37 J. Gairdner, *The Collections of A Citizen of London*, The Camden Society, 1876, p206

38 Ibid

39 CPR, *Henry VI, Vol VI 1452–1461*, Kraus Reprint, 1971, p542

40 Ibid, p515

41 See http://faculty.goucher.edu/eng240/early_english_currency.htm for a currency guide. A mark was 2/3 of a £, or 13s 4d

Fear and Sorrow

1 *Calendar of State Papers of Milan, 1461*. 'Milan: 1461', in Calendar of State Papers and Manuscripts in the Archives and Collections of Milan 1385–1618, ed. Allen B Hinds (London, 1912), pp. 37–106. British History Online http://www.british-history.ac.uk/cal-state-papers/milan/1385–1618/pp37–106 [accessed 12/12/17]. Item 63

2 Rev J.S. Davies, *An English Chronicle*, The Camden Society, 1856, p85

3 J. Gairdner, *The Paston Letters, Vol I, 1872*, p505–6

4 Rev J.S. Davies, An English Chronicle, The Camden Socety, 1856, p85

5 Ibid, pp86–90 for the complete articles sent. It is generally a standard attack on those around the king, containing accusations of abuses against the Church and of financial mismanagement.

6 Ibid, p91

7 Ibid, pp91–4 for the entire ballad. This verse appears on p93.

8 J. Gairdner, *The Paston Letters, Vol I, 1872*, p525

9   'Henry VI: October 1460', in *Parliament Rolls of Medieval England*, ed. Chris Given-Wilson, Paul Brand, Seymour Phillips, Mark Ormrod, Geoffrey Martin, Anne Curry and Rosemary Horrox (Woodbridge, 2005), British History Online http://www.british-history.ac.uk/no-series/parliament-rolls-medieval/october-1460 [accessed 16/12/17]. Item 8 details the reversal of the Coventry Parliament. The Act concluded that 'the said parliament held at your said city of Coventry is invalid and not to be considered a parliament; and that all the acts, statutes and ordinances made by authority of the same be reversed, annulled, cancelled, invalidated, repealed, revoked, void and of no force or effect.'

10 The word Parliament first appears in 1236. The first use of elected officials occurred in 1254 and Simon de Monfort's Parliament sat in 1265. De Montfort used elected officials largely because the nobility and Church opposed his seizure of the king. The novel aspect of this sitting was that it was the first time Parliament was summoned by someone other than the monarch. See http://www.parliament.uk/about/living-heritage/evolutionofparliament/originsofparliament/birthofparliament/keydates/1215to1399/

11 'Henry VI: October 1460', in *Parliament Rolls of Medieval England*, ed. Chris Given-Wilson, Paul Brand, Seymour Phillips, Mark Ormrod, Geoffrey Martin, Anne Curry and Rosemary Horrox (Woodbridge, 2005), British History Online http://www.british-history.ac.uk/no-series/parliament-rolls-medieval/october-1460 [accessed 16/12/17]. Item 10 begins the detailing of York's claim, which continues into Item 11. Item 12 describes York's claim being shown to Henry VI before Item 13 provides the objections offered by the Lords. York's answers to these are recorded in Items 14, 15, 16 and 17. The decision of the Lords is detailed in Item 18 and following that are the minutiae of the settlement. The obvious terror and buck-passing is frankly hilarious and warrants reading in its own right, probably with a nice glass of red wine.

12 York was invested as Princes of Wales and Henry VI's heir, with his own heirs to follow him. York was now next in line to the throne, followed by his as-yet childless sons Edward, Edmund, George and then Richard.

13 'Henry VI: October 1460', in *Parliament Rolls of Medieval England*, ed. Chris Given-Wilson, Paul Brand, Seymour Phillips, Mark Ormrod, Geoffrey Martin, Anne Curry and Rosemary Horrox (Woodbridge, 2005), British History Online http://www.british-history.ac.uk/no-series/parliament-rolls-medieval/october-1460 [accessed 16/12/17]. Item 24 states 'if any person or persons scheme or plot the death of the said duke, and are provenly convicted of overt action against him by their peers, that it shall be deemed and adjudged high treason.'

14 J. Gairdner, *The Collections of A Citizen of London*, The Camden Society, 1876, p210

15 Rev J.S. Davies, *An English Chronicle*, The Camden Society, 1856, p106

16 J. Gairdner, *The Collections of A Citizen of London*, The Camden Society, 1876, p210

17 H. Kleineke, 'Alice Martyn, Widow of London', *The Ricardian 14*, 2004, p34

18 J. Gairdner, *The Collections of A Citizen of London*, The Camden Society, 1876, p210

19 George would become the Duke of Clarence and Richard the Duke of Gloucester.

20 Public Record Office, PSO1/23, no. 1247B. In H. Kleineke, 'Alice Martyn, Widow of London', *The Ricardian 14, 2004*, pp32–6. Alice's grant was cancelled by an Act of Resumption in 1465.

21 CPR *Edward IV 1461–1467*, Public Record Office, p52

22 *Letters and Papers Illustrative of the Reign of King Henry the Sixth*, HM Treasury, 1857, p160. An example of York's negotiations with Charles VII for a marriage between his son Edward and Charles' daughter Princess Magdalene can be found here. When York was replaced as Lieutenant-General by Edmund Beaufort, Duke of Somerset, Charles wrote to Henry VI to complain about Edmund's attitude. Charles's envoys had refused to carry letters from Somerset to Charles because 'they were in a style derogatory to the honour of the king, and different from what had been used in time passed by the duke of York and other lords of the blood of the said prince [his] nephew.' This letter is at Ibid pp209–20, p214

23 ed. C.L. Kingsford, *Chronicles of London*, Clarendon Press, 1905, p174. The 'ffeeld', or battle, referred to here is the Second Battle of St Albans on 17 February, suggesting that Warwick's defeat there was the catalyst that caused Cecily to send her sons overseas.

24 J. Gairdner, *The Collections of A Citizen of London*, The Camden Society, 1876, p215

25 ed. C.L. Kingsford, *Chronicles of London*, Clarendon Press, 1905, p173–4

26 Ibid, p174

27 Ibid

28 Rev J.S. Davies, *An English Chronicle*, The Camden Society, 1856, p110

29 *The Chronicles of the White Rose*, James Bohn, 1845, p8

30 J. Gairdner, *The Collections of A Citizen of London*, The Camden Society, 1876, p215

31 Crowland, p424

32 J. Gairdner, *The Collections of A Citizen of London*, The Camden Society, 1876, p218

33 'Milan: 1461', in *Calendar of State Papers and Manuscripts in the Archives and Collections of Milan 1385–1618,* ed. Allen B Hinds (London, 1912), pp. 37–106. British History Online http://www.british-history.ac.uk/cal-state-papers/milan/1385–1618/pp37–106 [accessed 12/12/17]. Item 82. The reference to Charles probably means Philip's son Charles the Bold, whose daughter Mary was then four years old.

34 Ibid, Item 88

35 Ibid, Item 91

36 Ibid, Item 90

To The King's Brother

1 CPR, *Edward IV, 1461–1467,* Public Record Office, 1897, p214

2 ed. C.L. Kingsford, *Chronicles of London,* Clarendon Press, 1905, p176 and *The Chronicles of the White Rose,* James Bohn, 1845, p10. Here, Hearne's Fragment gives the same dates but makes 26 June 1461 a Thursday, when it was in fact a Friday.

3 Ibid, though Hearne's Fragment in *The Chronicles of the White Rose* states that 32 Knights of the Bath were made.

4 *The Chronicles of the White Rose,* James Bohn, 1845, p10

5 ed. C.L. Kingsford, *Chronicles of London,* Clarendon Press, 1905, p176

6 T.D. Hardy, *Rymer's Foedera, Vol II,* Longman and Co, 1873, p692

7 Edward IV: November 1461', in *Parliament Rolls of Medieval England,* ed. Chris Given-Wilson, Paul Brand, Seymour Phillips, Mark Ormrod, Geoffrey Martin, Anne Curry and Rosemary Horrox (Woodbridge, 2005), British History Online http://www.british-history.ac.uk/no-series/parliament-rolls-medieval/november-1461 [accessed 01/01/18], Item 10.

8 T.D. Hardy, *Rymer's Foedera, Vol II,* Longman and Co, 1873, p692

9 CPR, *Edward IV 1461–1467,* Public Record Office, p66

10 J. Ashdown-Hill, *The Third Plantagenet,* The History Press, 2014, p70

11 CPR, *Edward IV 1461–1467,* Public Record Office, p214

12 Ibid, p197

13 R. Somerville, *History of the Duchy of Lancaster, 1953,* p257 (DL 37/34/3)

14 C. Skidmore, *Richard III,* W&N, 2017, p36, from The National Archive DL 37/31/36

15 CPR, *Edward IV 1467–1477,* Public Record Office, pp295–6

16 CPR, *Edward IV 1461–1467,* Public Record Office pp307–8

17 Ibid, p292

18 Ibid, p387

19 Ibid, p391
20 The Tellers' Roll, Michelmas, 5 Edw IV, no 36
21 C.L. Scofield, *The Life and Reign of Edward IV*, Vol I, London, 1923, p216
22 *The Calendar of State Papers of Milan* in particular refer to Edward and Warwick as an inseparable unit ruling the country, rarely speaking of one without the other. Antonio de la Torre, English envoy to the Papal Court and to the Duke of Milan described Warwick in 1461 as 'like another Caesar in these parts'. 'Milan: 1461', in *Calendar of State Papers and Manuscripts in the Archives and Collections of Milan 1385–1618,* ed. Allen B Hinds (London, 1912), pp. 37–106. British History Online http://www.british-history.ac.uk/cal-state-papers/milan/1385–1618/pp37–106 [accessed 03/01/18], Item 58
23 C.L. Scofield, *The Life and Reign of Edward IV, Vol II*, London 1923, p. 384
24 'Milan: 1464', in *Calendar of State Papers and Manuscripts in the Archives and Collections of Milan 1385–1618*, ed. Allen B Hinds (London, 1912), pp. 110–114. British History Online http://www.british-history.ac.uk/cal-state-papers/milan/1385–1618/pp110–114 [accessed 03/01/18], Item 137
25 Ibid, Item 138
26 Ibid, Item 139
27 ed. C.L. Kingsford, *Chronicles of London*, Clarendon Press, 1905, p179
28 *The Chronicles of the White Rose*, James Bohn, 1845, pp15–6
29 J. Gairdner, *The Collections of A Citizen of London,* The Camden Society, 1876, pp226–7
30 Crowland, p439–40
31 J. Ashdown-Hill, *The Third Plantagenet*, The History Press, 2014, p73
32 *Leland's Collectanea, Vol VI,* London, 1770, pp2–14 contains full details of the enthronement feast and food prepared for it.
33 A tun usually contained 252 gallons, though the measure could vary slightly, particularly when unscrupulous merchants sought to extend their profits.

The Loyal Brother

1 https://www.british-history.ac.uk/cal-state-papers/milan/1385–1618/pp117–122 [accessed 12/12/17] Item 155
2 CPR, *Edward IV, 1461–1467*, Public Record Office, 1897, p530
3 https://www.british-history.ac.uk/cal-state-papers/milan/1385–1618/pp117–122 [accessed 12/12/17] Item 149

4 Ibid

5 J. Barker, *Agincourt*, Abacus, 2006, pp160–1 shows a real-world application of this ideal between Sir John Cornwaille and William Porter during the Agincourt campaign.

6 See 'Henry VI: February 1445', in *Parliament Rolls of Medieval England*, ed. Chris Given-Wilson, Paul Brand, Seymour Phillips, Mark Ormrod, Geoffrey Martin, Anne Curry and Rosemary Horrox (Woodbridge, 2005), British History Online http://www.british-history.ac.uk/no-series/parliament-rolls-medieval/february-1445 [accessed 09/01/2018] at Item 19. Suffolk sought to secure for himself a protection from any repercussions from the king's marriage and the handover of Maine and Anjou. Although it is possible his influence over Henry caused the king to take this route, his willingness to excuse Suffolk from any blame suggests otherwise: 'the thirde day of Juyn than next folowyng, to the said communes in thair house accustumed, in the presence of certayne lordes spirituell and temporell there then beyng present, oponed and declared; prayng all the communes, that they wold have this in their rememberaunce, that in the wyse afore said, what so ever fell for defaute of provision for that londe, that thus he hadde acquite hym to the kyng a part, and to all the lordes, and hereof he desyred an acte to be entred in the parlement rolle. The whiche was graunted hym.'

7 'Milan: 1467', in *Calendar of State Papers and Manuscripts in the Archives and Collections of Milan 1385–1618*, ed. Allen B Hinds (London, 1912), pp. 117–122. British History Online http://www. british-history.ac.uk/cal-state-papers/milan/1385–1618/pp117–122 [accessed 12/12/17] Item 149

8 Ibid

9 Ibid

10 Crowland, p457

11 Ibid

12 'Milan: 1467', in *Calendar of State Papers and Manuscripts in the Archives and Collections of Milan 1385–1618*, ed. Allen B Hinds (London, 1912), pp. 117–122. British History Online http://www. british-history.ac.uk/cal-state-papers/milan/1385–1618/pp117–122 [accessed 12/12/17] Item 151

13 Ibid

14 Ibid, Item154

15 Ibid, Item 156

16 CPR, *Edward IV, 1467–77*, Public Record Office, 1900, pp94–5

17 Ibid, p139

18 Ibid, p128

19 ed J. Gairdner, *The Paston Letters*, Vol II, John Grant, Edinburgh, 1910, pp317–319, no 585 is a letter from John Paston the Younger

to Margaret Paston giving his eye-witness account of the festivities to celebrate Margaret's marriage.

20 CPR, *Edward IV, 1467–77*, Public Record Office, 1900, pp170–1

21 BL, Cotton Julius B xii, ff. 115v–116v, *The Ricardian*, Volume XXVI, 2016, *Richard of Gloucester 1461–70: Income, Lands and Associates. His Whereabouts*, A.F. Sutton, pp60–1, n75

22 'Henry VI: October 1460', in *Parliament Rolls of Medieval England*, ed. Chris Given-Wilson, Paul Brand, Seymour Phillips, Mark Ormrod, Geoffrey Martin, Anne Curry and Rosemary Horrox (Woodbridge, 2005), British History Online http://www.british-history.ac.uk/no-series/parliament-rolls-medieval/october-1460 [accessed 13/01/2018], Item 23

23 BL, Cotton Julius B xii, ff. 115v–116v

24 'Henry VI: November 1459', in *Parliament Rolls of Medieval England*, ed. Chris Given-Wilson, Paul Brand, Seymour Phillips, Mark Ormrod, Geoffrey Martin, Anne Curry and Rosemary Horrox (Woodbridge, 2005), British History Online http://www.british-history.ac.uk/no-series/parliament-rolls-medieval/november-1459 [accessed 13/01/2018] Item 38. For reasons best known to himself, Henry VI left this request from his Commons unresolved, deciding instead to consider the matter further.

25 H. Ellis, *Letters Illustrative of English History, Second Series, Vol 1*, Harding and Lepard, 1827, pp143–4

26 ed J. Halliwell, *A Chronicle of the First Thirteen Years of the Reign of King Edward IV* by John Warkworth, London, 1839, p6

27 J. Fenn, *Original Letters Written During the Reigns of Henry VI, Edward IV and Richard III, Vol II*, London, 1787, pp40–2 for all three letters.

28 Bodleian MS Dugdale 15 f. 75 quoted in M. Barnfield, Diriment Impediments, Dispensations and Divorce: Richard III and Matrimony, *The Ricardian*, 2007, Vol 17, n21

29 Crowland, p458

30 'Milan: 1469', in *Calendar of State Papers and Manuscripts in the Archives and Collections of Milan 1385–1618*, ed. Allen B Hinds (London, 1912), pp. 128–134. British History Online http://www.british-history.ac.uk/cal-state-papers/milan/1385–1618/pp128–134 [accessed 03/01/18] Item 173

31 Crowland, p458

32 Ibid

33 J. Gairdner, *The Paston Letters, Vol II*, 1910, p389

34 Ibid

35 Ibid, p390

36 J. Ashdown-Hill, *The Mythology of Richard III*, Amberley, 2015 p91

37 CPR, *Edward IV, 1467–77*, Public Record Office, p178

38 BL Cotton Julius B xii, f. 121v, quoted in *The Ricardian, Vol XXVI*, 2016, p63

39 T.D. Hardy, *Rymer's Foedera*, Vol II, Longman and Co, 1873, p699

40 Calendar of Close Rolls 1468–76 p100, Item 403 *and* 'Close Rolls, Edward IV: 1468–1470', in Calendar of Close Rolls, Edward IV: Volume 2, 1468–1476, ed. W H B Bird and K H Ledward (London, 1953), pp. 94–103. British History Online http://www.british-history.ac.uk/cal-close-rolls/edw4/vol2/pp94–103 [accessed 07/01/2018], Item 403

41 DL 37/38/22

42 CPR, *Edward IV, 1467–77*, Public Record Office, p179

43 'Close Rolls, Edward IV: 1468–1470', *in Calendar of Close Rolls, Edward IV: Volume 2, 1468–1476*, ed. W H B Bird and K H Ledward (London, 1953), pp. 94–103. British History Online http://www.british-history.ac.uk/cal-close-rolls/edw4/vol2/pp94–103 [accessed 15/01/2018] Item 409

44 CPR, *Edward IV, 1467–77,* Public Record Office, p179

45 Ibid, p180

46 E 404/73/2/76 quoted in M. Hicks, False, Fleeting, Perjur'd Clarence: George, Duke of Clarence, 1449–78, Headstart History Publishing, 1992, p55, note 9

A Willing Exile

1 Longleat, MS257

2 New York Public Library, MS De Ricci 67

3 Worcester Record Office, 009:1/BA2636/174/92473 quoted in *The Ricardian, Vol XXVI,* 2016, A.F. Sutton, *Richard of Gloucester...*, p41, note 1

4 Transactions of the Shropshire Archaeological Society, 2nd Series, Vol I, 1889, p237, quoted in the above article, note 2.

5 Ibid

6 R. Horrox & P.W. Hammond, British Library Harleian Manuscript 433, The Richard III Society, 1979, Vol I, p271

7 M. Hicks, *Anne Neville*, Tempus Publishing, 2007, p157

8 R. Horrox, *Richard III: A Study in Service*, Cambridge University Press, 1991, p81

9 CPR, *Edward IV, 1467–77*, Public Record Office, p198

10 ed C. L. Kingsford, *The Stonor Letters and Papers, Vol II*, London, 1919, p70

11 CPR, *Edward IV, 1467–77*, Public Record Office, p185

12 ed J. Halliwell, *A Chronicle of the First Thirteen Years of the Reign of King Edward IV* by John Warkworth, London, 1839, pp51–9 offers evidence regarding the insurrection led by Welles but instigated by George and Warwick

13 *The Ricardian, Vol XXVI*, 2016, A.F. Sutton, *Richard of Gloucester...*, p75

14 J. Gairdner, The Paston Letters, Vol II, 1910, p392

15 Surviving copies can be found in Bodleian Library, MS Rawlinson Poet 143.11, British Library, MS Harley 541 and British Library MS Additional 5830

16 'Close Rolls, Edward IV: March 1470', in *Calendar of Close Rolls, Edward IV: Volume 2, 1468–1476*, ed. W H B Bird and K H Ledward (London, 1953), pp. 133–138. British History Online http://www.british-history.ac.uk/cal-close-rolls/edw4/vol2/pp133–138 [accessed 16/01/2018] Item 535

17 J. Gairdner, *The Paston Letters, Vol II*, 1910, pp395–6

18 CPR, *Edward IV, 1467–77*, Public Record Office, p211

19 'Close Rolls, Edward IV: March 1470', in *Calendar of Close Rolls, Edward IV: Volume 2, 1468–1476*, ed. W H B Bird and K H Ledward (London, 1953), pp. 133–138. British History Online http://www.british-history.ac.uk/cal-close-rolls/edw4/vol2/pp133–138 [accessed 16/01/2018] Item 529.

20 ed A.R. Scoble, *The Memoirs of Philip de Commines, Vol I*, George Bell & Sons, 1906, pp184–5 for Commines account of Warwick's attempt to enter Calais and the loss of Isabel and George's child, though Commines recorded that it was a boy.

21 CPR, Edward IV, 1467–77, Public Record Office, pp219–20

22 Ibid, p205

23 'Edward IV: January 1478', in *Parliament Rolls of Medieval England*, ed. Chris Given-Wilson, Paul Brand, Seymour Phillips, Mark Ormrod, Geoffrey Martin, Anne Curry and Rosemary Horrox (Woodbridge, 2005), British History Online http://www.british-history.ac.uk/no-series/parliament-rolls-medieval/january-1478 [accessed 16/01/2018], Item 16 for the degradation of George Neville in 1478, nominally on the basis that he 'does not and may not have by inheritance any livelihood to support the said name'. In other words, George was unable to live as a duke and so lost his title, leaving him with nothing. The dispossession of the Neville family was effectively completed by this measure.

24 ed J. Halliwell, *A Chronicle of the First Thirteen Years of the Reign of King Edward IV* by John Warkworth, London, 1839, p9

25 CPR, *Edward IV, 1467–77*, Public Record Office, p221

26 Ibid

27 T.D. Hardy, *Rymer's Foedera, Vol II*, Longman and Co, 1873, p700

28 'Milan: 1470', in *Calendar of State Papers and Manuscripts in the Archives and Collections of Milan 1385–1618*, ed. Allen B Hinds (London, 1912), pp. 134–145. British History Online http://www.british-history.ac.uk/cal-state-papers/milan/1385–1618/pp134–145

[accessed 16/01/2018], Items 188–95 chart the negotiations between Warwick and Margaret and details of the marriage of their children. Item 194 explains that Warwick had gone to sea before the wedding took place.

29 ed J. Halliwell, *A Chronicle of the First Thirteen Years of the Reign of King Edward IV* by John Warkworth, London, 1839, p10

30 Crowland, p462

31 Norfolk Records Office, KL/C 7/4, King's Lynn Hall Book 1452–97, p284 quoted in *The Ricardian Vol XVI*, 2016, A.F. Sutton, *Richard of Gloucester...*, p84, note 203

32 ed A.R. Scoble, *The Memoirs of Philip de Commines, Vol I*, George Bell & Sons, 1906, p194

33 Ibid, p192

34 Ibid, p194 It is possible that Commines conflates events, or simply that he assumed Gloucester was with Edward. He is the only lord Commines mentions, though, so it remains possible that they arrived together despite departing from different ports.

35 Ibid

36 *The Ricardian, Vol VI*, 1983, L. Visser-Fuchs, *Richard in Holland 1470–1*, p221, note 6

37 Ibid, p223

38 Ibid, p221, note 10

39 Ibid, note 11

40 Ibid, note 12

41 Ibid, p222, note 18

42 Ibid, p221

43 *The Ricardian, Vol III*, 1974, M. Lulofs, *King Edward IV in Exile*, p10

44 P.W. Hammond, *The Battles of Barnet and Tewkesbury*, Alan Sutton Publishing, 1990, p44, note 24

45 Ibid, pp49–50, note 36

46 *The Ricardian, Vol VI*, 1983, L. Visser-Fuchs, *Richard in Holland 1470–1*, p223, note 23

47 P.W. Hammond, *The Battles of Barnet and Tewkesbury*, Alan Sutton Publishing, 1990, p52

48 R. Vaughan, *Charles the Bold*, London, 1973, p71 *and* ed G.F von der Ropp, Hanserecesse, 1431–1476, series 2, Vol 6, 1890, p404

49 The Ricardian, Vol VI, 1983, L. Visser-Fuchs, *Richard in Holland 1470–1*, p225, note 42

50 J.B.B. van Praet, *Recherches sur Louis de Bruges*, Seigneur de Gruthuyse, Paris, 1831, p11

51 ed A.R. Scoble, *The Memoirs of Philip de Commines, Vol I*, George Bell & Sons, 1906, p192

52 ed J. Halliwell, *A Chronicle of the First Thirteen Years of the Reign of King Edward IV* by John Warkworth, London, 1839, ppxix–xx

The Trials of Battle

1 *The Arrivall,* p1
2 Ibid, p2
3 'Milan: 1471', in *Calendar of State Papers and Manuscripts in the Archives and Collections of Milan 1385–1618,* ed. Allen B Hinds (London, 1912), pp. 145–162. British History Online http://www.british-history.ac.uk/cal-state-papers/milan/1385–1618/pp145–162 [accessed 15 January 2018], Item 210
4 Ibid
5 J. Fenn, *Original Letters Written During the Reigns of Henry VI, Edward IV and Richard III, Vol II,* London, 1787, pp54–6
6 *The Arrivall,* p2
7 Ibid
8 J. Fenn, *Original Letters Written During the Reigns of Henry VI, Edward IV and Richard III, Vol II,* London, 1787, pp58–60
9 *The Arrivall,* p3
10 Ibid
11 Ibid
12 Ibid
13 Ibid, p4
14 Ibid
15 Ibid
16 Ibid, p5
17 ed J. Halliwell, *A Chronicle of the First Thirteen Years of the Reign of King Edward IV* by John Warkworth, London, 1839, pp13–4. Warkworth here identifies a Sir John Westerdale, a priest, who led the men of Holderness against Edward when he landed and that Northumberland's letters, along with the story that he meant only to claim the duchy of York, caused the men to let him pass.
18 *The Arrivall,* p6
19 Ibid, p7 notes that some joined Edward at Wakefield, in his father's former lands, 'but not so many as he supposed wolde have comen'.
20 Ibid, pp7–8
21 Ibid, p8
22 Ibid, p9
23 ed A.R. Scoble, *The Memoirs of Philip de Commines, Vol I,* George Bell & Sons, 1906, pp188–9
24 *The Arrivall* pp9–10
25 Ibid, p11
26 Ibid, p13. The writer leaves a full description of what was obviously considered a momentous moment in the campaign to regain the throne. I am tempted to wonder whether it did happen; the cold church suddenly filled to overflowing with warm bodies and the

temperature change causing the wood to expand and split along a joint. Whatever the cause, Edward was quick to snatch at the PR opportunity and made the most of it.

27 ed J. Halliwell, *A Chronicle of the First Thirteen Years of the Reign of King Edward IV* by John Warkworth, London, 1839, p15
28 Ibid
29 Ibid
30 ed A.R. Scoble, *The Memoirs of Philip de Commines, Vol I*, George Bell & Sons, 1906, p200
31 Ibid, pp17–8
32 Ibid, p18
33 Ibid
34 ed J. Halliwell, *A Chronicle of the First Thirteen Years of the Reign of King Edward IV* by John Warkworth, London, 1839, p15
35 Ibid, p16–7 *and* The Arrivall, pp19–20 provide the accounts of the battle and the detail that follows.
36 It was typical for men encumbered by armour to break these long periods of a battle into chunks of intense fighting punctured by periods of rest when fluid might be taken on. No one could stand in full harness and swing their weapon for six hours solidly. The armies would therefore frequently disengage and press again for an advantage in a series of mini battles. It would nevertheless have been a physically sapping experience.
37 G. von der Ropp, ed., *Hanserecesse, 1431–1476, vol. 6*, Leipzig, 1890, pp. 415–18 *and* The Ricardian, Vol 16, 2006, H. Kleineke, Gerhard von Wese's *Newletter from England, 17 April 1471*, pp9–10. Lord Scales refers to Anthony Woodville, Earl Rivers. He had been known as Lord Scales before his father's death and is here referred to by the older title.
38 *The Arrivall,* p21
39 T.D. Hardy, *Rymer's Foedera, Vol II*, Longman and Co, 1873, p702
40 Ibid, p701
41 *The Arrivall* 1838, p24
42 Ibid, p28, 'that Fryday, which was right-an-hot day, xxx myle and ore; whiche his people might nat finde, in all the way, horse-mete, ne mans-meate, ne so moche as drynke for theyr horses, save in one little broke'.
43 Ibid, p29
44 Ibid, pp28–31 gives *The Arrivall's* full account of the Battle of Tewkesbury.
45 Crowland, p466
46 ed J. Halliwell, *A Chronicle of the First Thirteen Years of the Reign of King Edward IV* by John Warkworth, London, 1839, pp18–9
47 W. Shakespeare, *The Third Part of King Henry the Sixth, Act V, Scene V*

48 ed H. Ellis, *Three Books of Polydore Vergil's English History*, London, 1844, p152

49 *The Arrivall*, p30

50 ed J. Halliwell, *A Chronicle of the First Thirteen Years of the Reign of King Edward IV* by John Warkworth, London, 1839, p18

51 Crowland, p466

52 Ibid

53 ed T. Wright, *Political Poems and Songs Relating to English History, Vol II*, London, 1861, p280

54 Ibid, pp466–7 *and* ed J. Halliwell, *A Chronicle of the First Thirteen Years of the Reign of King Edward IV* by John Warkworth, London, 1839, pp19–20 and *The Arrivall*, pp33–5 for a full account of the Bastard of Fauconberg's assault on London. There was a strong sense that he vastly outnumbered Edward and would have posed a far greater threat than the king had faced either at Barnet or Tewkesbury.

55 *The Arrivall*, pp38–9

56 ed J. Halliwell, *A Chronicle of the First Thirteen Years of the Reign of King Edward IV* by John Warkworth, London, 1839, p20

57 J. Gairdner, *The Paston Letters, Vol II*, 1910, p17

58 W. Shakespeare, *The Third Part of King Henry the Sixth, Act V, Scene VI*

59 *The Arrivall* p38

60 ed J. Halliwell, *A Chronicle of the First Thirteen Years of the Reign of King Edward IV* by John Warkworth, London, 1839, p11. Warkworth describes Henry when taken out of the Tower in 1470 as 'not worschipfully arrayed as a prince, and not so clenly kepte as schuld seme suche a Prynce'. That he remained uninspiring can be seen in the reaction to his progress around London with George Neville that effectively made up the city's mind to let Edward in.

61 Robert Fabyan's *The New Chronicles of England and France*, London, 1811, p662

62 ed J. Halliwell, *A Chronicle of the First Thirteen Years of the Reign of King Edward IV* by John Warkworth, London, 1839, p21

63 Crowland, p468. Note 21 provides H.T. Riley's assertion that the reference to a tyrant was 'a hint of Edward's complicity'.

64 'Milan: 1471', in *Calendar of State Papers and Manuscripts in the Archives and Collections of Milan 1385–1618*, ed. Allen B Hinds (London, 1912), pp. 145–162. British History Online http://www.british-history.ac.uk/cal-state-papers/milan/1385–1618/pp145–162 [accessed 18 February 2018], Item 220

65 I know that Ricardians will baulk at the suggestion, but please bear with me. The possible truth of moments like this fed into the man Richard became and by ignoring possibilities, minds are closed in a way Ricardians have fought against for centuries. Guilt in

one accusation does not translate to universal guilt. That is the traditionalist, Tudor view for Richard. I return to my belief that the white knight must be set aside in order to truly dispel the black legend.

66 W.G. Searle, *The History of the Queen's College of St Margaret and St Bernard in the University of Cambridge 1446–1560,* Cambridge, 1867, p90. pp87–92 give full details of the grant.

The Heir of Warwick

1 J. Fenn, *Original Letters Written During the Reigns of Henry VI, Edward IV and Richard III, Vol II,* London, 1787, pp90–2

2 The Anglo-Burgundian alliance had been behind much of Henry V's success, though a French lack of leadership and unity played a part too. The Treaty of Troyes in 1420 had seen Henry V married to Catherine of Valois, King Charles VI's daughter, and legally proclaimed heir to the French throne. The dissection of Burgundy from England in the mid-1430s, when John, Duke of Bedford's second marriage caused offence to Duke Philip the Good can be considered a key turning point in the English occupation on France.

3 I suggest this based on George's willingness to return to the Yorkist fold after what appeared to be a successful coup in 1470.

4 CPR, *Edward IV, 1467–77,* Public Record Office, p262

5 Anyone holding any property would be directly affected by this. How many kept a weather eye on the fluctuating situation amidst everything else is unclear, but the collection and bequeathing of an inheritance was a preoccupation of medieval men with any means. In 1399, a large part of the backlash against Richard II that swept Henry IV to power lay in Richard II's subversion of the laws of inheritance to try to acquire the vastly wealthy Duchy of Lancaster for himself on the death of his uncle, John of Gaunt.

6 CPR, *Edward IV, 1467–77,* Public Record Office, p266

7 Ibid, p260

8 Ibid, p283

9 Ibid

10 Ibid, p297

11 Crowland, p469

12 Ibid, pp469–70

13 Ibid, p470

14 'Edward IV: October 1472, Third Roll', in *Parliament Rolls of Medieval England,* ed. Chris Given-Wilson, Paul Brand, Seymour Phillips, Mark Ormrod, Geoffrey Martin, Anne Curry and Rosemary Horrox (Woodbridge, 2005), British History Online http://www.british-history.

ac.uk/no-series/parliament-rolls-medieval/october-1472-third-roll [accessed 12 February 2018], Item 16

15 Ibid

16 Ibid

17 ' Edward IV: October 1472, Second Roll', in *Parliament Rolls of Medieval England*, ed. Chris Given-Wilson, Paul Brand, Seymour Phillips, Mark Ormrod, Geoffrey Martin, Anne Curry and Rosemary Horrox (Woodbridge, 2005), British History Online http://www.british-history.ac.uk/no-series/parliament-rolls-medieval/october-1472-second-roll [accessed 12 February 2018], Item 20

18 Ibid, Item 23

19 M.A. Everett Wood, *Letters of Royal and Illustrious Ladies of Great Britain, Vol I,* London, 1846, pp100-4

20 J. Gairdner, *The Paston Letters, Vol III,* 1910, pp92–3. The letter, from Sir John Paston to John Paston, is dated 3 June 1473 and relates that 'the Cowntesse off Warwyk is now owt off Beweley Seyntwarye, and Sir James Tyrell conveyth hyr northward, men seye by the Kynges assent, wherto som men seye that the Duke off Clarance is not agreyd.'

21 A. Hanham, *Richard III and His Early Historians 1483–1535,* Clarendon Press, 1975, p121

22 J. Gairdner, *The Paston Letters, Vol III,* 1910, p98

23 Ibid. Sir John wrote that 'som men thynke that undre thys ther sholde be som other thynge entendyd, and som treason conspyred'. Whatever George's real intention, it is plain from this that his every action was being viewed with suspicion and ulterior, treasonous motives looked for.

24 CPR, *Edward IV, 1467–77,* Public Record Office, p408

25 Ibid, p102

26 'Henry VII: November 1485, Part 1', in *Parliament Rolls of Medieval England*, ed. Chris Given-Wilson, Paul Brand, Seymour Phillips, Mark Ormrod, Geoffrey Martin, Anne Curry and Rosemary Horrox (Woodbridge, 2005), British History Online http://www.british-history.ac.uk/no-series/parliament-rolls-medieval/november-1485-pt-1 [accessed 13 February 2018], 'Furthermore, Elizabeth, late countess of Oxford, [now] dead, mother of the said John de Vere, whose heir he is, for the true and faithful allegiance and service which she, as well as the same John de Vere, owed and did the aforesaid most blessed prince King Henry, was so threatened, put in fear of her life and imprisoned by Richard III, late in deed and not by right king of England, while he was duke of Gloucester, when the same John de Vere was not at his liberty but in prison, that for fear and by means of the same, the same countess, in order to save her life, was compelled to do and make, and to cause her feoffees to do and make,

such estates, releases, confirmations and other things to the said late duke of Gloucester and others to his use of various lordships, manors, lands, tenements and hereditaments of her inheritance, on the instructions of the same late duke and his council, as is notorious and publicly known, against all reason and good conscience; whereby the said John de Vere is likely to be disinherited of a great part of his inheritance unless some remedy is provided for him by authority of parliament in this matter.'

27 J. Ross, *The Ricardian*, 2005, Richard, *Duke of Gloucester and the De Vere Estates*, pp20–32

28 P.D. Clarke, *English Historical Review, vol. 120, English royal marriages and the Papal Penitentiary in the fifteenth century*, 2006, p1028

29 It's flaming complicated, isn't it!?!

30 'Milan: 1469', in *Calendar of State Papers and Manuscripts in the Archives and Collections of Milan 1385–1618*, ed. Allen B Hinds (London, 1912), pp. 128–134. British History Online http://www.british-history.ac.uk/cal-state-papers/milan/1385–1618/pp128–134 [accessed 13 February 2018], Item 173

31 I could write an entire book on the inability to prove things in relation to Richard throughout his life which ought, in my opinion, to be accepted as truth. Denying them is often an act of faith every bit as much as accepting them and it epitomises the problem of arguing a case in favour of or in opposition to Richard in many of the events of his life. For as long as these issues remain unresolved, the debate will be forced onwards, with neither side willing to concede to the other.

32 Crowland, p470

The Lord of the North

1 'Edward IV: October 1472, First Roll', in *Parliament Rolls of Medieval England*, ed. Chris Given-Wilson, Paul Brand, Seymour Phillips, Mark Ormrod, Geoffrey Martin, Anne Curry and Rosemary Horrox (Woodbridge, 2005), British History Online http://www.british-history.ac.uk/no-series/parliament-rolls-medieval/october-1472-first-roll [accessed 13 February 2018], Item 39 for all that follows.

2 J.L. Laynesmith, *Cecily Duchess of York*, Bloomsbury, 2017, pp134–6 and Notes 30–46 for detailed references of the following dispute. Details of the case are cited at Essex Record Office D/DQ/14/124/3/41 & 42

3 CPR, *Edward IV, 1467–77*, Public Record Office, p317

4 Ibid, p338

5 Ibid

6 Ibid, p329
7 Ibid, p339
8 'Milan: 1472', in *Calendar of State Papers and Manuscripts in the Archives and Collections of Milan 1385–1618*, ed. Allen B Hinds (London, 1912), pp. 162–172. British History Online http://www.british-history.ac.uk/cal-state-papers/milan/1385–1618/pp162–172 [accessed 12/12/2017], Item 237
9 The relationship between the Crown and Parliament is fascinating throughout the medieval period. I would argue that there was a constant effort from the Conquest onward to restrict the authority of the Crown and to return Parliament to something like the role of the Anglo-Saxon Witan, which had reserved for itself the authority to elect and appoint kings. Magna Carta was a crisis point in this movement that endured throughout the thirteenth century. The Wars of the Roses was a high-water mark in Parliament's authority in this regard. It became the arbitrator of competing rights and the vehicle for legitimisation of royal titles. To Henry VIII, it would be a method of imposing and approving his control of the Church and a posthumous obsession with the line of succession that was deemed to override the will of Edward VI on the matter. The next crisis would arrive when Charles I took an attitude to Parliament not dissimilar to Edward IV's and Parliament's desire to enforce what it considered its rights led to the Civil War. There's a book in here somewhere, I'm certain.
10 CPR, *Edward IV, 1467–77*, Public Record Office, p366
11 Ibid, p426
12 Ibid
13 C. Ross, *Richard III*, Methuen, 1990, p50
14 Ibid, Warwick had paid a fee of £13 6s 8d and Richard increased this to £20, perhaps as a sweetener to Conyers' continued service.
15 Sixth Report of the Royal Commission on Historical Manuscripts, Part 1, London, 1877, pp223–4
16 CPR, *Edward IV, 1467–77*, Public Record Office, p464
17 Ibid, p505
18 Ibid, pp466–7
19 Ibid, p549
20 Ibid, p556
21 T.D. Hardy, *Rymer's Foedera, Vol II*, Longman and Co, 1873, p704
22 Ibid, p705. The treaty was ratified by Edward and James III on 3 November 1474.
23 Ibid, p705. On 26 October a notarial attestation was recorded of the marriage. A proxy ceremony had taken place in which David Lindesaye, Earl of Crawford had represented the Scottish king and John, Lord Scrope the English. John, 5th Baron Scrope of Bolton was

based at Bolton Castle in Wensleydale, less than 10 miles north-west of Middleham. He was well known to Richard and became a close associate, so Richard may have been involved in securing this appointment for him.

24 Ibid, p706. On 3 December 1474, Edward received an indenture from Richard Langport to deliver the dowry. James granted the safe conducts on 16 January 1475 and a receipt for the payment was noted on 3 February 1475.

25 Ibid, pp704–6. The items are provided in chronological order on these pages, so I have avoided referencing them individually, telling myself that you, the reader won't mind, but in fact, perhaps being a bit lazy.

26 Ibid, p706 for the above items, again in chronological order on the page.

27 F. Devon, *Issues of the Exchequer*, London, 1837, p498: 'To Richard, Duke of Gloucester, for the wages of 116 men at arms, including himself ; viz. as Duke, at 13s. 4d. per day, 60*l*. 13s. 4d.; 6 knights, to each of them 2s. per day – 54*l*. 12s.; and to each of the remainder of the said 116 men at arms, 12c*l*. per day and 6d. per day as a reward,—743*l*. 18s. 6 d.; and to 950 archers in his retinue, to each of them 6d. per day, — 2161*l*. 5s.'

28 C.L Scofield, *The Life and Reign of Edward the Fourth*, Volume II, Fonthill, 2016, p117, note 2. The Teller's Roll recorded payment to Richard of an additional £666 13s 4d because of the extra men he had provided.

29 Sizes of medieval armies are rarely known with precision. This figure represents the most likely rough calculation based on indentures, wages paid and contemporary reports, but it cannot be a precise number.

30 ed A. Wiggins & R. Field, *Guy of Warwick: Icon and Ancestor*, D.S.Brewer, 2007, p164

31 I would suggest that there are no contemporary accounts of Richard's scoliosis made during his lifetime. Rous mentions it, but only after 1485 when he wrote his derogatory account of Richard. He may have been reporting something that was known but rarely discussed publicly out of fear or respect for Richard, but equally the curvature of his spine may only have become known to some after Bosworth, when his boy was stripped and taken to Leicester. With his clothing and any compensating padding removed, the effects of the scoliosis would have been clear to see. Still it was not widely reported even then.

32 ed J. Bristocke Sheppard, *The Letter Books of the Monastery of Christ Church, Canterbury*, Vol III, London, 1889, pp274–85 for the entire speech. It is standard late medieval rhetoric, but demonstrates

both the preoccupation with war in Edward's mind and the benefits to the nation of engaging in an offensive campaign in France.

33 ed J.G. Nichols, *The Book of Noblesse*, 2010, p49
34 Ibid, p50
35 I have inferred this from several pieces of suggestive evidence. That Richard held his father and brother in high esteem is suggested by his prominent part in their reburial, which will be examined later, and foundations to pray for their souls, which will also follow. An interest in delivering the Yorkist manifesto is discernible in his demonstrable commitment to justice and equity and I believe he had developed as a child a form of hero worship of his brother Edward, though this may have become tarnished a little by now, and certainly would be by the end of the French campaign. In these regards, it is possible to see Richard as the conscience of the Yorkist regime, trying to deliver his father's promises in an attempt to ensure the stability of the dynasty. This sense of responsibility may have fed into later events in 1483. This is, of course, all supposition, but it is feasible in an attempt to discover a three-dimensional Richard.

Tarnished Glory

1 British Library BL Add MS 48031, folio 187 and *The Politics of Fifteenth Century England: John Vale's Book*, Alan Sutton Publishing, 1995, p266. This letter, on the eve of the invasion of France, echoes sentiments used by Henry V in 1415 and implies a determination to fight on Edward's part, though it is also traditional rhetoric in the build up to an attack.
2 Ibid
3 ed A.R. Scoble, *The Memoirs of Philip de Commines, Lord of Argenton*, Vol I, London, 1906, p252
4 Ibid p251. For the account of the invasion of France I have relied heavily on Cora Scofield's *The Life and Reign of Edward the Fourth* and Philip de Commines' *Memoirs*. Although Commines is probably not reliable on the landing of Edward in Holland in 1470, he was an eye witness to much of what occurred during the English invasion of France. Having transferred his allegiance from Burgundy to France, Commines was close to Louis XI and present during the negotiations for peace that followed.
5 C. L. Scofield, *The Life and Reign of Edward the Fourth*, Vol II, Fonthill Media, 2016 (originally published 1923), p132
6 Ibid
7 ed A.R. Scoble, *The Memoirs of Philip de Commines, Lord of Argenton, Vol I*, London, 1906, p257
8 Ibid, pp257–8

Richard III

9 Ibid, p258

10 Ibid, p261

11 Ibid, p253

12 This is slightly odd, I think. Edward would no doubt want this viewed as a personal victory, for he had to polish this immediate capitulation somehow, so the pension was to be tied to him personally. If the English ejected him, the country would lose the money, but England might have been okay about losing French bribes. There was the risk of creating a problem in this measure too, since Louis' easiest and best route to being rid of the cost and possible embarrassment was to be rid of Edward, thus bringing the contract to an end.

13 ed A.R. Scoble, *The Memoirs of Philip de Commines, Lord of Argenton*, Vol I, London, 1906, pp263–4 and C. L. Scofield, *The Life and Reign of Edward the Fourth*, Vol II, Fonthill Media, 2016 (originally published 1923), p136

14 C. L. Scofield, *The Life and Reign of Edward the Fourth*, Vol II, Fonthill Media, 2016 (originally published 1923), pp136–7

15 ed A.R. Scoble, *The Memoirs of Philip de Commines, Lord of Argenton*, Vol I, London, 1906, p264

16 Ibid, p268

17 Ibid

18 C. L. Scofield, *The Life and Reign of Edward the Fourth*, Vol II, Fonthill Media, 2016 (originally published 1923), p139. Commines gives 300 carts, but this may be his propensity to exaggerate at work again.

19 ed A.R. Scoble, *The Memoirs of Philip de Commines, Lord of Argenton*, Vol I, London, 1906, p269. pp269–72 give an account of the English soldiers' behaviour at Amiens, which sounds a lot like English football fans abroad today. Drink led to violence and brought shame on the country.

20 Ibid, p275

21 Ibid, p278

22 Ibid p277

23 Ibid

24 Ibid, p267

25 ed A.R. Scoble, *The Memoirs of Philip de Commines, Lord of Argenton*, Vol II, London, 1856, p6

26 ed A.R. Scoble, *The Memoirs of Philip de Commines, Lord of Argenton*, Vol I, London, 1906, p279

27 'Milan: 1475', in *Calendar of State Papers and Manuscripts in the Archives and Collections of Milan 1385–1618*, ed. Allen B Hinds (London, 1912), pp. 189–220. British History Online http://www.british-history.ac.uk/cal-state-papers/milan/1385–1618/pp189–220 [accessed 21 February 2018], Item 319: 'When the King of England

was returning by sea from London to Calais, he had the Duke of Xestre thrown into the sea, whom he had previously kept a prisoner, according to what the duke told me, who resented the action.'

28 T.D. Hardy, *Rymer's Foedera, Vol II*, Longman and Co, 1873, p707 and C. L. Scofield, *The Life and Reign of Edward the Fourth, Vol II*, Fonthill Media, 2016 (originally published 1923), pp157–8

29 'Milan: 1475', in *Calendar of State Papers and Manuscripts in the Archives and Collections of Milan 1385–1618*, ed. Allen B Hinds (London, 1912), pp. 189–220. British History Online http://www. british-history.ac.uk/cal-state-papers/milan/1385–1618/pp189–220 [accessed 21 February 2018], Item 304

30 Ibid, Item 313

31 Crowland, p474

32 C. L. Scofield, *The Life and Reign of Edward the Fourth, Vol II*, Fonthill Media, 2016, p156

33 York Books, pp8–9

34 Ibid

35 'Milan: 1475', in *Calendar of State Papers and Manuscripts in the Archives and Collections of Milan 1385–1618*, ed. Allen B Hinds (London, 1912), pp. 189–220. British History Online http://www. british-history.ac.uk/cal-state-papers/milan/1385–1618/pp189–220 [accessed 22 February 2018], Item 316

36 Crowland, pp473–4

37 Ibid, p474

38 Ibid

39 'Edward IV: January 1478', in *Parliament Rolls of Medieval England*, ed. Chris Given-Wilson, Paul Brand, Seymour Phillips, Mark Ormrod, Geoffrey Martin, Anne Curry and Rosemary Horrox (Woodbridge, 2005), British History Online http://www.british-history.ac.uk/ no-series/parliament-rolls-medieval/january-1478 [accessed 23 February 2018], Item 16

40 In the case of George, Richard clearly had a vested interest in keeping him safe. His care for Anne Beauchamp when it brought no such benefit to him suggests that there may have been a less selfish motive at work too. Richard was, by now, established as the successor to the Neville lands, power and allegiances. It is reasonable that he may have felt some sense of responsibility to protect vulnerable victims of the family's fall who were not culpable for it, such as young George Neville. He seems to have remained close to John Neville's widow, George Neville's mother, as she joined the Corpus Christi Guild in York at the same time as Richard and Anne, and one of Richard's indented men Thomas, Lord Scrope of Masham was married to one of John Neville's daughters (see later for both events). Neither would it hurt his

standing amongst those with a lingering affection for the family to be seen as their salvation. Nevertheless, Richard needed George Neville alive and producing heirs to protect himself. If George died in poverty somewhere, unable to secure a marriage, Richard lost the ability to pass the Neville inheritance to his own son.

41 Milan: 1476', in *Calendar of State Papers and Manuscripts in the Archives and Collections of Milan 1385–1618*, ed. Allen B Hinds (London, 1912), pp. 220–229. British History Online http://www.british-history.ac.uk/cal-state-papers/milan/1385–1618/pp220–229 [accessed 23 February 2018], Item 322

42 CPR, *Edward IV, 1467–77*, Public Record Office, p583

43 I am wary of romanticising Richard's role, but it is entirely possible that this was part of the same kind of fascination with self and personal heritage that drives the modern interest in genealogy. Richard was only eight when his father and brother died, so may not have known them well, but this might have only added to the need to feel connected to them. It was his father's decade or more of work that had positioned Edward to take the throne and put Richard where he was now. For Richard, this was a chance to honour his father in a way he had never been able to before and to bring closure to the darkest chapter of his life.

44 C. Ross, *Richard III*, Methuen, 1981, p29, Note 22 for some reference to the potential dates of birth.

45 This is my assessment of George. I sense that he always wanted to be Edward, hence his willingness to abandon his brothers when Warwick promised him the throne and his swift volte-face when he found his prospects relegated behind Henry VI, Edward of Westminster and any children that prince had. His constant willingness to oppose his brother openly suggests resentment, despite being a royal duke and one of the wealthiest, best landed nobles in the country. It was never quite enough. Perhaps almost a decade as Edward's heir took a toll and George found himself unable to let go of the prospect as his brother had more and more children, and a son seemed an increasingly likely threat to George. This is my personal opinion of George, and I find him an endlessly fascinating enigma, hell-bent on self-destruction.

46 H. Schnitmer, *Margaret of York*, Richard III & Yorkist History Trust and Shaun Tyas, 2016, p71

47 Crowland, p478

48 I suggest that Hastings was opposed to the peace because of the previously discussed issue of his failure to provide a receipt for his pension.

49 J. Fenn, *Original Letters Written During the Reigns of Henry VI, Edward IV and Richard III*, Vol II, London, 1787, pp204–7

50 H. Ellis, *Original Letters Illustrative of English History*, Vol I, Hardin, Triphook and Lepard, 1824, pp16–7

After E., G Should Reign

1 A. Hanham, *Richard III and His Early Historians 1483–1535*, Clarendon Press, 1975, p121
2 York Books, p9
3 Ibid, p10
4 Ibid, p129
5 Ibid, p130
6 Ibid
7 Ibid, pp268–9
8 Ibid, pp46–7
9 Ibid, p44
10 Ibid, p48
11 Ibid, p78
12 See later during George's attainder in Parliament.
13 'Edward IV: January 1478', in *Parliament Rolls of Medieval England*, ed. Chris Given-Wilson, Paul Brand, Seymour Phillips, Mark Ormrod, Geoffrey Martin, Anne Curry and Rosemary Horrox (Woodbridge, 2005), British History Online http://www.british-history.ac.uk/no-series/parliament-rolls-medieval/january-1478 [accessed 27 February 2018], Item 17 for the account of Ankarette's treatment. This version was provided by her family as they tried to clear her name of the charges laid against her.
14 Crowland, p478
15 Ibid
16 *Rotuli Parliamentorum*, Vol VI, London, 1777, p193. pp193–5 provides the transcript of an original copy from the Tower of London. For the avoidance of referencing each one, all subsequent extracts of the attainder can be found in these pages. I will only add a footnote where the page changes. This attainder is significantly longer and more detailed than the version available at British History Online.
17 Ibid, p194
18 Ibid, p195
19 Mancini, p63
20 ed J. Gairdner, *Letters and Papers Illustrative of the Reigns of Richard III and Henry VII*, Vol I, London, 1861, p68
21 Mancini, p63
22 *Illustrations of Ancient State and Chivalry*, London, 1811, p29. pp27–40 contains a detailed account of the marriage on which I have relied here.

23 Ibid, p30

24 Ibid, p31. The editor notes that the reference to 'my Lord of Richmond' being in attendance was Henry Tudor, Earl of Richmond, later King Henry VII. This is not possible. Henry was in Brittany at this point and the subject of efforts by Edward to secure his custody. In 1472, George had been granted access to the lands and properties of the 'earldom, honour and lordship of Richmond', the reversion of which he held from the queen's father and mother (CPR, *Edward IV, 1467–77*, Public Record Office, p342). It is possible the Richmond referred to here was George's son Edward, using a courtesy title, since the wedding was just before George's attainder was passed through Parliament. In March, Richard would receive the castle and town of Richmond (see later), so it may also be a reference to his son Edward of Middleham as a courtesy title.

25 Ibid, pp32–4. Sir Robert Clifford is worthy of note amongst those taking part in the jousts. He would later loudly proclaim across the Continent that Perkin Warbeck was the real Richard, Duke of York, and it is clear that he was in prince's company on this occasion at the very least.

26 'Edward IV: January 1478', in *Parliament Rolls of Medieval England*, ed. Chris Given-Wilson, Paul Brand, Seymour Phillips, Mark Ormrod, Geoffrey Martin, Anne Curry and Rosemary Horrox (Woodbridge, 2005), British History Online http://www.british-history.ac.uk/no-series/parliament-rolls-medieval/january-1478 [accessed 27 February 2018], Items 10–11 for the settlement of the Mowbray inheritance.

27 Ibid, Item 11

28 Crowland, p481

29 I make this assumption from the swift return of the Norfolk inheritance to John, Lord Howard, later Duke of Norfolk, in 1483. As shall be discussed later, Howard was Anne Mowbray's legal heir and Richard was quick to put this legal injustice right. For some, his motive was a cynical bid to win support, but I don't think that stands up to the facts that will follow when that part of the story is reached.

30 CPR, *Edward IV, 1476–85*, Public Record Office, p67

31 Ibid

32 'Edward IV: January 1478', in *Parliament Rolls of Medieval England*, ed. Chris Given-Wilson, Paul Brand, Seymour Phillips, Mark Ormrod, Geoffrey Martin, Anne Curry and Rosemary Horrox (Woodbridge, 2005), British History Online http://www.british-history.ac.uk/no-series/parliament-rolls-medieval/january-1478 [accessed 27 February 2018], Item 13

33 CPR, *Edward IV, 1476–85*, Public Record Office, p90

34 Ibid, p112

35 Raine, J, 'The statutes ordained by Richard Duke of Gloucester for the College of Middleham, 1478', *Archaeological Journal*, 14, 1857, pp160–70 for the complete document of the statutes. This reference is at p160, and I shall footnote only changes of page again (I know, still lazy!)

36 Ibid, p161

37 Ibid, p163

38 Ibid, p164

39 Ibid, p166

40 Ibid, p167

41 Ibid, pp168–9 The full list of saints is: St John the Baptist, St John the Evangelist, St Peter, St Paul, St Simon, St Jude, St Michael, St Anne, St Elizabeth, St Fabian, St Sebastian, St Anthony, St Christopher, St Dionysius, St Blaise, St Thomas, St Alban, St Giles, St Eustace, St Erasmus, St Loy, St Leonard, St Martin, St William of York, St Wifred of Rippon, St Catherine, St Margaret, St Barbara, St Martha, St Winefrid, St Ursula, St Dorothy, St Radagund, St Agnes, St Agatha, St Apollonia, St Cithe, St Clare and St Mary Magdalene.

War in the North

1 'Venice: 1481–1485', in *Calendar of State Papers Relating To English Affairs in the Archives of Venice*, Volume 1, 1202–1509, ed. Rawdon Brown (London, 1864), pp. 141–159. British History Online http://www.british-history.ac.uk/cal-state-papers/venice/vol1/pp141–159 [accessed 12 December 2017], Item 483

2 Mancini, p63 states that after George's execution 'he came very rarely to court'. It is a view that has stuck that Richard shunned his last remaining brother after George's execution, but it is demonstrably untrue.

3 CPR, *Edward IV, 1476–85*, Public Record Office, p133

4 Ibid, p154

5 Ibid, p166

6 North Riding County Record Office, Clervaux Cartulary, ZQH 1, fos 155–6 quoted in A.J. Pollard, *Richard III and the Princes in the Tower*, Bramley Books, 1997, Appendix 1, pp234–6

7 Washington DC, Library of Congress, Thatcher, 1004 quoted in A.J. Pollard, *Richard III and the Princes in the Tower*, Bramley Books, 1997, Appendix 2, p237

8 York Books, p255

9 See M. Lewis, *Richard, Duke of York: King By Right* for my views of Richard's father and the notions that drove him into opposition to Henry VI. A sense amongst the nobility that they had an obligation to use their position to protect those in their care as well as to further

their own temporal and dynastic aims is easy to dismiss but lay at the heart of the chivalric ideals we have seen Richard being exposed to in books such as Ipomedon. There is, of course, a diametrically opposed interpretation of both father and son available. And I know. Citing my own book. Loser.

10 Scofield is essential and very detailed reading on these events, which would take up too much space here. The section entitled 'Louis XI's Pensioner' explains Edward's position and actions in far more depth that a biography of Richard can justify.

11 These payments can be seen at regular points throughout Rymer's Foedera from 1474.

12 Crowland, p481

13 CPR, *Edward IV, 1476–85*, Public Record Office, p183

14 Ibid, p205

15 Ibid, pp213–4

16 York Books, pp220–1

17 *A Chronicle of London From 1089 to 1483*, Longman, Rees, Orme, Brown and Green, 1827, p147. 'And this yere the duke of Gloucestre, and therle of Northumberland reisid grete people agein the Scottes, which fledded and wold not bide.'

18 F. Devon, *Issues of the Exchequer*, London, 1837, p499

19 Ibid, p501

20 York Books, p223. York sent one of their aldermen to see Richard at Sheriff Hutton.

21 Scofield, p320, note 1

22 ed J. Bain, *Calendar of Documents Relating to Scotland*, Vol IV, Edinburgh, 1888, p300

23 Ibid

24 'Venice: 1481–1485', in *Calendar of State Papers Relating To English Affairs in the Archives of Venice*, Volume 1, 1202–1509, ed. Rawdon Brown (London, 1864), pp. 141–159. British History Online http://www.british-history.ac.uk/cal-state-papers/venice/vol1/pp141–159 [accessed 12 March 2018], Item 475

25 CPR, *Edward IV, 1476–85*, Public Record Office, p254

26 Scofield, pp303–5

27 CPR, *Edward IV, 1476–85*, Public Record Office, p343

28 Scofield, p334, note 3: *Duchy of Lancaster, Entry Books of Decrees and Orders, Vol I, p62*

29 York Books, p251

30 Ibid, p252

31 ed H.E. Malden, *The Cely Papers*, Longman, Green and Co, 1900, p105

32 York Books, p256

33 T.D. Hardy, *Rymer's Foedera*, Vol II, Longman and Co, 1873, p713

34 P.M. Kendall, *Richard the Third*, Norton, 1955, p166

35 T.D. Hardy, *Rymer's Foedera*, Vol II, Longman and Co, 1873, p713

36 F. Devon, *Issues of the Exchequer*, London, 1837, p502

37 York Books, p259

38 E. Hall, *Hall's Chronicle*, London, 1809, p332 provides a list of the towns and villages burned.

39 'Rymer's Foedera with Syllabus: July–December 1482', in *Rymer's Foedera* Volume 12, ed. Thomas Rymer (London, 1739–1745), pp. 159–172. British History Online http://www.british-history.ac.uk/rymer-foedera/vol12/pp159-172 [accessed 13 March 2018]

40 E. Hall, *Hall's Chronicle*, London, 1809, pp332–3. Hall appears to have had access to some documents that no longer exist, though there is little reason to doubt his veracity in referring to them here.

41 Ibid. Again, it seems to be accepted that Hall was working from original documents that no longer survive. His version could, therefore, be erroneous, but it seems to fit with the aftermath.

42 'Rymer's Foedera with Syllabus: July–December 1482', in *Rymer's Foedera* Volume 12, ed. Thomas Rymer (London, 1739–1745), pp. 159–172. British History Online http://www.british-history.ac.uk/rymer-foedera/vol12/pp159-172 [accessed 13 March 2018]

43 F. Devon, *Issues of the Exchequer*, London, 1837, p502

44 Ibid, p501

45 Scofield, pp347–8

46 W.A. Shaw, *The Knights of England*, Vol II, London, 1906, pp19–21

47 Ibid, pp17–8

48 'Venice: 1481–1485', in *Calendar of State Papers Relating To English Affairs in the Archives of Venice*, Volume 1, 1202–1509, ed. Rawdon Brown (London, 1864), pp. 141–159. British History Online http://www.british-history.ac.uk/cal-state-papers/venice/vol1/pp141-159 [accessed 12 December 2017], Item 483

49 Crowland, p481

50 T.D. Hardy, *Rymer's Foedera*, Vol II, Longman and Co, 1873, p713 for 12 October decision to abandon the marriage and p714 for 27 October notification of the decision to the provost and citizens of Edinburgh.

51 York Books, pp248–9

52 Ibid p250

53 *Rotuli Parliamentorum*, Vol VI, London, 1777, p204

54 Ibid, p205

55 Scofield, p359 describes Parliament as being 'completely under Gloucester's thumb' and that Edward's illness 'had so weakened his judgment and understanding that he did not realise what he was doing'. This seems, to me, to be building a scenario to excuse something that in fact had benefit to the king and was warranted by Richard's services.

The King Is Dead

1 H.T. Riley, *Ingulph's Chronicle of the Abbey of Croyland*, George Bell and Sons, 1908, p482

2 Ibid, pp481–2

3 Ibid, p483

4 L.C. Attreed, *The York House Books*, Vol I, Alan Sutton Publishing, 1991, pp281–2

5 A. Carson, *Richard Duke of Gloucester as Lord Protector and High Constable of England*, Imprimis Imprimatur, 2015, p48, note 145 citing BL Sloane MS 3479 fos 53v–58r and Appendix IX for full translated text.

6 Ibid, p97

7 E. Ives, 'Andrew Dymmock and the papers of Rivers', p229

8 Ibid

9 ed C.A.J. Armstrong, *The Usurpation of Richard III by Dominic Mancini*, Alan Sutton Publishing, 1984, pp71–3

10 Ibid, pp65–7

11 *Grafton's Chronicle*, Vol II, London, 1809, p83

12 P. & F. Strong, 'The Last Will and Codicils of Henry V.' *The English Historical Review*, vol. 96, no. 378, 1981, pp. 79–102. JSTOR, www.jstor.org/stable/568386. Also A. Carson, *Richard Duke of Gloucester as Lord Protector and High Constable of England*, Imprimis Imprimatur, 2015, pp13–16 for further discussion.

13 See previously and CPRs, *Edward IV, 1467–77*, Public Record Office, p366

14 ed C.A.J. Armstrong, *The Usurpation of Richard III by Dominic Mancini*, Alan Sutton Publishing, 1984, p71

15 Ibid

16 Ibid

17 Ibid

8 Ibid, p73

9 ed H. Ellis, *Three Books of Polydore Vergil's English History*, London, 1844, p173

20 ed C.A.J. Armstrong, *The Usurpation of Richard III by Dominic Mancini*, Alan Sutton Publishing, 1984, p73

21 Ibid, p75

22 H.T. Riley, *Ingulph's Chronicle of the Abbey of Croyland*, George Bell and Sons, 1908, p485

23 Ibid

24 Ibid

25 Ibid, p486

26 Ibid

27 Ibid

28 Ibid, pp486–7 and ed C.A.J. Armstrong, *The Usurpation of Richard III by Dominic Mancini*, Alan Sutton Publishing, 1984, pp75–7 for details of this episode.

29 'Rymer's Foedera with Syllabus: July–December 1471', in *Rymer's Foedera* Volume 11, ed. Thomas Rymer (London, 1739–1745), pp. 714–733. British History Online http://www.british-history.ac.uk/rymer-foedera/vol11/pp714–733 [accessed 19 March 2018] *and* C. Scofield, *The Life and Reign of Edward the Fourth*, Vol II, Fonthill, 2016, p4

30 ed C.A.J. Armstrong, *The Usurpation of Richard III by Dominic Mancini*, Alan Sutton Publishing, 1984, p79

31 H.T. Riley, *Ingulph's Chronicle of the Abbey of Croyland*, George Bell and Sons, 1908, p487

32 ed C.A.J. Armstrong, *The Usurpation of Richard III by Dominic Mancini*, Alan Sutton Publishing, 1984, p77

33 H.T. Riley, *Ingulph's Chronicle of the Abbey of Croyland*, George Bell and Sons, 1908, p487

34 Cotton Vespasian F XIII

35 ed R. Horrox & P.W. Hammond, BL Harleian MS 433, Volume 1, The Richard III Society, 1979, pp3–4. The entry is undated but was made at St Albans. The assumption that Geffrey was a man familiar to and liked by the king is made from the description of him as 'our beloved in Christ'.

36 ed C.A.J. Armstrong, *The Usurpation of Richard III by Dominic Mancini*, Alan Sutton Publishing, 1984, p83

37 Robert Fabyan's *The New Chronicles of England and France*, London, 1811, p668

38 ed C.A.J. Armstrong, *The Usurpation of Richard III by Dominic Mancini*, Alan Sutton Publishing, 1984, p83

39 H.T. Riley, *Ingulph's Chronicle of the Abbey of Croyland*, George Bell and Sons, 1908, p487

40 R.R. Sharpe, *London and the Kingdom*, London, 1894, p320

41 ed A.R. Scoble, *The Memoirs of Philip de Commines*, Vol I, George Bell & Sons, 1906, p187

Protector

1 Crowland, p488

2 S. Bentley, *Excerpta Historica*, London, 1831, pp366–9

3 ed F.R.H. du Boulay, *Registrum Thome Bourchier*, Canterbury & York Society, 1957, pp52–3

4 Mancini, p85

5 Crowland, p487. Crowland interestingly refers to this meeting as 'Parliament', which it clearly was not. Why he would use the word is something of a mystery.

6 Ibid

7 Ibid, p488

8 Ibid, p487

9 Ibid, pp487–8

10 Mancini, p85

11 Take my word for it, or read Mancini's account in full if you would rather, but bear in mind as you do who his sources must have been. Gossips and Woodville sympathisers seem to have been the only voices reaching his ears.

12 Robert Fabyan's *The New Chronicles of England and France*, London, 1811, p668

13 R. Grafton, *Grafton's Chronicle*, Vol I, Johnson et al, 1809, pp86–8

14 ed H. Ellis, Three Books of Polydore Vergil's English History, London, 1844, pp176–7

15 Mancini, p81

16 R. Horrox, *Richard III: A Study in Service*, Cambridge University Press, 1991, p91. The efforts to prepare against the French threat alone had cost Edward IV £3,670.

17 ed R. Horrox, **Financial Memoranda of the Reign of Edward V**, Camden Miscellany Vol XXIX, 1987, p211 and 216

18 Crowland, p488

19 Ibid

20 Grants etc, pp1–2

21 Ibid, p2

22 Ibid, p3

23 Ibid, p2

24 Ibid, p5

25 Ibid

26 Ibid, pp31–2

27 Ibid, pp49–50

28 Ibid, p12

29 Ibid, p15

30 Ibid, pp63–4

31 Ibid, pp69–70

32 York Books, pp283–4

33 Grants etc, p68

34 R. Davies, *Extracts from the Municipal Records of the City of York*, London, 1843, pp149–50

35 Mancini, p91

36 C. Lethbridge Kingsford, *The Stonor Letters and Papers*, Vol II, London, 1919, pp159–60

37 By now I am aware that this will sound like the ravings of a rampant, unrestrained apologist for Richard. I am not that, but rather I challenge the belief in unsubstantiated stories that have clung about

Richard's reputation: when the facts are examined, the myths often fall away if an open mind can be applied. Ready? Let's go.

38   Mancini, p91

39   R.F. Green, 'Historical Notes of a London Citizen 1483–4', *English Historical Review*, Vol 96, 1981, p588

40   Crowland, p488

41   Mancini, p91

42   R.F. Green, 'Historical Notes of a London Citizen 1483–4', *English Historical Review*, Vol 96, 1981, p588

43   See previous discussion of the powers of the Constable above.

44   Crowland, p488

45   ed H. Ellis, *Three Books of Polydore Vergil's English History*, London, 1844, p175

46   T. More, 'History of King Richard III', in *The Great Debate*, The Folio Society, 1965, p71

47   Ibid, p69

48   The meaning of strawberries in Catholicism can be found in several locations (e.g. http://www.catholictradition.org/Saints/signs4.htm). More's motives are hard to discern, as are his reasons for setting his work aside. Did he discover that what he had been told by Morton was untrue? Was his work a deliberate attempt to obscure the truth? At least one theory places More as a central figure in protecting the sons of King Edward IV well into the Tudor era.

49   T. More, 'History of King Richard III', in *The Great Debate*, The Folio Society, 1965, p68

50   N. Amin, *The House of Beaufort*, Amberley Publishing, 2017, pp36–8

A Question of Legitimacy

1   Mancini, p93

2   Crowland, pp488–9

3   Mancini, p89

4   Ibid

5   Grants etc, pp xxxix–xlix. The speech is hard to make a great deal of sense of and demonstrates why attendees are prone to fall asleep in Parliament. There are some key themes that emerge by the end, though. All quotes are taken from these pages.

6   M. Beard, *SPQR*, Profile Books, 2015, p338

7   For definitions, see http://digitalcommons.law.yale.edu/cgi/viewcontent.cgi?article=5447&context=fss_papers or https://onlinelibrary.wiley.com/doi/pdf/10.1002/9781444338386.wbeah13254

8   H. Ellis, *Original Letters Illustrative of English History*, Vol I, Harding and Lepard, 1827, pp150–1

9 This is entirely my opinion. I see little evidence of subtlety in any other area of his life. He seems to me straightforward, and one who expected the same from others. It is a serious flaw in his character that would soon cost him in a way that makes such delicate manoeuvring in 1483 seem very unlikely.

10 Mancini, p95

11 York Books, p285

12 C. Lethbridge Kingsford, *The Stonor Letters and Papers*, Vol II, London, 1919, pp160–1

13 Mancini, p95

14 ed A.R. Scoble, *The Memoirs of Philip de Commines, Lord of Argenton*, Vol I, London, 1906, p265

15 Crowland, p489

16 ed A.R. Scoble, *The Memoirs of Philip de Commines, Lord of Argenton*, Vol I, London, 1906, p200

17 *Rotuli Parliamentorum*, Vol VI, London, 1777, p193

18 Ibid, p194

19 Ibid

20 ed A.R. Scoble, *The Memoirs of Philip de Commines, Lord of Argenton*, Vol II, London, 1856, pp63–4

21 T.D. Hardy, *Rymer's Foedera*, Vol II, Longman and Co, 1873, p710

22 Mancini, p63

23 C. Lethbridge Kingsford, *The Stonor Letters and Papers*, Vol II, London, 1919, pp160–1

24 J. Ashdown-Hill, *Eleanor: The Secret Queen*, The History Press, 2016, pp42–3

25 Ibid, p188

26 ed P.W Hammond, 'Richard III: Loyalty, Lordship and Law', Richard III and Yorkist History Trust, 1986, 'The Sons of Edward IV: A Canonical Assessment of the Claim that they were Illegitimate', R.H. Helmholz, pp106–70 provides an in-depth study of the nature of the canon law of illegitimacy and its impact on this case.

27 M. Levine, *Speculum*, Vol 34, 1958, 'Richard III – Usurper or Lawful King', pp391–401 presents the widely accepted view of the flaws in Richard's case which R.H. Helmholz examines.

28 Helmholz, p110, notes 10 and 11.

29 Ibid, pp111–3

30 Ibid, pp114–5

31 *Rotuli Parliamentorum*, Vol VI, London, 1777, p241

32 Helmholz, p116, note 33

33 Crowland, p496

34 See https://dictionary.cambridge.org/dictionary/english/usurp

35 See https://en.oxforddictionaries.com/definition/usurp. This definition provides the example '*Richard usurped the throne*', demonstrating the

hold this notion retains despite the flaws in it as a legal charge. Other similar examples are at https://www.thefreedictionary.com/usurp and https://www.collinsdictionary.com/dictionary/english/usurp

King Richard III

1 ed J. Halliwell, *Letters of the Kings of England*, Vol I, London, 1848, pp153–4
2 Crowland, p489
3 Mancini, pp91–3
4 J. Rous, *Historia Regum Angliae*, Oxford, 1745, pp213–4, translated in P.W. Hammond & A.F. Sutton, *Richard III: The Road to Bosworth*, Guild Publishing, 1985, p111
5 S. Bentley, *Excerpta Historica*, London, 1831, pp246–8 reproduces the will in full.
6 Ibid, p246
7 Ibid, pp246–7
8 Ibid, pp247–8
9 Ibid, p247
10 Ibid, p248
11 MSS433 Vol III, 1982, p29
12 Mancini, p99
13 *Acts of the Court of the Mercers' Company 1453–1527*, Cambridge, 1936, pp155–6
14 Ibid
15 Mancini, p101
16 Ibid
17 L.G. Wickham Legg, *English Coronation Records*, Archibald Constable & Co, 1901, pp193–7 for full details taken from Bodl. Ashm. MS. 863, p437. There is some evidence (p219) that Henry VII's Little Device for the Coronation was lifted directly from Richard III's coronation, since some of the officers described officiated at Richard's, but not at Henry's.
18 Ibid, p193
19 Henry II and Eleanor of Aquitaine on 19 December 1154, Edward I and Eleanor of Castile on 19 August 1274 and Edward II and Isabella of France on 25 February 1308.
20 Herbert was stripped of the Earldom of Pembroke by Edward IV in 1479 and given the title Earl of Huntingdon instead.
21 Precisely who carried this is unclear. The document gives the Earl of Bedford without listing any such person amongst the attendees earlier. Arundel (unless he was amongst the Barons of the Cinque Ports as Warden), Nottingham and Warwick (George's son Edward, it must be assumed) were in attendance but not listed with a specific

duty. It may be that this was an error caused by the reuse of an earlier document, used to formulate this coronation.

22 A golden sceptre appears in the list of royal regalia in an inventory of relics at Westminster Abbey compiled in 1450. I have assumed that the sceptre referred to is this one. Ibid, pp191–2

23 Ibid, p229. This is taken from the Little Device for Henry VII, but the document has been crossed through at the point of calling Richard's name and Henry's inserted instead, suggesting that the formula used by Henry was directly lifted from Richard's coronation. Given the dubious nature by which Richard was later deemed to have taken the throne, it is striking that Henry sought to copy it in such detail. The address by the archbishop included the phrase 'Sirs here is present Henry rightfull and indoubted enheritor by the Lawes of god and man to the Crowne and royal dignitie of Englande with all thinges thereunto annexid and apperteigning elect chosen and required by all three estates of this same Lande to take upon him the said crown and royall dignitie'. This sounds far more like Richard's accession than Henry's which was more properly by right of conquest.

24 Ibid, p230. This is also taken from Henry VII's Little Device on the basis that it mirrored Richard's coronation.

25 MSS433 Vol I, p3

26 R.R. Sharpe, *London and the Kingdom*, London, 1894, p323. The cup became the subject of a dispute when a later mayor tried to claim it as his own property. 'Item it is aggreed this day by the Court that where Hugh Brice Mair of this Citie, hathe in his Kepyng a Cuppe of gold, garneised with perle and precious stone of the gifte of Richard, late in ded and not of right, Kyng of Englond, which gifte was to thuse of the Cominaltie of the said Citee, that if the saide Cuppe be stolen or taken away by thevys out of his possession, or elles by the casualtie of Fire hereafter it shall hapne the same Cuppe to be brent or lost, that the same Hugh Brice hereafter shall not be hurt or impeched therfore.' (Journal 9, fo. 114b) The appearance is that the explicit grant by Richard was extraordinary and citable, a possible comment of the view of his legacy in July 1486.

27 Itinerary, pp4–10 covers Richard's royal progress. It is striking that he does not return London until November 1483, a full four months after his coronation.

28 A. Hanham, *Richard III and His Early Historians 1483–1535*, Clarendon Press, 1975, p122

29 I think this is amply demonstrated by the fear reported in London of a northern army in 1483 as well as other recent events, including the barring of the gates of London against Queen Margaret in 1461, though she also had a contingent of Scots that contributed to the terror then.

30 N.M. Herbert, The 1483 Gloucester Charter in *History, Gloucester,*
    1983, 'Charter of Richard III to Gloucester', pp9–15
31 MSS433 Vol II, p10
32 A. Hanham, *Richard III and His Early Historians 1483–1535,*
    Clarendon Press, 1975, p121
33 ed J.B. Sheppard, *Christ Church Letters,* The Camden Society, 1877,
    p46
34 Ibid, pp45–6
35 ed J. Gairdner, *Letters and Papers Illustrative of the Reigns of*
    Richard III and Henry VII, Vol I, London, 1861, p25
36 Ibid, pp34–5
37 Ibid, pp35–6
38 Ibid, pp31–3
39 Ibid, pp37–43
40 MSS433 Vol III, p38
41 Ibid, pp36–7
42 Ibid, pp108–9
43 See Dr J. Ashdown Hill www.richardiii.net/downloads/
    Ricardian/2005_vol15_Earl_Desmond_Execution.pdf for further
    details of the build up to the incident.
44 York Books, p286
45 Ibid, p287
46 Ibid
47 Ibid, pp287–8. The final colour is 'musterdivyles', which was
    musterdevillers, a mixed woollen cloth of grey.
48 Ibid, p289
49 Ibid
50 Ibid, pp291–2
51 Itinerary, p6
52 P.W. Hammond & A.F. Sutton, *Richard III: The Road to Bosworth,*
    Guild Publishing, 1985, p140 from York Minster Library, Bedern
    College Statute Book, p48
53 MSS433 Vol I, pp82–3
54 MSS433 Vol II, pp42–3
55 W.A. Shaw, *The Knights of England,* London, 1906, p21
56 P.W. Hammond & A.F. Sutton, *Richard III: The Road to Bosworth,*
    Guild Publishing, 1985, pp140–1 from York Minster Library, Bedern
    College Statute Book, p48

The October Rebellions

1 R. Davies, *Extracts from the Municipal Records of the City of York,*
   London, 1843, p179
2 Crowland, p490

3 Ibid
4 R. Green, *The English Historical Review*, Vol 96, No 380, 'Historical Notes of a London Citizen', 1981, pp585–90
5 P.W. Hammond & A.F. Sutton, *Richard III: The Road to Bosworth*, Guild Publishing, 1985, p125
6 Crowland, p491
7 Ibid
8 J. Stowe, *The Annals of England*, 1603, p767
9 Crowland, p491
10 Mancini, p93
11 Ibid
12 R. Horrox, *Richard III: A Study in Service*, Cambridge, 1989, p151
13 MSS433 Vol II, p19
14 R. Horrox, *Richard III: A Study in Service*, Cambridge, 1989, p151
15 H. Ellis, *Original Letters Illustrative of English History*, Vol I, Harding and Lepard, 1827, pp159–60
16 Ibid, p160
17 Crowland, pp491–2
18 C.L. Kingsford, *The Stonor Letters and Papers*, Vol II, London, 1919, p163
19 R. Davies, *Extracts from the Municipal Records of the City of York*, London, 1843, p177
20 J. Gairdner, *The Paston Letters*, Vol VI, London, 1904, p73 and J. Fenn, Original Letters Written During the Reigns of Henry VI, Edward IV and Richard III, Vol II, London, 1787, pp314–6
21 'Close Rolls, Richard III: 1483–1484', in *Calendar of Close Rolls, Edward IV, Edward V, Richard III 1476–1485*, ed. K H Ledward (London, 1954), pp. 332–355. British History Online http://www.british-history.ac.uk/cal-close-rolls/edw4/1476–85/pp332–355 [accessed 29 March 2018], Item 1171. Richard retained the Great Seal until 26 November, when it was returned to Chancellor Russell at Westminster in the Star Chamber. This handover was witnessed by Thomas Rotherham, Archbishop of York (by that point out of the king's disfavour), the Bishops of Bath and Wells, Durham, St Asaph and Menevia, John Gunthorpe, Keeper of the Privy Seal, Thomas Barowe, the Duke of Norfolk, the Earls of Arundel and Northumberland, Francis Lovell, Thomas Stanley and Sir Richard Ratcliffe as well as other members of the Council. The Chancellor received a sealed bag and then deposited the Great Seal at St Andrew's in Holborn.
22 'Rymer's Foedera with Syllabus: July–December 1483', in *Rymer's Foedera* Volume 12, ed. Thomas Rymer (London, 1739–1745), pp. 192–209. British History Online http://www.british-history.ac.uk/rymer-foedera/vol12/pp192–209 [accessed 29 March 2018]

23 Ibid

24 Ibid

25 Ibid

26 *Rotuli Parliamentorum*, Vol VI, London, 1777, pp244–9

27 MSS433 Vol II, pp48–9

28 'Close Rolls, Richard III: 1483–1484', in *Calendar of Close Rolls, Edward IV, Edward V, Richard III 1476–1485*, ed. K H Ledward (London, 1954), pp. 332–355. British History Online http://www.british-history.ac.uk/cal-close-rolls/edw4/1476-85/pp332–355 [accessed 29 March 2018], Item 1152

29 ed H. Ellis, *Three Books of Polydore Vergil's English History*, London, 1844, p203

30 Crowland, p496

31 R. Horrox, *Richard III: A Study in Service*, Cambridge, 1989, pp178–205 provides an in-depth study of the appointments made and their significance upon which I have relied.

32 Ibid, p191

33 MSS433 Vol I, p3

34 K. Hillier, *The Ricardian*, Vol III, No 49, 'William Colyngbourne', June 1975, pp5–9

35 E. Hall, *Chronicle Containing the History of England*, London, 1809, p398

The King in Parliament

1 S.H. Gem, *An Anglo-Saxon Abbot: Aelfric of Eynsham*, Edinburgh, 1912, p119

2 Grants etc, l–lvi

3 Ibid, li

4 Ibid, lii

5 Luke 15:8–9

6 Grants etc, lvi

7 Ibid, lviii–lxiii

8 Ibid, lviii

9 Ibid, lviii

10 Ibid, lxi

11 *Rotuli Parliamentorum*, Vol VI, London, 1777, p238–63

12 Ibid, pp238–40

13 Ibid, pp240–2

14 Ibid, p240

15 Ibid

16 Ibid, p241

17 Ibid, p242

18 Ibid, pp2444–50

19 Ibid, p250
20 Ibid
21 Ibid, pp250–1
22 Ibid, p250
23 Ibid
24 Ibid, p251
25 Ibid, pp251–2
26 Ibid, pp254–5
27 Ibid, pp252–4
28 D. Pickering, *The Statutes at Large*, Vol IV, Cambridge, 1763, p2
29 Ibid
30 eg J. Galt, *Life of Cardinal Wolsey*, London, 1846, p90
31 D. Pickering, *The Statutes at Large*, Vol IV, Cambridge, 1763, pp9–13
32 Ibid, p9
33 Ibid, p17
34 Ibid, p18
35 Ibid, p13
36 Ibid, p15
37 Ibid, p16
38 Ibid, p17
39 Ibid
40 Ibid, p18
41 Ibid
42 Ibid, pp19–21
43 Ibid, pp1–2
44 Ibid, pp2–3
45 Ibid, p3
46 Ibid, pp4–5
47 Ibid, p21
48 Ibid
49 Crowland, p496
50 MSS433 Vol III, p190
51 A. Williamson, *The Mystery of the Princes*, Alan Sutton, 1978, p122

The Cords of Death

1 P.W. Hammond & A.F. Sutton, *Richard III: The Road to Bosworth*, Guild Publishing, 1985, pp191–3, this quote p192. The prayer was written into Richard's Book of Hours held at Lambeth Palace Library MS 474, ff. 181–3
2 ed M. Hemmant, *Select Cases in the Exchequer Chamber before all the Justices of England*, Vol II, Seldon Society, 1948, pp86–90 reproduced in Ibid pp182–4

3 Ibid

4 CPR, *Edward IV, 1476–85*, Public Record Office, p422. Cold Harbour would be taken from the College of Arms and given to Margaret Beaufort when her son became king. The College was left homeless for seventy years until Queen Mary gave them Derby Place. That building was destroyed in the Great Fire of London in 1666 and the building that stands on that site today, where the College is still based, dates from the following decade.

5 J.O. Halliwell, *Letters of the Kings of England* Vol I, London, 1848, pp153–5

6 Ibid, pp160–1

7 ed J. Gairdner, *Letters and Papers Illustrative of the Reigns of Richard III and Henry VII*, Vol I, London, 1861, pp3–51 for the full instructions. This quote pp4–5

8 Ibid, p4

9 Ibid, p22

10 Ibid, p23

11 Mancini, p22 and Note 3

12 Ibid, p23

13 P.W. Hammond & A.F. Sutton, *Richard III: The Road to Bosworth*, Guild Publishing, 1985, pp167–8, quoting British Library, Harleian MS 258, f. 11b

14 CPR, *Edward IV, 1476–85*, Public Record Office, pp405, 416, 418, 512 for examples

15 For further discussion of this, see H. Kleineke, *The Ricardian*, Vol 17, 'Richard III and the Origins of the Court of Requests', 2007, pp22–32

16 CPR, *Edward IV, 1476–85*, Public Record Office, p458 for Richard's annuity and 467 for Ralph's confirmation. Ralph had lost some offices in the months after his brother's execution, but it is unclear whether that was because he was under suspicion or replaced by more competent men. By mid-1484, he was clearly confirmed in several posts.

17 Crowland, pp496–7

18 A. Hanham, *Richard III and His Early Historians 1483–1535*, Clarendon Press, 1975, p123

19 Itinerary, pp18–9

20 Ibid, pp18–22

21 MSS433 Vol I, p3

22 MSS433 Vol III, p114

23 MSS433 Vol II, p211

24 P.W. Hammond & A.F. Sutton, *Richard III: The Road to Bosworth*, Guild Publishing, 1985, p203

25 I do not have confidence that the remains currently within the urn in the Lady Chapel at Westminster Abbey are, in fact, those of the

Princes in the Tower. I have previously written on this in *The Survival of the Princes in the Tower*, The History Press, 2017, pp31–5

26 CPR, *Edward IV, 1476–85*, Public Record Office p493

27 R.R. Sharpe, London and the Kingdom, London, 1894, p326

28 J. Ashdown-Hill, *The Last Days of Richard III*, The History Press, 2010, p53

29 Itinerary, p23

30 ed R. Brown, *Calendar of State Papers of Venice*, London, 1864, p147

31 Ibid, p148

32 MSS433 Vol III, pp124–5 or H. Ellis, *Original Letters Illustrative of English History*, Vol I, Harding and Lepard, 1827, pp1162–6 or J. Fenn, *Original Letters Written During the Reigns of Henry VI, Edward IV and Richard III*, Vol II, London, 1787, pp318–26

33 'Rymer's Foedera with Syllabus: January–June 1484', in *Rymer's Foedera* Volume 12, ed. Thomas Rymer (London, 1739–1745), pp. 210–229. British History Online http://www.british-history.ac.uk/rymer-foedera/vol12/pp210–229 [accessed 2 April 2018]

34 S.B. Chrimes, *Henry VII*, Yale University Press, 1999, p29

35 CPR, *Edward IV, 1476–85*, Public Record Office, p526 for 75 pardons issued '*Pro soldariis de Hammes de pardonacione*'. The list was headed by Thomas Brandon and included William Blount and his wife Elizabeth.

36 Ibid, p535

37 Crowland, p498

38 Ibid, p499

39 Ibid

40 *Acts of the Court of the Mercers' Company 1453–1527*, Cambridge University Press, 1936, pp173–4

41 Crowland, p499

42 ed A.N. Kincaid, *The History of King Richard III* by Sir George Buck, Master of the Revels, Gloucester, 1979, p191

The Battle of Bosworth Field

1 J. Fenn, *Original Letters Written During the Reigns of Henry VI, Edward IV and Richard III*, Vol II, London, 1787, pp334–5

2 P.W. Hammond & A.F. Sutton, *Richard III: The Road to Bosworth*, Guild Publishing, 1985, pp201–2 for examples

3 J.O. Halliwell, *Letters of the Kings of England*, Vol I, London, 1848, p161

4 York Books, pp359–60

5 Crowland, p500

6 Itinerary, pp36–9

7 Crowland, p501

8 Ibid, p501

9 *The Manuscripts of His Grace The Duke of Rutland*, Vol I, Her Majesty's Stationery Office, 1888, pp7–8

10 J. Fenn, *Original Letters Written During the Reigns of Henry VI, Edward IV and Richard III*, Vol II, London, 1787, pp334–5

11 York Books, pp367–8

12 Many accounts of the military aspects of the Battle of Bosworth exist to draw together these disparate and unclear perspectives. I do not propose to rewrite the battle here, but to draw on those experts available. I recommend M. Ingram, *Bosworth 1485: Battle Story*, the History Press, 2015, Bennett, *The Battle of Bosworth*, The History Press, 2008 *or* C. Skidmore, *Bosworth: The Birth of the Tudors*, Weidenfield &Nicholson, 2013 *or* H. Bicheno, *Blood Royal*, Head of Zeus, 2016 for full accounts of the manoeuvres that day.

13 Crowland, p503

14 Ibid

15 For details of the injuries to Richard's skeleton, see https://www.cambridge.org/core/journals/antiquity/article/king-in-the-car-park-new-light-on-the-death-and-burial-of-richard-iii-in-the-grey-friars-church-leicester-in-1485/EB678293FE20EF21D246D149766A95F4

16 ed P.L. Hughes & J.P. Larkin, *Tudor Royal Proclamations*, Vol I, New Haven, 1964, p3

17 W. Shakespeare, *Richard III*, Act V, Scene IV

18 Crowland, p504

19 A. Hanham, *Richard III and His Early Historians 1483–1535*, Clarendon Press, 1975, p123

20 G. Wheeler, *The Ricardian*, Vol 2, No 36, 'A Spanish Account of the Battle of Bosworth', 1972, p2

21 ed. G. Doutrepont and O. Jodogne, *Chroniques de Jean Molinet (1474–1506)*, 1937, p435, though Molinet does go on to report a story that Richard tried to flee before being cut down.

22 ed H. Ellis, *Three Books of Polydore Vergil's English History*, London, 1844, p224

23 York Books, pp368–9

Index